The Cambridge Companion to the Rule of Law

The Cambridge Companion to the Rule of Law introduces students, scholars, and practitioners to the theory and history of the rule of law, one of the most frequently invoked – and least understood – ideas of legal and political thought and policy practice. It offers a comprehensive re-assessment by leading scholars of one of the world's most cherished traditions. This high-profile collection provides the first global and interdisciplinary account of the histories, moralities, pathologies and trajectories of the rule of law. Unique in conception, and critical in its approach, it evaluates, breaks down, and subverts conventional wisdom about the rule of law for the twenty-first century

Jens Meierhenrich is Associate Professor of International Relations at the London School of Economics and Political Science and previously taught at Harvard University. His books include *The Legacies of Law* (2008), *The Remnants of the Rechtsstaat* (2018), *The Violence of Law* (2021), and, as co-editor, *The Oxford Handbook of Carl Schmitt* (2016).

Martin Loughlin is Professor of Public Law at the London School of Economics and Political Science and previously taught at the University of Glasgow and at the University of Manchester. His books include *Sword and Scales* (2000), *The Idea of Public Law* (2003), *Foundations of Public Law* (2010), and, as co-editor, *The Paradox of Constitutionalism* (2007).

Cambridge Companions to Law

Cambridge Companions to Law

Cambridge Companions to Law offers thought-provoking introductions to different legal disciplines, invaluable to both the student and the scholar. Edited by world-leading academics, each offers a collection of essays which both map out the subject and allow the reader to delve deeper. Critical and enlightening, the Companions library represents legal scholarship at its best.

The Cambridge Companion to European Union Private Law
Edited by Christian Twigg-Flesner

The Cambridge Companion to International Law
Edited by James Crawford and Martti Koskenniemi

The Cambridge Companion to Comparative Law
Edited by Mauro Bussani and Ugo Mattei

The Cambridge Companion to Human Rights Law
Edited by Conor Gearty and Costas Douzinas

The Cambridge Companion to Public Law
Edited by Mark Elliott and David Feldman

The Cambridge Companion to International Criminal Law
Edited by William A. Schabas

The Cambridge Companion to Natural Law Jurisprudence
Edited by George Duke and Robert P. George

The Cambridge Companion to Comparative Family Law
Edited by Shazia Choudhry and Jonathan Herring

The Cambridge Companion to Comparative Constitutional Law
Edited by Roger Masterman and Robert Schütze

The Cambridge Companion to the First Amendment and Religious Liberty
Edited by Michael D. Breidenbach and Owen Anderson

The Cambridge Companion to the Philosophy of Law
Edited by John Tasioulas

The Cambridge Companion to Legal Positivism
Edited by Torben Spaak and Patricia Mindus

The Cambridge Companion to Hugo Grotius
Edited by Randall Lesaffer and Janne E. Nijman

The Cambridge Companion to International Arbitration
Edited by Chin Leng Lim

The Cambridge Companion to the Rule of Law

Edited by

Jens Meierhenrich
London School of Economics and Political Science
Martin Loughlin
London School of Economics and Political Science

CAMBRIDGE
UNIVERSITY PRESS

University Printing House, Cambridge CB2 8BS, United Kingdom

One Liberty Plaza, 20th Floor, New York, NY 10006, USA

477 Williamstown Road, Port Melbourne, VIC 3207, Australia

314–321, 3rd Floor, Plot 3, Splendor Forum, Jasola District Centre, New Delhi – 110025, India

103 Penang Road, #05–06/07, Visioncrest Commercial, Singapore 238467

Cambridge University Press is part of the University of Cambridge.

It furthers the University's mission by disseminating knowledge in the pursuit of education, learning, and research at the highest international levels of excellence.

www.cambridge.org
Information on this title: www.cambridge.org/9781316512135
DOI: 10.1017/9781108600569

First published 2021

A catalogue record for this publication is available from the British Library.

ISBN 978-1-316-51213-5 Hardback
ISBN 978-1-108-45443-8 Paperback

Contents

Contributors

Seyla Benhabib is the Eugene Meyer Professor of Political Science and Philosophy Emerita at Yale University.

Lauren Benton is the Barton M. Biggs Professor of History and Professor of Law at Yale University.

Khiara M. Bridges is Professor of Law at the University of California, Berkeley.

Peter C. Caldwell is the Samuel G. McCann Professor of History at Rice University.

Shane Chalmers is McKenzie Research Fellow and Program Director in Law and Art at the Institute for International Law and the Humanities at Melbourne Law School.

David Dyzenhaus is University Professor of Law and Philosophy at the University of Toronto.

Lindsay Farmer is Professor of Law at the University of Glasgow.

Lisa Ford is Professor of History at the University of New South Wales.

Roberto Gargarella is Professor of Constitutional Theory and Political Philosophy at the Universidad de Buenos Aires and at the Universidad Torcuato Di Tella, Argentina.

Tom Ginsburg is the Leo Spitz Professor of International Law at the University of Chicago Law School, and a Research Professor at the American Bar Foundation.

Gillian K. Hadfield is the Schwartz Reisman Chair in Technology and Society, Professor of Law, and Professor of Strategic Management at the University of Toronto.

Douglas Hay is Professor Emeritus of Law and History at York University, Canada.

Stephen Humphreys is Associate Professor of Law at the London School of Economics and Political Science.

Sharon R. Krause is the William R. Kenan, Jr. University Professor of Political Science at Brown University.

Martin Krygier is the Gordon Samuels Professor of Law and Social Theory at the University of New South Wales.

Nicola Lacey is School Professor of Law, Gender, and Social Policy at the London School of Economics and Political Science.

Adriaan Lanni is the Touroff-Glueck Professor of Law at Harvard Law School.

Paul Linden-Retek is Lecturer in Law and Society, University at Buffalo School of Law, State University of New York.

Martin Loughlin is Professor of Public Law at the London School of Economics and Political Science.

Jens Meierhenrich is Director of the Centre for International Studies at the London School of Economics and Political Science and a Visiting Professor of Law at Harvard Law School.

Vanessa E. Munro is Professor of Law at the University of Warwick.

Anne Orford is the Redmond Barry Distinguished Professor and the Michael D. Kirby Chair of International Law at Melbourne Law School.

Sundhya Pahuja is Professor and Director of Melbourne Law School's Institute for International Law and the Humanities.

Lawrence Rosen is the William Nelson Cromwell Professor of Anthropology Emeritus at Princeton University.

Kristen Rundle is Professor of Law at Melbourne Law School.

William E. Scheuerman is the James H. Rudy Professor of Political Science and International Studies at Indiana University.

Jane E. Stromseth is the Francis Cabell Brown Professor of International Law at Georgetown University.

Brian Z. Tamanaha is the John S. Lehmann University Professor at Washington University School of Law.

Mark Tushnet is William Nelson Cromwell Professor of Law Emeritus at Harvard Law School.

Mila Versteeg is Professor of Law at the University of Virginia School of Law and Director of the Human Rights Program.

Jeremy Waldron is University Professor at New York University School of Law.

Mark D. Walters is Professor and Dean of Law at Queen's University, Canada.

Barry R. Weingast is the Ward C. Krebs Family Professor in the Department of Political Science at Stanford University.

Part I

Introduction

Thinking about the Rule of Law

Jens Meierhenrich and Martin Loughlin

Introduction

This Companion provides an introduction to the theory and history of the rule of law, and thus to one of the most frequently invoked – and least understood – ideas of legal and political thought. Not so long ago, the "rule of law" was regarded as a rather esoteric expression, one employed by common lawyers – alongside such expressions as the *Rechtsstaat*, *État de droit*, and *Stato di diritto* that their continental confrères invoked – to identify certain technical features of the legal systems in which they worked. Over the last several decades, however, its usage has expanded rapidly and has now become a key phrase in the vulgar tongue of contentious politics, domestic and international. And in the process, it seems to have been converted from a technical phrase into a rhetorical slogan – an expression of such generality that it can be filled with whatever values the heart desires. For this reason, the rule of law now circulates in the marketplace of ideas as a debased currency.

This being so, ours is an opportune time for a major exercise in reappraisal. Several questions are addressed: What is the rule of law? What should it be? Whatever it might be, is it worth having if it cannot sustain the liberty of all citizens? Is it worth promoting if it can be used not just to bolster democracy but also authoritarian varieties of rule? What can be done about the rule of law? What can be done *with* it? What are the virtues of the rule of law? What of its vices? Our volume speaks to the meanings and machinations, to the values and violence, of the rule of law. We present it as "a noble but flawed ideal," a phrase we borrow from Martha Nussbaum, who recently found wanting another cherished tradition in the Western canon.[1]

[1] Martha C. Nussbaum, *The Cosmopolitan Tradition: A Noble but Flawed Ideal* (Cambridge: Belknap Press of Harvard University Press, 2019).

During another stock-taking two decades ago, José Mará Maravall and Adam Przeworski opined that the "normative conception of the rule of law was a figment of the imagination of jurists," one that was both "implausible as a description" and "incomplete as an explanation."[2] We agree, but our way of approaching the rule of law is not as rigidly rationalist as theirs. We come to it from an interdisciplinary perspective, one that draws on the scholarship of anthropologists, historians, philosophers, sociologists, and political scientists as well as lawyers, so that, with a bit of luck, our way of seeing the rule of law will be commensurable with both nomothetic *and* ideographic modes of reasoning.[3] To this end, we have invited a wide range of leading scholars to examine specific aspects of this topic, in the hope that will help us reassess both the promise of the rule of law and its limits.

Our contributors ask thorny questions about the appropriateness as well as the utility of the rule of law as a social imaginary for tackling the most pressing issues of our times. Our conviction is that in order to make sense of the rule of law today – both literally and figuratively – we need to view it as a social phenomenon with diverse and contradictory instantiations. To bring it into sharper focus, we commissioned chapters to reconsider key *histories* (Part II) and *moralities* (Part III) of the rule of law, and to trace notable *pathologies* (Part IV) and *trajectories* (Part V) thereof. In a substantial concluding chapter (Part VI), one of us reflects critically on the insights gleaned from surveying the landscape of the rule of law in the four preceding parts. The far-ranging analysis, which doubles as a very short introduction to the topic, culminates in a call for a realistic theory of the rule of law.

Allow us to say a little more about the organization of what is to come – and why, and how, the arguments of our distinguished contributors are relevant to thinking about the rule of law.

[2] José María Maravall and Adam Przeworski, "Introduction," in idem, eds., *Democracy and the Rule of Law* (Cambridge: Cambridge University Press, 2003), p. 1.

[3] On the methodological divide, and for one influential proposal of how to bridge it, see Robert H. Bates, Avner Greif, Margaret Levi, Jean-Laurent Rosenthal, and Barry R. Weingast, *Analytic Narratives* (Princeton: Princeton University Press, 1998), p. 12. For a trenchant critique of this proposal, see Jon Elster, "Rational Choice History: A Case of Excessive Ambition," *American Political Science Review*, 94 (2000), 685–695.

Histories

An argumentative thread running through our collection is the claim that we are better off to speak of *rules of law*, in the plural, than to imagine the rule of law as a singular phenomenon. Part II consists of five chapters that speak to the motif of multiples. Adriaan Lanni, Jens Meierhenrich, Luc Heuschling, Lawrence Rosen, Lauren Benton, and Lisa Ford introduce us to alternate realities of the rule of law. They alert us, if you will, to the changing character of the rule of law. Moving deftly across space and time – as well as cultures and legal traditions – this set of perspectives highlights not only the need to think about the variety of practices that over the centuries have come to be associated with the expression of the rule of law, but also the importance of historicizing, locally, its plethora of meanings.

To start us off, Lanni corrects significant misconceptions about the prehistory of the rule of law. Reconstructing from court practices and written texts of the period, she explains how the law ruled in ancient Athens. We also learn why Plato and Aristotle regarded with disdain these radically democratic Athenian practices. Less concerned with what worked in practice, and more with what they thought should apply in principle, Plato and Aristotle advocated more robust conceptions of the rule of law, with a stricter application of written law, than the city-state actually practised to sustain its exclusionary social order.

Meierhenrich, next, demonstrates that the difference between the concept of the *Rechtsstaat* and the rule of law is more than a variation on a theme. He argues that, globally speaking, the idea of the *Rechtsstaat* has been no less influential than the idea of the rule of law. Comprising a distinct meaning, the *Rechtsstaat* has left its institutional imprint on societies far and near. This continental European idea – which he calls "rule under law" – pre-dated the Dicyean conception of the rule of law by at least half a century. As a global phenomenon, the *Rechtsstaat* tradition has long rivalled that of the rule of law, which over time, and in certain parts of the world, it has grown to resemble. Given the practical importance of the *Rechtsstaat* tradition from the long nineteenth century to the present, Meierhenrich believes it imperative not to equate it – and the manifold everyday practices it has since inspired – with the rule of law tradition. Local histories of convergence, he cautions, must not distract us from the fundamental differences – historical, philosophical, conceptual – at the heart of these two contending ways of thinking about the concept of law and the manner of its rule.

Heuschling picks up the thread of the *Rechtsstaat* from Meierhenrich and weaves it into a historical narrative about the "Gallicization" of the neologism. What, he asks, did the French stand to gain from importing the German way of law? He develops an answer by analyzing the antecedents – and the aftermath – of the transplantation of the *Rechtstaat* during the Third Republic. Heuschling explains what prompted Léon Duguit in 1907 to come up with the concept of the *État de droit*, France's variation on the German idea of freedom. His chapter tells a story of legal change. From the Third to the Fifth Republic, Heuschling traces the meandering logic and effects of a little-known legal transfer and reconstructs the discursive formations involved and the resistances encountered.

Lawrence Rosen's chapter leads from the *Rechtsstaat* tradition to Islamic conceptions of the rule of law. After introducing histories of the rule of law – as this chapter understands the term – in Islam and the development of Islamic legal thought over the centuries, Rosen identifies common cultural themes that cut across rival approaches to law in the Islamic world. He relates the principal ideas of classical legal thought – with their focus on the Quran, the Traditions of the Prophet, and the four main schools of law – to the role of custom *('urf, adat)*, which, Rosen argues, in practical terms is often the prevailing source of law. From the Malays of Sumatra to the Berbers of North Africa local custom *is shari'a* – and not infrequently it acts as a constraint on the strict application of formal law. In his phenomenological account, Rosen also highlights the significance in Islamic conceptions of the rule of law of norms such as bargaining and equivalence, institutions such as the marketplace and the judiciary, and procedures such as rules of evidence, all of which commonly function as enabling constraints. Viewed from the vantage point of the everyday, Rosen notes, a considerable overlap between Muslim and non-Muslim visions of the rule of law exists. His chapter reinforces the sense that the exploration of singularities is thus a necessary precondition not only to theorizing the rule of law but also to evaluating its social performance, in all senses of that term.[4]

[4] On the performative dimensions of the rule of law, see, for example, Jens Meierhenrich and Catherine Cole, "In the Theater of the Rule of Law: Performing the Rivonia Trial in South Africa, 1963–1964," in Jens Meierhenrich and Devin O. Pendas, eds., *Political Trials in*

Benton and Ford also agree that there is more than one history of the rule of law to be told. They address "empire's neat but jarring place in the history of the rule of law,", thus acquainting readers with the dark sides of virtue. Noting that the rise in rule of law rhetoric coincides with the moment "when European jurists surveyed that world's laws and found all but their own wanting," they nevertheless remain alert to the need to avoid a reductionist portrayal of this jurisprudence of power. Benton and Ford show imperial legal orders were fluid, layered, and, above all, plural. With special reference to the British Empire, they contrast strategies of "imperial legal ordering," these techniques of authoritarian rule, with the variegated rights regimes that local conditions demanded. Although the rule of law emerges as a shadowy figure in their account, Benton and Ford caution that no unified idea of an "imperial rule of law" ever existed.

Moralities

Turning from histories to moralities, the third part of our collection explores the intelligibility of the concept of the rule of law. Our contributors here review the work of some of most important theories – and theorists – of the rule of law in the Western canon.

Jeremy Waldron sets the scene by reprising his well-known argument about the rule of law as an "essentially contested concept," which is the label the British philosopher Walter Bryce Gallie used to describe a term so vague that its diverse meanings are symptomatic of a chronic condition that cannot be healed conceptually. Gallie maintained that "displaying a certain kind of semantic vagueness, essentially contested concepts make it necessary to resort to historical considerations as a way to settle the disputes over their meaning."[5] Gallie's hermeneutical enterprise charts "a middle ground between a radical form of historicism, which sees all symbolic phenomena as the product of contingent historical trajectories, and an antihistorical form of realism, according to which the meaning of

Theory and History (Cambridge: Cambridge University Press, 2016), pp. 229–262. See also Bruno Latour, *The Making of Law: An Ethnography of the Conseil d'État*, trans. Marina Brilman and Alain Pottage (Cambridge: Polity, [2002] 2010).

[5] Tullio Viola, "From Vague Symbols to Contested Concepts: Peirce, W. B. Gallie, and History," *History and Theory*, 58 (2019), 246.

concepts and standards are fixed and just waiting to be discovered."[6] In Chapter 6, Waldron explains the relevance of this argument for thinking about the rule of law. His application of Gallie to discursive formations related to the rule of law sets the scene for the more detailed investigations of individual moralities that follow.

In those chapters, by Sharon Krause, Mark Walters, Martin Loughlin, Kristen Rundle, and Douglas Hay take turns to assess some of the most influential arguments in defense of the rule of law as a moral idea. Krause introduces us to Montesquieu's masterwork of 1748, *The Spirit of the Laws*. We learn why Montesquieu placed his faith in the role of institutions to curb arbitrary power, and what convinced him that these institutions were essential to achieving the rule of law, that is, to crafting standing rules. "[J] ust as the sea, which seems to want to cover all the earth, is constrained by the grasses and the smallest rocks that are found on the shore," Montesquieu wrote, "so monarchs whose power seems to be without limits, are constrained by the smallest obstacles."[7]

In addition to advocating intermediate constraints, Montesquieu was a proponent of using "fundamental laws" to curtail the reach and rule of the prince. Krause notes how important it was for him that the institutions of legality, and the laws they produced, were responsive to the "spirit" of the nation and the dispositions of the people *as well as* to the laws of nature and to such virtues as equity, proportionality, and moderation. These were *sense-giving features* of the rule of law, and so for him were moral psychology and everyday practices. According to, Montesquieu, the rule of law was a cocktail of the right passions. The rule of law, as he saw it, had to be general *and* flexible. It was a concrete abstraction, if you will: contingent on local mores, but answerable to universal values. As Krause's chapter makes plain, Montesquieu's vision of the rule of law was one of the first to treat legality and legitimacy as indivisible – and as indispensable to the protection of liberty.

Albert Venn Dicey followed Montesquieu in emphasizing the vital significance of maintaining a spirit of legality, as Walters shows in Chapter 8. He explains what makes Dicey's account of the rule of law quintessentially Anglo-Saxon, and why it was more than the unfortunate outburst of parochialism Judith Shklar believed it to be. Dicey's treatment of the rule

[6] Viola, "From Vague Symbols to Contested Concepts," 251.

[7] As quoted in Sharon Krause, "The Rule of Law in Montesquieu," in this volume, p. 142.

of law, a term to which he gave systematic meaning but did not invent, was one of the first integrated accounts of what Alexis de Tocqueville thought of with admiration as the legality of English habits. Dicey, writes Walters, was seized of the ambition to give the vague assumptions that Tocqueville and other foreign scholars were making about English governing practices formal legal expression – and under the banner of the rule of law.

The idea of the rule of law that runs through Dicey's *Introduction to the Study of the Law of the Constitution* of 1885 hinges on the importance of parliamentary sovereignty and on the supremacy of the ordinary law. In this common law conception of constitutionalism, Walters explains, the attribute of the rule of law Dicey regarded as definitive was the requirement that governmental powers have parliamentary authorization. Safeguarding this requirement was the revered institution of the judiciary. By marching in lockstep, parliament and the courts would hold prerogative rule in check.

Dicey's account extrapolates from sources he knew best. He was at pains to distinguish the English case, sometimes chauvinistically, from what he perceived to be France's perverse constitutionalism, as represented by the idea of the *droit administratif.* Walters tells us that formal requirements such as generality, prospectivity, clarity, and intelligibility, were of secondary importance in Dicey's scheme. He was a nationalist first, and a formalist second, and he valued concreteness over abstraction. For this reason, we should not read Dicey out of context. His conception of the rule of law is decidedly local – a theory of the rule of law in the vernacular. He was uniquely attuned to the rule of law as a social imaginary, which is why reading him in the twenty-first century can be rewarding, especially when thinking about cultures of legality, which for good reason is now *de rigueur.*[8] "A significant strength of Dicey's account," one commentator recently noted, "is that he does not confine the rule of law to the conduct of state officials."[9] But on the negative side, as Judith Shklar highlights, by equating the concept of the rule of law to the English practice, he essentialized the idea. And that explains why Dicey's *magnum opus* remains an influential but dispensable morality tale about the rule of law.

[8] See, for example, Paul W. Kahn, *The Cultural Study of Law: Reconstructing Legal Scholarship* (Chicago: University of Chicago Press, 1999); and Jean Comaroff and John L. Comaroff, eds., *Law and Disorder in the Postcolony* (Chicago: University of Chicago Press, 2006).

[9] N. W. Barber, *The Principles of Constitutionalism* (Oxford: Oxford University Press, 2018), p. 89.

In Chapter 9, Loughlin examines Michael Oakeshott's argument that the rule of law expresses the idea of the state as a moral association. Oakeshott's account is rather different from Dicey's, and Loughlin explains why. He highlights Oakeshott's debt to Roman legal thought, especially to the concept of *respublica*, and explains why he conceived the rule of law to be an essential ingredient of "the civil condition." Loughlin also unpacks what Oakeshott's ineffable idea of the *jus* of *lex* entails. Re-reading Oakeshott, he concludes that ultimately it represents a republican conception of the rule of law, one that is, above all else, "a self-sustaining model of association identified in terms of the ascertainable authenticity of *lex*."[10]

Morality was also an important theme for Lon Fuller, although he eschewed the term itself in his relational account of the rule of law. Rundle reminds us that the meaning Fuller wanted to convey by speaking of "morality" in relation to the concept of law was very specific and must be distinguished from other, broader rule of law moralities. Chapter 10, then, addresses the task of uncovering the morality of the rule of law as Fuller understood it. His mission, Rundle explains, was to articulate the moral demands appropriate to the structuring of one particular relationship: that between the lawgiver and the subjects of law. The logic of their interactions, Fuller believed, cut to the heart of what it meant to govern through law, which is why he set out to capture it as precisely as he knew how. Rundle explains how Fuller did this, how he fared against such interlocutors as H. L. A. Hart and Joseph Raz, and what import his argument about the internal morality of (the rule of) law has for our time.

In Chapter 11, Douglas Hay provides an intellectual biography of E. P. Thompson, whose argument about the rule of law is widely known but rarely studied. Most scholars and practitioners of the rule of law are familiar with chapter 10, section iv of *Whigs and Hunters*, the 1975 book in which Thompson famously – and controversially – asserted that the rule of law was "an unqualified human good." Few, however, are familiar with the 258 pages of fine microhistory that preceded it, and fewer still with Thompson's pioneering social historical work of which that book forms but one part.[11] Hay, a student of his teacher's, situates Thompson's

[10] Martin Loughlin, "Michael Oakeshott's Republican Theory of the Rule of Law," in this volume, p. 181.

[11] E. P. Thompson, *Whigs and Hunters: The Origin of the Black Act* (New York: Pantheon, 1975), p. 266.

argument within the Marxist debates of the 1970s and explains why we should care about the Black Act of 1723.[12] We learn that, unlike Dicey, Thompson did not hold the English judiciary in high regard, neither those of the eighteenth century whose actions and cases he studied in the archives, nor those from the twentieth century who, he argued, aided and abetted the modern security state. By inviting us into his collaborator's world, Hay helps us to see Thompson's argument about the rule of law in a new light and to appreciate its continuing relevance to analogous debates in the twenty-first century.

When *Whigs and Hunters* was published, Thompson, the world's leading historian of class and one of the founders of the "first" New Left, received a considerable degree of criticism from certain strands of Marxism. One such barrage came from scholars in Critical Legal Studies (CLS), the progressive movement that formed in several US law schools in the mid-1970s.[13] Morton Horwitz, the doyen of critical legal historians in the United States – in what may well be the most cited book review ever published – was incredulous.[14] Hay, in his contribution to this collection, explains what all the fuss was about, why Thompson's argument has stood the test of time, and why it ought to be read by those who do not know it – and re-read by those who think they do.

The final two chapters in Part III of our Companion switch gears and turn from influential theorists to influential *theories* of the rule of law. Brian Tamanaha gives functional theories of the rule of law their due, and Gillian Hadfield, Jens Meierhenrich, and Barry Weingast consider the payoffs from using game theory to think more formally about the rule of law.

Tamanaha examines the kinds of things that the rule of law is used for. Thinking about the functions of the rule of law for him is not about foregrounding the ends of law, but, rather, the kinds of contributions it has been shown to make in people's lives. Tamanaha distinguishes between manifest functions, such as the provision of security and the imposition of constraints, and latent functions, from the elevation of legal specialists to the entrenchment of powerful interests. The rhetorical invocation of these

[12] See Douglas Hay, Peter Linebaugh, John G. Rule, E. P. Thompson, and Cal Winslow, *Albion's Fatal Tree: Crime and Society in Eighteenth-Century England*, 2nd ed. (London: Verso, 2011).

[13] See also Mark Tushnet, "Critical Legal Studies and the Rule of Law," in this volume.

[14] Morton J. Horwitz, "The Rule of Law: An Unqualified Human Good?" *Yale Law Journal*, 86 (1977), 561–566.

and related functions of the rule of law, says Tamanaha, is often a sign that the rule of law matters, that it has social relevance. Indeed, there must be something special going on if socialists like E. P. Thompson, establishment lawyers like Lord Bingham, libertarians like Friedrich Hayek (who went to great lengths to deny that he was a conservative), and authoritarians like Viktor Orbán, the Prime Minister of Hungary, *all* are able to imagine the functions of the rule of law to be compatible with their vastly divergent social imaginaries.[15]

The question that Hadfield, Meierhenrich, and Weingast address in Chapter 13 is deceptively simple: What, reduced to its essence, is the rule of law, and under what conditions does it become a self-reinforcing, stable order? Missing from the various literatures that have attempted to answer it, they argue, is a satisfying account of the microfoundations of the behaviors that generate – and sustain – a distinctively legal order. A cognitive manifesto in hand, they show that existing approaches to the rule of law – both philosophical and applied – have neglected the question of what, *exactly*, is distinct about law's rule as contrasted to other forms of rule. We do not yet know enough, they argue, about what sets legal ordering apart from other strategies of ordering, be they economic or violent. Their chapter begins to fill this gap. In it, Hadfield, Meierhenrich, and Weingast advance a positive theory of the rule of law.

Pathologies

The next part continues with our examination of theorists and theories of the rule of law. But the perspectives we showcase are decidedly more critical. Whereas the focus in Part III is on the virtues of the rule of law, Part IV concerns its vices. We assembled seven critiques in total. Two revolve around critical thinkers – Thomas Hobbes and Judith Shklar – the remainder around the most important schools of critical thought, both conservative and progressive.

David Dyzenhaus enters the fray with an inquiry into the idea of rule *by* law. Those fond of it distinguish the notion from that of the rule of law. Many who are, see an ally in Thomas Hobbes. Hobbes thought rather

[15] See also Jens Meierhenrich, "The Rule of Law Imaginary: Regarding *Iustitia*," in Michael Sevel, ed., *The Routledge Handbook of the Rule of Law* (London: Routledge, forthcoming).

differently about the law than Sir Edward Coke, the seventeenth-century standard bearer of the rule of law tradition in English legal thought. But it would be wrong, Dyzenhaus maintains, to regard Hobbes as an intellectual forerunner of Jeremy Bentham and John Austin whose command theories held that law is what the *sovereign* makes of it. Dyzenhaus argues that Hobbes did have faith in the law – and he provided an attractive, though widely misunderstood, account of the rule of law. For Hobbes, the achievement of governing through – and under – law was also a moral achievement, writes Dyzenhaus, because it was a political achievement.[16] His analysis shows that Hobbes advanced not so much a critique of the rule of law *tout court*. He actually critiqued the rule of law as contemporaries drawn to the natural law tradition, like Coke, were imagining it. Hobbes's response to this common law conception of the rule of law was constructive – and he intended it as such. If a label were needed, says Dyzenhaus. Hobbes's was the first *political* theory of the rule of law in the West.

Conservative critics of the rule of law in the nineteenth and twentieth centuries, of which Peter Caldwell singles out four, also framed the rule of law politically. They theorized it – and the related ideas of the *Rechtsstaat* and the *État de droit* – in existential terms. In Chapter 15, Caldwell parses the counterrevolutionary writings of Joseph de Maistre and Heinrich von Treitschke alongside those of Carl Schmitt and Ernst Forsthoff, together with a brief commentary on Edmund Burke, the least radical of the conservatives in this set of counter-Enlightenment thinkers. Perturbed by the French Revolution of 1789, Maistre, Caldwell shows, regarded the rule of law as an expression of the sovereign state as an existential order. The rule of law emanated from, and was responsive to, divine will. Reason had nothing to do with it. The "political constitutions" Maistre defended were grounded in a metaphysics of rule, a belief in the supremacy of the state as an organically grown, culturally rooted superiority. Treitschke also endorsed this argument from foundational values, describing the state as a transhistorical necessity. According to these theorists, the state made law, and the law – so long as liberals were involved in making it – was vacuous. Responding to the growing influence of rights-based liberalism in the theory of institutional design, they clamored for alternatives to the formalism and relativism they associated with procedural conceptions of the

[16] On the idea of "rule under law," and its relation to the rule by law tradition, see also Jens Meierhenrich, "*Rechtsstaat* versus the Rule of Law," in this volume, esp. pp. 47–65.

rule of law, the *Rechtsstaat*, and *État de droit*. And it was for this reason that Carl Schmitt, under the influence of the German Revolution of 1918/19, in Weimar Germany declared legality the enemy of legitimacy.[17]

Like Ernst Forsthoff, with whom he served the Nazi dictatorship, Schmitt believed liberalism's concern with universality and abstraction was inherently incompatible with the homogeneity and concreteness he, like Burke, regarded as the cement of society. Hierarchy, all three thinkers maintained, was conducive, equality corrosive, to any viable social order. Maistre and Treitschke, Schmitt, and Forsthoff, were theorists of "the total state," the kind of state in which law rules absolutely – in the service of *raison d'état*. In conservative conceptions, the rule of law (in whatever shade) is derivative of the state, not constitutive of it. The implication is stark: the rule of law is an inferior institution. In conservative legal thought, the rule of law has always been, first and foremost, an enabling device, not a limiting one.

Chapter 16, written by Seyla Benhabib and Paul Linden-Retek, revisits Judith Shklar's foundational work on legalism. In the 1960s, Shklar recognized that "a greater degree of social self-awareness" about rule of law practices would make legalism "a more effective social force, a more intelligible and defensible political ideology and a more useful concept in social theory."[18] Benhabib and Linden-Retek explore the genesis of Shklar's political thought and explain why she found wanting the kind of philosophical abstraction that had dominated the Hart-Fuller debate in that period. They relate Shklar's account about the rule of law to her earlier argument about legalism and explain why she set out "to unsettle" the "underlying presumptions and aspirations" of the rule of law – why she felt compelled to chart the history of legal thought as "a story of forgetting."[19]

Interestingly, Benhabib and Linden-Retek link Shklar's argument about the rule of law to Jürgen Habermas's discourse theory of law, which, with its focus on intersubjectivity, they interpret as an undertaking "deeply responsive to her concerns."[20] The invocation of

[17] For a recent reevaluation of Schmitt's political, legal, and literary thought, see Jens Meierhenrich and Oliver Simons, eds., *The Oxford Handbook of Carl Schmitt* (Oxford: Oxford University Press, 2016).

[18] Judith N. Shklar, "In Defense of Legalism," *Journal of Legal Education*, 19 (1966), 58.

[19] Seyla Benhabib and Paul Linden-Retek, "Judith Shklar's Critique of Legalism," in this volume, p. 308.

[20] Benhabib and Linden-Retek, "Judith Shklar's Critique of Legalism," p. 311.

Habermas, the most influential theorist to have graduated from the so-called Frankfurt School, provides a segue to William Scheuerman, who, in Chapter 17, engages with rule of law critiques that emanated from the German left. He conjures two rival visions of the *Rechtsstaat*, that of Habermas, and a more radical, older analysis by Franz Neumann, whose Marxist leanings culminated in a powerful critique of the liberal rule of law. Both critiques, Habermas's discourse theory and Neumann's critical theory, will forever be associated with the *Institut für Sozialforschung*, which had its beginnings in Frankfurt, where it saw the light of day in 1923, before it relocated to New York during the Nazi dictatorship, and was eventually revived in Germany in 1951. Scheuerman explains why Habermas's thinking about the rule of law (and about the *Rechtsstaat*) changed over time, and why we might want to think of it as "a creative response to many of Neumann's concerns" about the relationship between capitalism and the rule of law.[21]

This nexus – the frequently pathological relationship between the rule of law and its structural foundations in society – was also what troubled the "Critical Legal Studies" movement in the United States. With roots in American Legal Realism, a school of jurisprudence that flourished in the interwar period of the twentieth century, CLS theorists of the 1970s and 1980s, in the interest of creating "a more humane, egalitarian, and democratic society," sought to foreground the political in the rule of law.[22] The target, as Mark Tushnet recounts in Chapter 18, was formalism. CLS scholars argued that substantive conceptions of the rule of law were *transparently* ideological, which is why it was primarily procedural approaches that needed rebutting. The reason they proffered: power hides in procedures. Locating the violence of law in these hiding places – these deep structures – became the CLS mission.[23]

Like the legal realists into whose shoes they stepped, CLS scholars mistrusted all efforts to ground the rule of law in a fixed moral foundation. For them, there was no rule of law in the singular. Almost everyone associated

[21] William E. Scheuerman, "The Frankfurt School and the Rule of Law," in this volume, p. 327.

[22] Duncan Kennedy and Karl E. Klare, "A Bibliography of Critical Legal Studies," *Yale Law Journal*, 94 (1984), 461.

[23] On law's violence, see, most recently, Jens Meierhenrich, *The Violence of Law: The Formation and Deformation of* Gacaca *Courts in Rwanda, 1994–2019* (Cambridge: Cambridge University Press, 2021); and idem, *Lawfare: A Genealogy* (Cambridge: Cambridge University Press, forthcoming).

with the movement over the last forty years – CLS has withered domestically but successfully branched out into international law – has been dubious about moralities. Critical theorists do not think any morality can be trusted as a guide to the rule of law's meaning. The rule of law may exist, but it is so deeply intertwined with ideology that its norms and institutions are invariably facadist. Whoever claims otherwise, so their argument goes, is a liberal – and living a noble lie.

One aspect to which CLS inquiries into the pathologies of the rule of law gave short shrift was that of gender. Several generations of feminist legal theorists, albeit to varying degrees and in different ways, have punctured the liberal rule of law bubble in which most twentieth-century thinking about the rule of law took place. Perturbed by the marginalization of gendered realities of precarity in political and legal thought, scholars of feminist jurisprudence have long looked askance at rule of law promises. Vanessa Munro, in Chapter 19, surveys the terrain of feminist jurisprudence – and reviews prescriptions for treating law's pathological state. Her analysis focuses on three problem areas: (1) the "manipulability" of the functional notion, widely associated with rule of law thinking, of a public/private distinction; (2) the atomistic vision of rights-based liberalism and the often inadequate solutions to the problem of female subjectification that are the wont of liberal legalism; and (3) the fundamental limits of the rule of law as a tool of, and site for, progressive reform. Munro has serious reservations about the rule of law and its gendered practices. But unlike some radical feminist legal scholars, she does not give up entirely on the idea. She calls for a "permanent, unclosed perspective" on the rule of law, one that regards it realistically, with a keen eye for "the exclusions, excesses, and violence that law's rule has imposed and/or justified," especially against women.[24]

CLS was also insufficiently attentive to issues of race. And so, arguably, were feminist critiques of the rule of law. They, too, commonly glossed over "the problem of the color-line."[25] Critical Race Theory (CRT) arose in response to both of these lacunae in the critical study of law. A broad church, this intellectual movement has promoted the concept of intersectionality to come to terms with institutions of whiteness and their failings – including those of the rule of law. In Chapter 20, Khiara Bridges traces the

[24] Vanessa E. Munro, "Feminist Critiques of the Rule of Law," in this volume, p. 356.

[25] W. E. B. Du Bois, *The Souls of Black Folk*, ed. Brent Hayes Edwards (Oxford: Oxford University Press, [1903] 2007), p. 3.

evolution of race-based critiques of the rule of law from the 1970s to Black Lives Matter. She attends to the vices of the rule of law by problematizing the notion of "colorblindness," which has long been a cornerstone of liberalism's solution to the problem of race. CRT, by contrast, aims to make color *appear*, not disappear. Like most intellectual movements, its membership is far from homogeneous. Bridges traces major faultlines from Derrick Bell to Kimberlé Crenshaw, and from Francisco Valdes to Sumi Cho. Some who belong to the movement believe the pathologies of the rule of law to be just that – pathological states. For them, "the self-serving 'rule of law'" is irredeemable, not least because its norm entrepreneurs – in domestic politics and international affairs alike – "cruelly declared formal (racial and social) equality while simultaneously limiting its reach."[26] These scholars regard the rule of law as having been associated far too often with the advancement of white supremacy. Other critical race theorists think more instrumentally about the rule of law. They recognize its value (if not its virtue) even when it is soiled by racial prejudice.

Trajectories

Whether one believes in the rule of law is, ultimately, a question of what one thinks the idea is capable of. One way to arrive at plausible answers is to think from trajectories. Part V of our collection develops this approach. It is both retrospective and prospective It looks forward as well as back. Our authors take stock of what has – and has not – been achieved in the name of the rule of law. Their principal focus is on the modern world, especially on pathways in the twentieth and twenty-first centuries. The nine chapters of this penultimate part consider the achievements and agonies of the rule of law in relation to undertakings with which it has been deeply intertwined, from constitutionalism to economic development, and from democracy to populism.

Shane Chalmers and Sundhya Pahuja, in Chapter 21, begin with an account of the rule of law as a continuous civilizing mission. Based on a genealogical reading of modern international history, they find that the fervent commitment to rule of law advocacy in the twenty-first century "was

[26] Francisco Valdes and Sumi Cho, "Critical Race Materialism: Theorizing Justice in the Wake of Global Neoliberalism," *Connecticut Law Review*, 43 (2011), 1521.

forged in the experience of colonialism."[27] They illustrate their argument with evidence from Liberia, arguing that "beneath the post colonial veneer of the 'rule of law and development' project lies a colonial core."[28] This continuity – the affective overlap between nineteenth-century and twenty-first centuries rule of law imaginaries – expresses a universalizing morality and provides an example of dependence development. Both of these trajectories Chalmers and Pahuja view with trepidation.

The promotion of democracy is as deeply intertwined with the phenomenon of the rule of law as is the goal of (economic) development. In Chapter 22, Martin Krygier reminds us why democracy, like the rule of law, has attained the status of a "solution-concept" (a term Jeremy Waldron favors), and why it is important not to misunderstand the relationship between them.[29] After an analysis, with particular reference to the writings of Isaiah Berlin and Benjamin Constant, of the idea of liberty, Krygier tackles a thorny contradiction, one that has become prevalent again in the early twenty-first century: the pursuit of democracy *without* the rule of law. Against the background of recent developments in countries like Hungary and Poland, Krygier asks what, if anything, is to be done about this "tyranny of false polarities," as Stephen Holmes once called it?[30] The way Krygier sees it, democracy and the rule of law are "helpmates," in the sense that both are required for freedom as non-domination.[31] In his chapter, he explains why.

Roberto Gargarella, next, addresses a conceptual pairing one commonly encounters in debates about democracy promotion: that of constitutionalism and the rule of law. He does so by examining three tensions he believes characterize that relationship. They concern, respectively, the question of individual autonomy, the idea of private property, and the institution of judicial review. Building on his work about Latin American constitutionalism, Gargaralla calls for a majoritarian reading of the rule of law, one that re-imagines some of the most common – and conservative – principles that over the last few hundred years have come to be associated with the rule of law.[32]

27 Shane Chalmers and Sundhya Pahuja, "(Economic) Development and the Rule of Law," in this volume, p. 390.

28 Chalmers and Pahuja, "(Economic) Development and the Rule of Law," p. 404.

29 Jeremy Waldron, "The Rule of Law as an Essentially Contested Concept," in this volume, p. 133.

30 Stephen Holmes, *Passions and Constraint: On the Theory of Liberal Democracy* (Chicago: University of Chicago Press, 1995), p. 28.

31 Martin Krygier, "Democracy and the Rule of Law," in this volume, p. 423.

32 See, for example, Roberto Gargarella, *Latin American Constitutionalism, 1810–2010: The Engine Room of the Constitution* (Oxford: Oxford University Press, 2013).

He charts a future trajectory for the rule of law in which institutional safeguards – especially constitutional ones – reflect *less* the mores and preferences of elites (such as judges and legislators) and *more* "the people themselves."[33]

The liberty of individuals is also of concern to those who think about punishment under the rule of law. Lindsay Farmer is among them. In Chapter 24, he traces the evolution of state-led retribution through the ages, beginning with the principle of moderation that Cesare Beccaria put forth in *Dei delitti e delle pene* (1764), the first modern argument for constraining the penal state. *On Crimes and Punishments* inspired other normative theories of punishment designed to curtail the arbitrariness of penal practices, including those of William Blackstone and Jeremy Bentham. Farmer explains how, at the end of the eighteenth century, these clarion calls for moderation ushered in one of the most fundamental principles of the rule of law: *nulla poena sine lege*. This maxim – which prohibits punishment without law – is a defining feature of the principle of legality. Farmer, with reference to recent case law, explores how this deceptively simple injunction has performed across various legal jurisdictions and traditions. He finds much to admire. But he also recognizes that rule of law restrictions in the democratic penal state have been more successful at defining unauthorized and disproportionate forms of punishment than in preventing injustice.

The perception of injustice lies at the heart of various populist movements that of late have engulfed not only the Global North (for example, Germany, Hungary, Poland, the United States) but also a large swath the Global South (for example, Argentina, Brazil, Turkey, South Africa, and Venezuela).[34] In Chapter 25, Nicola Lacey asks under what conditions populism might be a threat to the rule of law. She explains why impatience with the rule of law is a defining feature of populism, and what it can do to a social fabric. Lacey distinguishes several mechanisms by which populism can subvert the rule of law. They range from populist constitutionalism to "convention trashing" to

33 Roberto Gargarella, "Constitutionalism and the Rule of Law," in this volume, p. 442.

34 See, for example, S. Erdem Aytaç and Ziya Őniş, "Varieties of Populism in a Changing Global Context: The Divergent Paths of Erdoğan and Kirchnerismo," *Comparative Politics*, 47 (2014), 41–59; Dom Phillips, Jason Burke; and Paul Lewis, "How Brazil and South Africa became the World's most Populist Countries," *The Guardian*, May 1, 2019. See also Jan-Werner Müller, *What Is Populism?* (London: Penguin, 2017); Federico Finkelstein, *From Fascism to Populism in History* (Berkeley: University of California Press, 2017); and Paul Lewis, Caelainn Barr, Seán Clarke, Antonio Voce, Cath Levett, and Pablo Gutiérrez, "The Rise and Rise of Populist Rhetoric," *The Guardian*, March 6, 2019, a longitudinal study of 40 countries over two decades.

penal populism. Lacey maintains that populism will *always* be pushing in an "anti-rule of law direction."[35] But she is equally convinced that, absent a detailed mapping of the *actual* terrain where populists are contesting – and coopting – the rule of law, it will be impossible to say anything meaningful, let alone policy-relevant, about how this struggle for the soul of the state will play out in the end.

Is it possible to build the rule of law where it doesn't yet exist? This is the question at the heart of Chapter 26. Here, Stephen Humphreys critically examines the so-called rule of law movement that sprang up in the twentieth century and has adherents the world over. Taking a leaf from Oakeshott, he chides the movement for gravely misunderstanding what the rule of law is or can be. Training his sights on the World Justice Project, one of the most visible rule of law entrepreneurs, Humphreys examines the claims associated with international efforts to build, promote, or otherwise support the rule of law. Arguing that few such efforts have led to sustainable development, advanced human rights, or reduced poverty, he maintains that all are examples "of the ineradicable tendency to qualify, confuse, or deny the rule of law."[36] The reductionist approach prevailing among NGOs that see themselves in the vanguard of the international rule of law movement stands in contrast to Oakeshott's critique of entrepreneurial teleology. Humphreys draws out this contrast by weaving Oakeshott's concept of *societas* through his analysis of the so-called international rule of law movement. The end result is a critical intervention that warns of reducing the rule of law – in both theory and practice – to a form of managerialism.[37]

The international dimensions of the rule of law are also the subject of Chapter 27. Tom Ginsburg and Mila Versteeg are more sympathetic to recent international developments than Humphreys. They, too, analyze the work of the World Justice Project – alongside that of the World Bank, the Heritage Foundation, and Freedom House Theirs is a purely methodological analysis, however. These are the questions Ginsburg and Versteeg pose: How can the rule of law measured? What do the indicators that result from these efforts actually capture? How do rule of law measures compare? And how do these measures map onto the rule of law moralities to which

35 Nicola Lacey, "Populism and the Rule of Law," in this volume, p. 473.

36 Stephen Humphreys, "An 'International Rule of Law Movement'?," in this volume, p. 484.

37 On Oakeshott, see, in this volume, also Loughlin, "Michael Oakeshott's Republican Theory of the Rule of Law;" and Meierhenrich, "What the Rule of Law Is … and Is Not," esp. pp. 602–607.

we cling? They find, despite notable differences in the underlying conceptions of the rule of law, a high degree of correlation across the various measures. Their chapter adds key data points to the debate about the promise – and pathologies – of measuring the rule of law universally.[38] It also has implications for post-conflict rule of law.

In Chapter 28, Jane Stromseth takes stock of what on that score has been accomplished since the end of the Cold War, when international efforts to build the rule of law after military interventions went into overdrive. Her survey is more optimistic than many. Conceding that the track record of building the rule of law after conflict is "decidedly mixed," she argues, with Kathryn Sikkink, that there is "evidence for hope."[39] From women's empowerment through transitional justice to international criminal law, argues Stromseth, rule of law initiatives matter – and have made a positive impact. Against those who say international efforts of using might to make rights smack of "imperial utopianism" and spell "hubris," Stromseth defends the ambitions of liberal internationalism.[40] She confident that learning has taken place, and that the one-size-fits-all approach that once dominated international practices has given way to more appropriate ways of thinking about exporting the rule of law. Unlike Humphreys, Stromseth sees nothing *inherently* objectionable in the international movement that is trying to deliver post-conflict rule of law.

Anne Orford, in Chapter 29, sounds a more skeptical note. Describing the decade of the 1990s as "the high point for the project of liberal legalist international ordering," she inquires the backlash against global legalism that has seized especially the Global South.[41] Especially during the last decade, shows Orford, the effort to build a global rule of law, for example by strengthening, international adjudication in the areas of trade and investment law, has stalled. She makes a similar case about the project of international criminal law. Orford views critically the liberal vision of a Kantian international system forged through – and resting on – a universal rule of law. It is imperative, she

[38] Sally Engle Merry, Kevin Davis, and Benedict Kingsbury, eds., *The Quiet Power of Indicators: Measuring Governance, Corruption, and Rule of Law* (Cambridge: Cambridge University Press, 2015).

[39] Kathryn Sikkink, *Evidence for Hope: Making Human Rights Work in the 21st Century* (Princeton: Princeton University, 2017).

[40] Cf. Nehal Bhuta, "Democratisation, State-Building and Politics as Technology," in Brett Bowden, Hilary Charlesworth, and Jeremy Farrall, eds., *The Role of International Law in Rebuilding Societies after Conflict* (Cambridge: Cambridge University Press, 2009), p. 63.

[41] Anne Orford, "A Global Rule of Law," in this volume, p. 553.

argues, to recognize that "plural visions of the rule of law" exist and that the idea of a global rule of law is not a universally shared but an essentially contested vision.[42] Building the rule of law, Orford concludes, is impossible without moralizing it. But history has taught us, she says, that moralizing the rule of law invariably means politicizing it.

Conclusion

Our way of seeing the rule of law is – or so we like to think – realistic. To construct realistic theories of the rule of law, it is essential we consider the phenomenon "in its social totality."[43] Thinking about the rule of law realistically requires an ability to reason *both* abstractly *and* concretely. What we advocate is not a "downshift to naïve empiricism," but a willingness to see the world of law for what it is: large and murky and incredibly diverse.[44] Because history shows that law rules in all kinds of ways, we welcome the intellectual effort, renewed by a small band of anthropologists, historians, and political scientists a little over a decade ago, of studying *rules of law* – and in the real world. Meierhenrich elaborates on the motif of multiples in the final part of our Companion, thereby drawing the volume together.

Distilling and interrogating the insights of our contributors and setting their work in a broader context of notable scholarship, he makes a case for rethinking the rule of law – for fundamentally reassessing what passes for conventional wisdom in theory and practice. Through a critique of what he calls "criterial" conceptions of the rule of law, his chapter lays the intellectual foundations for a realistic theory of the rule of law.[45] Meierhenrich explains why he thinks the quest for what philosophers call the intelligibility of the rule of law is futile, and why a phenomenological approach – one centered on the study of practices, not premises – is more appropriate for thinking about the rule of law in the twenty-first century.

[42] Orford, "A Global Rule of Law," p. [564].

[43] Brian Z. Tamanaha, *A Realistic Theory of Law* (Cambridge: Cambridge University Press, 2017), p. 1. For an extended argument to this effect, see also Meierhenrich, "What the Rule of Law Is . . . and Is Not."

[44] See also Leslie Green, "The Forces of Law: Duty, Coercion, and Power," *Ratio Juris*, 29 (2016), 179.

[45] Meierhenrich, "What the Rule of Law Is . . . and Is Not," p. 582.

Part II

Histories

1 Classical Athens' Radical Democratic "Rule of Law"

Adriaan Lanni

Introduction

Herodotus' Persian debate – a fictional conversation between three noble Persians on the relative merits of rule by one, rule by the few, and rule by all – ironically provides one of our clearest statements of Greek democratic theory.[1] In the debate, Otanes, arguing for rule by all, highlights what are recognizable as the key features of Athenian democracy: *isonomia* (equality under the law); selection of magistrates by lot; accountability for officials; and decision-making in a deliberative popular Assembly.[2] These features suggest that the Athenians' core concern was preventing the accumulation of power by a tyrant or abusive officials; protecting individuals from the potentially oppressive judgment of the people was not a central feature of Athenian democracy. These values produced a distinctively limited and radically democratic approach to the "rule of law," one that focused on protection from abusive officials and equal treatment for all citizens under the law (*isonomia*) rather than ensuring that a stable and clear set of rules were consistently and predictably applied.

There is no surviving sustained statement of Athenian democratic legal theory. The theoretical texts we have – principally the works of Plato and Aristotle – are hostile to the democracy and offer little insight into the aims of the Athenian court system. Our best evidence for the Athenian approach to the rule of law comes from inferences from the structure and practices of the lawcourts themselves. After a brief survey of statements about the rule of law found in Athenian court speeches and literary texts, this chapter focuses on how Athenian legal institutions and court practice reflect

[1] Hdt. 3.80–82. All references to ancient sources use the abbreviations from the *Oxford Classical Dictionary*. For discussion, see Paul Cartledge, *Ancient Greek Political Thought in Practice* (Cambridge: Cambridge University Press, 2009), pp. 69–75. Translations from the Attic Orators come from the University of Texas Press's Oratory of Classical Greece series, with some modifications. All other translations come from the Loeb Classical Library.

[2] Hdt. 3.80.

a limited and democratic "rule of law." I conclude with a brief discussion of how Plato and Aristotle's writing on the rule of law responded to the Athenians' radically democratic approach.

1 Democratic Ideals

The rule of law and the related concept of equality before the law (*isonomia*) were central to Athenian democratic ideology. But the Athenian notion of "rule of law" seems to have been narrower and less robust than many modern variations.[3] Athenian texts juxtapose the rule of law in a democracy to being enslaved to the whim of a tyrant or monarch and emphasize the importance of equal access to judicial institutions and equal treatment for rich and poor citizens under the law. The notion that rules should be clear and should be consistently and predictably applied notably do not play a prominent role in encomia of Athens' adherence to law.[4]

Athens' democratic rule of law is often contrasted with the arbitrary and lawless rule of a tyrant. The orator Aeschines' remark is typical: "there are in the world three forms of government, autocracy, oligarchy, and democracy: autocracies are administered according to the tempers of their lords, but democratic states according to the established laws."[5] In a similar vein, Hyperides noted that "living in a democratic state where justice is established by the laws is different from passing into the power of one tyrant where the caprice of an individual is supreme."[6]

For the Athenians, the key feature of a democracy subject to the rule of law was *isonomia*, the ideal that rich and poor citizens are treated equally

[3] For discussion, see Sara Forsdyke, "Ancient and Modern Conceptions of the Rule of Law," in Mirko Canevaro, Andrew Erskine, Benjamin Gray, and Josiah Ober, eds., *Ancient Greek History and Contemporary Social Science* (Edinburgh: Edinburgh University Press, 2018), pp. 184–212; David Cohen, *Law, Violence, and Community in Classical Athens* (Cambridge: Cambridge University Press, 1995).

[4] As discussed below, in a series of legal reforms at the end of the fifth century the Athenians did make a short-lived attempt to clarify and remove the contradictions in their laws, but did not attempt to change the ad hoc and highly discretionary process of jury decision-making.

[5] Aesch. 1.4; see also Dem. 21.188; 24.75–76; 25.16; Eur. *Supp.* 429–437. Similarly, in the Persian debate, Otanes contrasts rule by many with rule under a tyrant, who "disrupts ancestral laws" and "puts men to death without trial" (Hdt. 3.80).

[6] Hyp. fr. 15. For discussion, see Paul Cartledge and Matt Edge, "'Rights,' Individuals, and Communities in Ancient Greece," in Ryan K. Balot, ed., *A Companion to Greek and Roman Political Thought* (Oxford: Wiley-Blackwell, 2009), p. 152.

under the law and that no one is above the law.[7] Equality before the law is singled out for praise in Thucydides' account of Pericles' funeral oration, and is frequently highlighted in Athenian court speeches.[8] Euripides' play *Suppliants* elaborates on this ideal: in contrast to a tyrant who can manipulate the law to his own interests, "when the laws have been written down, the weak and the rich have equal justice . . . and the weaker prevails over the great man if he has justice on his side."[9]

2 Democratic Practice

While the Athenian legal system clearly provided formal equality before the law[10] to male citizens and provided protections from the arbitrary exercise of power by officials,[11] scholars have intensely debated the question of whether Athens had a robust "rule of law" that included the consistent and predictable application of clear rules. Some scholars, primarily those of an anthropological bent, contend that the Athenian popular courts served primarily a social, political, or ritual role, and did not attempt to resolve disputes according to established rules or principles equally and impartially applied.[12] At the other extreme, some historians have argued that Athenian juries did strictly and predictably enforce the law.[13] Most recent scholarship takes an intermediate position, arguing that

[7] For discussion, see Forsdyke, "Ancient and Modern Conceptions of the Rule of Law."

[8] Thuc. 2.37; Dem. 21.188; 23.86; 25.16; 51.11; Aesch. 1.5. [9] Eur. *Supp.* 432–437.

[10] Just as in many legal systems, wealth and social status provided informal advantages in an Athenian court, most notably by permitting wealthy litigants to hire skilled speechwriters.

[11] Protections aimed at preventing official abuse included the use of boards of ten magistrates, with collective liability, as well required accountings and provisions for citizen complaints. For discussion of the various mechanisms of official accountability, see Mogens Herman Hansen, *The Athenian Democracy in the Age of Demosthenes* (Oxford: Blackwell, 1991), pp. 225–245.

[12] Cohen, *Law, Violence and Community in Classical Athens*, pp. 87–88, portrays Athenian litigation as a form of feuding behavior; Robin Osborne, "Law in Action in Classical Athens," *Journal of Hellenic Studies*, 105 (1985), 52 sees Athenian litigation as status competition; Werner Riess, *Performing Interpersonal Violence: Court, Curse, and Comedy in Fourth-Century BCE Athens* (Berlin: de Gruyter, 2012), pp. 143–145 views Athenian litigation as ritual performances that were "always unpredictable" and did not necessarily "operate rationally."

[13] Edward Harris, *The Rule of Law in Action in Democratic Athens* (Oxford: Oxford University Press, 2013); Harald Meyer-Laurin, *Gesetz und Billigkeit im attischen Prozess* (Weimar: Böhlaus Nachfolger, 1965); J. Meineke, "Gesetzinterpretation und Gesetzanwendung im Attischen Zivilprozess," *Revue Internationale des Droits de l'Antiquité*, 18 (1971),

while Athenian juries sought to reach a just outcome to the legal dispute before them, in doing so they had wide discretion that went beyond the consistent and predictable application of clear statutes, often considering a variety of other legal, equitable, and contextual considerations.[14] I outline below the features of the Athenian legal system that prevented the consistent and predictable application of clear rules. It seems that legal reasoning was considered only one of many possible strategies open to an Athenian litigant. Moreover, the lack of precise legal definitions and absence of binding precedent gave mass juries a great deal of discretion even when they were attempting to strictly apply the law. Perhaps most intriguing, it seems that the Athenians were aware of, and uneasy about, these features of their system but made a conscious choice in favor of a flexible, discretionary, and radically democratic approach to justice in their popular courts.

The Athenian legal system seems to have aimed primarily at making some form of redress available to amateur litigants rather than providing clear legal rules or making fine legal distinctions. Athenian statutes were notoriously vague; our surviving laws rarely define the offense or describe the essential characteristics of the behavior governed by the law. The surviving law of *hubris*, for example, offers no definition of this subjective term,[15] and the range of situations charged as impiety (*asabeia*) and bribery (*dorodokia*) suggest that these offenses may not have been clearly understood.[16] As a result, as Gagarin has pointed out, "a very wide range

275–360. Others (for example, Hansen, *The Athenian Democracy in the Age of Demosthenes*, pp. 161–177) have emphasized that the institutional reforms at the end of the fifth century signaled a shift from the sovereignty of the people to the sovereignty of law, without specifically arguing that Athenian juries faithfully and predictably applied statutes.

[14] Adriaan Lanni, *Law and Justice in the Courts of Classical Athens* (Cambridge: Cambridge University Press, 2006), pp. 2–3, 41–75, and 115–148; Matthew R. Christ, *The Litigious Athenian* (Baltimore: Johns Hopkins Press, 1998), pp. 195–196; Adele C. Scafuro, *The Forensic Stage: Settling Disputes in Graeco-Roman New Comedy* (Cambridge: Cambridge University Press, 1997), pp. 50–66; Forsdyke, "Ancient and Modern Conceptions of the Rule of Law"; see also Michael Gagarin, "Law, Politics, and the Question of Relevance in the Case on the Crown," *Classical Antiquity*, 31 (2012), 293–314, who notes that the Athenian concept of law "was broader than our own" and included "the broad set of customs or traditional rules that Athenians generally accepted whether or not they were enshrined in statute."

[15] Dem. 21.47.

[16] David Cohen, *Theft in Athenian Law* (Munich: C. H. Beck, 1983), pp. 203–210; Kellam Conover, "Bribery in Classical Athens," Ph.D. dissertation, Princeton University, 2010, pp. 21–64.

of conduct could be construed as wrongdoing under one of the broad categories of offenses in Athenian law."[17] It seems that magistrates – non-experts selected by lot for a one-year term – did not play an active role in shaping complaints; we have no evidence of a magistrate rejecting a complaint, and only two instances in which a magistrate compelled the prosecutor to amend his complaint.[18] Hagnon's proposal to try Pericles indicates how casual the Athenians could be about the legal basis of a lawsuit: according to Plutarch, he proposed that Pericles be tried before fifteen hundred jurors, "no matter whether it is called a prosecution for embezzlement (*klope*), bribery (*doron*), or a misdemeanor (*adikion*)."[19] In one treason case, the prosecutor admits that the defendant's conduct does not seem to be covered by the statute, but argues that the jury should act as law-givers (*nomothetai*) and convict anyway because the defendant's behavior was too heinous for a lawgiver to anticipate.[20]

Once in court, amateur prosecutors recounted their grievances against the defendant in layman's terms and did not necessarily attempt to carefully parse and apply the statute under which the case was brought. Athenian litigants at times cite an array of laws that do not govern the charges in the case, and at other times do not deem it relevant to discuss – or even mention – the law under which the suit was brought. The vagueness and lack of definition of the laws meant that even discussions of the specific charge left a great deal of discretion to the jury. There is evidence that some Athenians viewed the vagueness of the laws as a merit: the *Constitution of the Athenians* (a description of the history and institutions of Athens written by Aristotle or his students) reports that "some men think that [the lawgiver Solon] deliberately made the laws unclear in order that the demos would have power over the verdict."[21]

In the absence of legislative history or juristic commentary, litigants and jurors were left with little guidance on how to interpret vague statutes. At times litigants, doubtless assisted by speechwriters, made ingenious arguments supporting their interpretation of the law based on the putative "intent of the lawgiver," or on analogous statutes.[22] Jurors in individual

[17] Gagarin, "Law, Politics, and the Question of Relevance in the Case on the Crown," 311.

[18] Lys. 13.86; Is. 10.2. For discussion, see Gagarin, "Law, Politics, and the Question of Relevance in the Case on the Crown," 310.

[19] Plut., *Per.* 32. [20] Lyc. 1.9. [21] *Ath. Pol.* 9.2.

[22] See, for example, Is. 8.31–4; Hyp. 3.15–18. For discussion, see Lanni, *Law and Justice in the Courts of Classical Athens*, pp. 69–70; Steven Johnstone, *Disputes and Democracy:*

cases may have been swayed by these arguments on occasion, but there was no guarantee that a future jury would reach a similar conclusion. There was no doctrine of binding precedent obligating jurors to abide by previous verdicts. Records of past decisions were not easily available to litigants who wished to use them in their speeches, and even where litigants do cite previous verdicts, they rarely compare the cases in a way that would allow the jury to extract and apply a rule of decision from the prior case.[23]

Perhaps even more problematic than undefined statutory terms from the standpoint of predictability and consistency was the lack of statutory guidance regarding exceptions, defenses, and aggravating and mitigating factors. The presence of these types of arguments in our surviving speeches suggest that Athenian jurors sometimes considered them in reaching their verdicts,[24] and there is some evidence suggesting that jurors in particular cases were swayed by these arguments.[25] The difficulty is that there were no clear rules, written or unwritten, about when particular defenses or mitigating factors might trump the straightforward application of the statute.

So far, we have been discussing the lack of clarity and consistency regarding the application of what a modern would recognize as traditional "legal" considerations in Athenian courts – that is, the rules defining the offense and any defenses. But the predictability and consistency of verdicts was further hampered by the jury's consideration of what a modern would consider to be factors unrelated to whether the offense was committed.[26]

The Consequences of Litigation in Ancient Athens (Austin: University of Texas Press, 1999), p. 28.

[23] Adriaan Lanni, "Arguing from 'Precedent': Modern Perspectives Athenian Practice," in Edward M. Harris and Lene Rubinstein, eds., *The Law and the Courts in Ancient Greece* (London: Bristol Classical Press, 2004), pp. 159–171; Lanni, *Law and Justice in the Courts of Classical Athens*, pp. 118–128.

[24] For example, the speaker in Hyperides 3, *Against Athenogenes*, suggests an exception to the general rule that contracts should be binding. Riess, *Performing Interpersonal Violence*, pp. 22–101 sketches various aggravating and mitigating factors regarding violence that seem to have affected jurors, including public vs hidden violence, inebriation vs sobriety, old age vs youth, and escalation vs de-escalation. Harris, *The Rule of Law in Action in Democratic Athens*, pp. 285–291 lists several examples of equitable arguments in the orators.

[25] Din. 1.55–57; Dem. 21.71–76; for discussion, see Harris, *The Rule of Law in Action Democratic Athens*, pp. 292–300.

[26] For a more complete discussion, with references to primary sources, see Lanni, *Law and Justice in the Courts of Classical Athens*, pp. 42–64. On Athenian jurors' consideration of extra-legal considerations, see also Christ, *The Litigious Athenian*, pp. 40–44; Robert

From an Athenian point of view, of course, these arguments were just as relevant as statutory or mitigating arguments to reaching a just resolution of the case. I point out that moderns would view them as "extra-legal" considerations simply to highlight the fact that the number and types of factors that might influence an Athenian verdict was much larger than in a modern court. Athenian litigants routinely presented a highly contextualized picture of the dispute, describing the relationship and past interaction of the parties, including their behavior in the course of litigation; general arguments from fairness; the character and public services performed by the litigants and their families; and the effect that a penalty would have on the defendant and his family.[27] Moreover, litigants in cases that might appear to turn on a specific factual or technical question – for example, did a witness in a prior lawsuit perjure himself? had the statute of limitations run? was the suit barred in a *paragraphe* action? – typically attempt to convince the jury not only that the narrow issue should be resolved in their favor but that they are also in the right in the underlying substantive dispute.[28]

Will contests provide just one common example of how court speakers argue in favour of a contextualized notion of justice rather than the strict application of the law.[29] Speakers often attempt to reject a valid will based on general notions of fairness. Speakers compare their relationship to the deceased with that of their opponents in an effort to argue that they have the better claim on the estate: they present evidence that they were closer in affection to the deceased, performed his burial rites, or nursed him when he was ill, and suggest that their opponents were detested by the dead man and took no interest in his affairs until it was time to claim his estate.[30] One such litigant concludes with a summary of his arguments that places equitable considerations on an equal footing with the will and the law: he urges the jury to consider "first, my friendship with the men who have

W. Wallace, "When the Athenians did not Enforce their Laws," in Bernard Legras and Gerhard Thür, eds., *Symposion 2011: Vorträge zur grieschischen und hellenistischen Rechtsgeschichte* (Vienna: Austrian Academy of Sciences Press, 2012), p. 121.

27 Lanni, *Law and Justice in the Courts of Classical Athens*, pp. 42–64.

28 Lanni, *Law and Justice in the Courts of Classical Athens*, pp. 66–67.

29 For other examples of how litigants encouraged jurors to go beyond the letter of the law, see Christ, *The Litigious Athenian*, pp. 193–224.

30 See, for example, Is. 1.4, 17, 19, 20, 30, 33, 37, 42; 4.19; 5.36–38, 41–43; 6.51; 7.8, 11, 12, 33–37; 9.4, 27–42.

bequeathed the estate . . . then the many good deeds I did for them when they were down on their luck . . . in addition the will . . . further, the law."[31]

How did an Athenian jury go about evaluating the mass of information and argument, both contextual and legal, presented in a popular court case? Athenian juries offered no reasons for their verdicts and we rarely know the outcome of the cases for which speeches are preserved. One clue is the enigmatic and controversial phrase in the oath which was sworn each year by the panel of potential jurors. According to the standard reconstruction, the oath stated in part: "I shall vote according to the laws and decrees of the Athenian people and the Council of Five Hundred, but concerning things about which there are no laws, I shall decide to the best of my judgment, neither with favour nor enmity."[32] Although some scholars have viewed the juror's oath as evidence that the jury was limited to strictly applying the laws in all but the unusual case where there was no controlling statute, others have argued convincingly that the jurors' "best judgment" (*dikaiotate gnome*) necessarily played a much greater role in legal verdicts, noting particularly the broad discretion given to juries to interpret and apply laws that were often vague and ambiguous.[33]

We cannot know for certain how the average juror conceived his task, but surviving speeches suggest that even the relative importance of legal and contextual evidence in any individual case was open to dispute.[34] Individual Athenian court verdicts were the untraceable result of many individual jurors' complicated weighing of a variety of factors, both statutory and extra-statutory. This form of ad hoc, multi-factored decision-making meant that the popular courts rarely enforced the statute under which the case was brought in a predictable or consistent manner.

Does the absence of clear rules and consistent verdicts in the popular courts suggest that the Athenians were too primitive to conceive of a robust notion of the rule of law? On the contrary, the Athenians were all too aware of, and uneasy about, the lack of consistency in their legal system. At the end of the fifth century they embarked on a short-lived attempt to make their laws more coherent, though they stopped short of limiting the jury's wide discretion. Even more revealing, the Athenians did not employ the ad

[31] Isoc. 19.50. [32] Scafuro, *The Forensic Stage*, p. 50.

[33] For discussion of the various scholarly interpretations of the juror's oath, see Scafuro, *The Forensic Stage*, pp. 50–51.

[34] For discussion, see Lanni, *Law and Justice in the Courts of Classical Athens*, p. 72.

hoc, highly discretionary approach of the popular courts in all types of case: the rules in special homicide and commercial maritime procedures suggest a more robust notion of the rule of law in these cases.

At the end of the fifth century, in 411 and again in 404, the democracy was overthrown and replaced by short-lived oligarchic regimes. The revolutions revealed the fragility of the democratic constitution and the need for safeguards in the process of law-making to protect the most important Athenian laws from hasty repeal and amendment. The nature of the reforms also suggests an attempt to address the long-standing problem of inconsistency and uncertainty in the laws.[35] A board of magistrates was tasked with collecting the laws and correcting any inconsistencies to produce a single, consistent code of laws. The codification should have alleviated legal uncertainty in Athens to some degree by providing a single, authoritative collection of laws in a central location that could be consulted by litigants. But the law code is not mentioned again after 400. It seems that the Athenians did strive for legal codification in an attempt to increase consistency and coherence among their body of legal rules but seem to have abandoned the idea almost immediately. We cannot know for certain why the Athenians became so quickly disenchanted with codification. One attractive theory is that the public process of constant revision of the law code would highlight the reality that the laws were not, in fact, the unchanging ancestral laws of the law-givers Solon and Draco but were in constant flux.[36] The Athenians may have felt that the authority of the law was diminished rather than enhanced by codification and that the gains in legal certainty (which were in any case modest because the reforms did not change the ad hoc nature of jury decision-making) were outweighed by the reduction in respect for and authority of the laws.

The legal reforms also created a distinction between laws (*nomoi*) of general application included in the new law code, and decrees (*psephismata*), which were generally temporary or more specific enactments passed by the assembly and could not contravene a valid law. An elaborate process, *nomothesia*, was created that removed the power of amending or making a new law (*nomos*) from the popular Assembly. A board of

[35] For a detailed discussion of the legal reforms, with references to primary and secondary sources, see Lanni, *Law and Justice in the Courts of Classical Athens*, pp. 142–148.

[36] Stephen Todd, "Lysias Against Nikomachos: The Fate of the Expert in Athenian Law," in Lin Foxhall and A. D. E. Lewis, eds., *Greek Law in its Political Setting: Justifications not Justice* (Oxford: Oxford University Press, 1996), p. 130.

nomothetai (chosen by lot from the jury pool) heard arguments and decided whether to accept the proposed new law. A procedure that pre-dated the reforms, the *graphe paranomon*, permitted individuals to challenge any legislative proposal in the Assembly as *paranomon* ("contrary to law" or "unconstitutional"), and have a jury hear arguments for and against the law. While it is tempting to think of this procedure as akin to modern judicial review, in practice arguments in our surviving *graphe paranomon* cases are not limited to whether the proposed legislation does or does not contravene existing law but also includes political or policy arguments about whether the legislation is in the city's interest.[37] The Athenian procedures for reviewing legislation may have more in common with a second chamber in a bicameral system than modern judicial review, though this analogy is also imperfect.

Unlike the revision of the laws, *nomothesia* remained in force throughout the period of Athenian independence and, in some scholars' view, had a profound impact on the nature of Athenian democracy.[38] By taking the power to make laws out of the hands of the popular Assembly, so the argument goes, *nomothesia* contributed to a transition in the early fourth century from a radical to a more moderate democracy. However, the effect of *nomothesia* on the workings of the legal system was much more limited: although it may have fostered more consistency among the laws, this process did nothing to alleviate the uncertainty and inconsistency caused by the highly particularized, ad hoc nature of popular court decision-making.

The most suggestive evidence that the Athenians consciously chose a highly flexible, discretionary system over a robust rule of law is provided by the special homicide court procedures which served as a notional antithesis to the popular courts. The unusual procedures in the homicide courts, particularly a rule prohibiting irrelevant statements, made these courts (in theory and, to a lesser extent, in practice) more congenial to

[37] Adriaan Lanni, "Judicial Review and the Athenian Constitution," in Mogens Herman Hansen, ed., *Démocratie athénienne-démocratie modern: tradition et influences* (Geneva: Fondation Hardt, 2010), pp. 235–263.

[38] Hansen, *The Athenian Democracy in the Age of Demosthenes*, pp. 161–177; Martin Ostwald, *From Popular Sovereignty to the Sovereignty of Law: Law, Society and Politics in Fifth-Century Athens* (Berkeley: University of California Press, 1986), pp. 497–524; for an argument that the contrast between fifth- and fourth-century Athens is overdrawn, see Josiah Ober, *Mass and Elite in Democratic Athens: Rhetoric, Ideology, and the Power of the People* (Princeton: Princeton University Press, 1990), pp. 95ff.

formal legal argument. One homicide court speaker describes the special oath taken in homicide cases: "You had to swear the greatest and most powerful oath, . . . in very truth that you would accuse me only concerning the homicide itself, [arguing] that I killed, with the result that, had I done many bad acts, I would not be convicted for any reason other than the charge itself, and, had I done many good deeds, I would not be saved because of this good conduct."[39] The Athenians themselves perceived the homicide courts as focused on the factual allegations in the charge in a way that popular courts were not. Antiphon states, "the laws, the oaths, the sacrifices, the public announcements, and all the other things that happen in a homicide suit, are very different from other procedures because the facts themselves, concerning which the stakes are the greatest, must be known correctly."[40]

While the reasons for the homicide courts' special procedures is necessarily speculative, my own view is that homicide courts' more narrow focus on the homicide charge grew out of an urgent need to foster obedience of and respect for verdicts in a fledgling legal system that was just beginning to assert control over the private use of violence. By limiting the judges' discretion and discouraging evidence about the parties' character and social background, these procedures may have fostered a belief in the impartiality of the judges and thereby encouraged families to appeal to and abide by the results of the official homicide procedures. Moreover, by forcing families to cast their arguments in terms of the narrow question of the homicide, the homicide procedures promoted the view that the homicide was an isolated event to be resolved rather than simply one part of an ongoing and escalating cycle of violence that reached beyond the individual killer and victim to encompass their families as well.

The unusual homicide procedures suggest that the Athenians were capable of imagining a more formal legal approach but reserved this approach for a small minority of cases. At the same time, the idealization of the Areopagus, the main homicide court, as the finest court in Athens[41]

[39] Ant. 5.11. See also Lyc. 1.11–13. For discussion, see Lanni, *Law and Justice in the Courts of Classical Athens*, pp. 75–114.

[40] Ant. 6.6. For similar statements, see Lyc. 1.11–13; Dem. 23. 65–6; Xen. *Mem.* 3.5.20; Ant. 5.8–14; 6.6.

[41] See, for example, Xen. *Mem.* 3.5.20. For discussion, see Lanni, *Law and Justice in the Courts of Classical Athens*, pp. 75–114.

indicates anxiety and ambivalence about the choice to favor flexibility and discretion over consistency and predictability in the popular courts.

In the middle of the fourth century, special procedures were introduced for maritime commercial cases.[42] A written contract was required to bring this type of suit, and the surviving maritime speeches tend to focus more narrowly on the contractual dispute and less on the character of the litigants than similar nonmaritime commercial cases. These differences seem to stem from a need to facilitate trade by offering a predictable procedure for enforcing contracts and thereby to attract foreign merchants to Athens. Further, in judging claims of noncitizens, who made up a significant portion of the merchant litigants in maritime cases, Athenian jurors would be less eager to look beyond the terms of the contract to enforce social norms of fair dealing and good conduct. In this one area of law, the costs associated with flexible justice outweighed the benefits, and steps were taken to narrow the jury's approach in an effort to enhance the predictability of verdicts.

The distinctive procedures in homicide and maritime cases cannot be explained as part of an evolution towards a rule of law: the homicide procedures pre-date the popular courts, while the maritime procedures were introduced toward the end of the classical period. The jarring differences in the level of formality in these courts were the product not of progress but of ambivalence. The varied approach stems from a deep tension in the Athenian system between a desire for flexibility and wide-ranging jury discretion as opposed to consistency and predictability. The choice to favor flexibility in the vast majority of cases reflects not only a normative belief that a wide variety of contextual and equitable factors were often relevant to reaching a just decision but also a political commitment to popular decision-making in the direct democracy. Classical Athens thus serves as an example of a highly contextualized and radically democratic approach to the rule of law.

Conclusion

Greek political thinkers of the fourth century – most notably Plato and Aristotle – reacted against the Athenian democracy's radical approach to

[42] For discussion, see Lanni, *Law and Justice in the Courts of Classical Athens*, pp. 149–174.

the rule of law. Space does not permit a comprehensive treatment of the complicated, and often contradictory, approaches to the rule of law in these authors.[43] Instead, I will offer a few general observations about how these antidemocratic authors rejected the democracy's approach while nevertheless agreeing that flexibility in the interpretation of rules was necessary for justice.

In the *Republic,* Plato favored rule by a few enlightened individuals who are guided by reason and political expertise rather than bound by strict laws. In the *Statesman* he notes that laws are often too rigid and general to reach the best outcome in particular cases: "it is impossible to devise, for any given situation, a simple rule which will apply to everyone forever."[44] In the *Statesman* and the *Laws,* Plato admits that the ideal of rule by enlightened individuals is often not practical, and offers a strict rule of law as a second-best option.[45] In both these works, Plato conceives of a state where the laws are strictly applied and difficult to change; in the *Laws* he repeatedly states that all citizens should be 'slaves to the law.'[46] Yet compliance with law should come first and foremost through internalization of the norms embodied in law rather than through punishment and deterrence and statutes were to include preambles to persuade citizens of the law's virtue.

Aristotle similarly rejected the ad hoc approach of Athenian juries, criticizing radical democracies for their tendency to allow popular decision-making to override the law.[47] He concludes that law should be authoritative in most cases, but admits that they sometimes "go

[43] See, for example, Cartledge, *Ancient Political Thought in Practice,* pp. 96–106; Ryan K. Balot, ed., *A Companion to Greek Political Thought* (Oxford: Blackwell, 2006), pp. 177–265; Cohen, *Law Violence, and Community in Classical Athens,* pp. 34–57; Zena Hitz, "Plato on the Sovereignty of Law," in Ryan K. Balot, ed., *A Companion to Greek and Roman Political Thought* (Oxford: Blackwell, 2009), pp. 367–381. I am particularly indebted to the discussion in Forsdyke, "Ancient and Modern Conceptions of the Rule of Law."

[44] Plat. *Stat.* 294a; for discussion, see Forsdyke, "Ancient and Modern Conceptions of the Rule of Law."

[45] For discussion, see Hitz, "Plato on the Sovereignty of Law"; Balot, *Greek Political Thought,* pp. 212–220; Cohen, *Law, Violence, and Community in Classical Athens,* pp. 43–51.

[46] See, for example, Plat. *Laws,* 715c2–d4. For discussion of Plato's concept of "slavery to the law," see Julia Annas, "Virtue and Law in Plato," in Christopher Bobonich, ed., *Plato's Laws: A Critical Guide* (Cambridge: Cambridge University Press, 2010), pp. 72–73.

[47] Ar. *Pol.* 1292a4; for discussion, see Cohen, *Law, Violence, and Community in Classical Athens,* p. 41.

astray."[48] Elsewhere, he suggests that equity should temper the strict application of written law ("equity is justice that goes beyond the written law"), and that justice is a broader concept than written law: "justice consists in both that which is lawful and that which is fair."[49]

While both Plato and Aristotle advocate a more robust rule of law with a stricter application of written law than that practiced in Athens, both also notably acknowledge the desirability of providing flexibility to ensure justice in the individual case. In the spectrum of Athenian institutional and philosophical approaches to the rule of law we find, in the first legal system we know very much about, the fissure between following generalized rules and doing justice that has haunted debates over the rule of law ever since.

[48] Ar. *Pol.* 1286a23–24. For discussion, see Forsdyke, "Ancient and Modern Conceptions of the Rule of Law."

[49] Ar. *Rhet.* 1.13.13; *NE* 1129b. See also Forsdyke, "Ancient and Modern Conceptions of the Rule of Law."

Rechtsstaat versus the Rule of Law 2

Jens Meierhenrich

> A generous and elevated mind is distinguished by nothing more certainly than an eminent degree of curiosity; nor is that curiosity ever more agreeably or usefully employed, than in examining the laws and customs of foreign nations.
>
> Samuel Johnson[1]

Introduction

The difference between the idea of the *Rechtsstaat* and that of the rule of law is more than a variation on a theme. Theorists and practitioners of law's rule would do well not to equate – for analytical as well as practical reasons – the Anglo-American way of law with what Leonard Krieger called "the German idea of freedom."[2] And yet they have and will – to the detriment, I argue in this chapter, of understanding and prescription.

The eminent Scottish legal philosopher Neil MacCormick is among those who, erroneously, have claimed that "no significant difference" existed between the *Rechtsstaat* and the rule of law.[3] Given MacCormick's standing in the English-speaking world, his argument has been influential, and it is plausible, up to a point. Because the article in which he advanced it enjoys the status of a recurring – if rarely interrogated – footnote, I use it to frame my critique of extant accounts about how the *Rechtsstaat* and the

1 Samuel Johnson, as quoted in *Boswell's Life of Johnson*, vol. 1: *The Life (1709–1765)*, eds. George Birkbeck, Norman Hill, and L. F. Powell (Oxford: Oxford University Press, 1934), p. 89.

2 Leonard Krieger, *The German Idea of Freedom: History of a Political Tradition* (Boston: Beacon Press, 1957).

3 D. Neil MacCormick, "Der Rechtsstaat und die rule of law," *Juristenzeitung*, 39 (1984), 65.

rule of law conceptually relate.[4] The late MacCormick advanced several subsidiary claims, each of which, I submit, is problematic. I take issue with three of MacComick's propositions in particular: (1) that the concepts of the rule of law and the *Rechtsstaat* share the same foundational principles; (2) that the differences between them are merely semantic; and (3) that advocates of the *Rechtsstaat* and the rule of law have been committed to the same ideal of rule. By paying close attention to each of MacCormick's interpretive failings, I hope to provide readers with an improved understanding of the long gestation of the idea of the *Rechtsstaat*, how it relates to that of the rule of law, and why, in the twenty-first century, it may, globally, matter even more than the much-touted ideal of the Anglo-American way of law.

It is commonplace to equate the *Rechtsstaat* and the rule of law. Eminent legal scholars like T. R. S. Allan and Martin Krygier did so very recently.[5] Their inclination – and that of many others – to elide historical, philosophical, and conceptual differences when thinking about these contending visions of law's rule is understandable, sensible even. After all, the tradition of Germany's postwar *Rechtsstaat* – a form of rule that chastized elites invented after World War II to make amends for, and prevent a return to, dictatorship – is an impressive specimen of law-based rule. The constitutional patriotism that its diligent practice has inspired over the last seventy years does bespeak an intellectual convergence of sorts between this latest manifestation of that country's *Rechtsstaat* tradition and the kinds of rule of law practices we commonly associate with England and the United States. But the twenty-first century incarnation of Germany's *Rechtsstaat* is, in key respects, an *aberration* in the institutional evolution of the *Rechtsstaat*-tradition which it is said to represent. Therefore one ought not to generalize, on the basis of Germany's postwar experience alone, about the idea of the *Rechtsstaat* – and its relationship to the rule of law.

[4] That MacCormick's analysis appeared in Germany's leading law journal, the *Juristenzeitung*, founded in 1896, may help explain why he has received so little pushback. And this despite MacCormick's admission that his argument in 1984 contradicted "everything" he had ever read about the *Rechtsstaat*. See MacCormick, "Der Rechtsstaat und die rule of law," 67.

[5] T. R. S. Allan, "Rule of Law (Rechtsstaat)," in Edward Craig, ed., *The Routledge Encyclopedia of Philosophy*, vol. 8 (London: Routledge, 1998), pp. 388–391; Martin Krygier, "Rule of Law (and *Rechtsstaat*)," in James R. Silkenat, James E. Hickey, Jr., and Peter D. Barenboim, eds., *The Legal Doctrines of the Rule of Law and the Legal State (Rechtsstaat)* (New York: Springer, 2014), pp. 45–59.

The universe of the world's *Rechtsstaaten* is not an *n* of 1; it is considerably larger.[6] I submit it is historically, philosophically, and conceptually problematic to reduce the idea of the *Rechtsstaat* to that of the rule of law. Doing so distorts not only the convoluted history, both material and intellectual, of the *Rechtsstaat*'s gestation in Germany, but also, and more importantly, the many histories of its diffusion elsewhere. For there exists a global history of the *Rechtsstaat*. Only it has not yet been written, which is why so few can readily see it.[7] Wrapping one's head around this little-known history necessitates a contextual – rather than a purely conceptual – inquiry into what is a much-misunderstood tradition of governing through law. By examining, with Samuel Johnson, "the laws and customs of foreign nations," we stand to gain an improved understanding of what the *Rechtsstaat* tradition is, how it relates to that of the rule of law, and why this difference matters more than MacCormick thought.

1 *Rechtsstaat* beyond Borders

The idea of the *Rechtsstaat* has – globally speaking – been no less influential than the idea of the rule of law. It has left an institutional imprint on societies far and near, and it has done so for centuries. This continental idea – let us call it "rule under law" – pre-dated the Dicyean conception of the rule of law by half a century. It is widely known that the French term *État de droit* is a literal rendering of the *Rechtsstaat* concept. The French embrace of it represents a successful attempt at transplanting the original logic of the *Rechtsstaat* by way of institutional mimicry.[8] Less well known are other histories of institutional borrowing, many of them farther afield. They are well worth revisiting when it comes to thinking about (embarking on) transitions to – and from – the rule of law. Just as the English way of law found admirers beyond England's borders, there developed elsewhere a demand for the German idea of freedom.

The Afrikaans *regstaat* is derived from the *Rechtsstaat* tradition, as is the Dutch *rechtsstaat*, which, of course, influenced the development of the

[6] The same is true for the rule of law, as I have argued elsewhere. See Jens Meierhenrich, "What the Rule of Law Is . . . and Is Not," in this volume.

[7] I provide a brief sketch in Jens Meierhenrich, *The Idea of the Rechtsstaat: An Intellectual History* (Oxford: Oxford University Press, forthcoming).

[8] R. C. van Caenegem, *Legal History: A European Perspective* (London: Hambledon Press, 1991), p. 185. On this process of institutional borrowing, see also Luc Heuschling, "*État de droit*: The Gallicization of the *Rechtsstaat*," in this volume.

former. Also derivative of the idea of the *Rechtsstaat* are the Italian *Stato di diritto*, the Russian *pravovoe gosudarstvo*, the Polish *państwo prawa*, and the Spanish *estado de derecho*. As a global phenomenon, the *Rechtsstaat* tradition has long rivaled that of the rule of law, which, over the centuries, it has, in certain parts of the world, gradually come to resemble. Given the salience of the *Rechtsstaat* tradition in the history of legalism from the nineteenth century to the present, it is imperative not to equate it, and the manifold practices that it continues to inspire the world over, with the rule of law tradition. Nor must we let local histories of convergence distract us from the fundamental differences – historical, philosophical, conceptual – that long were (and in many cases continue to be) at the heart of these contending ways of thinking about law as rule.

I argue that both the rule *of* law tradition and the *Rechtsstaat* tradition – which I will also refer to, more generally, as the rule *under* law tradition so as to acknowledge the many non-German variants that have sprung up – came to be invented as responses to the rule *by* law tradition. The invention of these traditions took place at around the same time, but in response to very different local exigencies, differences that MacCormick acknowledges, but which he does not take into account.

2 Visions of Politics

To illuminate the differences between the *Rechtsstaat* and the rule of law traditions, I trace their origins to three alternative ways of seeing politics. Let us call them, for simplicity's sake, *absolutism*, *paternalism*, and *liberalism*. Each of these "visions of politics," to use Quentin Skinner's term, provides a fundamentally different perspective on the relationship between state and society. Skinner has spelled out the key disagreements between two of these traditions, absolutism and liberalism:

> One speaks of sovereignty as a property of the people, the other sees it as the possession of the state. One gives centrality to the figure of the virtuous citizen, the other to the sovereign as representative of the state. One assigns priority to the duties of citizens, the other to their rights. It hardly needs stressing that the question of how to reconcile these divergent perspectives remains a central problem in contemporary political thought.[9]

[9] Quentin Skinner, *Visions of Politics*, vol. 3: *Renaissance Virtues* (Cambridge: Cambridge University Press, 2002), p. xi.

Skinner glossed over a third vision of politics, however. I call this vision *paternalism*. My use of the term "paternalism" is anachronistic, but, like absolutism and liberalism, it captures aptly the essence of this third nineteenth-century vision of politics.[10]

All definitions of paternalism center on the interference of a state (or an individual) in the affairs of another. As an exercise of power, this interference takes place against the will of the other, and thus amounts to an intervention in domestic affairs. Paternalism, generally speaking, is founded on the assumption that individuals, whether subjects or citizens, are not capable of acting in their own best interests.[11] Acting on this condescending view of society's members, a subset of rulers in the nineteenth-century, especially in continental Europe, adjusted their vision of politics accordingly. They charted a pathway to rule by blending elements of absolutism and liberalism. Some altered course out of necessity (to stave off revolution), others out of conviction (to initiate reform).

In the case of post-revolutionary France, for instance, "[t]he constitutional arrangements of 1814 marked a positive attempt to invent a workable combination of royal and parliamentary authority."[12] There, an "aristocratic liberalism" developed in the wake of revolutionary defeat.[13] France's royalists were clamoring to sustain the empire by other means. Led by the likes of René de Chateaubriand, Charles Cottu, and Vicomte Jean-Baptiste Martignac, the enlightened wing of the country's

[10] For a defense of Mill's rejection of paternalism, see Richard J. Arneson, "Mill versus Paternalism," *Ethics*, 90 (1980), 470–489.

[11] The range of scholarship is immense. See, among others, Joel Feinberg, "Legal Paternalism," *Canadian Journal of Philosophy*, 1 (1971), 105–124; Douglas N. Husak, "Paternalism and Autonomy," *Philosophy and Public Affairs*, 10 (1981), 27–46; Cass R. Sunstein and Richard H. Thaler, "Libertarian Paternalism Is Not an Oxymoron," *University of Chicago Law Review*, 70 (2003), 1159–1202; Gerald Dworkin, "Moral Paternalism," *Law and Philosophy*, 24 (2005), 305–319; Russ Shafer-Landau, "Liberalism and Paternalism," *Legal Theory*, 11 (2005), 169–191; Jessica Begon, "Paternalism," *Analysis*, 76 (2016), 355–373. See also Christian Coons and Michael Weber, eds., *Paternalism: Theory and Practice* (Cambridge: Cambridge University Press, 2013).

[12] Pamela Pilbeam, *The Constitutional Monarchy in France, 1814–48* (London: Routledge, 2000), p. 3. For a non-European example of a constitutional monarchy, see Tom Ginsburg, "Constitutional Afterlife: The Continuing Impact of Thailand's Postpolitical Constitution," *International Journal of Constitutional Law*, 7 (2009), 83–105. On the common law world, see Cris Shore, "The Crown as Proxy for the State? Opening up the Black Box of Constitutional Monarchy," *The Round Table*, 107 (2018), 401–416.

[13] Annelien de Dijn, "Aristocratic Liberalism in Post-Revolutionary France," *Historical Journal*, 48 (2005), 661–681.

royalist movement during the so-called Bourbon Restoration (1814–1830) dreamt up an institutional architecture to be erected on the foundations of both liberty *and* aristocracy. Their call for "intermediate bodies" – what Alexis de Tocqueville, influenced by the ideas of aristocratic liberalism, called "secondary powers" – designed, as they were, to halt the march of liberalism *and* the restoration of absolutism, also became a rallying cry of long-standing liberals like Charles Dupont-White who, in 1864, presented a case for "liberty along royalist lines."[14]

The fact that even staunch opponents of Napoleon III such as Dupont-White were converted to the cause of aristocratic liberalism goes to show that the country's royalists, save for a few dozen *ultraroyalistes* in the Chamber of Deputies, "were not the mindless reactionaries they are often made out to be."[15] To be sure, France's aristocratic liberals were not democrats; but neither were they defenders of the *ancien régime*. Inspired by Montesquieu's *Esprit des lois*, they favored, both philosophically and practically, a rudimentary form of constitutionalism. To advocates of limited self-binding, the idea of constitutional monarchy was very attractive indeed. As self-declared custodians of ancient (as opposed to modern) liberties, the goal of France's aristocrats was to hold in check the central government in Paris, to mediate between the sovereign and the people. Their authoritarian legalism (borne out of an aristocratic liberalism) vindicated certain demands of the Revolution. They accepted rules for the game of politics (as codified in, most influentially, the Code civil), which gave *citoyens* room for play, but they did not give away the game itself.

Although the European Enlightenment laid the seeds for two revolutions – the 1776 one of thirteen American colonies, and France's Revolution of 1789 – it also paved the way for its opposite. Especially in the German lands, an "enlightened" type of authoritarianism gained popularity. There, several sovereigns (though far from all) discovered reason (or *Vernunft* in German) as a tool of state-building. Rulers like Prussia's Frederick II, better known as Frederick the Great, purported to perfect their societies by maximizing utility, by pursuing reasons of state. To some observers, this "science" of government was a strategic ruse, a cooptation of Enlightenment values in the service of unfreedom.[16]

[14] de Dijn, "Aristocratic Liberalism," 680. [15] de Dijn, "Aristocratic Liberalism," 664.

[16] For an overview, see Charles Ingrao, "The Problem of 'Enlightened Absolutism' and the German States," *Journal of Modern History*, 58 (1986), S161–S180.

But not everyone demurred over this idealized state of affairs. Even the supposed first theorist of the *Rechtsstaat*, Immanuel Kant, took a shine to this third vision of politics. The godfather of nineteenth-century German liberalism wanted reasonable rule – but *not* at all costs. It was his radical followers, not the philosopher himself, who clamored for a revolutionary legalism.[17] It is not only a conceptual but also an empirical distortion to claim, as Hans-Joachim Lauth and Jennifer Sehring do, that the idea of the *Rechtsstaat* "*always* implies the inclusion of human rights."[18] It was not always thus. For most of the history of the *Rechtsstaat*, *rex* mattered more than rights. As Ingeborg Maus, the notable legal theorist, put it: "Kant's entirely contentless, purely formal conception of the *Rechtsstaat* was capable of withstanding post-Enlightenment regressions," by which she meant the injection of the concept with metaphysical or otherwise substantive notions of the public good, including human rights.[19] Attempts "to humanize the practice of law" in the German principalities unlike in France, were not the revolutionary byproduct of "a passion for freedom and a tempestuous demand for reform" by a large class of the citizenry.[20] Instead, they stemmed from "the altruistic paternalism of enlightened authorities eager to perform their duty."[21] Law ruled in this eighteenth-century vision of politics, as it did in France, but the fundamentals of its rule were structured very differently.

Most significantly, the German idea of freedom paid no heed to the principle of equality. The General Land Law for the Prussian States, the *Preußische Allgemeine Landrecht*, is a case in point. Inspired, like the Code civil in France, by Enlightenment thinkers' preferences for codification, the General Land Law left the unequal stratification of Prussian society untouched. "There is no suggestion in the Code that citizens should ever

[17] Reidar Maliks, "Revolutionary Epigones: Kant and his Radical Followers," *History of Political Thought*, 33 (2012), 647–671.

[18] Hans-Joachim Lauth and Jennifer Sehring, "Putting Deficient *Rechtsstaat* on the Research Agenda: Reflections on Diminished Subtypes," *Comparative Sociology*, 8 (2009), 177 (emphasis added).

[19] Ingeborg Maus, *Zur Aufklärung der Demokratietheorie: Rechts- und demokratietheoretische Überlegungen im Anschluß an Kant* (Frankfurt am Main: Suhrkamp, 1994), p. 274 (emphasis added).

[20] Konrad Zweigert and Hein Kötz, *Introduction to Comparative Law*, 3rd ed., trans. by Tony Weir (Oxford: Clarendon Press, 1998), p. 137.

[21] Zweigert and Kötz, *Introduction to Comparative Law*, p. 137.

be free from the tutelage of the state or given the opportunity to create his own social world in a responsible manner."[22]

This crucial difference aside, French legalism and German legalism in this period embodied the same logic of rule. No longer absolutist, but not yet liberal, in the eighteenth and nineteenth centuries the law of both lands was shot through with "paternalistic authoritarianism."[23] It was the age of enlightened despotism, an age that found philosophical justification in Hegel's defense of constitutional monarchy.[24] The institution of constitutional monarchy solved, for Hegel, the problem of social order. It was a way "to reconcile the subjective freedom of individuals with the free and rational direction of public affairs."[25]

Law ruled rather differently across the Channel. In England, liberalism, not paternalism, was the guiding vision of politics, and thus central to the construction of law as a social imaginary. In accordance with this construction, law was widely regarded as a check on – not channel of – sovereign power:

> The Common Law became a mighty weapon in the hands of the Parliamentary party in the struggle against the absolutist prerogatives of the King, for in its long history it had developed a certain tenacity, its very cumbrous and formalistic technique serving to make it less vulnerable to direct attack from above. Ever since then, Englishmen have thought of the Common Law as being the essential guarantee of freedom, serving to protect citizens against the arbitrary inroads of absolute authority.[26]

Although both the concept of the rule of law in England and that of the *Rechtsstaat* in the German-speaking territories were byproducts of rationalism's victory over Christianity's salvation narrative, their ideational and institutional development was owed to "rival Enlightenments."[27]

Nineteenth-century paternalism, as I conceive of it, was a liminal form of rule. Neither purely absolutist nor entirely liberal, it conjured a vision of politics *sui generis*, a vision betwixt and between absolutism and liberalism. It is from this vision of politics that the *Rechtsstaat* tradition sprang.

[22] Zweigert and Kötz, *Introduction to Comparative Law*, p. 137.

[23] Zweigert and Kötz, *Introduction to Comparative Law*, p. 86.

[24] G. W. F. Hegel, *Elements of the Philosophy of Right*, trans. H. B. Nisbet, ed. Allen W. Wood (Cambridge: Cambridge University Press, [1820] 1991).

[25] Bernard Yack, "The Rationality of Hegel's Concept of Monarchy," *American Political Science Review*, 74 (1980), 719.

[26] Konrad Zweigert and Hein Kötz, *Introduction to Comparative Law*, p. 195.

[27] Generally, see Ian Hunter, *Rival Enlightenments: Civil and Metaphysical Philosophy in Early Modern Germany* (Cambridge: Cambridge University Press, 2001).

To fully grasp this liminal moment in the evolution of law, a brief excursus on the rule by law tradition is in order. Why? Because the *Rechtsstaat* tradition has affinities not only with the rule of law tradition but also with the rule by law tradition. Common to all three ways of seeing is the goal of reducing arbitrariness. They view law as an institution capable of stabilizing expectations about social outcomes, of turning "absolute uncertainty" into "organized uncertainty."[28] What separates these visions of politics are the *specific* virtues they ascribe to law.

3 Rule by Law

Thomas Hobbes founded the rule by law tradition, if we believe David Dyzenhaus, "in opposition to the conception of the rule of law exemplified in the writings of Sir Edward Coke according to which the common law, as interpreted by judges, contains fundamental legal and moral principles which condition the content of enacted or statute law."[29] Hobbes had no qualms about authoritarian legalism. He considered it a moral good. For him *any* transformation of sovereign power into legal right was a worthy achievement – even if the state's infrastructural power in a given setting was such that it had the capacity, at any moment, to crush an established system of rights.

Hobbes saw virtue in tempering power, even if it could not be constrained. He did not think rule by law offered a solution to the problem of anarchy. But he did believe authoritarian legality could make life in the state of nature more bearable, hospitable even. As Dyzenhaus writes, "Hobbes makes room for much of what the rule of law tradition takes to be worthwhile about government according to law," but he does it in a "less parochial" and "theoretically and politically more convincing" fashion "than that tradition."[30] Hobbes, a few hundred years before Francis Fukuyama, was thinking about how to encourage transitions to the rule of law.[31] His answer was as simple as it is timeless and wise: expect less from the law and you might see it take on a life

[28] On types of uncertainty, the commitment problems associated with them in times of large-scale social change, and the role(s) law can play in attenuating them, see Jens Meierhenrich, *The Legacies of Law: Long-Run Consequences of Legal Development in South Africa, 1652–2000* (Cambridge: Cambridge University Press, 2008).

[29] David Dyzenhaus, "Thomas Hobbes and the Rule by Law Tradition," in this volume, p. 261.

[30] Dyzenhaus, "Thomas Hobbes and the Rule by Law Tradition," 262.

[31] Francis Fukuyama, "Transitions to the Rule of Law," *Journal of Democracy*, 21 (2010), 33–44.

of its own. Or, as the World Bank put it more recently: "Formal law is usually applied first to nonelites ('rule *by* law'); the shift to 'rule *of* law' occurs when the elites themselves accept the law's limitations."[32]

The concept of law – in the rule by law tradition – presupposes the concept of the state. In this legal imaginary, the sovereign – be it a monarch or government – ranks supreme. William Sherlock, in 1684, gave apt expression to what rule by law meant in the seventeenth and eighteenth centuries, when he declared that "a *Soveraign Prince* does not receive his authoritie from the laws, but the laws receive their authoritie from him."[33] A century and a half later, John Austin provided the philosophical foundation for Sherlock's sentiment, when, in 1832, he established the "scientific" study of law and gave it an auspicious name: legal positivism.

In the rule by law tradition, law is what sovereigns make of it. At their most extreme, they exercise "arbitrary executive powers" and abridge liberties at will.[34] It is a case of legalism as utility. "Rule by law carries scant connotation of legal *limitations* on government, which is the *sine qua non* of the rule of law tradition."[35] The argument goes that as long as a government acts through law – anywhere, anyhow – the rule by law obtains.

Let me relate this tradition to the vision of politics from which, on my account, it sprang. The rule by law tradition, in England and elsewhere, is historically tied up with varieties of absolutism. Addressing Parliament on September 17, 1656, Lord Protector Oliver Cromwell described in the starkest terms the state of law in his deeply divided country: "There is one general grievance in the nation. It it is the law."[36] England's "wicked and abominable laws," he urged, were in Parliament's power to alter.[37] By drawing attention to the arbitrariness of everyday law, Cromwell's opening speech captured an essential feature of the rule by law tradition, a violent

32 World Bank, *World Development Report 2017: Governance and the Law* (Washington: World Bank, 2017), p. 15.

33 William Sherlock, *The Case of Resistance of the Supreme Powers Stated and Resolved, According to the Doctrine of the Holy Scriptures* (London: Gardiner, 1684), p. 196.

34 Charles I. Lugosi, "Rule of Law or Rule by Law: The Detention of Yaser Hamdi," *American Journal of Criminal Law*, 30 (2003), 229 fn. 17.

35 Brian Z. Tamanaha, *On the Rule of Law: History, Politics, Theory* (Cambridge: Cambridge University Press, 2004), p. 92.

36 Oliver Cromwell, *The Writings and Speeches of Oliver Cromwell*, vol. 4: *The Protectorate 1655–1658*, ed. Wilbur Cortez Abbott (Cambridge: Harvard University Press, 1947), p. 270.

37 Cromwell, *The Writings and Speeches of Oliver Cromwell*, vol. 4, p. 270.

tradition that he, ironically, himself kept alive. For Cromwell "deeply distrusted human institutions," which is why he, as an anti-formalist, never developed any expressive attachment to law.[38] Law for him was a means to an end, nothing less but certainly nothing more. As Cromwell thundered in his 1656 speech: "[I]f nothing should ever be done but what is according to law, the throat of the nation may be cut while we send for some to make a law."[39] Cromwell believed in the instrumental function of law. He considered neither morality nor legality one of law's virtues. As contemptible human forms, they were to him nothing but "dross and dung."[40] The way Cromwell saw it, the role of law was incidental, not central, to the creation and maintenance of social order.

The rule by law tradition, as I have sketched it, is relevant to understanding the similarities – and differences – between the two intellectual movements that sought to rein it in: the rule of law tradition and the *Rechtsstaat* tradition. Cognizant of the latter's global reach, and taking my cue from the late Harold Berman, I also refer to the latter as "the rule under law tradition." But let me start with the better-known of the two traditions.

4 *Lex, Rex*

Brian Tamanaha thinks it essential – Jeremy Waldron does not – to distinguish the rule by law tradition from the rule of law tradition. "The emptiness of formal legality," writes Tamanaha,

> runs contrary to the long tradition of the rule of law, the historical inspiration of which has been the restraint of tyranny by the sovereign. Such restraint went beyond the idea that the government must enact and abide by laws that take on the proper form of rules, to include the understanding that there were certain things the government or sovereign could not do. The limits imposed by law were substantive, based upon natural law, shared customs, Christian morality, or the good of the community. Formal legality discards this orientation. Consistent with formal legality, the government can do as it wishes, so long as it is able to pursue those desires in terms consistent with (general, clear, certain, and public) legal rules declared in

[38] David L. Smith, "Editor's Introduction," in idem, ed., *Cromwell and the Interregnum: The Essential Readings* (Oxford: Blackwell, 2003), pp. 4–5.

[39] Oliver Cromwell, *The Letters and Speeches of Oliver Cromwell, with Elucidations by Thomas Carlyle*, vol. 2, ed. S. C. Lomas (London: Methuen, 1904), p. 543.

[40] Oliver Cromwell, *The Letters and Speeches of Oliver Cromwell, with Elucidations by Thomas Carlyle*, vol. 3, ed. S. C. Lomas (London: Methuen, 1904), p. 373.

advance. If the government is moved to do something not legally permitted, it must simply change the law first, making sure to meet the requirement of the legal form. With this in mind, it is correct to conclude that formal legality has more in common with the idea of rule *by* law than with the historical rule of law tradition.[41]

In the rule of law tradition, the concept of the state presupposes the concept of law. This is an inversion of the rule by law tradition, against which advocates of the rule of law, like Sir Edward Coke, railed. In that tradition, as we have seen, the state comes first, and the law follows. Such was also the situation in early modern England.[42] The transition from rule *by* law to rule *of* law there got underway in the sixteenth century, during the reign of King James I, when "the English crown vastly extended its reach – its capacity to motivate its servants – by an appeal to the prestige of English positive law."[43] The turn to law was a calculated move: the Crown was blighted not only by a lack of "coercive power" but also by weak "bureaucratic muscle."[44] The sovereign's attempt to rule through law absolutely had unintended consequences because

> it provided means by which its power could be limited. The country's legalistic Reformation helped to encourage the belief that English common law was in a strict sense omnipotent, that is, was capable of finding answers to every social and political question, including questions that concerned the powers of the church and the monarch. This high view of the common law in general strengthened kings, but as soon as royal policies conflicted with expectations of the legal system, it had the effect of stiffening resistance. By the late 1620s, it had produced a parliamentary deadlock that a much subtler king than Charles would have had difficulty resolving.[45]

England was a dual state, consisting of two halves: a prerogative state and a normative state.[46] Under the Stuart monarchy, the two institutions became direct competitors, a schizophrenic state of affairs that led to the emergence in the realm of what I have elsewhere theorized as

[41] Tamanaha, *On the Rule of Law*, p. 96.

[42] For a more critical account of the rule of law tradition, see Meierhenrich, "What the Rule of Law Is . . . and Is Not."

[43] Alan Cromartie, *The Constitutionalist Revolution: An Essay on the History of England, 1450–1642* (Cambridge: Cambridge University Press, 2006).

[44] John Morrill, "The Stuarts (1603–1688)," in Kenneth O. Morgan, ed., *The Oxford Illustrated History of Britain* (Oxford: Oxford University Press, 1984), p. 301.

[45] Cromartie, *The Constitutionalist Revolution*, p. 33.

[46] More generally, see Jens Meierhenrich, ed., *Dual States: A Global History* (Cambridge: Cambridge University Press, forthcoming).

"authoritarian rule of law."[47] As Alan Cromartie writes, "within the professional world of the lawyers themselves, ideas were being developed that could absorb the royal absolute power within the sphere of legal processes."[48] In other words, seventeenth-century England had more to show for than rule *by* law, but it did not yet possess the rule *of* law.

We can glimpse the antecedents of the rule of law in everyday life. There, the sense of law's omnipotence was amplified by a rise among the English in the demand for litigation and an exponential growth of the legal profession. Between the 1520s and the 1620s, for example, the number of active barristers increased from about fifty to around five hundred. The legalization of everyday life came unexpected to most. An acquaintance of Thomas Hobbes, the Earl of Newcastle, registered his surprise: "[A]fter the Reformation, and dissolution of the abbeys, then the Law crept up, and at last grew to be so numerous, and to such a vast body, as it swelled to be too big for the kingdom."[49]

Despite such misgivings from the landed gentry, respect for the law in the kingdom was at an all-time high. The expanded and increasingly professionalized education of lawyers led to their re-socialization. Henceforth, they exhibited "an increasing readiness to think of common law as general custom, that is, as a set of determinate rules, created by the people. This picture of the law was well adapted to limiting the powers of the monarch," which is why, at that moment in English history, the rule of law tradition was on the precipice of invention.[50]

Thompson called the invention of the rule of law "a cultural achievement of universal significance."[51] And he was right, "the imposing of effective

[47] For the original concept of the dual state, see Ernst Fraenkel, *The Dual State: A Contribution to the Theory of Dictatorship*, trans. E. A. Shils, with an Introduction by Jens Meierhenrich (Oxford: Oxford University Press, [1941] 2017). I here rely on a reformulated version of the concept, as developed in Meierhenrich, *The Remnants of the Rechtsstaat*, where I also elaborate at length the concept of "the authoritarian rule of law," a useful heuristic in dire need of careful conceptualization. For recent usage, and the first proper, if not entirely successful, attempt to operationalize the term, see Yuhua Wang, *Tying the Autocrat's Hand: The Rise of the Rule of Law in China* (Cambridge: Cambridge University Press, 2015), pp. 16–49. For a perfunctory use of the term, see Jothie Rajah, *Authoritarian Rule of Law: Legislation, Discourse and Legitimacy in Singapore* (Cambridge: Cambridge University Press, 2012).

[48] Cromartie, *The Constitutionalist Revolution*, p. 108.

[49] Cromartie, *The Constitutionalist Revolution*, p. 179.

[50] Cromartie, *The Constitutionalist Revolution*, p. 182.

[51] E. P. Thompson, *Whigs and Hunters: The Origin of the Black Act* (New York: Pantheon, 1975), p. 265.

inhibitions upon power and the defence of citizens from power's all intrusive claims," first successfully attempted in England, was a remarkable accomplishment.[52] The jury is still out as to whether the rule of law is "an unqualified human good," as Thompson, controversially, also claimed. But the line of those keen to tell the tale is long. The term itself, as Otto Kirchheimer observed, "is a token of gratitude to a political success story."[53] John Phillip Reid shares that sentiment, though he reminds us that the idea "belonged to the seventeenth and eighteenth centuries. It was the gravid doctrine that formed the cornerstone of the jurisprudence of liberty in the years when liberty was struggling to survive."[54] What is the import of this for understanding the relationship between the *Rechtsstaat* and the rule of law?

Enter Friedrich Hayek. The libertarian Nobel Laureate in economics grew up with the *Rechtsstaat* in his native Austria but became an ardent advocate of the rule of law. Hayek thought the institution of the rule of law superior to that of the *Rechtsstaat.* This in itself raises questions about MacCormick's claim that the *Rechtsstaat* and the rule of law are nigh identical. In *The Constitution of Liberty*, Hayek described with awe the "great event" that he believed set England on its path toward the rule of law: the abolition in 1641 of the country's so-called prerogative courts. "In the debates of the following twenty years," Hayek wrote, "the central issue became increasingly the prevention of arbitrary action of government."[55] Throughout these debates, he noted, "the governing idea was that the law should be king."[56] Hayek found a formula for this idea: "*Lex, Rex.*"

Borrowed from Samuel Rutherford's 1644 treatise by the same title, Hayek used it to heap praise on the English rule of law, specifically on attributes that he thought had been purged from the *Rechtsstaat* tradition in the long nineteenth century.[57] He laid the blame squarely at the door of legal positivism, which, he complained,

[52] Thompson, *Whigs and Hunters*, p. 266. See also Douglas Hay, "E. P. Thompson and the Rule of Law: Qualifying the 'Unqualified Good,'" in this volume.

[53] Otto Kirchheimer, "The *Rechtsstaat* as Magic Wall," in William E. Scheuerman, ed., *The Rule of Law under Siege: Selected Essays of Franz L. Neumann and Otto Kirchheimer* (Berkeley: University of California Press, [1967] 1996), p. 244.

[54] John Phillip Reid, *Rule of Law: The Jurisprudence of Liberty in the Seventeenth and Eighteenth Centuries* (DeKalb: Northern Illinois University Press, 2004), p. 93.

[55] Friedrich A. Hayek, *The Collected Works of F. A. Hayek*, vol. 17: *The Constitution of Liberty*, ed. Ronald Hamowy (Chicago: University of Chicago Press, [1960] 2011), p. 250.

[56] Hayek, *The Collected Works of F. A. Hayek*, vol. 17, p. 250.

[57] Samuel Rutherford, *Lex, Rex: The Law and the Prince* (London: John Field, 1644).

from the very beginning could have no sympathy with and no use for those meta-legal principles which underlie the rule of law or the *Rechtsstaat* in the original meaning of this concept, for those principles which imply a limitation upon the power of legislation. In no other country did this positivism gain such undisputed sway in the second half of the last century as it did in Germany. It was consequently here that the ideal of the rule of law was first deprived of real content. The substantive conception of the *Rechtsstaat*, which required that the rules of law possess definite properties, was displaced by a purely formal concept which required merely that all action of the state be authorized by the legislature. In short, a "law" was that which merely stated that whatever a certain authority did should be legal. The problem thus became one of mere legality.[58]

5 *Rex, Lex*

What Hayek dismissed as "mere legality," most theorists of the *Rechtsstaat* long regarded as the institution's cardinal virtue, certainly up until 1945. After the initial perversion and eventual destruction of the previous *Rechtsstaat* tradition during the Nazi dictatorship, a reinvention, in Germany at least, was attempted. It was a successful experiment in legal reimagination. In this period, the postwar-*Rechtsstaat* began to resemble the rule of law, which is why the likes of MacCormick and Allan and Krygier are in the habit of equating the *Rechtsstaat* and the rule of law, of thinking both concepts express "the same ideal."[59] They do not, except in normative accounts that generalize about the idea of the *Rechtsstaat* solely on the basis of its late modern instantiation.[60]

The constitutional entrenchment of morals in the law by way of the 1949 *Grundgesetz*, while bringing the *Rechtsstaat* in a substantive alignment with the rule of law, did not alter the centrality of the state – its phenomenological significance – in Germany's social imaginary.[61] MacCormick made a crucial observation that becomes relevant here: When German

[58] Hayek, *The Collected Works of F. A. Hayek*, vol. 17, p. 346.

[59] MacCormick, "Der Rechtsstaat und die rule of law," 67.

[60] Martino Mona, "The Normative Content of the Notion of the *Rechtsstaat* in Late Modernity," *Punishment and Society*, 15 (2013), 412–419.

[61] For an early analysis of the moralization of the *Rechtsstaat* during the making of the *Grundgesetz*, see Friedrich Klein, "Bonner Grundgesetz und Rechtsstaat," *Zeitschrift für die gesamte Staatswissenschaft*, 106 (1950), 390–411. On the phenomenology of the rule of law, and Charles Taylor's concept of social imaginaries, see Meierhenrich, "What the Rule of Law Is . . . and Is Not."

constitutional lawyers speak of "the state," he observed, their British counterparts will speak of "the Crown" because "the state" is not an idea relevant to their understanding of the concept of law. It is for this reason, as Nicholas Barber writes, that "the rule of law can pass over one of the core concerns of the *Rechtsstaat*: how to achieve harmony between the state and the law."[62] Despite a convergence in legal practices, the issue Barber highlights is critical to grasping a fundamental difference between the traditions of the *Rechtsstaat* and of the rule of law.

In Germany, the concept of *Recht* (law) stands and falls with the state (*Staat*) – even in the twenty-first century. In the *Rechtsstaat* tradition, law derives from the state. If a shorthand were needed, *Rex, Lex* would be it. The sovereign – whether in the form of a monarch or the people – is law's overlord. A persistent feature in the long and winding history of the German *Rechtsstaat*, Girish Bhat writes, is the "fixed, continuous, and consistently influential role of state power in German aspirations towards a true *Rechtsstaat*."[63] A few years before the end of apartheid, Loammi Blaau reflected on the relationship between the *Rechtsstaat* and the rule of law from a South African perspective. In that country's mixed legal tradition, the idea of the *Rechtsstaat* was well known, as *regstaat* in Afrikaans and as *rechtsstaat* in Dutch. With the future of South Africa in mind, Blaau makes the important observation that in England "from the seventeenth century on the rule of law was a symbol of resistance against attempts by the Stuart kings to institutionalize an absolutist regime."[64] The hallmark of the rule of law tradition, as I use the term, is a belief in the morality of formally enacted rules, in their rightness. In contradistinction to the belief in the utility of formally enacted rules – their usefulness – that I took to be a defining characteristic of the rule by law tradition, in the rule of law tradition the legitimacy of law matters just as much as the legality of law.

In the *Rechtsstaat* tradition, this was not always the case. The invention of the concept began as a play on words. In 1798, Johann Wilhelm Petersen

[62] N. W. Barber, "The *Rechtsstaat* and the Rule of Law," *University of Toronto Law Journal*, 53 (2003), 450.

[63] Girish N. Bhat, "Recovering the Historical *Rechtsstaat*," *Review of Central and East European Law*, 32 (2007), 91.

[64] Loammi C. Blaau, "The *Rechtsstaat* Idea Compared with the Rule of Law as a Paradigm for Protecting Rights," *South African Law Journal*, 107 (1990), 89. See also Reinhard Zimmermann and Daniel Visser, eds., *Southern Cross: Civil Law and Common Law in South Africa* (Oxford: Clarendon Press, 1996).

published *Litteratur der Staatslehre.*[65] It was an effort to describe and defend what he called "the science of the principles according to which a polity should be founded, arranged, and governed" ("*die Wissenschaft der Grundsätze, nach welchen ein gemeines Wesen gegründet, eingerichtet und regiert werden soll*").[66] A disciple of Kant's, Petersen, who is better known under his pseudonym Placidus, endeavored to invert the study of law in the German lands, to popularize a new way of seeing public law. To this end, he made a quip. He heaped a measure of ridicule on the distinguished professors of public law, the "*Staats-Rechts-Lehrer*," by comparing their conservative mores unfavorably with those of a new brand of enlightened thinker, the "*Rechts-Staats-Lehrer.*"

As early as 1796, another of Kant's disciples, Georg Samuel Albert Mellin, made mention of the idea of a "*rechtlicher Staat*" ("legal state"), a German translation of Kant's concept of the "*status iuridicus,*" which appears in several of the latter's writings, including *Zum ewigen Frieden* (*Perpetual Peace*). Recent scholarship has shown that Kant's concept of law was fully formed as early as 1784, more than a decade before the publication of *Einleitung in die Rechtslehre* (1797), which is why at the beginning of the *Rechtsstaat* there stands, as so often in the annals of German political thought, Immanuel Kant.[67] Although Robert von Mohl is credited with coining the term itself, Kant's concept of the *status iuridicus* is widely regarded as the earliest articulation of the idea of the *Rechtsstaat.*

But it is important not to lose sight of key differences in the institutional trajectories of the *Rechtsstaat* and the rule of law: "In contrast to the placid career of the [r]ule of [l]aw throughout the nineteenth century, the German *Rechtsstaat* retained some elements of a snake charmer's performance, remaining an index of partly fulfilled and partly outstanding claims."[68] What dubious features did Kirchheimer have in mind? He, like many other critics of the *Rechtsstaat* – Hans Kelsen prominent among them – was keenly attuned to the danger that the principle of individual liberty could gradually recede into the background and "the liberty of the social collective" ("*die Freiheit des sozialen Kollektivums*") move to center stage.[69]

[65] Johann Wilhelm Placidus, *Litteratur der Staatslehre: Ein Versuch* (Stuttgart: Metzler, 1798).

[66] Placidus, *Litteratur der Staatslehre*, p. 4.

[67] Philipp-Alexander Hirsch, *Freiheit und Staatlichkeit bei Kant: Die autonomietheoretische Begründung von Recht und Staat und das Widerstandsproblem* (Berlin: de Gruyter, 2017).

[68] Kirchheimer, "The *Rechtsstaat* as Magic Wall," p. 245.

[69] Hans Kelsen, *Vom Wesen der Demokratie* (Tübingen: Mohr, 1920), p. 10.

Kirchheimer, with good reason, feared, given the institution's counter-revolutionary history, that rule by *Rechtsstaat* was dangerously susceptible to illiberalism. Leonard Krieger thought the same. He linked the idea of the *Rechtsstaat* to a vision of politics committed to "conservation as well as liberalization."[70] In this vision, no really existing *Rechtsstaat* was "univocally liberal."[71] In contrast to the doctrine of the rule of law, that of the *Rechtsstaat* has always been "concerned more with the redefinition than with the limitation of the state."[72]

Of great significance for the ideational development of the *Rechtsstaat* tradition, Kant aside, were Georg Wilhelm Friedrich Hegel and especially Johann Gottlieb Fichte. The details of their belief systems need not concern us here. Suffice to say, both embraced the distinction between what Kant, in *The Metaphysics of Morals*, called *"Legalität (Gesetzmäßigkeit)"* and *"Moralität (Sittlichkeit)."*[73] Although not new, the separation of law and morals in their philosophical writings gained new traction in that each theorist considered them to be separate but equal categories of analysis. Kant held that the eradication of "*Willkür*," or arbitrariness, was an important step toward freedom. It hinged, he argued, on the provision of legality, not of morality *as such*. Fichte went even further in emphasizing the priority of legality. On his argument, the legality of law can, under certain circumstances, even render law's rule legitimate. A legitimate *Rechtsstaat*, because it contributes to the maintenance of social order, Fichte surmised, was valuable for creating moral citizens.

6 Rule under Law

Instead of seizing upon *rights* as a means of politics, as rule of law theorists were wont to do, the early theorists of the *Rechtsstaat* favored the promotion of *rules*. Instead of elevating, by way of law, the status of individuals, they lowered the status of the state. The codification of rules tempered sovereigns, it did not tame them. And yet the legalization of politics meant that, over time, the arbitrariness of prerogative rule was

70 Krieger, *The German Idea of Freedom*, p. 261.

71 Krieger, *The German Idea of Freedom*, p. 253.

72 Krieger, *The German Idea of Freedom*, p. 253.

73 Immanuel Kant, *Werkausgabe*, vol. 8: *Die Metaphysik der Sitten*, ed. Wilhelm Weischedel (Frankfurt am Main: Suhrkamp, [1797] 1977), p. 324.

becoming a thing of the past. Sovereigns ruled not just *by* law; they also ruled *through* law. *Rex, Lex* was the order of the day.

Whereas in the rule of law tradition, the law has always tended to function as a *limit* to politics, in the *Rechtsstaat* tradition, the law has been both *lever* and *language* of politics. The difference is not trivial. In the former legal imaginary, the law is a constraint on rule, in the latter a conduit of rule. This fundamental difference brings us back to the theoretical relationship between state and society – and the implications of alternative visions of politics. "Liberty," in the *Rechtsstaat* tradition, "is not presupposed by the law but is considered as a product of the law. The distinctive mode of the *Rechtsstaat* lies in the connection between authority vested in the conservative aristocratic state, and protection of the new civil liberties: the latter being understood as a service offered through the state."[74] What we encounter here is the distinction between individual liberty and political liberty, as theorized by Benjamin Constant. The distinction, of which more below, is tied up with the history of the early modern state. The formation of national states in Western Europe went hand in hand with "their progressive appropriation of the means of producing law."[75] The birth of leviathan was accompanied by "a transition from law as a *limitation* on the state to law as a *product* of the state," a development in the history of ideas that had its origins in the decline of the natural law tradition and the rise of command theories of law.[76] Put differently, the facticity of "state law" created the intellectual space for thinking about the "law state," which is how the idea of the *Rechtsstaat* gained in popularity on the continent:

> This occurred in the field of jurisdiction with the growth of courts of justice belonging to the state and their exclusive, rival, or controlling jurisdiction, and also in the legislative field, with the extension of statutes both horizontally – to cover more ground: both public law and private law – and vertically, upwards and downwards. Upwards, for whilst the medieval and proto-modern conception of law placed the highest and theoretically unescapable order of divine and natural law above positive laws, the modern conception acknowledged as "law" only that

[74] Gianluigi Palombella, "The Rule of Law and Its Core," in Gianluigi Palombella and Neil Walker, eds., *Relocating the Rule of Law* (Oxford: Hart 2009), pp. 19–20.

[75] Antonio Padoa-Schioppa, "Conclusions: Models, Instruments, Principles," in idem, ed., *The Origins of the Modern State in Europe, 13th to 18th Centuries*, vol. 3: *Legislation and Justice* (Oxford: Clarendon Press, 1997), p. 365.

[76] Padoa-Schioppa, "Conclusions," p. 365.

which is positively sanctioned by the supreme political authority, the state. Downwards, as in place of the medieval system – which not only recognized independent bodies as something intrinsically legitimate in so far as they were *universitates* or "juridical persons," but also admitted customs and legal doctrines as proper sources of law – we find in the modern era a different principle, by virtue of which it is the state, and only the state, which grants to inferior bodies and social groups the right to create norms – customary or codified – the validity of which is acknowledged in law. The state becomes the first and potentially exclusive source of law: law becomes the law of the state.[77]

In the postrevolutionary period of the nineteenth century, these years of authoritarian renewal, a reactionary idea of the *Rechtsstaat* took hold of Germany. The concern for law and liberty, this hallmark of the liberal variant of the *Rechtsstaat*, was pushed to the margins of legal and political thought. No longer an interventionist state, as Mohl had envisaged it, the *Rechtsstaat* was reimagined as a purveyor of form – not substance. Ernst-Wolfgang Böckenförde thinks this transformation in the discourse about the *Rechtsstaat* was fueled by the fact that some of the goals of its liberal proponents had been achieved.[78] Indeed, there is merit to the claim that the demand for administrative law led to the proliferation of formal (instead of substantive) conceptions of the *Rechtsstaat* in this period. However, the influence of conservative legal thought cannot be gainsaid. We must factor in both material and ideational factors to understand the rise of the reactionary *Rechtsstaat* in the late nineteenth century. Two of its most influential theorists were Friedrich Julius Stahl and Rudolf Gneist.

The religious Stahl, detested the revolutionary furor of 1830 and 1848. And he was an intellectual enemy of Mohl's. More than a few of his contemporaries regarded him as an arch conservative advocate of a Christian state, as someone who administered freedom only in "homeopathic drips" ("*homöopathischen Tropfenteilchen*"). Stahl's definition of the *Rechtsstaat* is, more than anything, proceduralist: "The state shall be a *Rechtsstaat*, that is the slogan, and in reality, also the impulse of our time. It shall determine with precision and firmly secure the nature and boundaries of its reach as well as the free sphere of its citizens … That is the

[77] Padoa-Schioppa, "Conclusions," p. 365.

[78] Ernst-Wolfgang Böckenförde, "Entstehung und Wandel des Rechtsstaatsbegriffs," in idem, *Recht, Staat, Freiheit: Studien zu Rechtsphilosophie, Staatstheorie und Verfassungsgeschichte*, expanded ed. (Frankfurt am Main: Suhrkamp, [1969] 2006), p. 151.

concept of the *Rechtsstaat* ... It does not at all denote the goal (*Ziel*) and content (*Inhalt*) of the state, but only the nature (*Art*) and character (*Character*) required to realize them," that is, the state's substance.[79] Taking a leaf from Stahl, Gneist called for "government by law" ("*Regierung nach Gesetzen*").[80] He helped popularize the notion that the achievement of procedural justice was more important than the pursuit of more far-reaching, substantive forms of justice. Gneist is most famous for conceiving and promoting a system of administrative law courts, what became known as *Verwaltungsgerichtsbarkeit.* That institutional design was progressive without being radical. But despite this liberty-enhancing response to the supremacy of bureaucracy, Gneist was an unapologetic statist who condoned few of the revolutionary ideas of 1789.[81] Kenneth Ledford has summarized well the effects of the failed revolution of 1848: "After 1850, German thought conceived of the *Rechtsstaat* as the 'state of well-ordered administrative law,' including the availability of meaningful review of all administrative actions in judicial form."[82]

A new era of the *Rechtsstaat* began in the late 1870s.[83] Increased state interventionism spelled a rapid expansion of public law that lasted up until World War I. The authoritarian *Rechtsstaat,* with its quest for law and order, became the preferred institutional design of the times. Born of concerted resistance by reactionary forces in the German empire to the idea of the rule of law, as they saw it performed in the kingdoms of England and Scotland, it became a *counterideal.*

Acting as norm entrepreneur was also Paul Laband. The influential jurist distinguished the concept of the *Rechtsstaat* from what he believed to be its

[79] Friedrich Julius Stahl, *Die Philosophie des Rechts,* vol. 2: *Rechts- und Staatslehre auf der Grundlage christlicher Weltanschauung,* 3rd ed. (Heidelberg: Mohr, 1856), §30. The critical characterization comes from Friedrich Christoph Dahlmann, as quoted in Klaus von Beyme, *Politische Theorien im Zeitalter der Ideologien* (Wiesbaden: Verlag für Sozialwissenschaften, 2002), p. 477.

[80] Rudolf Gneist, *Der Rechtsstaat und die Verwaltungsgerichte in Deutschland,* 2nd ed. (Berlin: Springer, 1879), pp. 286–270.

[81] Rudolf Gneist, *Verwaltung–Justiz–Rechtsweg: Staatsverwaltung und Selbstverwaltung nach englischen und deutschen Verhältnissen mit besonderer Rücksicht auf Verwaltungsformen und Kreis-Ordnungen in Preußen* (Berlin: Springer, 1869), esp. p. 57. See also Böckenförde, "Entstehung und Wandel des Rechtsstaatsbegriffs," p. 153.

[82] Kenneth Ledford, "Formalizing the Rule of Law in Prussia: The Supreme Administrative Law Court, 1876–1914," *Central European History,* 37 (2004), 207.

[83] Michael Stolleis, *Geschichte des öffentlichen Rechts in Deutschland,* vol. 2: *Staatsrechtslehre und Verwaltungswissenschaft 1800–1914* (Munich: C. H. Beck, 1992), p. 457.

antonym: despotism (*Despotie*). Whereas rules of law ("*Rechtsregeln*") governed the *Rechtsstaat*, arbitrariness ("*Willkühr*") held sway in a despotic state.[84] And yet, Laband was no liberal reformer. For him, as for most other German-speaking theorists of this period, the *Rechtsstaat* was a state of law, but not necessarily one of morals. Characteristically, Laband wrote of "subjects" ("*Unterthanen*"), not "citizens" ("*Bürger*"), as Mohl had. Laband deemed their station in life subordinate to that of the state and its officials: "The state does not face its members as an equal subject, but as a gentleman equipped with *imperium*," by which Laband meant the power to command.[85] In this formative era, conservative intellectuals stripped the concept of the *Rechtsstaat* of most of the substance with which liberal theorists had equipped it just a few decades earlier. "Beginning with Carl Friedrich von Gerber, passing through Paul Laband up to Georg Jellinek, the conception of the *Rechtsstaat* underwent a profound transformation that marked the definitive defeat of the liberal standpoint."[86] Rights continued to matter, but, as Martin Loughlin explains, "[w]ithin the frame of this positivist jurisprudence, rights are created only through objective law: they therefore are entirely conventional concepts. Once this manoeuvre was set in place, the concept of [the] *Rechtsstaat* itself could be subsumed in the concept of *Staatsrecht*."[87]

To the extent that the rise of the rule of law neutered the sovereign state in England, the principle of the *Rechtsstaat* in the rest of nineteenth-century Europe merely channeled it. When the rhetoric of the *Rechtsstaat* seized the legal imaginations of the chattering classes, the days of the interventionist *Polizeistaat*, and the wanton and condescending rule that was its wont in the sixteenth and seventeenth centuries – especially in the Russia of Peter the Great and the Austria of Joseph II – were numbered. But, again, it would be a mistake to think that law turned liberal with the arrival of the *Rechtsstaat*, let alone democratic, as a result of it. The idea of the *Rechtsstaat*, as Brian Tamanaha reminds us, *predated* liberalism. It was a preexisting

[84] Paul Laband, *Das Staatsrecht des Deutschen Reiches*, vol. 2 (Tübingen: Laupp, 1878), p. 202.

[85] Laband, *Das Staatsrecht des Deutschen Reiches*, vol. 2, p. 202.

[86] Gustavo Gozzi, "*Rechtsstaat* and Individual Rights in German Constitutional History," in Pietro Costa and Danilo Zolo, eds., *The Rule of Law: History, Theory and Criticism* (Dordrecht: Springer, 2007), p. 247.

[87] Martin Loughlin, *Foundations of Public Law* (Oxford: Oxford University Press, 2010), p. 320.

condition, if you will. Unlike the idea of the rule of law, "it is not inherently tied to liberal societies, or to liberal forms of government."[88]

Harold Berman, for example, traced the idea back to the Papal Revolution of 1075–1122, this epic struggle between ecclesiastical and secular forces over the nature of rule. On the European continent, this "total transformation," as he called it, was not limited "to such issues as the struggle for papal control over the church and for the freedom of the church, under the papacy, from secular domination."[89] A whole lot more was accomplished, including, as Joseph Strayer reminds us, "the invention of the concept of the State."[90] The revolution in law that Pope Gregory VII's ultimately failed quest for papal supremacy unleashed was

> closely connected with the revolution *in* the church and the revolution *of* the church, which in turn were closely connected with the revolution in agriculture and commerce, the rise of cities and of kingdoms as autonomous territorial polities, the rise of the universities and of scholastic thought, and other major transformations which accompanied the birth of the West, as it thought of itself – and as it was thought of by others – during the next eight centuries and more.[91]

The medieval revolution in law had long-run consequences for legal development in Europe, especially on the territory of what would become modern Germany, where it established the intellectual antecedents for the rise of the *Rechtsstaat*. As Berman explains,

> The idea of a secular state, which was implicit in the Papal Revolution from its inception, and the reality of the secular state, which emerged out of the historical struggle between ecclesiastical and secular forces that constituted the Papal Revolution were in essence the idea and the reality of a state ruled by law, a "law state" (*Rechtsstaat*). This meant, first, that the respective heads of each body, the ecclesiastical and the secular, would introduce and maintain their own legal systems, that is, would regularly enact laws, establish judicial systems, organize government departments, and, in general, rule *by* law. Second, it meant that the respective heads of each body would be bound by the law which they themselves had enacted; they could change it lawfully but until they did so they must obey it – they must rule *under* law.[92]

88 Tamanaha, *On the Rule of Law*, p. 137.

89 Harold J. Berman, *Law and Revolution: The Formation of the Western Legal Tradition* (Cambridge: Harvard University Press, 1983), p. 23.

90 Joseph R. Strayer, *On the Medieval Origins of the Modern State* (Princeton: Princeton University Press, 1970), p. 22.

91 Berman, *Law and Revolution*, p. 23.

92 Berman, *Law and Revolution*, p. 292.

The *Rechtsstaat* tradition, invented seven centuries after the Papal Revolution, rests, more than anything, on a belief in the *legality* of formally enacted rules, in their lawfulness. Whereas the rule of law, ties in with the concept of the "state-in-society," as Joel Migdal's uses the term, the idea of the *Rechtsstaat* certainly in the nineteenth century and early twentieth century, enabled "the rule of the state *over* society."[93] In this rule under law tradition, as Berman has called it, "[l]aw is the specific voice of the state and expresses its own will: law is not the constraint but rather the 'form' of the state's will."[94]

This brings me to another difference that – historically and philosophically – has set the idea of the *Rechtsstaat* apart from the rule of law tradition. From the outset, the latter turned on the hinge of *individual liberty.* The *Rechtsstaat* tradition, by contrast, was premised on the realization of *political liberty.* Or, as Benjamin Constant put it, "Individual liberty ... is the true modern liberty. Political liberty is its guarantee, consequently political liberty is indispensable."[95] Most nineteenth-century theorists of the *Rechtsstaat*, including those who sought to import, export, or otherwise transplant the institution, were advocating a legalism that guaranteed, first and foremost, political liberty. They were far less concerned than the English (or liberty-seeking Americans) about due process protections for individuals. Whereas in the rule of law tradition, the individual made the state, in the *Rechtsstaat* tradition, the state made the individual, which explains why the majority of theorists and practitioners of the *Rechtsstaat*, up until the middle of the twentieth century, paid more heed to the legality of rules than to their morality.

The Anglo-American way of law was too revolutionary for many on the continent, especially for the absolutist and aristocratic hardliners who were clinging for dear life to governmental power in the old regimes. The rise of that form of paternalism we now call "enlightened absolutism" ushered in a tradition of law that ruled without morals. This counterrevolutionary effort, as Marc Raeff writes,

93 Joel S. Migdal, *The State in Society: Studying How States and Societies Transform and Constitute One Another* (Cambridge: Cambridge University Press, 2001). Palombella, "The Rule of Law and Its Core," p. 20 (emphasis added).

94 Palombella, "The Rule of Law and Its Core," p. 20; Padoa-Schioppa, "Conclusions," p. 366.

95 Benjamin Constant, "The Liberty of the Ancients Compared with that of the Moderns," in idem, *Political Writings*, trans. and ed. Biancamaria Fontana (Cambridge: Cambridge University Press, [1819] 1988), p. 323.

took the form of the codification of law, so as to provide a harmonious, regular, uniform, and stable legal framework within which the dynamic forces of modernity, which had been prodded into being by the *Polizeistaat*, might find their full scope and expression.[96]

During the second half of the eighteenth century, the codification of the *Rechtsstaat* seized the European continent. From one country to the next, sovereigns were "emphasizing the individual's duties at the expense of his rights."[97] The vigorous institutionalization of Europe's *Rechtsstaaten* amplified "the leadership role of the state, that is, of the political power."[98] It is important to not lose sight of the path-dependent effects of these legal developments on the continent. In the late nineteenth century, "every citizen was put to serve the state's requirement of ongoing modernization. It was the last step in the conversion of the single individual from a creative force into an instrument of modernity for the benefit of the state."[99] This history of paternalism, as I have called it, retarded transitions from authoritarian rule and interfered with transitions to democracy. At the same time, it created the conditions for the emergence of the welfare state in the late nineteenth century.

State *dirigisme* – so integral to the German idea of freedom – is anathema to the Anglo-American way of law, which is why Hayek resented the *Rechtsstaat* and was "dreaming the rule of law."[100] In his normative account of the rule of law, Hayek endeavored to subordinate *rex* to *lex*. The way he saw it, the concept of the rule of law was preferable to that of the *Rechtsstaat* because it successfully stood the idea of the latter on its head. Hayek applauded this reversal in the ordering of *rex* and *lex*. Nineteenth-century advocates of legalism, he argued in the 1950s, had on the European continent been faced from the very beginning with "the

96 Marc Raeff, "The Well-Ordered Police State and the Development of Modernity in Seventeenth- and Eighteenth-Century Europe: An Attempt at a Comparative Approach," *American Historical Review*, 80 (1975), 1240.

97 Raeff, "The Well-Ordered Police State and the Development of Modernity in Seventeenth- and Eighteenth-Century Europe," 1240.

98 Raeff, "The Well-Ordered Police State and the Development of Modernity in Seventeenth- and Eighteenth-Century Europe," 1240.

99 Raeff, "The Well-Ordered Police State and the Development of Modernity in Seventeenth- and Eighteenth-Century Europe," 1242.

100 The phrase is David Dyzenhaus's. See his "Dreaming the Rule of Law," in David Dyzenhaus and Thomas Poole, eds., *Law, Liberty and State: Oakeshot, Hayek and Schmitt on the Rule of Law* (Cambridge: Cambridge University Press, 2015), pp. 234–260.

existence of a highly developed central administrative apparatus," one that "had grown up unfettered by the restrictions which the [r]ule of [l]aw places on the discretionary use of coercion. Since these countries were not willing to dispense with its machinery, it was clear that the main problem was how to subject the administrative power to judicial control."[101]

The key difference between the *Rechtsstaat* tradition, with its deep roots on the European continent, and the rule of law tradition, with its Anglo-American heritage, has to do with the question of where the rights of individuals originate. Long-standing differences in legal styles – differences that pre-dated the nineteenth-century discourses about the *Rechtsstaat* and the rule of law – also mattered. They are important to take into account when comparing the two traditions. Konrad Zweigert and Hein Kötz have summarized them succinctly: "Common Law comes from the court, [c]ontinental law from the study; the great jurists of England were judges, on the [c]ontinent professors."[102] In the civil law tradition, to which the idea of the *Rechtsstaat* will forever be tied, "lawyers think abstractly, in terms of institutions; in England concretely, in terms of cases, the relationship of the parties, 'rights and duties.'"[103] Because these differences in legal reasoning do correspond to actual differences "in the [c]ontinental and English mentalities, attributable to different historical developments," one ought to inquire into their moralities and trajectories before rushing to conflate the *Rechtsstaat* and the rule of law.[104]

Similarities notwithstanding, the differences between these legal imaginaries are not trivial. The idea of the *Rechtsstaat* is the less legalistic of the two. Its inherently political – and thus impure – conception caused Hans Kelsen to reject the idea. He, like Hayek, dreamt of a state constituted by law. Kelsen's was an attempt to ground *rex* in *lex* by way of "a wonderful abstract representation of a pyramidal legal system" in which every legal

[101] Friedrich A. Hayek, "Decline of the Rule of Law, Part 2," *The Freeman*, May 4, 1953.

[102] Zweigert and Kötz, *Introduction to Comparative Law*, p. 69.

[103] Zweigert and Kötz, *Introduction to Comparative Law*, p. 69.

[104] Zweigert and Kötz, *Introduction to Comparative Law*, p. 70. See also Paul W. Kahn, *The Cultural Study of Law: Reconstructing Legal Scholarship* (Chicago: University of Chicago Press, 1999). See also Jeffrey C. Alexander, *The Meanings of Social Life: A Cultural Sociology* (Oxford: Oxford University Press, 2003).

norm derived from another legal norm.[105] In the perfectly law-governed state Kelsen conjured, these norms ultimately derived their validity from one "basic norm," the *Grundnorm.*[106] Like Hayek, Kelsen had no use for the concept of the *Rechtsstaat.* Kelsen rejected the "political" assumptions associated with the idea. For him the concept was fatally premised on the state's legal personality – and as such on misguided faith in the supremacy of *rex* over *lex.*[107] An effort to banish the state from the concept of law, Kelsen's pure theory of law, however, had little effect on theories of the *Rechtsstaat* in the 1920s and 1930s. In this time of great disorder, thinkers from Herman Heller on the left to Carl Schmitt on the right were clamoring for a "new statism."[108]

Whereas the idea of the *Rechtsstaat* has long been philosophically and historically intertwined with the theory of the state, the rule of law has not. In conventional usage, the rule of law is more akin to "a quality of, or theory about, legal order."[109] From the perspective of transplantation, this lack of a necessary connection with *rex*, thinks Barber, "may prove a source of strength for conceptions of the rule of law."[110] Whether it is – and under what conditions – is a question for another day.

Conclusion

The supremacy of *rex* over *lex* is not germane to the German variant of the *Rechtsstaat.* The state performs a similar role in the French *État de droit*, and it occupies an elevated position in the Russian concept of *pravovoe gosudarstvo.* It also dominates the law in the Italian *Stato di diritto* and is central to the Spanish *estado de derecho.* Given the global reach of these five languages alone – German, French, Russian, Italian, and Spanish –

105 Mireille Hildebrandt, "Radbruch's *Rechtsstaat* and Schmitt's Legal Order: Legalism, Legality, and the Institution of Law," *Critical Analysis of Law*, 2 (2015), 45.

106 Hans Kelsen, *General Theory of Law and State*, trans. Anders Wedberg (Cambridge: Harvard University Press, [1925] 1949).

107 Giorgio Bongiovanni, "*Rechtsstaat* and Constitutional Justice in Austria: Hans Kelsen's Contribution," in Pietro Costa and Danilo Zolo, eds., *The Rule of Law: History, Theory and Criticism* (Dordrecht: Springer, 2007), pp. 293–319.

108 Meierhenrich, *The Remnants of the Rechtsstaat*, p. 99.

109 N. W. Barber, "The *Rechtsstaat* and the Rule of Law," *University of Toronto Law Journal*, 53 (2003), 444.

110 Barber, "The *Rechtsstaat* and the Rule of Law," 452.

could it be that, contrary to MacCormick's claim, differences in naming are not just semantic? It stands to reason that they are indicative – and constitutive – of more fundamental differences in the social imaginaries that guide us in thinking about the rule of law, and, as such, are worthy of investigation not elision.

The idea of the *Rechtsstaat*, like that of the rule of law, is an invented tradition. In this chapter, I have tried to recover *some* of the logics of its invention. I have tried to sketch in the really existing differences that distinguished in centuries past the *Rechtsstaat* tradition and that of the rule of law – these rival ideas of freedom. The fairly recent rapprochement of these traditions – in their Anglo-American and Franco-German variants – must not cause us to fall prey to retrospective determinism, to settle for a convenient but reductionist view of the *Rechtsstaat* and the rule of law that glosses over the competing visions of politics from which they sprang.

The *Rechtsstaat* tradition, not unlike that of the rule of law, has been anything but static. Rather, it has been subject to reinvention from the get-go. In the nineteenth century, as we have seen, procedural conceptions of the *Rechtsstaat* held sway. In the twentieth century, especially in its latter half, these formal conceptions of the *Rechtsstaat* gradually gave way, in both theory and practice, to substantive understandings of what it means to govern by way of law. In postwar Germany, this has meant that conceptions of the *Rechtsstaat* and of the rule of law have, for all intents and purposes, converged, a trend that has continued in the twenty-first century. It is this recent convergence that likely convinced MacCormick to equate the idea of the *Rechtsstaat* with that of the rule of law. His monochromatic snapshot, however, was just that – a rendering in black and white that concealed the colorful histories of the *Rechtsstaat*, in Germany and elsewhere.

The global reach of the *Rechtsstaat* – rarely acknowledged and barely studied – is in need of comparative historical analysis for reasons theoretical and practical. Instead of lumping together the ideas of the *Rechtsstaat* and the rule of law, legal theorists, intellectual historians, and socio-legal scholars ought to take each idea seriously in its own right – theoretically, empirically, and practically. Studying the world's *Rechtsstaaten* – in the plural and the vernacular – would be a welcome and long overdue contribution to the phenomenology of the rule of law.[111] As one scholar not long ago put it, with Russia in mind,

[111] Meierhenrich, "What the Rule of Law Is . . . and Is Not."

to regard contemporary Germany and the rest of the continental, civil-law-derived Europe, even if implicitly, as polities on an evolutionary common law path, fails to acknowledge the enduring diversity of Western law. Consequently, in order to assess more accurately the prospects of the Anglo-American rule of law in transitional, traditionally statis polities such as today's Russia, a crucial starting-point would be greater intellectual fidelity to the German *Rechtsstaat* as a historical concept.[112]

[112] Bhat, "Recovering the Historical *Rechtsstaat*," 96–97.

3 *État de droit*: The Gallicization of the *Rechtsstaat*

Luc Heuschling

Introduction

This chapter will analyse the discourse in France on the relatively new French expression *État de droit*.[1] After an unsuccessful first rise in its use at the beginning of the twentieth century (1907–1930s), the term has since 1977 progressively informed the language of French constitutional law scholars and even penetrated the language of specialists of other legal disciplines, politicians, journalists, and, to some extent, of ordinary citizens.

1 The International Success Story of a German Term

In French, the term *État de droit* (generally written with a capital "E"), was originally coined in the second half of the nineteenth century (with the first documented use in 1868) as a direct translation of the German term *Rechtsstaat*, coined by Placidus in 1798. When capitalized, *État* means "State" (in German, "*Staat*"), and "*droit*" (in German, "*Recht*") signifies "law." In English, the term *Rechtsstaat* and its various foreign replicas are translated either as "rule of law" (for example, in the EU Treaties), which is quite a broad translation, or, more literally, by "Law State," "Legal State," or "Rule of Law State." I would also propose "Lawful State," having regard to Locke's classic expression of "Lawful Government." It should be noted, however, that some French scholars, such as Maurice Hauriou and Mireille Delmas-Marty, and some international law experts prefer to write *État de droit* with a small "e," especially in the context of international law. Thus, they delete any reference to the "State," a complex term that is central in the

[1] Due to space constraints, the use of the *État de droit* term in other French-speaking places (Belgium, Switzerland, Luxembourg, Canada, Africa, etc.) or in international law cannot be analyzed. For a more comprehensive treatment, including an exhaustive bibliography, see especially Luc Heuschling, *État de droit, Rechtsstaat, Rule of Law* (Paris: Dalloz, 2002).

classic legal scholarship of continental Europe but ignored in the English tradition. Using the term *état* with a small "e," which simply signifies "situation" or "status," suggests that the expression "*état de droit*" can be applied to any situation, to States, of course, but also to polities that do not qualify as such (for example, international organizations).

Although centered on France, this chapter has a broader scope: it raises some general questions regarding the globalization or, to put it more cautiously, the internationalization of the German *Rechtsstaat* discourse. Since the 1990s, that discourse has taken a strong lead – at least in the Western debate – on matters of "nomocracy", an expression here used as a culturally neutral, generic term. Often, the western debate tends to be reduced to two models: on the one side, the *Rechtsstaat* intellectual tradition and its current implementation in German positive law and, on the other, the so-called rule of law model, in which, notwithstanding some fundamental differences, especially regarding judicial review of statutes and the very concept of Constitution, the English and US traditions are merged. Other (Western or non-Western) traditions are neglected or marginalized.

The term *Rechtsstaat* is one of the most successfully exported items of German legal scholarship: since the end of the nineteenth century, it has been adopted in almost all European languages and even outside Europe. It gave birth, for example, to "*Stato di diritto*" in Italian, "*Rättsstat*" in Swedish, "*Państwo prawne*" in Polish, "*pravovoe gosudarstvo* (правовое государство)" in Russian, "*shteti i të drejtës*" in Albanian, "*hukuk devleti*" in Turkish, "*Estado de derecho*" in Spanish, "*dawlet al-qanoun*" in Arabic, and "*Hôchikokka*" or "*Hôchikoku*" in Japanese. Each discourse was inspired either directly by the German model or by the use of a literal replica by some other system; the use of *État de droit* in French-speaking African countries, for example, has been strongly influenced by the approach of France and such international organizations as the EU and the World Bank. In some jurisdictions, the impact of this "global" diffusion of German legal terms – another illustrative example is the success of the term "*Grundrechte*" (fundamental rights), instead of "*droits de l'homme*" – and German solutions (for example, the institution of the *Bundesverfassungsgericht*, its case law on human dignity or on "*Solange*," the eternity clause of Article 79(3) *Grundgesetz*, militant democracy)[2] is such that scholars start to, for example, speak

[2] For a first insight into this vast field: Ulrich Battis et al., eds., *Das Grundgesetz im internationalen Wirkungszusammenhang der Verfassungen: 40 Jahre Grundgesetz* (Berlin: Duncker und

about the "Germanization" of constitutional law and of constitutional law scholarship.[3] Certainly, an increasing number of jurists around the world use the expression *Rechtsstaat* or, more frequently, its local translation. Their *language* may be Germanized, but has their *mindset* as legal practitioner or scientific scholar also been influenced by German ideas?

One would expect so, as words – unless they are synonyms or lies – are not neutral (i.e., not interchangeable): they convey certain specific meanings. Law is expressed by language: to change the former, the easiest and most direct way is to change the latter; one rewrites the text, for example, by inserting the domestic translation of the term *Rechtsstaat* at the fore-front of the Constitution.[4] By changing the words people use when thinking about, or interpreting, legal texts, one may change their preconceptions thereof and, thus, indirectly, change the law. Yet, however reasonable it might appear, the working hypothesis that equates the Germanization of juridical language with the Germanization of the local legal mentality and/or legal norms is not always valid. This is obvious in the French *État de droit* discussion initiated by Léon Duguit: While the phrase, as he used it, stemmed from the German word, none of its meaning did. One may wonder whether part of the current international success of the term *Rechtsstaat* is just a fashion or a new buzzword.

If, however, the Germanization of the terminology amounts to a substantial change inspired by German views – as has happened in France in several cases – *why*, *how*, and to what *extent* did this change take

Humblot, 1990); Christian Starck, ed., *Grundgesetz und deutsche Verfassungsrechtsprechung im Spiegel ausländischer Verfassungsentwicklung* (Nomos: Baden-Baden, 1990); Klaus Stern, ed., *60 Jahre Grundgesetz* (München: C. H. Beck, 2010); Uwe Kischel, ed., *Der Einfluss des deutschen Verfassungsrechtsdenkens in der Welt. Bedeutung, Grenzen, Zukunftsperspektiven* (Tübingen: Mohr Siebeck, 2014); Constance Grewe, "Les influences du droit allemand des droits fondamentaux sur le droit français: le rôle médiateur de la jurisprudence de la Cour européenne des droits de l'homme," *Revue universelle des droits de l'homme*, 16 (2004), 26–32.

[3] Regarding Spain, see, for example, Pedro Cruz Villalón, "Das Grundgesetz im internationalen Wirkungszusammenhang der Verfassungen: Bericht Spanien," in Ulrich Battis, Ernst Gottfried Mahrenholz, and Dimitris Tsatsos, eds., *Das Grundgesetz im internationalen Wirkungszusammenhang der Verfassungen: 40 Jahre Grundgesetz* (Berlin: Duncker und Humblot, 1990), p. 93.

[4] Begun in Bavaria after World War II (Constitution of 1946, art. 3; on federal level: art. 28 *Grundgesetz* 1949), the constitutionalization of the term *Rechtsstaat* has occurred in Turkey (Constitution of 1961, art. 2), then in Portugal and Spain in the 1970s, and then in Brazil in 1988, before becoming an international trend after the fall of the Berlin Wall (see, among others, Romania, Bulgaria, Slovenia, Poland, Estonia, Russia, Switzerland, Finland, Benin, Togo, Burkina Faso, Madagascar, and the Democratic Republic of Congo. For a recent European example, see also the 1814 Constitution of Norway, as amended in 2012.

place? Is it possible to induce a change of law – even a paradigmatic one – by simply adding to a given legal system a new, catchy phrase taken from abroad, such as *Rechtsstaat*? What is the power of this particular term? In France, as in some other countries, scholars, not legislators, were the driving force behind the transplantation of the *Rechtsstaat* term, which, at least at the beginning, was totally external to positive law, as the term was not part of the latter's official terminology. What was the function of this scholarly notion? Was it merely descriptive, serving, for scientific investigators, as an external analytical tool in order to screen, identify, and classify the given content of one or all legal systems? Or was it prescriptive, serving politicians, judges, citizens, and scholars in their endeavor to conserve the status quo, to re-read open-textured provisions in light thereof, or to radically re-write the law? Or was it both descriptive *and* prescriptive?

Through the emblematic, albeit not totally representative, example of France – France stands here for the type of countries with a long-standing, liberal and democratic nomocratic tradition, as opposed to new democracies evolving from a dictatorial past – this chapter provides a first, necessarily incomplete insight into the "shadow side" (i.e., the often-overlooked side that some may even call the "inglorious" side) of the internationalization of the German *Rechtsstaat* discourse. Yet, this shadow side matters, for various reasons. Although the two "global" models mentioned above largely outshine the French *État de droit* (specifically, its system of judicial review that lags behind),[5] French public law still serves as a source of inspiration to certain regimes, be they former colonies or not, that are not necessarily looking for the most liberal solution.[6] France has also contributed to the worldwide diffusion of the term *Rechtsstaat*, by conditioning, since the Conference of La Baule (1990), its support to African countries, *inter alia*, on their *État de droit*. Furthermore, speaking of models and their diffusion presupposes an understanding not only of how, but also to what extent the German discourse has been adopted abroad. From this perspective, this chapter analyses both the

[5] Michel Fromont, "Les mythes du droit public français: séparation des pouvoirs et État de droit," in Patrick Charlot, ed., *Utopies: Études en hommages à Claude Courvoisier* (Dijon: Éditions universitaires, 2005), pp. 293–302; Olivier Jouanjan, "Le Conseil constitutionnel est-il une institution libérale?" *Droits*, 43 (2006), 73–90.

[6] See, for example, the Constitutional Council of Kazakhstan (Const. 1995, art. 71 ff). In the Democracy Index established by *The Economist* (2017), Kazakhstan is ranked 141 out of a total of 167 countries; it is qualified as an "authoritarian regime." On the reception of the *Rechtsstaat* term in Italy, see Eric Carpano, *État de droit et droits européens* (Paris: L'Harmattan, 2006).

displacement and resistance (be it micro- or macro-resistance) of the former French nomocracy tradition, a tradition that some English-speaking scholars would call "political constitutionalism" as opposed to "legal constitutionalism." Indeed, most of the pre-*État de droit* theories in France conveyed, at least since 1789, a strong distrust of the power and independence of courts; it favored non-judicial (political) organs to be the guardians of the supremacy of the Constitution – an idea that, now, appears rather strange to many people around the world because courts are frequently considered the "natural" bulwark of the law, including the Constitution. The most influential definition of the new *État de droit* phrase, that is, the concept that emerged in the 1920s and was later unearthed after 1977, established precisely this strong link between the existence of a legal norm and its protection by a court. It paved the way for a radically new vision of the judges' role in democracy, an issue that was – and still is – particularly sensitive in Montesquieu's home country. From this historical angle, this chapter also offers a broader picture of the diversity of (Western) understandings of nomocracy.

2 An Analytical Framework

Legal transfers are highly complex phenomena. When applied to such an elusive object as *Rechtsstaat* and its many meanings, the complexity is even greater.

First, even when freely chosen (as was the case with France's and with most other countries' importation of *Rechtsstaat*), legal transfers are rarely complete. That limitation applies where the object at stake is a small set of technical provisions of some code (i.e., some "rules") and even more so when the transfer concerns a multifaceted and elusive intellectual construct such as the *Rechtsstaat* discourse, a "principle" or even "meta and macro-principle" with several series of components and subcomponents. In the transfer, some elements or nuances may be deleted, transformed, or added; its scope (or target) may be reduced, expanded or reconfigured. The translation is creative or partial. It seems highly difficult – Pierre Legrand even considers it impossible – to transplant (or, more precisely, to recreate) the cultural and social background of the transferred object.[7] Thus, how far

[7] Pierre Legrand, "The Impossibility of 'Legal Transplants,'" *Maastricht Journal of European and Comparative Law*, 4 (1997), 111–124. For an assessment of this debate, see Günter

does the French *État de droit* discourse, and similar discussions in other countries, diverge from its German origin? As already mentioned, some French scholars chose to change the French version's spelling (and, thus, its sense/scope), by using a small "e." However, even when the term was exactly the same (*État de droit* with a capital E), its content has always been transformed and adapted. The most extreme example is the enucleation process operated by Duguit, the first to use the French phrase *État de droit* as a notion applicable to French law: he stripped the German term *Rechtsstaat* of all its German content, keeping just the (attractive) shell. Carré de Malberg and Hauriou imported certain German reasoning along with the term, but, at the same time, gave it a more radical turn.

Secondly, a transfer may consist in an almost immediate break (i.e., the legislature copies some specific foreign rules and ensures their implementation) or be the result of a more-or-less long "infiltration" process. If the object at stake has many facets and is, itself, evolving over time, as is the case with the German discourse surrounding the term *Rechtsstaat*, a first part of this larger set of ideas may be introduced, at some point, by some German-speaking law professors who diffuse it amongst colleagues and, later, practitioners. Once this first transfer has taken root, the transplantation either stops there (a one-shot Germanization) or acts as a cultural bridge that opens the way for future transfers from Germany. Such latter transfers may be either: (a) sporadic (enrichments and evolutions of the new key term, once transplanted from Germany, are mainly home grown or are influenced by some other foreign system); (b) frequent; or (c) structural (Germanization amounts to an exclusive reorientation of national scholars and practitioners toward German legal thinking). France's *État de droit* discourse is currently somewhere between hypotheses (a) and (b), with hypothesis (c) definitely not being applicable.[8]

Thirdly, as botanists well know, grafts may be rejected. The success of a transfer, especially one that concerns a change to a fundamental issue (as one would expect to be the case here), depends on various parameters.

Frankenberg, ed., *Order from Transfer: Comparative Constitutional Design and Legal Culture* (Cheltenham: Edward Elgar, 2013).

[8] See Olivier Beaud and Erk Volkmar Heyen, eds., *Eine deutsch-französische Rechtswissenschaft? Une science juridique franco-allemande?* (Baden-Baden: Nomos, 1999); my book review thereof in *Revue internationale de droit comparé*, 55 (2003), 995–1000; Constance Grewe, "Das deutsche Grundgesetz aus französischer Sicht," *Jahrbuch des öffentlichen Rechts der Gegenwart*, 58 (2010), 1–14.

Roughly, supply and demand must meet. What is offered by the German side, under the heading of *Rechtsstaat*, and what a certain country is looking for, given its own needs and constraints, must more or less correspond. The *Rechtsstaat* package must be attractive, not necessarily *in se*, but for that country's elite at that particular moment. The probability of a transfer decreases if the country in need of a solution (the potential "importer") has, in general, an ethnocentric attitude and if the authority of the potential "exporter" is low. After the fall of the Berlin wall, the countries of Central and Eastern Europe were keen to abandon their (communist) tradition and to look towards the West. German Constitutional law was, then, a highly esteemed model of how to overcome a dictatorial experience. In comparison, the conditions for Germanization in France were much more difficult. From 1789 until at least the end of the nineteenth century, France was at the forefront of modern progress in matters of nomocracy; France was proud of its own genius and tradition, and often saw itself not as an importer, but as an exporter, of its law and legal scholarship. When, during the Third Republic (1870–1940), some elements of the various German *Rechtsstaat* theories found their way into parts of the French constitutional scholarship, the conditions for such a transfer were seemingly the worst possible: at crucial moments during this long infiltration process (in 1870, 1914, and 1939), Germany was France's military and civilizational arch-enemy. Yet, one aim of the Gallicization of the *Rechtsstaat* discourse was to subvert a central and long-standing feature of France's Constitution and legal system.

3 The Gallicization of the *Rechtsstaat*: Three Historical Stages

Looking at it from a certain historical perspective, the current international success of the *Rechtsstaat* term is astonishing. In the eighteenth and nineteenth centuries, the driving liberal models in constitutional law were, mainly, England, the United States, and France. What *liberal* politician, philosopher, or law professor would have been interested in German law or legal scholarship at that time, as both lagged behind the standards set by the others? In 1881, in a famous letter to the Prussian Minister Gustav von Gossler, Bismarck mocked the elusiveness of the "artificial term" ("*Kunstausdruck*") *Rechtsstaat* (not a particularly original criticism); more interestingly, he pointed out that the term had yet to be translated into any foreign language, which was quite true. What, then, made foreign jurists change their attitude? Regarding its reception in France, three crucial periods can be distinguished: the nineteenth century, the early twentieth century (the so-called golden era of classic public law scholarship during the Third Republic), and the period since 1977.

First stage

During most of nineteenth century, until the coming of the Third Republic (1870–1940), the various *Rechtsstaat* debates did not give rise to any transfers in France. Although the (normative) concept of *Rechtsstaat*, as defined by Rotteck, Welcker, and Mohl during the *Vormärz* Era (1815–1848), was known, at least to some extent, in France, it had not attracted any sufficient interest leading to its importation. Indeed, most of their books on the subject found their way to the shelves of public libraries in Paris. Even though French constitutional discussions were very often focused on national history (before and after 1789) and the English model, exchanges between French and German liberals and scholars took place. In 1844, Mohl's famous work *Die Polizeiwissenschaft nach den Grundsätzen des Rechtsstaats* was even reviewed in a prominent French legal journal, where the term *Rechtsstaat* was translated by *État légal* ("*légal*" in that case meaning "statutory"). What was missing was not so much the supply, but the demand: no French thinker was interested in transplanting the German term into French discourse on French law. Indeed, it is one thing to translate a German term into French and use that translation to present *German* debates about *German* law (this occurred in France in 1844, 1868, 1877, 1901, 1903, etc.); it is quite another to apply the newly coined French phrase to *French* law (this first happened in 1907, with Duguit). This second step enables that French phrase to be used to *rethink*, in light of some German (normative) concepts, *French* law, as was later to happen with Carré de Malberg and Hauriou. The German *Rechtsstaat* theory during the *Vormärz* period was clearly a normative, natural law construct. It was used by liberal forces to seek (liberal) changes to positive law and to legitimize them once they were achieved. Yet, its substantive content was inspired by, or was similar to, Western (especially French) ideals of modern constitutionalism, with one major qualification: German liberalism, as conveyed by the *Rechtsstaat* discourse, was less liberal (less "aggressive") than French liberalism with regard to: the right to resist, the principle of national sovereignty, and the parliament's power vis-à-vis the monarch. This explains the lack of interest, or silence, on the French side.

But if the French rejected the phrase *Rechtsstaat*, which key term(s) did they use to convey their own understanding of nomocracy? The question matters in order to identify the French intellectual landscape of the pre-*État de droit* period and to measure how far that terminology and mind-set has, or has not, changed after 1907. Theories about nomocracy are expressed not only by thousands of words, sentences, and texts – book shelves are full of them – but, very often, their essence, or even their entire message, is supposed to be encapsulated in a single word, a key term or a catchy phrase. The latter both informs and reflects people's reflection in the field: by changing the paradigmatic words, scholars may indirectly trigger a change in human reality on a paradigmatic issue; by looking at those words, especially when a new one pops up, an observer may also detect an incoming-yet-invisible tide.

An historical and comparative discourse study shows that, regarding the matter of nomocracy, the language of legal thinkers and practitioners in Europe has, since the Enlightenment, encompassed not fewer than four types of key terms.[9] Quite often, they were synonyms, or, if their content differed substantially, they served the same function: each type conveys a certain idea of a polity subject to, and regulated by, law (i.e., nomocracy, as a generic term). The first category of terms refers to a well-ordered polity in which the *res publica* matters and the common good is strongly linked to law, i.e., the key term "*République*" in French (Rousseau), "*Republik*" in German (Kant), and "Commonwealth" or "Republic" in English (for example, Locke, Coke). The second type of key term encompasses the term "*État*," "*Staat*," or "State" in the sense of a State defined as an artificial person (for example, Hobbes, Gerber, Jellinek, Esmein, and Carré de Malberg), and, as such, informed by law (positive law and, sometimes even on a higher level, the social contract, i.e. natural law). The third type is inspired by the classical Greek and Roman terminology: Aristotle's "*nomon archein*," Pindar's "*nomos basileus*," Titus Livius' "*imperia legum*," the Digest's "*lex est omnium regina*." It gave birth, inter alia, in English to "government of law(s)," "rule of law," "due process of law," "reign of law" (the alternative key term proposed by Ivor Jennings), "empire of laws," "nomocracy," and, more recently, "principle of legality." Equivalent terms are: in French, "*règne de la loi*," "*principe de légalité*," "*Loyaume*" (instead of "*Royaume*"), "*prééminence du droit*," in German "*Herrschaft der Gesetze*," "*Rechtszustand*," and some others. The fourth type is a combination of the terms "State/*Staat*/*État*" and "law/*Recht*/

[9] Heuschling, *État de droit, Rechtsstaat, Rule of Law*, pp. 35ff, 49ff, 169ff, 323ff, 343ff.

droit": the most iconic example is, of course, *Rechtsstaat* together with some similar terms such as "*Verfassungsstaat*" (Constitutional State) and "*Gesetzesstaat*" (State bound by statutes). But, even in the past, before its translation into foreign languages, the German *Rechtsstaat* was not unique.[10] In France, Bodin, in his famous treaty *Les six livres de la République* (1576), defined "*Republique*" as a "*droit gouvernement*," "*gouvernement*" being understood not in a strict sense as it is usual today (meaning the cabinet), but in a larger sense (encompassing all public authorities, i.e., the State). Bodin's expression was translated by his English translator in 1600 as "lawful government," an expression that, later, was also put forward by Locke. Yet, Bodin's and Locke's attempts to introduce this potential key term into the lexicon failed, unlike the German (and now worldwide) success story of *Rechtsstaat*, which, in the context of the EEC and EU, gave rise to analogous terms like "*Rechtsgemeinschaft/Communauté de droit* (Lawful Community)" and "*Union de droit* (Lawful Union)."

In any given society, it may happen that, within this vast field, there exists only one consensual – even sacred – key word that is an absolute "Hurrah! Word."[11] Of course, many people may, for various reasons, understand this key term in different ways: referring to the same word does not imply a reference to the same concept or meaning. This situation may be observed, for example, in England, although with qualification, since Dicey popularized the term "rule of law" in the late nineteenth century. Similarly in Germany where, after 1945, the notion of the "*Rechtsstaat*" became the unrivalled iconic term, even though it had fallen into oblivion by the end of the preceding century. (It had, for example, been largely absent in the classic constitutional law writings of Laband, Gerber, and Jellinek, who focused on the term *Staat*, defined as a legal person, and,

[10] Cf. Ernst-Wolfgang Böckenförde, "The Origin and Development of the Concept of the Rechtsstaat," in his *State, Society and Liberty: Studies in Political Theory and Constitutional Law*, trans. J. A. Underwood (New York: Berg, 1991), p. 48: "Rechtsstaat is a term peculiar to the German-speaking world; it has no equivalent in any other language . . . French legal terminology has no comparable words or concepts whatever."

[11] The term is borrowed from C. K. Ogden and I. A. Richards, *The Meaning of Meaning: A Study of the Influence of Language upon Thought and of the Science of Symbolism*, 2nd ed. (London: Kegan Paul, 1927), as quoted in Stéphane Beaulac, "The Rule of Law in International Law Today," in Gianluigi Palombella and Neil Walker, eds., *Relocating the Rule of Law* (Oxford: Hart, 2009), p. 222.

later, under the Weimar Republic, with respect to such prominent scholars as Smend or Kelsen.) Key terms may fall out of fashion; the conceptual framework legal scholars use in order to systemize and inform the study of legal materials may vary greatly. Therefore, the collective reflection on nomocracy may be split into different strains, each one fighting under its own flagship term. Competing terms are met with open skepticism or even harsh criticism as a "Boo! Word"; each key term only reflects the ideas of one segment of the discussants, even though some convergences may be observed.[12]

Indeed, in France, before 1907, there was not one, but several key terms: in administrative law, the case law of the famous *Conseil d'État* and the administrative law scholarship (which in France preexisted the academic discipline of constitutional law) turned on the phrase "*principe de légalité.*" In French political thought and constitutional law scholarship, the central expressions used were, mainly, "*État,*" defined as a legal person, and "*République.*"

Second stage

The transplantation of *Rechtsstaat* took place during the Third Republic or, more precisely, in the period from 1907 to the 1930s. The conditions for that transfer were rather complex because, in some ways, they were easier and in others more difficult.

On the German side, the "supply" both decreased and changed. After 1870, the *Rechtsstaat* discourse disappeared almost entirely from the classic German constitutional law scholarship. As already mentioned, in the leading works of Gerber, Laband, and Jellinek, the term *Rechtsstaat* was overshadowed and marginalized by the key term *Staat,* defined as a state, required only to obey its own positive laws according to the self-limitation theory. Following the influential writings of Otto Bähr, Rudolf Gneist, and Otto Mayer, the *Rechtsstaat* term migrated to the then-nascent administrative law scholarship, where it operated to support a well-functioning system of administrative justice run by specialized courts and to protect the subjective rights of individuals.

On the French side, reactions to German legal thought were ambivalent. After the military disaster of 1870, a crucial mission of the entirely reorganized French university system was to reinvigorate the nation's forces by

[12] Ogden and Richards, *The Meaning of Meaning.*

"learning from the enemy." Most of the influential scholars, who are still considered the founding fathers of French constitutional law scholarship (Duguit, Carré de Malberg, Hauriou; but not Esmein), focused on the German debates, albeit with mixed feelings. Like many public lawyers in continental Europe, they were fascinated by the depth and richness of the German *Staatsrechtslehre* and *Staatslehre*. Yet, at the same time, for epistemological and patriotic reasons, they often adopted a critical, if not hostile, stance. Value neutrality and legal positivism were rejected by most French public law scholars, who, until the 1930s, clung to various natural law doctrines. The moral values they cherished, especially in the context of the growing tensions with Wilhelmine Germany, were those of France; any scholar who was considered to have come too near to German ideas had to face harsh criticism, as happened to Duguit and Carré de Malberg.

In Italy, in the 1880s, scholars and politicians had transplanted the term *Rechtsstaat* into Italian in order to reimagine their own (inefficient) system of judicial review of administration in light of the German discourse developed in the field of administrative law by Gneist, Mayer, and others.[13] In France, the home of the famous and often copied *Conseil d'État*, whose judicial review of administration was based, conceptually, on the idea of the protection not of subjective rights (as in Germany), but of objective law, such a transplant was simply unthinkable. In France, something different was at stake in the Gallicization of the *Rechtsstaat* discourse. Two approaches can be distinguished.

Fascinated by, and yet fiercely critical of, the powerful intellectual system of German scholarship, Duguit was the first to introduce, in 1907, the term *État de droit* as a concept applicable to French law. Yet, if one looks at it closely, this transfer was rather peculiar because Duguit transplanted the German *term* but rejected *all the meanings* that, at that time or before, were attached to it in Germany. He rejected the positivist theory of self-limitation of the State (Jellinek, Ihering) and the definition of the State as a legal person (*personne morale*); he was not particularly interested in Gneist's ideas on administrative courts nor in any of the previous *Rechtsstaat* theories (such as those of Mohl and Stahl). So, why did Duguit transplant the German term? Two possible reasons may be advanced. First, the term *Rechtsstaat/État de droit* perfectly fit into

[13] On the reception of the *Rechtsstaat* term in Italy, see Eric Carpano, *État de droit et droits européens* (Paris: L'Harmattan, 2006).

Duguit's intellectual system, the latter being entirely focused on the subjection of the "*État*," defined as a pure phenomenon of might external to any law, to the "*droit*," the law, which Duguit defined by referring both to positive law and, on a higher level, to the ideal of social solidarity. To neatly summarize it in the language of mathematics: "*État*" + "*droit*" = "*État de droit*." Secondly, as Duguit stated explicitly, all his writings were geared to fight German scholarship. He saw himself competing with Georg Jellinek, one of the finest legal minds of the time, for intellectual leadership in Europe. Taking over the German term *Rechtsstaat* and redefining it entirely with ideas stemming from "France" (i.e., for Duguit with ideas of a more liberal, democratic, and, especially, social flavour) was a strategic masterstroke. Yet, although Duguit had many disciples, his use of *État de droit* had no lasting impact. After World War II, French administrative law scholars continued to refer to Duguit's doctrine of *service public*, but they totally rejected his key term *État de droit* as the all-encompassing fundamental concept of French public law. Instead, the idea of *service public* was nested within the alternative fundamental concepts of *État*, defined as a legal person – a concept totally rejected by Duguit – and, above all, "principle of legality," the key term in the case law of the French *Conseil d'État*.

Under the Third Republic, a second logic of transplantation of the *Rechtsstaat* discourse took place. This aimed to transplant not only the German term but also some of the underlying German ideas. Carré de Malberg, as one of the rare legal positivists amongst constitutional lawyers, associated the term *État de droit* with the famous German theory of self-limitation of the State. But that use of the French phrase was quite rare and had no lasting impact as, in both Carré de Malberg's and the German writings, the theory of self-limitation of the State was mainly encapsulated in the key term *État* (*Staat*), and not in *État de droit* or *Rechtsstaat*. More importantly, Carré de Malberg and some other scholars, such as Hauriou, used the term *État de droit*/*état de droit* in order to convey a much thinner, albeit highly incisive, normative concept related to the role of courts in the French democracy.

In the German debate on judicial review of administration, a new definition of the term *Rechtsstaat* term emerged, whose core idea depended on a certain definition of law: law was intrinsically linked to courts since a rule only qualified as a legal rule if it could be applied by a judge who was able to sanction its infringement (as was the case in private law, which served as model for this definition). Strictly speaking, any rule lacking a judicial guarantee was not considered a legal rule, even though it may have been enacted in a formal legal text and could be protected by some nonjudicial organ; it was reduced to the status of a moral rule.

Such a definition of law, which might look rather obvious to English lawyers (cf. the dictum "no right without a remedy," Austin's theory of law, Dicey's distinction between "law" and "conventions"), was far less familiar on the continent, at least for public law specialists: many rules of international, constitutional, and even administrative law lacked any judicial guarantee at the time. In France, this restrictive definition of "law" had no major critical impact in the field of administrative law, due to the existence of its *Conseil d'État*, which became a true, independent court under the Third Republic. But, it was explosive with regard to the subjection of Parliament to the entrenched Constitution.

At the end of the nineteenth century, while German liberals mainly continued to worry about the dangers flowing from an executive that was still in the hands of the monarchical forces with no serious parliamentary checks, French liberal scholars started to fear the abuses, in their eyes, of an overly powerful Parliament. In this context, some scholars mobilized the newly coined phrase *État de droit.* They ascribed to it, as had Bähr and Mayer to the term *Rechtsstaat*, a conceptual link between law and judicial protection. But the French scholars applied it not to the administration, as in Germany, but to the Parliament. By Gallicizing a certain *Rechtsstaat* debate, they gave it a more radical turn for the purpose of adapting it to the practical needs of France. In the writings of Carré de Malberg, Hauriou, and some others, the term *État de droit* became a slogan intended to support judicial review of the constitutionality of Acts of Parliament. It was used to trigger a total break with French tradition that had, since 1789, rejected any judicial review thereof and, instead, promoted the idea of nonjudicial (political) guardians of the Constitution.

Yet, this graft, or cultural break, failed. Whereas Hauriou argued that, in light of this new concept of *état de droit*, the silence of the French Constitution of 1875 on the matter of judicial review of statutes ought to be interpreted as allowing all courts to undertake such review, the French *Cour de cassation* and the *Conseil d'état* read its silence in light of the French tradition hostile to judicial power. In Parliament, all proposals to introduce some type of judicial review of statutes, either by all courts or by some special, constitutional court, were rejected. Significantly, whereas the discourse in favor of the *État de droit* all but died out by the end of the 1930s – it had no descriptive function and its main normative function failed – the polemical term *Gouvernement des juges* (government by the judiciary; translated today as "juristocracy"), having been imported in 1921 by Edouard Lambert from the United States, was definitely adopted into the French culture. From the 1930s on, especially during the so-called *Révolution Duverger* after World War II, a new generation of constitutional law scholars preferred to concentrate on empirical studies instead of studying the formal text of the Constitution that, anyway, being not judiciable, proved to be relatively ineffective. Political reality mattered more than legal rules. Thus, constitutional law studies were merged with, and dominated by, political science studies.

Third stage

At the end of the 1970s, under the Fifth Republic, the discourse on the *État de droit* took on new life. In the meantime, a major shift had taken place in positive law. In 1958, the *Conseil constitutionnel* was established. In 1971, in its seminal decision on *Liberté d'association*, that body intensified and enlarged its own role. The *État de droit* discourse of Carré de Malberg or Hauriou and, a fortiori, the new German post-1945 *Rechtsstaat* discourse centred on protection of fundamental rights by the Federal Constitutional Court had no influence at all, or only a marginal influence, on these ground-breaking changes. The 1958 caesura was due to, and informed by, President de Gaulle's political will to protect the executive against Parliament, whose power was considered to be the main cause of France's weakness.

In this context the *État de droit* discourse was reactivated and enriched for two main purposes. First, the discourse was mobilized to describe these radical transformations via a new analytical tool, even if the necessity and adequacy of this function was questioned by those who considered that these transformations could be perfectly reflected by the traditional scientific categories. Secondly, and more importantly, it was used to justify, enhance, and even reorient (in a more liberal sense) the ongoing, still-fragile, and malleable transformation process. In 1977, against the ongoing criticism of *gouvernement des juges*, President Valéry Giscard d'Estaing celebrated the function of the *Conseil constitutionnel* by referring to the ideal of *État de droit*, a regime in which the hierarchy of norms would be implemented, at each level, by courts. The 1971 decision was hailed by the law professor Olivier Cayla in 1998, not as a "*coup d'État*," as some critics thought of it, but as a "*coup d'État de droit*" (the term *État de droit* referring, here, to the need for judicial protection of human rights).

Louis Favoreu, one of the first researchers on the *Conseil constitutionnel*, and founder of the influential "school of Aix," which specialized in the comparative study of constitutional adjudication, considered *État de droit* to be the new paradigm of the new constitutional law in France and in Europe. Thus, the phrase *État droit* was upgraded to the central concept in the writings of this school of thought. On the most abstract level, the term *État de droit* was equated with the hierarchy of norms, as developed by the Vienna School. More concisely, it was supposed to reflect (but also, as some would say, to inform) the new central role of the Constitution, which became, in 1958, a true legal norm due to the existence of judicial review, and even the highest and most important norm in the legal system (the so-called constitutionalization of the legal system). The term also served to convey a new, more favourable view of the constitutional courts, and, more generally, of all courts as guardians not only of statutory provisions (rules) but of a society's values, such as fundamental rights (principles). That, in turn, encouraged other scholars and activists to try to enlarge the scope of the *État de droit* discourse, by fighting for more independence and more financial means for the judiciary, a very sensitive issue in France given its long tradition of judicial dependence.[14]

As a normative, open-textured tool, the term *État de droit* may pop up in various debates, be it on judicial review of constitutional amendments, the status of prosecutors, the formal quality of legal norms, the state of emergency, etc. Even though the term's extension is, per se, virtually limitless and is effectively increasing – its precise topography is beyond the scope of this chapter – one should, however, note that not all scholars, practitioners, or other people use it. Some still prefer traditional references

[14] Luc Heuschling, "Why Should Judges Be Independent? Reflections on Coke, Montesquieu and the French Tradition of Judicial Dependence," in Katja Ziegler, Denis Baranger, and Anthony Bradley, eds., *Constitutionalism and the Role of Parliaments* (Oxford: Hart, 2007), pp. 199–223. For a historical account on French judiciary, see Jacques Krynen, *L'État de justice. France, XIIIe-XXe siècle*, 2 vols. (Paris: Gallimard, 2009 and 2012); Jean Pierre Royer et al., *Histoire de la justice en France du XVIIIe siècle à nos jours*, 5th ed. (Paris: PUF, 2016).

(*État*, *République*[15], *principe de légalité*). The academic sources of its content remain varied. Carré de Malberg served, at the beginning, as a strong (French!) reference point; but increasingly the term was fuelled by, and combined with, many other doctrines, starting with Kelsen's *Reine Rechtslehre* (notwithstanding Kelsen's well-known criticism of the term *Rechtsstaat*), the model of southern European Constitutional courts (Italy, Spain, Portugal) which were relatively open to German influences, European law, and, during the 1990s, the post-1945 German *Rechtsstaat* discourse. The last of these became influential as German *Staatsrechtslehre* was rediscovered in France by such prominent scholars as Michel Fromont, Constance Grewe, Olivier Beaud, and Olivier Jouanjan. Today, via the terms *État de droit* and similar *Rechtsstaat* replicas in other languages, the German understanding of nomocracy has become, at least to some extent, part of the intellectual landscape for many jurists outside Germany, including France.

Conclusion

Speaking of Germanization should not, however, mislead: there is no uniformity. Differences between the current French and German situations are numerous. The phrase *État de droit* is neither embedded in the French constitutional texts nor used in the constitutional case law as a legal norm. The French legal system did not, via the *État de droit* discourse, abandon its traditional doctrine of monism with regard to international law in favor of the traditional German approach of dualism. It is hardly conceivable that France will ever abandon the particular institutional model of its *Conseil d'État*, which, in sharp contrast to the German understanding of an administrative court, is both an adviser to the executive and a judicial body whose members have been trained at some *grandes écoles* rather than at law faculties. With regard to its *Conseil constitutionnel*, although some of its national, unorthodox peculiarities have already been "normalized" (for example, repealed in the 2008 reform), there are still some unique features. French constitutional scholars and judges have not adopted as the cultural background of their legal reasoning natural law theories that, in contrast,

[15] Although not frequently used in law, the iconic term *République* remains very popular among ordinary people and politicians, as it is identified with such "republican values" as *liberté*, *égalité*, *fraternité*, and *laïcité*.

played a crucial role in the establishment and life of the post-World War II German *Rechtsstaat.* The *Conseil constitutionnel* in Paris is much less activist than the *Bundesverfassungsgericht* in Karlsruhe. Even the way their decisions are written and justified remain opposites (for example, extensive vs short, dissenting opinions vs single statement of the majority). Their respective academic debates on constitutional interpretation take quite different lines with regard to both interpretation methods (a rich literature exists in Germany on this issue, while relative silence prevails in France) and its concept (to over-simplify it, Robert Alexy's natural law infused theory of principles vs Michel Troper's realist theory of interpretation). Last, but not least, whereas most other Western countries, especially Germany, subject general norms adopted by citizens themselves, via referendum, to judicial constitutional review, France still clings to its stance that ordinary statutes or even constitutional amendments adopted by the "*peuple*," based on Article 11 of the French Constitution, are nonjudiciable. According to the seminal 1962 decision of the *Conseil constitutionnel*, norms approved by electors are the "direct expression of national sovereignty."[16] The *État de droit* discourse here faces a major cultural obstacle: the tradition, going back to Napoleon[17] via de Gaulle, of a "dialogue" between the head of state (who raises a question) and the citizens (who deliver, hopefully, the expected answer), that escapes any judicial review, as the people are, according to de Gaulle, the "Supreme Court." By virtue of Article 11, and as happened in 1962, the Constitution can be openly violated if a majority of voters agree.

[16] This reasoning has been transplanted by some former French colonies. See Gabon, art. 110 of the Statute on the Constitutional Court of 1991. In the Democracy Index 2017, Gabon is qualified as authoritarian regime and is ranked 126.

[17] On the concept of "caesarian democracy (*démocratie césarienne*)" as developed and implemented under Napoleon III, see Pierre Rosanvallon, *La démocratie inachevée. Histoire de la souveraineté du people en France* (Paris: Gallimard, 2000), ch. 5, pp. 181ff.

4 Islamic Conceptions of the Rule of Law

Lawrence Rosen

Introduction

To speak of "the rule of law" in many of the Muslim countries of the world at present may seem, not only to Westerners but to many citizens of the Islamic world, at best hypocritical and at worst a cruel joke. How, after all, can one speak of the rule of law when a woman may be killed for a marriage not approved by her father or brother, when a constitution can be changed at the whim of a ruler, or when corruption is so pervasive as to leave much of the citizenry feeling dirtied and disaffected? And yet the rule of law remains more than an ideal, more than a vague concept, and more than a useless analytic concept employed only by academic lawyers. For if we try to understand the rule of law not as a universal concept but for what it means in the context of any particular cultural tradition and its system of law, it may be possible to discern features that are not incompatible with the sense in which this phrase is commonly employed.

Admittedly, "the rule of law" is (to soften a more salacious analogue) a veritable courtesan among concepts: it shamelessly associates with whatever seems to it most profitable and basks in whatever plaudits can cover its more questionable associations. To many it simply lacks any real substance. Justice Rosalie Silberman Abella of the Canadian Supreme Court has said that "Rule of Law is a euphemism no one understands" and one dictionary can only offer the tautology that the rule of law is "a state of order in which events conform to the law."

The meaning of the phrase has long been contested, as we can see for example in the debate among the contributors to the 1994 volume entitled *The Rule of Law*.[1] Thus, some of the analysts argue that scope for differing points of view (even arising to the level of civil disobedience) is vital to any rule of law, while others suggest that what is required are measures that

[1] Ian Shapiro, ed., *The Rule of Law: NOMOS XXXVI* (New York: New York University Press, 1994).

resolve the contradiction between majority rule and majoritarian dominance. Several others, continuing the debate between H. L. A. Hart and Ronald Dworkin, disagree over whether specific tests or only general principles can determine when and how moral versus legal precepts should govern. Still others ask: Does the rule of law require that rules be the result of rational choice, or does it demand the careful incorporation of (or studied distance from) binding institutions?

Such characterizations of the rule of law in the literature have long been central to Western discussions. Medieval thinkers resorted to law when they began to question unlimited monarchic power, while those of the early modern era (Montesquieu, Locke, and Paine among them) boldly proclaimed that the law is king, rather than the other way around. So, too, the American Founders modified the ancient Greek emphasis on the rule of law as rule by the best of men when they employed the concept of virtue (at least as embodied in those who shared common constraints for being white, male, free, and landowning) as a necessary adjunct to any formal distribution of powers.[2] Definitions have sometimes closed in on certain features. *The Oxford English Dictionary*, for example, speaks of the rule of law as a governor on individual behavior, all persons being "equally subject to publicly disclosed legal codes and processes." But the universal attributes noted by philosophers and lexicographers may themselves beggar precision, especially when they are really attached to a specific concept of human nature and public tranquility and when they cannot always be reconciled with the concept of justice that may be found in different cultural traditions.

What is true in Western jurisprudence and philosophy is no less true in the Islamic world. For while one could list any number of works in which religiously inflected ideas of the rule of law have been the source for endless debate among the literati, those debates may, as in the West, have as much to do with power struggles as with philosophical rigour. And yet, as in the history of any religious or political argument, the terms of discourse may have a characteristic quality however much the internal variation and reconfiguration may have been the source of great debate, if not indeed great crimes, among those favoring one view over another. Thus, in turning to the specifics of the idea of the rule of law (or its

[2] The issues are briefly outlined in Lawrence Rosen, *Islam and the Rule of Justice: Image and Reality in Muslim Law and Culture* (Chicago: University of Chicago Press, 2018), pp. 178–180.

functional equivalents) in countries where Islam is the predominant religion one must necessarily speak in terms of themes and variations rather than pretend to a singular voice informing every nuance or alternative that may have been put forth over so vast a timeframe and distance as the Muslim world embraces.

Put somewhat differently, can we discern some common denominators in what, for want of a better phrase, may be thought of as the range of precepts that may be covered under the rubric of the rule of law? Indeed, are there indigenous equivalents to this concept in Islam and, if so, what are their constituent features? If, as students of social history and not just the history of the legal scholars, we also look to popular conceptualizations of persons, time and conduct, can we triangulate in on something like a sense of the rule of law that is deeply embedded in Muslim cultures more generally? In doing so, we will want to have recourse initially to the ideas of those Muslim scholars who have addressed the issue, as well as to propositions that appear to inform the daily lives of ordinary believers.

1 Principles of Islamic Law

Looking at some of the key writers who have thought about and debated the place of the law in a society and polity informed by Islamic principles several themes stand out: that no worldly leader may stand above the Sacred Law (*shari'a*) yet may be responsible for determining its applicability; that as a matter of cultural common sense one cannot (and for that reason, should not) assume that the law can be applied without recourse to the wisdom and credibility of those who bespeak it; that justice requires assessing the claims made upon power by an individual who is himself taken as a whole social person; that equivalence rather than abstract rights is the measure of fairness; that no entitlement exists when one fails constantly to service one's claims; and that the law is not a body of positive rules but of situated appraisals of social repercussions applied through procedures that are consistent with what is known about human nature and what holds a society together. While these "cultural postulates" will have to be unpacked in their everyday manifestations we can see how they also suffuse – again, in a theme-and-variation sense – many of the formal commentaries, judgments, and debates that have characterized Islamic jurisprudence over the centuries.[3]

To most Islamic legal thinkers the preservation of a community of believers (*umma*) free from social chaos (*fitna*) is a foremost consideration and toward that end the founders of the four main schools of Islamic law were quite prepared to defer to political authority and to rely for substantive guidance on analogies drawn from provisions in the Quran and the accepted collections of the Prophet's sayings and acts (*hadith*, *sunna*). Personal reasoning (*ijtihad*) – whether of the majority or a particularly well-regarded scholar articulating a minority position – is recognized as a valuable addendum to the Quran and the Traditions of the Prophet by many scholars, provided it sounds in the practices of the people or the public good. Some, like the tenth-century writers al-Farabi and al-Razi, influenced by Greek ideas, rely on the "first chief" to guide the community, the constraints of personal virtue being paramount in avoiding the injustice that follows upon the failure to balance contending interests. Avicenna (Ibn Sina, 980–1037) is only one among many who, in his approach to legal constraints, stresses the importance of reciprocity in actual or partner-like relationships. Other commenters of the same era (including al-Mawardi) pick up on the Prophetic saying that "my community will not agree in error" to emphasize the role of consensus and consultation both as a restraint on leadership and as a form of social bonding. Like many of his predecessors, al-Ghazzali (1058–1111) does not focus on institutional ways to constrain misguided leaders noting, as does Averroes (Ibn Rushd, 1126–1198), that necessity commands obedience either to a ruler or learned man, while the more autocratic Ibn Taymiyya (1263–1328) vests almost unlimited power in a leader if he strives to hold people strictly to the tenets of the faith. Later thinkers, such as Nasir ad-Din Tusi (1201–1274), like their forbearers, resort to the concept of balance as equivalence without specifying precisely how this accounting should proceed other than as an emanation from a just ruler. And while Ibn Khaldun (1332–1406), notwithstanding his role as judge and political adviser, is not usually thought of mainly as a legal philosopher, his approach is consistent with that of many jurisprudential scholars in its emphasis on social solidarity, the need of men to be dominated by superior leaders, and the belief that

[3] See generally Wael Hallaq, *A History of Islamic Legal Theories* (Cambridge: Cambridge University Press, 1999).

religious law does not censure the role of the authoritative figure as such, only the evils that a particular tyrant may perpetrate.

It does no violence to the distinctive nature of these and many other Islamic commenters on the role of the law to suggest some common cultural themes that transcend their individual approaches and the times within which they were set. Preeminent among these features is the dependence on the ruler as a person rather than as the depersonalized occupant of an institution. Perhaps the absence of a clear line of succession to the Prophet himself – indeed perhaps owing in part to the murder of several early caliphs and the schism of the community into the Sunni and Shiite branches – reinforced the focus on the personality of the one who has taken hold of a given office. But it would be a mistake to think that this represents either some inherent taste for absolutism, the incompatibility of Islam and the rule of law, or that there was not, in fact, a broad array of limitations placed on the power of the ruling figure. Admittedly, some of the constraints may have been more in the nature of idealized practices than actual behavior. Islam distinguishes between those tasks (like prayer) that each individual must perform for him or herself and those that must be done by someone on behalf of the community of believers as a whole. This has led some Muslims to refuse service, say, as a prayer leader or religious judge (*qadi*) lest they mislead the community by even inadvertently failing to perform that role properly. Others, like an Egyptian qadi in the ninth century CE, argued that new court officials should be appointed every six months to avoid tempting corruption.[4] Notwithstanding such ideals, the concept of independent judges and scholars, as we shall see, is not without some reality. That many commenters have stressed the ideal qualities that a judge should possess and that institutional constraints should receive less consideration than personal virtues is consistent, therefore, with that cultural ethos that situates the main source of confidence in the pursuit of justly enacted powers in identifiable persons rather than impersonal structures.

Two possibilities, then, exist: that the rule of law depends on virtuous persons applying it, or that the rule of law requires counterbalancing mechanisms that limit the power of those who apply it. While most of the writings of classical Islamic law scholars would, as we have seen, suggest

[4] See Ghulam Murtaza Azad, "Conduct and Qualities of a Qadi," *Islamic Studies*, 24 (1985), 51–61.

that reliance on the virtuous law-enforcer is by far the dominant orientation, a more accurate picture emerges when both possibilities are considered. For while the religious scholars – whether Sunni or Shiite, Arab or Persian, Asian or Middle Eastern – almost always emphasize the just ruler who is faithful to the letter and spirit of the *shari'a*, there have almost always been countervailing forces that need to be considered. Primary among them are the other players in the marketplace, the procedures and presumptions employed by the judiciary, the legal consults (*ulama*) whose opinions on particular cases may be solicited by contending litigants, and the alternative dispute resolution mechanisms to which disputants may have recourse.

2 The Role of the Marketplace

The Prophet was a merchant, as was his wife. And, as in the marketplace, Islam places great stress on the principles of contractual relationships and reciprocity. Provided that none of the relatively few propositions of a law-like nature contained in the Quran is violated, Allah has designated as one of the rights of mankind (*haqq al-insan*) the ability to arrange their own agreements. This does not mean that all such relationships will go smoothly; indeed, there is a saying that "God placed contentiousness among men that they may know one another," and it is in just such dealings that one must attend to the distinctiveness of the other, his cultural ways, and his own network of social attachments. Moreover, while scholars – both Muslim and Western – tend to cite as the sources of Islamic law only the Quran, the Traditions of the Prophet, and the approaches of the four main schools of law, the fact is that custom (*'urf, adat*) is the unmarked category and, quite often, the prevailing source of law. In every age and every part of the Muslim world one thus finds some version of the proposition that a contractual stipulation takes precedence even over the *shari'a* and that local custom *is shari'a*, not something separate from it. Whether it is matrilineal Malays from Sumatra or the Berbers of North Africa who regard their distinctive inheritance practices *as* Islamic, custom is popularly seen not as something separate from *shari'a* law but as an integral aspect of it. As such, custom serves as a check on the strict application of textbook *shari'a* and, in many instances, as a factor that an autocratic ruler ignores at his peril.

We tend to think of religion as lodged in the place of worship, the law as housed in the courts, and the seat of philosophy as exclusive to the academy. But not only do ordinary people lead intellectual lives, they live their religion, their law, and their philosophy in the public realm. Thus, to view the marketplace, for example, as solely the realm of the economic is to possess a highly truncated view of how Islamic law and its inbuilt constraints may operate in everyday life. For the market is not only the natural environ of every Muslim from the Prophet on but a domain in which the rule of law is also given expression. Consider just a few practices. Contracts must be expressed in the present tense, not as something that has yet to achieve performance. This means that such an agreement is really the validation of an existing and negotiated arrangement, evidence not only of the terms of a deal but of a relationship – indeed a relationship that has consequences for the networks of indebtedness possessed by others, the totality of which both define and order society. By creating and sustaining, in a highly publicized manner, the connections one has forged with others, a man demonstrates that he is fulfilling his God-given capacity to arrange his ties to others through the employment of his reasoning powers and that he is contributing to keeping the community of believers whole by applying these precepts in his most ordinary of daily activities.

At the same time that one bargains in the marketplace one is also putting certain constraints on the centralization of power. For while it is true that most regimes have controlled the marketplace through inspectors, taxation, and regulatory schemes, it is also true that the application of custom, the arrangement of interpersonal obligations, and the system by which agreements are formed constitute ways in which power is dispersed, the regularization of relationships is given substantive form, and a key aspect of the rule of law – the more-or-less even application of principles both widely recognized and informally sanctioned – is given actual effect.

3 Judges and Jurists

The same may be said of the role of the judiciary. Here, one could speak of the formal elements of power distribution and, perhaps more importantly in the Muslim context, the mechanisms that may not seem to be overtly oriented toward the limitation of power yet have, directly or indirectly, that effect. Traditionally, Muslim judges were appointed by the powers that be.

Yet there are numerous reports of local people rejecting someone sent from the capital or simply finding ways of avoiding his disposition of cases. In theory, the ruler's own decisions were separate from those reached by a qadi, though it would be naïve to claim that the influence of the former on the latter was not, in most instances, profound. Still, litigants sometimes had a choice of venues where they could be heard. Moreover, scholarly opinions (sing. *fatwa*) were frequently sought and presented to the court. Because a judge's reputation and personal following were essential to his overall credibility, both his own judgments and his use of the proffered fatwas was at once a hedge on his own decisions and yet another vehicle through which the dispersal of power reinforced local conceptualizations of a rule of law.

Judicial decisions, though usually brief and unpublished, did not really set precedents. Nevertheless, it is not inaccurate to think of Islamic law as a variant on common law systems of law.[5] Here the key ingredients of a common law approach are that facts are adduced from the bottom up by local witnesses and experts and a system of variable categories is developed by reference to a range of specific cases. The result, intentional or not, is to once again distribute power in such a way that it is difficult for any one person or institution permanently to cumulate power to the exclusion of other avenues and challengers to its implementation.

Traditionally, no formal system of appeals existed in Muslim court structures. The purported theory was that no human could decide a matter with absolute certainty, hence an array of approaches by localized qadis, rather than a definitive statement of the law by a high court, was consistent with the belief that if similar processes of attending to cases were applied diverse results were acceptable. Indeed, because many Muslim judges to this day argue that cases are never identical, the proposition that similar cases should be decided similarly is not consistent with their emphasis on the unique relationships and personalities each case involves. From this perspective, a rule of law that treats things as if they were identical would violate common sense and the belief that justice demands a focus on the unique features of each case. If, however, a similar style of considering evidence and a shared sense of the criteria

[5] This argument is elaborated in Lawrence Rosen, *The Justice of Islam: Comparative Perspectives on Islamic Law and Society* (Oxford: Oxford University Press, 2000), pp. 38–68.

by which the sound judgment of a virtuous judge is applied, then justice – and what Westerners might call the rule of law – will have been honoured.

Islamic law is often regarded as containing a body of positive law and, to the extent that scholars published manuals and treatises in support of particular approaches to particular types of situations, that characterization is not inaccurate. But it is, at best, only part of the story. For the proposition that, as Noel Coulson argued, in Islam the chair (of the scholar) is more important than the bench (of the jurist) can be misleading.[6] Unlike continental systems of law, from which most Western scholars have projected their image of Islamic law, neither codes nor scholarly treatises were the predominant, much less the sole, basis for judgments. As we have seen, custom has always played a key role – particularly since it is regarded as not incompatible with the *shari'a* but part of it. Even more important has been the role of legal procedures.

Judicial procedures – including the rules of evidence, legal presumptions, and the role of witnesses and expert testimony – are important for their capacity to resonate with commonsense assumptions within a given culture and because procedural regularities may also reflect the role of the state and the limits of its powers.[7] In Islamic law the emphasis on personalism over institutions comes through quite clearly in the rules of procedure. Thus, tremendous emphasis is placed on witnesses who themselves have been recognized as reliable by virtue of their overall reputation in the community, which itself is a function of how well embedded they are in a set of kinship, local, and negotiated ties to others. Experts are witnesses whose special knowledge – whether of the marketplace, irrigation, medicine, or the likely ways people of different locales arrange their contractual relations – are vital to judicial decision-making. But note, too, that in the emphasis on these personal qualities the state is also being limited by knowledgeable persons. Just as the jury in the Anglo-American world gets the state off the hook for deciding against individuals, so too in most Islamic legal regimes the use of local people bringing information to the court takes some of the responsibility – as well as some of the power – away from the ruler and places it firmly in the hands of others.

[6] See Noel Coulson, *A History of Islamic Law* (Edinburgh: Edinburgh University Press, 1965).

[7] See the essays in Baudoin Dupret, ed., *Standing Trial: Law and the Person in the Modern Middle East* (London: I. B. Tauris, 2004).

Similarly, rules of procedure not only aid in determining what actually happened in a given dispute but reflect views of human nature that are integral to the distribution of powers through law. Thus, for example, if the person to whom certain items are usually attached (for example, the household goods to a wife) is assumed, the law is underscoring: (a) that justice requires an accounting of an individual's status and a judgment based on seeing persons in their proper category as well as for whatever additional attributes they may have taken on; and (b) that the state may not punish people for what may be in their minds if their actions, visible to all and retrievable by judicial process, do not bear out that interpretation. So, too, if an oath is to be used to settle the facts in a case the person entitled to take that oath first and thus cut off the other's claim is being allowed to step outside of presumptions the state could have enforced through the law by applying to a power higher than a human official. And when the distribution of oath-taking is based on a cultural assumption of who is most likely to know where the truth actually lies, it is through such views of humankind that individuals are both empowered against an arbitrary state and the values of the collective are reinforced.

4 Justice as Equivalence

That a person's status and overall set of connections should weigh significantly in most Islamic legal proceedings might seem antithetical to the rule of law as treating all persons equally. But consider this: Is it a violation of equality if women who are deeply committed to Catholicism believe that only men should serve as priests, or that similar views should inform the approaches of Orthodox Jewish women to being called up to the reading of the Torah, or Muslim women to serving as prayer leaders? Or, from their perspective, do these women believe that the religiously informed tasks they perform, whether in the home or through segregated rituals, are of equivalent importance to those undertaken by men? If they do, then what may be at work is a concept of justice not as equality or identical treatment of men and women but that the distinctive nature of each demands that they be treated true to their category and thus equivalently. If rights are the keynote of many Western conceptions of the rule of law, justice (*'adl*) is clearly the concept that is central for many Muslims and that concept does not imply absolutely identical treatment of persons in every situation but a clear assessment of the whole person, including his or her distinctive nature. And when equivalence – however assessed – is the focus of judgment, and when that process is pursued according to precepts broadly shared within the culture, it is impossible to characterize the results as failing to abide by some sense of a rule of law even if it is not the one that is put forth in other societies and religions. Culture thus can, alongside formal structures, serve as a check on the power of the state.

5 Informal Arbiters

However centralized power has been in Islamic states – whether in the person of a sultan or a big man who has employed pseudo-democratic means to gain office – not all legal power is at every moment under the ruler's control. Legal scholars (*ulama*) may vary in their impact, whether they serve alongside the head of a regime or as consults in individual cases. But they do possess an alternate source of legitimacy which – depending almost entirely (as in all other aspects of these cultures) on their personal forcefulness, their individual capacity to build networks of dependence, and their ability to capture through language the terms by which a matter may be addressed – can at times be interposed against the powers of the central authority. And since their intervention may itself partake of characteristic features for establishing their legitimacy, one can properly speak of their contribution as part of the rule of law.

The ulama are, however, by no means the only players who may generate a dispersal of power regularized by social convention and hence contribute to the rule of law as seen through local eyes. Often, disputants will go to people outside of the formal legal structure to have their differences addressed. The go-between (*wasita*) is more than an informal arbiter: this individual – whether a kinsman, neighbour, or other respected figure – at once intercedes (even usurps) the power of the state to decide issues but does so in such a way as to reinforce local conventions and customary practices. Moreover, their approach actually resonates with that taken by formal courts in many parts of the Muslim world. For if one asks what the goal is that such forums seek to achieve, the answer is often not that of Western courts – to assess facts and determine rights – but to put the parties into a position where they are most likely to negotiate their own differences. Once again, the ability to use social values – seen as Islamic values – and local people to achieve a degree of peaceful resolution of a dispute is not just a matter of legal pluralism in some abstract sense but of limiting state power and establishing regularity through local personnel and local conceptualizations. That, too, is partaking of a rule of law.

Consider, too, the fact that, contrary to Western stereotypes, if they pursue their family law cases to judicial decision women throughout the Muslim world win all or much of their lawsuits anywhere from 65 to 95 percent of the time.[8] The reasons appear to include that the cases they pursue tend to be clearly favorable to them, that Islamic law has long favored the poor, that the rules of evidence do not uniformly disadvantage women, and that pressures are often brought to bear on men to settle their wives' lawsuits. Once again, legal presumptions and the role of court experts do not simply work against the interests of women. And the image of women as reluctant to argue their own interests is seriously problematized by viewing such documentaries as Ziba Mir Hossein's *Divorce Iranian Style* or a film that follows a judge in Niger entitled *Justice at Agadez.*

Westerners, too, have often characterized Islamic legal decision-making as largely dependent on the unbounded discretion of the qadi. Max Weber, who spoke of *Kadijustiz* in these terms, is often cited here even though Weber was careful to state that his was an ideal type construct and that he knew actual Islamic legal adjudication was not simply arbitrary. In fact, careful studies of such discretion suggest that while judgment is indeed connected with the range of inquiry to which any judge may subject litigants, there are clear precepts and limits to which judges commonly adhere. Foremost, as we have suggested, are the procedural rules for adducing and weighing evidence, the presumptions that allot burdens of proof, and the preferred aim of creating some sort of workable continuity to an existing relationship. Though less apparent, perhaps, than a formal structure of divided powers, these features are crucial to the local variant of an Islamic rule of law.

6 Corruption

It would, however, be naïve to ignore the threat of corruption in any legal system. Assessing its role in Muslim adjudication is difficult to quantify

[8] The data supporting this assertion is detailed in Rosen, *Islam and the Rule of Justice*, pp. 28–62.

and still more difficult to separate from other aspects of the political and social forces in each country involved. What we do know with reasonable certainty is that the separation of the judiciary from governmental influence (if not direction) is far from perfect.

Examples abound. Thus, in June of 2015, President Abdel Fattah el-Sisi publicly browbeat the Egyptian judges who he said were failing to move against the Muslim Brothers he accused of assassinating a public prosecutor. In one particularly intriguing case a court in the state of Texas was called upon to decide a claim by an American oil company arguing that a decision reached against them in a Moroccan court was improperly influenced by the palace and should therefore not be enforced by the American court.[9] At the trial level the court did indeed find that there was such influence and that the Moroccan judiciary was insufficiently independent for its rulings to be given effect. However, the court of appeals found to the contrary and ruled in favor of granting comity to the foreign judgment, thus creating an interesting question as to what kind of influence goes beyond the bounds of a rule of law.

7 Constitutions and Human Rights Conventions

At various times many Muslim countries have addressed the balance of powers and the rule of law through the adoption of national constitutions and codes, many of which followed European models. What gets incorporated in any nation's foundational charter or codified laws, of course, reflects both the circumstances that apply at the time of their adoption and the broader concept of power that they embrace. In India, the British effectively created a body of substantive Islamic law that had not previously existed, while the French in North Africa redacted case law and treated it like a code. Following independence many of these codes persisted, especially in criminal and commercial law, sometimes alongside modified codes of personal status that ranged from those remaining very close to traditional Islamic law in the countries of the Arabian Peninsula to the highly Westernized laws of Tunisia. Certainly, revisions in some codes do seek to equalize the status of men and women. Notwithstanding massive

[9] See the discussion of the case at Karka Dieseldorff, "US Court Says Morocco's Justice is 'Fundamentally Fair'," *Morocco World News*, October 7, 2015.

protest marches in 2000 for and against its adoption, the Moroccan Code of Personal Status (*Moudawwana*) now provides that marriage is 'under the direction of both spouses,' that both parties can seek a divorce on equal grounds, that a woman does not lose child custody upon remarriage, and that a woman does not require the permission of a marital guardian to wed.

Most Muslim countries have not only centralized their law codes but the organization of their judiciary as well. Where once any respected scholar might be able to certify another as sufficiently learned that he might apply the *shari'a*, now government-controlled educational programs predominate; where once a qadi might be somewhat independent of the ruler, now the Ministry of Justice assigns posts and controls advancement, thus potentially jeopardizing judicial independence. However, on occasion judges have protested against governmental interference, and lawyers in Egypt, Tunisia, and Morocco have taken to the streets to make their views known. At best, lawyers and judges wish to be able to practise their professions independently; at worst, they are badgered or threatened into following direction from above.

More recently, international human rights conventions pose the question whether the standards of Western nations can be said to command worldwide adherence or whether these resolutions run counter to Islamic law. When, for example, the United Nations Universal Declaration of Human Rights was offered for adoption, Saudi Arabia refrained from acceptance – but then even the American Anthropological Association opposed it as an imposition of Western values. Bilateral treaties on the laws governing migrants from Muslim countries to Europe serve to regularize the status of those who live and work outside of their home countries. And although religious law courts have remained a voluntary option for religious adherents in a number of instances in North America and Europe, the aftereffects of the Salman Rushdie affair, 9/11, and various terrorist attacks have led to a backlash against Islamic law in the West. Thus, the Archbishop of Canterbury was roundly criticized for suggesting that some personal status matters might best be handled by Muslims in their own religious law courts, while various jurisdictions in the United States and Canada attempted to pass laws forbidding the application of *shari'a* within their territories. The result is, to some degree, to deprive religious Muslims of the rule of law they understand and to replace it with one whose substance and methods may run counter to their perceived sense of order and justice.

Conclusion

Ultimately, we are confronted with a series of concepts about how and in what manner one can speak of a rule of law when cultures and religions vary quite widely. Where many Muslims may see the identical treatment of persons as a failure to recognize legitimate differences or place their confidence in those persons whose relationships they believe serve as a more credible basis for constraint than impersonal institutions, Westerners may see systems that violate their idea of the rule of law as one that should be blind to just such features. At one level there is great overlap between Muslim and many non-Muslim visions of the rule of law – that fairness demands attending to all the facts, that no one individual should have unchallenged and unlimited power over another, that truth does not lie within the ambit of the powerful but with sources that transcend any one momentary possessor of control – while at the same time they exhibit quite different approaches to the distribution of power and the criteria by which authority should be acknowledged. One need not, therefore, be an unrepentant relativist or a claimant of universal values to nevertheless respect the organizing principles by which others place limits on power and treat one another with that degree of consideration to which they would expect any valid system of law to treat them as well.

Empires and the Rule of Law: Arbitrary Justice and Imperial Legal Ordering 5

Lauren Benton and Lisa Ford

Introduction

As composite polities, empires were plural legal orders. Conquest, settlement, and rule depended on elaborate arrangements to manage the relation of imperial law to local or indigenous law. Calls for impartial justice in empires emerged in the context of intricate legal conflicts over order and rights, with varied institutional trajectories as the result. The rule of law in empires must be approached as part of the history of legal politics in fluid, fragmented systems of law.

Jurisdictional complexity structured a good deal of imperial legal politics. Empires regularly adjusted structures of legal pluralism, intervening to tidy jurisdictional orders and to assert authority over new subjects and territories. Many reforms to imperial law were advanced in the name of containing petty despotism or protecting subjects, while others aimed at making court systems and legal procedures work more efficiently to enhance imperial power and wealth. The counterpart to this ordering impulse of empires was strategic maneuvering by subordinate groups to mobilize jurisdictional conflicts for their own benefit, often at the expense of other groups. Conquered populations adjusted quickly and used colonizers' courts to defend their own property interests and access to resources. Strategies of legal engagement ranged from litigation to outright challenges to the legitimacy of imperial courts to violent rebellion.

Efforts to propel legal change from above and below activated discourses about arbitrary justice. It was common for sovereigns to exercise legal authority in ritualized ways, purposely highlighting their vast discretionary judicial power, for example by ordering executions, dispensing mercy, and receiving subjects' petitions. Yet, even for empires with ideologies of world power in which all aliens represented potential imperial subjects, the very legitimacy of imperial rule still depended on demonstrations of impartial justice.[1] Inferior authorities were even more exposed to complaints of arbitrary justice. Cries of petty despotism flowed like an electric currents through empires, converting colonial scandals into highly charged moments of imperial reordering.

Such histories unsettle narratives of the rise of the rule of law as a universal historical tendency. Imperial legal orders exhibited some shared patterns of change and adopted some similar institutional designs, but they also encompassed an enormous variety of doctrines, discourses, and administrative structures. Borderland legal conflicts, intra-imperial jurisdictional struggles, fluid constitutional debates, and judicial and extrajudicial violence – such processes engendered deep imperial anxieties about arbitrary justice without producing a singular solution. Moves to promote consistency in the administration of law in empires upheld variegated rights regimes as a quality of imperial rule.[2] And as some participants in legal conflicts invoked fairness and called for due process and equal access to justice, institutional change in empires often worked to facilitate instability, spark violence, and create new sources of injustice.

Still, this is not just a history of endless complexity. In the long nineteenth century and beyond, processes of imperial legal ordering brought a handful of shared problems into full view, including struggles to define the legal relationship between imperial centers and old or new peripheries. At a minimum, imperial legal orders had to fix limits on power held by local legal authorities and clarify their standing in the imperial bureaucracy. Ongoing legal disputes, meanwhile, forced imperial governments to address and adjust the status and rights of various types of subjects, a process that led them to reference legal projects in other empires, including constitutional movements and authoritarian gambits. For many legal

[1] On universal monarchy in the Spanish Empire, see Anthony Pagden, *Lords of All the World: Ideologies of Empire in Spain, Britain and France c. 1500–1800* (New Haven: Yale University Press, 1995), ch. 2; on legal pluralism in Rome, see Clifford Ando, *Law, Language, and Empire in the Roman Tradition* (Philadelphia: University of Pennsylvania Press, 2011). A classic work on mercy relevant in imperial settings is Douglas Hay, "Property, Authority and the Criminal Law," in Douglas Hay, Peter Linebaugh, John G. Rule, E. P. Thompson, and Cal Winslow, *Albion's Fatal Tree: Crime and Society in Eighteenth-Century England* (London: Allen Lane, 1975), pp. 17–63. On mercy in empires, see Lauren Benton, *A Search for Sovereignty: Law and Geography in European Empires, 1400–1900* (Cambridge: Cambridge University Press, 2010), ch. 2.

[2] Imperial histories stand against a progressive narrative of rights. See esp. Jane Burbank, "An Imperial Rights Regime: Law and Citizenship in the Russian Empire," *Kritika*, 7 (2006), 397–431.

actors in empires, structures of legal pluralism offered opportunities for strategic maneuvering while presenting limited alternatives. Over time, legal politics gradually composed a widely recurring framework for law in empires that preserved legal diversity while affirming and expanding imperial authority.

In this chapter, we explore this complex history of the rule of law in empires. We trace some of the myriad ways in which jurisdictional complexity in empires resembled, but should not be mistaken for, the rule of law. We show that attempts to tidy colonial legal orders and to limit the scope of subordinate jurisdictions often utilized the language of fairness while working to enhance judicial power at the center and encompassing extrajudicial violence. Likewise, we suggest that appeals by colonial subjects and interlocutors for equal justice often had unintended consequences. We first examine legal politics across early modern European empires before turning to the example of the nineteenth-century British Empire's project of reordering its world through law. The rule of law in empires, we show, composed one element of a broader process of legal politics and institutional change.

1 Legal Pluralism in Empires

Empires throughout the early modern world contained legal orders comprised of multiple jurisdictions. Religious authorities, heads of households and estates, leaders of merchant communities, and many others held different measures of legal authority. The boundaries of jurisdictions could be legally defined by membership in religious or political communities, by the regulation of types of activities or disputes, or by a combination. Rulers held legal authority in tension with a multiplicity of other authorities, and empires were unevenly strident and successful in claiming hegemony over highly fragmented legal orders.[3]

The acquisition of new territories often exacerbated jurisdictional tensions. Leaders of military and reconnaissance expeditions received authority to adjudicate and punish their immediate followers and to preside as judges over fledgling settlements, but their vague and often

[3] Lauren Benton, *Law and Colonial Cultures: Legal Regimes in World History, 1400–1900* (Cambridge: Cambridge University Press, 2001).

formulaic instructions left them to innovate and to adopt legal measures that imperial sponsors later opposed. Empires could not hold sway over distant and diverse populations without delegating legal authority to their own agents and to locals, who in turn sought to expand their own prerogatives. Indigenous elites often preserved considerable authority over their own communities even while following directives to refer certain sorts of disputes to imperial officials. It was commonplace for imperial agents and settlers to assert legal power in an ad hoc fashion, in the hope that their authority would be recognized later by metropolitan governments.[4]

In these fluid and layered legal orders, pressures to clarify jurisdictional boundaries arose at multiple levels. From the top, imperial officials sought to expand their jurisdictions: for example, in the Spanish Empire royal officials regarded New World colonization as an opportunity to shrink the jurisdiction of the Church and the importance of canon law, in part by assuming authority to appoint Church officials in the New World. From the bottom, vulnerable subjects maneuvered legally with considerable sophistication: for example, Indians in New Spain flooded Spanish courts with petitions and litigation in the first generation after the conquest, and Indians in the eighteenth-century Andes appealed to the distant *audiencia*, or royal court, to contest their treatment by local elites. By appealing for justice to a distant crown, these communities effectively called for greater sovereign control over subordinate legal orders in order to enhance their own protection. From the middle, imperial agents propped up their own legal authority against local institutions and rival imperial agents: in the British Empire, for example, nineteenth-century conflicts between royal governors and judges generated a wave of scandals that titivated London politicians and altered imperial policy.[5]

Participants in such conflicts engaged a variety of familiar strategies. Some used "forum shopping" to try to place disputes before the most sympathetic court. Others tried "forum hopping" by bringing the same

[4] Jane Burbank and Fred Cooper, *Empires in World History: Power and the Politics of Difference* (Princeton: Princeton University Press, 2010); Benton, *Law and Colonial Cultures*.

[5] For examples, see Brian Owensby, *Empire of Law and Indian Justice in Colonial Mexico* (Stanford: Stanford University Press, 2008); Sergio Serulnikov, *Subverting Colonial Authority: Challenges to Spanish Rule in Eighteenth-Century Southern Andes* (Durham: Duke University Press, 2003); James Epstein, *Scandal of Colonial Rule: Power and Subversion in the British Atlantic During the Age of Revolution* (Cambridge: Cambridge University Press, 2012).

case in sequence to multiple forums – in adjacent colonial jurisdictions, in multiple jurisdictions in imperial centers, or across imperial borders. In criminal cases, too, jurisdiction was anything but clear cut. In borderlands where settlers and indigenous people competed for resources, efforts to try perpetrators of frontier violence produced disputes about the nature and boundaries of indigenous political communities and settler sovereignty.[6] Many of these contests rested on allegations of despotism, abuse of office and unfairness.

Jurisdictional jockeying reminds us that justice was a relative affair. By delivering transparent justice for some, colonial legal institutions could do great harm to others. Colonial settlers squatting on crown land lobbied for laws to confirm shaky tenure, at the expense of indigenous people.[7] Land Commissions in the Pacific carefully defined indigenous tenures in ways that made indigenous land available for mass settler purchase.[8] In some cases, shifting inter-imperial relations changed the political valence of legal conflicts. For example, empires encouraged privateering by creating networks of prize courts, then in peacetime turned to the same courts to punish piracy as a threat to imperial commerce. Elsewhere, the perceived disorderliness of various subjects operated as a trigger for legal change. In India, for example, British East India officials responded to an increase in rural banditry by criminalizing entire ethnic groups, and they empowered magistrates to punish unruly British sojourners and settlers.[9]

[6] On jurisdictional disputes involving settlers and indigenous groups, see Lisa Ford, *Settler Sovereignty: Jurisdiction and Indigenous People in America and Australia, 1788–1836* (Cambridge: Harvard University Press, 2010); and Nancy O. Gallman and Alan Taylor, "Covering Blood and Graves: Murder and Law on Imperial Margins," in Brian P. Owensby and Richard J. Ross, eds., *Justice in a New World: Negotiating Legal Intelligibility in British, Iberian, and Indigenous America* (New York: New York University Press, 2018), pp. 213–237. On cases in a multiplicity of jurisdictions within an empire, see Helen Dewar, "Litigating Empire: The Role of French Courts in Establishing Colonial Sovereignties", in Lauren Benton and Richard J. Ross, eds. *Legal Pluralism and Empires, 1500–1850* (New York: New York University Press, 2013), pp. 49–80; on cases moving across imperial lines, see Linda Rupert, *Creolization and Contraband: Curaçao in the Early Modern Atlantic World* (Athens: University of Georgia Press, 2012); Guillaume Calafat, "Jurisdictional Pluralism in a Litigious Sea (1590–1630): Hard Case, Multi-Sited Trials and Legal Enforcement between North Africa and Italy," *Past and Present*, 242 (2019), 142–178.

[7] S. H. Roberts, *The Squatting Age in Australia, 1788–1820* (Melbourne: Macmillan, 1968).

[8] Stuart Banner, *Possessing the Pacific: Land, Settlers, and Indigenous People from Australia to Alaska* (Cambridge: Harvard University Press, 2007).

[9] Lauren Benton, "Legal Spaces of Empire: Piracy and the Origins of Ocean Regionalism," *Comparative Studies in Society and History*, 47 (2005), 700–724; Mark G. Hanna, *Pirate*

Efforts to use law to protect and define property exemplify empires' neat but jarring place in the history of the rule of law. The desire for judgments to be reliably enforced sometimes created odd bedfellows, as it did in the Ottoman Empire when Jews shifted disputes about property from religious to secular courts, helping to make the imperial government responsible for the regulation of property across the empire and diminishing the role of Jewish courts.[10] Jurisdictional disputes had the capacity to alter even the deep structures and foundations of imperial law, for example, by transforming the initially very modest jurisdictional aspirations of trading factories into expansive claims for jurisdiction over unbounded territories that included many foreigners. The results were not necessarily permanent changes, or even stable policies. In Lagos, for example, British colonial officials introduced policies to formalize an existing market in land, then reversed some of those policies in order to shore up the power of hinterland elites who might serve as imperial agents.[11]

We should not consider that jurisdictional tensions between imperial powers and indigenous polities were quickly resolved. Recent studies point to the endurance of indigenous legal autonomy; in North and South America, for example, indigenous enclaves persisted as quasi-autonomous legal communities within nation states.[12] In India, even at the height of British power, empire coexisted with hundreds of princely states where the British held influence without asserting jurisdiction over most criminal and many civil cases.[13] Such arrangements were sometimes the direct result of empires' attempts to limit metropolitan responsibility for administering

Nests and the Ruse of the British Empire, 1570–1740 (Chapel Hill: University of North Carolina Press, 2015); Radhika Singha, *A Despotism of Law: Crime and Justice in Early Colonial India* (New York: Oxford University Press, 1998); Elizabeth Kolsky, *Colonial Justice in British India: White Violence and the Rule of Law* (Cambridge: Cambridge University Press, 2010).

10 Karen Barkey, "Aspects of Legal Pluralism in the Ottoman Empire," in Lauren Benton and Richard J. Ross, *Legal Pluralism and Empires, 1500–1850* (New York: New York University Press, 2013).

11 Barkey, "Aspects of Legal Pluralism in the Ottoman Empire"; Kristin Mann, "African and European Initiatives in the Transformation of Land Tenure in Colonial Lagos," in Saliha Belmessous, ed., *Native Claims: Indigenous Law against Empire, 1500–1920* (Oxford: Oxford University Press, 2012).

12 See, for example, Jordana Dym, *From Sovereign Villages to National States: City, State, and Federation in Central America, 1759–1839* (Albuquerque: University of New Mexico Press, 2006).

13 Benton, *A Search for Sovereignty*, ch. 5.

justice on chaotic peripheries. In some places, too, creating or preserving the jurisdictional autonomy of indigenous groups worked to prepare the way for the gradual erosion of their power. In the French Empire, for example, the deterioration of legal control by religious and ethnic communities took many forms; it occurred in New France when colonial elites found ways to chip away at property rights attached to indigenous enclaves, and it happened later when French "modernization" of the Moroccan legal system left Jews with fewer, less desirable jurisdictional options.[14]

Another cluster of legal problems arose from the delegation of legislative authority to colonies. A first problem arose from the open-ended relation of metropolitan to colonial law. Typically, the legal administration of empire fell to bureaucracies that were not empowered to sort out vexing questions such as whether legislation enacted in the metropole applied throughout the empire, whether legislative bodies in the colonies had the power to diverge from metropolitan law, or whether colonial courts were obliged to follow metropolitan procedures and standards. Even procedures for appeal were often unclear or threaded only small numbers of cases through tight judicial pathways.[15] Blackstone's schematic stipulations about how metropolitan law differed in its application to conquered and settled colonies sounded simple, but it did not clear up ambiguities about which English laws applied in the colonies.[16] As we shall see below, a vague principle that colonies should make no law repugnant to the laws of England left a great deal of scope for interpretation and ample room to deviate from English law between the seventeenth and twentieth

[14] Allan Greer, *Property and Dispossession: Natives, Empires and Land in Early Modern North America* (Cambridge: Cambridge University Press, 2018); Jessica M. Marglin, *Across Legal Lines: Jews and Muslims in Modern Morocco* (New Haven: Yale University Press, 2016), p. 16.

[15] The recognition but irresolution of these issues are salient in the early British empire. See esp. Ken MacMillan, *The Atlantic Imperial Constitution: Center and Periphery in the English Atlantic World* (New York: Palgrave Macmillan, 2011); Daniel Hulsebosch, *Constituting Empire: New York and the Transformation of Constitutionalism in the Atlantic World, 1664–1830* (Chapel Hill: University of North Carolina Press, 2006); Joseph Henry Smith, *Appeals to the Privy Council from the American Plantations* (New York: Columbia University Press, 1950).

[16] Lisa Ford and David Andrew Roberts, "'Mr Peel's Amendments' in New South Wales: Imperial Criminal Reform in a Distant Penal Colony," *Journal of Legal History*, 37 (2016), 198–214. Nor was this vagueness remedied in Judge Mansfield's ruling in *Campbell* v. *Hall*. See Lauren Benton and Lisa Ford, *Rage for Order: The British Empire and the Origins of International Law, 1800–1850* (Cambridge: Harvard University Press, 2016), pp. 41, 238, n. 67

centuries. In many places, legal procedures transposed from metropolitan centers took on different significance in colonies. The category of legal non-personhood emerged in *ancien régime* France and then proved useful in the penal colony of French Guiana, where the category hardened into a status of perpetual punishment and legal limbo.[17]

If colonies were sometimes defined as legally exceptional or anomalous, they were also at times subject to systemic, if unsystematic, pan-imperial efforts to impose consistency. The Atlantic revolutions of the late eighteenth century corresponded to a wave of legal reform measures in European overseas empires, from attempts to ameliorate (rather than immediately replace) the Code Noir in revolutionary Haiti to the effort to reconcile monarchism and liberalism in constitutional form for the Spanish Empire in the Cádiz Constitution.[18] Reflecting its ascendance as a global military power, its territorial gains, and its growing commercial influence, the British Empire undertook a truly global project of imperial legal reform in the early nineteenth century that epitomizes these processes. It did so at the very moment when legal politics in England were giving rise to the rule of law as a principle of metropolitan governance. Although some London officials were vocal in advocating the creation of a coherent framework for imperial law, Britain's imperial reform project in fact proceeded mainly from scattered crises of order that began in the colonies. Mid-level officials, in particular, called for strengthening governors' legal authority and shrinking the jurisdictional powers of local elites, whether indigenous lords or colonial slave holders.[19]

The resulting global constitutional ordering projects had two characteristics that make them worthy of special attention as we ponder the relation

[17] Mary Sarah Bilder, *The Transatlantic Constitution: Colonial Legal Culture and the Empire* (Cambridge: Harvard University Press, 2008); Miranda Spieler, *Empire and Underworld: Captivity in French Guiana* (Cambridge: Harvard University Press, 2012).

[18] Malick Ghachem, *The Old Regime and the Haitian Revolution* (Cambridge/New York: Cambridge University Press, 2012); Matthew Mirow, *Latin American Constitutions: The Constitution of Cádiz and its Legacy in Spanish America* (New York: Cambridge University Press, 2015).

[19] See the next section and also Lauren Benton and Lisa Ford, "Magistrates in Empire: Convicts, Slaves, and the Remaking of the Plural Legal Order in the British Empire," in Benton and Ross, eds., *Legal Pluralism and Empires, 1500–1850*, pp. 173–198. See also Brendan Gillis, "Conduits of Justice: Magistrates and the British Imperial State, 1732–1834," Ph.D. dissertation, Indiana University, 2015.

of imperial law to the rule of law. First, even when conditions across empires had the effect of strengthening imperial authority and placing subordinate jurisdictions formally under the imperial government's purview, executive legal authority was always exercised through a layered bureaucracy that could further, thwart or complicate efforts to bring empires to order. Secondly, precisely because empires were composite polities long engaged in articulating multiple jurisdictions and authorities, imperial law reform provoked and responded to intense debates over the dangers of arbitrary justice and the proper way to contain it through institutional reform.

2 "Rule of Law" in the Nineteenth-Century British Empire

The phrase "the rule of law" was not often spoken in the early nineteenth-century British Empire. But its emergence as a catchphrase later in the century is bound up with British imperial and colonial efforts to order legal administration on the fringes of empire from 1800 to 1840. Indeed, reforms to law in the British Empire in this period defined imperial power in relation to self-legitimating appeals to due process, the repugnancy of colonial legislation, the competence of colonial judges, and the despotism of foreign legal systems. Reordering law in the empire served to increase central control over colonial subjects of all sorts, usually in ways that drew subtle (and not so subtle) lines between metropolitan and colonial subjecthood. Claims of despotism justified imperial aggression and demands for extraterritorial jurisdiction. At the same time, orderly and nested colonial legal forums created deeply uneven meeting points where some, but not all, colonized subjects could craft claims in appropriately deferential forms. It is not surprising that in the aftermath of the American Revolution the increase of crown prerogative or parliamentary power was often sought by disaffected people, including many new British subjects, on colonial peripheries.[20]

Many modalities for ordering British colonial law in the nineteenth century were not new. The doctrine of repugnancy, for example, had

[20] This is a central point in Benton and Ford, *Rage for Order*.

long been the bedrock of imperial rule.[21] Self-governing peripheries could legislate as they chose so long as their laws did not contravene fundamental (and applicable) English law.[22] The use of repugnancy to bring empire to order waxed and waned – indeed, in Jamaica the supervision of legislation lessened over time.[23] However, from the 1820s the Colonial Office wielded repugnancy in new ways, to force old, self-governing colonies to ameliorate harsh slave laws and, after 1833, to control the misuse of vagrancy laws invoked against former slaves. Repugnancy was also the only real form of imperial control over settler colonies after 1840 when the empire capitulated to demands for local, elected legislatures in Canada, Australia and the Cape.[24] This was a flawed governance strategy. Some colonies responded, cannily, by passing obnoxious laws of very short duration that expired before they could be disallowed.[25]

Many other strategies appear less coercive but were not so. From its earliest days, imperial officials repackaged familiar jurisdictional gambits to extend their control. In India, European notions of some jurisdictional autonomy for religious communities informed the strategy of crafting a plural legal order after 1765, when the East India Company assumed the *diwani* (rights to collect revenue delegated by the Mughal Empire) over Bengal, Bihar and Orissa. In this plan, Company agents would fall under British jurisdiction, and Hindu and Muslim subjects would be ruled under their own law, a seemingly simple scheme that gave rise to innumerable complexities and led the British to privilege written sources for Hindu law

[21] One of the best accounts of repugnancy in the early British Empire remains Mary Bilder's excellent chapter, "English Settlement and Local Governance," in Michael Grossberg and Christopher Tomlins, eds., *The Cambridge History of Law in America*, vol. 1: *Early America (1580–1815)* (Cambridge: Cambridge University Press, 2008), pp. 63–103.

[22] The applicability of law rested on the complex and understudied question of when, how and to what degree English law automatically pertained in various colonies: B. H. McPherson, *The Reception of English Law Abroad* (Brisbane: Supreme Court Library of Queensland, 2007).

[23] Aaron Graham, "Jamaican Legislation and the Transatlantic Constitution, 1664–1839," *The Historical Journal*, 61 (2018), 327–355.

[24] Russell Smandych, "'To Soften the Extreme Rigor of Their Bondage': James Stephen's Attempt to Reform the Criminal Slave Laws of the West Indies, 1813–1833," *Law and History Review*, 23 (2005), 537–588; Damen Ward, "Legislation, Repugnancy and the Disallowance of Colonial Laws: The Legal Structure of Empire and Lloyd's Case (1844)," *Victoria University of Wellington Law Review*, 41 (2010), 381–402.

[25] Graham, "Jamaican Legislation," 352.

over custom in ways that were deeply distorting.[26] Elsewhere, colonial officials plucked from canon law the idea of a special obligation to protect the weak – a principle used to justify potentially controversial efforts to claim control over various peoples and territories. The most obvious example is the Crown's assertion that the need to protect North American Indians as subjects and/or allies justified its restriction of English settlement in Indian country in the Proclamation of 1763.[27] "Protection talk" amplified calls for incorporative strategies in early nineteenth-century imperial law reform. In 1815, it was used with only a modicum of embarrassment to justify the conquest of the Kingdom of Kandy, an independent kingdom in the center of the new crown colony of Ceylon. Governor Robert Brownrigg not only alleged that the King of Kandy had harassed Ceylonese traders formally classed as British subjects but also asserted that Kandyan subjects needed British protection from the unjust tyranny of their king. Deploying similar language, Britain used its formal role under treaty as 'protecting sovereign' of the Ionian Islands to justify constitutional meddling within the islands and to assert its right to define unilaterally who counted as British subjects and when they deserved protection.[28]

One of the most important ways in which law-talk about protecting subjects projected imperial power was through the negotiation of extraterritorial courts in foreign jurisdictions. Such arrangements were not initially founded in imperial power. Along with other foreign agents, English ambassadors had long exercised consular jurisdiction in the Ottoman Empire under agreements that, in Ottoman eyes, reflected the power of the Porte to grant legal privileges. Such mechanisms of law were much less benign by the nineteenth century.[29] When Chinese imperial commissioner Lin Zexu confined British traders in their Canton factories in 1839 and demanded that the British hand over 20,000 chests of opium, Britain declared war on the grounds that Chinese legal disorder threatened

[26] J. D. M. Derrett, "The Administration of Hindu Law by the British," *Comparative Studies in Society and History*, 4 (1961), 10–52.

[27] Benton and Ford, *Rage for Order*, p. 85; Colin G. Calloway, *The Scratch of a Pen: 1763 and the Transformation of America* (New York: Oxford University Press, 2007).

[28] Benton and Ford, *Rage for Order*, pp. 98–100.

[29] Maurits Boogert, *The Capitulations and the Ottoman Legal System: Qadis, Consuls and Beraths in the 18th Century* (Leiden: Brill, 2005); Umut Özsu, "The Ottoman Empire, the Origins of Extraterritoriality, and International Legal Theory," in Anne Orford and Florian Hoffmann, eds., *The Oxford Handbook of the Theory of International Law*, Part 1 (Oxford: Oxford University Press, 2016), pp. 124–137.

"British life, liberty, and property ... against the dignity of the British Crown."[30] In the aftermath, with other European powers, Britain wrested territorial jurisdiction in a string of trading cities in China where their merchants could not only trade freely but could do so under the criminal and civil jurisdiction of British judges exercising their own law. While these jurisdictions were not as foreign to Chinese imperial law as many thought, and while they provided a truncated and biased forum shopping opportunity for some Chinese litigants, the courts worked chiefly to give unfair advantage to European and Japanese traders by the end of the century – all in the name of defending foreign subjects in China against despotic Chinese law.[31] It is no surprise, then, that rule of law discourse took the world by storm at the very moment when European jurists surveyed the world's laws and found all but their own wanting. The rule of law and high imperialism were mutually constitutive.[32]

Foreign despots were not the only threat to legal order. Perhaps the most important historical trend in emerging ideas about the rule of law in empires was the dramatic increase in crown efforts to order legal regimes within British colonies after the American Revolution.[33] Some spectacular (and winning) instances of such interventions include the trials of Lt Governor Joseph Wall of Gorée and Governor Thomas Picton of Trinidad for extra-judicial violence and/or illegal torture at the turn of the nineteenth century. Lieutenant Governor Joseph Wall was tried and eventually executed for killing a soldier without trial in Gorée in 1782.[34] Governor Thomas Picton

[30] Superintendent of Trade, Charles Elliot, as quoted in Li Chen, *Chinese Law in Imperial Eyes: Sovereignty, Justice, and Transcultural Politics* (New York: Columbia University Press, 2016), pp. 205, 201–242.

[31] Par Cassell, *Grounds of Judgment: Extraterritoriality and Imperial Power in Nineteenth-Century China and Japan* (Oxford: Oxford University Press, 2012), pp. 15–84; Jürgen Osterhammel, "Britain and China, 1842–1914," in Andrew Porter, ed., *The Oxford History of the British Empire*, vol. 3: *The Nineteenth Century*, (Oxford: Oxford University Press, 2009), pp. 146–169; Chen, *Chinese Law in Imperial Eyes.*

[32] Antony Anghie, *Imperialism, Sovereignty, and the Making of International Law* (Cambridge: Cambridge University Press, 2005); Turan Kayaoglu, *Legal Imperialism: Sovereignty and Extraterritoriality in Japan, the Ottoman Empire, and China* (Cambridge: Cambridge University Press, 2014).

[33] Christopher Bayly, *Imperial Meridian: The British Empire and the World, 1780–1830* (London: Longman, 1989).

[34] *The Trial of Joseph Wall, Esq., Late Governor of Goree, for the Wilful Murder of Benjamin Armstrong, a Serjeant [sic] of the African Corps, at the Old Bailey, on Wednesday, January 20, 1802* (London: A. Macpherson, 1802); David Dean, "Joseph Wall of Goree Island," *African Affairs*, 57 (1958), 295–301.

escaped censure by the Privy Council for ordering the extrajudicial killing of twenty-nine British subjects during his short stay in Trinidad from 1797 to 1803, but he was convicted at King's Bench for torturing a free black girl suspected of theft in 1806.[35] The Crown tried to show, in cases like these, that even its most senior colonial officials were not above the law.

The most sweeping demonstration of the entwining of moves to strengthen imperial power with calls to impose transparent laws and due process in the colonies was the British Empire's dispatch of commissions of legal inquiry to remake the imperial constitution between 1819 and 1838. Commissions aimed at reforming all aspects of British governance in the early nineteenth century. Inside the United Kingdom, royal commissions were a well-worn instrument of investigation that for centuries had touched on virtually all aspects of social and political life.[36] Even so, the two dozen or so reports penned about the colonies in the early nineteenth century stand out for their breadth and ambition. Instructions to commissioners charged them with amassing information about every aspect of the structure and function of colonial legal regimes and, in the process, incorporating new and old colonial legal systems "everywhere, all at once" into a comprehensive imperial constitution.[37]

If the project sounds dreary and obvious, that is because we recognize its forms, reading backwards through the rule of law. The commissions carried (mostly) London-appointed lawyers to investigate and diagnose the system of legal administration from the Caribbean to Malta. Britain had acquired new colonies in its long war against Napoleon, and these were governed under an array of foreign laws, overlaid with make-shift and often autocratic infrastructures of government. The commissions were tasked with bringing these seemingly exotic colonies within the constitutional fold, but their interest also extended much further. The imperial government (and sometimes the commissioners themselves) seized the moment to take a look at older, self-governing slave colonies of the Caribbean. A wave of

[35] James Epstein, *Scandal of Colonial Rule: Power and Subversion in the British Atlantic during the Age of Revolution* (Cambridge: Cambridge University Press, 2012).

[36] Oz Frankel, *States of Inquiry: Social Investigations and Print Culture in Nineteenth-Century Britain and the United States* (Baltimore: Johns Hopkins University Press, 2006); Hugh McDowall Clokie and J. William Robinson, *Royal Commissions of Inquiry* (Stanford: Stanford University Press, 1937).

[37] Phrase taken from an article about 1838, by Kate Boehme, Peter Mitchell and Alan Lester, "Reforming Everywhere and All at Once: Transitioning to Free Labor across the British Empire, 1837–1838," *Comparative Studies in Society and History*, 60 (2018), 688–718.

scandals and legal panics originating in these colonies had made them emblematic of the corruption of law across the empire and had generated calls for the imperial power to 'police' colonial governments and protect vulnerable subjects from the meddling of self-interested colonial elites.[38]

Everywhere they went, commissions were inundated with unsolicited evidence, much of which advocated greater intervention in colonial law and courts. In new colonies, commissioners called for the maintenance of foreign civil law administered by centrally appointed judges and governors in council.[39] In colonies where English law prevailed, officials demanded its increased supervision, publication, and modernization, all under the much more watchful eye of the center. This effort to bind a plural global empire was neither simply autocratic nor decidedly liberal. The project to fit foreign legal regimes into the poorly articulated "fundamental principles" of British imperial constitutional law genuinely attempted to make colonial legal systems and legal processes less despotic and more fair.[40] Yet, at the same time, commissions operated knowingly to diminish the rights and responsibilities of colonial subjects. They showed in the process how legal reform and due process fit neatly into the project of crafting an autocratic empire for the times.

The British Empire's "rage for order" shows the imperial alchemy of juxtaposing due process and arbitrary justice. The doctrine of repugnancy suggested that nested colonial law was a premise of empire long before the British center set about creating the necessary bureaucracies to supervise its empire effectively.[41] In the nineteenth century, the discourse of imperial order was broader, and it was wielded parsimoniously but effectively to

[38] The need to "police" corrupt slave legislatures was raised by key pundits from the American Revolutionary period onwards: Christopher Leslie Brown, *Moral Capital: Foundations of British Abolitionism* (Chapel Hill: University of North Carolina Press, 2006), pp. 27, 209–258; see also Christopher Leslie Brown, "Empire without Slaves: British Concepts of Emancipation in the Age of the American Revolution," *William and Mary Quarterly*, 56 (1999), 273–306; Lauren Benton and Lisa Ford, "Time and Imperial Justice: Slavery, Legal Panics, and the Constitution of Empire," in Dan Edelstein, Stefanos Geroulanos, and Natasha Wheatley, eds., *Power and Time: Temporalities in Conflict and the Making of History* (Chicago: University of Chicago Press, 2020).

[39] The commissions often recommended imposing British criminal law.

[40] Bigge in New South Wales a notable exception, but the center gave NSW a real court and a legislative council anyway: New South Wales Act, 1823 (4 Geo. IV, c. 96).

[41] Compare John Brewer, *Sinews of Power: War Money and the English State, 1688–1783* (Cambridge: Harvard University Press, 1990), which notes the early sophistication of Britain's financial and military controls.

attack the jurisdictional privileges of local elites, especially the private jurisdiction of slave owners. At other times, allegations of arbitrary justice supported the annexation of new territories and the expansion of extraterritorial jurisdictions from the Mediterranean to China. The binary of due process and arbitrary justice created enormous buy-in: colonists everywhere called for increased central power to control the despotism of middling officials or foreign powers. In the process many collaborated in a marked shift towards autocratic colonial governance managed through "the rule of law."

This multisided support for reform efforts did not construct a liberal empire. As many British subjects in India already knew by 1800 and many others would discover before decolonization in the 1950s, transparent and orderly legal structures did not deliver equal justice for all. They preserved variegated rights regimes. They also set the foundations for episodes of martial law – effusions of state-sponsored violence that exposed the differentiated legal treatment of various parts of the empire and different kinds (and races) of subjects.[42] Legal reforms were as much about neo-authoritarianism as they were foundational to global liberalism. In the context of the British Empire they provided cover for vast economic dislocation, rising racial discrimination, and real violence.[43]

Conclusion

Both internal imperial reform and projections of imperial power as bearers of procedural consistency and fairness formed the backdrop to the heady rhetoric and deep chauvinism of Western legal universalism in the late nineteenth century. By the 1880s, international lawyers saw only legal chaos and backwardness in places not controlled by Europe. As European states gobbled up African states and Pacific Islands, often in blatant projects of national aggrandizement, in meeting after meeting they promised to bring legal order – and with it the prospect of inclusion into supposedly universal legal norms and practices – to the ends of the earth.

Imperial historians have for a long time argued against the older narrative of smooth and ubiquitous transitions from empires to

[42] R. W. Kostal, *A Jurisprudence of Power: Victorian Empire and the Rule of Law* (Oxford: Oxford University Press, 2005); Benton, *A Search for Sovereignty*, ch. 4.

[43] Singha, *A Despotism of Law*; Kolsky, *Colonial Justice in British India*.

nation-states in world history. Empires persisted as powerful forms of political organization, and the category remains meaningful in understanding "national" strategies of global expansion and integration.[44] Histories of legal change in empires add to this reframing of world history by highlighting variations in the evolution of empires. Efforts to reconcile ambitions of imperial ordering with political, ethnic, legal, and racial diversity produced different patterns of institutional change and left many legal puzzles unsolved. Debates about British imperial federation and conflicts over citizenship in the French empire overlapped and shared some characteristics, but we cannot collapse them into a single narrative of an imperial rule of law.[45]

Does this diversity mean that the idea of the rule of law is not useful in analyzing imperial history? We have tried to show here that the rule of law framework is relevant, but in limited ways. First, elements of a discourse of the rule of law were associated with ongoing attempts to contain arbitrary justice – through imperial legal reform, jurisdictional gambits, projections of and appeals to "protective" imperial power, and an array of other legal strategies deployed by imperial centers and their peripheral interlocutors. Such attempts were often flawed and even more often had unintended consequences, but it would be wrong to view them as either based on misunderstandings or merely as epiphenomena of a deeper structural logic of change. In this sense, imperial legal histories align with E. P. Thompson's view that a modicum of justice acted as a powerful incentive for individuals and groups to participate in legal politics and, in the process, to seek to influence imperial legal reordering.[46]

[44] Mark Mazower, *No Enchanted Palace: The End of Empire and the Ideological Origins of the United Nations* (Princeton: Princeton University Press, 2009).

[45] Duncan Bell, *The Idea of Greater Britain: Empire and the Future of World Order, 1860–1900* (Princeton: Princeton University Press, 2007); Frederick Cooper, *Citizenship between Empire and Nation: Remaking France and French Africa, 1945–1960* (Princeton: Princeton University Press, 2014); Jane Burbank and Fred Cooper, "Rules of Law, Politics of Empire," in Benton and Ross, eds., *Legal Pluralism and Empires, 1500–1850*, pp. 279–294.

[46] We do not need to accept E. P. Thompson's defense of the rule of law as an "unqualified human good" or to overlook other shortcomings of his analysis in order to appreciate the point he makes about occasional fairness as a powerful inducement to participation in the law, even for eighteenth-century commoners undergoing dispossession. See E. P. Thompson, *Whigs and Hunters: The Origin of the Black Act* (New York: Pantheon, 1975), p. 263; and for a discussion of Thompson and the rule of law in empires, Benton, *Law and Colonial Cultures*, ch. 7.

Secondly, broad patterns of change in empires included shifts in the nature of claims about the systemic qualities of law and the hegemony of the state with regard to subpolities and subordinate jurisdictions. This not the same as showing that an imperial rule of law took root. The shifts we are describing emerged from jurisdictional politics and often amplified imperial legal anomalies. Still, we cannot overlook the trend toward more explicit and more expansive claims that the legal order itself represented a medium of governance and that imperial power involved special responsibilities for systemic ordering. These claims had real and often painful consequences.[47]

Viewed through these processes of conflict and projects of global ordering, the rule of law in empires emerges as a figure in the shadow of other and institutional change. Yet, its shadowy form was not without influence, as participants in legal conflicts and reforms could point to the virtues of legal order with powerful effect, and feel the brunt or benefit of it in the course of ongoing struggles for justice. Even when they referenced the rule of law indirectly under the more explicit banners of combating arbitrary justice and resolving constitutional crises at a distance, imperial rulers and subjects represented empires as systems of law that facilitated, contained, and defined the exercise of power.

[47] Ocko and Gilmartin make a persuasive plea to broaden study of the rule of law to include non-Western empires, but they preserve a sharp distinction between discourses of legitimacy and legal politics – one we are seeking to collapse here. Jonathan K. Ocko and David Gilmartin, "State, Sovereignty, and the People: A Comparison of the 'Rule of Law' in China and India," *Journal of Asian Studies*, 68 (2009), 55–100; and see the commentary in the forum on Asia and the rule of law in the same issue.

Part III

Moralities

The Rule of Law as an Essentially Contested Concept 6

Jeremy Waldron

Introduction

That a concept in common use, such as *the rule of law*, may be called essentially contested is not a criticism of that concept. Quite the contrary: "essentially contested" is a theoretical designation that draws attention to the way in which arguments about the meaning of a given concept contribute to our understanding and evaluation of the systems, practices, and actions to which the concept is applied.

It is true that some conceptual contestation just bogs us down in confusion. But not always. The philosopher who can claim to have been the first to draw essential contestability to our attention – W. B. Gallie – cited the concept of *democracy* as one of his examples and said that a key question to ask was whether "continuous competition for acknowledgement between rival uses of the popular concept of *democracy* seems likely to lead to an optimum development of the vague aims and confused achievements of the democratic tradition?"[1] If the answer is "Yes," then *democracy* is an essentially contested concept and we should not despair of its use just because there is no agreement about definitions. So it is also, we can argue, with *the rule of law*. There are many different definitions of *the rule of law* and none of them can claim to be canonical. But contestation between these rival conceptions works to enrich rather than impoverish our understanding of the heritage that has been associated over the centuries with legal and political uses of *the rule of law*.[2] We are in a better position to deploy *the rule of law* as a political ideal than

[1] W. B. Gallie, "Essentially Contested Concepts," *Proceedings of the Aristotelian Society*, 56 (1956), 186.

[2] For the contrast between concept and conceptions in the context of essential contestability, see Ronald Dworkin, *Taking Rights Seriously* (Cambridge: Harvard University Press, 1977), p. 134.

we would have been had it come to us with a single uncontested definition.

It is worth mentioning this at the outset because the idea of an essentially contested concept has sometimes been understood pessimistically, as an imperfection that takes us in the direction of relativism. "Essentially contested" may be taken to mean "very, very contested" – as though "essentially" were just an intensifier – a characterization that is supposed to steer clear thinkers away from the concept in question. Hopefully, we can show that this understanding is a mistake, and that drawing attention to the "essential contestedness" of *the rule of law* is not a reason for condemning the concept, but a way of showing how the heritage of disputation associated with it enriches and promotes some or all of the purposes for which *the rule of law* is cited in legal and political argument.

1 Types of Contestation

What kind of contestation affects (or afflicts) the concept of the rule of law? Contestation arises in a number of different ways.

First, the best known controversy concerns the breadth or narrowness – thickness or thinness – of *the rule of law*. On many accounts, *the rule of law* encompasses political ideals like human rights. For example, the World Justice Project (WJP) in its "Rule of Law Index" includes not only factors such as "Constraints on Government Powers" and the quality of "Civil Justice" and "Criminal Justice" in a society, but also "Open Government" and "Fundamental Rights." Under the last of these, it factors into the assessment of each nation's standing in the Rule of Law Index adherence to rights like the right to life, freedom of expression, freedom of religion, the right to privacy, fundamental labor rights, including the prohibition of child labor, and the elimination of discrimination. The inclusion of these factors is based on a conviction "that a system of positive law that fails to respect core human rights established under international law . . . does not deserve to be called a rule of law system." At the same time the WJP adds the following comment:

> Since there are many other indices that address human rights, and as it would be impossible for the Index to assess adherence to the full range of rights, this factor focuses on a relatively modest menu of rights that are firmly established under the

Universal Declaration [of Human Rights] and are most closely related to rule of law concerns.[3]

The last observation apparently concedes that "rule of law concerns" do not necessarily include human rights, but affirms that some human rights are worth including because they are more closely related to genuine rule of law concerns than others. That concession is necessary because many academic conceptions of the rule of law do not include any such substantive elements.

Thin conceptions of the rule of law confine themselves to formal and procedural aspects of legality – for example, the clarity, generality, prospectivity, consistency, and stability of the norms by which a society is governed and the integrity of the procedures and institutions by which they are enforced and through which disputes about their application are resolved. Joseph Raz is famous for insisting on this narrower understanding. The factors he mentions in his thin account of the rule of law include principles like these: all laws should be prospective, open, clear and relatively stable; the making of particular legal orders should be guided by general rules; the independence of the judiciary must be guaranteed; the courts should be easily accessible; and the principles of natural justice (like open and fair hearings, and absence of bias) must be observed. There is nothing about human rights on this list of formal and procedural elements, and Raz acknowledges that this omission may seem "alarming" to some. But he defends it by saying that:

the rule of law is just one of the virtues which a legal system may possess and by which it is to be judged. It is not to be confused with democracy, justice, equality (before the law or otherwise), human rights of any kind or respect for persons or for the dignity of man. A non-democratic legal system, based on the denial of human rights, on extensive poverty, on racial segregation, sexual inequalities, and religious persecution may, in principle, conform to the requirements of the rule of law better than any of the legal systems of the more enlightened Western democracies. This does not mean that it will be better than those Western democracies. It will be an immeasurably worse legal system, but it will excel in one respect: in its conformity to the rule of law.[4]

[3] See World Justice Project, *Rule of Law Index 2017–2018*, available at http://worldjusticeproject.org/factors.

[4] Joseph Raz, "The Rule of Law and its Virtue," in his *The Authority of Law: Essays on Law and Morality* (Oxford: Clarendon Press, 1979), p. 210.

Raz is anxious that "the rule of law" should not be used as a general stand-in for everything good one could ever want from a political system. He fears that would make our political evaluations less articulate. But not everyone is convinced. Tom Bingham, former Lord Chief Justice of England and Wales, writes in his book, *The Rule of Law*, that even though he recognizes the logical force of Raz's contention, he would "roundly reject it in favour of a thick definition, embracing the protection of human rights within its scope."[5] When battle lines are drawn in this manner, it is unlikely that contestation will end anytime soon.

The general controversy over thick and thin versions of the rule of law is mirrored also in detailed contestation about particular rule of law principles. Consider, for example, the principle of generality: people should be ruled by general norms not particular edicts. The requirement that norms be general in form and application does not in and of itself preclude discrimination. General laws phrased conditionally may impose special burdens or disabilities on certain disfavored groups such as racial groups or groups defined by gender or sexuality. Some will say that this shows that a requirement of formal generality is useless unless accompanied by a substantive prohibition on discrimination. Others respond, however, that the thin requirement of formal generality is not unimportant. If there are going to be practices of official discrimination, said one South African scholar during the apartheid era, "it is still preferable that they be stated as rules of law rather than that the power to discriminate be left to the discretion of an individual, for that would mean even greater arbitrariness."[6]

A second dispute that pervades discussion of *the rule of law* has to do with the kinds of norms it sponsors or favors. *The rule of law* requires certainty in the way a society is governed; that much is conceded. It respects everyone's need to know where they stand so far as the law is concerned and to know exactly how to modify their conduct to conform to its demands. But does *the rule of law* require clarity in the form of mechanically applicable rules, such as numerical speed limits? Does it preclude the use of what jurists call standards, like the prohibitions on "excessive" bail, "cruel" punishments, and "unreasonable" searches and seizures in the American Bill of Rights? Some say no. Cass Sunstein points

[5] Tom Bingham, *The Rule of Law* (London: Penguin, 2010), p. 67.

[6] Ben Beinart, "The Rule of Law," *Acta Juridica* (1962), 107.

out, quite rightly, that standards like these have always been devices available in the law's toolbox; they cannot be disassociated from the rule of law.[7] One need only think of the "reasonable care" standard in tort law. Others insist, with Antonin Scalia, that the rule of law has to be a law of rules, whose purpose it is to preclude the kind of discretion that the application of standards inevitably involves.[8] F. A. Hayek said that "[o]ne could write a history of the decline of the Rule of Law ... in terms of the progressive introduction of these vague formulas into legislation and jurisdiction."[9]

A third dispute goes directly to this issue of discretion. Does *the rule of law* prohibit the exercise of official discretion – the focused use of individual or collective intelligence for particular cases in a way that is not dictated by general rules – in the administration of a society? Those, like A. V. Dicey, who say that it does preclude the use of discretion do so because they see the rule of law as a necessary restriction on arbitrary government.[10] But those who say it does not preclude discretion say so because they believe discretion can be authorized and guided by law even if it is not wholly dominated by rules. They worry that a more restrictive conception of *the rule of law* will make it obsolete – completely incompatible with the modern administrative state.[11]

Fourthly, in modern constitutionalism, some of these issues crop up in the form of a debate about the nature of judicial authority. The idea of constitutional government taking place entirely under the control of a body of fundamental law continues to attract and fascinate us. But constitutional constraints, we know, cannot apply themselves. They work most effectively when officials and government agencies can be hauled before courts to have their conduct evaluated by the judiciary according to constitutional principles. This raises questions about the role of judges, particularly when the meaning or bearing of

[7] Cass R. Sunstein, "Rules and Rulelessness," Coase-Sandor Institute for Law and Economics Working Paper No. 27, University of Chicago Law School, 1994.

[8] Antonin Scalia, "The Rule of Law as a Law of Rules," *University of Chicago Law Review*, 56 (1989), 1175.

[9] Friedrich A. Hayek, *The Road to Serfdom* (Chicago: University of Chicago Press, 1972), p. 78.

[10] A. V. Dicey, *Introduction to the Study of the Law of the Constitution*, 8th ed. (London: Macmillan, 1915).

[11] Kenneth Culp Davis, *Discretionary Justice: A Preliminary Inquiry* (Baton Rouge: Louisiana State University Press, 1969), pp. 27–42.

a constitutional constraint is controversial. If courts are to have the last word in such controversies, can that really be regarded as *the rule of law* – as though a Supreme or Constitutional Court were nothing but the mouthpiece of the law? Or does it rather mean that we are still ruled by men – albeit men in black robes or men in wigs? This remains a live issue in the United States as jurists swing uneasily between the view that *the rule of law* requires that the Supreme Court have the final say in any constitutional crisis, and the position that judicial supremacy is as offensive to *the rule of law* as any other form of unreviewable supremacy in a constitutional regime.

A final point to note: there is a broader controversy behind all this. Historically, *the rule of law* has been associated with the belief that a salutary addition may be made to the classical menu of constitutional forms: as well as rule by one man, rule by the few, and rule by the many – monarchy, oligarchy, and democracy – there is also the possibility of *the rule of laws, not men.* That we might be ruled by the law itself rather than by any number of men is a prominent theme in Aristotle's discussion of law in the *Politics*;[12] it was a common topic in medieval political philosophy;[13] and it survived into the modern era in constitutionalist answers to Hobbesian absolutism.[14]

Now, most legal positivists regard the idea of *the rule of laws not men* as a nonstarter. Since laws are made, interpreted, and administered by men, there is really no contrast between *the rule of law* and *the rule of men.* To the extent that men *are* involved, we should still want to know whether we are dealing with (say) a legislative democracy, a legislative oligarchy, or a legislative monarchy. We should be under no illusion that it is possible to find a legalistic escape from human rule. The most we can hope for, say the legal positivists, is men ruling us through the medium of law – which means conforming their edicts to the forms and procedures noted above in the thinnest conception.

[12] Aristotle, *The Politics*, trans. Stephen Everson (Cambridge: Cambridge University Press, 1988), Bk III.

[13] See, for example, James of Viterbo, "Is It Better to Be Ruled by the Best Man than by the Best Laws?" in Arthur Stephen McGrade, John Kilcullen, and Matthew Kempshall, eds., *The Cambridge Translations of Medieval Philosophical Texts*, vol. 2: *Ethics and Political Philosophy* (Cambridge: Cambridge University Press, [1295–1296] 2001), pp. 321–325.

[14] Cf. Thomas Hobbes, *Leviathan*, ed. Richard Tuck (Cambridge: Cambridge University Press, [1652] 1997), ch. 26.

But the idea of being ruled by law itself has never been completely debunked. It survives in the form of the modern contrast between the rule of law and rule *by* law. *Rule by law* is said to be characteristic of authoritarians who use the forms and procedures of law as tools of power.[15] *Rule by law* does not involve the subordination of the highest echelon of government to legal control. Under *the rule of law*, by contrast, the human element in government is constrained by laws that somehow do not represent in themselves a form of human control. Of course, no one denies that there is always a human aspect (unless we are talking about natural law or divine law). But even on earth, certain kinds of law push the element of human power into the background, either because the laws in question were laid down centuries ago and so do not represent the exercise of power by a current generation of rulers, or because the laws that constrain government now can be seen as an unplanned resultant of a myriad of human decisions (by common law judges, for example) rather than as a deliberately imposed constraint. Law can mean many things and, as these examples illustrate, under pressure of controversy *the rule of law* sometimes comes to privilege some forms of law rather than others - custom or common law, for example, rather than legislation.[16]

2 Has the Concept Lost Clear Meaning?

So there is all this contestation – and more.[17] Philosophers sometimes write as though the phrase "the rule of law" once had a clear meaning, but now lamentably it has lost it through misuse occasioned by well-meaning but muddled enthusiasm. This lamentation over lost clarity is a common trope in the rhetoric of philosophical analysis. But it is usually a myth. The terms whose ordinary usage we now deplore as confused, the terms we accuse our contemporaries of misusing, have almost always been perplexing. They have always resisted the analyst's corral.

15 See Tom Ginsburg and Tamir Moustafa, eds., *Rule by Law: The Politics of Courts in Authoritarian Regimes* (Cambridge: Cambridge University Press, 2008).

16 Friedrich A. Hayek, *Law, Legislation and Liberty*, vol. 1: *Rules and Order* (Chicago: University of Chicago Press, 1973), pp. 94ff.

17 For further examples, see Jeremy Waldron, "Is the Rule of Law an Essentially Contested Concept (in Florida)?" *Law and Philosophy*, 21 (2002), 137.

So what are we to say? If street-level use were completely confused, we would have no alternative but to pronounce the term meaningless. This is Judith Shklar's verdict:

> It would not be very difficult to show that the phrase "the Rule of Law" has become meaningless thanks to ideological abuse and general over-use. It may well have become just another one of those self-congratulatory rhetorical devices that grace the public utterances of Anglo-American politicians. No intellectual effort need ... be wasted on this bit of ruling-class chatter.[18]

Some concepts are just "radically confused": we would do better disengaging on the basis of the redefinition of terms or the invention of new ones. At that stage, the best we could do would be to substitute for "the rule of law" a well-defined technical term, which would serve us for analytic and theoretical purposes.[19] But of course such strategies seldom work. Well-defined technical terms hardly ever succeed in replacing the loose usage they are intended to supersede. Since the loose term of ordinary language coexists with the theorist's replacement, the latter usage has to be attended with constant reminders that it is not to be confused with its promiscuous and disorderly homonym on the streets. And anyway, there is seldom ever just one technical stipulation: usually there are dozens, each put forward by a well-meaning philosopher hoping to clear up ordinary usage by the introduction of his own (controversial) conception. The result might be a situation among theorists which is as confused and equivocal in its way as the situation on the streets.

Moreover motives are not always pure in this debate. For one reason or another, "the rule of law" is a phrase with powerful overtones of positive evaluation. It is tempting for ideologues to appropriate the benefit of those overtones by associating the phrase tendentiously with their own political or economic agendas. So, for example, if one wants to persuade governments to respect property and the principle of market freedom, one does one's best to associate those values with "the rule of law." This strategy is often quite deliberate and cynical.[20]

[18] Judith N. Shklar, "Political Theory and the Rule of Law," in Allan Hutchinson and Patrick Monahan, eds., *The Rule of Law: Ideal or Ideology* (Toronto: Carswell, 1987), p. 1.

[19] For a defense of this general approach to conceptual disputation, see Felix Oppenheim, *Political Concepts: A Reconstruction* (Oxford: Blackwell, 1981), pp. 177 ff.

[20] See the discussion in Jeremy Waldron, *The Rule of Law and the Measure of Property* (Cambridge: Cambridge University Press, 2012), pp. 49–50.

We must therefore ask: can the idea of essential contestability characterize disputes about *the rule of law* in a more respectable way than this?

3 Fallon and Beyond

In 1997, Richard Fallon set out a number of features that make it especially difficult to reach consensus about the meaning of "the rule of law."[21] He pointed out, first, that even though there is some consensus about the basic principles of the rule of law, they are all understood quite vaguely and there is no easy consensus on the application of terms like the clarity of laws or their constancy. It is difficult moreover to reach agreement on how to determine the relative significance of acknowledged departures from what the Rule of Law is said to require. As Fallon put it:

> If administrative agencies can mix executive, lawmaking, and judicial functions in implementing vague statutory mandates; if courts are bound by the originally understood or intended meaning of authoritative legal texts; and if rules do not determine outcomes, then what, if anything, could be left of the Rule of Law?[22]

Not only that, but as long as we lack a consensus on standards of judicial interpretation, it is hard to agree about when or whether judges are constrained by law in making their decisions.[23] At best, Fallon says we must acknowledge that the rule of law tangles together a number of different strands of evaluation: different values jostle and compete with one another in this domain. Sometimes they present themselves as complementary. But their interplay is never straightforward, and we are often puzzled by others' use of the concept while at the same time exhibiting too much confidence in our own particular conceptions. "Invocations of the Rule of Law," says Fallon, "are sufficiently meaningful to deserve attention, but today are typically too vague and conclusory to dispel lingering puzzlement. We should strive to do better."[24]

[21] Richard Fallon, "'The Rule of Law' as a Concept in Constitutional Discourse," *Columbia Law Review*, 97 (1997) 1, 9–10.

[22] Fallon, "'The Rule of Law' as a Concept in Constitutional Discourse," 4.

[23] Fallon, "'The Rule of Law' as a Concept in Constitutional Discourse," 9.

[24] Fallon, "'The Rule of Law' as a Concept in Constitutional Discourse," 55–56.

Against this background, Fallon asks whether *the rule of law* should be regarded as an essentially contested concept in the technical sense of that term.[25] Fallon was alluding to an idea introduced in philosophical circles forty years earlier by W. B. Gallie to describe concepts like *art* and *democracy*, that seem to be both meaningful and at the same time the locus of endemic contestation. As I have indicated, I think Fallon is on to something. Unfortunately, he did not pursue the details of Gallie's characterization as it might be applied to this particular concept. So let us see, as Fallon says, whether we can do better.

What makes a contested concept – a concept that people disagree about – into an *essentially* contested concept? Gallie said a number of things. The first is that the prospect of contestation is bound up with the very essence of the concept. There are certain concepts, Gallie said, "the proper use of which inevitably involves endless disputes about their proper uses on the part of their users."[26] One does not understand these terms without understanding the inevitability of contestation. To think that the concept in question is clear is to make a mistake about its meaning.

A second way of getting at Gallie's idea is to say that the term "essentially' refers to the *location* of the disagreement: it is contestation at the core, not just at the borderlines of a concept. We all know about vagueness: some things are green, some are blue; and on the borderlines there are blue/green cases of indeterminacy. By contrast, a concept such as *democracy* evokes disagreement not only about marginal cases but also about paradigm or core cases. For some, the United States is a paradigm case of democracy: if the US is not a democracy nothing is. For others, the US is not a good paradigm, not only because of things like low voter-turnout, lack of proportional representation, and compromises with various aristocratic ideals (like judicial review), but also because it lacks important features of social democracy – for instance, the empowerment, in something more than merely formal terms, of the worst-off members of society. The disagreement between those who define *democracy* purely in terms of formal electoral arrangements and those who insist on a social element is disagreement about the essence of the concept. It is essence-related contestation.

[25] Fallon, "'The Rule of Law' as a Concept in Constitutional Discourse," 6.
[26] Gallie, "Essentially Contested Concepts," 169.

As well as these explanations of what makes conceptual contestation "essential," Gallie also listed a number of features that a concept must possess in order to count as an essentially contested concept. It must be a normative concept, used to refer to some sort of valued or outstanding achievement. That achievement in turn must be a complex one having to do with the presence of a number of different aspects or attributes. But the attributes do not figure in a rigidly understood list of necessary or sufficient conditions. Though everyone agrees the achievement is complex, "there is nothing absurd or self-contradictory in any one of a number of possible rival descriptions of its total worth, one such description setting its component parts or features in one order of importance, a second setting them in a second order, and so on ... [T]he accredited achievement is initially variously describable."[27] Moreover, it is accepted on all sides that a concept of this kind is sensitive in different ways to changes in the subject matter to which it is applied. Everyone acknowledges that the achievement is "of a kind that admits of considerable modification in the light of changing circumstances; and such modification cannot be prescribed or predicted in advance."[28] But those who grasp the concept understand that it may be applied in various ways to the new circumstances that it faces.

It is not hard to apply all this to *the rule of law*. *The rule of law* is plainly an appraisive concept: it is deployed by almost all of its users to enter a favorable evaluation of the regimes or practices to which it applies.[29] Its complexity is pretty evident as well. In Anglo-American jurisprudence, the phrase "the rule of law" is used to conjure up a laundry list of features that a healthy legal system should exhibit. These are mostly variations on the eight desiderata of Lon Fuller's "internal morality of law": laws should be (1) general, (2) publicly promulgated, (3) prospective, (4) intelligible, (5) consistent, (6) practicable, (7) not too frequently changeable, and (8) congruent with the behavior of officials.[30]

27 Gallie, "Essentially Contested Concepts," 172.

28 Gallie, "Essentially Contested Concepts," 172.

29 There are one or two thinkers who disparage the rule of law. See, for example, Morton J. Horwitz, "The Rule of Law: An Unqualified Human Good?" *Yale Law Journal*, 86 (1977) 566: "I do not see how a Man of the Left can describe the rule of law as 'an unqualified human good.'" This was in response to the discussion in Thompson, *Whigs and Hunters*, p. 266.

30 Lon L. Fuller, *The Morality of Law* (New Haven: Yale University Press, 1964), p. 39.

Actually this may not be the complexity that the contestedness of *the rule of law* involves. Rival conceptions of the ideal are not formed by listing Fuller's eight principles in different orders of inclusion or priority. Most contestation arises (as we have already seen) out of attempts to supplement Fuller's list with elements of different kinds. Some conceptions, modestly, add certain procedural and institutional elements: Raz does this with his reference to natural justice (procedural due process) and the independence of the judiciary.[31] Others do it more radically, insisting on substantive considerations, like human rights, or by insisting on an explicit link between the rule of law and the defense of private property.[32] But Gallie's suggestion that our understanding of this concept and our ordering of its various priorities is bound to change over time is certainly satisfied. As governance changes, as the practice of law changes, so also will we expect changes and contestation about changes in the rule of law.

In the midst of this contestation, what holds the conceptual debate together? What ensures that the disputants are not just talking past one another? In his 1958 article, Gallie suggested that what holds an essentially contested concept together is the implicit reference back, on the part of all the competing users, to the achievement of an exemplar and to different ways in which that achievement might be characterized or offered as a model in current circumstances. Essential contestability was associated with the existence of an original exemplar, whose achievement the rival conceptions sought to characterize and develop. (He cited, as an example here, the contested concept of *the Christian way of life*.)

But such reference back to the achievement of a single exemplar may be too narrow an account of what gives unity to such a concept. For some of his other examples, such as *democracy*, Gallie cites a heritage of thought and understanding. There is no original exemplar of *democracy* – not even ancient Athens – that we are all trying to characterize and apply in the modern world. But there has come down to us a recognizable heritage of democratic thought, and that is what the various conceptions are trying to make sense of. And so I think it is with *the rule of law*.

[31] See Raz, "The Rule of Law and its Virtue," pp. 214–219; John Finnis, *Natural Law and Natural Rights* (Oxford: Oxford University Press, 1980), p. 270; and Jeremy Waldron, "The Rule of Law and the Importance of Procedure," in James Fleming, ed., *Getting to the Rule of Law: NOMOS L* (New York: New York University Press, 2011), p. 3.

[32] Bingham, *The Rule of Law*, pp. 66ff.

Perhaps there is no original exemplar of *the rule of law*. But there is certainly a problem that has preoccupied us for 2,500 years: How can we make law rule in a state full of powerful men? On this account the rule of law is a solution-concept, not an achievement-concept; it is the concept of a solution to a problem – *it is a conceptual answer to a problem* – we are unsure how to solve; and rival conceptions are rival proposals for solving it or proposals for doing the best we can, given that the problem is insoluble.

4 *Essential* Contestability

How does the designation of a concept as essentially contested affect the way we argue about it? John Gray has raised the question of whether there might not be "a radical fault in the very notion of a contest which cannot by its nature be won or lost."[33] How can there be argument about something which (in Gallie's words) is "not resolvable by argument of any kind"?[34] If it is true that "no one clearly definable general use of any of [the concept in question] can be set up as the correct or standard use,"[35] then there does not seem to be anything for the disagreement to be *about*. How can people contribute to a debate if, as Gallie says, it is part of the proper understanding of the concept that the disagreement will never go away?

The characterization in terms of essential contestability seems to misrepresent what it is like to engage in such contestation. To a participant, surely nothing matters more than that his definition be sustained and his opponent's one refuted. He is not saying simply, "Here's one more view about *the rule of law* to put in the catalogue." Surely each proponent is saying, "This is what *the rule of law* really is. This, and not those other views, captures the true essence of the concept." An observer, however, with Gallie's article in his back pocket, will say: "JW thinks he's going to win, but he must know in the back of his mind that the discussion is unwinnable. So why is he making so much fuss? There are no right answers here: *the rule of law* is an essentially contested concept." Can these perspectives be combined in a sort of

[33] John Gray, "Political Power, Social Theory, and Essential Contestability," in David Miller and Larry Siedentop, eds., *The Nature of Political Theory* (Oxford: Oxford University Press, 1983), p. 75.

[34] Gallie, "Essentially Contested Concepts," 169.

[35] Gallie, "Essentially Contested Concepts," 168.

double consciousness? At the level of the well-informed theorist, we may ask: Is it possible to engage in one of these debates as a partisan of a particular view but also and at the same time as a theorist who knows why disputes of this kind are intractable? Can one acknowledge that a concept is essentially contested and still claim that one's own view is right and one's opponent's view wrong?

This remains the chief difficulty for Gallie's idea. I think the most one can say is that realistically one's participation in such a dispute is predicated on the hope that the contestation will be the better for one's intervention.

Conclusion

So we return to the point with which we began. Can we say that calling a concept – such as the rule of law – essentially contested is not a way of disparaging it? Can we say that the contestation actually helps with the enrichment of the concept and advances the quality of argumentation that uses it? Gallie thinks we can:

> Recognition of a given concept as essentially contested implies recognition of rival uses of it (such as oneself repudiates) as not only logically possible and humanly "likely," but as of permanent critical value to one's own use or interpretation of the concept in question . . . One very desirable consequence of the required recognition in any proper instance of essential contestedness might therefore be expected to be a marked raising of the level of quality of arguments in the disputes of the contestant parties.[36]

In other words, the contestation between rival conceptions deepens and enriches all sides' understanding of the area of value that the contested concept marks out.

"Essential contestability" is about a way in which certain ideals are present to us. Some ideals are present in clear and well-defined form – the economists' term "wealth-maximization," for example. In that case controversies tend to center on strategies and implementation, and the weight that the ideal should have against other competing values. But in the case of essentially contested concepts, they are present to us only in the

[36] Gallie, "Essentially Contested Concepts," 193.

form of contestation about what the ideal really involves. And that kind of presence can promise theoretical enrichment.

For *the rule of law*, this enrichment has happened in a number of areas. Let me end with three examples.

As a first example, consider recent debates about legal certainty. Though *the rule of law* has often been associated with a demand for predictability, we have seen a number of subtle attempts to reconceive the role that predictability plays in our understanding of the value of law and to relate it to different forms of legal reasoning and argumentation. We see this, for example, in Ronald Dworkin's response to what he calls "legal conventionalism" in *Law's Empire*,[37] and we see it too as a dialectic internal to the work of Friedrich Hayek over time.[38]

A second example concerns the critique by theorists of the modern administrative state of the rule of law criteria set out in Lon Fuller's work.[39] Edward Rubin has argued that we need to reconsider and rebuild our understanding of *the rule of law* for an age where we are not just talking about courts' administering determinate statutes, but about agencies and institutions of the state communicating with one another and mediating at several different levels between law-makers and citizens.[40] Rubin does not want to argue that *the rule of law* is an archaic irrelevance in the age of the administrative state. But he does believe it needs to be rethought, particularly in its requirements of publicity and clarity.

A third example invites us to consider the way in which *the rule of law* might operate in the international realm. Some jurists simply transpose traditional criteria of clarity and certainty and affirm that these matter as much in international governance as they do in the municipal sphere.[41] Others acknowledge that the different position of states as subjects or agencies of international law calls for different epistemic relations

[37] Ronald Dworkin, *Law's Empire* (Cambridge: Harvard University Press, 1986), ch. 4.

[38] Compare the conception of predictability set out in Friedrich A. Hayek, *The Constitution of Liberty* (London: Routledge, 1960) with the quite different and much more subtle understanding thirteen years later in Hayek, *Law, Legislation and Liberty*, vol. 1.

[39] Fuller, *The Morality of Law*, p. 39.

[40] Edward Rubin, "Law and Legislation in the Administrative State," *Columbia Law Review*, 89 (1989), 369.

[41] See, for example, Simon Chesterman, "An International Rule of Law?" *American Journal of Comparative Law*, 56 (2008), 331.

toward governing norms.[42] Once again, those who participate in these controversies may seem to be talking past each other. But by deploying subtly or considerably different conceptions of *the rule of law* against each other, they lay the conditions for each conception to be enriched by elements that are not initially given as part of its content.

[42] See Jeremy Waldron, "Are Sovereigns Entitled to the Benefit of the Rule of Law?" *European Journal of International Law*, 22 (2011), 315.

The Rule of Law in Montesquieu 7

Sharon R. Krause

Introduction

The rule of law is a central theme of Montesquieu's major work, *The Spirit of the Laws* (1748), and in many respects it forms the conceptual core of his political theory. For Montesquieu, the rule of law means that the use of political power is subject to the formal constraint of standing rules that are codified in the positive laws of the land. It means that no one is above the law and that the actions of the state must conform in a consistent way to publicly known standards. The rule of law is the single most important factor, as Montesquieu sees it, in establishing moderation in government and therefore in protecting political liberty. Political liberty is the primary standard of measure that Montesquieu employs in his wide-ranging assessment of rulers and regimes from ancient Greece and Rome to medieval Europe to eighteenth-century France and England to the far-flung societies of China, Persia, and Russia. Interpreters disagree about some aspects of Montesquieu's work, including whether he preferred the regime of monarchy represented by modern France or the commercial republic exemplified by England,[1] whether or not he was a proponent of natural

[1] There is a reasonable debate between those who regard Montesquieu as favoring republicanism and those who see him as a defender of monarchy. Mark Hulliung defends the former position in *Montesquieu and the Old Regime* (Berkeley: University of California Press, 1976). Others who read Montesquieu as a defender of republicanism (whether classical or contemporary) include Paul Rahe, *Montesquieu and the Logic of Liberty* (New Haven: Yale University Press, 2010); and Thomas Pangle, *Montesquieu's Philosophy of Liberalism: A Commentary on The Spirit of the Laws* (Chicago: University of Chicago Press, 1973). Those who read Montesquieu as favoring the monarchical form of government include Annelien De Dijn, "Montesquieu's Controversial Context: *The Spirit of the Laws* as a Monarchist Tract," *History of Political Thought*, 34 (2013), 66–88; Robin Douglass, "Montesquieu and Modern Republicanism," *Political Studies*, 60 (2012), 703–719; Michael A. Mosher, "Monarchy's Paradox: Honor in the Face of Sovereign Power," in David W. Carrithers, Michael Mosher, and Paul Rahe, eds., *Montesquieu's Science of Politics: Essays on The Spirit of Laws* (Lanham: Rowman & Littlefield, 2001), pp. 214–218; Jean Ehrard, *Politique de Montesquieu* (Paris: Armand Colin, 1965), p. 35;

law,[2] and if he can fairly be described as an Orientalist.[3] Yet there is little disagreement about the central role that the rule of law plays within his political thought.

At the same time, the depth and originality of Montesquieu's distinctive understanding of the rule of law has received less attention than it deserves. Three features of his view are especially significant. The first is his focus on the diverse dimensions of the rule of law as a political practice. This diversity includes institutional mechanisms such as the separation of powers, human passions such as honor and self-interest, and multiple forms of contestation across competing sites of power – economic, social, and religious as well as political. The second distinctive feature of Montesquieu's view is the multidimensionality of law as he conceives it. For the rule of law to be in effect, political power must answer not only to law as the formally codified outputs of legislative processes but also to what Montesquieu calls "the spirit of the laws." By this he means that power should be exercised consonant with the broader background of norms, values, and social practices that constitute a particular people's way of life and should be consistent with natural law and the standard of natural equity. The rule of law in Montesquieu links positive law to law in these other forms. The third distinctive feature of Montesquieu's approach is the emphasis he places on the independence of the judicial branch of government and on moderation in the content and application of civil and criminal laws. Together these features of Montesquieu's view suggest that that the rule of law is best understood not in exclusively legalistic terms and not as the fixed backdrop of politics but as a multidimensional, dynamic political practice that must be continuously reenacted, drawing support from a broad array of sources.

and Emile Faguet, *La politique comparée de Montesquieu, Rousseau et Voltaire* (Paris: Société Française d'Imprimérie et de Librairie, 1902), pp. 46–47.

[2] See, for example, David L. Williams, "Political Ontology and Institutional Design in Montesquieu and Rousseau," *American Journal of Political Science*, 54 (2010), 527–531; Michael Zuckert, "Natural Law, Natural Rights, and Classical Liberalism: Montesquieu's Critique of Hobbes," *Social Philosophy and Policy*, 18 (2001), 227–251; C. P. Courtney, "Montesquieu and Natural Law," in Carrithers, Mosher, and Rahe, eds., *Montesquieu's Science of Politics*, pp. 41–68; Simone Goyard-Fabre, *La philosophie du droit de Montesquieu* (Paris: Librairie C. Klincksieck, 1973); Mark Waddicor, *Montesquieu and the Philosophy of Natural Law* (The Hague: Martinus Nijhoff, 1970); and Tzvetan Todorov, *On Human* Diversity, trans. Catherine Porter (Cambridge: Harvard University Press, 1993), pp. 369–372.

[3] For discussion of Montesquieu and Orientalism, see Sharon R. Krause, "Despotism in *The Spirit of Laws*," in Carrithers, Mosher, and Rahe, eds., *Montesquieu's Science of Politics*, pp. 249–272.

The next section of this chapter lays out the meaning of the rule of law as it emerges in *The Spirit of the Laws* and examines the institutional conditions, moral psychology, and forms of contestation that Montesquieu believed necessary to sustain it.[4] The text then explores how the rule of law incorporates the "spirit of the laws" in its multiple forms as well as natural law and natural equity. The penultimate section elaborates the importance of an independent judiciary for maintaining the rule of law, along with Montesquieu's emphasis on moderation in civil and criminal law. In concluding, I return to the role of the rule of law in sustaining Montesquieu's guiding principle of political liberty.

1 The Meaning and Conditions of the Rule of Law

Although the term "rule of law" is not a mainstay of Montesquieu's political thought, the concept permeates *The Spirit of the Laws*. It is a key variable in his typology of regimes, a fundamental criterion for distinguishing monarchy from both republics and despotism. On his view, government admits of three main forms: republics in which "the people as a body, or . . . a part of the people, have sovereign power"; despotism, in which "one alone, without law and without rule, drives everything by his will and his caprices"; and monarchies, in which "one alone governs, but by fixed and established laws" (II.1, 239). Despotism is the *bête noire* of

[4] In addition to *The Spirit of the Laws*, Montesquieu's other important works include *Persian Letters* (1721) and *Considerations on the Causes of the Greatness of the Romans and their Decline* (1734). He also kept extensive notebooks, *Mes Pensées* (1899–1901), which contain seeds of ideas developed elsewhere. *The Spirit of the Laws* is without doubt his *magnum opus*, however, written over a period of twenty years and completed just seven years before his death. He says in the preface to the work that in the course of writing the book, "I discovered my principles . . . the histories of all nations being only their consequences" Montesquieu, *De l'esprit des lois*, in *Oeuvres complètes*, ed. Roger Caillois (Paris: Pléiade, 1951), vol. 2, Preface, pp. 231, 229. As one commentator puts it, Montesquieu was "a man who put all he knew into . . . one book." Anne M. Cohler, "Introduction," in Montesquieu, *The Spirit of the Laws*, trans. and ed. by Anne M. Cohler, Basia Carolyn Miller, and Harold Samuel Stone (Cambridge: Cambridge University Press, [1748] 1989), p. xi. Given the comprehensiveness of *The Spirit of the Laws* and its centrality within Montesquieu's political thought, the present analysis focuses on this work. Hereafter references to *SL* will appear parenthetically in the text, citing book, chapter, and page number of the Pléiade edition. Translations are my own, although I have consulted the translation by Cohler et al., cited above.

Montesquieu's political theory, the always-present danger that his work shows us how to resist. It is government by will and caprice, perpetually unpredictable, running on fear, spawning violence and destruction, and tending inevitably toward its own dissolution.[5] It is the antithesis of the rule of law. Republican government is not the black hole that Montesquieu conceives despotism to be and in his view some republics have managed to achieve moderation and liberty. Yet republics are unreliable in this regard because the rule of law is not endemic to them. The structure of republican government is defined solely in terms of the sovereign power of the people (or a part of the people, depending on whether the republic takes a democratic or an aristocratic form), without reference to the presence of fixed laws that would serve to limit this power. In contrast to monarchies, in which "the laws have provided for the constitution" and "the principle of government constrains the monarch," when a citizen in a republic "gives himself exorbitant power, the abuse of this power is greater because the laws ... have done nothing to constrain it" (II.3, 245). More generally, because the power of the people is not checked by fixed and fundamental laws, republics tend to swing unpredictably between permissiveness and tyranny. Thus Montesquieu insists that those who identify republican government with liberty are wrong. In republics, he says, "the people seem roughly to do what they want," but to conclude from this fact that republics are necessarily free is a mistake. One must not confuse "the power of the people" with "the liberty of the people"; the two are by no means equivalent (XI.2, 394). Republics "are not free states by their nature" because the rule of law is not a constitutive feature of this form of government (XI.4, 395), and the rule of law is the measure of a free state.

[5] For further discussion of despotism in Montesquieu, see Vickie B. Sullivan, *Montesquieu and the Despotic Ideas of Europe* (Chicago: University of Chicago Press, 2017); Françoise Weil, "Montesquieu et le Despotisme," in Françoise Weil, *Actes du congrès Montesquieu réuni à Bordeaux du 23 au 26 mai 1955 pour commémorer le deuxièm centenaire de la mort de Montesquieu* (Bordeaux: Imprimeries Delmas, 1956), pp. 191–215; Alain Grosrichard, *Structure du sérail: La fiction du despotisme asiatique dans l'occident classique* (Paris: Éditions du Seuil, 1979); Roger Boesche, "Fearing Monarchs and Merchants: Montesquieu's Two Theories of Despotism," *Western Political Science Quarterly*, 43 (1990), 741–761; Badreddine Kassem, *Décadence et absolutisme dans l'oeuvre de Montesquieu* (Paris: Librairie Minard, 1960); David Young, "Montesquieu's View of Despotism and His Use of Travel Literature," *Review of Politics*, 40 (1978), 392–405; and Krause, "Despotism in *The Spirit of Laws*."

Among the three primary types of government, the rule of law figures constitutively only in the regime of monarchy.[6] Here it is found both in the presence of "fundamental laws" that check the will of the monarch and in the "intermediate" powers such as the clergy and the nobility, whose constitutionally entrenched status, social standing, and wealth make them formidable "obstacles" to the potentially encroaching power of the crown (II.4, 247–248). Montesquieu does concede that "in a monarchy, the prince is the source of all political and civil power," and consequently he describes the intermediate bodies as "subordinate and dependent" rather than as equi-sovereign. At the same time, however, he insists that these bodies, above all the nobility, are "in the essence of monarchy." Indeed, the "fundamental maxim" of this form of government is "no monarch, no nobility: no nobility, no monarch; instead one has a despot" (II.4, 247). The intermediary bodies are constitutive of the regime of monarchy not merely supplements to it because they help establish the rule of law there.

They include the military branch of the nobility (the *noblesse d'épée*) and the clergy but Montesquieu associates them especially with what he calls the "political bodies" that administer the "fundamental laws," staffed mainly by members of the administrative branch of the nobility (the *noblesse de robe*) (II.4, 248). These bodies function as "a depository of laws" that "announce the laws when they are made, and recall them when they are forgotten" (II.4, 249). Crucially, their independent status insulates them from the "momentary will of the prince," in contrast to "the prince's council," which is directly dependent on the prince and therefore "is not a suitable depository" (II.4, 249). The *noblesse de robe* was comprised of lawyers, judges, members of the *parlements*, and local officials. Technically, their role was to carry out the prince's laws, but in practice this role made it possible for them sometimes to obstruct the prince's will. The *parlements*, for example, enjoyed a right of remonstrance that enabled them to delay registration of a law while presenting a formal objection about it to the crown. Likewise, local officials could slow, alter, and impede the execution of decrees issued by the prince when implementing them in their domains.[7]

[6] The rule of law also figures in the mixed regime of England, with its constitutionally established separation of powers (XI.6; XIX.27). England is discussed in what follows.

[7] For discussion of the role of the nobility in this regard, see Jacob Levy, "Montesquieu's Constitutional Legacies," in Rebecca Kingston, ed., *Montesquieu and His Legacy* (Albany: State University of New York Press, 2008), pp. 115–138; Pierre Barrière, *Un grand provincial: Charles-Louis de Secondat baron de La Brède et de Montesquieu* (Bordeaux: Delmas,

Montesquieu regards this capacity to obstruct as immensely valuable. As he puts it, "the bodies that are the depository of the laws never obey better than when they move slowly and carry into the affairs of the prince that reflection which one can scarcely expect given the dearth of enlightenment of the court about the laws of the state" (V.10, 289–290). So even though Montesquieu ostensibly insists on the sovereignty of the prince, the regime of monarchy is constituted in its nature by innumerable pockets of resistance to the prince. Consequently, "just as the sea, which seems to want to cover all the earth, is constrained by the grasses and the smallest rocks that are found on the shore, so monarchs, whose power seems to be without limits, are constrained by the smallest obstacles" (II.4, 248). The dividedness of the regime, and the periodic resistance from independent, intermediary bodies charged with administering the laws of the land, are how the rule of law works in monarchy.[8]

The rule of law is therefore closely tied to the principle of separate or balanced powers that Montesquieu made famous and that was so influential for the American founders. In view of the "eternal experience that every man who has power is led to abuse it" and will continue "until he finds limits," effective constraints on the abuse of power must be built into the structure of government, meaning that "by the arrangement of things power must constrain power" (XI.4, 395). French monarchy is one way to achieve this balance, with its combination of king and intermediary bodies such as the nobility. England's constitution, which formally divides power between executive, legislative, and judicial branches, offers a different approach to the same idea, and Montesquieu's most influential remarks

1946), pp. 119–130; Melvin Richter, "Montesquieu and the Concept of Civil Society," *The European Legacy*, 3 (1998), 35; Rebecca Kingston, *Montesquieu and the Parlement of Bordeaux* (Geneva: Librairie Droz, 1996); and Franklin Ford, *Robe and Sword: The Regrouping of the French Aristocracy after Louis* XIV (Cambridge: Harvard University Press, 1953). There was a sizable literature in the early eighteenth century on the constitutional standing of the French nobility and the status of their legislative and judicial rights. Books XXVIII and XXX–XXXI of *The Spirit of the Laws* comprise Montesquieu's contribution to those debates. For further discussion, see Iris Cox, *Montesquieu and the History of French Laws* (Oxford: Voltaire Foundation, 1983).

[8] Isaiah Berlin once noted that, for Montesquieu, free societies are necessarily "in a constant state of agitation." See *Against the Current: Essays in the History of Ideas* (New York: Viking, 1980), p. 158. On this point, see also Judith Shklar, *Montesquieu* (Oxford: Oxford University Press, 1987), p. 59; and Nannerl O. Keohane, *Philosophy and the State in France* (Princeton: Princeton University Press, 1980), p. 398.

on the separation of powers come from his chapters on England (XI.6; XIX.27).

Yet the constitutional form of a division and balance of powers is incomplete, on Montesquieu's view, without an accompanying moral psychology. Indeed, his typology of regimes pairs the "nature" of each government, meaning "its particular structure," with a specific "principle," meaning "that which makes it act" (III.1, 250). The principle of each government is its distinctive moral psychology, the "human passions that make it move" (III.1, 251). The principle of republics is civic virtue, the principle of despotism is fear, and the principle of monarchy is honor. These principles are never the only motives in play but in each case the principle of government has a special salience for the regime and contributes in a distinctive way to maintaining its institutional structure. Popular self-government is only possible over the long term if the citizenry is, on the whole, motivated to love the republic, and to prioritize the common good over private interests (V.2, 274). For despotism to sustain itself, widespread fear is required "to beat down all courage and put out even the least feeling of ambition" that might generate challenges to the prince (III.9, 258–259). In monarchy, it is honor that "makes all the parts of the body politic move" (III.7, 257). Honor is "the prejudice of each person and each condition" (III.6, 256), meaning an attachment to one's position and the political prerogatives that attend it. Honor marries the desire for personal distinction to a particular code that takes the form of a set of "law" and "consistent rules" (III.8, 258). This spirited combination motivates the members of the intermediary bodies to oppose actions by the crown that run contrary to their constitutional prerogatives and to established law. This results in "necessary modifications of obedience" to the crown (III.10, 260) and upholds the rule of law. As Montesquieu puts it, honor "gives life" not only to "the whole body politic" but also – perhaps above all – "to the laws" (III.8, 258).[9] Under the right conditions, self-interest also can support the rule of law. In Montesquieu's depiction of the government of England, for example, the interests of the various groups (the king, the nobility, and the people) associated with the different branches of government

[9] For a fuller elaboration of the meaning and role of honor in Montesquieu, see Sharon R. Krause, *Liberalism with Honor* (Cambridge: Harvard University Press, 2002), pp. 32–66; and Michael Mosher, "Monarchy's Paradox: Honor in the Face of Sovereign Power," in Carrithers, Mosher, and Rahe, eds., *Montesquieu's Science of Politics*, pp. 159–230.

(executive, legislative, judicial) motivate them to defend their political prerogatives against encroachments from the other branches (XIX.27). This resistance supports the separation of powers and helps sustain the rule of law. Establishing the rule of law therefore requires both the right institutions and the right passions.

Other factors also can help. Montesquieu regarded commerce as potentially valuable in this regard, in part because it generates extrapolitical sources of influence from which the potentially abusive power of a prince can be contested. Commerce "has taken away the great acts of authority" on the part of monarchs by establishing powerful countervailing forces (XXII.13, 671).[10] As a result of commerce, princes have begun "to be cured of Machiavellianism" and "have had to govern themselves with more wisdom than they themselves would have thought" (XXI.20, 641). Religion too can provide grounds for resistance to the abuse of power, even under despotism. It "can sometimes oppose the will of the prince" insofar as it proscribes his subjects from doing what he commands. "One will abandon one's father, one will even kill him, if the prince orders it," Montesquieu says, but if religious texts forbid the consumption of alcohol "one will not drink wine [even] if the prince wants it and orders it. The laws of religion are part of a higher precept" (III.10, 260). Religion can therefore support political resistance to a monarch. It can also constrain the monarch directly:

> A prince who loves religion and who fears it is a lion who cedes to the hand that strokes him or to the voice that appeases him; the one who fears religion and who hates it is like the wild beasts who bite the chain that prevents them from pouncing on those who pass; one who has no religion at all is that terrible animal that feels its liberty only when it tears up and devours (XXIV.2, 715–716).

Thus "even if it were useless that subjects have a religion," Montesquieu says, 'it would not be useless for princes to have one and to whiten with foam the only brake that those who fear no human laws can have" (XXIV.2, 715). Commerce and religion cannot on their own guarantee the rule of law but insofar as they provide mechanisms for checking and balancing

[10] Thomas Pangle emphasizes how commerce can counter a despot's power in *The Theological Basis of Liberal Modernity in Montesquieu's Spirit of the Laws* (Chicago: University of Chicago Press, 2010), pp. 99–100. On Montesquieu's treatment of commerce, see also Catherine Larrère, "Montesquieu on Economics and Commerce," in Carrithers, Mosher, and Rahe, eds., *Montesquieu's Science of Politics*, pp. 335–374.

political power they can support the rule of law. Along with the right passions and political institutions, they can help to establish and maintain a regime in which political power is bounded by the rule of law as a continuing political practice.

2 The Multiplicity of Law

A distinctive aspect of the rule of law in Montesquieu is his insistence that political power answer not only to established positive laws but also to the broader standard entailed by "the spirit of the laws." To speak of the rule of law in this context is to invoke an ideal of governance that is responsive to "the disposition of the people for whom it has been established" (I.3, 237). The spirit of the laws refers to the "relations" between a country's laws and a myriad of factors that help define its character, including "the *physique* of the country" (its climate, terrain, location, and extent of territory), as well as "the form of life of the people," their religion, "their inclinations, their wealth, their number, their commerce, their mores and their manners" (I.3, 238). Governments are "most in conformity with nature" when their institutions are suited in this way to the disposition of their people (I.3, 237). Indeed, laws "ought to be so appropriate to the people for whom they are made that it is a very great accident if those of one nation can be fitting for another" (I.3, 237). Thus while Montesquieu clearly favors the rule of law as a general principle, in view of the multiplicity of *esprits des loix* the application of this principle will yield a diversity of regimes and legal codes rather than generating uniformity across societies.[11]

At the same time, the rule of law is tied to Montesquieu's distinctive conceptions of natural law and natural equity. The laws of nature have a universal reach because "they derive uniquely from the constitution of our being" (I.1, 235). Considering man "before the establishment of societies," Montesquieu finds that the primary human condition is for the individual to "feel above all his feebleness" before others, which motivates him to seek peace, "the first natural law" (I.2, 235). The second law follows from "the sentiment of his needs," which "inspire" him "to seek nourishment" (I.2, 236). The third law is the "natural entreaty" that comes from

[11] On Montesquieu's "particularism" as it bears on the rule of law, see Keegan Callanan, "Liberal Constitutionalism and Political Particularism in Montesquieu's *Spirit of the Laws*," *Political Research Quarterly*, 67 (2014), 589–602.

"the charm the two sexes inspire in each other" (I.2, 236). Finally, "the desire to live in society is a fourth natural law" (I.2, 236). Because the laws of nature embody consistent patterns of behavior on the part of the human species, some commentators have interpreted them descriptively as simply "man's natural and inherent inclinations."[12] It is true that natural law in Montesquieu does not fit the mould of traditional accounts, where the laws of nature were conceived as "the intentions or commands of God built into [the human] frame," directing people to follow God's will.[13] Still, the laws of nature have normative significance and not merely descriptive value because they articulate fundamental human needs and desires, which Montesquieu thinks positive laws and political rulers should respect. Indeed, natural laws underlie in a general way the spirit of the laws of every particular people in the sense that the spirit of the laws represents each country's manner of enacting basic human needs and desires.

A principle of natural equity, meaning that persons are by nature free and equal, is part and parcel of the laws of nature. Although Montesquieu was critical of "extreme equality" in politics (VIII.2, 349) and generally did not defend political egalitarianism, he did insist that "all men are born equal" in terms of their moral status and that persons are by nature free (XV.7, 496; XVII.5, 528). Elsewhere he makes direct reference to the principle of natural "independence" (XXVI.15, 767) and explicitly invokes a universal natural right to self-defense grounded in self-ownership ("because my life is mine") (X.2, 377).[14] Consequently, despotism is always a violation of human nature (II.4, 248; VIII.8, 356; VII.21, 366). The standard of natural equity is also in play when Montesquieu rejects the idea that slavery is justified by its usefulness (XV.9, 497). Slavery surely is useful for those who are masters but to determine whether "the desires of

[12] David Lowenthal, "Book I of Montesquieu's *The Spirit of the Laws*," *American Political Science Review*, 53 (1959), 492; and see Zuckert, "Natural Law, Natural Rights, and Classical Liberalism," 238–241.

[13] Lowenthal, "Book I of Montesquieu's *The Spirit of the Laws*," 492; see also Robert Shackleton, *Montesquieu: A Critical Biography* (Oxford: Oxford University Press, 1961), p. 252; Emile Callot, *La philosophie de la vie au XVIIIe siècle* (Paris: Éditions Marcel Rivière, 1965), p. 84; and Courtney, "Montesquieu and Natural Law," 43. On the meaning of natural law in Montesquieu, see also Dennis Rasmussen, *The Pragmatic Enlightenment* (Cambridge: Cambridge University Press, 2014), esp. ch. 2; and Sharon R. Krause, "Laws, Passions, and the Attractions of Right Action in Montesquieu," *Philosophy and Social Criticism*, 32 (2006), 211–230.

[14] Zuckert, "Natural Law, Natural Rights, and Classical Liberalism," 247–250.

each are legitimate" in such matters one must "examine the desires of all" (XV.9, 497). He also makes reference to "the law of natural enlightenment," which "wants us to do to others what we would want to have done to us" (X.3, 378). The standard of natural equity suffuses Montesquieu's analysis of rulers and regimes and informs his assessment of particular positive laws. For him, the rule of law means the rule of *legitimate* laws, or laws that answer to natural law and the standard of natural equity.

Still, these universal norms are always in practice entwined with local manners, mores, and customs, so that the natural desire for society with our fellows naturally takes many different forms in terms of family structures and other social relations. Likewise, the desire for self-preservation is served by different kinds of economic practices, and the desire for peace can be supported through any number of cultural forms, religions, and political institutions. The fact that natural law and natural equity are always mediated by society explains Montesquieu's insistence that "the government most in conformity to nature" is the one most responsive to the country's *esprit* (I.3, 237). To thwart the dispositions of one's people is a form of tyranny (XIX.3, 557; XIX.14, 564). Thus the rule of law answers both to natural law and natural equity, on the one hand, and to the spirit of the laws, on the other. This dual responsiveness makes the rule of law in Montesquieu a standard that is at once general and flexible,[15] and which, because the content of the laws also matters, requires more than mere adherence to the settled, standing laws.

3 Independence and Moderation

As a member of the *noblesse de robe* Montesquieu practiced law for a time, serving as *magistrat au parlement de Bordeaux* from 1714 until 1726, the last ten years as *président à mortier* of that body.[16] He understood that the courts are where the ordinary individual confronts the power of the state most directly and he was alive to the deep vulnerability endemic to this

[15] As Todorov puts it, Montesquieu's "universal principles" are found in natural law, yet his account of natural law contains "no absolute values" because Montesquieu's only absolute value is that "power should not be absolute." Todorov, *On Human* Diversity, pp. 369, 372, and 374.

[16] See Rebecca Kingston, "Parlement de Bordeaux," in Catherine Volpilhac-Auger, ed., *Dictionnaire Montesquieu* (Lyons: ENS, 2013), available at http://dictionnaire-montesquieu.ens-lyon.fr/fr/article/1377636809/fr/

experience. To ensure liberty, he thought it necessary to establish procedural independence and impartiality in the judicial branch and to insist on moderation in the content and application of the civil and criminal laws. The independence of the judiciary is one aspect of the separation of powers. In each state, Montesquieu says, "there are three sorts of powers": legislative power, executive power, and "the power to judge" (XI.6, 396–397). There can be "no liberty" unless the power of judging is separated from both legislative and executive powers because "if it were joined to legislative power, the power over the life and liberty of citizens would be arbitrary, for the judge would be the legislator," and "if it were joined to executive power, the judge could have the force of an oppressor" (XI.6, 397). Montesquieu emphasizes in particular that a monarch holds the power of judging only in despotic states: "He cannot judge in monarchies; the constitution would be destroyed, the intermediate dependent powers annihilated; one would see all the formalities of judgment cease; fear would invade all spirits" (VI.5, 314).

The formalities of law are crucial; they "increase in relation to the significance placed on the honour, fortune, life, and liberty of the citizens" (VI.2, 311). Adhering to these formalities ensures that "one judges today as one judged yesterday . . . so that the property and life of citizens are secure and fixed like the constitution of the state itself" (VI.1, 307). Montesquieu acknowledges that these formalities sometimes are inefficient. "If you examine the formalities of justice in relation to the trouble of a citizen in having his property returned or to obtain satisfaction for some insult," he says, "you will find them without doubt to be too many" (VI.2, 310). On the other hand, "if you consider them in the relation they have to the liberty and security of citizens, you will often find them too few." The truth is that the formalities of justice – including the penalties, expenses, and delays they often entail – are "the price each citizen pays for his liberty" (VI.2, 310). Formalities facilitate consistency and reflect adherence to standing rules rather than capture by individual wills; they are thus the antithesis of arbitrariness. The independence of the judicial power helps protect the power of formalities, which protects the liberty of subjects and the security of the constitution.

In keeping with his idea that the rule of law must answer to the distinctive *esprits* of different peoples, Montesquieu gives us multiple models for conceiving an independent judiciary. On the model of French monarchy, the judicial function is in the hands of the nobility who are charged not only with recording and administering the king's laws but also with adjudicating them. The independence of the nobility in this regard is a function of the fact that their appointments are largely insulated from direct intervention by the monarch, as we have seen. The judicial power is constructed somewhat differently in England, which Montesquieu treats as a commercial republic, albeit one "that hides itself under the form of monarchy," in view of both its more egalitarian social structure and the predominance of its representative legislature relative to the monarch (V.19, 304). Here "the power to judge should not be given to a permanent" body but instead "should be drawn from the body of the people" (XI.6, 398). A selection process should be conducted "at certain times of the year in a manner prescribed by law to form a tribunal that lasts only as long as necessity requires" (XI.6, 398). The key is that "the judges must be of the same condition as the accused, or his peers, so that it cannot enter his mind that he has fallen into the hands of people motivated to do him violence" (XI.6, 399). Moreover, judges in this context are to interpret the law in a strict way so that judgments "are never anything but a precise text of the law" (XI.6, 399). Together these considerations ensure that "the power to judge, so terrible among men, being attached neither to a certain state nor to a certain profession becomes, so to speak, invisible and null" (XI.6, 398). They depersonalize the judicial function so that "one fears the magistracy, not the magistrates" (XI.6, 398).

Montesquieu's treatment of the rule of law also includes attention to the specific content of civil and criminal laws, and to practices of punishment. Once again, he allows for a significant measure of diversity resulting from the distinctive conditions and *esprits* of different peoples. Yet there are limits. On the one hand, civil and criminal laws are not to be confused with mores or with religion (XXVI.1, 750–751). The former should aim to regulate only "the actions of the citizen" not the moral character of "the man"; they should focus on external conduct rather than the individual's inner life (XIX.16, 566; XXVI.9, 759). Although "religion, even a false one, is the best guarantee that men can have of the integrity of men" (XXIV.8, 720), enforcing religious belief directly should not be the subject of civil laws or criminal penalties because moral "perfection," the subject of religion, "does not concern men or things in a universal way" (XXIV.7, 720). Hence forcing the matter is bound to undermine liberty.[17] The rule of law is

[17] On this point, see Mosher, "What Montesquieu Taught: 'Perfection Does not Concern Men or Things Universally'," in Kingston, ed., *Montesquieu and His Legacy*, p. 7.

to be distinguished not simply from the arbitrary rule of despots, then, but also from the direct rule of religion and morality. Montesquieu's discussion of civil and criminal law also reminds us that the rule of law is intended to bind ordinary citizens as well as political sovereigns.[18]

In his assessment of civil and criminal laws, Montesquieu weighs in on a wide range of issues, from civil and domestic slavery to taxation and finance, marriage and divorce, incest, education, personal debt, and welfare. A common theme is that punishment ought to be proportional to the crime and that it should not be excessively severe. "It is the triumph of liberty," Montesquieu says, "when criminal laws draw each penalty from the particular nature of the crime. All arbitrariness ceases; the penalty does not derive from the caprice of the legislator but from the nature of the thing, and man does not at all do violence to man" (XII.4, 433). Excessive punishments are a mark of despotism. In fact, "every penalty that does not derive from necessity is tyrannical. The law is not a pure act of power" (XIX.14, 565). Disproportionate and unnecessary punishments are not only a violation of liberty but also undermine the efficacy of the law. To the extent that "immoderate penalties" tend to engender "terror in [people's] spirits," they make it difficult to find anyone "to accuse or condemn; whereas, with modest penalties, one would have both judges and accusers" (VI.14, 325). In Japan, Montesquieu remarks, the "extravagance" of punishments led to "the powerless of Japanese laws" (VI. 13, 322) as people covered up crimes to protect themselves and others from unwarranted bloodshed. "Atrocity in the laws" is antithetical to the rule of law because it "prevents their execution. When the penalty is without measure, one is often obliged to prefer impunity" (VI.13, 324).

Thus although Montesquieu allows for – even champions – a significant measure of diversity among societies, he consistently defends the ideal of moderation with respect to the content and application of the laws. Indeed, late in *The Spirit of the Laws* he remarks that "I have written this work only to prove" that "the spirit of moderation should be that of the legislator; the political good, like the moral good, is found always between two limits"

[18] As Georges Benrekassa points out, it is above all "the relationship of the citizen to the law that makes liberty," and this relationship is "more complex than merely a constitutional mechanism." Benrekassa, *Montesquieu: La liberté et l'histoire* (Paris: Librairie Générale Française, 1987), p. 149.

(XXIX.1, 865).[19] So the rule of law in Montesquieu is not simply about the structure of government in an abstract sense, meaning how the power of political sovereigns is to be bounded and constrained. It also concerns how ordinary persons actually experience the power that government exercises over them, and about how their own actions are to be ruled by the laws of the land. Montesquieu's treatment of independence and moderation in the practice of law presses these important points.

Conclusion

For Montesquieu, the structural limitation of political power and the personal practice of living in accordance with established laws are the flip sides of the single coin that constitutes political liberty. As we have seen, he distinguishes political liberty from simply "doing what one wants" (XI.3, 395), saying that those who equate political liberty with democracy, where the people seem to do what they want, confuse "the power of the people" with "the liberty of the people" (XI.2–3, 394–395). Doing what one wants is not liberty but "independence" (XI.3, 395).[20] Where independence reigns no one is truly free because all are vulnerable to the unlimited wills of others (XI.3, 395) "and what results from this is the oppression of all" (XI.5, 396). By contrast, when power checks power "by the arrangement of things" the citizen is protected from both the will of the political sovereign and the wills of other citizens. His freedom consists in "the right to do all that the laws permit" (XI.3, 395) while not being forced to do things that the laws do not require (XI.4, 395). Political liberty at its core is protection against arbitrary power, and the meaning and necessary condition of this protection is the rule of law. To live under the rule of law is what freedom

[19] On the role of moderation in Montesquieu's treatment of law, see Paul Carrese, *Democracy in Moderation* (Cambridge: Cambridge University Press, 2016), esp. ch. 1.
See also David W. Carrithers, "Montesquieu's Philosophy of Punishment," *History of Political Thought*, 19 (1998), 213–240; and Vickie Sullivan, "Criminal Procedure as the Most Important Knowledge and the Distinction between Human and Divine Justice in Montesquieu's *Spirit of the Laws*," in Ann Ward and Lee Ward, eds., *Natural Right and Political Philosophy: Essays in Honor of Catherine Zuckert and Michael Zuckert* (Notre Dame, Notre Dame University Press, 2017), pp. 153–173.

[20] Binoche draws a parallel between Montesquieu's concept of "independence" and Locke's idea of "licence" on the grounds that both were intended to contrast with liberty. Bertrand Binoche, *Introduction à De l'esprit des lois de Montesquieu* (Paris: PUF, 1998), pp. 258–259.

means or, as Montesquieu puts it, "we are free because we live under civil laws" (XXVI.20, 772) and are "subject only to the power of law" (XI.6, 399).

But simple conformity to positive law is not sufficient to constitute the rule of law or to establish political liberty. The content of the laws and how they are applied also matter. The laws must be responsive to the spirit of the nation and the dispositions of the people, to the laws of nature and the standard of natural equity, and to the ideals of proportionality and moderation. Moreover, to be viable over time the rule of law must be understood as more than just a normative ideal; it must come to be a continuing political practice. It must be embedded in the right institutions and supported by appropriate passions, and it requires regular contestation from a variety of sources, including the different branches of government and various social groups, as well as commerce, religion, and individual citizens themselves. And while the rule of law as a general principle is one that Montesquieu endorses without qualification, it allows for a substantial measure of diversity among societies.

Montesquieu's analysis of the rule of law remains relevant today because, as he emphasized, the abuse of power constitutes a perpetual threat to all forms of government and a danger to liberty everywhere. The continuing relevance of Montesquieu's account comes partly from the forceful way he makes us feel the connection between liberty and law, partly from how effectively he demonstrates the multiple sources and practices that sustain this connection, and partly from how he reconciles the singular force of the rule of law with an abiding commitment to pluralism. For all these reasons, not to mention the luminosity and grace of his presentation, the rule of law in Montesquieu richly repays revisiting today – and likely always will.

The Spirit of Legality: A. V. Dicey and the Rule of Law 8

Mark D. Walters

> By every path we come round to the same conclusion, that parliamentary sovereignty has favoured the rule of law, and that the supremacy of the law of the land both calls forth the exertion of parliamentary sovereignty, and leads to its being exercised in a spirit of legality.
>
> A. V. Dicey[1]

Introduction

With the publication of his lectures on constitutional law in 1885, A. V. Dicey introduced an account of the rule of law that would have, for better or worse, a powerful influence. His book, *Law of the Constitution*, is an extended essay on how the law of the English or British constitution is the expression of two basic principles, the rule of law and parliamentary sovereignty. These ideas were not new to English legal writing, but Dicey succeeded with impressive literary flourish to elevate them to the status of *the* organizing principles of the constitution. One result was to expose fault lines at the centre of the ideal of constitutionalism. His attempt to define the relationship between sovereignty and legality can be seen to raise larger questions about the relationship between reason and will, principle and policy, right and might, *jus* and *lex*, justice and power, rule and discretion, and so on, questions that are at the heart of what it means for a 'Commonwealth' to be 'an Empire of Lawes and not of Men.'[2]

Dicey's book raised large theoretical questions, but it was not a work of general legal theory. Dicey wrote about the law of a particular people. His statements about the rule of law are revealing: "with us" no one may be

[1] A. V. Dicey, *Lectures Introductory to the Study of the Law of the Constitution* (London: Macmillan, 1885), p. 340.

[2] James Harrington, *The Common-Wealth of Oceana* (London: J. Streater, 1656), p. 11. This chapter develops ideas explored in my book *A. V. Dicey and the Common Law Constitutional Tradition: A Legal Turn of Mind* (Cambridge: Cambridge University Press, 2020).

punished except under ordinary law; "with us" everyone is equal before the law; "with us" the constitution is found in judicial decisions rather than in a code.[3] It has been said that Dicey's account of the rule of law was an "unfortunate outburst of Anglo-Saxon parochialism."[4] This claim is not entirely fair, but it is accurate in one respect. Dicey's rule of law *is* Anglo-Saxon. His claim that the rule of law means the "rule or supremacy . . . of *ordinary* law"[5] reflected his conviction that the continental view of public law as the special preserve of the executive was inconsistent with English notions of liberty and legality. But his argument was hardly an outburst. Dicey's work on constitutionalism is best understood as part of a long tradition of legal literature that portrays both legality and sovereignty as enveloped within a *common law* interpretive discourse.

Law of the Constitution is a complex book that can be read in different ways. Whether Dicey's argument about the rule of law speaks to us today – and here I have a more inclusive *us* in mind than he did – will depend upon which reading we regard as most important. After introducing Dicey's basic argument, I will consider three critical readings of his work – the *formalist*, the *ideological*, and the *nationalist* readings – before turning to a redemptive reading, which may be called the *spiritual* reading, based on Dicey's own association of the rule of law with a *spirit of legality*.

1 Dicey's *Law of the Constitution*

Albert Venn Dicey (1835–1922) was born into a family of antislavery campaigners and he recalled that constitutional politics were "in the air" when he was young, his parents being "very sound Whigs."[6] After being elected to the Vinerian Professorship of English Law at Oxford in 1882, he wrote, "I naturally took mainly to the constitutional side thereof as it was the part of our law in which from having been brought up in a very good Whig circle, I had been from my youth perpetually though unconsciously

3 A. V. Dicey, *Introduction to the Study of the Law of the Constitution*, 8th ed. (London: Macmillan, 1915), pp. 189, 191, 198. References to *Law of the Constitution*, hereafter referred to as *LOTC*, will be to this edition – the last edition prepared by Dicey himself.

4 J. N. Shklar, "Political Theory and the Rule of Law," in Allan C. Hutchinson and Patrick Monahan, eds., *The Rule of Law: Ideal or Ideology* (Toronto: Carswell, 1987), p. 5.

5 *LOTC*, p. 34 (emphasis added).

6 R. S. Rait, *Memorials of Albert Venn Dicey, Being Chiefly Letters and Diaries* (London: Macmillan, 1925), p. 22.

educated."[7] Defining what "Whig" meant in the days of Dicey's youth is not easy.[8] It is fair to say, however, that Whigs at this time generally believed in the connection between rights of liberty and values of legality, and in particular they celebrated the alliance between common lawyers and parliamentarians against crown and royal prerogative that culminated with the Glorious Revolution of 1688.

Conflict in seventeenth-century England was religious, social, and economic, but it was also about competing conceptions of law. One conception was reflected in arguments made by crown lawyers that there was a *law of state*, separate from the ordinary common and statute laws, clothing the king and his council with extraordinary powers to act at will in cases of state necessity on the assumption that the *salus populi suprema lex est*. These arguments gained some traction in the courts, but they were bitterly contested.[9] Opponents built upon a well-established trope within English legal literature that associated broad claims of prerogative power with Roman or civil law, a foreign law to be rejected in favor of an ancient Anglo-Saxon constitution of liberty under which prerogative power was tamed by the common law.[10] From within Parliament, common lawyers would produce grand statements reflecting this conception of law, the Petition of Right 1628 and the Bill of Rights 1689, statutes that, as Dicey would say, had "a certain affinity to judicial decisions."[11] When arguments for an extraordinary "law of State" were resurrected in the 1760s, they were quickly rejected: the common law, it was said in *Entick* v. *Carrington*, "does not understand that kind of reasoning."[12] The firm line drawn by the civilian legal tradition between public law and prerogative power on the one hand and ordinary law and ordinary courts on the other was rejected by Whigs in favor of a common law conception of constitutionalism. In this sense, at least, Dicey was a Whig.

[7] A. V. Dicey to O. W. Holmes, Jr., December 10, 1921, Oliver Wendell Holmes, Jr. Papers, Box 42–8, Harvard Law Library Special Collections.

[8] J. W. Burrow, *Whigs and Liberals: Continuity and Change in English Political Thought* (Oxford: Clarendon Press, 1988).

[9] Martin Loughlin, *Foundations of Public Law* (Oxford: Oxford University Press, 2010), pp. 378–383.

[10] The outlines of this argument can be traced to the fifteenth century: John Fortescue, *De Laudibus Legum Anglie* [1471], ed. S. B. Chrimes (Cambridge: Cambridge University Press, 1949). For a classic overview, see J. G. A. Pocock, *The Ancient Constitution and the Feudal Law* (Cambridge: Cambridge University Press, 1957).

[11] *LOTC*, p. 191 fn. 2.

[12] *Entick* v. *Carrington* (1765) 19 St Tr 1029, at 1073.

Dicey's ideas on this point are revealed in his early work. Dicey was not starry-eyed enough to accept the Whiggish myth of an ancient pre-Norman constitution. Nor did he believe in "natural rights" – the theory had been destroyed, he said, by the "cool and deadly analysis of Bentham."[13] Instead, he argued that the roots of liberty and legality in England were to be found in the rigid and consistent administration of justice during the centuries following the Norman conquest. Over time people came to expect and then demand strict adherence to common law in regular courts, and this public sentiment was reinforced by common lawyers who resisted executive encroachment upon the judicial terrain and the infiltration of Roman civil law.[14] Although the Chancery and Star Chamber would in time exercise discretionary power similar to that of the Roman *prœtor* to set ordinary law aside, often to secure justice in specific cases, Dicey concluded that because of their close connection to the king these institutions had a tendency "to substitute the will of the sovereign for the government of law," a tendency which he thought common lawyers had commendably resisted.[15] Dicey concluded in an 1875 essay that, given this history, the "spirit" rather than the "form" of English institutions "may be expressed in the assertion that their one essential merit has been to secure the rule of law," and indeed "through a fortunate combination of circumstances, the rule of law was established in England at a time when it was unknown in every other great country of Europe."[16] The "rule of law" was thus an idea deeply embedded within a story of national, social, political, and institutional development.

This was perhaps Dicey's first use of the term "rule of law." He had previously referred to "government by law," which was by then a common expression,[17] and he was aware of references to "dominion of law"[18] and

[13] A. V. Dicey, "Woman Suffrage," *Quarterly Review*, 210 (1909), 277.

[14] A. V. Dicey, *The Privy Council: The Arnold Prize Essay, 1860* (Oxford: T. & G. Shrimpton, 1860), pp. 11, 35.

[15] A. V. Dicey, "The Development of the Common Law," *Macmillan's Magazine*, 24 (May/Oct 1871), 296.

[16] [A. V. Dicey], "Stubbs's Constitutional History of England," *Nation*, 20 (March 1875), 153, 154.

[17] Jeremy Bentham, *A Fragment on Government* (London: T. Payne, P. Elmsly, and E. Brooke, 1776), pp. xiii–xiv; John Austin, *Lectures on Jurisprudence* (London: John Murray, 1863), vol. 2, p. 191; J. S. Mill, *Considerations on Representative Government* (London: Parker, Son, & Bourn, 1861), p. 38.

[18] William Stubbs, *The Constitutional History of England in Its Origin and Development* (London: Macmillan & Co., 1874), vol. 1, p. 248. Dicey admired this book: see Dicey, "Stubb's Constitutional History of England."

"supremacy of law"[19] by others. In fact, English legal writers had referred in passing to the rule of law before,[20] and the expression would soon be found in a leading translation of Aristotle's *Politics*.[21] Dicey did not invent the "rule of law." However, with his book he would succeed in popularizing the term and dominating debates about its meaning.[22]

Dicey's basic objective in writing *Law of the Constitution* was to demonstrate that within the amorphous collection of rules, customs and conventions that made up the unwritten British constitution there was indeed a *law* of the constitution. He began by offering a (superficially) simple definition of law as rules "enforced by the Courts," and concluded that constitutional law is therefore those rules relating to government and individual rights that the courts enforce.[23] He then explained this law in light of two general legal principles. The first part of his book examined the first principle, parliamentary sovereignty, the idea that Parliament has the right to make or unmake any law whatever and that no person or entity has the right to set its statutes aside.[24] The second part of the book explained the second principle – the rule of law.

Dicey began his discussion by observing that "foreign" writers like Tocqueville were struck by the "legality of English habits," but when they tried to define this "trait of national character" they confused together "the habit of self-government, the love of order, the respect for justice and a legal turn of mind."[25] Dicey's rule of law was an attempt to give these vague assumptions about national character concrete legal shape. He proceeded to explain that the rule of law means the following three things:

(1) no one can be punished or deprived of liberty or property except for a breach of law established in the "ordinary" legal manner before the "ordinary" courts, and thus the rule of law is inconsistent with "the exercise by persons in authority of wide, arbitrary, or discretionary powers of constraint";[26]

19 W. E. Hearn, *The Government of England: Its Structure and its Development* (London: Longmans, Green, Reader, & Dyer, 1867), pp. 88, 99, 549. Dicey relied heavily upon this book: H. W. Arndt, "The Origins of Dicey's Concept of the Rule of Law," *Australian Law Journal*, 31 (1957), 117.

20 David Rowland, *Manual of the English Constitution* (London: John Murray, 1859), p. 439.

21 J. E. C. Welldon, *The Politics of Aristotle* (London: Macmillan & Co., 1883), p. 154.

22 W. Burnett Harvey, "The Rule of Law in Historical Perspective," *Michigan Law Review*, 59 (1961), 487, at 491.

23 *LOTC*, p. 23. 24 *LOTC*, pp. 37–38. 25 *LOTC*, pp. 180, 185. 26 *LOTC*, pp. 183–184.

(2) "no man is above the law" but rather "every official, from the Prime Minister down to a constable" is subject to "the ordinary law" and "the ordinary tribunals," and this "equality before the law" means that there can be nothing in England "corresponding to the 'administrative law' (*droit administratif*) or the 'administrative tribunals' (*tribunaux administratifs*) of France";[27] and

(3) "general principles of the constitution," including rights to liberty, are the result of "judicial decisions determining the rights of private persons in particular cases"; unlike "foreign" constitutions in which rights are "deduced" from a legislated code that can be suspended or repealed, in England rights are "inductions" drawn from judicial decisions in which "private law" is applied to everyone, even public officials, with the result that the constitution is "judge-made" and part of "the ordinary law of the land," and in this sense it may be understood as a "spontaneous growth closely bound up with the life of a people" that cannot be suspended or repealed without a "revolution."[28]

Dicey would elaborate upon the rule of law in the next nine chapters of his book. As we shall see, however, criticism of his ideas has tended to focus upon these three initial points.

The first point is, in one sense, not surprising. It can be seen as a restatement of the idea captured by what Dicey elsewhere called the "celebrated thirty-ninth article of the Magna Carta" that no man may be deprived of life or liberty except according to the law of the land – a classic principle of legality.[29] However, in making this point Dicey appeared to conflate discretionary with arbitrary power, and this would prove deeply controversial. The second point also looks familiar. It is simply a re-statement of the common law ideal of constitutionalism secured during the seventeenth century that denied a separate law of state of the kind found in the continental or civilian legal tradition placing executive prerogative above ordinary law – and indeed *Entick v. Carrington* is cited as authority.[30] But Dicey's insistence that the rule of law is therefore inconsistent with continental administrative law would provide another source of contention. The third point is a novel variation on an old theme. Here Dicey advanced a theory of inherent rather than

[27] *LOTC*, pp. 189, 198. [28] *LOTC*, pp. 191, 192–193, 197, 199. [29] *LOTC*, p. 202.
[30] *LOTC*, p. 189 fn. 3.

legislated rights of individual liberty. In asserting that "individual freedom" is "inherent in the ordinary law of the land,"[31] a law that being inferred from judicial decisions in individual cases appears organically integral to the life of the community, Dicey presented a complex yet ambiguous set of ideas. However, we can at least appreciate why he might have thought that if rights are threaded into the web of private relationships defining communal life they could not be pulled apart and denied without a revolution in the very character of the nation. Indeed, it might be said that this was Dicey's version of the ancient constitution.[32]

In light of subsequent developments in rule of law theory, the three points are perhaps somewhat curious. Dicey gave little attention to the formal qualities of generality, prospectivity, clarity, stability, intelligibility, consistency, and so on, that theorists like Lon Fuller and Joseph Raz would later identify with the rule of law.[33] Likewise, there is little direct support for the idea, later advanced by theorists like Ronald Dworkin, that the rule of law is ultimately manifested through a distinctive style of normative reason or interpretation based upon ideals of integrity or coherence.[34] We return to these points in the final part of this essay. First, however, we consider the central arguments against Dicey's rule of law.

2 Critiques of Dicey's Rule of Law

The first critique of Dicey's rule of law to consider is the *formalist* critique. According to this reading, Dicey was a legal positivist inspired by John Austin who sought to write a black-letter textbook presenting law as a system of formal rules isolated from history or morality.[35] Dicey's three points about the rule of law were therefore *rules* about the rule of law. As

31 *LOTC*, pp. 191, 197.

32 Martin Loughlin, *Public Law and Political Theory* (Oxford: Clarendon Press, 1992), pp. 147–153.

33 Lon Fuller, *The Morality of Law* 2nd rev. ed. (New Haven: Yale University Press, 1969); Joseph Raz, "The Rule of Law and Its Virtue," *Law Quarterly Review*, 93 (1977), 195.

34 Ronald Dworkin, *Law's Empire* (Cambridge: Belknap Press of Harvard University Press, 1986).

35 Loughlin, *Public Law and Political Theory*, pp. 17, 18, 47, 140; David Sugarman, "The Legal Boundaries of Liberty: Dicey, Liberalism and Legal Science," *Modern Law Review*, 46 (1983), 102, at 107, 110.

such, however, the three points were easily shown to be inaccurate. It was pointed out that government in Britain sometimes exercised discretionary power, rights were sometimes adjudicated by administrators not judges, officials were sometimes immune from suit, and so on.[36] Of course, these powers and immunities all had to be authorized by statute – but this led to a deeper problem. Dicey's rule of law was intended to be substantive rather than just formal. "If the sovereignty of Parliament gives the form," he wrote, "the supremacy of the law of the land determines the substance of our constitution."[37] Indeed, Dicey's rule of law purported to be far more substantive than Fuller's rule of law would be. The "rule of law" or the "supremacy of law" means, he said, "the security given under the English constitution to the rights of individuals" and to "the maintenance of freedom."[38] Dicey's rule of law seemed to be a full-blown unwritten bill of rights. But of course Dicey also advanced the idea of parliamentary sovereignty. What prevented the ruling law made by the legislature from violating the rule of law? Upon closer inspection, it seemed that the rule of law for Dicey boiled down to just one procedural rule: governmental power must have parliamentary authorization. His statements about the rule of law were thus revealed to be a series of truisms: "A subject's person or property may not be interfered with – unless it may. A person is not liable for what he speaks or writes – unless he is. No liability attaches to one who takes part in a public meeting – unless it does."[39] Dicey's rule of law was simply and disappointingly rule *by* law – a formal or procedural rule of law.[40] Indeed, in light of Dicey's conclusion that illegal executive acts may be legalized by statute after the fact,[41] even formal principles of legality regarding prospectivity and generality in law appeared to be ignored. On this reading, Fuller seemed justified in his conclusion that Dicey "disregard[ed] completely the realities of creating and administering a legal system."[42]

[36] W. Ivor Jennings, *Local Government in the Modern Constitution* (London: University of London Press, 1931), pp. 33–35; E. C. S. Wade and G. Godfrey Phillips, *Constitutional Law* (London: Longmans, Green, & Co., 1931), pp. 79–88.

[37] *LOTC*, p. 466. [38] *LOTC*, pp. 180, 295.

[39] O. Hood Phillips, *The Principles of English Law and the Constitution* (London: Sweet & Maxwell, 1939), p. 62.

[40] Geoffrey Marshall, *Constitutional Theory* (Oxford: Clarendon Press, 1971), p. 138; Paul Craig, "Formal and Substantive Conceptions of the Rule of Law: An Analytical Framework," *Public Law* (1997), 467.

[41] *LOTC*, p. 48. [42] Fuller, *Morality of Law*, p. 116.

The second prominent critique of Dicey's rule of law is the *ideological* critique. As Ivor Jennings put it, the rule of law as articulated in *Law of the Constitution* is "the subconscious reaction of Dicey's Whig mind against the intervention of the State in economic life,"[43] and thus his rule of law is nothing but "a rule of action for Whigs and may be ignored by others."[44] On this view, Dicey's constitution was fit for a quaint England of sturdy individuals enjoying ancient common law liberties and limited government, a nation of shopkeepers, artisans, publicans, and vicars whose only meaningful contact with the state was through occasional encounters with the village constable, the magistrate, or the local member of Parliament. Denied the levers of administrative discretion by the rule of law, the central government was precluded from carrying out the collectivist policies associated with the modern welfare state – the "new despotism" that Dicey's arch-conservative admirers feared so much.[45] But of course this was, even by Dicey's day, an imaginary country. A new administrative state *was* emerging, and Dicey's rule of law was thus caught flat-footed, its conflation of discretionary with arbitrary power leaving it incapable of explaining how modern techniques of governance might be reconciled with principles of legality. The continued influence of a rule of law framed for an age of *laissez faire* individualism thus became a problem. The "dead hand of Dicey" held back the development of a modern and functional public law within Britain and other common law jurisdictions throughout the world.[46]

This second critique blends into a third critique – the *nationalist* reading of Dicey. His rule of law obstructed modern public law in part because it purported to deny the existence of administrative law, and it did so in terms that betrayed nationalist chauvinism. Dicey insisted that the "true nature" of the rule of law "as it exists in England," and in countries which, like the

[43] W. Ivor Jennings, "Courts and Administrative Law: The Experience of English Housing Legislation," *Harvard Law Review*, 49 (1936), 430.

[44] W. Ivor Jennings, *The Law and the Constitution* (London: University of London Press, 1933), p. 256.

[45] Lord Hewart, *The New Despotism* (London: Ernest Benn, 1929); Friedrich A. Hayek, *The Road to Serfdom* (London: George Routledge & Sons, 1944).

[46] William Robson, "The Report of the Committee on Ministers' Powers," *Political Quarterly*, 3 (1932), 347. See also, for example, John Willis, "Three Approaches to Administrative Law: The Judicial, the Conceptual, and the Functional," *University of Toronto Law Journal*, 1 (1935), 53. See in general Martin Loughlin, "The Functionalist Style in Public Law," *University of Toronto Law Journal*, 55 (2005), 361.

United States, "derive their civilisation from English sources," could be illustrated "by contrast with the idea of *droit administratif*, or administrative law, which prevails in many continental countries."[47] His specific target was France. In that country, matters of public law were removed entirely from the ordinary courts and left to the administration itself, with abuses of official power addressed by a system of official or administrative tribunals and ultimately by the highest executive body within the state, the *Conseil d'État*. For Dicey, this was basically prerogative absolutism through star-chamber justice – a betrayal of everything the Whig constitutional settlement of the seventeenth century had achieved in England and the very opposite of the rule of law.

What Dicey initially missed, however, was the remarkable transformations in the French administrative system after 1872. The *Conseil d'État* had developed an impressive case law that in many respects outpaced public law remedies in English law.[48] The French experience thus involved a paradox: an effective public law had been forged from *within* the administration and *not* by independent judges.[49] Once Dicey realized this, he re-wrote his chapter on *droit administratif*.[50] However, he could not bring himself to withdraw his claim about the rule of law.[51] While *droit administratif* comes "very near" to being "law" and is "utterly different from the capricious prerogatives of despotic power," it still could not be reconciled with "our English rule of law" with its insistence on subjecting public officials to ordinary courts. In his gentle critique, the French public law scholar Maurice Hauriou said that Dicey was to be commended for his innovative comparative analysis, even if he had missed the fact that the French system also claimed to respect "le règne de la loi."[52] Indeed, Hauriou even suggested that "les conceptions anglo-saxonnes sur le *règne de la loi*"

[47] *LOTC*, pp. 199, 326.

[48] Spyridon Flogaïtis, *Administrative law et droit administratif* (Paris: R. Pichon et R. Durand-Auzias, 1986).

[49] C. J. Hamson, *Executive Discretion and Judicial Control: An Aspect of the French Conseil d'État* (London: Stevens & Sons, 1954), pp. 66–71.

[50] Mark D. Walters, "Public Law and Ordinary Legal Method: Revisiting Dicey's Approach to *Droit Administratif*," *University of Toronto Law Journal*, 66 (2016), 53.

[51] Roger Errera, "Dicey and French Administrative Law," *Public Law* (1985), 706; Augustin Simard, "Tocqueville, Dicey et le 'problème' du droit administratif," *Tocqueville Review*, 38 (2017), 270.

[52] Maurice Hauriou, *Précis de droit administratif et droit* public, 8th ed. (Paris: Recueil Sirey, 1914), p. 34 fn. 1.

advanced by Dicey and others had contributed to positive developments in this respect within French administrative jurisprudence.[53] Had Dicey been criticized for failing to appreciate changes in French law that he himself had helped to produce? This might be going too far. The point is that Dicey never stepped back to reflect upon the possibility that the rule of law could be a general principle capable of transcending institutional differences between the common law and continental systems. He spoke of an *English* rule of law. What about a *French* rule of law? What about a *general* rule of law? Although he denied claiming that the French system was "inferior" or "unsuited for a civilised and free people,"[54] Dicey's preferences were clear: "Our rigid rule of law has immense and undeniable merits" for "[i]ndividual freedom is thereby more thoroughly protected in England against oppression by the government than in any other European country."[55]

3 Dicey's Spirit of Legality

Each of the three critical readings of Dicey summarized above contain important truths about the Diceyan account of the rule of law. However, on their own these readings leave an incomplete impression. A more rounded understanding requires that we attend to the connections that Dicey himself made between the rule of law and something that he called the "spirit of legality." We turn, then, to what I shall call the *spiritual* reading of Dicey.

To begin, it is important to observe that the formalist, ideological, and nationalist readings pull Dicey in two different directions. Dicey is either a democratic-authoritarian whose rule of law is an empty vessel ready to be filled by whatever legislators wish or Dicey is a liberal-communitarian whose rule of law is a trojan horse containing a set of substantive individual rights emanating from the relationships that he thinks define the community. Dicey is thus pulled towards conflicting formal and substantive conceptions of legality, one oriented around legislative will, the other around common law reason, a tension, one might say, between modern and ancient understandings of law.[56] Indeed, these two conceptions can be

[53] Maurice Hauriou, *La jurisprudence administrative de 1892 à 1929*, Vol. 1 (Paris: Recueil Sirey, 1929), p. 47.
[54] *LOTC*, pp. 364, 390–391. [55] *LOTC*, p. 389.
[56] Loughlin, *Public Law and Political Theory*, p. 153.

seen to track the distinction that Dicey made, in his epic survey of law and public opinion, between "Benthamism" and "Blackstonianism," or, that is, the positivist idea of law as an instrument of democratic reform advanced by Jeremy Bentham on the one hand and the non-positivist idea of law as the embodiment of the inherent rights and liberties of the people defended by Sir William Blackstone on the other hand.[57] From this perspective, Dicey is both ancient and modern, Blackstonian and Benthamite, and thus theoretically confused and lost.

In contrast, the spiritual reading looks for normative direction in Dicey. Perhaps the place to begin is with the charge of Benthamism. Like most mid-Victorian English jurists, Dicey was influenced to a certain extent by the jurisprudence of Bentham and his disciple Austin. Nevertheless, he rejected the Benthamite-Austianian framework for understanding constitutional law. Following Bentham, Austin defined law as the command of the sovereign and he concluded that sovereign power and the constitutional rules that define it therefore exist outside or above the law within the world of political or social fact.[58] In contrast, Dicey, as we have seen, defined law as rules enforced by courts, and he concluded that it is because courts enforce statutes over other sources of law that Parliament is sovereign. For this reason, Dicey was able to assert that parliamentary sovereignty is not just a "legal" rather than a "political" principle, but a legal principle defined by the ordinary "law of England."[59] The inclusion of sovereignty *within* the law has profound implications for the rule of law. In the Benthamite-Austinian frame, the contest between legality and sovereignty is a contest between a legal principle on the one hand and an *extra*-legal political or social fact on the other. In their separate domains, legality and sovereignty will, from this perspective, always remain in some sense irreconcilable. In the Diceyan frame, however, the contest between legality and sovereignty is a contest between two legal principles, and the

[57] A. V. Dicey, *Law and Public Opinion in England during the Nineteenth Century* (London: Macmillan, 1905), pp. 82–83, 305–306. See on this comparison, David Dyzenhaus, "The Politics of Deference: Judicial Review and Democracy," in Michael Taggart, ed., *The Province of Administrative Law* (Oxford: Hart, 1997), p. 280; David Dyzenhaus, "Form and Substance in the Rule of Law: A Democratic Justification for Judicial Review," in Christopher Forsyth, ed., *Judicial Review and the Constitution* (Oxford: Hart, 2000), p. 151.

[58] John Austin, *The Province of Jurisprudence Determined*, 2nd ed. (London: John Murray, 1861).

[59] *LOTC*, pp. 37–38, 70–71.

relationship between these two principles is itself one to be defined by ordinary law. Reconciliation becomes theoretically possible. Given that he was nurtured within a Whig ethos that celebrated the historical alliance between parliamentarians and common lawyers, it was perhaps only natural that Dicey would assume the soundness of a theoretical alliance between parliamentary sovereignty and the rule of law.

Of course, if the rule of law and parliamentary sovereignty are treated as all-or-nothing rules, then the tension between them will still be irresolvable even if they are both *legal* rules (unless one is subordinated to the other). But Dicey thought that they were legal *principles* not rules. We must therefore supplement the formalist reading of Dicey. Dicey *did* think that English law can be understood as a coherent body of legal rules – but only because he thought those rules can be shown to be animated by a limited number of general principles. Principles in his view are "essentially generalisations" that lack the "accuracy and precision" of rules but "indicate the direction" in which rules of law "tend," giving "rational meaning" to rules that by themselves might appear "arbitrary."[60] In this way, principles reveal the symmetry or coherence of law.[61] Like all general principles of normative value, legality and sovereignty pull in different directions when considered abstractly. However, Dicey assumed that the concrete system of rules that principles animate can, indeed must, be understood as exhibiting a sense of normative unity or symmetry, and so in their application or manifestation in any particular case principles like sovereignty and legality *will* be reconciled. Given the very nature of legal interpretation, there can be no a priori or general ranking of the two principles. Both are substantive and coequal principles the meanings of which will, in effect, play out only as a principled legal narrative involving their integration unfolds on a case-by-case basis.

It is from this perspective that Dicey's explanation of how the rule of law and parliamentary sovereignty relate to each other, presented in chapter thirteen of his book, should be considered. Dicey began his explanation by acknowledging that parliamentary sovereignty and the rule of law "appear to stand in opposition to each other" or appear to be "at best only counterbalancing forces" – but he insisted that "this appearance is delusive."[62] The

[60] A. V. Dicey, *A Digest of the Law of England with reference to the Conflict of Laws* (London: Stevens & Son, 1896), pp. 61, 62.

[61] Dicey, *Law and Public Opinion in England during the Nineteenth Century*, pp. 362–363.

[62] *LOTC*, p. 402.

two principles are, he concluded, mutually reinforcing ideas. His basic argument is that parliamentary sovereignty is *legislative* sovereignty only, and this is a powerful constraint upon its exercise. He thus argued that the "commands" of Parliament can be expressed only through an Act of Parliament and so must "always take the shape of formal and deliberate legislation," a requirement of form that is "no mere matter of form."[63] Formality and deliberateness serve to check "arbitrary" decisions and prevent "those inroads upon the law of the land" that a despotic king might effect through "ordinances or decrees."[64] The need for a statute also means that the sovereign's command will immediately be subject to "interpretation" by an independent judge.[65]

Parliamentary sovereignty is also legislative in substance. Dicey states that Parliament never exercises "direct executive power" or issues "a direct order" to executive officials, and so "Parliament, though sovereign, unlike a sovereign monarch who is not only a legislator but a ruler, that is, head of the executive government, has never hitherto been able to use the powers of the government as a means of interfering with the regular course of law."[66] In other words, the sovereign in a common law system may be legally unlimited in making laws, but it is otherwise completely bereft of legal power; meanwhile, the governmental actors who *do* have authority to administer or execute laws and who might otherwise be a position to interfere with the regular course of law, do not have any sovereign powers or capacities to so interfere. Power has been spliced in the common law system so that *nobody* is left with the power to interfere with the regular course of law.

Of course, Dicey acknowledged that Parliament can grant broad discretionary powers to the executive. Indeed, his acknowledgment of the rise of new forms of administrative governance and even an "English" administrative law undermines at least elements of the ideological critique.[67] However, he insisted that the very requirement that the executive obtain powers through a statute illustrates the inseparable connection between the rule of law and parliamentary sovereignty. The requirement of statutory authorization in such cases is not, he insists, "merely formal" or "a

63 *LOTC*, pp. 402–403. 64 *LOTC*, p. 403 fn. 1. 65 *LOTC*, p. 403.

66 *LOTC*, pp. 404, 405.

67 A. V. Dicey, "*Droit Administratif* in Modern French Law," *Law Quarterly Review*, 17 (1901), 304–306; *LOTC*, pp. 384–385, 409; A. V. Dicey, "The Development of Administrative Law in England," *Law Quarterly Review*, 31 (1915), 152.

substitution of the despotism of Parliament for the prerogative of the Crown."[68] In one of the most important passages in his book, Dicey states that because the executive can only exercise powers under an Act of Parliament, governmental power will always be under the supervision of the courts, and, no matter how extraordinary the powers conferred are, the legal range of those powers will always be determined by judges: "judges, who are influenced by the feelings of magistrates no less than by the general spirit of the common law" and who will thus be "disposed to construe statutory exceptions to common law principles in a mode which would not commend itself either to a body of officials or to the Houses of Parliament, if the Houses were called upon to interpret their own enactments."[69] Dicey concludes chapter thirteen with the passage that opened this essay: "By every path we come round to the same conclusion, that parliamentary sovereignty has favoured the rule of law, and that the supremacy of the law of the land both calls forth the exertion of parliamentary sovereignty, and leads to its being exercised in a spirit of legality."[70]

Dicey's argument for the union of the rule of law and parliamentary sovereignty within a spirit of legality is brief and leaves many loose ends. However, it is possible to identify two parts to the argument that correspond roughly with two principal ways in which the rule of law came to be understood over the second half of the twentieth century. First, Dicey's argument only makes sense if Parliament acts through *law* and not *decree* – through general rules rather than *ad hoc* and individualized orders. Within Dicey's analysis are thus the ingredients of the now-classic Fullerian account of the rule of law. It follows that parliamentary sovereignty must be exercised in a manner or form that meets, at some basic level at least, the requirements of generality, prospectivity, clarity, publicity, intelligibility, stability, and so on, that Fuller associated with the rule of law. Perhaps Fuller judged Dicey too quickly.

When read in this way, however, Dicey's position is open to the same argument that Raz made against Fuller: laws that meet the formal requirements of legality can still be substantively unjust. The second part to Dicey's argument can be seen as an attempt to meet this kind of claim. Here Dicey argued that insofar as sovereignty is exercised through laws and not decrees, it will be moulded through a distinctive style of

[68] *LOTC*, pp. 408–409. [69] *LOTC*, p. 409. [70] *LOTC*, p. 409.

interpretive discourse that aspires for normative unity or consistency throughout the law – that positive or statute law must be integrated through interpretation with the "general spirit of the common law."[71] Here, then, is something that begins to resemble the approach to legality or the rule of law based upon interpretation and principled coherence that Ronald Dworkin would later articulate.[72] Writing in terms that Dworkin would have appreciated, Dicey observed that *if* the French were moving toward the rule of law it was *because* decision-makers within their administrative system had begun to think more about "the consistency of the law than its expediency" and were thus open to influence by the "theorist" who could demonstrate "that a mass of isolated decisions can be regarded as illustrations of some few leading principles."[73] The spirit of legality is the product of a particular interpretive attitude – a "legal turn of mind."[74] The legal turn of mind for Dicey was evidenced not exclusively but perhaps most effectively by the interpretive attitude adopted by ordinary judges. Indeed, Dicey insisted that "reverence" for the rule of law is "at once the cause and the effect of reverence for our judges."[75]

Conclusion

The spirit of legality arises from a synthesis of rule of law values and the exercise of legislative sovereignty through the development of a distinctive legal narrative that is, in the end, just an example of ordinary legal interpretation. Whether this vision of the rule of law is attractive to "us" today will depend upon whether we are attracted to interpretivist theories of law and legality. The origins of this style of constitutionalism may lie in an idiosyncratic common law history – in

[71] For the most sustained exploration of Dicey in this respect, see T. R. S. Allan, *Law, Liberty, and Justice: The Legal Foundations of British Constitutionalism* (Oxford: Clarendon Press, 1993); T. R. S. Allan, *Constitutional Justice: A Liberal Theory of the Rule of Law* (Oxford: Oxford University Press, 2001); T. R. S. Allan, *The Sovereignty of Law: Freedom, Constitution, and Common Law* (Oxford: Oxford University Press, 2013).

[72] Indeed, Dworkin himself cited Dicey: Ronald Dworkin, *Justice in Robes* (Cambridge: Belknap Press of Harvard University Press, 2006), pp. 176–177. On the link between Dicey and Dworkin, see Neil MacCormick, "Jurisprudence and the Constitution," *Current Legal Problems*, 36 (1983), 13; and T. R. S. Allan, "Dworkin and Dicey: The Rule of Law as Integrity," *Oxford Journal of Legal Studies*, 8 (1988), 266.

[73] A. V. Dicey, "*Droit Administratif* in Modern French Law," *Law Quarterly Review*, 17 (1901), 312.

[74] *LOTC*, p. 183. [75] *LOTC*, p. 390.

the struggle by common lawyers and parliamentarians against crown prerogative and star-chamber justice – and Dicey offered only brief observations upon its relevance beyond the common law world. However, there are, I think, sound reasons for defending a general theory of legality that subsumes sovereign power within law through forms of legal interpretation that seek principled coherence, an approach to the rule of law that could be universal in its ambitions.[76] Granted, this general theory of legality would have to shed the parochial elements found in Dicey. In doing so, it would also have to address concerns about the judge-centric tendencies that this approach to the rule of law implies.

In this respect, we may close simply by recalling how Dicey consistently linked the rule of law to broader societal attitudes and practices. His understanding of legality as a cultural trait forged through practice and emerging social expectations was evident in his early work. It remained evident in *Law of the Constitution*. The third of his three rule of law points was that legislation cannot destroy the rights inherent in ordinary law because they are embedded within the organic lines of normative order that give the community its identity – or at least such legislation cannot be made without effecting a "revolution" in the basic character of the nation. It may be possible to say, then, that Dicey's "spirit of legality" is embedded within the culture of a people – that it is a *culture of legality*. "[T]he existence for centuries of a regular and uniform body of law" premised upon "singular deference" to "decided cases" had, he suggested, "affected the tone of mind and modes of thought prevalent among the English people" such that "in every department of speculation, in politics, in theology, in ethics, and in historical criticism, English modes of thought and feeling have been profoundly affected by the habits and associations produced by the English law."[77] Lamenting the use of arbitrary power in response to civil disorder in Ireland, Dicey wrote about the social conditions necessary to ensure that the "paths of legality" remain open, and he invoked the work of Rudolph von Jhering in concluding that a true legal order means that both rulers and subjects feel engaged in a common struggle

[76] Mark D. Walters, "The Unwritten Constitution as a Legal Concept," in David Dyzenhaus and Malcolm Thorburn, eds., *The Philosophical Foundations of Constitutional Law* (Oxford: Oxford University Press, 2016), pp. 33–52.

[77] [A. V. Dicey], "Digby on History of English Law," *Nation*, 21 (Dec. 1875), 374.

for justice.[78] If we look past Dicey's nationalism and his reverence of judges, he is saying, rightly I think, that a community will honor the rule of law only if its members themselves internalize the distinctive values associated with a spirit of legality.

[78] A. V. Dicey, "How Is the Law to be Enforced in Ireland?" *Fortnightly Review*, 30 (Nov. 1881), 540. See Rudolph von Jhering, *The Struggle for Law*, trans. J. J. Lalor, 5th ed. (Chicago: Callaghan, 1879).

9 Michael Oakeshott's Republican Theory of the Rule of Law

Martin Loughlin

Introduction

In his lectures on the history of political thought given at the London School of Economics and Political Science (LSE), Michael Oakeshott, the most important English political philosopher of the twentieth century, emphasized the remarkable accomplishments of the Romans. While they may not have produced philosophers of such distinction as Plato and Aristotle, the Romans had shown "a genuine genius for government and politics."[1] The fruits of this political genius were evident in the establishment of "a political community, a *civitas*, a state, out of tribal societies," in "creating the Roman people, the *populus Romanus*, out of a miscellany of different peoples," and in generating the sense of a people united in a distinctive mode of association.[2] This political community was distinctive because it was united not in pursuit of some common enterprise but in a shared respect for its ancient customs and laws. He called this special type of association, unknown to the ancient Greeks, "civil association."[3] And it is the identification of the state as a civil association, he later argued, that provides the basis for understanding how "the rule of law" is not simply rhetorical; it is a coherent concept.[4]

Oakeshott recognized that, although commonly invoked when seeking to describe the character of a modern European state, the "rule of law" remains an "ambiguous and obscure" expression.[5] He therefore sought to

[1] Michael Oakeshott, *Lectures in the History of Political Thought*, ed. Terry Nardin and Luke O'Sullivan (Exeter: Imprint Academic, 2006), p. 176. Oakeshott held the chair of political science at LSE from 1951 until his retirement in 1969. These lectures were given during the 1960s, but were prepared for publication from typescript notes only after his death in 1990.

[2] Oakeshott, *Lectures in the History of Political Thought*, p. 193.

[3] Oakeshott, *Lectures in the History of Political Thought*, p. 212.

[4] Michael Oakeshott, *On Human Conduct* (Oxford: Clarendon Press, 1975), ch. 2.

[5] Michael Oakeshott, "The Rule of Law," in idem, *On History and Other Essays* (Indianapolis: Liberty Fund [1983] 1999), p. 129.

explain "what it *must* mean, leaving out of the account the desirability or otherwise of the condition it describes and neglecting what it may or may not be made to mean when used as an ideological slogan."[6] Acknowledging that it identifies a distinct type of human association, he conceived the rule of law as an expression of the idea of the state (*civitas*) as civil association. This derived from his deep appreciation of the Roman genius for statecraft, demonstrated over the several centuries of the Roman republic. His account, I will argue, presents a republican conception of the rule of law.

1 The Roman Inheritance

Of central importance to Oakeshott's claim about the rule of law is the Roman concept of *respublica.* Although sometimes translated as "the state," he suggests that this is not accurate. After all, the Romans had a more precise word for the state: *civitas*, an expression of the political community to which all Romans belonged. *Respublica*, by contrast, referred to the "public thing" or the "public concern"; it represented "the 'concern' or the 'affair' in which all Romans believed themselves to be united: the public activity of the *populus Romanus.*"[7] *Respublica* was an expression of the conditions shaping the identity of the community as a *civitas.*

Respublica denotes a distinction that the ancient Greeks had never managed to make, that is, "a *political* distinction between 'public' and 'private.'"[8] It is by virtue of this distinction that the Romans could specify more precisely the activity of governing. Government required "the care and custody of *res publica*, the public concern in terms of which all Romans were united."[9] And "the 'ruler', whoever he might be, or whatever the name given to his office, was the custodian of the *res publica Romana.*"[10] The activity of governing carried with it the fulfilment of important public responsibilities.

In *On Human Conduct*, Oakeshott's most important work on this subject, he examined the concept of *respublica* in greater depth. It refers to those rules of conduct that must be subscribed to in civil association. *Respublica* "does not define or even describe a common substantive purpose, interest,

6 Oakeshott, "The Rule of Law," p. 119.
7 Oakeshott, *Lectures in the History of Political Thought*, p. 222.
8 Oakeshott, *Lectures in the History of Political Thought*, p. 223.
9 Oakeshott, *Lectures in the History of Political Thought*, p. 223.
10 Oakeshott, *Lectures in the History of Political Thought*, p. 223.

or 'good'" of the association and it can be seen as "an object of want" only when the association might be threatened with extinction.[11] In civil association, citizens (*cives*) relate to one another only "in the acknowledgment of the authority of *respublica* and the recognition of subscription to its conditions as an obligation."[12]

Oakeshott then extended this account of *respublica* and associated concepts to present a general theory of the state. In doing so, he was not content to work with the common stock of concepts drawn from modern political philosophy. As he explained elsewhere, he was concerned that "the words and expressions used in recognizing the character and identifying the characteristics of a modern European state" were being invoked in a confusing manner and have "for long enough been at the mercy of often negligent users."[13] Rejecting contemporary terminology, he turned instead to the original source materials. Contending that "the political dwellings European peoples have since lived in have been built out of materials which were left lying about when the political experience of the Romans disintegrated,"[14] he wanted to restore the work of the pioneers of these practices and construct a theory of the state from concepts the Romans had bequeathed. In place of "the state," Oakeshott adopts *civitas* or "the civil condition"; in place of "subjects" or "citizens" he retains the Latin *cives*; in designating the comprehensive conditions of association he resurrects the concept of *respublica*; and as an expression of the relationships established by this mode of association he invokes the Roman expression for law: *lex*.

Although the Romans had given us a precise terminology alongside a set of practices generated by a thousand years of political experience, that practical knowledge had never been "turned into a coherent system of abstract ideas."[15] His intention, then, was to present the fruits of that experience in the form of an ideal character, "not in the sense of being a wished-for perfect condition of things but in being abstracted from the contingencies and ambiguities of actual goings-on in the world."[16] The virtue of doing so is that "the condition and relationship [these terms]

[11] Oakeshott, *On Human Conduct*, p. 147. [12] Oakeshott, *On Human Conduct*, p. 149.

[13] Michael Oakeshott, "The Vocabulary of a Modern European State," *Political Studies*, 23 (1975), 319, 320.

[14] Oakeshott, *Lectures in the History of Political Thought*, p. 206.

[15] Oakeshott, *Lectures in the History of Political Thought*, p. 208.

[16] Oakeshott, *On Human Conduct*, p. 109.

plausibly distinguish are neither quite so narrow as those pointed to in the words 'legal' and 'legally', nor so indiscriminate as those commonly (but I think unfortunately) understood by the words 'political' and 'politically.'"[17] The relationships to be considered in explicating the nature of the civil condition, he was suggesting, may blend legal and political considerations but they are intrinsically juridical.

This essential feature of the civil condition originates with the Romans. It was they who "set a very high value upon something which the Athenians valued very little and scarcely understood, namely, legality," and although legality was only one of several civic values they were "most unwilling to sacrifice legality in favour of other values."[18] The great achievement of the Romans was to have developed "by far the most comprehensive and elaborate system of law that any people, save in modern times, ever generated for themselves."[19] Conceiving law as "what is right and wrong in conduct,"[20] they quickly came to distinguish between that which is derived from divine or religious sources (*fas*), that which is derived from the customs and mores of a people (*jus*), and the stricter, more positive, sense of law as that which is made at a certain time and produced in written form (*lex*). Consequently, the Romans not only placed a high value on legality: they also had a remarkably clear sense of its various sources of authority.

The idea of law as *lex* has a special significance. It provides us with the earliest clear sense of law as a human artifact whose authority derives not from the reasonableness of those enactments but simply from having been made through an established law-making process. As written law, *lex* is published, operates prospectively, and acquires the authority to modify and even abolish ancient customs. Its authority in Roman thought culminates in the enactment of the Twelve Tables of Roman law which were engraved on metal panels, displayed in the Forum, and revered as their fundamental laws. "It was in virtue of the high value the Romans placed upon legality and their understanding of what this meant," Oakeshott states, "that the Roman *civitas* became and was what may be called a civil association," a community "joined in the recognition of a law to which they, all alike, owed obedience."[21]

[17] Oakeshott, *On Human Conduct*, p. 108.
[18] Oakeshott, *Lectures in the History of Political Thought*, p. 237.
[19] Oakeshott, *Lectures in the History of Political Thought*, p. 237.
[20] Oakeshott, *Lectures in the History of Political Thought*, p. 238.
[21] Oakeshott, *Lectures in the History of Political Thought*, p. 247.

It is this remarkable Roman inheritance, then, that provides us with the foundation for understanding the rule of law as a coherent concept.

2 Identifying the Rule of Law

The rule of law, says Oakeshott, is an essential feature of the type of association he calls "the civil condition." What, then, does the civil condition entail? Oakeshott refers to it as a "mode of association." By this, he means that it is "a categorially distinct kind of relationship, specifiable in terms of its own conditions."[22] People have various types of relationships with others, including legal, commercial, and professional relationships, as well as those of love or friendship. But when we seek to specify the *nature* of any particular mode of relationship we are obliged to conceive of people as abstractions, that is, as *personae*, persons related to one another only in terms of certain conditions. To grasp the meaning of the rule of law, we must first identify "a *persona* related to others of the same modal character."[23] Only then can we identify the conditions of this mode of association.

This is no simple exercise, not least because human relationships exist prior to any conscious reflection on the conditions of such conduct. It is for this reason that the rule of law "stands for a mode of human relationship that has been glimpsed, sketched in a practice, unreflectively and intermittently enjoyed, half-understood, left indistinct."[24] The best way of reflecting on this, Oakeshott suggests, is indirectly, by making contrasts. He draws out what the rule of law entails by considering a series of different modes of association, focusing specifically on transactional association, rule association, and moral association. These are sketched in turn.

3 Transactional Association

Transactional association is the mode in which persons engage with one another for the purpose of satisfying particular needs or desires. In certain circumstances, moral or legal considerations may of course enter into the actual operations of particular transactions. But such considerations can

[22] Oakeshott, "The Rule of Law," p. 119. [23] Oakeshott, "The Rule of Law," p. 120.
[24] Oakeshott, "The Rule of Law," p. 120.

have no bearing on categorial integrity: in essence, transactional association is geared purely to the satisfaction of substantive wants.

We recognize this mode of association most readily in the contract for services between buyer and seller. This is intrinsically a power relationship, being dependent on the ability to make or refuse offers to transact. But the transactional mode also exists when agents join together to promote some common interest, such as when an organization is established with the purpose of achieving a desired state of affairs. This, says Oakeshott, "is the assemblage of an aggregate of power to compose a corporate or an associational identity designed to procure a wished-for satisfaction."[25]

In order to realize particular ends, formal organizational structures, such as articles of association, offices of responsibility, and the making of a constitution, may be required. But such arrangements "are no more than the prudential disposition of the available resources, instrumental to the pursuit of the common purpose and desirable in terms of their utility, which itself lies in their uninterrupted functionality."[26] And the fact that associates recognize that there are certain moral or legal aspects does not qualify it as a distinct mode of association: as a *mode* of association "there is only Purpose, Plan, Policy, and Power."[27]

4 Rule Association

The transactional mode of association may be contrasted with the relationship entailed in the playing of games. If those involved in a game are regarded as competitors, then the game can be viewed as a purposive enterprise. Since the objective is to win, it involves the pursuit of a desired substantive satisfaction. Since competitors relate to one another in terms of relative skill needed to achieve success, it also involves a power relationship. While the skill needed for success can be formulated in rules ("always hold the bat straight"), these are invariably prudential considerations; the essence of the skill needed for success is conveyed by way of instrumental precepts.

A game can therefore be seen as a purposeful enterprise. But in addition to understanding it in this way, it is also just a game. Rather than treating the rules as the means to some substantive end, the game can be

[25] Oakeshott, "The Rule of Law," p. 123. [26] Oakeshott, "The Rule of Law," p. 124.
[27] Oakeshott, "The Rule of Law," p. 125.

understood solely in terms of the authenticity of its rules. Once that is appreciated, players of a game can be seen to be related in two categorially distinct modes of association. One is an actual and limited relationship between real contestants in which they seek a substantive outcome: to win. The other is an ideal relationship that exists independently of any particular contest: it is the mode of association understood expressly and exclusively in terms of the recognition of rules. Oakeshott's point is that, once we focus on the latter mode, we can glimpse what is entailed in the concept of the rule of law.

The idea of a game understood purely in terms of its rules provides a simple illustration of the mode of association which is the rule of law. But there are important differences. First, playing a game is intermittent and a matter of choice. Secondly, the engagement in a game provides a kind of purely transient satisfaction. Thirdly, actions to which the rules of a game relate are generally few and simple, as are the rules themselves. Finally, the rules are the arbitrary conditions of an autonomous engagement, making any inquiry into the authenticity of the rules a difficult, even pointless, exercise. Oakeshott maintains that these limited conditions of game-playing do not apply with respect to a rule-based understanding of the civil condition. To get a better sense of what is entailed in "rule of law" association, we therefore need to reflect on the conditions of a less intermittent mode of association than game-playing. We need to consider what he terms "moral association."

5 Moral Association

As Oakeshott defines it, moral association involves the relationship of human beings "in terms of the mutual recognition of certain conditions which not only specify moral right and wrong in conduct, but are prescriptions of obligations."[28] Agents may be related transactionally in realizing their wants, but they may also have an obligation to observe conditions that are not instrumental to the satisfaction of wants. This noninstrumental sense of right or wrong is the basis of moral association.

A morality "is not a list of licences and prohibitions but an everyday practice." It is, rather, "a vernacular language of intercourse" which, like all

[28] Oakeshott, "The Rule of Law," p. 132.

language in use, "is neither fixed nor finished." It may be "criticized and amended in detail" but it can "never be rejected *in toto*." Moral conduct, "conduct in respect of its recognition of the conditions of a morality," is, Oakeshott argues, "a kind of literacy." And "just as considerations of literacy do not themselves compose utterances, and just as a practice can never itself be performed, so we may act morally but no actual performance can be specified in moral terms."[29]

The critical point is that a morality is not entirely constituted by its rules. A moral practice may often be abridged and presented as a set of rules, but this is a source of confusion. If a moral practice is reduced to rules, moral considerations are likely to be converted into "mere protocol."[30] This makes it difficult to identifying moral practice as a distinct mode of association. Perhaps the most complicated aspect is "the difficulty of determining the authenticity of an alleged moral rule and of distinguishing this from the recognition of the 'rightness' of the conditions it prescribes."[31] This type of difficulty does not exist with respect to games, where the question of authenticity is resolved by simply consulting the rulebook. But "in respect of a morality reduced to rules, where both authenticity and 'rightness' are prime and contentious considerations, there is no easy solution."[32] In such circumstances, a moralist is likely to abandon authenticity – adherence to the rule – and adhere to some notion of "rightness" as the grounds for moral obligation.

6 The Rule of Law

Oakeshott examines the distinctive character of each of these various modes of association in order to be able to specify more precisely what the rule of law entails. Drawing on the illustration of moral association he suggests that "we may carry with us the perception that it must be a mode of association in which *lex* (a rule understood in terms of its authenticity) and *jus* (a rule understood in terms of the 'rightness' or 'justice' of what it prescribes) are both recognized but not confused."[33] But he then states that, taken precisely, the rule of law "stands for a mode of moral association exclusively in terms of the recognition of the authority of known,

[29] Oakeshott, "The Rule of Law," p. 133.
[30] Oakeshott, "The Rule of Law," p. 134.
[31] Oakeshott, "The Rule of Law," p. 135.
[32] Oakeshott, "The Rule of Law," p. 135.
[33] Oakeshott, "The Rule of Law," p. 136.

noninstrumental rules (that is, laws) which impose obligations to subscribe to adverbial conditions in the performance of self-chosen actions of all who fall within their jurisdiction."[34]

Oakeshott here gives a purely formal definition of the rule of law as a mode of association. It cannot be association to promote a substantive satisfaction. It cannot be association reduced to the simplicity or pointlessness of a game. And it cannot be association based on the common acceptance of some quality of rightness, justice, or reasonableness that laws may be understood to possess. "The sole terms of this relationship," he concludes, "are the recognition of the authority or authenticity of the laws."[35]

The most basic criteria for this mode of association are that associates know what the laws are and that a procedure exists for determining their authenticity. These criteria are met only when laws have been deliberately enacted and can be repealed. This therefore requires the existence of a "sovereign" office of the legislature. The rule of law requires that this office exists but does not prescribe any particular constitution. It requires only that the legislature's authority be an endowment of the office itself and not a consequence of the wisdom, charisma, or virtue of its occupants.

Oakeshott's account may seem formal and legalistic, but it is less so when he explicates its meaning. Although the authority of law derives from the authenticity of its enactment, the conditions that laws impose on conduct have other qualities. The most important of these is that of the justice of their requirements. This he calls "the *jus* of *lex*." This claim, which parallels his point about the complexity of identifying moral association as a code of rules, is central to his argument. He is clear that the way in which the legislative office is established (such as through a democratic procedure) is of no concern to the *jus* of *lex*. Nor can the *jus* of *lex* be identified with the promotion of the common good. Neither is it related to the universal recognition of certain basic goods (such as bodily integrity, freedom of speech, etc.) claimed as conditions of human flourishing. The *jus* of *lex*, Oakeshott maintains, can only comprise noninstrumental considerations of rightness.

Do such noninstrumental considerations include the necessity for laws to be publicly promulgated, prospectively formulated, and general in character? Oakeshott maintains that strictly speaking these are not

[34] Oakeshott, "The Rule of Law," p. 136. [35] Oakeshott, "The Rule of Law," p. 137.

considerations of *jus*; they are inherent in the idea of *lex*. So what might these considerations comprise? He recognizes that at this point many theorists fall back on some inherently "higher" law, whether found in rational moral deliberation or in the will of some divine legislator. But he is adamant that the *jus* of *lex* cannot involve the search for overarching "fundamental values" or any inviolable set of "human rights" because this would transform considerations of *jus* into substantive satisfactions.

He concludes, then, that the search for unambiguous and universal criteria of the *jus* of *lex* is beside the point; it is an unnecessary and unattainable exercise. The rule of law draws a distinction between *jus* and the procedural considerations for determining the authenticity of *lex*. Beyond this, the rule of law "may float upon the acknowledgement that the considerations in terms of which the *jus* of *lex* may be discerned are neither arbitrary, nor unchanging, nor uncontentious, and that they are the product of a moral experience which is never without tensions and internal discrepancies."[36] The *jus* of *lex*, it turns out, is "not a set of abstract criteria." Rather, it is

> an appropriately argumentative form of discourse in which to deliberate the matter; that is, a form of moral discourse, not concerned generally with right and wrong in human conduct, but focused narrowly upon the kind of conditional obligations a law may impose, undistracted by prudential and consequentialist considerations, and insulated from the spurious claims of conscientious objection, of minorities for exceptional treatment and, so far as may be, from current moral idiocies.[37]

This leads to his conclusion that laws "are unavoidably indeterminate prescriptions of general adverbial obligations" which "subsist in advance and in necessary ignorance of the future contingent situations to which they may be found to relate."[38] Since laws cannot disclose their meaning in respect of any circumstantial situation, in addition to the legislator, there must also be an office with authority to rule on actual situations solely in respect of their legality. This is the office of judicature, in which a court reaches a conclusion on whether the law has been breached with respect to some actual occurrence. Judicial deliberation, Oakeshott contends, involves an "exercise in retrospective casuistry" which, like all casuistical enterprise, "is a devious engagement."[39] Its saving grace is that the exercise is governed by rules and conventions designed to focus on the relevant

[36] Oakeshott, "The Rule of Law," p. 143.
[37] Oakeshott, "The Rule of Law," p. 143.
[38] Oakeshott, "The Rule of Law," p. 144.
[39] Oakeshott, "The Rule of Law," p. 145.

considerations. The office of the judiciary may not regard itself as the custodian of public policy and "knows nothing of a 'public interest' save the sum of the obligations imposed by law."[40]

The rule of law, then, is a distinct mode of association denoting a relationship both strict and unexacting: unexacting because it needs no inquiry into motives or intentions, but strict in that it does require fidelity to enacted laws. It does not seek to procure substantive satisfactions; rather, it requires common adherence to a set of noninstrumental rules recognized not in terms of their rationality, fairness, or justice but only of their validity. The rule of law acknowledges a clear distinction between *jus* (rightness of conduct) and *lex* (rule as enacted). Although it incorporates the establishment of a moral discourse that seeks to determine the *jus* of *lex* (the rightness of the rule), it is, above all else, a self-sustaining mode of association identified in terms of the ascertainable authenticity of *lex*.

7 The Rule of Law in European Thought and Practice

The rule of law is a mode of association created by human imagination. But is it purely the product of thought? That is, does it express a mode of human association that exists in practice? What place, asks Oakeshott, has the rule of law "occupied in the hopes and expectations of the creation of the states of modern Europe?"[41]

Turning to the European experience, we see that the modern state emerged from a variety of medieval empires, realms, and principalities. Although there were many forms of association on which to draw, including patrimonial ideas of feudal lordship or a corporate enterprise pursuing a common purpose, there was still "a lively tradition, deriving from ancient Rome, . . . which centred upon the notion of the rule of law."[42] Vestiges of this tradition are to be found in the recognition of rulership as an office with responsibilities rather as than a proprietorial inheritance, or in the conviction that government can only maintain its authority by standing above civil strife and removing itself from questions about ultimate truth.

[40] Oakeshott, "The Rule of Law," p. 146. Oakeshott also recognizes the need for the establishment of an executive power "equipped with procedures composed of rules and authorized to compel the performance of the substantive actions commanded by a court of law" and authorized to act as "custodians of 'the peace.'" Oakeshott, "The Rule of Law," p. 148.

[41] Oakeshott, "The Rule of Law," p. 151.

[42] Oakeshott, "The Rule of Law," p. 151.

But there is no avoiding the fact that the modern state had no architect and was not a product of design. The character of a state, Oakeshott notes, "is not a model"; it can only be "what the effort to understand this experience has made of it."[43]

Oakeshott examines the nature of the modern state in detail in *On Human Conduct*. He suggests that, notwithstanding the variability of origins, there are two sets of ideas around which the character of the modern state has continuously revolved. These are identified by invoking two terms which derive from Roman law and which express two different modes of human association: *societas* (partnership) and *universitas* (corporation).[44] The parallels with his analysis of modes of association in his essay on the rule of law are obvious.

Societas is a mode of association that "was understood to be the product of a pact or agreement, not to act in concert but to acknowledge the authority of certain conditions in acting."[45] It treats the state as "a formal relationship in terms of rules, not a substantive relationship in terms of common action" and citizens relate to one another simply "in the common acknowledgement of the authority of rules of conduct indifferent to the pursuit or the achievement of any purpose."[46] Oakeshott argues further that a *societas* expresses a moral relationship in which the conditions of association are specified by a system of law. The ruler is to be seen simply as "the custodian of the loyalties of the association."[47] Such a state is "a *civitas*, and its government (whatever its constitution) is a nomocracy whose laws are to be understood as conditions of conduct, not devices instrumental to the satisfaction of preferred wants."[48] *Societas* is the term Oakeshott uses to identify the state as a mode of association based on the rule of law.

Universitas, by contrast, is a state conceived as a corporate entity. In this conception, the state is treated as a corporation aggregate, an association of persons pursuing some common purpose, and endowed with particular powers and privileges. In the state as *universitas* the many become one "in the joint pursuit of a common substantive purpose and in the enjoyment of

43 Michael Oakeshott, "On the Character of a Modern European State," in his *On Human Conduct*, p. 198.
44 Oakeshott, "On the Character of a Modern European State," pp. 199–206.
45 Oakeshott, "On the Character of a Modern European State," p. 201.
46 Oakeshott, "On the Character of a Modern European State," p. 201.
47 Oakeshott, "On the Character of a Modern European State," p. 202.
48 Oakeshott, "On the Character of a Modern European State," p. 203.

the means necessary for undertaking the managerial decisions entailed." The rulers make rules that are instrumental to this common undertaking and in this sense the governing function "may be said to be teleocratic, the management of a purposive concern."[49] *Universitas* evidently is the portrayal of the state as a transactional association.

Oakeshott's argument is not that each of these modes is to be read as alternative accounts of the nature of the state. Although they are irreducible and cannot be combined, they are to be understood as the "specification of the self-division of this ambiguous character."[50] The modern state represents "an unresolved tension between the two irreconcilable dispositions represented by the words *societas* and *universitas*."[51] The idea of a state animated by adherence to the rule of law may be deeply rooted in European history but it occupies a thoroughly ambivalent position in the workings of the state today.

Oakeshott suggests that the vision of a modern state as a law-governed association was first developed by such jurists as Bodin and Hobbes. Its character and presuppositions were then "fully explored in the writings of Hegel," who rejected the idea of natural law as a way of measuring the justice of the laws. And the presuppositions of these scholars can then be seen operating in "a slimmed-down version in the writings of the jurist Georg Jellinek" and in some of the positivist modern jurists.[52] Notwithstanding the power of the image of the state which they portray, he accepts that "the circumstances of modern Europe have always made it impossible for any state (except, perhaps, Andorra) to achieve this condition without qualification or interruption."[53] The main qualification evidently is that modern states have felt it necessary to superimpose on the authority to make laws the authority also to pursue policies.

Conclusion

In an unpublished note found among his papers, Oakeshott acknowledged that while the rule of law "has long been an element in European political

[49] Oakeshott, "On the Character of a Modern European State," pp. 205–206.
[50] Oakeshott, "On the Character of a Modern European State," p. 200.
[51] Oakeshott, "On the Character of a Modern European State," pp. 200–201.
[52] Ibid., 162. See Georg Jellinek, *Allgemeine Staatslehre*, 3rd ed. (Berlin: Springer, 1921).
[53] Oakeshott, "The Rule of Law," p. 162.

thought," a "State of this character has never in fact existed and it could never subsist without qualification."[54] He similarly noted in the conclusion to his essay on the rule of law that a state founded on this concept "bakes no bread, it is unable to distribute loaves or fishes (it has none), and cannot protect itself against external assault." But he emphasized that it nonetheless "remains the most civilized and least burdensome conception of a state yet to be devised." And he reiterated finally that we owe the expression of this distinctive mode of political association "not to the theorists, but to the two peoples who, above all others, have shown a genius for ruling: the Romans and the Normans."[55]

Once we recognize just how much his analysis rests on an examination of the contemporary significance of that Roman inheritance, we can see that the distinct mode of association he explicates is in fact a republican conception of the rule of law. This might seem a surprising conclusion: not many would associate Oakeshott with republicanism and his work has been entirely ignored by those who have recently sought to revive republican political thought.[56] Nevertheless, the traces of republicanism are clearly present.

Despite the lack of clarity over the values of modern republicanism, the core tenets are well understood. These include the legal and political equality of the individual, a conception of freedom as nondomination, the necessity of guarding against arbitrariness in the exercise of public power, the need to restrain the power of factions, and the importance of fostering a political culture that encourages the virtuous to take on the tasks of leadership. Although Oakeshott presents his account of the rule of law in rather austere terms, these values shine through his investigations. He also shares with republican thinkers acknowledgment of just how

[54] Michael Oakeshott, "Law," in his *What is History? and Other Essays*, ed. Luke O'Sullivan (Exeter: Imprint Academic, 2004), p. 426.

[55] Oakeshott, "The Rule of Law." p. 164.

[56] So far as I can ascertain, Oakeshott does not figure at all in any of the leading works of the republican revival in political and legal theory, including: Philip Pettit, *Republicanism: A Theory of Freedom and Government* (Oxford: Oxford University Press, 1997); Quentin Skinner, *Liberty before Liberalism* (Cambridge: Cambridge University Press, 1998); Maurizio Viroli, *Republicanism* (New York: Hill & Wang, 2002); Cécile Laborde and John Maynor, eds., *Republicanism and Political Theory* (Oxford: Blackwell, 2007); Samantha Besson and José Luis Martí, eds., *Legal Republicanism: National and International Perspectives* (Oxford: Oxford University Press, 2009). The republican basis of Oakeshott's conception is, however, intimated in David Boucher, "The Rule of Law in the Modern European State: Oakeshott and the Enlargement of Europe," *European Journal of Political Theory*, 4 (2005), 89–107.

precarious the achievement of the civil condition is. Far from being natural endowments, the basic rights protected in the civil condition are established and maintained only through institutions, laws and customs. The citizen of a republic, notes Maurizio Viroli, held "civil and political rights that derived from belonging to a *res publica*, or *civitas*, that is, a *political* community, whose goal was to allow individuals to live together in justice and liberty under the rule of law."[57] And a republic, Viroli emphasizes, "is not a profit-seeking corporation but a way of living in common that aims to ensure the equal dignity of its citizens."[58]

The precarious status of a republic is manifest in the tensions Oakeshott identifies as pervading the character of the modern state. In this respect he echoes Rousseau's claim that "any state which is ruled by law I call a 'republic', whatever the form of its constitution," because "only then, and then alone, does the public interest govern and then alone is the 'public thing' – the *res publica* – a reality."[59] They both recognized just how rigorous those conditions are.[60] Rousseau explained that "putting the law above man is a problem in politics which I liken to that of squaring the circle in geometry"; if achieved, we have the rule of law but if not "it will be men who will be ruling."[61] Oakeshott then presents the most systematic account of what the rule of law as a mode of association actually entails. But ultimately both also demonstrate precisely why the rule of law can never actually be the main principle animating modern political regimes.

[57] Viroli, *Republicanism*, p. 65. [58] Viroli, *Republicanism*, p. 67.

[59] Jean-Jacques Rousseau, *The Social Contract* [1762] in *The Social Contract and other later Political Writings*, ed. Victor Gourevitch (Cambridge: Cambridge University Press, 1997), pp. 39–152, 67.

[60] Rousseau also argued that the ideal places in which to realize the rule of law were small city-states, suggesting that the only European country capable of achieving this was Corsica: Rousseau, *The Social Contract*, p. 78. Cf. Oakeshott's pointed reference to Andorra being the only state in modern Europe with the conditions for realizing the rule of law: n. 53 above.

[61] Jean-Jacques Rousseau, *Considerations on the Government of Poland* [1772] in his *The Social Contract*, pp. 177–260, 179.

10 The Morality of the Rule of Law: Lon L. Fuller

Kristen Rundle

Introduction

For readers of legal philosophy, the title of this entry is likely to generate an expectation of a discussion that runs something like this. In the mid-twentieth century, the idea of the rule of law began to figure prominently and problematically within the long-standing debate between legal positivists and natural lawyers about the connections between law and morality. The question that presented itself for answering was the following. Could the positivist "separability thesis" – the argument that there is no necessary connection between law and morality – be said to hold with respect to the connection (if any) between the concept of "law" and the concept of "the rule of law"?

Though a very willing participant in the debate that emerged in response, the protagonist of the present entry – the mid-twentieth century American legal philosopher, Lon L. Fuller – would never have posed the question in such conceptually circumscribed terms. To his eyes, the kind of inquiry needed to explore the moral dimensions of the rule of law defied the conceptual strictures dictated by orthodox frames of legal philosophical debate and was substantially disserved by them. The aim of this entry, accordingly, is to shed light on the idea of the "morality" of the rule of law as it presented in Fuller's thought, both within and beyond that debate.

At the outset, however, it is important to note that Fuller never set out to provide a theory of the rule of law per se. The term "the rule of law" actually only appears occasionally in his writings. Fuller was instead concerned to develop and defend the idea that the practice of governing through law contains an "internal morality." It is therefore necessary to understand what he had in mind by this "internal morality" idea before its implications for the idea of "the morality of rule of law" can be appreciated. To that end, I begin in section 1 by briefly recounting Fuller's tale of King Rex and his eight failures to make law that has long been read as supplying the foundations of his jurisprudence on the rule of law.

I then offer an extended discussion in section 2 of what Fuller sought to indicate through that tale about the morality of the rule of law. This "morality" is to be distinguished from other possible moral dimensions of the rule of law that might be suggested by legal philosophers, such as whether laws made in accordance with the principles of the rule of law will necessarily be moral in terms of the rightness or justice of their content or *ends*. Fuller's jurisprudence does display some interest in this possible moral dimension of the rule of law as an arguably observable empirical reality.[1] But his writings make clear that the meaning he sought to convey through the use of the term "morality" was very different. Fuller was concerned, above all, to articulate the moral *demands* appropriate to the particular *relationship* between lawgiver and legal subject(s) that he saw as constitutive to the enterprise of governing through law. It is his preoccupation with these demands that illuminates the distinctly moralized conception of *reciprocity* between lawgiver and legal subject that Fuller saw to be constitutive to the practice of the rule of law. At his pen this condition of reciprocity is never exhausted in the sociological fact of interaction per se. It is meant to signal a conscious ethos of respect and responsibility toward those over whom legal authority is claimed.

Fuller's account of the moral demands of the rule of law stands as a leading contribution to theorizing the rule of law in its own right. But as I explain in section 3, an appreciation of the breadth and depth of that contribution is necessarily strengthened by an understanding of how it emerged in the context of his effort to discredit the positivist insistence that law and morality are necessarily conceptually separable. Understanding how Fuller's efforts in that larger debate were answered by the two leading legal positivist philosophers of the twentieth century, H. L. A. Hart and Joseph Raz, is equally important to grasp if we are to see how the treatment of the idea of the rule of law within the analytical frame set by positivism disserved and arguably continues to disserve a proper understanding of the message of Fuller's distinctive rule of law jurisprudence. This disservice has registered above all in how the dominant lines of that treatment have

[1] Lon L. Fuller, "Reply to Professors Cohen and Dworkin," *Villanova Law Review*, 10 (1965), 664.

encouraged a distorted "checklist" reading of Fuller's eight principles of the internal morality of law while marginalizing his central concern for the relational demands between asymmetrically positioned legal participants that he regarded as constitutive to a condition of the rule of law.

Appreciating Fuller's contribution to theorizing the rule of law thus necessarily involves an exercise in reclamation and clarification. Once this exercise is undertaken, new possibilities for how we are to understand him as a theorist of the rule of law emerge. In particular, a wider view of what Fuller offered to the project of theorizing the rule of law opens up novel possibilities for the application of his insights to contemporary challenges of the rule of law. I close the entry in section 4 with a brief consideration of these new questions.

1 Learning from Rex: Uncovering the Morality of the Rule of Law

Fuller probably never expected that his playful tale of the hapless King Rex who failed in eight ways to make law would make his name as one of the leading theorists of the rule of law in the Anglo-American tradition. Such, however, proved to be the case. We meet the beleaguered Rex in the book *The Morality of Law*, in a chapter tellingly titled "The Morality that Makes Law Possible."[2]

As Fuller tells Rex's story, the well-intentioned monarch came to the throne determined to make his name in history as a great lawgiver. Rex's dream, sadly, was short-lived. First he failed to achieve appropriate generality in the rules he issued. Then some of his laws were kept secret from his subjects while others operated retroactively. He proved in turn to be a hopeless legislative draftsman, with his laws suffering from obscurity and perpetuating confusion in their contradictory demands. He changed his laws far too often, and some were impossible for his subjects to comply with. Finally, adding insult to injury, Rex's judicial opinions bore little relation to the enacted rules on which they were allegedly based. Disillusioned with the legal enterprise and facing revolt from his subjects, Rex gave up on law and died a miserable king. The first act of his successor,

[2] Lon L. Fuller, *The Morality of Law*, 2nd rev. ed. (New Haven: Yale University Press, 1969), ch. 2.

Rex II, was to take the powers of government away from lawyers and put them in the hands of psychiatrists and experts in public relations so that his people could be made happy without rules.[3]

Rex might have been a hopeless lawgiver, but, Fuller insists, we have much to learn from his failures. By exemplifying how *not* to create and administer a legal system, the pathologies of Rex's efforts invite reflection on the constitutive demands of the endeavor that he undertook. These demands are described by Fuller as "eight kinds of excellence towards which a system of rules may strive": that law be (1) general; (2) publicly promulgated; (3) non-retroactive; (4) sufficiently clear; (5) non-contradictory; (6) possible to comply with; (7) relatively constant through time; and (8) that there be congruence between official action and declared rule. These eight desiderata have long been accepted as comprising the basic elements of a "formal" conception of the rule of law: that is, a conception that goes to the *form* through which legal norms should be expressed, rather than to the substantive *content* of those norms. To have the rule of law, the idea runs, is to have laws and a legal system that exhibit the features contained in Fuller's "account," or some close cousin thereof. Fuller's own point, however, was that together these eight principles comprised the "internal morality" of law.[4] It is therefore necessary to understand what he meant – and what he did not mean – by this description if we are to grasp the idea of the "morality" of the rule of law that is associated with his thought.

On the question of what idea of *law* animates Fuller's "internal morality of law," the closest thing he ever offered to a definition of "law" – "the enterprise of subjecting human conduct to the governance of rules"[5] – makes clear that his focus lay with the "enterprise" much more than with the "rules."[6] This point is important. Fuller repeatedly complained in his private correspondence about the confusions surrounding the reception of his arguments in *The Morality of Law*, a point to which I return in section 3. To him, the book stood above all as "an attempt to discern what kind of job law-making is."[7] Following closely from this, the *internal* designation

[3] Fuller, *The Morality of Law*, pp. 33–38. [4] Fuller, *The Morality of Law*, p. 41.

[5] Fuller, *The Morality of Law*, p. 96.

[6] This question of the confinement of these demands to the modality of "rules" is further explored in section 5, below.

[7] In the same private correspondence Fuller admitted that he might have "fared better with my critics if I had been able to give my book some such title as The Morality of Lawing":

indicates that the orientation of Fuller's principles is not to the external substantive *ends* of law, but to the inner constitutive structure of the activity of governing through law. Fuller's eight principles distil the features of this internal structure with respect to "the enterprise of subjecting human conduct to the governance of rules." But in what sense are these principles *moral*? This question warrants an extended answer.

2 The Moral Demands of the Rule of Law

The overarching inquiry that animated Fuller's scholarship for over three decades was his effort to uncover how, and in what ways, the human interactions constitutive to different "forms of social order" generate distinctly moral demands on their agents.[8] The seeds of this inquiry can be seen in some of his earliest attempts to illuminate the "natural laws" or "compulsions necessarily contained in certain ways of organising men's relations with one another,"[9] and the required comportment of those responsible for creating and maintaining these forms of social order.[10] The tale of Rex is an expression of these enduring preoccupations with respect to the special burdens that attach to creating and maintaining a condition of governance through legal rules. The "morality" of Fuller's eight principles of the internal morality of law is therefore best understood as the *role morality* appropriate to the relationship between lawgiver and legal subject(s) that he saw as constitutive to that enterprise.[11]

Foundational to the demands of this role morality is the need to see that to rule through law is a practice that relies for its very existence on a "cooperative effort – an effective and responsible interaction – between lawgiver and subject."[12] Each of these terms deserves attention if we are to understand why the principles of Fuller's internal morality of law reflect

Letter to O. Lewis, March 11, 1966, *The Papers of Lon L. Fuller,* Harvard Law School Library, Box 5, Folder 2 (Correspondence).

8 By "forms of social order" Fuller meant to include "rules, procedures, and institutions": see Lon L. Fuller, "Human Purpose and Natural Law," *Journal of Philosophy*, 53 (1956), 697, 704.

9 Lon L. Fuller, "American Legal Philosophy at Mid-Century: A Review of Edwin W. Patterson's *Jurisprudence, Men and Ideas of the Law*," *Journal of Legal Education*, 6 (1954), 476.

10 Lon L. Fuller, "Reason and Fiat in Case Law," *Harvard Law Review*, 59 (1946), 378.

11 Fuller, *The Morality of Law*, p. 239.

12 Fuller, *The Morality of Law*, p. 216.

distinctly moral demands. Beginning with the idea of "interaction," though legal direction might emanate from "above" in terms of the respective positioning of lawgiver and legal subject, for Fuller the creation and maintenance of a condition of governance through law can never be a top-down project. In this commitment alone his jurisprudence departs significantly from the concept of a legal system associated with Hartian iterations of legal positivism.[13] But Fuller's insistence that this interaction involves a "cooperative effort" between lawgiver and subject, and that this "cooperative effort" must not only be "effective" in terms of bringing about some desired end but also "responsible," takes this point of departure much further.

Here it is important to highlight that there is nothing amiss in reading Fuller's use of the term "effective" as an indication of his concern for the effectiveness of lawgiving technique. No conception of the demands of governance through law could be coherent without attention to how to achieve the best possible instantiation of its medium. Still, caution is needed here. As I elaborate in section 3, the idea that Fuller's eight principles orient *only* to the efficacy of laws produced in accordance with their observance proved to be the dominant reading of the purpose and value of those principles on the part of positivist legal philosophers – and, crucially, the source of their denial that there is anything necessarily "moral" about them. Fuller himself, however, was very clear that efficacy is only ever part of the story. At his pen the principles of the internal morality of law speak not just to "the pride of the craftsman" who seeks to command his toolkit effectively towards some or other desired end, but also to a "sense of trusteeship" for the fate of persons.[14] Lawgiving not only involves a relationship *with* persons, but responsibilities *to* them.

It is in this idea that governing through law implicates special kinds of responsibility that the depth of the moral demands of Fuller's rule of law jurisprudence become apparent. By explicitly locating those moral demands within the lawgiver's relationship to persons occupying the position of (putative) legal subjects, their distinctly relational character is brought into sharper focus. But how are we to conceptualize the person to whom these demands are owed? Fuller elaborates this point later in *The Morality of Law* in his

[13] Fuller's heavily annotated personal copies of *The Morality of Law* contain multiple references to there being "no cooperation in Hart."

[14] Fuller, *The Morality of Law*, p. 43.

discussion of "the conception of the person implicit in legality."[15] Here he argues that to embark on the enterprise of subjecting human conduct to the governance of rules "involves of necessity a commitment to the view that man is, or can become, a responsible agent, capable of following rules and answerable for his defaults."[16] Calling upon two of his principles of the internal morality of law to illustrate the point, Fuller suggests that to judge a person's actions by unpublished or retrospective laws "is no longer an affront, for there is nothing left to affront – indeed, even the verb 'to judge' becomes itself incongruous in this context; we no longer judge a man, we act upon him."[17]

It is important to emphasize the two directions in which this analysis runs. The first is the simple idea that certain capacities are needed in order to be ready to participate in legal relations. The [putative] legal subject must be a "responsible agent, capable of following rules, and answerable for his defaults." But as a species of agency *presupposed* by law, this acknowledgment of the subject as an agent quickly translates in Fuller's jurisprudence into a demand about how she must be treated. The short point is that, if a condition of law is to take root and function, it must maintain conditions and communicate respect for these necessary capacities on the part of the legal subject. Jeremy Waldron has nicely captured this point in his statement that "law itself may be an enterprise unintelligible apart from the function of treating humans as dignified and responsible agents capable of self-control" and "unscrupulous rulers must make what they can of that fact when they decide, for reasons of their own, to buy into the 'legal' way of doing things."[18]

Yet to accept that certain capacities are presupposed by the enterprise of subjecting human conduct to the governance of rules does not, on its own, fully illuminate the weight of the principles of the internal morality of law as a set of *moral* demands. Here a second argument is needed. What is morally at stake in the practice of the rule of law is not just respect for and indeed reliance on the capacities of persons as "pre-legal" beings, but the distinctive kind of agency that law itself *creates*. This kind of agency possessed by the legal subject is that which arises because of law and is inseparable from it. It might be described in different ways, such as giving those in possession of it such things as relative security of expectations and protection from domination

[15] Fuller, *The Morality of Law*, p. 162. [16] Fuller, *The Morality of Law*, p. 162.

[17] Fuller, *The Morality of Law*, p. 163.

[18] Jeremy Waldron, "Positivism and Legality: Hart's Equivocal Response to Fuller," *New York University Law Review*, 83 (2008), 1167.

and arbitrary action. But the point to emphasise for present purposes is that this is the kind of agency – the "positive" freedom that speaks to conditions of action – which Fuller sees as constituted in the person within an appropriately realized condition of the rule of law. An especially good formulation of this point is recorded in a working note associated with Fuller's defense of his claims against the objections of his critics (about which more below):

> A legal system does not succeed or achieve "efficacy" simply because the citizen is willing to obey orders. It succeeds if it creates a stable order by which the citizen can orient his conduct towards his fellows ... a functioning society is its goal, *not a subservient populace ready to do what they are told to do.* This is not some extra-legal purpose assigned to law from without; it is intrinsic to the very notion that government act towards the citizen only in compliance with previously announced general rules.[19]

It is therefore not possible to grasp the notion of the "morality" of the rule of law as Fuller understood it without witnessing the significance that he attributes to the agency and responsiveness of the legal subject within the enterprise of governing through law.[20] If laws are to be addressed to such persons, and if such persons are to cooperate with those in possession of legal authority with respect to those laws, then the moral demands of the *relational form* of the enterprise must be met.[21] Once this is grasped, it is not hard to see why Rex ultimately never produced any law, never became a lawgiver and, by extension, never ruled over any legal subjects. Rex failed to understand, and still more to discharge, the demands of the (role) morality that is prior to the possibility of governance through law.

Reciprocity

These relational demands of legal governance are often described – including by Fuller himself – through the language of "reciprocity." But

[19] Undated and untitled document, *The Papers of Lon L. Fuller,* Harvard Law School Library, Box 12, Folder 1 (Notes for the "Reply to Critics").

[20] Intriguingly, in private correspondence Fuller suggested that his statement of the demands of the internal morality of law could be understood as "a kind of minimum bill of rights derived from the simple proposition that law is a means of subjecting human conduct to the control of rules": Letter to Dr Hans Klinghoffer, November 10, 1964, *The Papers of Lon L. Fuller,* Harvard Law School Library, Box 4, Folder 12 (Correspondence).

[21] Further, see Kristen Rundle, "Fuller's Relationships," in Hirohide Takikawa, ed., *The Rule of Law and Democracy: The 12th Kobe Lecture and the 1st IVR Japan International Conference, Kyoto, July 2018* (Stuttgart: Franz Steiner Verlag, 2020), pp. 17–40. The collection is a special supplement of the *Archiv für Rechts- und Sozialphilosophie.*

in order to appreciate *why* this idea of reciprocity was so central to the message of his jurisprudence, it is necessary to situate it within the larger landscape of questions of legal philosophy with which Fuller was concerned when he developed and defended his idea of the internal morality of law. The relevant connections become apparent in Fuller's analysis of the lessons to be learned from the tale of Rex. Here he makes a strong and unapologetically normative claim: a total failure to meet the demands of the principles of the internal morality of law does not simply result in a bad system of law, but something "that is not properly called a legal system at all."[22] This apparent conceptual claim about the constitutive requirements of a legal system is immediately linked to the traditional concern of natural law theory toward the basis of a legal subject's obligation to obey law. As Fuller puts the point, "there can be no rational ground for asserting that a man can have a moral obligation to obey a law that does not exist, or is kept secret from him, or that came into existence only after he had acted, or was unintelligible, or was contradicted by another rule of the same system, or commanded the impossible, or changed every minute."[23]

The argument here is not that it is necessarily impossible, in practical terms, to obey a law enacted or administered in violation of one or more of the eight principles of the internal morality of law. The argument is instead that in the face of a formally debased legal order – one in which there has been a significant failure to meet the moral demands of the eight principles – the question of the subject's obligation should remain open. This is because the legal subject's obligation to obey law should arise only in response to, or in anticipation of, the corresponding effort of the lawgiver. To secure the subject's fidelity to law, Fuller insists, the lawgiver must enter into a relationship of "reciprocity" with her.[24] And if this bond of reciprocity is finally or completely ruptured, "nothing is left on which to ground the citizen's duty to observe the lawgiver's rules."[25]

Again, it is helpful to return to the tale of Rex to situate this reciprocity dimension of the morality of the rule of law. What lay in the balance of Rex's failures was not just disrespect for his subjects as self-determining agents, but the absence of any basis for those subjects to convey their acceptance of the authority that Rex sought to claim over

[22] Fuller, *The Morality of Law*, p. 39. [23] Fuller, *The Morality of Law*, p. 40.
[24] Fuller, *The Morality of Law*, pp. 39–40. [25] Fuller, *The Morality of Law*, p. 40.

them through the medium of legal rules.[26] Adapting another long-standing normative commitment of the natural law tradition, Fuller insists that this has implications for the existence of law itself.[27] The underlying message is that what cannot be obeyed – or for which there is no basis for an obligation to obey – cannot itself be "law" in the proper sense. It cannot be said to exist.

Fuller's claims thus locate the relational demands of the activity of governing through law deep within enduring questions of jurisprudence. As such, their content reflects much more than a reproduction of the insights of the work of the early twentieth century German sociologist, Georg Simmel, whose thought profoundly influenced the development of Fuller's thinking on this point. Of foremost significance to Fuller was Simmel's insistence that the form of the authority structure of legal governance is constitutively relational even though it might appear to be top-down and unilateral.[28] It is therefore not hard to see why Fuller added a footnote – one of only a handful accompanying his analysis of the lessons to be learned from Rex's eight failures to make law – alerting "those concerned with defining the conditions under which the ideal of the 'the rule of law' can be realized" to Simmel's writings. Of particular interest to Fuller was Simmel's analysis of "Interaction in the Idea of Law," as well his account of the form of social relations that attach to the sociological phenomenon of "Subordination Under a Principle."[29] Simmel's point here is strikingly close to Fuller's in the idea that "the *inner form of law* brings it about that the law-giver, in giving the law, subordinates himself to it as a person, in the same way as all others."[30] But it was solely Fuller's turn of thought to develop the *moral* or *ethos* demands of that relational structure as a novel site of legal theory.

[26] The same message is conveyed in Fuller's famous analysis of the defects of Nazi law *as* law: Lon L. Fuller, "Positivism and Fidelity to Law – A Reply to Professor Hart," *Harvard Law Review*, 71 (1958), 646.

[27] See further Kristen Rundle, "Opening the Doors of Inquiry: Lon Fuller and the Natural Law Tradition," in Robert P. George and George Duke, eds., *The Cambridge Companion to Natural Law Jurisprudence* (Cambridge: Cambridge University Press, 2017), ch. 16.

[28] Fuller, *The Morality of Law*, p. 39 fn. 1.

[29] Fuller, *The Morality of Law*, p. 39 fn. 1, referring to Simmel's "Interaction in the Idea of Law" and "Subordination a Principle" in Kurt H. Wolff, *The Sociology of Georg Simmel* (New York: Simon & Schuster, 1950), pp. 186–189 and 250–267.

[30] Wolff, *The Sociology of Georg Simmel*, p. 263 (emphasis added).

3 Fuller and the Rule of Law Debate

Meeting the relational demands of legal governance was, to Fuller's eyes, a precondition for law itself to exist. It was this view that saw him take his place as the central protagonist in the debate about the necessary connections between law and morality that, in its mid-twentieth century incarnation, took an unexpected rule of law turn. Put briefly, Fuller's challenge to positivism's "separability thesis" ran along two closely related lines. The first went to the possibility that the concept of "law" can be insulated from the concept of the "internal morality of law": or, for our purposes, from the principles of "the rule of law." Here, against positivism, Fuller insisted that a (putative) legal system that fails to meet the demands of his internal morality of law is not just a bad legal system but something not properly to be called a legal system at all. The second limb of Fuller's position is his claim that these principles are moral in character. It is the combination of these two arguments that creates a problem for positivism. If the demands of the rule of law are moral in character, *and* if they are part of the very idea of law rather than a contingent ideal separable from it, then *law itself* must necessarily contain some moral dimension.

It is therefore necessary for positivists to neutralise the alleged constitutive significance to the existence of law itself of the claimed "moral" dimensions of Fuller's eight principles if the separability thesis is to be defended. An argument designed to do precisely this work was quickly provided by Fuller's most famous interlocutor, H. L. A. Hart.[31] Akin to an "internal morality of poisoning" – principles that, when followed, aid the poisoner to poison well – Hart argued that observance of Fuller's eight principles simply makes the end-product of law more effective in the pursuit of its ends. As this aid to efficacy is just as likely to assist the realization of morally evil laws as it is morally good ones, there is nothing of "moral" interest. Rather, Fuller's principles are merely neutral instrumental aids to the effectiveness of the lawgiving task.

This "efficacy" reading of the value of the principles of the internal morality of law has had an enormous impact on how Fuller's jurisprudence has been received by legal philosophers. Yet on closer inspection it can be

[31] H. L. A. Hart, "Book Review: *The Morality of Law* by Lon L. Fuller," *Harvard Law Review*, 78 (1965), 1281–1296, reprinted in H. L. A. Hart, *Essays in Jurisprudence and Philosophy* (Oxford: Clarendon Press, 1983), p. 363.

seen that Hart's response is at best an incomplete reply to the arguments that Fuller actually made. The only kind of "moral" dimension to Fuller's principles that Hart appears to consider relevant to debates about the connections between law and morality is their consequence for the moral quality of law's *ends*. But this was not the domain of Fuller's argument: he never advanced any conceptual claim about the connection between observance of his eight principles and the moral quality of legal ends of the kind that Hart's reply speaks to. As earlier noted, Fuller's writings at most entertained a connection between the observance of the internal morality of law and the substantive justice of laws as something likely, but not necessarily, to be observed in practice.[32] He was also explicit that his eight principles were "neutral over a wide range of ethical issues."[33]

The more sophisticated positivist response to Fuller's claims can be traced to Joseph Raz. In Fuller's favor, Raz's essay, "The Rule of Law and its Virtue," did much to strengthen the association between Fuller's principles of the internal morality of law and the idea of the rule of law with the result that, among contemporary legal philosophers, the two have basically become interchangeable.[34] Raz also accepts in the essay that the rule of law is a morally valuable ideal, above all to those who benefit from its observance. But much more problematically for Fuller, Raz repackaged in much more sophisticated form Hart's claim that the principles of the so-called "internal morality of law" are merely nonmoral aids to the instrumental efficacy of laws produced in accordance with them. As Raz argues the efficacy point, the rule of law is the "virtue" of law in the same way that sharpness is the virtue of the knife: its "good-making" quality.[35]

But it is through two further arguments that Raz is widely regarded as having disposed entirely of Fuller's challenge to the separability thesis. The "minimal compliance" argument contends that although all legal systems require rules to establish the institutions that will constitute the legal system itself, the level of compliance with the ideal of the rule of law needed to achieve these rules is minimal. The intended inference from this "minimal compliance" argument, it would seem, is that this minimal level of compliance is so small as to be morally insignificant, and thus presents

[32] Fuller, "Reply to Professors Cohen and Dworkin," 664.

[33] Fuller, *The Morality of Law*, p. 162.

[34] Joseph Raz, "The Rule of Law and its Virtue," in idem, *The Authority of Law: Essays on Law and Morality* (Oxford: Clarendon Press, 1979), ch. 11.

[35] Raz, "The Rule of Law and its Virtue," p. 225.

no real challenge to the positivist insistence that there is no necessary connection between law and morality. But should someone interject that, though minimal, this is nonetheless still compliance with something that Raz himself recognizes as morally significant – the ideal of the rule of law – a second argument is at the ready. The rule of law, Raz argues, is ultimately a "negative" virtue. It merely offsets or corrects evils that only law could have created.[36]

Numerous scholars sympathetic to Fuller's jurisprudence have sought to highlight the various ways in which Raz's "negative virtue" argument is problematic both as a response to Fuller and in its own right. These need not be detailed here.[37] For present purposes the important point lies in how the avowedly instrumental orientation of the positivist response to Fuller's claims – designed to serve the conceptual separation of the idea of "law" from the idea of "the rule of law" – has generated conditions for the distortion rather than illumination of Fuller's position. In particular this instrumental orientation has complemented and compounded the "checklist" reading that has come to be widely associated with Fuller's eight principles as a measure of the existence of the rule of law. On this account, the eight principles are to be understood as a model of eight rule of law "criteria" that should be met in all cases. Such an approach to understanding the conditions necessary for the rule of law invariably diverts attention from the much more important idea that Fuller actually sought to convey about the moral demands of the relationship between lawgiver and subject that are reflected in his eight principles. Indeed, Fuller was clear that sometimes the rule of law might actually be better served by departures from rather than compliance with certain principles if to do so was needed to serve the wider health of a condition of legality.[38] This insight, however, can find no place in

[36] Raz, "The Rule of Law and its Virtue," p. 224.

[37] See, for example, Kristen Rundle, "Form and Agency in Raz's Legal Positivism," *Law and Philosophy*, 32 (2013), 767, 778–781; Nigel Simmonds, "Reply: The Nature and Virtue of Law," *Jurisprudence*, 1 (2010), 277, 285; Martin Krygier, "The Hart–Fuller Debate, Transitional Societies and the Rule of Law," in Peter Cane, ed., *The Hart–Fuller Debate in the Twenty-First Century* (Oxford: Hart, 2009), p. 117; Jeremy Waldron, "The Concept and the Rule of Law," *Georgia Law Review*, 43 (2008) 1, 11; Colleen Murphy, "Lon Fuller and the Moral Value of the Rule of Law," *Law and Philosophy*, 24 (2005), 239, 246–252.

[38] This point is made especially strongly in Fuller's analysis of the principle of nonretroactivity. Fuller argues that a retroactive statute can, in certain instances, be an important curative measure in repairing the "various kinds of shipwreck" in which a legal system

a "checklist" reading of the principles of the internal morality of law. It makes sense only within the wider frame of relational demands that Fuller saw as intrinsic to the rule of law project.

Conclusion

The rule of law in Fuller's jurisprudence is thus not a thing or "concept" to be analyzed, but an activity. Being an activity, as a subject the rule of law presents certain challenges to the theorist who approaches it. Fuller embraced these challenges with open arms; indeed, he relished them as a way of demonstrating the limitations of alternate approaches to theorizing law. Taking aim especially at legal positivism,[39] to Fuller there could be no purity in the business of theorizing the rule of law, and still less in realizing it. The existence of a legal system was and is "always a matter of degree."[40]

Reflecting on this fundamental tenet of Fuller's rule of law jurisprudence invites consideration of how his thinking might translate to certain challenges of contemporary rule of law governance.[41] Two which might be briefly mentioned are the now widespread practice of rule of law transplantation and measurement, and the transferability of the principles of the internal morality of law to the variety of modalities that might feature in contemporary rule of law practice.

On the first point, one might suppose that we here have an excellent match. Especially with respect to the rule of law measurement project, support for this conclusion might be found in how Fuller clearly intended his principles of the internal morality of law to provide standards against which the degree of attainment of a condition of legality could be evaluated. The picture, however, is likely to be much more complex. In his own elaboration of the idea of the internal morality of law, Fuller readily

might find itself. The complexity of the requirement of nonretroactivity thus arises from how and when to know the difference: that is, how to know when its breach represents a tolerable sacrifice of legality, as opposed to when such would be an abuse of the feature of prospectivity that otherwise makes sense of the enterprise of governing through rules: Fuller, *The Morality of Law*, pp. 53–54.

39 See, for example, Fuller's comments on the methodology of his theoretical approach in *The Morality of Law*, pp. 92 and 147–148.

40 Fuller, *The Morality of Law*, p. 122.

41 See further Rundle, "Fuller's Relationships," pp. 32–36.

acknowledged that the realization of his principles would (rightly) be subject to considerable variation across different contexts. But still more instructively, acquaintance with the larger body of Fuller's work makes obvious his enduring preoccupation with the suitability of different "forms of social ordering" to the problems they were directed to solve and the context within which they were expected to operate.[42] For Fuller, there could never be a "one size fits all" solution to problems of human governance. Insofar that this position might problematize the relationship between his rule of law jurisprudence and contemporary practices of rule of law transplantation and measurement, Fuller's sense of the moral dilemmas inherent in such practices ought also to be kept in mind. The assumption that "the newly emerging nations" are "fundamentally just like ourselves" and thus "need the same political and legal institutions that we do" could, Fuller thought, amount to a "cruel self-centredness, a cruel blindness towards the views of others" in its application.[43] With such indications in view, it seems likely that Fuller would have expressed more than passing skepticism toward at least some contemporary practices of rule of law transplantation and measurement.

On the second point, however, one might equally speculate that Fuller would have welcomed the task of determining how the fundamental commitments of his jurisprudence could be transferrable to the great variety of legal and nonlegal forms that feature in contemporary rule of law practice. Without question, being explicitly connected to rules, Fuller's eight principles of the internal morality of law are most readily associated with the modality of legislation. Yet there is no reason to think that the *demands* that those principles are designed to reflect – demands of role integrity, participation, insight, and effort toward the relationships and purposes of governance through law – ought to be tied exclusively to the legislative form. To be sure, working out how to meet those demands in contemporary rule of law practice might require some imagination. But the need for imagination is not

[42] Among the most famous of Fuller's treatments of this issue is in an essay ultimately unpublished during his lifetime, "The Forms and Limits of Adjudication" (later published in *Harvard Law Review*, 92 (1978), 353). This kind of inquiry lies at the heart of Fuller's unfinished "eunomics" project – his "science or theory of good order and workable social arrangements" – which was motivated by his lament of the neglect by contemporary legal philosophers of these questions of institutional design as questions worthy of deep theoretical reflection. See Fuller, "American Legal Philosophy at Mid-Century."

[43] Notes for an undated talk, "The Rule of Law – Who Wants It?" *The Papers of Lon L. Fuller*, Harvard Law School Library, Box 14, Folder 14.

itself a measure of misalignment. At the heart of the idea of "the morality of the rule of law" in Fuller's conception is the impetus to acknowledge and to meet the relational and agentic demands of legal governance, however convened. Which is to say, the mode might change, but the demands will not.

11 E.P. Thompson and the Rule of Law: Qualifying the Unqualified Good

Douglas Hay*

> [T]he rule of law itself, the imposing of effective inhibitions upon power and the defence of the citizen from power's all-inclusive claims, seems to me to be an unqualified human good ... And if the actuality of the law's operation in class-divided societies has, again and again, fallen short of its own rhetoric of equity, yet the notion of the rule of law is an unqualified good.
>
> E. P. Thompson[1]

Introduction

These words appear in a short eleven-page passage headed "The rule of law" in E. P. Thompson's 300-page historical study of one British statute enacted in May 1723. Yet the passage, and particularly the quoted words, received enormous attention at the time and since, provoking widespread criticism as well as praise.[2] Edward Palmer Thompson (1924–1993) was

* Thanks for suggestions from Stephen Brooke, Peter Linebaugh, Bryan Palmer, Christine Sypnowich, and the editors. A longer version appears at https://works.bepress.com/douglas_hay/

1 E. P. Thompson, *Whigs and Hunters: The Origin of the Black Act* (Harmondsworth: Penguin, 1977), pp. 266, 267.

2 A sampling: Morton J. Horwitz, "The Rule of Law: An Unqualified Human Good?" *Yale Law Journal*, 86 (1977), 561–566; Inga Clendinnen, "Understanding the Heathen at Home: E. P. Thompson and His School," *Historical Studies*, 18 (1979), 435–440; Adrian Merritt, "The Nature and Function of Law: A Criticism of E. P. Thompson's 'Whigs and Hunters'," *British Journal of Law and Society*, 7 (1980), 194–214; Perry Anderson, *Arguments Within English Marxism* (London: Verso, 1980), pp. 69–73, 197–215; Harvey J. Kaye, *The British Marxist Historians* (London: Macmillan, [1984] 1995), pp. 194–7, 199, 203–5; Mitchell C. Stein, "Bringing Professors Hay and Thompson to the Bargaining Table," *Boston University Law Review*, 68 (1988), 621-651; Robert Fine, "The Rule of Law and Muggletonian Marxism: The Perplexities of Edward Thompson," *Journal of Law and Society*, 21 (1994), 193–213; Robert Fine, *Democracy and the Rule of Law: Liberal Ideals and Marxist Critiques* (London: Pluto Press, 1984), pp. 169–189; Robert W. Gordon, "E. P. Thompson's Legacies," *Georgetown Law Journal*, 82 (1994), 2005–2011; Daniel H. Cole,

probably the best-known British historian of the second half of the twentieth century, acclaimed for *The Making of the English Working Class.*[3] Those eleven pages were rooted first in his life-long attempt to understand, celebrate, and promote a distinctive British socialist tradition; secondly, in his hostility to Stalinism for both its tyranny and its caricature of Marx's thought; and finally in his rage at what he deplored as the contempt for civil liberties of Britain's late-twentieth-century security state. British imperialism, Soviet Communism, World War II, postwar security "emergencies," and the arms race of the Cold War – all, in different ways, raised three questions. When is state law legitimate? What is its relevance to social justice? And how can we understand law's wider role in societies past and present – and in any future socialist ones?

The answers he proposed were drawn from a deep historical investigation into 350 years of English popular movements and their experience of statute and common law. The law's relation to the state that was coeval with it, and the opposition of both to popular demands for justice, recur throughout his work. Unlike most who write on the rule of law he found his arguments in detailed historical research, informed by a passionate commitment to recover the voices and the ideas of the "real men and women" who made those demands for justice. Such people – radical democrats in the 1640s and the 1790s; protesting laborers, spinners, weavers, and early factory workers during the first industrial revolution; the Chartists of the 1830s and 1840s; British admirers of Marx like William Morris – are largely invisible in most legal histories and philosophies. Thompson used their voices to inform the public and chastise the politicians of twentieth-century Britain, while making class central to all adequate future histories of law. Class necessarily led to law, both in the past and in the twentieth

"'An Unqualified Human Good': E. P. Thompson and the Rule of Law," *Journal of Law and Society*, 28 (2001), 177–203; Paddy Ireland, "History, Critical Legal Studies, and the Mysterious Disappearance of Capitalism," *Modern Law Review*, 65 (2002), 120–140; Mark Brown, "'An Unqualified Human Good'? On Rule of Law, Globalization, and Imperialism," *Law and Social Inquiry*, 43 (2018), 1391–1426.

3 E. P. Thompson, *The Making of the English Working Class* (London: Victor Gollancz, 1963); 2nd ed. with a postscript (Harmondsworth: Penguin, 1968); 3rd ed. with a new preface (Penguin, 1980). In the 1980s Thompson was reported by the *Arts and Humanities Citation Index* to be the most-often cited historian in the world, and among the 250 most cited authors ever: Eric Hobsbawm, "E.P. Thompson," *The Observer*, August 29, 1993 and *Radical History Review*, 58 (1994) 157. See the select bibliography of his work by Harvey J. Kaye and Keith McClelland in John Rule and Robert Malcolmson, eds., *Protest and Survival: Essays for E. P. Thompson* (New York: The New Press, 1993), pp. 417–421.

century.[4] His answers came from both politics and history, his thoughts expressed in vivid prose. But what did he mean by "the rule of law"? And how did it fit with Marxist – or any socialist – theory?

1 Politics

Thompson's socialism was, like his later reflections on the rule of law, deeply influenced by his experience of the war. Going up to Cambridge on a scholarship, he soon left to enlist in an elite regiment, becoming a tank commander at the age of 18 and returning to Cambridge a war veteran aged 22.[5] He shared the lives and hopes of many men and women in the volunteer army and civilian life for a postwar future of greater social equality. Equally important were the adult education classes he then taught for seventeen years in Yorkshire for Leeds University.[6] His political and intellectual relationships in the Communist Party of Great Britain (CPGB), which he had joined during the war, were also critical. But perhaps most important was his deepening knowledge of British labor and social and political history. His political activity gave him insights, not found among many academic historians, into how radical movements survived during the early nineteenth century, when democracy was treated by the state as treason. In the history of the British socialist and labor movements, and his relationships within the rank and file of the CPGB in Yorkshire, he saw "real men and women" who had fought labor's battles and faced the power of capital.

By 1947 Thompson was deeply critical of Labour as its leadership moved to full support of American cold war strategies.[7] He had also

[4] It appears from correspondence after his death that Thompson's eleven pages on rule of law were an afterthought. "According to Dorothy Thompson, his collaboration on [*Albion's Fatal Tree*] left him deeply pessimistic about the role of law in society. She engaged him in a 'very heated discussion,' during which she suggested that 'he was leaning too far in the direction taken by some of the contributors to *Albion's Fatal Tree* in dismissing the law simply as an instrument of class power. He took time to re-think the question and added the famous afterword to *Wh and H*.'" Cole, "'An unqualified human good'", 181 fn. 18, 183 fn. 31.

[5] For Thompson's war see "Overture to Cassino," in *Double Exposure* (London: Merlin Press, 1985) and "Drava Bridge," in *The Heavy Dancers* (London: Merlin Press, 1985), pp. 231–237.

[6] *The Essential E. P. Thompson*, ed. Dorothy Thompson (New York: The New Press, 2001), p. ix; Peter Searby, John Rule, and Robert Malcolmson, "Edward Thompson as a Teacher: Yorkshire and Warwick," in Rule and Malcolmson, eds., *Protest and Survival*, pp. 1–23.

[7] Michael Kenny, *The First New Left: British Intellectuals After Stalin* (London: Lawrence & Wishart, 1995), p. 145; "Mr Attlee and the Gadarene swine," in Thompson, *The Heavy Dancers*, p. 242.

expressed dislike about many aspects of the Communist Party, including its rigid ideology, its authoritarian bureaucracy, and its complete defense of Stalinism. And in 1956, following Khrushchev's "secret" speech in February 1956 on Stalin's terror and then the Soviet invasion of Hungary, he left the CPGB. Before doing so, he had been invited to take part in a CP School on the "History of our Labour Movement." He had suggested a session on "The Free-Born Englishman" showing "*the illusions and realities* of our democratic tradition" but it was not included in the main program.[8] Later, in his polemics against the leadership, he quoted Milton and Lilburne, invoked Winstanley, Cobbett, Oastler, Ernest Jones, William Morris, Keir Hardie, and Tom Mann, and concluded:

> Bourgeois democracy, we know, is a liar and a cheat. But it is a libel on our proudest history to say that all our liberties are illusions, the "fig-leaf" of absolutism. It is a libel upon the British working class to suggest that they would exchange these liberties for a higher standard of life.[9]

The predictable Party riposte, "A caricature of our Party,"[10] prompted Thompson's article in the first issue of *The Reasoner*, the internal unapproved review he started with John Saville. In it he attacked the dogma of Party doctrine ("we get, do we not, some analogy with Holy Church?"), its reluctance to examine Khrushchev's revelations, and its stultified version of Marxist theory. The moral bankruptcy of the CPGB was complete:

> What impresses the British people is that for twenty-odd years we have been eagerly justifying as "the highest form of democracy" a society [the Soviet Union] in which there is no real freedom of the press – whether for the publication of information, opinion, or creative writing – no freedom from arbitrary arrest, and no contested elections.

He concluded that he was not proud of the Party or its record, and "I am *not* proud of the silence which I and others have kept too long over these and other matters."[11]

[8] (emphasis added)

[9] E. P. Thompson, "Winter Wheat in Omsk," *World News*, June 30, 1956, reprinted in Paul Flewers and John McIlroy, eds., *1956: John Saville, EP Thompson and The Reasoner* (London: Merlin Press, 2016), pp. 110–112.

[10] George Matthews in *World News*, June 30, 1956 reprinted in Flewers and McIlroy, eds., *1956*, pp. 114ff.

[11] E. P. Thompson, "Reply to George Matthews," *The Reasoner*, July 1, 1956, reprinted in Flewers and McIlroy, eds., *1956*, pp. 150–155. See also E. P. Thompson, The Poverty of Theory and Other Essays (London: Merlin Press, 1978), p. 324.

These themes resonated through all of Thompson's subsequent political and historical work; he returned to them again and again, to the end of his life. There is the celebration of civil liberties claimed by democratic radicals since at least the seventeenth century, including a free press, democratic elections, and protection from arbitrary state power by legal institutions – notably, the jury. There is the hope that a "humanist" socialism can be attained, ideally by political action on a wide united front. There is a clear rejection of violence. All these beliefs deeply informed the "notion" of the rule of law found in his history and excursions into theory.

2 History

Thompson's first book, a study of William Morris (1834–1896), appalled some reviewers: as well as the celebrated artist and designer, romantic poet, and wealthy businessman, here was the revolutionary socialist agitator.[12] Morris crossed "the river of fire" to committed and indefatigable activism in 1883: he immersed himself in factional decisions, endless speaking engagements, bruising political confrontations. Repudiating both Fabian state planning and the parliamentarism of Hyndman's Social-Democratic Federation as compromises with capitalism, he fought for a socialism of workers. Earlier biographers, when they noticed this part of his life, insisted he was no Marxist. Thompson showed Morris's admiration for Marx's insight that surplus value was the result of labor's oppression, and how admirers of Morris the artist had slighted or misrepresented those convictions. The passages on Morris's hatred of British imperialism, capitalist exploitation of labor, Victorian hypocrisy about sex and hunger and "merriment," are splendidly represented by extensive quotation, joined to Thompson's own pungent prose. His considered conclusion was that Morris was a revolutionary utopian socialist, committed to the idea and reality of class conflict, who united English Romanticism's savage critique of capitalism with the insights of Marx's ideas.

Thompson celebrated Morris's decency, his love of life and art and friends, his radical democracy and hatred of class distinctions, his enormous energy and devotion to the cause of socialism and social justice, his full commitment to equality for women, his generous encouragement of

[12] E. P. Thompson, *William Morris: Romantic to Revolutionary*, rev. ed. (Pontypool: Merlin Press, [1955] 2011).

young workers and artists.[13] He emphasized Morris's insistence that moral values, above all respect for human life and freedom and desires – denied by capitalism – had to be the essence of socialism.

He remarked years later how good a companion Morris had been to him, but Morris's view of the law was not to be Thompson's. Morris's account of law in his own society, capitalist late-nineteenth-century England, confirmed his view that capital was ruthless in its use of law, and that parliamentary roads to socialism were dead ends.[14] For Morris, law was *the* origin of fraud and class oppression, the principal cause of man-made suffering in the nineteenth century. Capitalism, he wrote, is "the Law-Courts, backed up by the executive, which [handle] the brute force that the deluded people [allow] them to use for their own purposes . . . the army, navy, and police." Morris's contempt for English law was profound.[15]

In 1963 Thompson published *The Making of the English Working Class*, the work which made him famous and transformed social history in England and many other countries. Thompson had traced Morris's friendships with aged Chartists, whose radical democratic demands in the 1830s and 1840s could be connected back to Tom Paine in the 1790s, and beyond that to the Levellers. *The Making* showed those links – and the importance of law.[16] Struggles against legal repression, in court cases brought by radical or sympathetic lawyers, were everywhere in *The Making*. Juries were critical points of opposition to repressive laws, which is why English governments went to extraordinary lengths to secretly pack them with trustworthy men who would find guilty verdicts.

The book opens with the trial and acquittal for treason of the London Corresponding Society leaders in 1794. State trials for sedition and treason punctuate the narrative of struggle for popular democratic rights, as a self-conscious working class emerged. Thompson explored the class character of state law in sedition charges, executions of rioters and unsuccessful revolutionaries, criminal penalties against trade unions, enclosures of common lands by a parliament of landlords ("class robbery"), spying by

13 In my experience as his student, all qualities of EPT himself.

14 Thompson, *William Morris*, pp. 488ff.

15 William Morris, *News From Nowhere*, ed. James Redmond (London: Routledge and Kegan Paul, [1890] 1970), pp. 34, 65, 71, 98.

16 In *Witness Against the Beast: William Blake and the Moral Law* (Cambridge: Cambridge University Press, 1993), he traced a possible link between the civil war and the 1790s through the Muggletonian sect.

police informers, and refusal to prosecute or punish the middle-class mounted "Volunteers" who sabered to death peaceful demonstrators at "Peterloo" in 1819. Artisanal riots and sabotage of gig-mills and other new machinery that was once forbidden by law were met by new capital statutes, exemplary mass hangings, and repeal of the ancient laws. All attempts by labor to reinstate some of the Tudor-Stuart protections it had enjoyed under the Elizabethan Statute of Artificers (5 Eliz. c. 4, 1562) were repulsed by a parliament of landowners and industrialists in the early nineteenth century.

Against state law Thompson counterpoised the popular beliefs in customary legal rights that he developed in his later work on the "moral economy" of food rioters, the "sale" of wives by the poor, and such common rights as grazing and gleaning for the poor.[17] All entailed popular ideas of legal right, ideas also enacted in medieval, Tudor, and Stuart statute, or imbedded in ancient manorial custom. And again, both parliament and the judges (and troops and the newly invented police of the nineteenth century) were used by capital and its state to expunge those popular claims and erase them from the law of England.[18]

Whigs and Hunters, famous for the eleven pages on the rule of law, actually made the argument through meticulous archival work that law was a principal instrument of power – the power of a state controlled by a rapacious agrarian capitalist class. The Waltham Blacks episode was

[17] Mentioned in *The Making of the English Working Class*, fully developed in *Customs in Common* (London: Merlin Press, 1991), chs. 4, 5, 7.

[18] Thompson perhaps understated the degree to which both wife sales and the moral economy of markets were parasitic on state law. The form of plebeian divorce in the wife sale referenced the fact that sale of a beast in "open market" was a guarantee of the new owner's title, even if a horse had been stolen. Statutes of 1555 and 1588 (2&3 Philip & Mary c. 7, 31 Eliz. c. 12) set out that guarantee. Copying their terms explains some incidents of wife sales: weighing the woman, using the halter around her neck, sometimes entering the sale in a market tollbook, even creating a written contract (Thompson, *Customs in Common*, p. 421). This is not to deny that a wife was often the instigator of such a sale, leaving her husband for a lover, as Thompson explains. The point is that popular custom justified itself by closely copying analogous statute law as legitimation for the otherwise impermissible change of ownership by theft (and was not a wife "property"?). The practice was ended by the new police of the nineteenth century. In food markets, not until the high court judges accepted the arguments of Adam Smith did law repudiate moral economy: Douglas Hay, "The State and the Market: Lord Kenyon and Mr Waddington," *Past and Present*, 162 (1999), 101–162; Douglas Hay, "Moral Economy, Political Economy, and Law," in Adrian Randall and Andrew Charlesworth, eds., *Moral Economy and Popular Protest: Crowds, Conflict and Authority* (Manchester: Manchester University Press, 1999), pp. 93–122.

a conflict between holders of local customary rights over land, and a parasitic upper class at the heart of the state prepared to use the most coercive of state powers, capital punishment, to reap profit at the expense of middling and plebeian commoners. Parliament passed the "Black Act" (9 Geo. I, c. 22) in their interest. The high court judges interpreted the Act expansively, contrary to the dictum that penal statutes, particularly those punishing with death, should be read narrowly. Possibly sympathetic local juries were circumvented by the unusual provision in the Act that cases could be tried in any county, allowing the state to prosecute one group of Blacks in Westminster Hall, and to have them executed in London. Whig crowds there did not sympathize with the Blacks, tainted with the suspicion of Jacobitism. Backed by a sophisticated understanding of Hanoverian land law as well as criminal law, the argument led Thompson to greatly qualify what he meant by the "rule of law" in those eleven famous pages at the end. Law had to seem to be just in order to have purchase: "indeed, *on occasion*, by actually *being* just." The legal ideologies of the powerful "struck root in a soil, *however shallow*, of actuality." Rules of law "*may curb*" power. "In a context of gross inequalities, the equity of the law must *always* be in some part a sham." "The forms and rhetoric of law acquire a distinct identity which *may, on occasion* inhibit power and afford some protection to the powerless."[19]

The importance of conflicts over definitions of property, legal and popular, was expanded in his subsequent work. For lawyers, custom was a source of law. General custom was the notional source of the common law; local manorial custom, limited to particular places, was recognized by the high courts; London had a custom of its own; custom formed part of legal contract terms in individual trades and employment.[20] On the land, "common rights," multiple use-rights over the same piece land – by lords of manors, copyholders, and commoners – were recognized in law from medieval times. Manorial custom ensured the rights of commoners and copyholders (including widows' right of occupation of land by right of

[19] Thompson, *Whigs and Hunters*, pp. 262–267 (emphases added).

[20] E. P. Thompson, "The Grid of Inheritance: A Comment," in Jack Goody, Joan Thirsk, and E. P. Thompson, eds., *Family and Inheritance: Rural Society in Western Europe, 1200–1800* (Cambridge: Cambridge University Press, 1978), pp. 328–360; Thompson, *Customs in Common*, ch. 3. For a statement of the legal doctrine, see C. K. Allen, *Law in the Making*, 7th ed. (Oxford: Clarendon Press, 1964), ch. 2 and Appendix. For a summary of the social significance of the change, see Douglas Hay and Nicholas Rogers, *Eighteenth-Century English Society: Shuttles and Swords* (Oxford: Oxford University Press, 1997), chs. 6, 7.

"free bench") through an amalgam of ancient practice, preservation in written custumals and local memory, and occasional successful litigation when prosperous men went to the courts and sometimes encouraged their plebeian neighbors to riot against the pretentions of rich lords of the manor.[21]

That alliance weakened in the eighteenth century and disappeared at parliamentary enclosure. His argument about this long process combined a detailed analysis of case law with an equally detailed recovery of the lives, beliefs, and struggles – legal, political, and riotous – of those who claimed common rights. Rights in many parts of the country had extended to poorer inhabitants without property – by custom, and because it made economic and political sense. Gleaning of fields by the poor was only one instance. Thompson made the case that common rights – especially these possibly very extensive uncodified rights of the poor – were swept away not only by acts of parliamentary enclosure. They were eroded by social change, as wealthy men sought to create full property in severalty, without coincident use-rights. They were powerfully supported by judicial interpretation. He concluded that "it was the law which served as a superb instrument for enforcing the reification of right and for tearing down the remnants of the threadbare communal grid . . . The judges sought to reduce use-rights to an equivalent in things or in money, and hence to bring them within the universal currency of capitalist ownership." In many cases they did this by importing into the law the tenets of classical political economy.[22] "If it is pretended that the law was impartial, deriving its rules from its own self-extrapolating logic, then we must reply that this pretence was class fraud."[23]

Finally, in two brilliant articles Thompson explored the way in which eighteenth-century law, and the upper-class rule that created and applied it, was an instance of hegemonic rule, a constantly recreated but contested ruling-class ideology in the Gramscian Marxist sense.[24] It fit with his earlier argument that Britain's class formations from the seventeenth to

[21] See also J. M. Neeson, *Commoners: Common Right, Enclosure and Social Change in England, 1700–1820* (Cambridge: Cambridge University Press, 1993), pp. 328–360.

[22] Thompson, "The Grid of Inheritance," pp. 339, 341; Thompson, *Customs in Common*, chs.1, 3.

[23] Thompson, *Customs in Common*, p. 176.

[24] E. P. Thompson, "Patrician Society, Plebian Culture," *Journal of Social History*, 7 (1974), 382–405; and idem, "Eighteenth-Century English Society: Class Struggle without Class," *Social History*, 3 (1978), 133–165.

the nineteenth century had been highly distinctive: notably an early, triumphant *agrarian* bourgeois capitalism, a category that European Marxist theorists, and Englishmen under their influence, found too unorthodox to accept.[25]

The modern security state was the subject of most of Thompson's writing throughout the later 1970s, and although he had given up writing history for a time (he returned to it near the end of his life), his polemical journalism constantly used historical arguments in an attempt to overcome citizens' amnesia about constitutional liberties, now under serious threat.[26] He saw a complaisant Labour government, then a radically neoliberal Tory regime, happily acquiescing in cold-war security demands from the intelligence services and their American counterparts. Parliament, judiciary and the police establishment aided and abetted the subversion of civil liberties and the rights of workers won by past popular struggles. He used history to lambast politicians, public officials, police and judges. He hoped to educate an electorate (and left activists) deplorably ignorant of their country's constitutional history. Beyond freedom of the press and habeas corpus he particularly emphasized the jury. A place of public participation in the law, a place where the letter of the law could be neutralized by popular opinion, the jury also educated citizens in their rights and their power.[27]

The 1970s saw huge legislated erosion of traditional trial by jury. Thompson invoked the coroner's juries used by the Victorian radical Dr Wakeley to attack the coroner and judges who tried to block an inquiry into the death of Blair Peach, a protestor killed by the police in 1979.[28] He pilloried law officers of the crown who secretly used the police to help choose politically "safe" jurors, and legislated to make the probable views of jurors harder for defense barristers to identify. He denounced the government for transferring offenses historically tried by juries, charges often arising out of street demonstrations, to the swift and certain summary convictions of magistrates' courts. He deplored the legislated 1974 change allowing jury verdicts based on majorities of ten to two or nine to one

[25] Thompson, "The Peculiarities of the English," *The Socialist Register*, reprinted in idem, *The Poverty of Theory and Other Essays* (London: Merlin Press, [1965] 1978), pp. 35–91.

[26] The most important are collected in Thompson, *Writing by Candlelight* (London: Merlin Press, 1980).

[27] E. P. Thompson, "Subduing the Jury," *London Review of Books*, December 4 and 18, 1986.

[28] For which the Metropolitan Police admitted responsibility in 2010.

rather than the historic unanimity of twelve. And he was scathing about the high court judges. They scurried to do the will of the government, they held deep-rooted establishment and right-wing prejudices, their reverence was more for the "Rights of Money" than the rights of the citizen. But then, "no British liberty has ever arisen from the decision of judges, although there have been occasions when these liberties have been judicially *defined*." For "the law today can be a profoundly corrupting profession," and judges drawn from such a profession would find it difficult to become guardians of the people's liberties: "it will be no easy matter for a professional law-breaker to mend his habits overnight."[29]

Thompson believed the 1970s to be an authoritarian moment, with a strong smell of Weimar. In writing the eleven pages, he countered the arguments of a vulgar current Marxism, but his mind was clearly somewhere else – in Hitler's Germany and Stalin's Soviet Union – and on the politics of class war and state secrecy that made him compare England in the 1970s and 1980s to the crisis of the 1930s.[30] State security services were out of control, police brutality was shielded by the legal establishment, and policing of demonstrations was all too similar to the tenderness shown to the British Union of Fascists in the 1930s. He accurately foresaw Thatcher's escalating attack on the unions, and a further "brutalizing of the common law." "This may be good class war, but it has nothing to do with the rule of law. The British ruling class has always been hazy about the distinction."[31]

The rule of law was not a settled thing. It had always been a contest. But the sectarian ultra-left seemed to be indifferent, consumed by academic Marxist theoretical debate that was doubly compromised: unconnected to any popular political movement, and unpleasantly reminiscent of the CPGB in its certitudes.[32] Behind everything stood the threat of catastrophe, nuclear war. The state intelligence services on both sides of the iron curtain stifled debate, whether by repression in the east, or the more subtle – sometimes not so subtle – subversion of civil liberties in the west. His

[29] Thompson, *Writing by Candlelight*, pp. 37, 99–111, 187, 192–193, 206–208, 211–223, 217–218, 220ff, 245.

[30] Thompson, *Writing by Candlelight*, pp. ix, x, 122, 254.

[31] *Writing By Candlelight*, pp. 197ff, 211, 213–214, 239, 242, 246, 251.

[32] E. P. Thompson, *Persons and Polemics* (London: Merlin Press, 1994) pp. 340–341.

polemical journalism of the later 1970s seems to spring directly from the famous eleven pages; it certainly was of a piece, but is far from a celebration of English justice.

3 Theory

Many supporters of liberal capitalism invoked Thompson's "rule of law" as a counter-Marxist argument, providentially delivered by a (reformed?) Marxist. We have seen that they could do so only by ignoring not only most of *Whigs and Hunters* but also the rest of his historical and political writing. Ironically, this mistaken judgement was shared by many readers who were Marxists, or scholars sympathetic to a class analysis of law. They thought Thompson had become an apologist for capitalist "justice." In fact, Thompson's focus on law is much narrower than some read him. In spite of his assertion in the quote at the opening of this article that law was a constraint on "power's all-inclusive claims," it is clear he meant the power of state actors. He concentrated on basic civil liberties issues, and especially on criminal procedure. Unfortunately the term "rule of law" is often vaguely defined, in academic as well as demotic usage. Sypnowich has remarked its many meanings, and Waldron how few jurists using the term have gone beyond rather abstract principles. In an attempt to give the term more content both have emphasized legal *procedure*.[33] That was also Thompson's focus.

To the liberal-left critics of "rule of law" rhetoric, Thompson seemed to be ignoring the enormous malleability or even indeterminacy of law. The legal issues most germane to capitalism today – the insulation of the corporation from regulation, the expansion of its intellectual property claims, its rights under international trade agreements to derail state regulation of either its capital or its workers – are also those where the shibboleths of "rule of law" are now most likely to be invoked by capital.[34] Thompson said relatively little about private law later than the eighteenth century, although it was much on the minds of his critics in the law schools,

[33] Christine Sypnowich, "Utopia and the Rule of Law," in David Dyzenhaus, ed., *Recrafting the Rule of Law: The Limits of Legal Order* (Oxford: Hart, 1999), pp. 178–195; Jeremy Waldron, "The Concept and the Rule of Law," *Georgia Law Review*, 43 (2008), 1–61.

[34] Joshua Barkan, *Corporate Sovereignty: Law and Government under Capitalism* (Minneapolis: University of Minnesota Press, 2013).

notably the (sometimes *marxisant*) critical legal studies theorists who were exploring the indeterminacy of law.[35] They thought Thompson failed to see the manifold ways, particularly in a common law tradition, that law can be opportunistically reshaped to serve capital and state. But we have seen that he was in fact acutely aware that the common law, and legislation, reflected the pressures of capitalist needs and ideologies in the eighteenth century, and in the twentieth. Deciding what "rule of law" meant was always decided by *political* struggle. The institutions that supposedly preserve civil liberties and the rule of law – juries, independent judges, parliamentary oversight – would do so only if the public valued them, and understood their historical importance. Otherwise the security state would progressively subvert them – and the judges and parliament and civil service and police would be the co-conspirators. The argument has resonance today.

For his Marxist critics, the theoretical arguments were about three things: whether law could ever restrain the power of a ruling class, since it was the creation of that class; whether a basis/superstructure argument explained law; whether law was only conceivable in capitalism, and would not exist in a truly socialist ("Communist?") future state. Implicit in all three was a judgement about the justifications (if any) for revolutionary violence. Thompson thought all three issues were contaminated and confused by a new enthusiasm for old dogmatic Marxist positions, expressed in obscure and pretentious theoretical language by a Paris-based circle with growing influence on the British left, including on Perry Anderson, who published a book that was an all-out attack (sometimes respectful, sometimes unfair) on Thompson's politics, history, and theory, including his view of law.

Anderson protested that "A tyranny can perfectly well rule by law: its own laws."[36] Thompson had made the point himself with respect to South Africa and the Communist bloc, and in all his histories. In his polemic against the "Parisian cabal," whom he believed largely Althusserian, he slyly suggested that their theories, irrelevant to England, were *perhaps*

[35] Horwitz, "Rule of Law"; Peter Gabel et al., "Critical Legal Studies Symposium," *Stanford Law Review*, 36 (1984), 1–674; Roberto Unger, *The Critical Legal Studies Movement* (Cambridge: Harvard University Press, 1986). Cf. Thompson's apparent belief that "rules of law . . . are exactly defined" (see "Conclusion" below).

[36] Anderson, *Arguments Within English Marxism*, pp. 69–73, 197–215.

more germane to "Other Countries."[37] Thompson put the English jury at the very heart of his defense of law: what was enforceable law in England was defined in significant measure by popular consent, and popular participation. "Other Countries," we notice, did not have the jury.[38] And it was with such institutions as the jury, habeas corpus appeals, and coroners' inquests that ruling-class outrages had been contested over the centuries: law was a site of struggle, not a thing.

Thompson had always intensely disliked the "Marxist" idea that law was only "superstructural," a sort of epiphenomenon of an economic, mode-of-production "basis." It was an article of faith for Stalinists, but ambiguous in Marx. Thompson quoted instead Marx's statement in the *Grundrisse* that:

> In all forms of society it is a determinate production and its relations which assign every other production and its relations their rank and influence. It is a general illumination in which all other colours are plunged and which modifies their specific tonalities. It is a special ether which defines the specific gravity of everything found in it.[39]

Law, like all institutions, was bathed in the light of a mode of production, not mechanically determined by it. But there was no really apposite metaphor. Critically, Thompson argued that law also necessarily *shaped* economic class relations. Law determined the bounds of markets, ownership, property relations – it was in fact "everywhere," at every level, in the economic relations of society.[40] There, too, it could lead to resistance. This repudiation of the basis/superstructure metaphor had great political as well

[37] Anderson defended Althusser, but with criticisms, and argued that Thompson ironically made similar, if opposite, theoretical errors. He declared Althusser no Stalinist; for Thompson it was enough that Althusser was long an ideologue and apologist of the French Communist Party, and conceded his intellectual debt to Stalin: Anderson, *Arguments*, pp. 113ff; Thompson, *Poverty of Theory*, pp. 271–272 and *passim*. Thompson thought Anderson himself was not an Althusserian, although he had adopted some of his "concepts and modes": Henry Abelove, Betsy Blackmar, Peter Dimock, and Jonathan Schneer, eds., *Visions of History* (Manchester: Manchester University Press, 1983), p. 17.

[38] Or imported the manly English model only to emasculate it: Bernard Schnapper, *Voies nouvelles en histoire du droit: la justice, la famille, la répression pénale (XVIème – XXème siècles)* (Paris: Presses Universitaires de France, 1991); James M. Donovan, *Juries and the Transformation of Criminal Justice in France in the Nineteenth and Twentieth Centuries* (Chapel Hill: University of North Carolina Press, 2010).

[39] Thompson, *Poverty of Theory*, pp. 39, 52, 79ff; Thompson, "Class Struggle without Class," 151–152; Thompson, *Customs in Common*, pp. 73, 84.

[40] Thompson, *Whigs and Hunters*, p. 261; Thompson, *Poverty of Theory*, p. 288; Thompson, *Persons and Polemics*, p. 222.

as analytic importance for Thompson. Vulgar Marxist denigration of bourgeois law as secondary to economic class relations led inexorably, for Stalin and Stalinists, to denigration of all those civil liberties gained and extended by popular, not just aristocratic or bourgeois, resistance over centuries. For Stalinists law was simply an expression of class power – bourgeois law under capitalism, proletarian law under Soviet Communism.[41] Thompson never forgot the bitter experience of Stalinist apologetics and its contempt for "bourgeois" law.

Part of Thompson's dislike of the basis/superstructure model was his distrust of models *tout court*. His Marxist critics said he was erecting straw men, living in the past, that vulgar Marxism of the Stalinist variety had been entirely superseded by a nuanced understanding of the relationship of law to productive relations, notably in the notion of the "relative autonomy" of law. And they accused Thompson of ignoring the ineluctable ties of law to the mode of production.[42] His reply was that abstract models needed testing in historical research, research that had not been done by the "new Cartesians" and other dogmatists. Not only Marxists, but also enthusiasts for capitalist "modernization theory" (which he derided as imperialist propaganda) abandoned early, or did not even begin, the work necessary to validate their models. Attempts to salvage basis/superstructure under the guise of Poulantzas's "relative autonomy" did not impress him.[43] Models were both abstract and static – yet economies, class relations, and political contexts were in constant movement, and only close historical work could discover, and perhaps explain, their movement and interaction. To pretend there was a magic theoretical key was self-delusion.

Thompson deplored the sleight of hand by which Althusserian structuralism retained economic determinism in the theory while allowing absolute contingency in practice (empirical, historical) without ever doing any history. He excoriated Althusser's ignorant dismissals of actual historical practice, exemplified by such statements as "The truth of history cannot be read in its manifest discourse, because the text of history is not a text in which a voice (the Logos) speaks, but the inaudible and illegible notation of

[41] Christine Sypnowich, *The Concept of Socialist Law* (Oxford: Clarendon Press, 1990), pp. 17–23.

[42] See, for example, Merritt, "The Nature and Function of Law."

[43] Thompson, *Poverty of Theory*, pp. 78, 260, 288ff, 404.

the effects of a structure of structures."[44] Any politics based on delusion and over-simple models had been shown, in Stalinism, to be a moral and human disaster. He did find Gramsci's idea of hegemony fruitful (but was told by some on the left that he misunderstood it). And he never abandoned his belief that, as Marx held, historical materialism was the only foundation for socialist analysis.[45]

On the third theoretical issue, whether there would be law in a classless society, Thompson had no doubts. William Morris had believed that law would wither away with the state under Communism, that the end of private property, and shared abundance, would end the need for formal law. Thompson never thought so, probably because the abandonment of legal norms had so often been a pernicious escape from having to justify means as well as ends under Stalinism and fascism. In the late twentieth century to abandon such norms was "a desperate error of intellectual abstraction." It would never be wise, or possible, to "dispense with the negative restrictions of bourgeois legalism." Of such "utopian projections," he declared, a historian "can bring in support of them no historical evidence whatsoever."[46] That some "utopians" were also apologists for revolutionary violence was probably important to him. Not only sectarian left groups but the Parisian "cabal" (and hence their English admirers) were guilty. He was incensed by Jean-Paul Sartre's preface to Frantz Fanon's *Les damnés de la terre* (1961).[47] What are we to make, he demanded, of its "emotional parasitism on the drama of revolution, its refurbishing of neo-Sorelian mystiques of violence? Of its preoccupation with mammoth intellectual apologias?" He pointed to Belsen, Stalinist labor camps, the invasion of Budapest, and the atrocity of nuclear warfare. What might be relevant to a colonial resistance movement was dangerously misleading for British (and

44 As quoted in Thompson, *Poverty of Theory*, p. 207. See E. P. Thompson, "An Open Letter to Leszek Kolakowski," in his *Poverty of Theory*, pp. 139, 141; and Ellen Meiksins Wood, "Falling through the Cracks: E. P. Thompson and the Debate on Base and Superstructure," in Harvey J. Kaye and Keith McClelland, eds., *E. P. Thompson: Critical Perspectives* (Cambridge: Polity, 1990), ch. 5, pp. 125–152.

45 Bryan D. Palmer, *E. P. Thompson: Objections and Oppositions* (London: Verso, 1994), ch. 4.

46 Thompson, *Whigs and Hunters*, p. 266. Sypnowich, *Concept of Socialist Law* presents a sustained argument, citing Thompson at several points, for the continued necessity of law in any future classless society.

47 Jean-Paul Sartre, "Preface," in Frantz Fanon, *The Wretched of the Earth*, trans. Constance Farrington (London: Penguin [1961] 1990), pp. 7–26.

French) socialists.[48] In 1978 he wrote, in words echoing his stance in 1956, "As a Marxist (or a Marxist-fragment) in the Labour Party [which he had rejoined in 1978], I have always tried to envisage a politics that will enable us, in this country, to effect a transition to a socialist society ... without rupturing the humane and tolerant disposition for which our working class has been noted."[49]

The argument in *Whigs and Hunters* is hardly mentioned, certainly not engaged, by many Marxist critics of Thompson's work. Over the years many were more preoccupied with whether he understood Trotskyism (he saw it as an "anti-popery" to Stalinism, and loathed its supporters' tactics), or whether (as they said) he was a deluded enthusiast of Popular Front rather than "proper" class politics, or was uncomradely in accusing Althusser of Stalinism, or had ditched the economic explanation of class for a "culturalist" one, or had been bested by Perry Anderson in explaining England's class history and the allegedly defective British inheritance of socialism, or had (perhaps) come to practice a Gramscian structuralism while denouncing the Althusserian variety. And Thompson's appeals from 1956 on for a "socialist humanism" were almost always passed off as deluded romanticism. He believed Althusser was particularly and personally dismissive, although others also stressed Thompson's roots in the English romantic tradition, and cited his failure to reconcile Morris and Marx, or find a strategy in the 1960s to emulate the Popular Front of the 1930s. Often the rule of law passage is mentioned only in passing, in a hasty summary of his historical writing that betrays lack of knowledge of English history, or of the varieties of historical materialism. And for those wedded to a basis/superstructure explanation of law, Thompson was now simply a bourgeois liberal.[50]

Ultimately, Thompson abandoned Marxist polemics after 1979, when a rancorous debate at a History Workshop conference emphasized these differences. Perhaps more important was the wider political context. He had hoped through the late 1960s and the 1970s that the "new left" could

[48] "Where Are We Now?" Memo written for the *New Left Review* meeting at which Thompson left the journal, April 1963, as quoted in Scott Hamilton, *The Crisis of Theory: E. P. Thompson, the New Left, and Postwar British Politics* (Manchester: Manchester University Press, 2011), p. 103.

[49] Thompson, *Writing by Candlelight*, p. 185.

[50] Thompson, "Socialist Humanism," *New Reasoner*, 1 (1957), 105–143; *Poverty of Theory*, pp. 321–326; Christos Efstathiou, *E. P. Thompson: A Twentieth-Century Romantic* (London: Merlin Press, 2015). On Trotskyism and Popular Front politics, see Thompson, *Poverty of Theory*, pp. 76, 122, 124; Flewers and McIlroy, eds., *1956*, pp. 410ff.

make civil liberties a way to confront an increasingly authoritarian state, and he had actively collaborated with the National Council for Civil Liberties, and such groups as State Research during the notorious "ABC trial" (1978) of three journalists under the Official Secrets Act 1911.[51] Through the 1970s and Thatcher's victory (1979) and government, his conviction grew that Britain increasingly resembled the Weimar Republic, with a government that was destroying civil liberties and waging class war, while the sectarian Marxist left was consumed by dogmatic abstractions and tempted toward violence.[52] And the danger of nuclear annihilation made all else moot. In the 1980s he devoted almost all his energy to the European movement for nuclear disarmament, while remaining supportive of the struggle for civil liberties in Britain. At the end of his life he turned back to his long-neglected study of Blake, and Blake's indictment of the laws of both religions and states for denying human justice.[53] Thompson, some say, was at heart, like Blake, a visionary rather than a vanguardist. Or a modern Muggletonian who struggled with the unresolvable antinomies of law and justice throughout his life.[54]

Conclusion

In the early twenty-first century, more than two decades after Thompson's death, the specter of fascism – rather than Stalinism – again informs the debate. It was not only a Stalinist Soviet Union that made the forms and rules and procedures of law a fraud – so too did Nazi Germany, and apartheid South Africa, to name only two where the facade of formalist law was preserved – and where the judiciary, for the most part, played their ideological roles – and preserved the interests of their class.[55]

[51] Christopher Moores, *Civil Liberties and Human Rights in Twentieth-Century Britain* (Cambridge: Cambridge University Press, 2017), pp. 145, 150–151, 166, 210, 211, 214.

[52] Palmer, *Thompson*, pp. 123–125 suggests his willingness to debate Marxist theory was ebbing and ended with the History Workshop debate of 1979; Hamilton, *The Crisis of Theory* pp. 160–163, emphasizes Thompson's huge dismay at Indira Gandhi's authoritarian rule during a visit he made in 1977/78; Koditschek, "The Possibilities of Theory," p. 94 fn. 33. sees it in the categories of Thompson's *Customs in Common.*

[53] Thompson, *Witness Against the Beast.*

[54] Hamilton, *The Crisis of Theory* p. 194; Robert Fine, "The Rule of Law and Muggletonian Marxism: The Perplexities of Edward Thompson," *Journal of Law and Society*, 21 (1994), 193–213.

[55] Ingo Müller, *Hitler's Justice: The Courts of the Third Reich* (Cambridge: Harvard University Press, [1987] 1991); Jens Meierhenrich, *The Remnants of the Rechtsstaat: An Ethnography*

To those anxious to recruit him to the rule of law brigade, or to Marxist abstractions that he distrusted, Thompson's reply was that old institutions such as the jury

> have been the locus of intense historic struggles, the swaying to-and-fro motions of the contest between social classes. Each precedent signifies a contest between privilege and liberty, lost, gained, or held in the balance; and certain precedents have been signed in blood . . . They are rules which may sometimes seem to trammel and limit us, but at the same time they limit the powers of those who would rule us and push us about. They are at one and the same time rules of conduct and the places where we fight about those rules.
>
> . . . There is no such abstract entity as the Rule of Law, if by this we mean some ideal presence aloof from the ruck of history, which it is the business of judges to "administer" and of policemen to "enforce." That is all ideology. It used to be the ideology of kings and despots. It is now the ideology of the authoritarian state.
>
> If I have argued elsewhere that the rule of law is an "unqualified human good" . . . I have done so as an historian and a materialist. The rule of law, in this sense, must always be historically, culturally, and, in general, nationally specific. It concerns the conduct of social life, and the regulations of conflicts, according to rules of law *which are exactly defined and have palpable and material evidences* – which rules attain toward consensual assent and are subject to interrogation and reform. That this itself is an ideal definition, which takes little account of social and ideological determinants of property and class, *and which has never been matched by social reality*, does not mean that the aspiration towards that state is not a human good.[56]

The weight one gives to each of those italicized passages will determine, for most readers, whether Thompson made a convincing case. He did make one other clarification. "Everything we have witnessed in this century," he wrote, "suggests that no serious socialist thinker can suppose that a rule of some kind of law – albeit, socialist law and not capitalist law – is not a profound human good."[57]

of Nazi Law (Oxford: Oxford University Press, 2018); Michael Lobban, *White Man's Justice: South African Political Trials in the Black Consciousness Era* (Oxford: Clarendon Press, 1996), pp. 252ff.; Jens Meierhenrich, *The Legacies of Law: Long-Run Consequences of Legal Development in South Africa, 1652–2000* (Cambridge: Cambridge University Press, 2008), pp. 112–174.

[56] Thompson, *Writing by Candlelight*, p. 230 (emphases added).

[57] Abelove et al., eds., *Visions of History*, p. 9.

Functions of the Rule of Law 12

Brian Z. Tamanaha

Introduction

Theorists often begin with the elements or features of the rule of law, frequently distinguishing formal and substantive versions.[1] Instead, I explore two other senses. The first sense is that the rule of law exists in a society when government officials and the populace are generally bound by and abide law. Framing the analysis in terms of a society subject to law enables a more expansive view of functions of the rule of law. The second sense construes "the rule of law" as an ideal and as rhetoric, asking what functions are served when people invoke it. Function is a complex notion with several permutations centered around the proposition that a function plays a role in the operation of a system or arrangement. In my usage, function is not necessarily a purpose or end (though it can be); function at base means "what it does" or "what it is used for."[2] Multiple functions will be identified from different angles and levels of generality. I also distinguish manifest functions from latent functions that usually go unrecognized or unmentioned.[3] In this essay, I identify several functions of the rule of law as a society under law and as an ideal and as rhetoric.

1 A Society under Law

The rule of law exists in a society when government officials and the populace are generally bound by and abide law. This statement requires several clarifications. "Government officials" include anyone acting in

[1] See Brian Z. Tamanaha, *On the Rule of Law: History, Politics, Theory* (Cambridge: Cambridge University Press 2004), pp. 91–113.

[2] See Arno Wouters, "The Function Debate in Philosophy," *Acta Biotheoretica*, 53 (2005), 123–151, 146.

[3] Robert K. Merton, *Social Theory and Social Structure* (New York: The Free Press 1957), pp. 19–84. I use a simplified version of Merton's original distinction.

a governmental capacity. "Populace" includes all natural and artificial persons within a territory. Though government officials count among the populace, they bear specific mention to emphasize the application of the rule of law to government actions. "Bound by" means under legal obligation, that is, subject to law's claim to compel or constrain (to bind) the populace. "Abide law" ranges from obeying, to accepting, to tolerating or putting up with, to not violating the law.

The latter meaning differs from the others in a salient respect. To obey or accept or tolerate the law, one must know what law is being obeyed, accepted, or tolerated. To not violate the law means not acting contrary to legal requirements, which is possible even without specific knowledge of the law. People who do not violate the law may do so consciously or may not know the law but nonetheless act in ways consistent with legal proscriptions (the relevance of this point will be indicated later).

2 Manifest Functions

Personal and Collective Security and Trust

A society in which the populace and government officials are generally bound by and abide law gives rise to an individual and collective sense of security and trust. People in advanced capitalist societies go about their daily affairs implicitly reassured by an assumed legal backdrop that provides them with a sense of security in their persons and in their social, cultural, economic, and political affairs.[4] Criminal laws protect people from violence or harm by others. Property laws preserve the fruits of their labor, enable exchanges, and allow the accumulation of assets. Contract laws facilitate economic transactions and arrangements. Tort laws provide remedies for injuries to person and damage to property. Family laws detail the rights and responsibilities of marital unions and care for offspring. Constitutions construct the polity, confer powers and duties, and impose restrictions on public actors. Election laws determine how officeholders are selected, and civil service laws cover the rights and responsibilities of public employees. Laws create, internally constitute (through contracts), and regulate corporations. Labor and employment

[4] See Brian Z. Tamanaha, *A Realistic Theory of Law* (Cambridge: Cambridge University Press, 2017), pp. 139–142.

laws protect employees. Health, sanitation, and fire safety laws promote public health and safety. Much more is covered by this legal backdrop, which permeates social, cultural, economic, and political arenas.

A seminal function of the rule of law is to provide a general sense among the populace of a well-organized background structure for activities, and the sense that a measure of legal redress exists should things go wrong (notwithstanding a general lack of knowledge of the details of law). This sense is especially necessary in mass urban societies when people rely on and come into contact with a multitude of strangers through extended networks of interaction. To appreciate the significance of this legal background, imagine if people were exposed to a high risk of assault or robbery, real property was not widely titled, contracts were hardly utilized, injuries to person and damage to property were left unaddressed, political and government offices were subject to capture and rent seeking, etc. – insecurity and uncertainty would color many interactions. Several or all of these conditions plague societies that lack the rule of law as well as marginalized subcommunities within largely rule of law societies. Other functionally equivalent social mechanisms might fulfill aspects of these functions (social norms, relationships, self-help, etc.), but only the rule of law fills all of them simultaneously through a connected set of government maintained legal institutions backed by coercion. When the populace and government officials are generally bound by and abide law, everyone benefits from the luxury of unthinkingly assuming that legal structures in place are substantially adhered to, which enhances the level and types of activities in which people engage.

Integration of Society

The legal phenomena that create a sense of security and trust for individuals are put in a different light when viewed in the structural-functionalist perspective of society as a social system. The function of law from this standpoint is to maintain social order through the integration of society. Structural-functionalism has been subjected to penetrating criticisms, but it remains an informative perspective when its postulates are softened.[5]

[5] For an overview of critiques of functionalism, see Alexander Rosenberg, *Philosophy of Social Science*, 3rd ed. (Boulder: Westview Press, 2008), pp. 141–168. An excellent

Though functionalist theory does not focus on the rule of law in particular, it does focus on societies in which the populace and government officials are bound by and abide law. Jonathan Turner elaborates:

> From very modest beginnings, law evolved into a complex system that regulates just about every facet of social life in post-industrial societies. Indeed ... law has become the principal integrative structure of a society that preserves, codifies, and translates key cultural symbols into specific rules defining what is deviant, while coordinating transactions among actors. Without law, each differentiated institutional complex in a modern society could not operate, nor could relations among institutional subsystems proceed smoothly. In the absence of law, then, a large and differentiated social structure is not viable; and if a specific legal system proves incapable of managing internal actions and relations within an institutional subsystem, as well as external relations among institutional subsystems, social structures and the cultural codes that guide them begin to disintegrate.[6]

Institutional subsystems, in his account, are the economy, kinship, religion, polity, education, science, medicine, and law. Law helps maintain order as a means of social integration at the societal (macro) level by coursing within and across subsystems, and by structuring and coordinating social action within and between organizations and networks (meso) and among individuals (micro).

One need not adopt the functionalist view of society as a discrete whole to recognize that legal institutions lay a comprehensive, common underlying infrastructure, which in its entirety functions to undergird and tether together differentiated mass societies. An emergent state of ubiquitous and routine law-abiding behavior, in turn, facilitates and encourages law-abiding behavior.[7] Another function of the rule of law, therefore, is to create the conditions for its own existence, thereby reproducing and perpetuating itself (though this self-reinforcing circle can break down).[8]

collection on functionalism is Don Martindale, ed., *Functionalism in the Social Sciences: The Strength and Limits of Functionalism in Anthropology, Economics, Political Science, and Sociology* (Philadelphia: American Academy of Political and Social Science, 1965).

6 Jonathan H. Turner, *Human Institutions: A Theory of Societal Evolution* (Lanham: Rowman & Littlefield, 2003), p. 243.

7 See Brian Z. Tamanaha, "Law's Evolving Emergent Phenomena: From Rules of Social Intercourse to Rule of Law Society," *Washington University Law Review*, 95 (2018), 1–39.

8 This process is analogous to genes and memes that replicate themselves. See Richard Dawkins, *The Selfish Gene*, 2nd ed. (Oxford: Oxford University Press, 1990).

Legal Restrictions on Officials

A primary function of the rule of law is to restrict arbitrary exercises of sovereign power – conveyed by the requirement that government officials are bound by and abide law. Prolific rule of law theorist Martin Krygier calls this "an immanent value of the rule of law, its telos."[9] This function traces back to classical times. Aristotle contrasted "the arbitrary rule of a sovereign power over all the citizens" with "the rule of law."[10] "Therefore he who bids the law rule may be deemed to bid God and Reason alone rule, but he who bids man rule adds an element of the beast; for desire is a wild beast, and passion perverts the minds of rulers, even when they are the best of men."[11] Montesquieu drew a parallel contrast: "monarchical government is that in which one alone governs, but by fixed and established laws; whereas, in despotic government, one alone, without law and without rule, draws everything along by his will and his caprices.[12] A ruler who acts free of legal constraints exposes the populace to untrammeled cupidity, whim, anger, spite, bias, perversion, stupidity, domination – all too familiar human tendencies and temptations.

The danger lies in the combination of human weaknesses with concentrated government power. As John Locke observed: "he being in a much worse condition, who is exposed to the arbitrary power of one man, who has the command of 100,000, than he that is exposed to the arbitrary power of 100,000 single men."[13] "And therefore, whatever form the commonwealth is under, the ruling power ought to govern by *declared* and *received laws*, and not by extemporary dictates and undetermined resolutions ... and the rulers too kept within their [legal] bounds, and not be tempted, by the power they have in their hands[.]"[14]

Rulers themselves, needless to say, do not readily recognize that it is crucial to protect the public from their potential abuses and depredations.

[9] Martin Krygier, "The Rule of Law: Pasts, Presents, and Two Possible Futures," *Annual Review of Law and Social Science*, 12 (2016), 216.

[10] Aristotle, *The Politics*, ed. Stephen Everson (Cambridge: Cambridge University Press, 1988), 1287a, p. 78.

[11] Aristotle, *The Politics*, p. 78.

[12] Montesquieu, *The Spirit of the Laws*, ed. Anne M. Cohler, Basia Carolyn Miller, and Harold Samuel Stone (Cambridge: Cambridge University Press, [1748] 1989), p. 10.

[13] John Locke, *Second Treatise of Government*, ed. C. B. Macpherson (Indianapolis: Hackett, [1689] 1980), section 137, p. 72.

[14] Locke, *Second Treatise of Government*, pp. 72–73.

Hence the origins and basis for legal restraints on government officials lies elsewhere – in long-standing, evolving cultural views. In early civilizations going back several millennia, "laws were often claimed to originate with the gods, who transmitted them to humans through the proclamations of rulers."[15] The legal order was said to be the product of higher metaphysical forces that identified law with justice and the natural order of things. "The Babylonian king Hammurabi," for instance, "claimed to have assembled his law code at the command of the god Utu, or Shamas, who, because as the sun god he saw everything that humans did, was also the patron deity of justice."[16] Rulers in Medieval Europe were seen as subject to customary law, natural law, and ecclesiastical law, a shared understanding expressed in coronation oaths. "These ceremonies, controlled and performed by the Church hierarchy, incorporated the secular Germanic idea that the king's chief duty was to be guardian of the community's law; in all the rituals the king promised to perform this duty faithfully."[17] Pepin said, "Inasmuch as we shall observe law toward everybody, we wish everybody to observe it toward us"; Charles the Bold swore, "I shall keep the law and justice"; Louis the Stammerer asserted, "I shall keep the customs and the laws of the nation."[18] Louis XIV stated in an ordinance in 1667, "Let it be not said that the sovereign is not subjected to the laws of his State; the contrary proposition is a truth of natural law ... what brings perfect felicity to a kingdom is the fact that the king is obeyed by his subjects and that he himself obeys the law."[19] Every US president, from George Washington in 1789 to Donald Trump in 2017, uttered: "I do solemnly swear that I will faithfully execute the office of the president of the United States, and will to the best of my ability, preserve, protect, and defend the Constitution of the United States."[20] Government officials at all levels take similar oaths to uphold the law.

The notion that government officials are bound by and abide law is a normative ideal, expectation, and orientation widely shared in society

[15] Bruce G. Trigger, *Understanding Early Civilizations* (Cambridge: Cambridge University Press, 2003), p. 221.

[16] Trigger, *Understanding Early Civilizations*, p. 222.

[17] John B. Morrall, *Political Thought in Medieval Times* (Toronto: University of Toronto Press, 1980), p. 24.

[18] Andre Tunc, "The Royal Will and the Rule of Law," in Arthur E. Sutherland, *Government under Law* (Cambridge: Harvard University Press, 1956), p. 404.

[19] Tunc, "The Royal Will and the Rule of Law," p. 408.

[20] This required oath is set forth in Article II, Section 1, of the US Constitution.

(including among officials themselves) about appropriate conduct, a key ingredient in producing the rule of law. In rule of law societies today, no genuine sovereign exists – just officeholders who come and go. What keeps government officials within legal limits – in addition to their personal commitment to abide law – are functioning bureaucratic legal institutions (prosecutorial, judicial) widely disbursed at various levels and settings of government, along with a vigilant civil society that demands officials abide law.

Liberty

Liberal theorists, from John Locke to Friedrich Hayek, have identified the preservation of liberty (and property) as the primary function of the rule of law.[21] "The Rule of Law was consciously evolved only during the liberal age," Hayek proclaimed, "and is one of its greatest achievements, not only as a safeguard but as the legal embodiment of freedom."[22] The rule of law, in his formulation, means "that government in all its actions is bound by rules fixed and announced beforehand – rules which make it possible to foresee with fair certainty how the authority will use its coercive powers in given circumstances and to plan one's individual affairs on the basis of this knowledge."[23] Locke made a similar point when asserting that government power "ought to be exercised by *established and promulgated laws*; that . . . the people may know their duty, and be safe and secure within the limits of law."[24] Advance knowledge of law encompasses exposure to criminal sanctions by government for conduct that violates legal proscriptions, as well as the legal implications of interaction with others in civil matters like contracts, torts, property, wills, and so forth. Having predictability about the legal consequences of one's actions empowers people to make choices and achieve their objectives.

21 See Brian Z. Tamanaha, "The Dark Side of the Relationship Between the Rule of Law and Liberalism," *New York University Journal of Law and Liberty*, 3 (2008), 516–547. The weaknesses of arguments by liberal theorists who tie property to the rule of law are demonstrated in Jeremy Waldron, *The Rule of Law and the Measure of Property* (Cambridge: Cambridge University Press, 2012).

22 Friedrich A. Hayek, *The Road to Serfdom* (Chicago: University of Chicago Press, 1944), p. 90.

23 Hayek, *The Road to Serfdom*, p. 80.

24 Locke, *Second Treatise of Government*, section 137, p. 73.

To enable people to plan, Hayek asserted, laws must be set out in advance, be made public, be phrased in general terms, be applied equally, and be certain and stable[25] – these are the elements of the formal rule of law identified with Lon Fuller and Joseph Raz.[26] Based on this formal understanding, Andrei Marmor asserts that the rule of law serves the "pivotal function of guiding human conduct."[27] "To the extent that certain features are functionally necessary for law to guide human conduct, and to the extent that the law purports to guide human conduct, these features of the rule of law make the law good, that is, good in guiding human conduct."[28]

The often-declared guidance function of the rule of law, however, is dogged by a puzzle. On the one hand, "people can only be *guided* by rules or prescriptions if they know about the existence of the rule or prescription";[29] on the other hand, "most people do not know the vast majority of the laws of their country."[30] Law is a highly specialized body of technical language, concepts, practices, and institutions that people without legal training cannot fully comprehend; on top of this, in modern legal systems the huge volume of rules and regulations, with complex subareas, is too much for anyone to know (including lawyers). This objection is "beside the point," Marmor asserts, because most laws do not affect individuals in their affairs and they can hire a lawyer if they need to know the law on a given matter.[31] His cavalier response notwithstanding, it is undeniable that law is generally opaque to the populace. Studies have found that lay beliefs about law on important matters, common law as well as statutory, are incorrect a significant percentage of time across a range of legal subjects.[32] And many people do not consult lawyers

[25] Friedrich A. Hayek, *The Constitution of Liberty* (Chicago: Chicago University Press, 1960), pp. 205–219.
[26] See Tamanaha, *On the Rule of Law*, pp. 91–101.
[27] Andrei Marmor, "The Rule of Law and Its Limits," *Law and Philosophy*, 24 (2004), 5.
[28] Marmor, "The Rule of Law and Its Limits," 7.
[29] Marmor, "The Rule of Law and Its Limits," 5.
[30] Marmor, "The Rule of Law and Its Limits," 16.
[31] Marmor, "The Rule of Law and Its Limits," 16.
[32] See Arden Rowell, "Legal Rules, Beliefs, and Aspirations," Unpublished paper, September 2017, whose survey research finds significant percentages of erroneous beliefs about law on ten subjects. See also Pauline T. Kim, "Bargaining with Imperfect Information: A Study of Worker Perceptions of Legal Protection in an At-Will World," *Cornell Law Review*, 83 (1998), 105 (showing that workers often harbour erroneous beliefs about legal

owing to the prohibitive cost of legal services, resulting in a high rate of unmet legal needs in civil and criminal matters.[33]

Hayek's portrayal of the common law supplies a partial answer to this conundrum (though he glossed over that common law judging does not fit his paradigm of general legal rules publicly declared in advance). Hayek asserted that common law judges render decisions based on existing social expectations and views of justice. "The aims of the rules must be to facilitate that matching or tallying of the expectations on which the plans of the individuals depend for their success."[34] Since the common law conforms to prevailing assumptions within the community, by his account, people know what the law is. His idealized account overlooks that communities have competing views of justice and policy, and that judicial decisions are also shaped by doctrinal, technical, and systematic legal constraints that can lead to outcomes contrary to lay expectations. But even if one grants Hayek's account, the point remains that people are not actually *guided* by the law but by prevailing social expectations and views of justice, which they assume are reflected in the law.

Theorists who emphasize the guidance function of law ignore that modern law is specialized, complex, obscure, contested, and extraordinarily voluminous – and that many people go without legal advice because it is too costly and burdensome to acquire. A centuries old common law maxim is "everyone is presumed to know the law."[35] Jurists have long acknowledged, however, that this proposition "is on its face absurd."[36] The

employment protections); John M. Darley, Kevin M. Carlsmith, and Paul H. Robinson, "The Ex Ante Function of the Criminal Law," *Law and Society Review*, 35 (2001), 181.

[33] See Tamanaha, *A Realistic Theory of Law*, pp. 145–146; Gillian K. Hadfield and Jamie Heine, "Law in the Law-Thick World: The Legal Resource Landscape for Ordinary Americans," in Samuel Estreicher and Joy Radice, eds., *Beyond Elite Law: Access to Civil Justice for Ordinary Americans* (Cambridge: Cambridge University Press, 2016), pp. 21–52.

[34] Friedrich A. Hayek, *Law, Legislation, and Liberty*, vol. 1: *Rules and Order* (Chicago: University of Chicago Press, 1973), p. 98.

[35] Richard E. Kohler, "Ignorance or Mistake of Law as a Defense in Criminal Cases," *Dickinson Law Review*, 40 (1935), 113.

[36] Edwin R. Keedy, "Ignorance and Mistake in the Criminal Law," *Harvard Law Review*, 22 (1908), 91; Livingston Hall and Selig J. Seligman, "Mistake of Law and Mens Rea," *University of Chicago Law Review*, 8 (1941), 641–683. ("It is easy to show that such a presumption is now indefensible as a statement of fact, even though it might have been substantially true in the very early days of the criminal law.") See also Ronald A. Cass, "Ignorance of the Law: A Maxim Reexamined," *William and Mary Law Review*, 17 (1976), 671–699.

justification for the maxim was not factual accuracy, but a prudential policy that incentivizes people to know the law and holds them responsible regardless.[37] Theorists who assert that legal rules guide the populace are in effect positing as true what is acknowledged to be a convenient fiction.

Rule of law societies in which the populace is bound by and abides law must be broken down into different categories of actors. Commercial actors and wealthy people with resources to retain lawyers to plan their affairs enjoy the liberty extolled by Hayek. But many others in society do not fall in these categories. People know basic matters like murder and theft are illegal, contracts are binding, and taxes must be paid, though the details of applicable doctrines and defenses are beyond their ken. Many people conduct their activities hardly thinking about law, or holding assumptions about law that they do not verify beforehand with a lawyer. Under these circumstances, people are not obeying the law or being guided by it; rather, they abide law in the negative sense specified at the outset: not violating it.

Liberty under the rule of law exists in a society, then, when widely held assumptions among the populace about legal proscriptions applicable to their conduct are not incorrect, that is, what people believe law dictates roughly corresponds to law de facto. (To count as liberty also presupposes that the range of free actions permitted by law is broad enough to allow people's strongest desires.) Law is predictable under these circumstances even though people literally do not know what the publicly declared law is. Then people are able to plan and carry out their projects based on their assumptions without routinely being surprised and disappointed when the law proves otherwise. What matters for this function of the rule of law to operate is that law substantially matches social expectations.

Economic Development

The rule of law functions to enable and enhance economic development, according to many economic theorists, political scientists, and development organizations. The *World Development Report 2017* declares:

> It has long been established that the *rule of law* – which at its core requires that government officials and citizens be bound by and act consistently with the law – is the very basis of the good governance needed to realize full social and economic potential. Empirical studies have revealed the importance of law and legal

[37] Hall and Seligman, "Mistake of Law and Mens Rea," 646–652.

institutions to improving the functioning of specific institutions, enhancing growth, promoting secure property rights, improving access to credit, and delivering justice in society.[38]

The crucial importance of the rule of law for economic development has been conventional wisdom among development agencies for over two decades. Billions of dollars have been expended on projects designed to build the rule of law during this period,[39] spent on judicial training, training lawyers and police, transplanting legal codes, upgrading court systems, titling property, and other law-building projects.[40] Despite many confident affirmations of the connection between the rule of law and economic development, however, the relationship is decidedly murky. "Correlations between indicators of the rule of law and income levels are high," the Report notes, "but the direction of causality and the mechanisms that determine this association are less well understood."[41] There are problems with defining the rule of law (thick or thin?), measuring the rule of law (competing indices combine various indicators, subjective and objective), and establishing a causal connection between rule of law and economic development.[42] (Never mind that no one knows how to successfully develop the rule of law.[43])

Max Weber provided the most influential account of the link between law and economic development. He contended, "the rationalization and systematization of the law in general and . . . the increasing calculability of the functioning of the legal process in particular, constituted one of the

[38] World Bank, *World Development Report 2017: Governance and the Law* (Washington: World Bank, 2017), p. 83. I should disclose that the language in the first sentence – "requires that government officials and citizens be bound by and act consistently with the law" – roughly matches the meaning of the rule of law in this essay because I served as a consultant on the Chapter.

[39] See Stephen Humphreys, *Theatre of the Rule of Law: Transnational Legal Intervention in Theory and Practice* (Cambridge: Cambridge University Press, 2010), pp. 128–132.

[40] See generally Brian Z. Tamanaha, "The Primacy of Society and the Failures of Law and Development," *Cornell International Law Journal*, 44 (2011), 216–247.

[41] World Bank, *World Development Report 2017*, pp. 95–96.

[42] For excellent overviews of the vexing issues in establishing this relationship, see Stephan Haggard, Andrew MacIntyre, and Lydia Tiede, "The Rule of Law and Economic Development," *Annual Review of Political Science*, 11 (2008), 205–234; Tom Ginsburg, "Pitfalls of Measuring the Rule of Law," *Hague Journal of the Rule of Law*, 3 (2011), 269–280; Stephan Haggard and Lydia Tiede, "The Rule of Law and Economic Growth: Where are We?" *World Development*, 39 (2011), 673–685.

[43] See Tamanaha, "The Primacy of Society and Failures of Law and Development."

most important conditions for the existence of economic enterprise intended to function with stability and, especially, of capitalist enterprise, which cannot do without legal security."[44] A stable regime of formal legal rules declared publicly in advance, applied by judges according to their terms, provides predictability for transactions.[45] In addition to a formal legal system carried out by an independent judiciary, property rights encourage productive activity by allowing people and commercial actors to reap the rewards of their labor and to accumulate capital that can be leveraged for economic purposes; contract law enables people to conduct transactions at a distance over time with strangers and expand the number of contracting partners, and allows them to reliably calculate the costs and benefits of prospective exchanges.

There is no doubt that the rule of law is an integral aspect of advanced capitalist societies that functions in multiple ways to further economic activities. However, if the rule of law is taken to include property rights, contract enforcement, and independent courts applying the law, then the claimed causal connection is hard to square with the fact that the Asian Tigers and China did not meet these legal prerequisites during their (respective) spectacular surges of economic growth.[46] (Nor, contra Weber, was the common law a formally rational system during England's economic takeoff.[47]) Predictability and security, assuming they are necessary for economic transactions, can be provided through alternative (informal) means other than formal rule of law. It might be the case, moreover, that the causal arrow goes in the other direction: in initial stages, economic development facilitates the development of the rule of law (via increasing public demands for effective legal regimes along with the acquisition by government of sufficient resources to build requisite educational and legal institutions), with both thereafter working together in a mutually supportive fashion.

[44] Max Weber, *Economy and Society: An Outline of Interpretive Sociology*, vol. 2, ed. Guenther Roth and Claus Wittich (Berkeley: University of California Press, [1922] 1978), p. 883.

[45] Weber, *Economy and Society*, p. 811.

[46] See Tom Ginsburg, "Does Law Matter for Economic Development?" *Law and Society Review*, 34 (2000), 829–856; Frank Upham, "Mythmaking in the Rule of Law Orthodoxy," in Thomas Carothers, ed., *Promoting the Rule of Law Abroad: In Search of Knowledge* (Washington: Carnegie Endowment for International Peace, 2006), pp. 75–104.

[47] For an illuminating discussion, see David M. Trubek, "Max Weber on Law and the Rise of Capitalism," *Wisconsin Law Review*, (1972), 720–753.

3 Latent Functions

A latent function of the rule of law is to secure a pivotal place for legal professionals who exercise a stranglehold on specialized legal knowledge, practices, and institutions utilized in the operation of the state legal system. Weber highlighted the dominant role of "legal honoratiores" in formally rational legal systems, providing essential services to the system while benefiting financially.[48] (Partners in elite US law firms today bill $1,000 per hour for their services.) Though not hidden, this is a latent function in that it receives scant attention in discussions of the rule of law.[49] A society in which the populace and government officials are bound by and abide law depends heavily on lawyers to carry through this arrangement, particularly judges. In some rule of law societies lawyers play more limited roles (Japan) than in others (US), and various legal tasks can be handled outside the profession – by civil servants, notaries, accountants, paralegals, legal technicians, computer programs, and others – but the operation of the legal system accords special status as well as gainful employment to trained lawyers. Consistent with this, rule of law projects carried out by development organizations, mentioned above, are dominated by lawyers and focus on building institutions manned by lawyers. A contemporary manifestation of the prominence of lawyers in rule of law systems is the expanding assertiveness of judges over political matters in constitutional and human rights cases.[50]

A second latent function of the rule of law is to constitute, entrench, and maintain power structures in society through a coercive system of law backed by force. Law does this in every society, rule of law and nonrule of law.[51] Depending on the society, these power structures operate along various lines, including economic class, racial or ethnic groups, caste distinctions, religious differences, gender relations, and other ways. In advanced capitalist societies, actors with economic power are able to disproportionately influence law by funneling money

[48] Weber, *Economy and Society*, pp. 784–808.

[49] An exception is Robert W. Gordon, "The Role of Lawyers in Producing the Rule of Law: Some Critical Reflections," *Theoretical Inquiries in Law*, 11 (2010), 441–468.

[50] See Ran Hirschl, *Towards Juristocracy: The Origins and Consequences of the New Constitutionalism* (Cambridge: Harvard University Press, 2004).

[51] See Tamanaha, *A Realistic Theory of Law*, pp. 82–117.

through the polity to obtain favorable legal regimes across a range of matters, from taxation to liability rules, effectuated via legislation, regulation, and the appointment of judges.[52] One might object that reflecting and maintaining power structures in society is a feature of law itself, not attributable to the rule of law per se. The rule of law, however, is law writ large throughout society, so a feature of law is necessarily a feature of the rule of law. Proponents of a substantive version of the rule of law, which incorporates human rights, equality, and other aspects of the good, might respond that pernicious forms of legal domination do not meet rule of law standards. Even granting their argument, however, which disqualifies only the worst offenders, the point remains that when a populace and government officials are bound by and abide law, power structures within society will be reflected and enforced in law. This must be kept in mind because the legitimating glow that attaches to the rule of law should not obscure that what matters ultimately is the justness of the law.

4 A Political Ideal and Rhetoric

A compelling argument can be made that the rule of law is not a social artifact like a table, or a bureaucratic organization, or indeed a legal system. When legal theorists, political scientists, development economists, political leaders, and others talk about the rule of law, there is no single set of constituent legal institutions to which it refers. Even independent courts, often identified as necessary to the rule of law, need not be present for the rule of law to exist.[53] Jurists who elaborate on the rule of law are largely engaged in selective invention centered on Western legal traditions.[54] There are myriad varying historically evolved social-

[52] See Brian Z. Tamanaha, *Law as a Means to an End: Threat to the Rule of Law* (Cambridge: Cambridge University Press, 2006).

[53] As Tom Ginsburg points out, courts in Japan are "highly deferential to the ruling political party," though it is a rule of law society. Ginsburg, "Pitfalls of Measuring the Rule of Law," p. 271. Serious questions are also raised by the highly politicized process of federal and state judicial appointments in the US. Tamanaha, *Law as a Means to an End*, pp. 172–189.

[54] Albert Dicey, responsible for giving modern currency to the phrase "rule of law," acknowledged that the meaning he accorded it is "peculiar to England, or to those countries which . . . have inherited English traditions." Albert V. Dicey, *Introduction to the Study of the Law of the Constitution* (London: Macmillan, 1889), p. 176.

legal arrangements, from which theorists pick and choose familiar and seemingly important aspects of law – appending the label "rule of law" to their preferred construction. Paring away layers of theoretical elaborations, the rule of law basically refers to a comprehensive system of law that works fairly well (as evaluated by various selected criteria). At bottom "the rule of law" functions as an ideal and as rhetoric, which people invoke for a variety of reasons in innumerable contexts to advocate the primacy of law.

To say "rule of law" is used as an ideal and as rhetoric is not to diminish its significance. Ideals are essential and rhetoric is powerful. Belief in the rule of law ideal is pivotal to the effective functioning of law, as described earlier. Striving to live up to the rule of law ideal has motivated lawyers, judges, and the public at critical moments to resist illegal activities by government officials. Invoking the rule of law ideal also functions as a normative standard to evaluate and criticize government officials. Since nearly all governments around the world today claim to live up to the rule of law, an accusation that the rule of law is being violated can prompt officials to explain why their actions are consistent with the rule of law or to change their conduct.

Rule of law *rhetoric* draws on and shades into the ideal; both may be present in a given instance. The rhetorical component functions to advance an agenda beyond merely maintaining a law bound government or society. Hayek invoked the rule of law to attack aspects of the social welfare state he disfavored, asserting "any policy aiming directly at a substantive ideal of distributive justice must lead to the destruction of the Rule of Law."[55] Mouthing "rule of law rhetoric," a number of authoritarian polities have touted their (relatively) independent courts to lend legitimacy to their regimes.[56] Neoliberal reforms emphasizing property rights, protection of foreign investments, limited regulation, and Western commercial laws have been promoted in the name of the rule of law.[57] Along with many progressives, Tom Bingham asserted the rule of

[55] Hayek, *The Road to Serfdom*, p. 83.

[56] Tom Ginsburg and Tamir Moustafa, "Introduction: The Functions of Courts in Authoritarian Politics," in Tamir Moustafa and Tom Ginsburg, eds., *Rule by Law: The Politics of Courts in Authoritarian Regimes* (Cambridge: Cambridge University Press, 2008), pp. 1–22, 5–7.

[57] See Tamanaha, "The Dark Side of the Relationship Between the Rule of Law and Liberalism," 537–541.

law includes respect for human rights and compliance with international law.[58] The examples are countless, from all political persuasions. As long as the rule of law ideal remains unprecedentedly popular worldwide, it will be invoked for rhetorical purposes.

[58] Tom Bingham, *The Rule of Law* (London: Penguin, 2011), pp. 66–84, 110–129.

13 A Positive Theory of the Rule of Law

Gillian K. Hadfield, Jens Meierhenrich, and Barry R. Weingast

Introduction

What is the rule of law, and under what conditions does it become a self-reinforcing, stable order? Missing from the various literatures that have attempted an answer is a coherent attempt to create a satisfying account of the microfoundations of the behaviors that generate and sustain a distinctively legal order. Whether philosophical or applied, existing approaches to the rule of law have neglected the question of what, exactly, is distinct about law's rule. We do not yet know enough about what sets *legal ordering* apart from other strategies of ordering, be they economic, political, or violent.[1] This chapter responds to this lacuna. In so doing it gives an account of the kinds of things required for a positive theory of the rule of law.

1 A Cognitive Manifesto

We assume that law, properly understood, is a manifestation of three interlocking elements: (1) interests; (2) institutions; and

[1] Lest we be misunderstood, we are painfully aware that alternative strategies of ordering are not mutually exclusive. We also acknowledge that legal ordering is often shot through with violence, and that other modes of ordering are similarly impure: all strategies of economic ordering have political dimensions, and violent ordering is inherently political and also typically governed by economic factors. On law's violence, see Robert M. Cover, "Violence and the Word," *Yale Law Journal*, 95 (1986), 1601–1629; and Jacques Derrida, "Force of Law: The Mystical Foundation of Authority," in Drucilla Cornell, Michael Rosenfeld, and David Gray Carlson, eds., *Deconstruction and the Possibility of Justice* (New York: Routledge, 1992), pp. 3–67. More recently, see Jens Meierhenrich, *Lawfare: A Genealogy* (Cambridge: Cambridge University Press, forthcoming). See also Lauren Benton and Lisa Ford, "Empires and the Rule of Law: Arbitrary Justice and Imperial Legal Ordering"; Mark Tushnet, "Critical Legal Studies and the Rule of Law"; Vanessa E. Munro, "Feminist Critiques of the Rule of Law," and Khiara M. Bridges, "Critical Race Theory and the Rule of Law"; all in this volume. Also relevant is Douglass C. North, John Joseph Wallis, and Barry R. Weingast, *Violence and Social Orders: A Conceptual Framework for Interpreting Recorded Human History* (Cambridge: Cambridge University Press, 2009).

(3) ideologies.[2] *Interests* must be part of any conception of law on account of the fact that law is a purposive activity. This assumption is at the heart of consequentialist conceptions of law.[3] *Institutions* such as courts shape the articulation and adjudication of law, and they affect the performance of law. *Ideologies*, lastly, refer to the normative underpinnings of the law, that is, the universe of beliefs associated with the meaning of law – law's real and imagined place in society. The mutually constitutive relationship among interests, institutions, and ideologies is captured in the following account: "From an external point of view, institutions are shared behavioral regularities or shared routines within a population. From an internal point of view, they are nothing more than shared mental models or shared solutions to recurrent problems of social interaction. Only because institutions are anchored in people's minds do they ever become behaviorally relevant. The elucidation of the internal aspect," to which this chapter is committed, "is the crucial aspect in *adequately* explaining the emergence, evolution, and effects of institutions."[4]

Although social scientists differ on what it means to take ideology seriously, constitutional political economists take the concept to denote "the shared framework of mental models that groups of individuals possess that provide both an interpretation of the environment and a prescription as to how that environment should be structured."[5]

Law is constituted by interests because it facilitates the solution of recurrent problems of social interaction. Law is constituted by institutions because institutions, as humanly devised constraints, structure incentives in social interaction.[6] Law is constituted by ideologies because it

[2] This section draws on Jens Meierhenrich, *The Legacies of Law: Long-Run Consequences of Legal Development in South Africa, 1652–2000* (Cambridge: Cambridge University Press, 2008), pp. 56–63.

[3] See, for example, Joseph Raz, *The Morality of Freedom* (Oxford: Oxford University Press, 1986). For, as Russell Hardin writes, "if law is to work it must serve people well. This is the minimal moral content of law not by definition but by causal requirement if law is to work well." See his "Law and Social Order," *Philosophical Issues*, 11 (2010), 80.

[4] C. Mantzavinos, Douglass C. North, and Syed Shariq, "Learning, Institutions, and Economic Performance," *Perspectives on Politics*, 2 (2004), p. 77 (emphasis added).

[5] Arthur T. Denzau and Douglass C. North, "Shared Mental Models: Ideologies and Institutions," *Kyklos*, 47 (1994), 4.

[6] The relationship between interests and institutions is straightforward: "Institutions [including legal institutions] are not necessarily or even usually created to be socially efficient; rather they, or at least the formal rules, are created to serve the interests of those with the

is cause – and consequence – of shared mental models as defined herein. Our focus on the ideological underpinnings of the law relates to recent advances in new institutional economics, where the cognitive dimensions of institutions have moved to the forefront of theories of institutional design. Inquiries into beliefs and the way their maintenance and change affects the operation of institutions – their emergence, evolution, and effects – have come to represent the cutting edge of the new institutionalism. The late Douglass North was among the trailblazers of this cognitive turn.[7] It is worth quoting at length from his cognitive manifesto:

> Beliefs and the way they evolve are the heart of the theoretical issues of this book. For the most part, economists, with a few important exceptions such as Friedrich Hayek, have ignored the role of ideas in making choices. The rationality assumption has served economists (and other social scientists) well for a limited range of issues in micro theory but is a shortcoming in dealing with the issues central to this study. Indeed the uncritical acceptance of the rationality assumption is devastating for most of the major issues confronting social scientists and is a major stumbling block in the path of future progress. The rationality assumption is not wrong, but such an acceptance forecloses a deeper understanding of the decision-making process in confronting the uncertainties of the complex world we have created.[8]

The preceding was North's diagnosis. Here is his prescription:

> The way we perceive the world [including the institutions within it] and construct our explanations about that world [and the institutions that populate it] requires that we delve into how the mind and brain work – the subject matter of cognitive science. This field is still in its infancy but already enough progress has been made to suggest important implications for exploring social phenomena.[9]

Among those who made progress in this emergent field was North himself.[10] Together with Arthur Denzau, he introduced a framework for the study of ideologies and institutions, one on which we draw in theorizing about the rule of law.

bargaining power to devise new rules." Douglass C. North, *Institutions, Institutional Change and Economic Performance* (Cambridge: Cambridge University Press, 1990), p. 16.

7 For a sustained analysis, see Douglass C. North, *Understanding the Process of Economic Change* (Princeton: Princeton University Press, 2005).

8 North, *Understanding the Process of Economic Change*, p. 5.

9 North, *Understanding the Process of Economic Change*, p. 5.

10 Denzau and North, "Shared Mental Models," 3–31.

Based on preliminary research, Denzau and North developed a model for theorizing the role of ideas in institutional development and political and economic performance. Their groundwork is of immediate relevance for the argument of this chapter. Consider the following discussion by Denzau and North:

> Ideas matter; and the way that ideas are communicated among people is crucial to theories that will enable us to deal with strong uncertainty problems at the individual level [such as the ones encountered in democratization]. For most of the interesting issues in political and economic markets, uncertainty, not risk, characterizes choice-making. Under conditions of uncertainty, individuals' interpretation of their environment will reflect their learning. Individuals with common cultural backgrounds and experiences will share reasonably convergent mental models, ideologies, and institutions; and individuals with different learning experiences (both cultural and environmental) will have different theories (models, ideologies) to interpret their environment.[11]

But what, *exactly*, is the relevance of this for modeling the rule of law? By taking cognition seriously, we refine rationalist explanations of the rule of law. Law, like institutions more generally, is about the stabilization of expectations of those within its reach.[12] Under the right conditions, which we formally specify below, law can reduce uncertainty by invoking common cultural backgrounds and experiences. This speaks to the role of common knowledge in strategic interaction. In instances where interacting adversaries share qua law reasonably convergent mental models, the resolution of the bargaining and uncertainty predicaments are likely to be less intractable.

This resonates with the learning model of Denzau and North, in which shared mental models provide "a set of concepts and language which makes communication easier. Better communication links would lead to the evolution of linked individuals' mental models converging rather than diverging as they continue to learn directly from the world."[13] The learning

[11] Denzau and North, "Shared Mental Models," 3–4.

[12] Niklas Luhmann, *Das Recht der Gesellschaft* (Frankfurt am Main: Suhrkamp, 1993), p. 136.

[13] Denzau and North, "Shared Mental Models," 18. Mantzavinos defines a mental model as "a coherent but transitory set of rules that enables the organism to form predictions of the environment based on the available knowledge." See C. Mantzavinos, *Individuals, Institutions, and Markets* (Cambridge: Cambridge University Press, 2001), p. 26. Mantzavinos, North, and Shariq further elaborated the nature of mental models: "Depending on whether the expectation formed is validated by the environmental

that results has been referred to as "cultural learning" in the new institutionalism. The term connotes that whenever the solution to a specific problem is obtained in the learning model, the norms and institutions that facilitated the solution will be strengthened. Recent scholarship believes that "[a] series of successful solutions to the same problem create what we call a routine. The essential characteristic of a *routine*," in institutional parlance, "is that it is employed to solve a problem without any prior reflection."[14] This is of immediate relevance for understanding the rule of law in the real world.

If we believe Denzau and North, the process of learning contributes to human interaction, in both ancient and modern societies, "the categories and concepts which enable members of that society to organize their experiences and be able to communicate with others about them," thereby creating the conditions for the emergence of routines.[15] Once norms and institutions – which economists lump together as rules – are employed repeatedly, and successfully so, for the solution of a problem, "they are successively strengthened and stored by the organism, and after a time they take the form of unconscious routines."[16]

The Denzau/North learning model is useful for understanding transitions to – and from – the rule of law in both consolidated and changing societies. To paraphrase the model's inventors: Law's performance in a given setting is a consequence, first and foremost, of the incentive structures that rulers have put into place; that is, the institutional framework of the polity, especially the institutional structure of the state. These incentive structures are in turn a function of the shared mental models and ideologies of the agents operating within the institutional framework.[17] Consider, for example, the value of the rule of law in transitions from

feedback, the mental model can be revised, refined, or rejected altogether. Learning is the complex modification of the mental models according to the feedback received from the environment." See Mantzavinos, North, and Shariq, "Learning, Institutions, and Economic Performance," 76. However, it is important to appreciate in this context that mental models are "not ready-made recipes employed every time the individual faces a problem in his environment. They are, moreover, flexible knowledge structures created anew every time from the ready-made material of the rules. They are to be understood as the final prediction or expectation that the organism makes about the environment before getting feedback from it." Mantzavinos, *Individuals, Institutions, and Markets*, p. 27 (emphasis omitted).

[14] Mantzavinos, *Individuals, Institutions, and Markets*, p. 29.

[15] Denzau and North, "Shared Mental Models," 15.

[16] Mantzavinos, *Individuals, Institutions, and Markets*, pp. 29–30.

[17] Denzau and North, "Shared Mental Models," 27.

authoritarian rule. Historical institutionalists have shown that law, especially formally rational law, can have instrumental and expressive value in democratization, and that this value has been neglected in the existing literature.[18] In instances where formally rational law is instrumental during authoritarian rule, it will likely become common knowledge. "This common knowledge basis may help discourage self-interested behavior that is harmful to the general welfare of society."[19] It is in this sense that ideologies of law can "help individuals frame complex and unfamiliar problems."[20] Framing can enable interacting adversaries to face strategic interaction with more ease. Law in times of democratization, but also at other times, can work as a supplement to the formal and informal enforcement of commitments.[21] If agents have confidence in the law, they can afford to take larger risks – believe despite uncertainty – in strategic interaction. If agents have reasonable confidence in the law, they have more reason to believe despite uncertainty. The formality of law is what appears to make it useful in democratization. This is so because "[l]egal rules do more than provide incentives, they change people."[22] As Oren Bar-Gill and Chaim Fershtman write,

> different legal systems may affect not just the behavior of individuals, but who they are. And since who you are also affects how you choose to behave, a new indirect influence on behavior is introduced. Such an approach expands the boundaries of law and economics, introducing the endogenous formation of preferences as part of the analysis.[23]

[18] Meierhenrich, *The Legacies of Law*; Kathryn Hendley, *Everyday Law in Russia* (Ithaca: Cornell University Press: 2017).

[19] Michael J. Ensley and Michael C. Munger, "Ideological Competition and Institutions: Why 'Cultural' Explanations of Development Patterns Are Not Nonsense," in Ram Mudambi, Pietro Navarra, and Giuseppe Sobbrio, eds., *Rules and Reason: Perspectives on Constitutional Political Economy* (Cambridge: Cambridge University Press, 2001), p. 116. See also Norman Schofield, "Anarchy, Altruism, and Cooperation: A Review," *Social Choice and Welfare*, 2 (1985), 207–219.

[20] Ensley and Munger, "Ideological Competition and Institutions," p. 116.

[21] For a brief discussion, see Robert Axelrod, *The Complexity of Cooperation: Agent-Based Models of Competition and Collaboration* (Princeton: Princeton University Press, 1997), pp. 60–61.

[22] Oren Bar-Gill and Chaim Fershtman, "Law and Preferences," *Journal of Law, Economics, and Organization*, 20 (2004), 331.

[23] Bar-Gill and Fershtman, "Law and Preferences," 332. For a related argument from law and the humanities, see Peter Goodrich, *Languages of Law: From Logics of Memory to Nomadic Masks* (Cambridge: Cambridge University Press, 1990). On the question of endogeneity

A habit of legality – not unlike soft law in the international realm – provides a reliable basis for the construction of credible commitments among interacting agents. This is beneficial in everyday life because humans generally long for reassurance:

> Humans attempt to use their perceptions about the world to structure their environment in order to reduce uncertainty in human interaction. But whose perceptions matter and how they get translated into transforming the human environment are consequences of the institutional structure, which is a combination of formal rules, informal constraints, and their enforcement characteristics. This structure of human interaction determines who are the entrepreneurs whose choices matter and how such choices get implemented by the decision rules of that structure. Institutional constraints cumulate through time, and the culture of a society is the cumulative structure of rules and norms (and beliefs) that we inherit from the past that shape our present and influence our future.[24]

The logic of transaction costs completes the argument as laid out thus far. Transaction costs condition what choices agents are likely to make. Transaction costs refer to an agent's opportunity costs in strategic interaction. Such opportunity costs arise for agents because strategic interaction involves the acquisition of three services: (1) the provision of information about the opportunities for interaction; (2) the negotiation of the terms of interaction; and (3) the determination of procedures for enforcing a struck agreement, or contract of interaction. The costs involved in the acquisition of the first service are frequently referred to as *search costs*; the costs involved in the acquisition of the second service as *negotiation costs*, and the costs involved in the acquisition of the third service as *enforcement costs*. The costs of providing all three services are called transaction costs. Transaction costs accrue to agents in strategic interaction for social, political, and economic advantage.[25] Transaction costs are subject to the performance of institutions. Institutions can reduce transaction costs and improve human interaction. The question of transaction costs occupies a central place in endgame situations.

raised by Bar-Gill and Fershtman, see Avner Greif and David D. Laitin, "A Theory of Endogenous Institutional Change," *American Political Science Review*, 98 (2004), 633–652.

24 North, *Understanding the Process of Economic Change*, p. 6.

25 For a seminal analysis of transaction costs in history, see Douglass C. North and Robert Paul Thomas, *The Rise of the Western World: A New Economic History* (Cambridge: Cambridge University Press, 1973), esp. p. 93.

The increasing returns from formally rational law can be considerable in the calculation of transaction costs, especially in democratization. When adversaries in strategic interaction believe that the other side will commit – and credibly so – to commitments reached, the prospects for cooperation and thus sustainable democracy are increased. This is regularly the case in instances where a rule-governed way of doing things – a habit of legality – survives the worst excesses of authoritarian rule. A habit of legality may strengthen the credibility, and thereby the viability, of democratic commitments.[26] If a polity in the past maintained a general fidelity to the law, by which we mean a fidelity to organizing social life (including politics and economics) by legal means, the collective memory of formally rational law is likely to be strong. In instances where legality – understood here in the sense of doing things in a formally rational way – has become a habit, we classify this state of affairs as the rule of law.[27] After these preliminaries, let us take a closer look at the microfoundations of the rule of law.

2 Microfoundations of the Rule of Law

Despite a veritable cottage industry dedicated to the construction and export of the rule of law, the phenomenon itself is rather poorly understood in the corridors of governments, international organizations, and NGOs. Practitioners tend to pay little attention to the question of what it means to "rule" by way of law. But scholars do not fare much better. Little in the political science and economics literature has successfully distinguished *legal* decision-making from other modes of decision-making such as those one finds in markets or legislatures. The judicial politics literature in the political-science-subfield of American politics, for example, largely treats

[26] Joel Migdal, "Studying the State," in Mark Irving Lichbach and Alan S. Zuckerman, eds., *Comparative Politics: Rationality, Culture, and Structure* (Cambridge: Cambridge University Press, 1997), p. 223.

[27] We borrowed the term "habit" from Francis A. Allen, *The Habits of Legality: Criminal Justice and the Rule of Law* (New York: Oxford University Press, 1996). On the idea of the normative state, as used herein, see, Ernst Fraenkel, *The Dual State: A Contribution to the Theory of Dictatorship*, trans. E. A. Shils, with an Introduction by Jens Meierhenrich (Oxford: Oxford University Press, [1941] 2017). For an account linking the idea of legal normativity to the new institutionalism in political science, see Jens Meierhenrich, *The Remnants of the Rechtsstaat: An Ethnography of Nazi Law* (Oxford: Oxford University Press, 2018), esp. ch. 8.

a judicial decision as a fundamentally political decision.[28] Much of this literature has no role for distinctive features of law, such as doctrine or precedent.[29] Similarly, economists treat judicial decisions as economic choices designed to select an outcome deemed optimal.[30] Nowhere do we see a recognition that if judges really did make decisions in the same way as politicians or economic actors, they would hardly be operating in a recognizable legal system along the lines that legal philosophers from Lon Fuller to Joseph Raz have theorized.

Fuller famously set out "eight kinds of excellence toward which a system of rules may strive," namely that law be general, publicly promulgated, nonretroactive, sufficiently clear, noncontradictory, possible to comply with, relatively constant through time, and that there be congruence between official action and declared rule.[31] Raz, from the opposing vantage point of legal positivism, argued that a "legal system can be conceived of as a system of reasons for action."[32] He went on to argue that two features were necessary to make a reason a legal one: "(1) They are reasons applied and recognized by a system of courts. (2) Those courts are bound to apply them in accordance with their own practices and customs. These features account for the institutional character of law: law is a system of reasons recognized and enforced by authoritative law-applying institutions."[33]

But, unlike Fuller, Raz was more circumspect when it came to the substance of law's rule:

> The rule of law is just one of the virtues which a legal system may possess and by which it is to be judged. It is not to be confused with democracy, justice, equality (before the law or otherwise), human rights of any kind or respect for persons or for the dignity of man. A non-democratic legal system, based on the denial of human rights, on extensive poverty, on racial segregation, sexual inequalities, and

[28] Jeffrey R. Lax, "Political Constraints on Legal Doctrine: How Hierarchy Shapes the Law," *Journal of Politics*, 74 (2012), 765–781.

[29] Barry Friedman, "Taking Law Seriously," *Perspectives on Politics*, 4 (2006), 261–276.

[30] Nicola Gennaioli, and Andrei Shleifer, "Overruling and the Instability of Law," *Journal of Comparative Economics*, 35 (2007), 309–328.

[31] Lon L. Fuller, *The Morality of Law*, 2nd rev. ed. (New Haven: Yale University Press, 1969), p. 41. For a comprehensive textual analysis, see Kristen Rundle, *Forms Liberate: Reclaiming the Jurisprudence of Lon L. Fuller* (Oxford: Hart, 2013), See also idem, "The Morality of the Rule of Law: Lon L. Fuller," in this volume.

[32] Joseph Raz, *The Concept of a Legal System: An Introduction to the Theory of a Legal System*, 2nd ed. (Oxford: Clarendon Press, 1980), p. 212.

[33] Raz, *The Concept of a Legal System*, p. 212.

religious persecution may, in principle, conform to the requirements of the rule of law better than any of the legal systems of the more enlightened Western democracries.[34]

Regardless of whether one finds Fuller more persuasive, or Raz, their normative interventions should give us pause. Their attempts to understand law as a form of rule *distinct* from the rule of politics on the one hand, and from the rule of economics on the other, point to the inherent limits of much game-theoretic rule of law scholarship in political science and economics. Having said that, neither Fuller nor Raz concerned himself with the empirically – and practically – equally significant question of how a legal order is able to achieve supremacy over other normative orders in which law plays no central role. Leaving the rule of law's violent trajectory entirely to one side, Fuller and Raz started with the assumption that the supremacy of law was a given, even though recorded history is abundant with evidence that transitions to legal rule have almost always been deeply contested. To cite but the most famous example, the road to the adoption of Magna Carta that King John of England agreed to at Runnymede in 1215, and which constrained the principle of *vis et voluntas*, or force and will, was paved with upheaval – and it caused large-scale violence in the immediate aftermath of its adoption. Given this experience, and many others like it, it is incumbent on scholars and practitioners alike to study what Francis Fukuyama has called "transition to the rule of law."[35]

The case of Magna Carta is interesting because it points to a starting point for one particular rule of law tradition that originated not with the state but came from below. The "Great Charter" was a formally recognized means of collectively coercing the King. The case stands, *pars pro toto*, for transitions to the rule of law in which legal norms and institutions are not unimaginatively imposed in accordance with general templates, universal toolkits, and hastily learned lessons from history, but in which they emerge as a form of spontaneous order.

Modeling the rule of law means normatively crafting it in terms of the values of an underlying society, then inculcating these values with all

[34] Joseph Raz, "The Rule of Law and Its Virtue," in idem, *The Authority of Law: Essays on Law and Morality* (Oxford: Clarendon Press, 1979), p. 211.

[35] Francis Fukuyama, "Transitions to the Rule of Law," *Journal of Democracy*, 21 (2010), 33–44.

deliberate speed, whether formally or informally. Fukuyama, taking a leaf from both Fuller and Raz, has come to a similar conclusion:

> Because we in the West now define law in purely positive and procedural terms, we tend to promote the visible procedural infrastructure of the law as it exists in developed countries – things like formal legal codes, computerized dockets, bar associations, efficient courtrooms, and the like. We tend to worry less about whether the imported law actually commands the respect of people in the society. The use of foreign models does not much matter when dealing with something like a commercial code, but on issues of personal status, family law, inheritance, and the like it can be far more problematic.[36]

These insights are not new, of course. Legal anthropologists have advanced them for more than a century. The rich literature on what is known as global pluralism has always paid close attention to the processes and attributes that distinguish law in particular settings. And yet, this literature is also known to have worked with underspecified assumptions about why social agents act and how institutions function. To be sure, thick descriptions of legal behavior derived from deep immersion in empirical settings have certainly focused on conduct and beliefs at the micro-level. However, they rarely provide an entirely convincing account of how individual choices and beliefs intertwine to produce aggregate outcomes. To put it more starkly: They tend to fail to assign a formal role to law as a conceptual variable.

Because insufficient attention continues to be paid, theoretically as well as empirically, to the institutional origins and development of the rule of law, we remain without the microfoundations required for constructing rule of law theory. Such theory, however, is a sine qua non for explaining – and predicting – why the rule of law matters, to whom, and when. To help remedy this failing, we offer a formal account of the rule of law, one that is rigorous without being reductionist. The goal is to come up with a shared standard for qualitative and quantitative research. We think of this standard as a Weberian ideal type. Few scholars have described Max Weber's method better than Fritz Ringer:

> This "construction" has a "utopian" character, in that it is obtained by conceptually "heightening" certain aspects of reality. Where we suspect the empirical presence of relationships resembling those emphasized in the "ideal type," the "type" can help

[36] Fukuyama, "Transitions to the Rule of Law," 41–42.

us to "understand" and to "portray" these connections. It can also guide our causal attributions; though *not itself a hypothesis*, it may *suggest* fruitful hypotheses.[37]

Ours is a contribution to a growing literature that combines positive and normative theory in studying the rule of law; it is also an effort to achieve a rapprochement between nomothetic and ideographic theorists of the rule of law. Neither deduction nor induction alone are capable of grasping the rule of law, of responding to the challenge of sustaining it, growing it, nurturing it, and transplanting it. We hope to accomplish two things in this chapter: first, to demonstrate what is to be gained from reducing the phenomenon of the rule of law to its conceptual essence; and, second, to contribute with our ideal typical model to a new understanding of the institutional foundations of the rule of law. For it is a mistake to presuppose that the state is an essential feature of law's rule. Across history a sizable number of legal orders developed and proved sustainable without the presence of a centralized coercive force; indeed, the organized state with a monopoly over the legitimate exercise of force is a relatively recent phenomenon.[38] Evidence from ancient Athens to medieval Iceland, and from merchants in medieval Europe to Melanesian islanders in the Trobriand Archipelago, shows that the state transforms the nature of legal order in multiple ways, but it is neither necessary for establishing the rule of law, nor essential to making it work.[39]

Legal anthropologists have rightly emphasized the analytical problems that arise when the phenomenon of the rule of law is not taken seriously as a phenomenon distinct from (albeit related to) the state. The idea that state is necessary for establishing the rule of law has in the past led to two erroneous beliefs: (1) that an increase in state coercion will lead to greater respect for the rule of law; and (2) that rule of law problems are the result of partial or complete state failure, be it lack of enforcement, an incompetent judiciary, or a related weakness of a state's coercive institutions. The incessant failures of rule of law projects in the twentieth and twenty-first centuries, many of which have revolved

[37] Fritz K. Ringer, *Max Weber's Methodology: The Unification of the Cultural and Social Sciences* (Cambridge: Harvard University Press, 1997), p. 111.

[38] Gillian K. Hadfield and Barry R. Weingast, "Law without the State: Legal Attributes and the Coordination of Decentralized Collective Punishment," *Journal of Law and Courts*, 1 (2013), 3–34.

[39] Hadfield and Weingast "Law without the State."

around the reform of judiciaries and enforcement agencies, attest to the error of this way of thinking.[40]

If law's rule is not about the enforcement of rules by a sovereign state, as so many literatures suppose, what is it? Building on the cognitive conception of law that we set out above, we argue that the rule of law is a type of normative social order.[41] A normative social order is an equilibrium characterized by conduct in a relevant community that is systematically patterned on community-based normative evaluations of behavior. The concept of social norms can be understood in this way: Social norms are community-based evaluations of behavior; they designate some behaviors as good or warranting approval, others as bad or warranting disapproval. The evaluations are not personal in the sense that they reside only in the private assessments of particular individuals. They are social in the sense that any representative member of the community is expected to share the evaluation. By modeling the rule of law on the basis of these assumptions, we hope to do justice to the analytical concerns of nomothetic and ideographic scholars alike.

3 A Formal Model

We assume a simple world of three agents whom we call two buyers and a seller. We could instead interpret the model to apply to any setting in which there are individuals – citizens, for example – who would like to prevent behavior engaged in by another individual, such as a sovereign.[42]

For concreteness we suppose that each buyer has the opportunity to enter into a contractual relationship with the seller each period in a repeated game. We also suppose that in each period in which the seller is in a contract with a buyer, the seller has an opportunity to take an action that benefits the seller but that could be costly to the buyer. Some of these costly actions will be considered by the buyer to be in breach of contract. We make the key assumption, however, that what counts as breach for an

[40] Gillian K. Hadfield, *Rules for a Flat World: Why Humans Invented Law and How to Reinvent It for a Complex Global Economy* (Oxford: Oxford University Press, 2017), esp. ch. 11.

[41] Gillian K. Hadfield and Barry R. Weingast, "What Is Law? A Coordination Model of the Characteristics of Legal Order," *Journal of Legal Analysis*, 4 (2012), 471–514.

[42] See Gillian K. Hadfield and Barry R. Weingast, "Microfoundations of the Rule of Law," *Annual Review of Political Science*, 17 (2014), 21–42.

individual buyer is a product of the buyer's personal evaluation scheme – what we call each buyer's idiosyncratic logic. We assume the buyer's personal evaluation scheme is completely private – neither the other buyer nor the seller can observe it. This assumption captures the presence of diversity in a community in which reasonable individuals can disagree about what constitutes good or bad behavior, such as what constitutes a valid contract and whether the seller was obliged to perform some action. We argue that a key role for law is to manage the diversity of views in a community about what constitutes good and bad behavior.

Each buyer would like to induce the seller to honor the contract rather than to breach it. We assume that, acting individually, however, the buyer does not possess the capacity to deter breach. The only action available to the buyer to punish the seller is a decision not to enter into a contract in the following period, but a one-buyer, one-period boycott is insufficient to deter breach. We assume that a decentralized collective punishment – specifically a two-buyer, one-period boycott – is sufficient to deter breach.

This setting generates a coordination problem. The buyers, whom we assume do not have any express means of communicating and coordinating (capturing the more general setting with more agents), need some mechanism for deciding individually when bad behavior has occurred and hence when to boycott the seller. We assume they observe all actions taken by the seller; but each needs to know how to classify actions taken by the seller.

We consider the introduction of an institution that classifies conduct as good or bad in order to coordinate the buyers' responses to seller behavior. We ask in particular what attributes the classification institution must possess in order to coordinate an equilibrium in which the seller was deterred from at least some behavior considered breach by a buyer. Intuitively, the classification institution must be a public institution in the sense that all agents can access the institution's classifications of the actions that count as breach and those that do not. More than this, it must be common knowledge that all agents consult the same classification institution to determine breach.[43] We call the classification scheme produced by the classification institution a common logic.

Under what conditions will both buyers be willing to boycott for one period when the seller takes an action classified as breach under the common logic, given their diversity of opinions? First, we observe that the

[43] See Michael Suk-Young Chwe, *Rational Ritual: Culture, Coordination, and Common Knowledge* (Princeton: Princeton University Press, 2001).

common logic is unlikely to be identical with either buyer's idiosyncratic logic. Secondly, intuitively, it must be that the common logic reaches the same classifications as an individual buyer's idiosyncratic logic sufficiently often that each buyer prefers the equilibrium in which actions classified as breach are deterred to one without deterrence. Boycotting is costly to the buyer. The cost is worth it if it helps to secure a result the buyer prefers to the alternative. We call the equilibrium with deterrence according to the common logic a legal order and the equilibrium without deterrence disorder.

This is our first implication: Buyers are unlikely to prefer just any legal order over disorder. Whether they do depends on whether the announced common logic deters the things they care about sufficiently often to warrant their participation by punishing bad conduct even if they are not the victim. This problem is therefore not a pure coordination game as we see in the existing literature.[44] The candidate common logic must be incentive compatible for the participants to follow. We say that the idiosyncratic logic and common logic are sufficiently convergent for an agent if this incentive compatibility constraint is met.

Our second implication stems from closer scrutiny of the incentive-compatibility constraint. Incentive compatibility is required for every agent who is essential to the enforcement mechanism. In our model, if either buyer is unwilling to participate in coordinated boycotts, then the classification institution fails to establish legal order; the seller is not deterred; and the equilibrium is disorder. So neither buyer's interests can be ignored.

We call this universality, and it is the first legal attribute that our model suggests must be implemented by the classification institution to achieve legal order. Achieving universality requires eliminating systems of privilege that differentiate among people, because such systems are unlikely to induce all players to support the candidate common logic.

The above considerations relate to the substance of the common logic. The remainder of the legal attributes we identify relate to the formal characteristics of the classification system. The classification institution's role is to coordinate boycotting behavior and to ensure that the common logic

[44] Gerald J. Postema, "Coordination and Convention at the Foundation of Law," *Journal of Legal Studies*, 11 (1982), 165–203, Kaushik Basu, *Prelude to Political Economy: A Study of the Social and Political Foundations of Economics* (Oxford: Oxford University Press, 2000); Richard H. McAdams, "An Attitudinal Theory of Expressive Law," *Oregon Law Review*, 79 (2000), 339–390; and Roger B. Myerson, "Justice, Institutions, and Multiple Equilibria," *Chicago Journal of International Law*, 5 (2004), 91–107.

satisfies the incentive-compatibility constraints. Assume that the substance of the common logic is incentive compatible in the sense that both buyers prefer a coordination equilibrium based on the common logic to the alternative disordered equilibrium. Incentive compatibility still requires that all three agents believe that coordination will be achieved. Neither buyer will boycott unless she expects the other buyer to boycott in a given period. Both buyers want to be sure that the seller believes that coordination will be achieved in future periods, because that is the horizon over which the benefits of coordination are enjoyed to compensate for the costs incurred in any period in which a boycott has to be carried out.

In our model the lack of deterrence is the only other possible equilibrium; we do not here consider alternative classification institutions. We emphasize that universality is qualified in the sense that the common logic must be capable of protecting the interests of not all agents but rather only those who are essential to making enforcement effective.[45]

Achieving this coordination – both as a practical matter to effectuate a two-buyer boycott and as a matter of shared beliefs about how all agents will behave – requires, we argue, that the classification institution have the following attributes, which we call legal attributes:

- publicity,
- clarity, noncontradiction, uniqueness: authoritative stewardship,
- stability,
- prospectivity and congruence,
- generality,
- impersonal, neutral, and independent reasoning, and
- public reasoning and open process.

Our list of attributes in many ways tracks those developed by legal philosophers such as Fuller and Raz. We think a critical lesson from these careful jurisprudential efforts to distinguish the rule of law from other normative social orders is the idea that legal institutions differ from other dispute-resolving or norm-giving social institutions. Unlike the philosophical literature, however, our list is not based on an intuitive assessment or on a priori normative commitments such as equality between persons or fairness. Instead, we derive the legal attributes from the characteristics we argue are necessary for a classification institution to be capable of

[45] See Hadfield and Weingast, "What Is Law?," p. 25, for a discussion.

establishing an equilibrium legal order in which behavior is patterned on the classifications emanating from the institution.

Our claim is that these attributes support the stability of an equilibrium under the rule of law. To understand why, imagine the reasoning of an individual buyer who has observed seller behavior in one period and is wondering whether to boycott in the next period. First the buyer needs to figure out what the common logic classification of the behavior is. We have already noted that this requires that the classifications be public. Publicness requires making available all materials and logic used by the classification institution's common logic to arrive at classifications, such as statements of principle or collections of exemplar classifications. To arrive at a binary classification – breach or not – and to feel confident that the other buyer will reach the same classification – that is, to achieve common knowledge classifications – requires that the common logic classify conduct in a way that is relatively clear and noncontradictory and that results in unique classifications. To achieve clarity, noncontradiction, and uniqueness requires that the common logic be under what we call authoritative stewardship. By this we mean that there is a common-knowledge mechanism for definitively resolving any ambiguity or inconsistencies in classifications. A variety of different institutions can serve in this role, for example, a court or a designated legal authority, such as the Law Speaker in medieval Iceland.[46] The buyer must also be confident that classifications will remain stable over a sufficiently long period, a necessary condition for the buyer to be better off when participating today in a costly boycott.

A potential source of unreliability arises in these calculations. The idiosyncrasy of the evaluation schemes of both buyers implies that a third-party classification institution will not be able to anticipate all the specific circumstances under which a buyer might privately judge conduct to be breach; the institution will not therefore be able to publish ex ante statements that address all of the possibilities the buyers care about. The inevitable incompleteness of law is a fact that has been recognized since at least Aristotle. The buyer who evaluates the value of future deterrence, therefore, needs to predict the classification of novel sets of circumstances – which perhaps can only be anticipated by the buyer – by reasoning from the common materials currently available. For this to be accomplished, these materials must be general or generalizable, allowing

[46] Hadfield and Weingast, "Law without the State."

someone to reason from either abstract language or the treatment of specific circumstances to the likely classification of new circumstances. Furthermore, making reasonably reliable predictions requires the buyer to have confidence that the classifications realized in the future will also be the product of reasoning from the currently available materials. This implies both that the common logic is prospective and that classifications that emerge are congruent with preexisting materials. Moreover, the common logic must also be based on impersonal reasoning, meaning that the operation of the logic on a set of facts is invariant to the identity of the person or entity engaged in the operation. The buyer needs to have confidence that the authoritative steward is independent and neutral, not influenced in ambiguity resolution by interests other than the project of maintaining a clear, coherent, and stable system of reasoning. Impersonal reasoning therefore reduces uncertainty by removing extraneous (and often hard to anticipate) factors from the buyer's prediction process.

The buyer must also have confidence that, in the event of a truly novel case, he or she will have an opportunity to present: (a) evidence about circumstances about which he or she possesses private information; and (b) reasons the common logic should be applied to reach a particular classification. These procedures give the buyer an opportunity to seek a classification that matches the predictions the buyer made. This analysis therefore implies the ongoing classification process must have two further characteristics: the existence of an open process – open to the evidence and arguments of the buyer; and a public reasoning process – so that both buyers can incorporate into their predictive materials any new information that emerges from the process of resolving ambiguity.

In summary, our model implies that the classification institution cannot devise ex ante a complete set of laws, including contingencies and exceptions. Incomplete information and the inability to specify all the relevant contingencies mean that the process must be designed to solicit and absorb information from those who have a stake in the system, producing new rules as new information and circumstances arise. In this sense, the model closely tracks Fuller's idea of law respecting the dignity and "active intelligence"[47] of participants in the legal system and Hayek's "adaptive efficiency."[48]

[47] Jeremy Waldron, "The Rule of Law and the Importance of Procedure", in James E. Fleming, ed., *Getting to the Rule of Law: Nomos L* (New York: New York University Press, 2011), p. 23.

[48] Friedrich A. Hayek, *The Collected Works of F. A. Hayek*, vol. 17: *The Constitution of Liberty*, ed. Ronald Hamowy (Chicago: University of Chicago Press, [1960] 2011).

We noted above that the legal attributes promote the capacity for a buyer contemplating a boycott to make reasonably reliable predictions about how future circumstances will be classified. We emphasize now that whereas clearly there is some scope for uncertainty in a law-driven regime, it cannot be large. This is not a consequence of any assumptions about risk aversion on the part of the buyer. Rather, it is a product of the requirement of common knowledge. It is insufficient for the buyer to predict classifications. The buyer also has to have confidence that the other buyer and the seller (who must know the actions deemed as breach before making choices) make the same predictions, and that they each expect the buyer to make these predictions, and so on. The degree of noise that the system can accommodate is thus much smaller than that based only on an individual agent's tolerance for uncertainty.

Our approach, we suggest, provides the microfoundations of legal order. It addresses many of the questions raised in the existing literature and reflects many of the insights of that literature. It studies the attributes that distinguish the rule of law from other normative social orders – be they political, economic, or violent – while dealing explicitly with the behavioral mechanisms at work in a wide variety of social settings. It creates a central place for an often-overlooked factor in standard analysis, namely common-knowledge belief systems. Lack of attention to this important factor in legal development, we believe, accounts for much of the misplaced confidence in the belief that creating a set of laws and establishing public enforcement institutions is sufficient for making the rule of law work.

The introduction of formal institutions of law, from codes to constitutions, must satisfy the incentive-compatibility constraint, and this requires common knowledge. We provide a way of analyzing the role of common-knowledge belief systems, however, without falling back on vague claims about culture or the need to educate people to hold different beliefs. Like many in the existing literature, we believe law fundamentally coordinates behavior and beliefs; but we go more deeply by identifying a critical role for incentive compatibility. Finally, by denying the equation of law with the state or an official enforcement apparatus, we create an analytical framework in which the impact of changing the nature of enforcement can be evaluated.

An important implication of our framework is that the nature and efficacy of enforcement can depend on the size and scope of the community of people who perceive themselves as benefiting from a particular legal order, and on the potential for individuals to observe and punish violations. An enforcement mechanism might become more stable and effective if the scope of the community and relevant behaviors is expanded. We see this idea, for example, in Acemoglu and Robinson's analysis of the role of the Glorious Revolution in securing a more stable legal order by protecting the interests of a wide array of groups.[49] Our framework is also consistent with Weingast's analysis of the need for a constitution to secure the interests of the groups necessary for effective retaliation against a transgressing rule.[50]

Conclusion

Despite considerable variation in histories of the rule of law, the empirical evidence to date suggests that most forms of *genuinely* law-based rule are, in the long-run, preferable to lawlessness because they are more likely to be self-reinforcing – and thus sustainable – than alternative strategies of rule.[51] But what does it take to model the rule of law?

Modeling the rule of law means crafting the most appropriate variant of the rule of law for a given society. The task is enormous: "The problem of figuring out what the people living in poor countries really need from law is probably one of the most complex the world has ever seen."[52] And the need, now more than ever, to avoid the trappings of international paternalism means the task is not only daunting from an institutional-design perspective but also from the perspective of diplomacy.[53] We have shown why, and how, formal theory can be of use in building the rule of law. We have thus far emphasized the importance of factoring in cognition. But a second factor is key: context.

The international community would be well advised to take with a grain of salt long-standing philosophical presuppositions, liberal or otherwise, about

[49] Daron Acemoglu and James A. Robinson, *Economic Origins of Dictatorship and Democracy* (Cambridge: Cambridge University Press, 2006).

[50] Barry R. Weingast, "The Political Foundations of Democracy and the Rule of the Law," *American Political Science Review*, 91 (1997), 245–263.

[51] For a comparative historical analysis of transitions to – and from – the rule of law, see Jens Meierhenrich, ed., *Dual States: A Global History* (Cambridge: Cambridge University Press, forthcoming).

[52] Hadfield, *Rules for a Flat World*, p. 285.

[53] Michael N. Barnett, *Paternalism beyond Borders* (Cambridge: Cambridge University Press, 2016).

what it takes to establish rule of law. It is undeniable that "[m]any successful democracies such as Israel and India deviate from modern liberal legal practice by accommodating traditional religiously-based rules, precisely in order to get buy-in from the communities involved."[54] Additional examples come to mind that lend credence to this finding. It is noteworthy in this respect that, in 2008, when the UN Commission for the Legal Empowerment of the Poor reported that four billion people around the world were excluded from the rule of law, it was less concerned with lack of progress on substantive achievements, from equality to dignity, and more with the widespread lack of "concrete on-the-ground legal rules and systems."[55]

By way of conclusion, it is worth articulating the minimalist understanding of the rule of law that underpins the model at the heart of this chapter, and our argument for thinking about the microfoundations of the rule of law – in *all* senses of the term:

> In this more grounded sense, being excluded from the rule of law means not having a legal identity that allows you to enter into binding agreements to pay for supplies or labor on credit or to hold others responsible for shoddy goods or dangerous working conditions. It means not being able to prove that you own the building, be it ever so humble, where you live and work and so being unable to use that property as collateral for a loan. It means lacking official authorization to operate a business – a market stall, a small workshop – and so being at risk of getting shut down on the whim of a local politician or person more powerful than you. It means having no recourse when a private company or a member of the local elite grabs all or part of the land your family has harvested for decades. It means having no choice but to pay whatever a customs official asks when you cross the border with your goods. It means having no protection against having the cash your earned from selling your goods in the market in town stolen on the way back to your village, and no way to send the money you earn as a migrant worker safely to your family back home. It means having nowhere to turn when those wages go unpaid, the promised job is given to someone else, or the factory collapses. This world without the basic ground rules for managing economic life is what many call the informal economy[56]

Establishing the supremacy of the rule of law in the informal economy, however, need *not* involve the sovereign state. For law to meaningfully rule, all kinds of institutional designs are conceivable, including

[54] Fukuyama, "Transitions to the Rule of Law," 42.
[55] Hadfield, *Rules for a Flat World*, p. 285.
[56] Hadfield, *Rules for a Flat World*, pp. 285–286.

decentralized enforcement. As Hadfield has shown, "the failure to think innovatively about how legal infrastructure can be built for the mundane operation of ground-level economic activity in . . . enormously complex settings – the exclusive focus on governments as the source of all legal infrastructure – is making the problem worse, not better."[57]

A positive theory of the rule of law – one fit for the twenty-first century – requires attunedness to context. This means bidding farewell to off-the-shelf models of legal order. A priori normative commitments, whether philosophical or otherwise, do not serve the project of rule of law well. To build a rule of law does not mean "to introduce law but to modify the operation of existing normative social orders – by expanding the scope of a relevant community or behaviors or changing the classification institution."[58] One can profitably think of the rule of law as a "rational ritual."[59] Or, to quote Oliver Wendell Holmes, Jr.'s famous adage: "The life of the law has not been logic; it has been experience."[60] Holmes was convinced that "[t]he law embodies the story of a nation's development through many centuries, and it cannot be dealt with as if it contained only the axioms and corollaries of a book of mathematics."[61] Modeling the rule of law is not just a matter of gaming institutions. It also requires a real-world understanding of common knowledge – these everyday systems of belief. The imperative to grasp the rule of the law not just abstractly, but also in the real world, returns us to where we began: the cognitive foundations of the rule of law. Absent a cognitive manifesto, building the rule of law is a fool's errand.

[57] Hadfield, *Rules for a Flat World*, p. 289.
[58] Hadfield and Weingast, "Microfoundations of the Rule of Law," 37.
[59] Chwe, *Rational Ritual*; Meierhenrich, *The Legacies of Law*.
[60] Oliver Wendell, Holmes, Jr., *The Common Law*, with an Introduction by G. Edward White (Cambridge: Belknap Press of Harvard University Press, [1881] 2009), p. 1.
[61] Holmes, Jr., *The Common Law*, p. 1.

Part IV

Pathologies

Thomas Hobbes and the Rule by Law Tradition 14

David Dyzenhaus

LAWYER:	You speak of the Statute Law, and I speak of the Common Law.
PHILOSOPHER:	I speak generally of Law.

Thomas Hobbes[1]

Introduction

Thomas Hobbes is the founder of the rule by law tradition in modern Western thought. It argues that there is no more to law than what the holder of supreme legislative power chooses to enact, whatever its content. Hobbes founds it in opposition to the conception of the rule of law exemplified in the writings of Sir Edward Coke according to which the common law, as interpreted by judges, contains fundamental legal and moral principles which condition the content of enacted or statute law. Coke and others in this rule by law tradition thus consider the rule of law to be a moral good.

Hobbes's main criticism of this conception is that its rule of law is really the rule of lawyers. It elevates their views above the supreme legislative power by extolling the virtues of judicial interpretation in determining the content of enacted law to make it consistent with the "reason" claimed to be embedded in the common law. In addition, it inevitably leads to the claim that consistency with such reason is a mark of the validity of enacted law so that an inconsistent statute is void.[2] If that tradition prevails, we do

[1] Thomas Hobbes, *A Dialogue Between a Philosopher and a Student, of the Common Laws of England*, in Alan Cromartie and Quentin Skinner, eds., *Thomas Hobbes: Writings on Common Law and Hereditary Right* (Oxford: Clarendon Press, 2005), p. 10.

[2] Coke in his judgment in Dr Bonham's case stated that "it appears in our books, that in many cases, the common law doth control Acts of Parliament, and sometimes adjudge them to be void; for when an act of Parliament is against Common right and reason, or repugnant, or impossible to be performed, the Common Law will control it, and adjudge such an Act to be

not get the rule of fundamental principles. Rather, we get the rule of the views of lawyers masquerading as objective moral and legal principle.

The contrast between the rule by law and the rule of law traditions is illuminating. Its basic themes echo in the criticism of the common law tradition by the English legal positivists Jeremy Bentham and John Austin in the eighteenth and nineteenth centuries and in the second half of the twentieth century in the debates between H. L. A. Hart, Bentham's main standard bearer, and the American legal theorists Lon L. Fuller and Ronald M. Dworkin, both of whom adopt what legal positivists regard as the disingenuous mysteries of the common law tradition as well as its natural law-like claim that inherent in the law are principles that condition its content.

But the contrast also obscures as much as it illuminates. Hobbes no less than the common lawyers thought that to have a political order governed by fundamental legal principles – his laws of nature – is a moral good, indeed, the only moral good upon which all rational individuals can agree.[3] Of course, in his political theory the claim about moral good is generally understood to have authoritarian implications. Because, or so his argument runs, all rational individuals will agree that life subject to the will of a supreme and absolute sovereign is preferable to the chaos of subjection in a state of nature to the private judgment of all other individuals, we do in fact agree and so accept that de facto sovereign power is de jure or legitimate authority.[4] But, as I shall argue below, within that argument Hobbes makes room for much of what the rule of law tradition takes to be worthwhile about government according to law. Moreover, he does so in a way that is both less parochial and theoretically and politically more convincing than that tradition.

As the philosopher in the dialogue with the lawyer – a "student of the common law" – tells us, Hobbes's theory is not an account of either statute law or the common law but "of law," more precisely of government according to law. His project is to show that in the modern era a well-designed legal state is necessary to establish the conditions for peaceful

void." *The Selected Writings and Speeches of Sir Edmund Coke*, vol. 1, ed. Steve Sheppard (Carmel: Liberty Fund, [1600] 2003), p. 275.

[3] Thomas Hobbes, *Leviathan*, ed. Richard Tuck (Cambridge: Cambridge University Press, [1652] 1997), p. 111, (hereafter *Leviathan*).

[4] *Leviathan*, pp. 120–121.

and stable interaction between those subject to its authority. Such subjects regard themselves as equally endowed with the capacity to judge right and wrong, while recognizing that there will be very different such judgments in any complex society and that, as a result, they must find some rational basis for submitting themselves to a common, public set of judgments about how to live together. They need to be able to understand how they can authorize the state to act in their name so that each can own what the state does as a matter of right, not a mere exertion of power.

The role of law in this project is to transform power into legal right – to constitute the state so that the acts of all public officials from the sovereign law-maker at the apex of the legal order down to the lowest public official charged with implementing the law can be owned in this way. While the coercive power of the sovereign is necessary for maintaining the state, it is not for Hobbes the reason for subjects to obey the sovereign. Rather, it is necessary to keep in line those who cannot appreciate Hobbes's argument that the basis of the sovereign's authority is, as he put it in the last lines of *Leviathan*, "the mutuall Relation between Protection and Obedience."[5] As a result, Hobbes does not so much present a critique of the rule of law as a theoretically sophisticated, morally and politically attractive account of it.

In a nutshell, my argument is that Hobbes's legal theory shows that any attempt to give an account of the authority of law must contain three elements. First, it will explain authority as compliance with fundamental principles of legality – the right-giving basis of the legal order. Secondly, the theory will give to judges and other officials a role in interpreting enacted law in the light of such principles. It thus must offer a theory of the role of interpretation in maintaining legal order. Thirdly, given one and two, the principles make up a "grammar of legality" in that enacted laws that cannot be interpreted in the light of the principles both have a shaky claim to be law and begin to shift the order from one of legal right to an order of unmediated coercive power. Here the idea of "interpretability" is crucial. Laws that are not interpretable in this way lose their claim to authority because they do not bear the marks of having been enacted with legal right.

I begin by showing that Hobbes's critique of Coke is more nuanced than the orthodox view suggests. My second section shows how that critique can only be properly understood when it is set within the context of Hobbes's

[5] *Leviathan*, p. 491.

account of judicial interpretation of statutes. The third section examines the implications for Hobbes's general political theory of the legal state.

1 Hobbes versus Coke

In chapter 26 of *Leviathan* – "Of Civill Lawes" – Hobbes takes three of Coke's propositions as the foil for his critique of the common law conception of the rule of law.

1. "That the Common Law, hath no Controuler but the Parlament."[6]
2. "[The law is] an Artificiall perfection of Reason, gotten by long study, observation, and experience."[7]
3. "If a man . . . that is Innocent, be accused of Felony, and for feare flyeth for the same; albeit he judicially acquitteth himselfe of the Felony; yet if it be found that he fled for the Felony, he shall notwithstanding his Innocency, Forfeit all his goods, chattells, debts, and duties. For as to the Forfeiture of them, the Law will admit no proofe against the Presumption in Law, grounded upon his flight."[8]

Hobbes perceives the threat in the first proposition to be that it seeks to make "the Legislative Power depend on private men, or subordinate judges."[9] The second proposition contains much the same threat. It answers the question of "whose Reason . . . shall be received for Law" by claiming that it is the reason of the lawyers because of their study of and experience in the practice of the law.[10]

The third proposition Hobbes treats with scorn, as an example of the absurdities that can arise when the "Presumption" of judges is taken to be a presumption of law.[11]

However, as I shall now show, Hobbes does not so much reject the first two propositions as heavily qualify them. And as I shall show in the next section, while he clearly rejects the third, his reasons for so doing undermine any attempt to place him neatly on the rule by law side of a rule by law/rule of law distinction.

The proposition that the common law has no controller but parliament on its face concedes that the common law is subordinate to parliament,

6 *Leviathan*, p. 186.
7 *Leviathan*, p. 187.
8 *Leviathan*, p. 193
9 *Leviathan*, p. 186.
10 *Leviathan*, p. 187.
11 *Leviathan*, p. 193.

though Hobbes seems to suspect that it opens the way to giving common law principles a higher status than statute. However, he chooses to take the proposition at face value and says that it is true, but not of legal order in general. Its truth is contingent on there being in place a particular kind of legal order, one in which parliament is the supreme legislative power in contrast, for example, with a legal order in which a monarch is sovereign.[12]

When it comes to the proposition about lawyers and the artificial reason of the law, Hobbes understands it as seeking to make sense of the lawyers' claim, with which he agrees, that "Law can never be against reason."[13] But he offers two objections to the claim that the reason is artificial. The first is already indicated – that the reason of lawyers and "subordinate judges" reduces to their views of right and wrong and that leads to "contradiction" and "discordance" in the law.[14] The only way to avoid this problem is to see that the reason of the law is the

> Reason of this our Artificiall Man the Common-wealth, and his Command, that maketh Law: And the Commonwealth being in their Representative but one Person, there cannot easily arise any contradiction in the Lawes; and when there doth, the same Reason is able, by interpretation, or alteration, to take it away.[15]

The second objection is that if the reason of the law is taken to be the artificial reason of lawyers, one must consider that the "long study" of the law may possibly "encrease, and confirm erroneous Sentences" and that "where men build on false grounds, the more they build, the greater is the ruine."[16] It is in some tension with the first because its focus is not discordance but concordance – judges as a group treating past (possibly bad) decisions as binding precedent.

Hobbes repeats this objection later in the chapter in his discussion of the judicial interpretation of statute law, set within the context of his general legal theory. It is in that context that he pours scorn on Coke's dictum about the legal presumption in the case of the innocent man who fled when charged with felony. This context is badly neglected by almost all Hobbes scholars. They generally skip over Hobbes's chapter on civil law, pausing only to notice his definition of law as the command of the sovereign,[17] the paragraph in which he sets out his view that the sovereign is legally

[12] *Leviathan*, p. 186. [13] *Leviathan*, pp. 186–187. [14] *Leviathan*, p. 187.
[15] *Leviathan*, p. 187. [16] *Leviathan*, p. 187. [17] *Leviathan*, p. 184.

unlimited,[18] and his puzzling claim that the "Law of Nature, and the Civill Law, contain each other, and are of equall extent."[19]

Such partial attention to chapter 26 produces its own and highly misleading context. The conjunction of claims that law is the command of the sovereign and that the sovereign is legally unlimited explain Hobbes's alleged place as the founder of the rule by law tradition. It does so by conceiving his legal theory as a precursor to Bentham and Austin's command theory of law, according to which law is the commands of the sovereign, the sovereign is identified by seeing who in a political community is habitually obeyed by the bulk of the population and is not subject to any other person or body, that is, is legally unlimited, and the motivation for obedience is fear of the sanctions that attach to each command.

Once Hobbes's theory is so conceived, the puzzle about his claim about the equal containment of civil and natural law is too easily solved. The nineteen laws of nature, which are discussed at length in chapters 14 and 15 of *Leviathan*, are held to be of equal extent with the civil law only in that the content of the civil law should be taken by legal subjects as an accurate guide to the content of natural law. Thus, as one philosopher has argued, if the sovereign orders all mediators to be killed on sight this must be taken as the correct interpretation of Law 15: "*That all men that mediate Peace, be allowed safe Conduct.*"[20] This position entails that the "true function" of Hobbes's extensive account of the laws of nature "and the only one that cannot be eliminated, is to provide the most absolute ground to the norm according to which there is no other valid law than positive law."[21] The function of the laws of nature is to give rise to the authoritarian conclusion that legal subjects must take the law of their sovereign to be binding, whatever its content.

This solution to the puzzle raised by the containment thesis is, however, at odds with Hobbes's response to Coke's dictum. In Hobbes's view, the dictum shows not the possibility but the actuality of what goes wrong when one adopts a slavish approach to precedent. Hobbes affirms that it is against the law of nature "To punish the Innocent; and Innocent is he that acquitteth himselfe Judicially, and is acknowledged for

[18] *Leviathan*, p. 186. [19] *Leviathan*, p. 185.

[20] *Leviathan*, p. 108. See Mark C. Murphy, "Was Hobbes a Legal Positivist?," *Ethics*, 105 (1995), 846–873.

[21] Norberto Bobbio, *Thomas Hobbes and the Natural Law Tradition*, trans. Daniela Gobetti (Chicago: Chicago University Press, 1993), p. 148.

Innocent by the Judge." He thus concludes that "there is no place in the world, where ... [Coke's dictum] can be an interpretation of a Law of Nature, or be made a Law by the Sentences of precedent Judges, that had done the same. For he that judged it first, judged unjustly; and no Injustice can be a pattern of Judgement to succeeding Judges."[22] And just in case his reader has not appreciated the point, he repeats it in even stronger terms.[23]

However, the point so far is only about precedent and judge-made law, not a statute, which leads Hobbes to contemplate a statutory intervention. He says that "a written Law may forbid innocent men to fly, and they may be punished for flying: But that flying for feare of injury, should be taken for presumption of guilt, after a man is already absolved of the crime Judicially, is contrary to the nature of a Presumption, which hath no place after Judgement given."[24] This example is instructive. For Hobbes, this is the only legitimate way the sovereign may regulate by law the actions of innocent people facing a criminal charge who may consider flight. Hobbes does not, then, confront the example of a law that explicitly enacted the objectionable presumption, though elsewhere in *Leviathan* he contemplates the possibility that the sovereign may violate the laws of nature. He also insists both that the sovereign is answerable for such commands only to God, not to his subjects,[25] and that the sovereign's agents, which includes subordinate judges, must implement the commands. Indeed, if they refuse to implement such a command they break Law 3 of the laws of nature, which forbids "breach of covenant"[26]and which Hobbes says in chapter 15 is "the Fountain and Originall of JUSTICE."[27] One could plausibly conclude that while it might be illegitimate for the sovereign to enact a statute that violates a law of nature, such illegitimacy is from God's perspective only, not from the perspective of either subjects or judges.

But as I shall now show, when these issues are placed within the context of Hobbes's legal theory, particularly his theory of the role of interpretation, we see that he is committed to an account of the rule of law that not only includes the essentials of the common law conception of the rule of law, but also provides a better explanation of them.

[22] *Leviathan*, p. 192. [23] *Leviathan*, p. 193. [24] *Leviathan*, pp. 192–193.
[25] *Leviathan*, p. 148. [26] *Leviathan*, p. 113. [27] *Leviathan*, p. 100.

2 The Grammar of Legality

Hobbes's legal theory presents some of the key elements of a command theory of law. Law is the commands of the sovereign, the sovereign is not subject to the law of any other body and is he who is in fact obeyed. However, one key element of the command theory is missing. Hobbes does not have as part of his definition of law that each command comes with a sanction to motivate compliance. Rather, he says that "Law in generall, is not Counsell, but Command; nor a Command of any man to any man; but only of him, whose Command is *addressed to one formerly obliged to obey him.*"[28] The basis of legal order is not therefore coercion but an obligation that derives from the social contract between the individuals in the state of nature whose agreement constitutes the state and authorizes the sovereign to act in their name.

Secondly, Hobbes says that when it comes to civil law it adds to his definition of law in general only "the name of the person Commanding, which is *Persona Civitatis*, the Person of the Common-wealth."[29] It adds, that is, the name of the sovereign, who is an artificial not a natural person – an artifact of the social contract.

As an artificial person, he takes on a role in which the laws of nature are implicated. For example: Law 11 is the law of equity, that "*if a man be trusted to judge between man and man*, it is a precept of the Law of Nature, *that he deal Equally between them*";[30] and because, says Hobbes, "every man is presumed to do all things in order to his own benefit, no man is a fit arbitrator in his own cause," which gives us Law 17;[31] for the same reason, Law 18 holds that no man is to be judge who "*has in him a natural cause of partiality*";[32] finally, Law 19 is that in controversies of fact, the judge must give credit to the witnesses.[33] These four laws are both procedural and substantive in that they affect, without determining, the content of any decision by a sovereign who is faithful to the moral discipline of his role.

This point brings me to my third, about the passage that is supposed to say that the sovereign is not subject to law.

The Soveraign of a Common-wealth, be it an Assembly, or one Man, is not Subject to the Civill Lawes. For having power to make, and repeale Lawes, he may when he pleaseth, free himselfe from that subjection, by repealing those Lawes that trouble

[28] *Leviathan*, p. 183 (emphasis added). [29] *Leviathan*, p. 183. [30] *Leviathan*, p. 108.
[31] *Leviathan*, p. 109. [32] *Leviathan*, p. 109. [33] *Leviathan*, p. 109.

him, and making of new; and consequently he was free before. For he is free, that can be free when he will: Nor is it possible for any person to be bound to himselfe; because he that can bind, can release; and therefore he that is bound to himselfe onely, is not bound.[34]

But this passage is far from the claim that the sovereign is legally unlimited. Hobbes is clear that for an artificial person to be free "when he will" he must *will* publicly. He must express himself in a way that is publicly accessible and recognizable to his subjects as an expression of will. Since the sovereign's will has to bear the "manifest signs" or formal marks of authority to be recognized as such,[35] he is subject to what I have called elsewhere the "validity proviso": it is a necessary but not sufficient condition of the sovereign's authority that when he exercises that authority he does so in a way that complies with the public criteria recognized by his audience for certifying that a law is valid.[36] Moreover, when Hobbes repeats the claim that the sovereign is not subject to civil law in chapter 29 he takes care to emphasize that the sovereign is subject to the laws of nature.[37] But if the sovereign is accountable for his violations of the laws of nature to God alone and judges and other officials are under a duty to implement a statute that violates the laws of nature, such subjection would not amount to anything. At most, he would be subject to the formal requirement that to change a law he must comply with criteria of validity.

However, as I have also argued, the sovereign is subject to a second, substantive "legality proviso": the laws of the sovereign must be interpreted, and so must be interpretable, in light of the laws of nature.[38] The idea of interpretability falls out of Hobbes's account of the role of judicial interpretation.

Hobbes begins that account by saying that before validly enacted laws can become binding there is another "very material" condition that must be met: the laws have to be given an "authentique Interpretation," a condition necessary because "All Laws, written, and unwritten, have need of Interpretation."[39] He does want that the interpreters "can be none but those, which the Soveraign" appoints lest "by the craft of an Interpreter,

[34] *Leviathan*, p. 184. [35] *Leviathan*, p. 189.

[36] David Dyzenhaus, "Hobbes on the Authority of Law," in David Dyzenhaus and Thomas Poole, eds., *Hobbes and the Law* (Cambridge: Cambridge University Press, 2012), p. 198.

[37] *Leviathan*, p. 224. [38] Dyzenhaus, "Hobbes on the Authority of Law," 199.

[39] *Leviathan*, p. 190.

the Law may be made to beare a sense, contrary to that of the Soveraign; by which means the Interpreter becomes the Legislator."[40]

But when it comes to the duties of the subordinate judges, that is, the interpreters appointed by the sovereign, Hobbes emphasizes that the judge's duty is to give a "reasonable interpretation," which is the interpretation that accords with the laws of nature lest the judge insult the sovereign by supposing that his intention could be other than "Equity." If the judge cannot reach a reasonable judgment, he should "respit Judgement till he have received more ample authority," that is, defer judgment and consult the sovereign.[41] Thus, legislative intention is for Hobbes a matter of construction by judges in light of their understanding of the laws of nature, which makes his account of judicial interpretation of statute law quite similar to that put forward by the common lawyers, save for Hobbes's hostility to precedent.[42]

But even that hostility is qualified because Hobbes does not oppose a doctrine of precedent when it comes to "mutable" laws or statutes.[43] Even a mistaken interpretation by a judge of statute law binds into the future. It is true that this force into the future depends on the sovereign permitting this state of affairs to persist. However, this marks no distinction with the common lawyers since they also think that the persistence of such precedent is conditional on the legislature not choosing to overrule the judgment. Nevertheless, Hobbes insists that there can be no precedent when it comes to interpretation of "immutable" laws – the laws of nature.[44] It is here that he offers Coke's dictum about the presumption of guilt as an example of why, with interpretation of the laws of nature, the judge's judgment has force only for the parties.

The implications of Hobbes's qualified hostility to precedent are immense. His theory of sovereignty is far from stripping judges of power. Rather, it proclaims that judges have the authority of their sovereign to interpret his laws in the light of the laws of nature even when the "bare words of a written Law" appear to suggest that such an interpretation is not

[40] *Leviathan*, p. 190. [41] *Leviathan*, p. 192.

[42] Elsewhere Hobbes insists again that it is natural or human reason, not Coke's idea of artificial reason, that is the "Life of the Law." But this cannot affect the point that the task of the interpreter of the law is to work out the content of the law that was made, not to impose his own view of the law that should have been made. See *A Dialogue Between a Philosopher and a Student, of the Common Laws of England*, in idem, *The Clarendon Edition of the Works of Thomas Hobbes*, vol 11: *Writings on Common Law and Hereditary Right*, ed. Alan Cromartie and Quentin Skinner (Oxford: Clarendon Press, [1681] 2005), p. 10.

[43] *Leviathan*, p. 192. [44] *Leviathan*, p. 192.

warranted.[45] This is as potent an authority as most lawyers in the common law tradition have ever claimed.[46]

Nevertheless, as Sir Hersch Lauterpacht once remarked, judges have "wielded" presumptions such as that the sovereign's intention should always be presumed to be equity as a "powerful weapon" and "with a determination which on occasions have come near to the denial of the supremacy of Parliament."[47] That, more than any actual assertion of the authority to void, explains why the claim that judges must interpret all statute law in the light of some set of fundamental principles leads to the suspicion that the person making the claim is elevating those principles above sovereign authority.

Hence, Hobbes does not state any real distinction between his theory and the common law conception of the rule of law when he says that while an "incommodity" that arises when a written law seems inconsistent with a law of nature should set the judge on the path to find a reasonable interpretation of the law, nevertheless, "no Incommodity can warrant a Sentence against the Law."[48] In addition, when he says that the sovereign's erroneous pronouncements about the laws of nature cannot prevail, he has in mind the sovereign acting as judge, not legislator; and judges must interpret legislation consistently with the laws of nature.[49]

The real distinctions between Hobbes and the common lawyers are as follows. First, Hobbes, unlike the common lawyers, explicitly advocates an institutional solution to problems that arise when judges cannot determine a reasonable interpretation for a statute. The judge, as we have seen him

45 *Leviathan*, p. 194.

46 Coke's dictum from Dr Bonham's case which declares the authority of judges to void statutes which are "against common right and reason" is exceptional. Moreover, it was said in a context where Coke ruled that the charter of the College of Physicians did not as a matter of statutory interpretation permit it to sanction Bonham – an unlicensed practitioner – in the ways that it had, and that more generally the College could not be a judge in its own cause. The authority to void statutes was not therefore in issue in the case.

47 Hersch Lauterpacht, "Is International Law a Part of the Law of England?" in idem, *International Law: Being the Collected Papers of Hersch Lauterpacht*, vol. 2: *The Law of Peace, Part I*, ed. Elihu Lauterpacht (Cambridge: Cambridge University Press, 1975), p. 544. The presumption Lauterpacht is discussing is the presumption that the sovereign must be taken by judges to intend to comply with international law. Lest this discussion seem not pertinent because of Hobbes's alleged "realism" about international relations (*Leviathan*, p. 90), see Theodore Christov, *Before Anarchy: Hobbes and His Critics in Modern International Thought* (Cambridge: Cambridge University Press, 2015).

48 *Leviathan*, p. 194. 49 *Leviathan*, pp. 192–193.

suggest, should suspend judgment until he has consulted the sovereign. The judge's question to the sovereign is: "Is a reasonable interpretation of the law possible, given that the 'bare words of a Written Law' are so obviously inconsistent with a law of nature?" Such consultation presents the sovereign with an option, either to give a kind of advisory opinion as to an interpretation that the judge could adopt or, because there is no way to avoid violating the law of nature while implementing the enacted law, to initiate legislative reform.

Secondly, Hobbes gets to this position not by working up an account of judicial interpretation from the existing practices of a particular jurisdiction, as for example the common lawyers did with the common law, and as Dworkin did with the constitutional decisions of the Warren Court. He does not, that is, offer a theory of interpretation, but of the role of judicial interpretation as part of a more general inquiry into the modern legal state in which the sovereign is he who rules by law. That inquiry is part of an even more general inquiry into the place of legal order in the construction of stable political order in a bid to answer what Bernard Williams calls the "Hobbesian question" of how to secure "order, protection, safety, trust, and the conditions of cooperation."[50] This, Williams says, is the "first" political question because "solving it is the condition of solving, indeed posing, any others."[51] Hobbes's theory of law is, then, first and foremost a political theory of legal order, as I shall now explain.

3 Hobbes on the Autonomy of "the Political"

Hobbes's sketch of how a legal order that can be part of the solution to the first political question is both rich and sparse. It is rich because a political order is characterized by authority relationships in contrast with relationships of unmediated coercive power. The point is not that a political order can do without coercive power, only that it wields power in a way that makes plausible a claim to have been authorized by those who are subject to that power. Any exercise of coercive power by the state must therefore be recognizable as an authoritative act, which entails that it must meet the

[50] Bernard Williams, "Realism and Moralism in Political Theory," in idem, *In the Beginning was the Deed: Realism and Moralism in Political Argument*, ed. Geoffrey Hawthorn (Princeton: Princeton University Press, 2005), p. 3.

[51] Williams, "Realism and Moralism in Political Theory," 3.

two provisos set out above. That puts an onus of justification on officials which, if it cannot be discharged, raises the question whether the subject is within the reciprocal relationship of protection and obedience, and so implies that the relationship is not political but one of hostility or unmediated coercion between more and less powerful natural individuals.

Put differently, while Hobbes's solution to the first political question is the injunction, "Obey the law, whatever its content," it is far from unmediated coercion. It is coercion mediated by legal right because the content must be put into legal form and then applied and interpreted in a way that discharges the onus of justification.[52]

This account of the role of legal order in sustaining political order subtly changes the understanding of the relationship between sovereignty and fundamental legal principles. The contest between the rule by law and rule of law traditions is usually understood in terms of a binary option. Either the sovereign is subject to *legal* principles with judges as their guardian or the principles are *political* principles and the sovereign as the ultimate law-maker is the sole judge of the content of the principles.[53]

Hobbes presents another option: fundamental principles are the political principles intrinsic to the rule by law project and should not be seen primarily as limiting sovereign authority. Rather, the principles constitute sovereign authority. They are the right-giving principles of the legal state. As such, the subordinate officials of the state – those who work at levels below the level of supreme legislative power – must concretize the law or complete the exercise of sovereignty consistently with those

[52] According to Williams, "Realism and Moralism in Political Theory," p. 4, it is a necessary condition of legitimacy that the state solves the first political question, which means that it must satisfy "the Basic Legitimation Demand" that every legitimate state must satisfy if it is to show that it wields authority rather than sheer coercive power over those subject to its rule. To meet that demand the state "has to be able to offer a justification of its power *to each subject*," which means to every individual in its power, "whom by its own lights it can rightfully coerce under its laws and institutions."

[53] Both traditions recognize that all laws require interpretation. This is not, of course, a problem for the rule of law tradition since to the extent that it puts forward a general theory of law, it is built up from a particular set of judicial practices of interpretation. It is a problem for the rule by law tradition, at least in its legal positivist version, which it can attempt to solve by designing legal order in a way that diminishes the scope for judicial interpretation to the greatest extent possible, as in Bentham's fantasy of a complete code of statute law, or just by calling for a frank acknowledgement that judges are exercising a quasi-legislative discretionary power, as in Hart's legal theory.

principles. Sovereignty, while often identified by Hobbes with the ultimate law-making power, is more complex than a one-off act because it involves a process of concretizing general laws until they can be applied to legal subjects consistently with the laws of nature.[54]

This understanding of the constitution of sovereignty does imply limits of a kind. First, Hobbes insists from the beginning of *Leviathan* that the individual human being as such is the subject of political order. In his view, there is only one prepolitical right, the right that every individual has to self-preservation, including the right to judge for oneself how to exercise that right.[55] In the state of nature, it is a worse than useless right since its existence contributes to the precariousness of that state, so it is rational for individuals to authorize a sovereign to govern them. It is thus also rational for anyone subject to such government to understand that he or she should be taken to have consented so to be governed. But it is rational only as long as the reciprocal relationship between protection and obedience is maintained in which protection is of the subject understood as a person who is free and equal before the law.

Hence, the prepolitical right to preserve oneself survives into the civil condition as a political right, for Hobbes the right of rights, which is the right to demand a justification from public officials for any exercise of coercive power in terms of the reciprocal relationship between protection and obedience. But it also survives as setting the limit of that political relationship by marking the point where justification runs out and political order turns into unmediated coercion, at which point the subject is no longer getting protection and is no longer bound to the sovereign.

But while rich in this way, Hobbes's account is also, as I said, sparse, though its very sparsity does lead to a second kind of limit that comes about through the institutional nature of his conception of sovereignty. His

[54] In this way, Hobbes's legal theory is the starting point for what I call in my work in progress "the long arc of legality," an arc that stretches from Hobbes through to the major legal philosophers of the twentieth century, most notably Hans Kelsen and Lon Fuller. This is an inquiry sparked by Michael Oakeshott's magnificent, Hobbes-inspired set of reflections on the rule of law: in particular, first, that Hobbes's laws of nature are "no more than an analytic breakdown of the intrinsic character of law, what I have called the *jus* inherent in genuine law which distinguishes it from a command addressed to an assignable agent or a managerial instruction concerned with the promotion of interests"; secondly, that such a conception of the legality "hovers over the reflections of many so-called 'positivist' modern jurists." See Michael Oakeshott, "The Rule of Law," in idem, *On History and Other Essays* (Carmel: Liberty Fund, [1983] 1999), pp. 172–173, 175.

[55] For example, *Leviathan*, pp. 93–94, 151–152, 214.

project is to construct a legal theory in service of a general political theory, one that explains the role of legal order in sustaining legitimate political authority, whatever the nature of the political regime – monarchy, democracy, or aristocracy. In this respect, he is well described as a "constitutional indifferentist,"[56] since he is a political and legal philosopher who thinks that the choice for one kind of constitutional order over another is to be made on pragmatic grounds.

The best example of Hobbes's indifferentism is that his argument for the superior nature of monarchy over democracy is not at the level of abstract political theory. Instead, he argues that the former is more likely than the latter to conduce both to stability and the overall good of the people.[57] His argument against precedent should be understood in the same light. A legal order should not adopt such a doctrine as a matter of abstract political theory, which can tell one only that law must be interpretable in the light of the fundamental principles of legality. Rather, the decision should be on the basis of whether the doctrine promotes conformity to fundamental principles from the perspective of a "very able architect" who wishes above all to avoid designing "a craisie building" that "must assuredly fall upon the heads of . . . posterity."[58]

Similarly, abstract political theory cannot decide what kind of institution should confront the problems that arise when statute law is not interpretable in the right way. But there must be some such institution lest the legal order be incapable of vindicating its commitment to its principles. Here there are various options. First, there is Hobbes's own option which requires a judicial reference to the sovereign. Secondly, there is the common law tradition's option, which gives judges an extensive interpretative authority, which Hobbes also adopts, save that he is clearly wary of the hint that the authority might extend to the voiding of flagrantly offensive laws. Indeed, it seems likely that the first option is intended to avoid judges finding themselves in a situation of institutional face-off because it channels the matter into the institutional structure of sovereignty.[59]

[56] Lars Vinx, "Constitutional Indifferentism and Republican Freedom," *Political Theory*, 38 (2010), 809–837.

[57] *Leviathan*, pp. 131–138.

[58] *Leviathan*, p. 221.

[59] This double-barreled institutional solution has an interesting contemporary analogue in the UK Human Rights Act (1998), which in section 3 requires that judges strain to interpret statutes to make them compatible with the human rights commitments of the statute, and in section 4 requires judges to make a declaration of incompatibility of the statute with the

A third option, which did not exist in Hobbes's time, and which it may seem he must reject, is the explicit grant of authority to judges to invalidate statutes on the basis of a bill of rights in an entrenched constitution. But even in this regard, his rejection might be nuanced. He explicitly says that a formally valid sovereign act that undermines the essential rights of sovereignty would be void *ab initio*.[60] Moreover, constitutional mechanisms that require judges to consider that limits on rights can be justified by the government in a proportionality analysis or that allow legislative overrides of judicial declarations of unconstitutionality, or even mechanisms of constitutional amendment that do not make amendment politically impossible, can plausibly be understood as consistent with the interpretation of Hobbesian sovereignty presented here.

Hobbes can then be understood as the founder of the rule by law tradition in modern political and legal theory. But he is also one of the founders of the modern political discourse of constitutionalism about the reciprocal relationship between, on the one hand, the sovereign person of the state and the officials who implement and interpret the law and, on the other hand, the persons who are subject to the law. The sovereign as an artificial person speaks to the subjects through law[61] and legal language has its own grammar that requires that subjects be addressed in a way that respects them as responsible agents, each endowed with equal capacity to judge right and wrong. Since such discourse is governed by fundamental principles of legality, it is, as I have argued, a mistake to see Hobbes as a critic of the rule of law. Rather, he has a particular critique of the common

human rights commitments, if they cannot find an interpretation under section 3; the declaration does not affect the validity of the statute.

60 *Leviathan*, p. 127.

61 This proposition commits me to the view that that all acts of sovereignty must comply with the law to be recognizable as acts of sovereignty. That view is at odds with many important passages in Hobbes, for example, the way he tells the story of David and Uriah, *Leviathan*, p. 148. But that way is totally inconsistent with his account of the sovereign as an artificial person, as I argue in "How Hobbes met the 'Hobbes Challenge,'" *Modern Law Review*, 72 (2009), 488–506. Hobbes also says that the subject may contest the sovereign's act when the sovereign relies on a law as the warrant for the act but not when the sovereign acts by "vertue of his Power": *Leviathan*, p. 153. But if subjects have to be able to identify what counts as a sovereign act by reference to publicly recognizable criteria, before an act of power can count as a sovereign act it must be attributable to the sovereign as an artificial person. For the argument against this interpretation, see Thomas Poole, "Hobbes on Law and Prerogative," in David Dyzenhaus and Thomas Poole, eds., *Hobbes and the Law*, pp. 68–96.

law conception of that rule. But, as I have tried to show, even that critique is nuanced and it displays Hobbes's legal theory as a superior articulation of, rather than an attempt to undermine, the idea that the rule of law is a moral good.

Perhaps even more important is that the rule of law is a moral good because it is a political good, one that helps to make it possible for individuals to live together on stable and peaceful terms despite their very different views of the moral good for themselves. One might say that a mark of this conception of the political is that political order is always legal order, in that the subjects of the law can demand of officials that they justify their coercive acts by showing that there is a basis or warrant in the law for these acts, not only in the positive or enacted law of the order, but also (where relevant) in the fundamental principles of that order. The claim imagines a realm of politics which is independent of any conception of the highest moral good for individuals. Its real rival is not the common law conception of the rule of law but those figures in the reason-of-state tradition who understand law's role as all about closing down political conflict by a legally unconstrained decision. Somewhat ironically, one can then argue that if Carl Schmitt was right that political theory needs a conception of the autonomy of the political,[62] one of the marks of such autonomy is that it requires that might be transformed into legal right.

[62] Carl Schmitt, *The Concept of the Political*, trans. George Schwab (New Brunswick: Rutgers University Press, [1932] 1976).

15 Conservative Critiques of the *Rechtsstaat*

Peter C. Caldwell

Introduction

Given the connection of "law and order" politics with conservatism, the idea of a conservative critique of the *Rechtsstaat* at first seems contradictory. After all, wasn't John Adams's insistence on defending the British soldiers involved in the Boston Massacre used as evidence for his conservatism? Didn't Burke's criticism of the French Revolution revolve around the preservation of law as part of a concrete order? But law and order are not identical and it is in the tension between the rule of law and the well ordered society that the possibility for conservative critique of the *Rechtsstaat* lies. In a time of revolutionary upheaval, furthermore, when revolutionaries proclaim the law, the legal side of "law and order" can come under fire as well.

The preservation of order, of course, is not just or even primarily a matter for the courts; it is a matter for political authorities from the executive to the army to the police. Preserving order against the perceived threat of chaos, whether from outside or from within a country, is related to the logic of "reason of state": in certain cases the "state" as an existential force for order can ignore positive law and rights. Closely associated with the logic of the reason of state is the counter-Enlightenment critique of the ability of humans to create laws for themselves at all, given the inherent and irremediable taint of evil in humanity, a logic made with special force by Joseph de Maistre after the French Revolution. The need for a "dictator" to protect public order (Alexander Hamilton invokes the notion in the *Federalist Papers*, Carl Schmitt in the early years of the Weimar Republic) further underlines the conservative critique of the *Rechtsstaat*: concrete measures and just as important human leaders are necessary to fuse the nation and to ensure order. The abstract rights of citizenship that apply to all citizens might, from the perspective of conservatives (and others) also apply to citizens who undermine the political order. The rights of women, for example, could undermine the natural authority of the father and with him the family as a bedrock of order; similarly, extending equal rights to minorities, the classic case being that of the Jews in Europe, could also be viewed as a threat to social order, to political legitimacy, and therefore a threat to the state itself.

None of these positions implied any necessary opposition to social policy: conservatism is not the same as authoritarian liberalism. Paternalism is part of the conservative tradition. (At least in theory; in practice, and as John Stuart Mill noted over 150 years ago, paternalism is an ideological mask for vested interests.[1]) But another school of conservatives dissociated social intervention from social rights that courts can adjudicate. Social interventions should be concrete actions by individuals or by state administrators to provide for the existence of those in need to protect against the potential for chaos. Such was the argument of Lorenz von Stein for a social monarchy; such was the argument of Ernst Forsthoff after 1945 for a strong executive and a professional administration that clearly distinguished social policy from the *Rechtsstaat*.

Germany in 1918, like France in 1789, experienced a revolution that toppled a monarch and implemented a democracy. But from its very beginning this democracy was under fire from left and right. Conservatism took on new forms in the context of a democratic *Rechtsstaat* that had overthrown an older order: critical of the new order as *not really* order, *not really* a barrier against chaos; searching for a new foundation that would provide legitimacy, not merely legality, to the system; experimenting with new forms of order that could point beyond the "formalism" and "relativism" of the rule of law.

1 Relativizing Law

The revolutions of 1776 and 1789 proclaimed a break with despotic rule, that is, rule unconstrained by law and rights, and the notion that laws agreed to by the people constituted the state itself. Unlike the prerevolutionary political system in which reforms might *modify* a preexisting state authority – and implicitly leave with the sovereign a residual right to stand above the rules – the constitutional revolution was about *creating* the

[1] John Stuart Mill, *The Subjection of Women* (Indianapolis: Hackett, [1869] 1988), p. 36.

state.[2] Thus the United States Constitution of 1787 laid out the laws that constituted state authority that began with citizens' right, directly or indirectly, to determine the content of laws and the limits of state power. Thus the French Declaration of the Rights of Man and Citizen of 1789 declared the basic rights that would both limit and determine the nature of state authority, and declared that only through a representative, legislative process (not yet determined) could rights be limited. Law constituted authority, a conception that also shaped the defense of the Rechtsstaat in early German liberalism. The *Rechtsstaat*, more than merely a formal statement that the state operated through laws, implied a substance protecting the rights and property of civil society.[3]

The harshest conservative criticism of the new revolutionary constitutions went beyond ad hominem attacks on the revolutionaries to hit at the basic premise that mere humans could create forms for themselves, much less constitute themselves as a political or civil body. Joseph de Maistre declared that "every particular form of government is a divine construction, just like sovereignty in general"; all institutions, he continued, are based on religion. Human reason, by contrast, merely produces skepticism and undermines morality and law.[4] Sovereignty in the end lies with God; the rules are sovereign in the sense of having no earthly limit, but derive their legitimate power from God. Laws themselves develop over time, and are not rights either demanded from below or produced in the form of rational systems; they are the product of circumstances and ultimately of God. Maistre condemned the "perfect stupidity . . . of those poor people who imagine that legislators are men, that laws are pieces of paper, and that nature can be created *by ink*."[5] By extension, the natural place of a person in a state is that of subject, even slave; the natural place of the sovereign is that of master. Christianity

[2] See esp. Dieter Grimm, *Deutsche Verfassungsgeschichte 1776–1866* (Frankfurt am Main: Suhrkamp, 1988), p. 57 and passim.

[3] These ideas echoed through the works of Welcker, Mohl, and Rotteck in the first half of the nineteenth century. See esp. Ernst-Wolfgang Böckenförde, "Entstehung und Wandel des Rechtsstaatsbegriffs," in idem, *Staat, Gesellschaft, Freiheit: Studien zur Staatstheorie und zum Verfassungsrecht* (Frankfurt am Main: Suhrkamp, 1976), pp. 65–92.

[4] Joseph de Maistre, "Study on Sovereignty," in idem, *The Works of Joseph de Maistre*, selected, trans., and with an Introduction by Jack Lively (New York: Schocken, 1971), pp. 107–108.

[5] Joseph de Maistre, "Essay on the Generative Principle of Political Constitutions," in idem, *The Works of Joseph de Maistre*, pp. 146, 157.

may have raised people up from slavery, but not because humans have any inherent rights; in such cases, humans have been raised up by supernatural rather than human or natural causes.[6]

Maistre's critique is of constitution-makers, but it applies as well to ideas of the *Rechtsstaat*. Even in its more conservative nineteenth-century variant, when the *Rechtsstaat* merely modified existing authority, it aimed to impose rules and procedures on the state that would require the state to act within law, to expose itself to rational discussion of whether an action was within the law, and so on; the *Rechtsstaat* also asserted basic principles about law, such as the principle that criminal laws could not be retroactive. In short, while not a doctrine of democratic sovereignty, the *Rechtsstaat* had constitutional implications, insofar as it determined the bounds of political authority and protected against the opposite of the *Rechtsstaat*, the *Policeystaat* (an executive that used its own judgment to reach goals promoting its citizens' welfare, moral and otherwise).[7] On Maistre's account, by contrast, the validity of laws resided in their existence over time, which proved their natural or divine origin beyond the world of men. Principles were secondary. A basic principle of the *Rechtsstaat* like habeas corpus, so important to the English legal system, was illusory; in reality, the government could and did suspend habeas corpus for long periods of time, which did not bother Maistre in the least.[8] Maistre relativized basic laws and principles of law, just as Robespierre on the left did, but without appeal to either reason or popular sovereignty. Within law, constitutional or otherwise, resided a reality of the state which, for Maistre, acted in accordance with a prelegal divine will.

The effect of Maistre's dictum that "the fundamentals of political constitutions exist before all written laws" is a valuable insight that potentially opens the way for an exploration of the social bases of constitutionalism; in this sense, he was developing problems for a political sociology. Its political and legal effect, however, was to relativize the new revolutionary

[6] Joseph de Maistre, "The Pope," in idem, *The Works of Joseph de Maistre*, p. 145.

[7] These opinions run though German liberal thought before 1848: see Karl-Georg Faber, "Macht, Gewalt: Liberale Lehre von der Staatsgewalt," in Otto Brunner, Werner Conze, and Reinhart Koselleck, eds., *Geschichtliche Grundbegriffe* (Studienausgabe), vol. 3 (Stuttgart: Klett-Cotta, 2004), pp. 917–918; connected to constitutionalism in Georg Haverkate, "Staat und Souveränität," in Brunner, Conze, and Koselleck, eds., *Geschichtliche Grundbegriffe*, vol. 6, pp. 75ff.

[8] Maistre, "Essay on the Generative Principle of Political Constitutions," p. 149.

constitutions in order to undermine the idea of the republic itself: it is not the people who found their republic, it is a prior divine force that does. The same tension between insights into the social and political prerequisites of constitutions and the so-called "bourgeois" *Rechtsstaat* is found in Carl Schmitt's writings following the Revolution of 1918. Schmitt expressed his intellectual debt to Maistre already in 1921, and Maistre's forms of thinking echo through Schmitt's work.[9] Like Maistre, Schmitt made the written constitution into a merely relative conception of the constitution overshadowed by the decisive, existential content of the "absolute constitution," that is, democracy; "constitutionalism" modified "democracy" just as the *Rechtsstaat* modified state power. The *Rechtsstaat* was a kind of parasite on the existential form, an expression of the bourgeoisie's striving to protect individual rights in the nineteenth century. Real political form, namely the existential power of the state (whether democratic or otherwise), was not about the *Rechtsstaat*, but rather sovereignty and the "power of real life."[10]

There is an apparent difference between Maistre and Schmitt, however, in that where Maistre sees the notion of a unified nation deciding on a constitution as absurd, Schmitt suggests that precisely such a basic and existential decision by the nation really exists – at times even echoing Robespierre! Schmitt's "populism," however, is a strange one, insofar as it both asserts a preexisting, prelegal, unified will of the nation (a concept that for a political thinker at other times critical of political romanticism and favoring realism seems rather naïve), and at times implies that a strong leader or state uses myth to create the feeling of national will. This dispute on Schmitt's basic intentions will remain unsettled. In either case, however, he, like Maistre, appealed to a real, underlying order, an order of facts that preexisted conscious human decisions or norms and thus relativized laws and rights, eventually subsuming the latter under the rubric of "mere" legality.[11] Maintaining this factual order required a different kind of reason than legal, a concrete, context-specific reason of state.

[9] Carl Schmitt, *Political Theology: Four Chapters on the Concept of Sovereignty*, trans. George Schwab (Cambridge: MIT Press, [1922] 1985), ch. 4.

[10] Carl Schmitt, *Constitutional Theory*, trans. and ed. Jeffrey Seitzer (Durham: Duke University Press, [1928] 2008), p. 169ff.; Schmitt, *Political Theology*, pp. 15.

[11] On the motif of deriving norms from existing facts in conservatism, see Karl Mannheim, *Konservatismus: Ein Beitrag zur Soziologie des Wissens* (Frankfurt am Main: Suhrkamp, 1984), p. 124.

2 *Raison d'État*

"*Raison d'état*" is a term with multiple meanings. On the one hand, as a purely descriptive term it has to do with the logic of actions taken within a system of politics differentiated from other social systems in the modern world, a demythologizing description of a tradition of political thinking from Machiavelli to the present.[12] On the other hand, *raison d'état* may be invoked to justify state actions taken without regard to law or rights, in the interest of preserving political order. The latter usage raises a critical question about the fundamental relationship between law and state: does the state as an entity preexist law? Or does law "constitute" the state, in the sense of organizing different forces and rules into a unit? As the previous section suggests, the radical conservative critique of the *Rechtsstaat* suggested that consciously made law could not constitute a state, given the fallen nature of humanity, and so the state, this prior and presupposed entity, had to act to preserve order. The logical difficulty in the latter position, developed so well by Hans Kelsen in the 1920s, lies in the assumption that a given set of individuals exerting power made up a state. A coercive action, even in the most ruthless dictatorship, is imputed logically and normatively to "the state," and precisely this act of imputation, Kelsen argued, was law. The logic of *raison d'état*, however, implied some foundational existential unity potentially outside of the legal order, though Kelsen would argue that even in this case legal logic was necessary to impute a violent action, logically and normatively, to the state in the first place.

What Kelsen termed a "theory of surplus value" of the state was the guiding justification for monarchical absolutism in the early modern world (although, as historians have pointed out, the actual power of "absolute" monarchs was in fact quite limited), and carried on as a political challenge to the *Rechtsstaat* and constitutionalism in the nineteenth century.[13] Precisely this logic remained in place in the German states following the introduction of constitutional rule in the mid-nineteenth century. The

[12] See, for example, Niklas Luhmann, *Politische Soziologie* (Berlin: Suhrkamp, 2010), pp. 86–87.

[13] Hans Kelsen, *General Theory of Law and State*, trans. Anders Wedberg (Cambridge: Harvard University Press, [1925] 1949), pp. 191–192; Hans Kelsen, *Introduction to the Problems of Legal Theory: A Translation of the First Edition of the Reine Rechtslehre or Pure Theory of Law*, trans. Bonnie Litchewski Paulson and Staney L. Paulson (Oxford: Clarendon Press, [1934] 1992), pp. 99–101.

constitutions were structured as decisions of the monarch and, in the work of a conservative jurist like Friedrich Julius Stahl, that prior power of monarchs remained in tension with the notion of a law-bound state.[14] The conservative historian Heinrich von Treitschke made the priority of the state into a principle of modern history writing: the state was a transhistorical necessity, it formed its people into a nation, it was subordinate to no higher earthly entity. Following the Prussian military victory that brought political unity to Germany, some German lawyers developed the same argument about the state in international law: in cases of emergency, the German state (and army) was only subordinate to its need to preserve itself and order: "necessity knows no law."[15]

The notion that the Germans did not follow international law became one of the justifications for the British and then US entry into World War I.[16] Violating international law was, of course, hardly peculiar to the Germans (although the specific nature of the violations in Belgium did constitute more than a mere pretext for war). More important is that the thought process justifying the violation of international law in times of emergency found its parallel in the realm of domestic law. During the Prussian Constitutional Conflict of 1862–1866, Otto von Bismarck, Prime Minister of Prussia, declared that when the representative assembly failed to approve a budget, the state would act to ensure political and military continuity by continuing to use the old budget. The state therefore acted as an entity operating separately from the laws that were to provide it with its lifeblood, taxes. This was the "theory of surplus value" of the state to which Kelsen referred. That logic of a prior state power continued to exist on the margins of political discourse throughout the German Empire, when Bismarck or later Kaiser William II hinted at a *coup d'état*, or when Hindenburg and Ludendorff hinted at the need for direct military control over society. These threats, even during World War I, never became reality, not least because of

[14] Haverkate, "Staat und Souveränität," pp. 76–77.

[15] Heinrich von Treitschke, *Politik*, ed. Max Cornicelius (Leipzig: W. Hirzl, 1897); Adolf Lasson, *Das Culturideal und der Krieg* (Berlin: Moeser, 1868).

[16] James Brown Scott, *A Survey of International Relations between the United States and Germany* (New York: Oxford University Press, 1917); Isabel V. Hull, *A Scrap of Paper: Breaking and Making International Law during the Great War* (Ithaca: Cornell University Press, 2014).

the fear of civil war; in fact, the state did not have this prior legitimacy that underlay the idea of a *coup d'état*.

3 From *Raison d'État* to *Coup d'État*: Legitimacy versus Legality

The idea of a separate *raison d'état* above mere law remained during the Weimar Republic, and found an articulate defender in Carl Schmitt, who translated the notion from constitutional monarchy to constitutional democracy. A more radical critique of the *Rechtsstaat* as a form of state premised on clear, formal rules for the production of laws and for the action of the administration within the bounds of law developed after 1928. Schmitt, working with the leadership of the German army, now openly juxtaposed real legitimacy to mere legality: the president of the republic, elected directly, commanded real legitimacy of the nation, which could only be conceptualized as a unity, whereas political parties in their multiplicity and diversity, protected by merely formal rights, could never represent the entire nation. For Schmitt, as for many other liberals and conservatives, the president embodied the existential unity that preexisted mere constitutionalism and the civil *Rechtsstaat*, the "defender of the constitution," a term directly borrowed from the constitutional jurisprudence of the German Empire, where it referred to the Kaiser.[17]

In *Legality and Legitimacy* of 1932, his last major work before the end of the Republic, Schmitt developed this argument at length. Now the *Rechtsstaat* became the open enemy. The *Rechtsstaat*, he argued, had been reduced to mere form, a mere set of rules and procedures without ethical content, which culminated in a machine for producing statutes. Legality's main purpose was that of "making superfluous and rejecting the legitimacy" of either monarch, or people, that is, of the concrete, factual sovereign underlying the political

[17] Carl Schmitt, "The Guardian of the Constitution," in Lars Vinx, ed., *The Guardian of the Constitution: Hans Kelsen and Carl Schmitt on the Limits of Constitutional Law* (Cambridge: Cambridge University Press, [1929] 2015), pp. 171–173; Peter C. Caldwell, *Popular Sovereignty and the Crisis of German Constitutional Law* (Durham: Duke University Press, 1997), p. 117; Gabriel Seiberth, *Anwalt des Reiches: Carl Schmitt und der Prozess "Preußen contra Reich" vor dem Staatsgerichtshof* (Berlin: Duncker und Humblot, 2001).

system.[18] The procedure for creating laws was purely mathematical, with no necessary foundation in morality or substantive political decision: a majority produced a statute, a 2/3 majority could change the constitution, allowing political victors to deny an equal chance to their opponents. Schmitt's description of the legislative state read like a comedy, where individual, interest-oriented parties plotted, connived, and haggled to produce laws for their benefit but without any sense of a higher order. The parties thereby deposed real authority and replaced it with raw power derived from the ballot box. Schmitt's argument was not directed only against radical parties, it was directed against all parties. His main example illustrates the point: the Social Democratic Party and the Center Party had altered the parliamentary procedure in the state of Prussia to require those voting no confidence (Nazis and Communists) to propose a new government with majority support in order for the no confidence vote to take effect, in other words to implement the "constructive vote of no confidence" currently in effect in the German Basic Law. This act was not a sincere attempt to protect democracy from dictatorial parties aimed at causing chaos, according to Schmitt; it was precisely the democratic parties trying to hinder chaos whom Schmitt accused of using "self-evident means of partisan power maintenance." Parties appeared in his last works of the Republic to be illegitimate as such.[19]

Mere legality contradicted legitimacy; mere legality involved individual rights, voting rights, political parties, pluralism, all of which Schmitt took to destroy real unity.[20] The alternative was "legitimacy." But years before, in his essay on Maistre, Schmitt had noted the problem that legitimacy became a real problem in postrevolutionary society, when it was no longer apparent who the legitimate sovereign was. The state became reduced "to a pure decision not based on reason and discussion and not justifying itself."[21] Where, then, could one start to locate that factual basis of legitimate rule? Schmitt's strategy in 1932 was to break the constitution into parts, declaring some parts merely reflective of the *Rechtsstaat*, constitutionalism, and legality, while others described legitimate rule.

18 Schmitt, *Legality and Legitimacy*, trans. and ed. Jeffrey Seitzer, introd. John P. McCormick (Durham: Duke University Press, [1932] 2004), pp. 3, 9, 10.

19 Schmitt, *Legality and Legitimacy*, pp. 35–36.

20 Schmitt, *Legality and Legitimacy*, p. 9.

21 Schmitt, *Political Theology*, p. 66.

The first part of the constitution was "merely" *rechtsstaatlich*, setting out the framework of rules and procedures for constitutional democracy. The second part described basic rights. Most rights, Schmitt argued, were also formal and *rechtsstaatlich* in nature. But some rights pointed toward a "presupposed homogeneity that is thorough and indivisible." These values were, as part of the factual order of the polity, inviolable and therefore in fact not susceptible to change by a mere 2/3 vote.[22] But what precisely were these foundational values? Schmitt ventured to name marriage, religion, and property as such values, all of course connected to traditional conservatism. The constitutional text, however, both defended marriage and asserted the equal rights of illegitimate children, both guaranteed freedom of religion and also guaranteed the choice of a nonreligious worldview, both upheld private property and seemed to open the way for workers' councils.[23] His "discovery" of a body of unchallenged values, in other words, ignored or set aside the broader complexity of the rights system of the merely legal Weimar Constitution.

Secondly, Schmitt distinguished between elections of representatives and the direct vote of the people in plebiscites. The latter, as the direct expression of the factual unity of the people, was closer to legitimacy, and in it the sovereign people "is directly present and not represented." These votes, which, as Schmitt noted, had to be posed in a yes/no form in the modern mass state, represented a "higher" power than the mere legislature.[24] The function of such a voting process was to neutralize the complex interests and considerations that go into legislation, that is, the content, while preserving the form of democratic decision-making. Legitimation in practice meant silencing and disempowering the many concrete voices of the people.

Thirdly, Schmitt looked to the emergency laws, which provided the directly elected president with extraordinary powers. Just as the assembly of the constitutional *Rechtsstaat* could intervene in all areas of life by statute, so could the president. Certainly some "organizational minimum" had to be protected. But as with the basic values that Schmitt claimed were the "real" constitution, he was not very clear about the content of that minimum. The modern state was at any rate already "total" in its ability to intervene anywhere. The whole point of neutralizing party-based

[22] Schmitt, *Legality and Legitimacy*, pp. 41, 51.
[23] Schmitt, *Legality and Legitimacy*, p. 46.
[24] Schmitt, *Legality and Legitimacy*, pp. 60, 62, 89.

democracy, participation, and the system of rights that limited the state was to reestablish legitimacy: “the total state needs a stable authority.”[25] Namely the president. That the president was also elected by a mathematical formula, that presidential elections in the Weimar Republic were also highly partisan affairs, Schmitt ignored.

Carl Schmitt justified what amounted to a presidential (and military) coup, in the form of plebiscitary rules and a civil service and military protected from political parties, in the name of an asserted, indeed mythic, national unity. In the interest of order, Schmitt advocated an authoritarian, even fascist solution, based on dismantling the inherently illegitimate *Rechtsstaat*.[26]

4 Against Abstract Rights

Edmund Burke denounced abstract rights as a revolutionary form that would undermine the organically developed social and political order of Great Britain. He was thinking in concrete terms. At issue were the rights of hereditary landowners to retain their privileged place in economy, society, and politics. Burke invoked the corrosive effects of abstract civil rights in several famous passages, asking whether Church lands were “to be sold to Jews or usurers,” and invoked a new generation of French “nobility” who “will resemble the artificers and clowns, and the money-jobbers and Jewish usurers, who will be always their fellows, sometimes their masters.”[27] The point of citing the passage is not to reveal Burke as a modern anti-Semite. His invocation of Jews was meant, I think, as an extreme example of someone who was not a traditional elite, to argue against the unlimited rights of all to buy or sell commodities like land, and as part of his general condemnation of lawyers, doctors, stock market speculators, and other representatives of urban society who had power through money. It was an argument first and foremost against rights granted without distinction to all members of the population. In Germany and continental Europe, the anti-Jewish motif became part of a conservative backlash against the general rights proclaimed by the French regime and indeed against played a role in the debate over whether Jews should be legally emancipated in the

[25] Schmitt, *Legality and Legitimacy*, p. 90.
[26] See esp. John McCormick's introduction to *Legality and Legitimacy*.
[27] Edmund Burke, *Reflections on the Revolution in France* (Indianapolis: Hackett, [1790] 1987), pp. 42, 47.

post-Napoleonic German states. When Germany finally unified, Jews were emancipated, and the principle of equality before the law put into practice. The debate, however, did not go away. It resurged in the 1870s, when the historian Treitschke reintroduced an older argument about whether Jews could ever become part of the German nation without giving up their Judaism, or whether they contributed to Germany's "misfortune," and came up again in the decades that followed as German anti-Semites attacked the immigration of Jews from eastern Europe.[28]

At issue was a principle connected with the *Rechtsstaat*: equality before the law. To be sure, that principle was not universally recognized in the nineteenth century in Europe, as the example of the systematic legal inequality of women shows. The very idea, however, that states should follow rules brought with it the notion that rights and rules should apply equally to all for whom they were relevant – at the very least as the guarantee of legal security. Legal equality did not mean political equality, nor did it signify social equality, as the socialists quickly pointed out. But it did mean civil rights. Jewish men should have the right to buy and sell goods just like German Christians, commoners or Junkers; Jews should have equal rights to publish books, join organizations, exactly what Burke and his German followers had feared. The political anti-Semitism that arose in the late nineteenth century was a rejection of abstract equality in the name of national identity (often coded in religious terms), to distinguish insiders and outsiders in communities, and to protect elites.

Fixating on an enemy could serve as one means of creating an "integral experience" unifying the collective, a state-oriented notion of politics. Carl Schmitt's *The Concept of the Political* describes this process in terms suggesting a foreign enemy challenging the existence of a policy, a conception that could, as Ernst-Wolfgang Böckenförde has suggested, be compatible with a *Rechtsstaat* based on the abstract equality of citizens before the law. But it could also serve to draw distinctions among those *within* the polity. In this sense, Schmitt's argument shifted from the state-

[28] Connecting Burke, von der Marwitz, and Treitschke: Jonathan Steinberg, *Bismarck: A Life* (New York: Oxford University Press, 2011), pp. 20–27, 388–397; Amos Elon, *The Pity of It All: A History of Jews in Germany, 1743–1933* (New York: Henry Holt, 2002); Shulamit Volkov, "Antisemitism as a Cultural Code," *Leo Baeck Institute Yearbook*, 23 (1978), 25–46. Cautioning against a clear line from Burke to the German context: Jonathan Allen Green, "Edmund Burke's German Readers at the End of Enlightenment, 1790–1815," Ph.D. dissertation, University of Cambridge, 2017.

oriented conservatism underlying his defense of the *coup d'état* to something else, to describing a kind of mythical "intensity" in society itself that created the political collectivity.[29] In earlier work, Schmitt cited the French theorist Georges Sorel, who focused on divisions between friend and enemy within a country not between countries. Sorel explicitly noted that the absolute division into friend and enemy in the violence of the general strike was possible only because the actors ignored the complexities of modern life that belied such a clear distinction among classes. Ignoring complexity in a sense permitted the formation of a mythical collective aimed at a vague but qualitatively different future. Indeed, *The Concept of the Political* is about both external and internal struggles against an enemy of the collective, which have the function of solidifying authority and order.[30]

Before 1933, Schmitt opposed pluralism because it undermined state authority, and after because it undermined national unity. That meant rejecting the abstract principle of equality before the law: some could not be equal in the interest of order. After Hitler came to power, Schmitt adopted the language of the National Socialists. Already in 1933 he launched an attack against the conservative defender of the *Rechtsstaat* Friedrich Julius Stahl; years before the Nazis required Jews to bear "Jewish" names, Schmitt asserted that "his true name is Joll Jolson." Similarly, Schmitt defended the purging of "*fremdgeartete Elemente*" or "elements of a foreign nature" – Jews as well as socialists and communists – from the civil service. The foundation of the new state was no longer the normative equality before the law, but the factual racial equality (*Artgleichheit*) that connected the masses to the Führer and by definition excluded the racial enemy.[31] Schmitt's 1936 call for the systematic

[29] Ernst-Wolfgang Böckenförde, "The Concept of the Political: A Key to Understanding Carl Schmitt's Constitutional Theory," in idem, *Constitutional and Political Theory: Selected Writings*, eds. Mirjam Künkler and Tine Stein (Oxford: Oxford University Press, [1988] 2018), pp. 69–85; Christoph Schönberger, "Der Begriff des Staates im *Begriff des Politischen*," in Reinhard Mehring, ed., *Carl Schmitt: Der Begriff des Politischen* (Berlin: Akademie Verlag, 2003), pp. 21–44. It seems to me that Schmitt oscillates between a statism and a belief that politics has gone beyond the state, which he never really resolves: his fascination with anarchism never really led him to an anarchist position, more to a nostalgia for the lost state.

[30] Georges Sorel, *Reflections on Violence*, trans. T. E. Hulme and J. Roth (Mineola: Dover, [1916] 2004), pp. 123–127, 132; Carl Schmitt, *The Crisis of Parliamentary Democracy*, trans. introd. Ellen Kennedy (Cambridge: MIT Press, [1923/1926] 1985), ch. 4.

[31] Carl Schmitt, *Staat, Bewegung, Volk: Die Dreigliederung der politischen Einheit* (Hamburg: Hanseatische Verlagsanstalt, 1933), pp. 30, 32, 42.

identification and exclusion of "Jewish" legal thought – associated with formalism, positivism, and the formal *Rechtsstaat* – was a tool both to attack equality before the law and to shore up the National Socialist political order.[32] After 1935, when he had supposedly withdrawn from public life and National Socialism, Schmitt restated the point: it was the "liberal Jew" Spinoza who inserted private rights into Hobbes's *Leviathan*, Moses Mendelssohn who extended the idea with "the unerring instinct for the undermining of state power that served to paralyze the alien and to emancipate his own Jewish folk," and "Stahl-Jolson" who did his work in "castrating a leviathan that had been full of vitality" in the name of the *Rechtsstaat.*[33]

5 The Providing State versus the *Rechtsstaat*

Anti-Semitism was central to the National Socialist revolution against the *Rechtsstaat* and involved replacing the formal values embedded in law (legal security, equality before the law, etc.) with a substantive notion of law that destroyed those formal values. But it was not just about anti-Semitism. At issue was the entire structure of the state that had contributed to a system of individual rights, procedures for creating law, representation of some kind, and a judiciary to ensure that executive actions remained within the bounds of approved law. There was a deep critique that claimed that the *Rechtsstaat* was unable to deal with the realities of twentieth-century society (*Blut*, i.e., the biological foundation of reproduction, and *Boden*, i.e., the natural basis of social reproduction) and had to give way to a different principle of order.

This claim, too, had its roots in the nineteenth century. Lorenz von Stein, whose critical writings on socialism in France ironically helped bring socialist ideas to the pre-1848 German states, viewed

[32] Carl Schmitt, "Die deutsche Rechtswissenschaft im Kampf gegen den jüdischen Geist," *Deutsche Juristen-Zeitung*, 41 (1936), 1193–1199. More on the undermining of the *Rechtsstaat* among jurists in Peter C. Caldwell, "National Socialism and Constitutional Law: Carl Schmitt, Otto Koellreutter, and the Debate over the Nature of the Nazi State," *Cardozo Law Review*, 16 (1994), 399–427, and deeper analysis of Schmitt's long-standing anti-Semitism and rejection of equality before the law in Raphael Gross, *Carl Schmitt and the Jews*, trans. Joel Golb (Madison: University of Wisconsin Press, 2007), pp. 32–67.

[33] Carl Schmitt, *The Leviathan in the State Theory of Thomas Hobbes: Meaning and Failure of a Political Symbol*, trans. George Schwab and Erna Hilfstein (Westport: Greenwood, [1938] 1996), pp. 57–58, 60, 69–70.

the liberal-democratic tradition as culminating in a state hemmed in by rights, its actions defined by laws approved by a representative assembly. The rights ensured, first and foremost, private property: the representative assembly by its very nature upheld the existing system of class rule. As a result, the *Rechtsstaat* and the constitutional state spurred the creation of a critical, revolutionary political movement from below, socialism. For Stein, the solution to this conflict could only come from outside of the system, and from some entity that still commanded legitimacy: the monarch. The "social monarchy" and its administration took action from its position above class society to ensure members of the lower class a "share" or "entitlement" in wealth.[34]

Stein's social monarch, floating over society, finds its echo in Carl Schmitt's notion of a "qualitative total state" that somehow regains its distinction from and place above civil society – its legitimacy in the era of the interventionist state.[35] Schmitt's student Ernst Forsthoff took the argument further as a justification for the Nazi state:

> Modern states, which have undergone the process of industrialization and technological transformation, are states of the masses [*Massenstaaten*] and will remain such for the foreseeable future. Where the population appears as a mass, bureaucratic forms of administration become necessary. For here the possibility of handling an individual as an individual and as an individual case is lost. Justice is to be found in the equality and generality of the rule according to which the conduct of the administration is differentiated. The most obvious example is public poor relief.[36]

Social provisioning was a matter for a bureaucracy, not a democracy. It was a matter for the total state, not for the deliberately limited *Rechtsstaat*. Between 1933 and 1935, Forsthoff defended the dictatorship as the solution to the problem. After the mid-1930s, he, like others arguably closer to

[34] See esp. Ernst-Wolfgang Böckenförde, "Lorenz von Stein als Theoretiker der Bewegung von Staat und Gesellschaft zum Sozialstaat," in idem, *Staat, Gesellschaft, Freiheit: Studien zur Staatstheorie und zum Verfassungsrecht* (Frankfurt am Main: Suhrkamp, 1976), esp. 160–165.

[35] Carl Schmitt, "Die Wendung zum totalen Staat," in idem, *Positionen und Begriffe im Kampf mit Weimar-Genf-Versailles* (Hanseatische Verlagsanstalt, 1940), pp. 146–157; Schmitt, *Legality and Legitimacy*, pp. 6, 35.

[36] Ernst Forsthoff, "Führung und Bürokratie: Einige grundsätzliche Erwägungen," *Deutsches Adelsblatt*, 53 (1935), 1339.

a state-oriented fascism than to Hitler's chaotic rule undermining the state, widened his criticism of mass states to include National Socialism.[37]

Forsthoff would return to these issues in post-1945 West Germany, reiterating many of the themes but in a postfascist context. Again, he declared that the *Rechtsstaat* could not come to terms with the real, concrete needs of modern society, which rendered individuals dependent on state services; that a welfare state (*Sozialstaat*) required a civil service, bound to provide equal services to all, but protected from the vagaries of individual rights, courts, and parliament; and that a strong leader able to exercise personal authority, perhaps in the form of a strengthened West German presidency, was necessary to bind the whole together – a kind of ersatz social monarch.[38] The same motif, juxtaposing order to law and legitimacy to legality, in order to maintain a stable social basis for the state, persists in these last works, even as Forsthoff gave up his political radicalism.

Conclusion

Certainly not all conservatives were National Socialists and anti-Semites. Many, including some who resisted, hated the movement. Burke would have been shocked by the movement's anti-traditionalism. But neither can conservatism simply write National Socialism off as "not really" conservative. Legal forms can come into conflict with the yearning for order, with the result that minorities can be deemed a threat to concrete order and not deserving of such rights. The systematic undermining of the *Rechtsstaat* through a combination of normal and extraordinary state activity, the former for racial comrades and the latter for the enemy, described so well

[37] For further references, see esp. Florian Meinel, *Der Jurist in der industriellen Gesellschaft: Ernst Forsthoff und seine Zeit* (Berlin: Akademie Verlag, 2011), and in English, Peter C. Caldwell, "Ernst Forsthoff in Frankfurt: Political Mobilization and the Abandonment of Scholarly Responsibility," in Moritz Epple, Johannes Fried, Raphael Gross, and Janus Gudian, eds., *"Politisierung der Wissenschaft": Jüdische Wissenschaftler und ihre Gegner an der Universität Frankfurt am Main vor und nach 1933* (Frankfurt am Main: Wallstein Verlag, 2014) pp. 249–283.

[38] See esp. Böckenförde, "Entstehung und Wandel des Rechtsstaatsbegriffs," pp. 76–78, and Forsthoff's key essays reprinted in *Rechtsstaatlichkeit und Sozialstaatlichkeit* (Darmstadt: Wissenschaftliche Buchgesellschaft, 1968), as well as Peter C. Caldwell, "Ernst Forsthoff and the Legacy of Radical Conservative State Theory in the Federal Republic of Germany," *History of Political Thought*, 15 (1994), 615–641.

by Ernst Fraenkel, is not entirely alien to a conservative rhetoric that seeks to suspend rights for suspect minority groups in the name of order and security. Indeed, if order and security are the main aims, abstract rights and abstract equality preserving a realm of human freedom become secondary concerns at best.[39]

This contribution has focused on a radical conservative critique of the *Rechtsstaat*, and used the radical examples of Maistre and Treitschke, Schmitt and Forsthoff to illustrate its points. The radical conclusions sometimes reached were not necessary conclusions. A "slippery slope" argument from Burke to Hitler is just as tendentious and abstract from reality as slippery slope arguments from nineteenth-century socialism to the gulag. There are, however, points of connection between conservative and radical criticisms of the *Rechtsstaat*. Law and rights for both do not always uphold order. Equal rights in business and in politics do not always reinforce elites, or for that matter even produce competent leaders. The challenges of political revolution and terrorism, on the agenda of the modern state for the past two centuries, lead to arguments about the need to suspend the rule of law, even to violate established norms of international law (torture, for example), in the interest of conserving order. Rhetorical attacks on political parties and rights in the name of a mythical, stable totality of the nation, arguments ultimately for rule by a single man representing the nation, have not disappeared from the political stage, and are arguments of those figures whose actual practice sometimes seems to draw as much from Robespierre and Lenin as from Maistre and Mussolini.

[39] On Fraenkel, see Jens Meierhenrich, *The Remnants of the Rechtsstaat: An Ethnography of Nazi Law* (Oxford: Oxford University Press, 2018).

Judith Shklar's Critique of Legalism 16

Seyla Benhabib and Paul Linden-Retek

Introduction

The origins, social function, and the legitimacy of law were life-long preoccupations for Judith Shklar. She was one of the first political philosophers in the Anglo-American tradition after World War II to devote intense attention to the role of law in liberal-democratic societies. In this respect, her work is more in line with European thinkers such as Max Weber, Franz Neumann and Harold Laski, and, of course, her adviser, Carl Friedrich, who was the first to recommend to her that she consider the topic of legalism.[1] From her 1964 book on *Legalism*[2] to her 1987 essay on "Political Theory and the Rule of Law,"[3] Shklar develops a contextualist analysis of law that situates it within socio-historical and cultural conditions, while seeking to avoid the normative skepticism to which such contextualism might lead. This tension between the socio-historical function of law and its normative content are the two poles around which her reflections vacillate, without quite reaching an equilibrium. In her work, "the facticity" and "the validity" of the law face each other as unreconciled dimensions.[4]

In this chapter we first consider Shklar's early book on *Legalism* in which she distinguishes among aspects of legalism as ideology, creative policy, and an ethos of the law. Shklar's critique of international criminal law, to which the second half of *Legalism* is devoted, is being revived today by

[1] Judith B. Walzer, "Oral History of Tenured Women in the Faculty of Arts and Sciences at Harvard University," Hadl. 1902.1/00709 Murray Research Archive (1988).

[2] Judith N. Shklar, *Legalism: An Essay on Law, Morals, and Politics* (Cambridge: Harvard University Press, 1964).

[3] Judith N. Shklar, "Political Theory and the Rule of Law," in idem, *Political Thought and Political Thinkers*, ed. Stanley Hoffmann (Chicago: University of Chicago Press, [1986] 1998), pp. 21–38.

[4] Jürgen Habermas, *Between Facts and Norms: Contributions to a Discourse Theory of Law and Democracy*, trans. William Rehg (Cambridge: MIT Press, [1992] 1996).

those who share her skepticism. But this revival misrepresents the subtleties of her position and needs to be balanced against her full-throated defense of the legitimacy of the Nuremberg Trials, which, we will argue, merits consideration along with Hannah Arendt's *Eichmann in Jerusalem*.

Over the years, Shklar sought to differentiate more precisely between "the rule of law," which she continued to defend rigorously and "legalism" as a mistaken theory and practice of it. The skepticism of her early work was tempered by her more nuanced analysis of the rule of law in later writings. We turn to an elaboration of this distinction in the latter half of this essay.

1 Legalism: An Essay on *Mentalité*

Written in the direct and acerbic style that would become her mark, Shklar states: "This is ... a polemical and opinionated book. It is, however, not meant to be destructive ... The object here is to stir up controversy by a clear confrontation of incompatible positions, not just to upset the genteel academic applecart."[5] Shklar's wish to stir up controversy was not fulfilled. At the time the book was largely ignored both by legal theorists[6] and political philosophers but it did signal the emergence of the singular voice of one younger than German-Jewish luminaries such as Hannah Arendt and Leo Strauss who had dominated American academia in political theory during those years.

With the memory of the Nuremberg trials and the McCarthy hearings in the United States still very much alive, Shklar positioned herself against too much self-congratulation on the part of liberal democracies. Drawing a sharp line between the ideologies of free market capitalism and the political essence of liberalism, she wrote of her work that:

> It is, at its simplest, a defense of social diversity, inspired by that bare bones liberalism which, having abandoned the theory of progress and every specific

[5] Shklar, *Legalism*, p. viii.

[6] Samuel Moyn observes how few reviews had appeared in legal journals, and contrasts this with increasing references to her work in recent years: Samuel Moyn, "Judith Shklar versus the International Criminal Court," *Humanity*, 4 (2013), p. 500, at 500 fn. 43. Early reviews of Shklar's book were: Francis R. Aumann, *Journal of Politics*, 27 (1965), 703–705; H. A. Bedau, *Philosophical Review*, 76 (1967), 129–130; and Brendan F. Brown, *University of Toronto Law Journal*, 17 (1967), 218–225.

scheme of economics, is committed only to the belief that tolerance is a primary virtue and that a diversity of opinions and habits is not only to be endured but to be cherished and encouraged. The assumption throughout is that social diversity is the prevailing condition of modern nation-states and that it ought to be promoted.[7]

What is legalism? Shklar defines it as "the ethical attitude that holds moral conduct to be a matter of rule following, and moral relationships to consist of duties and rights determined by rules."[8] This claim at first suggests that her concern is with moral philosophy of a certain kind and Shklar, who was to write a book on Hegel's *Phenomenology of Spirit*,[9] could have been thinking of Hegel's critique of the legalism and abstract rigour of Kant's moral philosophy. Yet although she devotes a few pages to a critique of Kantian morality,[10] she is not concerned with moral theory as such but rather with legalism as a way of thinking about the law that tries to insulate the law from morals as well as politics.

The first part of her book deals with a critique of analytical positivism – including the views of Hans Kelsen and H. L. A. Hart – as well as of natural law theories. Whereas analytical positivism attempts to distinguish law from both politics and morals by professing ideological neutrality and formalism, natural law approaches set a premium on law and moral agreement which, in turn, is incompatible with diversity and tolerance.[11] Shklar thinks that her critique of legalism applies equally well to both perspectives, but this is not convincing. The difficulty with natural law theories is not the *separation* but rather the *conflation* of law and morals, and even of law and politics.[12] The real target of her critique is the legal positivist tradition and in particular the relationship of legalism to liberalism as understood in this tradition. And along the way, she makes a number of distinctions concerning legalism that begin to blur the crispness of her original assertions.

Legalism is said to be the "ideology" of its practitioners in that they believe that the legal system consists of the rule of law and that law rests on formally correct rationality in the sense specified by Max Weber.[13] For her,

[7] Shklar, *Legalism*, p. 5. [8] Shklar, *Legalism*, p. 1.

[9] Judith N. Shklar, *Freedom and Independence: A Study of the Political Ideas of Hegel's Phenomenology of Mind* (Cambridge: Cambridge University Press, 1976). In her interview with Judith Walzer, Shklar states that this book was one she was least satisfied with. Walzer, "Oral History of Tenured Women."

[10] Shklar, *Legalism*, pp. 47–49, 57. [11] Shklar, *Legalism*, p. 5. [12] Shklar, *Legalism*, p. 8.

[13] Shklar, *Legalism*, p. 21.

this belief is ideological because law's coercive power as well as the fact that it is obeyed by those it addresses are not just matters of legal sanction and legal doctrine; rather the law must be seen to be "part of a social continuum."[14] This critique of legal formalism and her insistence that law ought to be considered in a social context have led some to call Shklar a "postmodernist,"[15] or, more plausibly, to classify her as a precursor of the Critical Legal Studies movement.[16] Neither classification can do justice to Shklar's own account of the relation of legalism to liberalism. She herself tried to capture this relationship in a paradoxical formula:

> The great paradox revealed here is that legalism as an *ideology* is too inflexible to recognize the enormous potential of legalism as a *creative policy* but exhausts itself in intoning traditional pieties and principles which are incapable of realization. This is, of course, the perennial character of ideologies. It should not, however, in this case, lead one to forget the greatness of legalism as an *ethos* when it expresses itself in the characteristic institutions of the law.[17]

Legalism then has at least three dimensions: it is an *ideology*; it is a *creative policy*; and it is an *ethos of the law*. It is indeed paradoxical that if legalism is an ideology it would also be accepted as creative policy as well as admired as an ethos. Practitioners prefer one policy to another and adopt one ethos rather than another precisely because they believe they have good and justified reasons to do so. If they thought that such a policy or ethos were *merely* ideological, they would be less sanguine in accepting them. Yet by "ideology" Shklar does not mean "false consciousness" or "distortion" in the Marxian sense but rather "a series of personal responses

[14] Shklar, *Legalism*, pp. 3, 35.

[15] Steven White, *Political Theory and Postmodernism* (New York: Cambridge University Press, 1991).

[16] Moyn, "Judith Shklar versus the International Criminal Court," 474. Shklar raised these observations about her own work in the Preface to the new edition of *Legalism: Law, Morals, and Political Trials* (Cambridge: Harvard University Press, 1986), pp. xi–xii. She also commented that "*Legalism*, which is my favorite of the books that I have written, went quickly from being a radical outrage to being a conventional commonplace, when compared to the 'assaults' of the Critical Legal Studies Movement." Judith Shklar, "A Life of Learning," in Bernard Yack, ed., *Liberalism without Illusions: Essays on Liberal Theory and the Political Vision of Judith N. Shklar* (Chicago: University of Chicago Press, 1996), pp. 274–275. See also Robin West, "Reconsidering Legalism," *Minnesota Law Review*, 88 (2003), 122: "In the forty years since Shklar's book was published, not all, but much of it has stood the test of time."

[17] Shklar, *Legalism*, p. 112 (emphases added).

to social experiences which come to color, quite insensibly often, all our categories of thought."[18]

Viewed as such, for the "historian of ideas," as she also calls herself,[19] legalism is ideological not because it is a form of false consciousness but because it reflects the inevitable perspective of the practitioner of "mature legal systems," as articulated in, for example, the theories of J. L. Austin, Kelsen and Hart.[20] In this sense "ideology" seems to mean something like the *inevitable presuppositions without which a practice may not make sense.* To use the language of the late Wittgenstein, some rules are constitutive of what it means to play poker or to do algebra, for example, and for the poker player as well as the one who solves algebra problems, a certain perspective is inevitable. Yet this is not what Shklar has in mind either since she denies that what is called the "inevitable perspective of the mature legal system," amounts to *the constitutive rules and practices* of a system without adopting which one cannot be a player or a problem solver; rather, she suggests that to separate law radically from morals and politics is a *choice,* and not an *epistemic inevitability.*

In an essay called "In Defense of Legalism," written shortly after her book was published, Shklar introduced yet a fourth dimension of this concept. "Legalism" refers here to a *theoretical* way of looking at the law by moral philosophers, jurists, and others. It is not so much the perspective of the practitioner of law that is emphasized but that of the outsider who is trying to *understand* legal systems. She asks: "What mature moral attitudes and political ideologies are and are not compatible with 'mature' legal systems? What are the social limits of legalistic mores?"[21] Observing that Max Weber had already discussed this question but that legal theorists have not paid him enough attention, she quotes Weber: "For the lawyer an order is either valid or not, but no such alternative exists for the sociologist. Fluid transitions exist between validity and non-validity."[22]

Nonetheless, as inevitable as contextualization and a sociological attitude may be in demystifying legalist theories of law, can we wholeheartedly recommend that legalism be adopted by the legal practitioner even

[18] Shklar, *Legalism*, p. 41. [19] Shklar, *Legalism*, p. vii.

[20] Judith Shklar, "In Defense of Legalism," *Journal of Legal Education*, 9 (1966), 51–58.

[21] Shklar, "In Defense of Legalism," 53.

[22] Shklar, "In Defense of Legalism," 53 fn. 5; see Max Weber, *On Law in Economy and Society* (Cambridge: Harvard University Press, 1954), pp. 4–5.

while we know it to be a historically contingent perspective reflecting the preferences of a certain social milieu alone? Shklar's intellectual honesty leads her to confront this question head-on. "Anyone who asserts that justice is a policy and that the judicial process is not the antithesis of politics, but just one form of political action among others, must expect to meet certain outraged accusations."[23] But the answer, she says, is that "there is politics and politics."[24] As opposed to victor's justice and sham political trials: "There are occasions when political trials may actually serve liberal ends, where they promote legalistic values in such a way as to contribute to constitutional politics and to a decent legal system. The Trial of the Major War Criminals by the International Military Tribunal at Nuremberg probably had that effect."[25] Is this answer satisfactory? Can Shklar really put to rest accusations of victor's justice ("*Siegerjustiz*") about the Nuremberg trials? Before turning to her account of the Nuremberg trials, let us stress the conceptual conundrums, and even impossibilities, of reconciling legalism as ideology, policy, and ethos. Even in the nonpejorative sense of ideology, it is hard to defend legalism as a *policy* and to recommend it as an *ethos* once it is demystified by the contextual work of the intellectual historian. Shklar's principal objective of reconciling liberalism and legalism remains remote and paradoxical.

Samuel Moyn concludes that legalism "not only does work but must work as *a noble lie:* philosophers, and perhaps associated guardians, know it is false but allow its many votaries to proceed as if it were true because only the myth makes their conduct possible."[26] Moyn radically disagrees with Shklar's somewhat cheery assessment of the influence of Nuremberg on postwar Germany and legal developments. He is skeptical that, having suffered the excessive politicization of law under the Nazi regime, the German people were ready to switch to a more humane and liberal politics, "by adopting a legalism they simultaneously knew was a myth but adopted purely and self-consciously as a matter of political utility."[27] Moyn adds that "[o]ne difficulty with legalist myths – whether it is fatal or not is a matter of dispute – is that the people will get wind of the truth."[28]

[23] Shklar, *Legalism*, p. 143. [24] Shklar, *Legalism*. p. 145. [25] Shklar, *Legalism*, p. 145.
[26] Moyn, "Judith Shklar versus the International Criminal Court," 494 (emphasis added).
[27] Moyn, "Judith Shklar versus the International Criminal Court," 494.
[28] Moyn, "Judith Shklar versus the International Criminal Court," 495.

We have to tread carefully here. For Shklar, legalism is not a lie, whether noble or not. She insists that her considerations "do not imply a criticism of legalism as an ethos or of law as an institution. It must be repeated that the hope is that a greater degree of social self-awareness will make legalism a more effective *social force*, a more intelligible and defensible *political ideology* and a more useful concept in *social theory*."[29] She may have been too sanguine in thinking that a "greater degree of social self-awareness" would not lead instead to a more skeptical and dismissive attitude toward legalism in all its dimensions, but to defend it as "a noble lie" was not her intention. Nowhere are the tensions among these complex dimensions more evident than in her analysis of the Nuremberg and Tokyo Trials.

2 International Criminal Law and Legalism

Shklar was one of the first to address the philosophical puzzles of international criminal law in the wake of World War II. "There was and is no system of international criminal law," she wrote, "just as there are no international community and international political institutions to formulate or regularly enforce criminal laws."[30] Despite this militant dismissal of international criminal law, she reaches the surprising conclusion that: "What makes the Nuremberg Trial so remarkable is that, in the absence of strict legal justification, it was a great legalistic

[29] Shklar, "In Defense of Legalism," 58 (emphasis added).

[30] Shklar, *Legalism*, p. 157. Shklar's observations about the conceptual absurdities of the Tokyo Trials, and her sardonic comments on the work of the chief prosecutor, Joseph Keenan, anticipate many postcolonial critiques of international law in our times: Shklar, *Legalism*, pp. 181ff. Commenting on Mr. Keenan's claim that the "Christian-Judaic absolutes of good and evil" had universal validity, Shklar exclaims: "What on earth could the Judeo-Christian ethic mean to the Japanese?" Ibid., p. 183. But was Shklar objecting to the obtuseness of the American prosecutor alone or did she have a more radical objection in mind such as the legitimacy of holding a trial for war criminals across such vast cultural divides at all? Why could one not see the Tokyo Trials as a form of "creative policy" much the same way as she did Nuremberg? After all, Japan was not as removed from and as uninformed about Western conceptions of legality as Shklar may have assumed. For a recent judicious account of the controversies concerning the legitimacy of the Tokyo War Crimes Trial in the light of new historical evidence, see Yuma Totani, *The Tokyo War Crimes Trial: The Pursuit of Justice in the Wake of World War II* (Cambridge: Harvard University Press, 2008). For a postcolonial critique of international law, see Antony Anghie, *Imperialism, Sovereignty, and the Making of International Law* (Cambridge: Cambridge University Press, 2005).

act, the most legalistic of all possible policies, and, as such, a powerful inspiration to legalistic ethos."[31] While the Trial was a political one in that it aimed to eliminate a political enemy and its ideology, "it need have given offense neither to legalistic nor to liberal values." And "[o]nly because the crimes against humanity were the moral center of the case that all this was possible."[32]

It is surprising that of the three charges considered in the Trial – crimes against the peace or waging aggressive war, war crimes, and crimes against humanity – Shklar should focus insistently on crimes against humanity. Her reasons were as follows: she thought that the first charge against the Nazis was justifiably subject to the argument *tu quoque*, that is, the leaders of states judging the Nazis had committed acts no less criminal against the peace than had the Nazis.[33] Regarding the charge that the Nazis had committed war crimes, Shklar's riposte is that, of course they had, but they had also engaged in acts that went far beyond the Hague Convention of 1907, which the French representative on the Tribunal wanted to consider as the binding document. Shklar, like Hannah Arendt, is convinced that what justifies the charge of crimes against humanity is the *novelty* of the acts in which the Nazis had engaged: "To say that the charge of crimes against humanity was unknown is therefore no argument against it."[34]

In *Eichmann in Jerusalem,* Hannah Arendt had argued that the Jerusalem Court erred in condemning Eichmann for "crimes against the Jewish people" in the first instance and by naming "crimes against humanity" only as the third and separate charge.[35] In the dramatic Epilogue to *Eichmann,* speaking in the voice of the Judges of Jerusalem, Arendt explained what crimes against humanity means for her.[36] Genocide, the highest of the crimes against humanity, is an attack upon the human status and human plurality, which is the condition "under which life on earth has

[31] Shklar, *Legalism*, p. 170; cf. West, "Reconsidering Legalism," 122–124; Tiphaine Dickson, "Shklar's Legalism and the Liberal Paradox," *Constellations*, 22 (2015), 193–194.

[32] Shklar, *Legalism*, p. 170. [33] Shklar, *Legalism*, p. 161. [34] Shklar, *Legalism*, p. 163.

[35] Hannah Arendt, *Eichmann in Jerusalem: A Report on the Banality of Evil*, rev. and enl. ed. (New York: Penguin, [1963] 1992), pp. 244–245. See Seyla Benhabib, "International Law and Human Plurality in the Shadow of Totalitarianism: Hannah Arendt and Raphael Lemkin," in idem, ed., *Dignity in Adversity: Human Rights in Troubled Times* (Cambridge: Polity, 2011), pp. 41–57.

[36] Arendt, *Eichmann in Jerusalem*, p. 277.

been given to man."[37] For Arendt, nothing less than a full-fledged ontological defense of human plurality could justify the significance of crimes against humanity and its pinnacle, genocide.

Shklar says nothing about the legal or moral justification of "crimes against humanity." Undoubtedly, she would dismiss Arendt's ontological anchoring of this concept in the human condition of plurality as a variant of natural law thinking. Can we rest satisfied, though, with the simple positing of a new criminal statute to deal with new and unprecedented acts? As is well-known, the German defense lawyers, both in Nuremberg and during the Eichmann Trial, kept raising the objection of *nulla crimen, nulla poene sine lege* ("no crime, no punishment without the law"), although none went so far as to claim that the mass slaughter of innocent civilians, women and children was a justifiable act of war. Rather, they maintained that the overall criminality of the regime left no choice but to consider the will of the Führer as the law of the land. In that sense, legality, in the Third Reich, meant criminality.

This form of perverted legalistic consciousness, exercised by the likes of Eichmann, clearly was what Shklar herself also had in mind by legalism, that is, blind obedience to orders and the law of the land, no matter how perverse and criminal. Yet by leaving the concept of "crimes against humanity" so unelaborated and philosophically unjustified, she left her own argument open to the charge of *Siegerjustiz*. "As for the Eichmann case it, too, does not really create new problems for legal theory," she writes. "Eichmann, alas, was always a Jewish problem."[38] From a nonlegal point of view, the trial had to be judged in terms of its political value for the various Jewish communities involved, but from a theoretical point of view, the problems being the same in Nuremberg and in the Eichmann Trial, there was no need to consider them separately.[39] We have reasons to doubt this conclusion because without the evidence concerning the Nazi genocide of the Jews, which was not all that central to the Nuremberg Trials, the category of crimes against humanity, hangs in mid-air. In this sense, the Eichmann Trial contributed far more to the project of international criminal law than Shklar may have been willing to admit.

[37] Hannah Arendt, *The Human Condition* (Chicago: University of Chicago Press, [1958] 1973), p. 7.

[38] Shklar, *Legalism*, p. 155. [39] Shklar, *Legalism*, p. 155.

3 The Morality of Law and the Hart–Fuller Debate

The morality and legality of the Hitler regime preoccupied not only Shklar herself. In his famous exchange with Lon Fuller, H. L. A. Hart discusses the case of a woman who in 1944, wishing to be rid of her husband, had denounced him to the authorities for insulting remarks he had made about Hitler.[40] The husband was arrested and sentenced to death, though he was not executed but sent to the front instead. In 1949, the woman was prosecuted in a West German court for "illegally depriving a person of his freedom." She pleaded that under Nazi laws, she had committed no crime. The court of appeal held that the wife was guilty because the Nazi statute was "contrary to the sound conscience and sense of justice of all decent human beings."[41] Hart observed wryly that: "The unqualified satisfaction with this result seems to me to be hysteria."[42] The 1958 Hart–Fuller debate is the hinge between Shklar's chapters on "Law and Morals" and on "Law and Politics."[43] Shklar considers this debate pivotal because if the rule of law is mistakenly understood merely as the equal application of rules to like cases, no matter how foundational or structural these might be, it would fail to register the persistent pluralism of normative values, the historical development of political institutions, and the deployment of public power. Yet for her the exchange is disappointingly illustrative of the regrettably "tiresome" state of debates between natural lawyers and legal positivists, and was "essentially a family quarrel among legalists."[44] Both sides affirmed the "necessity of following rules" but differed about what "fidelity to law" means.[45]

Shklar considers Hart's straightforwardly positivist position to be that the rule of law requires the judge to apply valid rules, as undesirable or unjust as they might be. To suspend or overturn an existing rule on account of its injustice would, for Hart, upend the very framework of legality. As

[40] H. L. A. Hart, "Positivism and the Separation of Law and Morals," *Harvard Law Review*, 71 (1958), 593–629; Lon L. Fuller, "Positivism and the Fidelity to Law – A Reply to Professor Hart," *Harvard Law Review*, 71 (1958), 630–672.

[41] The phrases in quotation marks are from Hart's recounting of the case: Hart, "Positivism and the Separation of Law and Morals," 619.

[42] Hart, "Positivism and the Separation of Law and Morals," 619.

[43] Shklar, *Legalism*, pp. 107–111.

[44] Shklar, *Legalism*, p. 106.

[45] Shklar, *Legalism*, p. 106.

Shklar sees it, positivism assigns to law a value distinct from its morality: a security of "expectations based on existing rules" for which, by definition, adherence to legalist morality as rule-following is essential.[46]

Countering Hart, Fuller famously argued that upholding legality required preserving the foundational "inner morality of the law," even if this involved retroactive punishment or other deviations from the ordinary course of positivistic rule-following in the proximate sense. At stake, Shklar writes, was the issue "whether law can be defined so as to exclude justice or not, or at least whether its partial inclusion commits one also to a notion of a morality inherent in law."[47] She finds "odd" Fuller's insistence of an "inner morality" constitutive of legality and immanent to law as such. Fuller, in her view, attempted unconvincingly to incorporate antipositivist insights into positivistic legality without recourse to the extralegal sources of natural law. The result, in any case, remained the same as Hart's: a pursuit of "legalistic morals," of "equal application of rules ... – pre-established, known, and accepted," in keeping with "the lawyerly habit of treating law as 'there.'"[48]

Fuller aimed to defend his principles as more than instrumental to effective legislation; they meant to express a basic "reciprocity between government and citizen with respect to the *observance of rules*."[49] Notwithstanding Fuller's insistence of their capacity to protect human dignity,[50] these principles were still strictly formal, and Fuller emphatically maintained that legality was connected to justice through form alone. In this respect, on Shklar's reading, Fuller replicates the abstract legalism of Kant's moral theory as critiqued by Hegel, and she chides Fuller for divorcing the judge from "normative and political context within which his ratiocinations take place."[51] Hart's retort – that Fuller's emphasis on law's formal consistency and rule-following were nevertheless "compatible with very great iniquity"[52] – seems to her to be obvious and inescapable.[53]

[46] Shklar, *Legalism*, p. 107. [47] Shklar, *Legalism*, p. 108 fn. 14.

[48] Shklar, *Legalism*, p. 109.

[49] Lon L. Fuller, *The Morality of Law*, 2nd rev. ed. (New Haven: Yale University Press, 1969), p. 39.

[50] Fuller, *The Morality of Law*, p. 162.

[51] Shklar, "Political Theory and the Rule of Law," p. 33.

[52] H. L. A. Hart, *The Concept of* Law, 2nd ed. (Oxford: Clarendon Press 1994), pp. 206–207.

[53] Shklar, *Legalism*, p. 109.

4 Political Theory and the Rule of Law

Two decades later Shklar returns to the distinction between legalism and the rule of law. Again she resists situating herself on the spectrum common to contemporary debates on the proper theoretical formulation of the "rule of law," conceived from formal to substantive, each with "thinner" or "thicker" alternatives. If formal conceptions attend to the "proper sources and form of legality," substantive theories additionally speak to "requirements about the content of the law."[54] Formal conceptions emphasize the proper promulgation or authorization of the law, and many, if not all, elements identified by Lon Fuller: law's clarity, generality or generalizability, publicity, the conformity of law to the principle of noncontradiction, its stability over time, and its prohibition against retroactivity and impracticability.[55] Together, these comprise a set of formal requirements that distinguish the rule of law as a particular mode of social organization. Indeed, "thicker" interpretations of this formal account of the rule of law identify an intrinsic discipline, and what Fuller called an "inner morality" that amounts to a "procedural natural law."[56]

Substantive theories, by contrast, do say something about these matters. Represented most prominently by the work of Ronald Dworkin, these theories deny that substantive justice is independent of legality, for they consider the formalistic demarcation of procedure from substance to be incoherent. They require, "as part of the ideal of law, that the rules in the book capture and enforce moral rights," as formulated in the final analysis by the judge on the basis of the principles of democracy, equality, liberty, individual rights, or other criteria of morality and justice.[57] Such substantive criteria underlie the concept of the rule of law itself, and they can thereby be used to distinguish "good" law from "bad."

Surveying the ongoing debate over precise delineations among formal, procedural, substantive, and natural law conceptions among Fuller, Raz, Dworkin and others through the mid-1980s, Shklar might have parsed these classifications and their frayed edges, pressing questions they leave open or only tenuously answer. But she chooses not to evaluate the

[54] Brian Tamanaha, *On the Rule of Law: History, Politics, Theory* (Cambridge: Cambridge University Press, 2004), p. 92.

[55] Fuller, *The Morality of Law*, ch. 2. [56] Fuller, *The Morality of* Law, p. 96.

[57] Ronald Dworkin, "Political Judges and the Rule of Law," *Proceedings of the British Academy*, 64 (1978), 262.

alternatives as the debate had presented them; rather, she indicted the terms of the debate itself. Shklar argues that the concept of "the rule of law" had lost its political vitality. It had become abstract, shorn of contact with its political, social, and historical context, because contemporary legal theories "have lost a sense of what the political objectives of the ideal of the Rule of Law originally were and have come up with no plausible restatement."[58] The conceptualizations of the rule of law between formalist and substantive approaches is itself a distortion, a product of the problem she diagnosed as "legalism" almost twenty years prior, the misguided attempt to insulate law from the context and purposes of morality and politics.

Just as she did in *Legalism*, Shklar enters the rule of law debate in order to reframe it, to unsettle its underlying presumptions and aspirations. Her guiding question is: what makes the ideal of the rule of law even worth pursuing? This is not equivalent to the question whether the rule of law is a politically or morally neutral concept, whether it is best expressed in formal or substantive terms. Shklar seeks an anterior, genealogical corrective and a reminder: she inquires into the conditions that render any conceptualization of the rule of law intelligible – indeed, politically relevant.

To answer this question, Shklar recalls "two quite distinct archetypes," two ideal types of the rule of law drawn from the history of political thought: Aristotle and Montesquieu. Aristotle's rule of law is the rule of reason in politics, a comprehensive ideal with "an enormous ethical and intellectual scope."[59] Its "single most important condition" was the impartial judgment of the wise, "the constant disposition to act fairly and lawfully" and to "reason syllogistically."[60] The health of the *polis* depends on the mediation of these powers of reasoning of the "judging agent," though they are admittedly confined to a limited subset of the population and, of course, are "perfectly compatible" with the slave society of ancient Athens and modern fascist or apartheid states alike.[61] Montesquieu, on the other hand, conceives the rule of law more narrowly as "those institutional restraints that prevent governmental agents from oppressing the rest of society."[62] Law here does not defend the good life but rather relieves the individual from the arbitrariness of those who rule. "[I]t fulfills only one

[58] Shklar, "Political Theory and the Rule of Law," p. 21.
[59] Shklar, "Political Theory and the Rule of Law," p. 21.
[60] Shklar, "Political Theory and the Rule of Law," p. 21.
[61] Shklar, "Political Theory and the Rule of Law," p. 21.
[62] Shklar, "Political Theory and the Rule of Law," p. 21.

fundamental aim: freedom from fear."[63] And, while in this sense it is more limited in its ambitions, Montesquieu's vision is also broader than Aristotle's, for it applies to (the benefit of) all. While contemporary accounts of the rule of law draw on these archetypes, they are in fact deformations, for they have forgotten "the political and historical contexts that gave the original archetypes their meaning."[64]

Conclusion

The history of legal thought is a series of moves toward formalization and philosophical abstraction that have obscured those original vices and virtues animating concern for the rule of law. What Shklar charts is a story of forgetting.

In the vein of Montesquieu, she indicts the work of Dicey, Hayek, and Unger. Dicey trivializes the original fear of arbitrary power instead as a parochial preoccupation with formal access to established English courts and to the assurance that all cases would be judged only by that same body of judges. In Dicey's formulations, Shklar writes, "[n]ot the structure or purposes of juridical rigor but only its forms became significant for freedom."[65] Likewise, she is dismayed by Hayek's substitution of fear of arbitrary oppression and persecution with a concern instead for the uncertain arbitrariness caused by human ignorance. Hayek's rule of law aims at general and prospective principles that would "facilitate the free market," allow individuals to internalize basic rules of social conduct to minimize conflict and inefficiency, and to do so without recourse to the kind of social planning that ends in totalitarianism. Shklar balks not only at the bare purposelessness of Hayek's rules for "spontaneous order" ("[t]hey adjust, they do not order"), but also at the ahistorical quality of those "unfalsifiable assumptions about human ignorance" on which Hayek's approach relies.[66] And equally, though in a mirror image, Shklar chides Roberto Unger, in his too quick debunking of liberal law's masked hierarchies and exploitations, for offering a facile reading of Max Weber in place of serious historical inquiry.[67] She ties Unger's

[63] Shklar, "Political Theory and the Rule of Law," p. 21.
[64] Shklar, "Political Theory and the Rule of Law," p. 21.
[65] Shklar, "Political Theory and the Rule of Law," p. 21.
[66] Shklar, "Political Theory and the Rule of Law," p. 21.
[67] Shklar, "Political Theory and the Rule of Law," p. 21.

neglect of historical argument also to his dangerous utopianism, which "shows little grasp of the fragilities of personal freedom which is the true and only province of the Rule of Law."[68]

Shklar next focuses on how the writings of Fuller and Dworkin exhibit analogous abstractions that trivialize and deform the "rationality of judging" by stripping it of the "ethical and political setting[s]" in which it might be realized.[69] She notes in particular that their accounts dramatically divorce the figure of the judge from the "normative and political context within which his ratiocinations take place." Unlike Aristotle, Fuller in his conception of law's "inner morality" "did not specify what sort of society would be ruled by such a legal system, nor did he offer a very clear picture of its other historical institutions for social control and coercion."[70] Likewise, Shklar notes that while Dworkin more adequately than Fuller situates his judge Hercules within the course of American political culture, he mistakenly claims for a circumscribed judiciary *alone* the privileged work of "reasoned decision making."[71] If syllogistic judicial reasoning from high principles might perhaps be a model for the rule of law, Shklar doubts that Dworkin succeeds in showing how Hercules can perform this role "considering the kinds of controversies and political structures in which [Dworkin's] program must inevitably embroil the judiciary."[72]

We can draw number of conclusions from this remarkable set of observations. A first aspect to note is that the liberal and Aristotelian archetypes as Shklar sketches them do not translate straightforwardly into considerations of, respectively, formal and substantive theorists. The inclusion of the formalist Fuller along with the substantive Dworkin within the Aristotelian model is the case in point. This indicates again that Shklar resists the received wisdom to systematize rule of law conceptions along the formal/substantive distinction and searches instead for a distinct line of critique, one tracking degrees of contextualism and attention to politics, institutions, sociology, and history. If the history of legal thinking about the rule of law, including recent attempts to systematize this history,[73] has

[68] Shklar, "Political Theory and the Rule of Law," p. 21.

[69] Shklar, "Political Theory and the Rule of Law," p. 21.

[70] Shklar, "Political Theory and the Rule of Law," p. 21.

[71] Shklar, "Political Theory and the Rule of Law," p. 21.

[72] Shklar, "Political Theory and the Rule of Law," p. 21.

[73] See, for example, Jørgen Møller and Svend-Erik Skaaning, "Systematizing Thin and Thick Conceptions of the Rule of Law," *Justice System Journal*, 33 (2012), 136–153.

obscured these dimensions, Shklar aims to recollect and revive them, whether in the form of Montesquieu's psychological justification for limited government and appropriate checks on power, for example, or Aristotle's account of the relation of rational judgment to processes of persuasion and coercive social control. Shklar concludes that the purpose and value of the rule of law cannot be understood apart from the institutions, social structures, and historical junctures within which law is embedded and its authority is to be practically realized.

Secondly, she maintains a creative ambivalence with respect to the uses and abuses to which the rule of law – just like legalism itself – can be put. If her reminder of law's embededness resists the vices of an abstracted legalism, her rebuke of Unger is a reminder of the opposite – of legality's virtues one ought not overlook too hastily. Indeed, this position places significant daylight between Shklar's critique of legalism and the much more reductive critique leveled by some in Critical Legal Studies of legal formalism and liberalism as mere hypocrisy.[74] Shklar's critique illuminates how the move towards philosophical abstraction yields a narrow discourse that is blind not only to the vices of legalism as mere rule-following but also to the possibly virtuous political ends that the *creative deployment* of law and legal institutions might achieve in redressing political fear, violence, and injustice – as Shklar indeed argued was the case at Nuremberg.

Thirdly, Shklar's critiques of Dworkin and Hayek taken together underscore her attention to the pluralism of politics and to the need for democratic political action and they help connect her work not only to Hannah Arendt's reflections on human plurality but also to Jürgen Habermas's critique of Dworkin's Hercules as a lonely, monologic thinker. While Shklar admittedly could not affirm Arendt's full-fledged ontological defense of human plurality, she grounds her critique of natural law in the existence and desirability of diverse ethical views and thus a need for toleration and more inclusive forms of civic belonging. And, indeed, her reproach of Dworkin for his mistaken isolation of the high court judges as the privileged source of authoritative political principles suggests her rejection of the high liberal tendency to entrench law and legal judgment within a comprehensive theory of justice.

The affirmation of political diversity, coupled with a defense of purposeful public action in her critique of Hayek, also point, in Shklar's

74 Cf. West, "Reconsidering Legalism."

understanding of law, to a nascent internal relationship between legality and democratic forms of opinion- and will-formation. Although she was never able to fully resolve the relationship between law and public reason as part of her critique of legalism, in crucial respects Shklar here anticipates, while not resolving, Habermas's positing of the internal relationship between facticity and validity. Responding to Dworkin's Hercules, Habermas denied that the question of normative principles could be anchored in the "ideal personality of a judge who distinguishes himself by his virtue and his privileged access to the truth."[75] Instead, Habermas sought to anchor such principles in the opinions and actions of a broader, politically constituted citizenry, where the subjectivity of the judge could be complemented by the intersubjectivity of a community of constitutional interpreters as part of his discourse theory of law.

Such a move seems in crucial respects deeply responsive to her concerns. Though much of this remains speculative, we might return to Shklar's thought to see embryonic strands of a legal theory that intertwines the facticity and validity of the law more convincingly. Indeed, while it is true that Shklar's critique leaves unresolved the many paradoxes of legalism as ideology, creative policy, and ethos, discourse theory might perhaps shed light on plausible linkages between the medium of law and those deliberative democratic processes of a kind more receptive to political context, institutions, and history, just as Shklar had hoped. And, conversely, if the dimensions of facticity and validity do remain unresolved in Shklar's theory, perhaps we would do well to appreciate that they remain so because of the richness of the way she conceived the different categories – ideology, creative policy, ethos – within which they concurrently function. Understanding her terms, then, is crucial in judging the adequacy, in turn, of the attempts of many contemporary theories to reconcile these dimensions.

[75] Habermas, *Between Facts and Norms*, p. 222.

17 The Frankfurt School and the Rule of Law

William E. Scheuerman

Introduction

Tucked away in a minor footnote to the final chapter of *Between Facts and Norms*, Jürgen Habermas (b. 1929), the Frankfurt School's premier second-generation representative, offers a tantalizing remark about Franz L. Neumann (1900–1954), his predecessor at the Institute for Social Research and its most impressive first-generation legal thinker. In Germany, Habermas claims, "the discussion over the generality of legal statutes is still colored by the rather extreme views found in Carl Schmitt's 1928 *Verfassungslehre* [*Constitutional Theory* (2008)]." This view, Habermas believes, "became influential in the Federal Republic through the direct efforts of Ernst Forsthoff [Schmitt's disciple] and indirectly through Franz Neumann. I did not escape this influence myself at the end of the fifties" in early writings such as *Student und Politik* (*Students and Politics* [1961]).[1]

Habermas's comments provide a useful launching pad for reexamining the Frankfurt School's critique of the rule of law.[2] In fact, Neumann occasionally relied on Schmitt when formulating his heterodox Neo-Marxist account of the *Rechtsstaat* or "rule of law."[3] As Habermas observes, for both Schmitt and Neumann the idea of the generality of the

1 Jürgen Habermas, *Between Facts and Norms: Contributions to a Discourse Theory of Law and Democracy*, trans. William Rehg (Cambridge: MIT Press, [1992] 1996), pp. 563–564 fn. 75.

2 The "Frankfurt School" refers to a group of scholars, including Theodor Adorno, Max Horkheimer, Herbert Marcuse, and Friedrich Pollock, based at the interdisciplinary, Neo-Marxist Institute for Social Research, whose original home was in Frankfurt (Germany) before being forced into political exile and relocating to New York City in the 1930s. In the 1950s, the Institute reopened its doors in Frankfurt, where its two leading figures, Horkheimer and Adorno, played leading organizational and intellectual roles. Habermas, its most important second-generation figure, was Adorno's student.

3 For my purposes here, the terms are treated as equivalent, though there are some important differences between them.

legal statute represented its very linchpin. Unless resting directly on a strict notion of general law, both writers believed, the rule of law becomes meaningless; its various components (for example, the independence of the judiciary) then no longer make sense. Habermas is also right to note that his own early publications, including his *Structural Transformation of the Public Sphere* (1989 [1962]), were influenced by the early Frankfurt School's dialogue with Schmitt. There he similarly interpreted liberal law's generality as its normative centrepiece and, like Neumann, worried about its decline under contemporary conditions. In his more recent writings, in contrast, Habermas has downplayed legal generality, in part because he believes that an "extreme" preoccupation with it risks producing a hostile, one-sidedly critical diagnosis of contemporary welfare state law, where the proliferation of amorphous standards (for example, "in good faith," "in the public interest") contravenes fidelity to clear general legal rules and the traditional separation of powers. Although Habermas still worries about unaccountable administrative and judicial discretion, he doubts that foregrounding law's generality gets us very far in making sense of either its sources or perils.

Yet Habermas's remark conveniently neglects other key parts of the story. Neumann not only reworked Schmitt's legal ideas but also specifically challenged his right-wing antipode's notion of general law. To suggest that Neumann simply imported Schmitt's model of law into postwar debates in Germany or elsewhere is misleading. The fact that Habermas unsympathetically relegates his Frankfurt predecessor to an obscure footnote might lead us to miss some additional parallels between his and Neumann's thinking. To his credit, Habermas jettisons problematic features of his Frankfurt predecessor's approach for a richer, more nuanced account of democracy and the rule of law. Nonetheless, his own contributions remain very much in the shadows of his Frankfurt School forerunner.

1 Law's Generality

While active in the Social Democratic Party (SDP), Neumann practiced and wrote widely about law, working fiercely with other left-wing lawyers, including his Berlin law partner Ernst Fraenkel, to defend Weimar against right-wing critics. Like others – most importantly, Otto Kirchheimer (1905–1965), another left-wing political and legal scholar with whom he later collaborated at the Institute for Social Research – Neumann closely followed Schmitt's theoretical trajectory, even attending seminars Schmitt conducted in Berlin in the early 1930s. Not surprisingly perhaps, Neumann's reflections, while serving diametrically opposed political and normative goals, occasionally tracked Schmitt's. Neumann's rendition of the rule of law, as laid out most completely in *The Rule of Law* and in essays originally penned for the Institute's *Zeitschrift für Sozialforschung* while in US exile, indeed mirrored some features of Schmitt's *Constitutional Theory.*[4]

Neumann followed Schmitt in describing the rule of law as the mainstay of a bourgeois-liberal worldview requiring of officials that they legitimize state intervention into a principally unlimited sphere of individual freedom. Because the burden of proof lies with government, state intervention can only transpire when based on clearly promulgated, public, general norms; everything government does needs to be traceable to strict general statutes. This simple idea could only carry sufficient normative weight, however, if general law offers adequate restrictions on state officials. "It is the most important and perhaps the decisive demand of liberalism that interference with the rights reserved to the individual is not permitted on the basis of individual but only on the basis of general laws."[5] When instead imprecisely defined to permit *any* conceivable activity by state officials, as Schmitt and Neumann accused legal positivists (for example, Hans Kelsen) of proposing, general law becomes empty: it can no longer check officials in even minimally necessary ways and entails its "complete dissolution."[6] Generality therefore requires that "the essential facts to which the norm refers are clearly defined" and references to vague or controversial moral standards (for example, "in good faith," "unconscionable") are minimized.[7]

4 See Franz L. Neumann, *Political Theory and the Legal System in Modern Society* (Leamington Spa: Berg, [1936] 1986). Neumann's original title for the LSE dissertation that formed the book's basis, and which Harold Laski supervised, was "The Governance of the Rule of Law: An Investigation into the Practical Theories, the Legal System, and the Social Background in the Competitive Society."

5 Franz L. Neumann, "The Change in the Function of Law in Modern Society," in William E. Scheuerman, ed., *The Rule of Law Under Siege* (Berkeley: University of California Press, [1937] 1996), p. 108.

6 Carl Schmitt, *Constitutional Theory*, trans. Jeffrey Seitzer (Durham: Duke University Press, [1928] 2008), p. 196. Schmitt's discussion of law's generality is mostly found at pp. 181–196.

7 Neumann, "The Change in the Function of Law in Modern Society," p. 106.

Generality is also indispensable to the separation of powers and especially to an independent judiciary. When statutes cease to constitute "a hypothetical judgment of the state regarding the future conduct of its subjects," but instead are retroactive or so vaguely formulated as to invite judges to single out individuals without reference to some rule, judges become akin to ad hoc administrators.[8] "The *independence of judges* from internal administrative commands, for example, has its essential correlate in the *dependence* of judges on the [general] *statute*. Dependence on the statute means something other than dependence on the commands and special instructions of a superior."[9] Law's generality represents a lasting normative remainder of classical ideas of natural law, ideas both thinkers viewed as untenable in a modern "disenchanted" moral universe.[10] To be sure, even a carefully crafted general rule can promote odious or unjust causes. Nonetheless, legal generality, when properly conceived, provides protections against arbitrary and unfair state action: it helps guarantee the principle of equality before the law and a minimum of basic liberty.[11]

Reproducing Schmitt's terminology, Neumann delineated "political" from "material" views of law, with the former referring to the "decisionist" idea that every measure of the state, whatever its content or character, constitutes law, and the latter to the notion that law must instead embody some striving for rationality. General law, when correctly defined as implying minimal restraints on state intervention, falls under the latter category.[12] Notwithstanding his strict ideas about legal generality, Schmitt was no legalist: *Constitutional Theory* describes the rule of law as a limited – and ultimately secondary – facet of the modern constitutional state. On Schmitt's terms, the bourgeois-liberal rule of law is implicitly predicated on the flawed "normativistic" quest to render *every* facet of political existence directly subject to general law. Liberalism obscures the crucial point that the rule of law can only flourish in the context of a viable

[8] Neumann, "The Change in the Function of Law in Modern Society," p. 106.

[9] Schmitt, *Constitutional Theory*, p. 195.

[10] Franz L. Neumann, "Types of Natural Law," [1940] in idem, *The Democratic and Authoritarian State* (New York: The Free Press, [1940] 1957), p. 90; Schmitt, *Constitutional Theory*, pp. 195–196.

[11] Neumann, "The Change in the Function of Law in Modern Society," pp. 117–118; Schmitt, *Constitutional Theory*, pp. 195–96.

[12] Schmitt, *Constitutional Theory*, pp. 184–185; Neumann, "The Change in the Function of Law in Modern Society," pp. 104–105; Neumann, *The Rule of Law*, pp. 45–46.

state or political order resting on a fundamentally "existential," but not legal-normative, collective decision in favor of a concrete "way of life" that needs to be able to preserve its identity against life-or-death challenges. For Schmitt, law ultimately represents nothing more than a limited element of modern politics: legal normativities mesh poorly with the laws of political existence. Not surprisingly, general rules cannot perform the ambitious tasks liberals ascribe to them, for example, during dire crises or emergencies. When push comes to shove, fundamentally political or "existential" elements of the modern constitutional state, resting on a logic unrelated to the bourgeois-liberal aspiration for strict general rules, necessarily prove more decisive.

Also viewing modern politics as plagued by a fundamental tension between sovereignty (or force) and law, and highlighting the rule of law's unfinished contours, Neumann initially appears to have followed Schmitt here as well. Throughout modernity, Neumann insisted, the liberal dream of a perfectly seamless system of strict general law has been interrupted. Why? Liberal-bourgeois society has never been "a rational one."[13] Even the nineteenth-century limited or "night-watchman's" state, for example, "conducted warfare and crushed strikes."[14] Jettisoning Schmitt's political existentialism for Neo-Marxism, Neumann's diagnosis ultimately diverged sharply from Schmitt's. The irrationalities and injustices of capitalism, not "the political" conceived as an existential battleground always pitting rival collectivities in life-or-death struggles, become the sources of irrational modes of nongeneral law.

2 Capitalism and Law

Like other scholars based at the Institute for Social Research pursuing interdisciplinary Neo-Marxist inquiries, Neumann interpreted fascism as ultimately rooted in the transformation of classical or competitive capitalism, "based on the assumption of a large number of entrepreneurs of about equal strength, freely competing with each other on the basis of freedom of contract and freedom of trade, with the entrepreneur investing his capital and his labor for the purpose of his economic ends, and bearing the risks involved," into contemporary "monopoly"

[13] Neumann, "The Change in the Function of Law in Modern Society," p. 117.
[14] Neumann, "The Change in the Function of Law in Modern Society," p. 101.

capitalism.[15] In the latter, huge corporations possess structural advantages in relation to small and medium-sized firms, cartels and other anticompetitive institutions become widespread, and the "self-regulating" market declines. Extensive state intervention becomes necessary and economic risks are eliminated for many large businesses.

Neumann's main contribution to Frankfurt theory was to chronicle the "change in the function of law" generated by capitalist transformation. Under classical capitalism, the rule of law performed key political, ideological, and economic functions. By privileging statutory legislation, it aided the cause of bourgeois groups that in Britain, France and elsewhere had successfully gained political influence in parliament. Invoking the idea of a "rule of law, not men," it also effectively veiled the fact that "in reality, men do rule, even when they rule within the framework of the law," and that it was the rising middle classes that increasingly called the shots.[16] Finally, the rule of law not only provided a liberal or free-market economy, as Max Weber and others had argued, with the requisite legal calculability and predictability. More to the point, general law directly corresponded to an economic scenario characterized by the existence of relatively equal competitors: law's generality helped ensure equal treatment before the law, a necessary legal component of any economic order committed to free and equal competition between and among roughly similarly situated players.

Despite his Marxist sympathies, Neumann also ascribed a historically transcendent *ethical* function to general law. A product of bourgeois-liberalism, the rule of law nonetheless provided legal protections potentially enjoyed by a broad array of social groups:

> The generality of laws and the independence of the judge guarantee a minimum of personal and political liberty ... Generality of the laws and independence of the judge, as well as the doctrine of the separation of powers, have therefore purposes that transcend the requirements of free competition ... Equality before the law is, to be sure, "formal," that is, negative. But Hegel, who clearly performed the purely-formal nature of liberty, already warned of the consequences of discarding it.[17]

This thesis not only distinguished Neumann from orthodox Marxists for whom the rule of law represented *nothing but* a veil or mere

[15] Franz L. Neumann, *Behemoth: The Structure and Practice of National Socialism, 1933–1944*, 2nd ed. (New York: Harper & Row, 1944), p. 258.

[16] Neumann, "The Change in the Function of Law in Modern Society," p. 115.

[17] Neumann, "The Change in the Function of Law in Modern Society," pp. 117–118.

"superstructure" for capitalism, but also from Schmitt, for whom it remained essentially – and perhaps exclusively – liberal-bourgeois in character.[18] Whereas Schmitt would later *celebrate* Nazi Germany's embrace of nonliberal law, apparently seeing in it the makings of an authentically *postliberal* order, Neumann would instead collaborate with his Institute colleague Kirchheimer during the 1930s and 40s in documenting Nazism's assault on liberal legal protections, protections that in their view represented far more than an obsolescent leftover from a dying liberal era.[19] In their writings on National Socialism, a "totalitarian monopoly capitalist" system exhibiting contemporary bourgeois society's worst pathologies, Neumann and Kirchheimer tirelessly documented the resulting dangers. For his part, Kirchheimer contributed with detailed research on various areas of Nazi law,[20] while Neumann wove its results into his mammoth *Behemoth.*[21]

From this perspective, the central dilemma was clear enough: the rule of law's economic presuppositions evaporated with the shift from competitive to monopoly capitalism. Although legal reality even in classical liberalism never meshed neatly with strict models of the rule of law, monopoly capitalism invited the proliferation of open-ended legal standards (*Generalklauseln),* inconsonant with strict notions of general law and conducive to particularized, discretionary legal rule. Monopoly capitalism fed an alarming "deformalization" of law destructive of a host of auxiliary legal institutions (for example, an independent judiciary). Empirical evidence, drawn in part from Neumann's own experience as a labor lawyer, suggested that the legal trends in question served privileged economic actors; they were typically best placed to exploit law's vague, open-ended contours.

In addition, when "the state is confronted only by a monopoly, it is pointless to regulate this monopoly by a general law."[22] If a specific case

[18] A claim, by the way, that anticipated E. P. Thompson's revisionist Marxist account of law in *Whigs and Hunters: The Origin of the Black Act* (London: Penguin, 1977).

[19] On Schmitt's embrace of Nazi law, see William E. Scheuerman, *The End of Law: Carl Schmitt in the Twenty-First Century* (London: Rowman & Littlefield, 2019), pp. 133–205.

[20] Frederick Burin and Kurt Schell, eds., *Politics, Law, and Social Change: Selected Essays of Otto Kirchheimer* (New York: Columbia University Press, 1969); Otto Kirchheimer, *Von der Weimarer Republik zum Faschismus: Die Auflösung der demokratischen Rechtsordnung* (Frankfurt am Main: Suhrkamp, 1976).

[21] Neumann, *Behemoth.*

[22] Neumann, "The Change in the Function of Law in Modern Society," p. 126.

(for example, a large bank or corporation) represents the only example of a one-member category or set, as inevitably occurs in an economy dominated by giant monopolies, a "general" legal application may legitimately call for what in fact constitutes an individualized legal intervention. Traditional attempts to distinguish general from "individual" law necessarily blur.

This simple observation – since echoed by others – encouraged Neumann to offer a more nuanced analysis of law's generality than the "rather extreme" view Habermas accurately attributes to Schmitt.[23] Whereas *Constitutional Theory* categorically rejects legislative acts directed against specific individuals or cases, Neumann suggested a more differentiated view.[24] On his analysis, non-general legal forms – for example, open-ended legal standards like those commonplace within the regulatory and welfare states – often pose dangers. The Nazi case, in particular, demonstrated their worst perils. However, when promulgated by democratic legislatures where subordinate social classes have gained a say and basic civil and political freedoms remain operative, nonclassical law's dangers can be effectively mitigated. If a freely elected legislature faces an economic monopoly whose regulation seems congruent with the public good, an "individual" measure may be "the only appropriate expression of the sovereign power. Such an individual measure neither violates the principle of equality before the law nor runs counter to the general idea of the law, as the legislator is confronted only with an individual situation." According to Neumann, Schmitt had instead dogmatically presupposed the controversial position "that the principle of legal equality relates not only to the administration and judiciary but also to the legislative power." But even if we endorse a view of general law as binding on legislative action, Schmitt had overlooked something else: equality before the law is by no means "attainable *only* through general laws."[25] That proposition only holds water, Neumann argued, when presupposing far-reaching economic and social equality, something absent from monopoly capitalism. When law-makers face vast inequalities in economic position, equality before the law may instead require, as it had in Weimar Germany,

[23] See, for example, Lon L. Fuller, *The Morality of Law*, 2nd rev. ed. (New Haven: Yale University Press, 1969), p. 47 fn. 4. Schmitt's "extreme view" of generality, I have argued elsewhere, *did* make its way into Friedrich Hayek's neoliberal model of the rule of law See Scheuerman, *The End of Law*, pp. 247–266.

[24] Schmitt, *Constitutional Theory*, pp. 190–193.

[25] Neumann, "The Change in the Function of Law in Modern Society," pp. 125–126.

individual legal interventions: "German legislation between 1919 and 1932 did indeed create special measures with regard to individual monopolistic enterprises."[26]

But why not follow Schmitt (and some radical left-wing jurists)[27] in marking general law as nothing more than a product of bourgeois-liberalism? Why underscore the existence of an "ethical" function that might seem, given contemporary social conditions, abstract and intangible? One reason has already been noted: even under present-day conditions, general law performs basic protective functions. A second, more speculative, reason derived from Neumann's sympathetic interpretation of Rousseau. On his view, Rousseau anticipated the prospect of an egalitarian postcapitalist order that might finally allow for the completion of the rule of law. Rousseau grasped that the supremacy of general law might best be realized under a system of socialized property.[28] Sovereignty and law necessarily conflict within the contours of capitalism. In a fully realized social democracy, however, the tension could perhaps be successfully resolved to law's advantage. In an egalitarian social context absent "differences between rich and poor, between owners of the means of production and dependent workers, between monopolists and non-monopolists," general law might reign supreme, and the legal order successfully cleansed of arbitrary measures.[29]

If capitalist irrationalities and injustices represent the main driving force behind vague standards of conduct favoring monopolies, socialism might prove up to the task of completing the rule of law. Only then might general law express an authentic democratic common good; only then would there no longer be any need for nonclassical law (directed, for example, at a specific bank or corporation).

By day's end, the idea of the rule of law's ethical function was meant to capture not only its protective role within *existing* capitalism, but also – and perhaps more fundamentally – its anticipation of a *future*, egalitarian socialist political community. Only there, Neumann inferred, might we successfully achieve the rule of law. Though a product of bourgeois-liberal

[26] Neumann, "The Change in the Function of Law in Modern Society," p. 126.

[27] See, for example, Roberto M. Unger, *Law in Modern Society* (New York: The Free Press, 1976). US-based Critical Legal Studies (CLS), in sharp contrast to Neumann (and Habermas), has always been much less appreciative of classical liberal law's normative potential.

[28] Neumann, *The Rule of Law*, pp. 135–137; Neumann, "The Change in the Function of Law in Modern Society," p. 126.

[29] Neumann, *The Rule of Law*, p. 136.

civilization, its successful realization awaited the construction of a very different socialist social order.

3 Beyond General Law?

Whatever its advantages vis-à-vis Schmitt's views, Neumann's Neo-Marxist theory built on some problematic tenets. It proffered a one-sidedly economistic interpretation of recent legal development that downplayed the multifaceted causes behind the proliferation of nonclassical legal forms. The transition from classical to organized capitalism is part of that story; other political and social processes have contributed to it as well. Neumann's Rousseau-inspired model of a socially homogeneous, postcapitalist social order is not only insufficiently attuned to the exigencies of modern social complexity but seems potentially antipluralistic. Too many basically orthodox Marxist assumptions about politics and law color an otherwise provocative left-wing account of the rule of law, one rightly critical – while also suitably appreciative – of its possibilities.

To Neumann's credit, he seems to have acknowledged some of the weaknesses. In essays from the early 1950s, penned while a professor at Columbia University's Department of Political Science, he distanced himself from Rousseau's troublesome, antipluralistic idea of democracy as resting on a "perfect identity of interests."[30] Correspondingly, he gave up his earlier, probably utopian vision of an egalitarian society where the rule of law might be rendered perfect and the reign of general law supreme. The strict legalist's dream of rendering every aspect of political life subject to clear general laws, he bluntly declared, "does not work. It never did and never could." Many have hoped, he pointed out, that "our social, economic, and political life were merely a system of rational, calculable relationships," potentially subsumed under strict rules, yet this dream was illusory and not just because of the regulatory dictates of monopoly capitalism.[31] Eminently noneconomic reasons – for example, emergencies in which the political community's security is threatened – render untenable the idea that political life could always accord with strict legality.

[30] Franz L. Neumann, "Labor Law in Modern Society," in Scheuerman, ed., *The Rule of Law Under Siege*, p. 235. The essay dates from 1951.

[31] Franz L. Neumann, "The Concept of Political Freedom," in Scheuerman, ed., *The Rule of Law under Siege*, p. 204. The essay was first published in 1953.

Yet the goal was hardly to concede analytic or political ground to Schmitt, whom Neumann continued to view as a fascist theorist committed to an unappealing vision of a "national community" predicated on the "the existence of an enemy whom one must be willing to exterminate physically."[32] Instead, Neumann asserted, the necessary inadequacies of liberal law would have to be compensated for by other features of political freedom, best disaggregated into separate legal (or judicial), cognitive, and volitional components. Only a political community permitting meaningful democratic participation (i.e., volitional freedom), while offering the citizenry real opportunities to make thoughtful choices about complex issues (i.e., cognitive freedom), could potentially make up for the necessarily incomplete contours of law (i.e., legal or judicial freedom). A flexible political machinery able "to cope with problems," resting on "the education of its citizens," might, he hoped, make sensible employment of legal trends that contradicted hitherto sacrosanct liberal ideas.[33] Law would need a thriving democracy and competent citizens, in part because liberalism's promise of perfect legal calculability and security could never be completed.

Unfortunately, existing liberal democracies were failing to pass the requisite tests. The rule of law seemed increasingly fragile, yet new possibilities for cognitive and volitional freedom had failed to materialize. Until they did so, liberal democracies faced a "crisis in political freedom." Although left cold by various neocorporatist experiments in governance, Neumann suggested that democracy's crisis required further institutional experimentation.[34] Legal theory, by implication, would need to go hand in hand with a critical-minded theory of contemporary democracy.

4 Democracy and the Rule of Law

Well before the publication of his legal-theoretical magnum opus, *Between Facts and Norms*, Jürgen Habermas wrote and theorized extensively about the rule of law. A far more impressive philosophical thinker, and always more attuned to the importance of a normatively robust theory of democratic politics, the overall trajectory of his legal thinking, in important

[32] Neumann, "The Concept of Political Freedom," p. 223.
[33] Neumann, "The Concept of Political Freedom," p. 217.
[34] Neumann, "The Concept of Political Freedom," pp. 220–222.

respects, nonetheless tracks Neumann's earlier path. Like Neumann, Habermas began with a model of the rule of law in which law's semantic generality loomed large, eventually abandoning it for a more multisided analysis. With echoes of Neumann, Habermas jettisoned an early Marxist-based *Verfallsgeschichte* (story of decline) about modern law for the thesis that strict general law's present-day fragility is potentially congruent with a more just and decent order. Whereas the young Habermas directly linked law's deformalization to capitalist transformation, his more recent self has thrown much of Marxism overboard. This shift has enabled him, far more clearly than ever transpired in Neumann's work, to engage constructively with liberal political and legal theory.

In *Student und Politik (Students and Politics)* (1961), Habermas took up Neumann's core thesis: the transition from competitive to monopoly or organized capitalism meant that the liberal rule of law – and especially the generality of legal statutes – was undergoing decay.[35] Similarly, *Structural Transformation* described contemporary capitalism as engendering unchecked administrative and judicial discretion and novel authoritarian types of decision-making. Like Neumann, Habermas interpreted the idea of the generality of law as the linchpin of the rule of law, a concept whose normative potential he highlighted and which he analogously depicted as building constructively on the rich legacy of modern natural law.[36] As Habermas revealingly lamented in a 1963 essay, Marx "went beyond Hegel to discredit so enduringly for Marxism both the idea of legality itself and the intention of Natural Law."[37] Unhappy with orthodox Marxism, he tried to correct for the oversight in part by emphasizing the rule of law's implicit normative prospects. Accordingly, *Structural Transformation* demonstrated how the rule of law and the crucial idea of legal generality not only contributed to the calculability and security of competitive capitalism but also represented the necessary basis for the classical bourgeois public sphere, something Habermas refused to view as a mere liberal anachronism. The liberal rule of law had proved critical to the bourgeois public

[35] Jürgen Habermas, "Zum Begriff der politischen Beteiligung," in Jürgen Habermas, Ludwig Friedeburg, Christoph von Oehler, and Friedrich Weltz, eds., *Student und Politik* (Neuwied: Luchterhand, 1966), pp. 13–55.

[36] Jürgen Habermas, *The Structural Transformation of the Public Sphere*, trans. Thomas Burgher (Cambridge: MIT Press, [1962] 1989), pp. 177–179, 284 fn. 88.

[37] Jürgen Habermas, "Natural Law and Revolution," in idem, *Theory and Practice*, trans. John Viertel (Boston: Beacon Press, [1963] 1974), p. 113.

sphere's implicitly emancipatory promise: "The bourgeois idea of a law based state, namely, the binding of all state activity to a system of norms legitimated by public opinion (a system that had no gaps, if possible), already aimed at abolishing the state as an instrument of domination altogether."[38] As Neumann had earlier inferred, one might begin to conceive of the possibility, given certain social conditions, of overcoming the perennial conflict between state sovereignty and law, or *voluntas* and *ratio*, in the process moving towards a rule of general law "in which domination itself was dissolved; *veritas non auctoritas facit legem*."[39]

To be sure, this ambitious agenda – for Habermas, as for his Frankfurt predecessor – necessarily remained unfulfilled in capitalism. Nonetheless, contemporary efforts at a radical overhaul of the social welfare state could still learn something from it. If a dramatic "minimizing of bureaucratic decisions and . . . relativizing of structural conflicts" could be achieved, the classical rule of law's implicit quest for a political order free of irrational domination might nonetheless survive, albeit in a novel postbourgeois, social democratic form.[40]

In short, Habermas regularly highlighted not just general law's protective and defensive functions, but its apparent status as modern law's *normative cornerstone*. Indeed, as late as 1976, Habermas described the quest for semantically general norms (and related prohibition on individual measures) as pivotal to the intuition that modern law gains its normative legitimacy from "universalizable interests."[41] Though conceding that radical critics had effectively deconstructed bourgeois formal law, Habermas insisted that their critique still presupposed modern law's implicit aspiration to provide a "rational basis" for state and society, an endeavor, he pointed out, that has been anticipated by natural law theories from Hobbes to Hegel.[42] A strict idea of legal generality, he again seemed to suggest, remained that legacy's lasting accomplishment.

This early conception of the rule of law, like his predecessor Neumann's, could be aptly categorized as falling under what Ronald Dworkin famously

[38] Habermas, *The Structural Transformation of the Public Sphere*, p. 82.

[39] Habermas, *The Structural Transformation of the Public Sphere*, p. 82.

[40] Habermas, *The Structural Transformation of the Public Sphere*, p. 235.

[41] Jürgen Habermas, *Rekonstruktion des Historischen Materialismus* (Frankfurt am Main: Suhrkamp, 1976), p. 265.

[42] Habermas, *Rekonstruktion des Historischen Materialismus*.

described as the rule of law as a "model of rules."[43] By the mid-1980s, however, Habermas, had begun to abandon this (general) rule-centered notion of the rule of law, a shift that ultimately crystallized in *Between Facts and Norms*. Why his growing skepticism about the generality of law?

First, *Theory of Communicative Action* relied on research in legal sociology to posit that *general* or *abstract* legal regulation sometimes counterproductively functioned as a means by which the "media-controlled subsystems of the economy and the state intervene with monetary and bureaucratic means" in ways that undermine rather than support autonomy.[44] Inappropriate modes of general law contributed to a worrisome "colonization" of the life-world in social spheres (for example, in the family and schools) where they weakened existing communicative structures. A pathological "juridification" (*Verrechtlichung*) sometimes resulted.

Secondly, his Tanner Lectures given at Harvard in October 1986 directly challenged notions of the rule of law linking modern law's universalistic normative bearings "too concretely ... to [law's] specific semantic features."[45] A proper understanding of law's universal (or general) normative energies should instead underscore general or universal processes of moral-practical rationality operative in processes of adjudication and especially democratic legislation. A normatively coherent notion of the rule of law, he concluded, would have to show how "legal procedures institutionalized for legislation and for the administration of justice guarantee impartial judgment and provide the channels through which practical reason gains entrance into law and politics."[46] Such a view, in any event, could no longer rely on overly concrete ideas of the rule of law that reduced its moral-practical universalism to law's *semantic* generality. Law's generality, in sum, was located *primarily* in the "general" processes of discourse and deliberation undergirding modern law and whose proper functioning provided normative legitimacy.

Between Facts and Norms then relied on a broadly Neo-Kantian reconstruction of contract theory and a proceduralist theory of (deliberative) democracy to rethink the rule of law. Synthesizing socio-theoretical and

[43] Ronald Dworkin, *Taking Rights Seriously* (Cambridge: Harvard University Press, 1978).

[44] Jürgen Habermas, *Theory of Communicative Action*, vol. 2, trans. Thomas McCarthy (Boston: Beacon Press, [1985] 1987), p. 356.

[45] Jürgen Habermas, "Law and Morality," in Sterling M. McMurrin, ed., *The Tanner Lectures on Human Values* (Salt Lake City: University of Utah Press, 1988), p. 242.

[46] Habermas, "Law and Morality," p. 279.

sociological legal theories with normative political and legal philosophy, Habermas built on the core idea, discussed in the volume's opening chapters, of a "co-primordiality" of popular sovereignty and human rights, of public and private autonomy. Although endorsing Dworkin's skepticism about rule-centered models of legality, Habermas did not privilege, as Dworkin's jurisprudence arguably did, liberal rights *over* democracy (and rules made by elected legislatures). Instead, he envisaged popular sovereignty and human rights as possessing an equal status, even as he followed Dworkin in making an ambitious theory of rights, interpreted in accordance with a theory of rational discourse, one of modern law's centerpieces. With the rule of law now viewed as inextricably linked to democratic deliberation and its semantic attributes deemphasized, *Between Facts and Norms* laid out a normatively demanding democratic theory of law. Far more ambitiously than Neumann, the mature Habermas was able to focus his impressive theoretical energies on the complex nexus between democracy and the rule of law.

For our purposes, one striking result was the claim that *both* classical liberal general (or formal) law *and* nonclassical welfare state law deny the mutual dependence – or coprimordiality – of democracy and rights, of public and private autonomy. Like its classical liberal predecessor, social welfare state-type legal institutions rest implicitly on a troublesome productivistic and economistic image of society: they privilege private over public autonomy. Just as classical liberalism favored the *bourgeois*, the modern welfare state too often sanctions passivity and civic privatism. With echoes of Neumann's 1950s writings, Habermas continued to express anxieties that contemporary liberal societies – and their dominant legal types – do far too little to counter them.

Consequently, a potentially more desirable *proceduralist* legal alternative should aspire to "secure the citizens' private and public autonomy *uno actu*: each legal act should at the same time be understood as a contribution to the politically autonomous elaboration of basic rights."[47] Specific addressees of legal regulation might conduct "public discourses in which they articulate the [relevant legal] standards and justify the relevant aspects" of possible state regulation to a greater degree than is presently achieved.[48] The law-maker might select from competing forms of legal

[47] Habermas, *Between Facts and Norms*, p. 410.

[48] Habermas, *Between Facts and Norms*, p. 425.

regulation (potentially including formal and materialized law) "according to the matter that requires regulation . . . Choosing among alternative legal forms reflexively does not permit one to privilege just one of these forms."[49] In sum: "Dealing with the law reflexively requires that parliamentary legislators first make meta-level decisions; whether they should decide at all; who should decide in the first place; and assuming they want to decide, what the consequences will be for the further legitimate processing of their broad legal programs."[50] Citizens and ultimately law-makers would deliberate about the specific regulatory tasks at hand and make meta-decisions about the best way to tackle them. In doing so, they might still opt to employ familiar (i.e., formal-general and materialized) legal means. Yet they might also experiment with novel types of legal and administrative oversight.

On this view, proceduralist law potentially performs a vital political function. If properly institutionalized, it might allow the welfare state to refurbish its democratic credentials while successfully working to "tame the capitalist economic system."[51]

Despite the substantial distance separating Habermas's reflections in *Between Facts and Norms* from those of his Frankfurt predecessor, his reform proposals can be interpreted as a creative response to many of Neumann's concerns about recent legal trends. According to Habermas, only radical reform – and far-reaching experiments with new modes of "proceduralist" regulation – can successfully preserve, albeit in a novel historical form, the noble ideal of the rule of law. Although a legitimate object for social critique, the rule of law, when properly conceived and reconstructed, transcends its origins in modern liberalism.

[49] Habermas, *Between Facts and Norms*, p. 425.
[50] Habermas, *Between Facts and Norms*, p. 439.
[51] Habermas, *Between Facts and Norms*, p. 410.

18 Critical Legal Studies and the Rule of Law

Mark Tushnet

Introduction

The World Justice Project publishes a "Rule of Law" Index. For 2016 the nations with the highest scores were Denmark, Norway, and Finland. Germany outranked Singapore, which in turn outranked the United States. Russia and Ecuador were tied at the relatively low 45th position, but both were above Bolivia (104) and Venezuela, which came in dead last. The Index attempts to measure compliance with what its sponsors identify as "universal principles of the rule of law." These are that "[t]he government and its officials and agents as well as individuals and private entities are accountable under the law," that "laws are clear, publicized, stable, and just, are applied evenly, and protect fundamental rights, including the security of persons and property," that "[t]he process by which the laws are enacted, administered, and enforced is accessible, fair, and efficient," and that "[j]ustice is delivered by competent, ethical and independent representatives and neutrals who are of sufficient number, have adequate resources and reflect the makeup of the communities they serve."[1] Some of these universal principles replicate in other terms Lon Fuller's famous list of elements of the rule of law; others go beyond Fuller's minimum requirements.

The Index breaks these general principles down into nine factors, and then specifies several components of each factor, leading to a list of forty-seven discrete measures incorporated into the overall assessment that produces the ranking. Significantly for present purposes, the first factor is "Constraints on Government Powers." And, also significant, when summarizing the importance of the rule of law "in everyday life," the Annual Report places first the "business environment," and asks the reader to "[i]magine an investor

[1] The material in the text is drawn from World Justice Project, *WJP Rule of Law Index 2016 Report*, available at https://worldjusticeproject.org/our-work/publications/rule-law-index-reports/wjp-rule-law-index%C2%AE-2016-report, https://perma.cc/VKG3-CP8Y.

seeking to commit resources abroad." Inadequacies in the rule of law would discourage her from those investments.

The Rule of Law Index is the product of a project closely associated with leaders of the American Bar Association.[2] From a critical legal studies perspective, the Index shows that the "rule of law" is an ideological project. Like all successful ideological projects, it identifies some things that are, in E.P. Thompson's famous words, "unqualified human good[s]."[3] The rule of law in this aspect guarantees that those holding power (perhaps only those holding government power) not act arbitrarily in adversely affecting the interests of others. Other aspects of the rule of law support the distinctive interests of the powerful, as indicated by the inclusion of property in the Index's list of universal principles. So, for example, supporters of this version of the rule of law invoke it against radicals who seek to replace regimes that fall within some "acceptable" range, while mounting no such objections to similar extralegal efforts to displace regimes outside that range (Iran in 1953, perhaps Venezuela today). What counts as "acceptable" is, again, ideologically defined.

1 The Rule of Law in Critical Legal Scholarship

The corpus usually identified as critical legal studies contains relatively few prominent discussions of the rule of law as such. Discussion of "the" or better "a" critical legal studies perspective on the rule of law requires taking some general themes in critical legal studies and extrapolating them to the topic.

The absence of express discussion of the rule of law in critical legal studies stems largely from the location of critical legal studies within the development of American legal thought.[4] Critical legal theory in the United States is best understood as a way of thinking affected by two features of the historical circumstances in the late 1960s. The first is political. The

[2] The ABA itself has a "rule of law initiative," which is less transparently ideological than the Rule of Law Index.

[3] E. P. Thompson, *Whigs and Hunters: The Origin of the Black Act* (New York: Pantheon, 1975).

[4] "American legal thought" is a category for historical and sociological analysis, and is distinct from systematic jurisprudence. Situating critical legal studies in American legal thought is another way of explaining why critical legal studies gave relatively little attention to jurisprudential ideas about the rule of law.

early critical legal theorists were participants in the civil rights movement and the movement against US involvement in war in Vietnam. They attributed the limitations of the legal response to the former, and essentially all of the latter, to self-described political liberals. One component of the liberal worldview was that the rule of law was a permanent achievement of liberal society. Yet, for critical legal scholars, if that were true, the liberal rule of law had to have some connection to – "responsibility for" – what they saw as the political landscape they confronted. And, because they found that landscape unattractive, they were interested not in examining the rule of law on its own terms, but only in examining it as an ideological project.

The second feature of critical legal theory's historical setting was the strong influence American Legal Realism had on legal thought in the United States.[5] Critical legal theorists saw legal theory as dialogic, with each intervention responding to a prior one and then generating dialectical responses. They saw Fuller's defense of the rule of law as a response to claims by American Legal Realists about the fact, as those Realists saw it, that legal materials were insufficient to generate determinate results in interesting cases. The dialogic response to Fuller was the restatement and elaboration of the Legal Realist claims, bolstered by references to contemporary social theory. In short, critical legal theorists had little interest in responding to liberal proponents of the rule of law on their own terms.

Notably, the critical legal studies perspective on the rule of law focuses on purely procedural versions of the rule of law. Infused with substantive content, the rule of law would become transparently an ideological project. The common inclusion of property rights within the rule of law, for example, makes its ideological content obvious. So would the inclusion of social welfare rights in the rule of law, though of course the ideological content would be different.

The most prominent portrayal of the rule of law in canonical critical legal studies works is a relatively brief discussion by Morton Horwitz of E. P. Thompson's claim quoted earlier. Horwitz found it impossible for "a man of the Left" to write what Thompson did. Taking the rule of law in the same way that the World Justice Project does, Horwitz wrote that the rule of law "undoubtedly restrains power, but it also prevents power's

[5] I refer to American Legal Realism throughout to ensure that referent not be confused with the Legal Realism associated with Alf Ross.

benevolent exercise." He agreed that it "creates formal equality . . . but it *promotes* substantive inequality by creating a consciousness that radically separates law from politics," and "[b]y promoting procedural justice it enables the shrewd, the calculating, and the wealthy to manipulate its forms to their own advantage. And it ratifies and legitimates an adversarial, competitive, and atomistic conception of human relations."[6]

We should disentangle two themes here. One deals with the substantive implications of the rule of law understood in purely procedural terms. Formal equality and mere procedural justice are said to promote undesirable outcomes by making it difficult for power to be exercised – presumably by governments representing the people – benevolently. This theme is consistent with those views of the rule of law that take property rights as a substantive component.

As already noted, though, a conception of the rule of law committed to substantive equality and social democracy seems entirely available – unless substantive equality is inconsistent with the rule of law. Friedrich Hayek may have believed that it was, at least at some points in his thinking about the rule of law. Substantive equality, Hayek may have thought, required arbitrary adjustments of previously acquired entitlements. Robert Nozick later offered a variant in his objection to patterned accounts of justice, that sustaining substantive equality would inevitably require essentially retrospective adjustments of entitlements. Yet, once the rule of law includes rules of change (as discussed below), it becomes difficult to see how those adjustments are in any interesting sense retrospective. Once a law of progressive taxation is in place, for example, adjustments in entitlements to achieve substantive equality do not seem to be either arbitrary or retrospective in a "rule of law" sense.

The second theme deals with consciousness. Here, Horwitz asserts, the very idea of the rule of law entails an "atomistic conception of human relations." This claim was rather clearly influenced by C. B. Macpherson's *Political Theory of Possessive Liberalism.*[7] Macpherson's claim, though, was historically specific; in the present context, we would say that it was about the conception of the rule of law associated with the liberal tradition.

[6] Morton J. Horwitz, "The Rule of Law: An Unqualified Human Good?" *Yale Law Journal*, 86 (1977), 561–566.

[7] C. B. Macpherson, *The Political Theory of Possessive Liberalism: From Hobbes to Locke* (Oxford: Oxford University Press, 1962).

To the extent that critical legal scholars were either embedded within or responding to that tradition, Horwitz's claim about the consciousness associated with the (liberal conception of) the rule of law was well-grounded and probably accurate. It was an interpretive claim about the consciousness then (and perhaps still) prevailing in liberal societies, and supporting the claim with what then (and probably now) counts as empirical evidence is difficult.[8]

2 A Critical Legal Studies Perspective on the Rule of Law

Earlier the World Justice Project's conception of the rule of law was described as liberal and ideological, but also as only one version of the rule of law. For, from a critical legal studies point of view, there is no "rule of law" in the singular. Rather, there are versions of the rule of law, each serving different ideological goals – a "rule of law with liberal characteristics," a "rule of law with Chinese characteristics," and so on through one's preferred list of ideological projects. The reason for this proliferation lies in the critical legal studies proposition known as the indeterminacy thesis – that all legal rules are either stated in such abstract terms that they can be given whatever content their interpreter prefers or are accompanied in the set of legal rules by other rules with which they can be combined to generate, once again, whatever content one prefers.[9]

The liberal version of the rule of law is captured in Fuller's familiar list and even better in Hayek's 1944 version: "government in all its action is bound by rules fixed and announced beforehand – rules which make it possible to foresee with fair certainty how the authority will use its coercive power in given circumstances."[10] The link between this formulation and the World Justice Project's attention to business planning is clear. Hayek's version compresses Fuller's items of generality, publicity, and prospectivity. Yet, that version omits an important item on Fuller's list – that the law be "relatively

[8] That difficulty might account for the attraction some critical legal scholars felt to the approach taken by the Frankfurt School, which they took to be committed to interpretive social science.

[9] For a discussion, see Mark Tushnet, "Defending the Indeterminacy Thesis," *Quinnipiac Law Review*, 16 (1996), 339–356. It may be worth noting that the indeterminacy thesis was either a restatement of an important American Legal Realist claim, or a stronger version of that claim.

[10] Friedrich A. Hayek, *The Road to Serfdom* (Chicago: University of Chicago Press, 1944), p. 72.

constant."[11] For Fuller, the rule of law requires – or at least is consistent with – a set of rules of legal change, as any sensible account must be.

Of course, the rules of change must be consistent with the rule of law itself – general, announced in advance, and down through the list. This is the leverage point for the critical legal perspective. That perspective directs attention not to the abstract and general terms Fuller and Hayek use, but to the institutional arrangements by which the rule of law is actually implemented – that is, to legislatures and courts.

With respect to legislatures, a strong theme in the US-focused discussions that generated critical legal studies was the claim that legislatures were vehicles for the expression of (mere) preferences. If they are, their output might not be reasonably stable but, instead, might be arbitrary. As parliamentary majorities shift from liberal to conservative, wild shifts in policy might ensue. When Hayek returned to consideration of the rule of law in 1973, that was his position.[12] Legislation, for him, tended to be troublingly retrospective. The implication for the modern administrative and social welfare state, pervaded by important statutes, was strongly libertarian, again demonstrating how the rule of law was ideologically structured. And yet, for many, not only those associated with critical legal studies, something must have gone awry with the argument if Hayek's conclusion followed from his premises. The simple fact is that social democracy has not led to serfdom or anything remotely like it.

One place where the argument might have gone wrong was in the premise that legislation was merely preference-based. Some critical legal scholars joined others not associated with that perspective in claiming that legislatures could be, and in many places were, instruments for a politics guided by principles that were consistent with the rule of law. The critical legal studies formulations, though, suggested that even on the view that politics could be principled and for that reason consistent with the rule of law, specific versions of the rule of law would remain ideological.

The difficulty critical legal scholars identified was that, Dworkin and similar scholars to the contrary notwithstanding, disputes over principles were irreducible, in a way similar to but significantly different from the

[11] Perhaps Hayek's "fair certainty" can be understood as a version of Fuller's idea of reasonable constancy.

[12] Friedrich A. Hayek, *Law, Legislation, and Liberty*, vol. 1: *Rules and Order* (Chicago: University of Chicago Press, 1973).

way in which disputes over mere preferences were irreducible. Mere preferences might have no deep structure; there are no reasons to think that people who like chocolate ice cream dislike modern art, for example. In contrast, principled politics in real world settings are believed to have a structure – there are liberals, conservatives, reactionaries, social democrats, and many more. These structures need not have some trans-historical content: at some times and places, social democrats might promote market-oriented reforms, and reactionaries support a robust social safety net. But in the critical legal studies view, at any one time and place the belief that disputes over principles were structured meant that they were ideological – and that that ideology seeped into the versions of the rule of law that were available then and there.

Another strand in critical legal studies accepted, at least provisionally, the critique that legislatures were preference-driven and turned attention to the courts. Drawing on their experience with the common law, they began with the point, obvious within a common law world, that the general rules to which Fuller and Hayek directed attention were not self-applying "in given circumstances," to repeat Hayek's words. Here critical legal studies was a direct descendant of one important component of American Legal Realism. It argued (or, as its proponents would have said, pointed out) that the common law taken as a whole contained rules that, at least on their face, contradicted each other, even if each could in some sense be given precise content. Contracts had to be honored, for example, but not if circumstances had changed, and judicial disagreement was pervasive over when circumstances had changed enough to relieve someone of the duty to honor a contract. That disagreement was not resolvable within the framework made available by the common law itself.

Yet, for some critical legal scholars disagreements among judges were not arbitrary or random. Rather, they had a structure, just as disagreements about political principle did. This argument was associated with the term "tilt."[13] It preserved the ideal of the rule of law, but at the "cost" of treating each version of the rule of law as ideological.

Another line of argument found the concept of "tilt" unnecessary and to some extent mistaken. The "indeterminacy thesis" held that the corpus of legal materials on which judges could properly rely always provided (at least) two answers, pointing in different directions, to any legal question.

[13] Wythe Holt, "Tilt," *George Washington Law Review*, 52 (1983), 280–288.

There were no resources within law to determine which answer was legally "correct" or even "better." This line of argument supported the proposition that the rule of law, understood as a way to constrain arbitrary exercises of power, was impossible: that X and not-X were equally available would seem to be the essence of arbitrariness.

Many scholars committed to the liberal version of the rule of law were skeptical about the claim that judges when applying the law in good faith would reach the one right answer, but were deeply uncomfortable with the possibility of pervasive arbitrariness, especially when attributed to judges. Some responded by shifting attention away from law-application "in given circumstances" and toward the overall set of institutional arrangements for determining the law. The argument, associated with Legal Process scholars such as Henry Hart and Al Sacks, had several components. First, Hart and Sacks and their followers accepted both the proposition that judges would inevitably have good faith disagreements about law-application and the proposition that those disagreements could not be resolved within the corpus of law that judges administered. Secondly, they argued that people in an organized society had a strong interest in accepting the resolution of their disagreements but (from the first argument) that the resources judges had were not in themselves sufficient to persuade dissenters to accept the judges' resolution. Thirdly, they argued that, in light of their interest in resolving disagreement, people *could* accept an overall set of institutional arrangements that allocated authoritative decision-making to different institutions.

The thought here was that disagreements about decisions made at the level of law-application – "in given circumstance," again – could be subsumed into a category "decisions made by institutions authorized to make them," and that agreement could be reached about which institutions should make which decisions even among people who disagreed about law-application. As a notable passage in the handbook of the Legal Process school put it in connection with the overall perspective: "Are the positions which have been taken thus far in these materials conventional and generally acceptable? Might a representative chairman of the Republican National Committee ... be expected to agree with them? ... A representative president of the United States Chamber of Commerce? ... A representative member of the Soviet Politburo?"[14]

[14] Henry M. Hart, Jr. and Albert M. Sacks, *The Legal Process: Basic Problems in the Making and Application of Law*, eds. William N. Eskridge, Jr. and Philip P. Frickey (Westbury:

The institutional allocation that Hart and Sacks favored had a highly technocratic aspect to it, which allowed them to trade on the idea that scientific-technocratic questions indeed did have right answers. The critical legal studies response was the assertion that moving to the institutional level replicated rather than avoided the question of ideology. The aggregate output of each institution, they argued, would have distinctive distributional consequences. So, for example, the outcomes in courts, taken as a whole, might favor relatively poorer (or richer) people, while legislative outcomes, also taken as a whole, might favor richer (or poorer) people. Those disadvantaged by the overall results of the allocations had no strong reason to accept the allocations: they could offer reasons, internal to the account of why specific institutions should make a category of decisions, explaining that courts should be preferred to legislatures (or vice versa) with respect to issues of interest to them. Institutional allocations no less than law-application, that is, had political content, and the defense of any specific allocation was supported by an ideology associated with that content.

As at every prior step in the critical legal studies argument defenders of the liberal version of the rule of law could refuse to go forward: they maintained that there were right answers discernible by legal reason, or correct allocations that good policy analysis could disclose. But even if these defenders went along with each step in the critical legal studies argument, they had one final defense. They contended that the strong version of the indeterminacy thesis implied that well-informed lawyers could not know what the outcome of law-application in given circumstances would be. That was belied by lawyers' daily experience. Lawyers readily identified strong and weak arguments, arguments that were likely to succeed and ones that were likely to fail – and, quite often, without regard to who the lawyers expected the judges to be. The weaker "tilt" version was also inconsistent with lawyers' experience. The answers to some, perhaps many, problems had no obvious ideological tilt, and lawyers knew of too many cases in which judges ruled in a way inconsistent with their presumed ideological inclinations for ideology to be doing much work.[15]

Foundation Press, 1994), p. 113. The work was circulated in mimeographed form for decades starting in 1958.

15 A good presentation of these arguments is Owen M. Fiss, "Death of the Law?" *Cornell Law Review*, 72 (1986), 1–16.

Sometimes critical legal scholars disputed these responses. Even cases with no ideological tilt on the surface, they argued, did have a deep structure with ideological content. Take an ordinary contract dispute between large businesses. The rules governing the resolution of that dispute rested, according to critical legal theory, on basic assumptions about individual choice. An ordinary contract dispute would not typically bring to the surface core questions about what "choice" meant. In the background, though, contract law always conditioned its analysis on the assumption that the case did not involve fraud, coercion, or incapacity. Yet, when those concepts came to the surface, the competing lines of analysis available within contract doctrine showed that the very concept of the "individual chooser" had important social – and ideological – dimensions: ideology determines when one party's concealment of private information from another counts as fraud, or whether refusal to accommodate a party's straitened economic circumstances counts as coercion.

Similarly, whether retrospective civil legislation – making tax laws applicable to transactions completed before the legislature completed its enactment, for example – is consistent with the rule of law receives an answer shaped in significant part by ideology. Classical liberals might find such legislation problematic in "rule of law" terms but perhaps permissible in narrow circumstances, while social democrats might find it consistent with the rule of law in a rather larger range. How much change pursuant to preannounced rules of legal change is consistent with "reasonable stability," in Fuller's terms, is also answered with reference to ideology. On this view, the ideological content of the rule of law would often be far in the background, but it was always there.

Critical legal theorist Duncan Kennedy offered another account of why the ideological content of the rule of law might not come to the surface.[16] He referred to the "stakes" of a controversy, and the "work" needed to be done to reach outcomes. Where the ideological stakes were low, no lawyer or judge would do much work on the problem. Were the stakes to be elevated, or high from the outset, though, lawyers would do a great deal of work to ensure that the result they and their clients preferred ensued. The cases that critics of critical legal studies pointed to as showing that the rule

[16] Duncan Kennedy, *A Critique of Adjudication:* fin de siècle (Cambridge: Harvard University Press, 1998).

of law was neither ideological nor tilted were typically low stakes ones and, for Kennedy, showed us little about the rule of law generally.

Other critical legal scholars approached the question of determinacy in practice from a different direction. Again drawing upon the American Legal Realist heritage, they pointed to Karl Llewellyn's idea that good lawyers and judges developed a "situation sense," a way of understanding cases and problems that was independent of the legal rules bearing on the cases. The practicing lawyer's ability to predict what a judge would do rested on that situation sense, not on calculations about the odds of having a liberal or conservative judge deal with the case, that is, without worrying about ideology. For Llewellyn, situation sense resulted from the ways lawyers were educated and from their experience in the practice of law.[17] In more modern and sociological terms, situation sense resulted from lawyers' socialization.

The sociological perspective explains why there are versions of the rule of law: in liberal societies lawyers are socialized into the liberal version of the rule of law, in social democratic ones into a social democratic version. If there is a process of legal socialization with Chinese characteristics, then there will be a rule of law with Chinese characteristics.

3 Ideology Critique Applied to the Rule of Law

As an ideology (or as ideologies), the rule of law capitalizes on the fact that nonarbitrariness is indeed an unqualified human good. From a critical legal studies perspective, every social order promotes the immediate interests (or values or desires or ...) of some at the expense of the immediate interests, values, desires, or whatever of others. Those adversely affected by some policy need a reason to comply with it or, more broadly, to accede to assertions of power that harm them in the short run. One such reason is fear of direct physical coercion. But, from the powerholders' point of view, coercion may be not be effective enough unless it is deployed on a scale so large as to eat away at the benefits the powerholders get from the order overall. Narratives that explain why those who are adversely affected in the short run will actually benefit from the social order in the long run are

[17] Karl Llewellyn, *The Bramble Bush: The Classic Lectures on the Law and Law School*, ed. Steve Sheppard (New York: Oxford University Press, [1951] 2008). The lectures were initially delivered to students at Columbia Law School in 1930.

sometimes more effective than coercion in securing compliance. Those narratives are the ideologies powerholders disseminate.

That a policy adversely affecting someone is not arbitrary can be one part of a narrative offering reasons for accepting the adverse effects. To adopt a term used in recent discussions of the role of proportionality in comparative constitutional law, the rule of law is (part of) a culture of justification: it requires that adverse effects be justified to the person affected. Typically, the form of justification will be that the action at issue is not arbitrary because it promotes the long-term interests, desires, values, or whatever of the person complaining. And, again, the requirement that action be justified in this sense does seem an unqualified good, at least when the justification is a "good" one in the sense that it provides a credible and reasonably accurate account of the long term.

Of course, different social orders will give varying content to the account of why the policy is beneficial in the long run. That is why there can be a rule of law with liberal characteristics or with Chinese characteristics or with social democratic characteristics. But within each of these orders the culture of justification – the rule of law's requirement that action not be arbitrary – reduces the order's need to coerce. That too is a human good, though not an unqualified one if the social order is seriously unjust.

Purely procedural accounts of the rule of law appear to be quite thin. The indeterminacy critique of some components of Fuller's list thins them down even more. And when the requirement of nonarbitrariness becomes only a requirement of justification according to some substantive ideological narrative, the rule of law is thinned down yet further – perhaps almost to the vanishing point. Yet, even in its weakest form, the rule of law, seen from a critical legal studies perspective, does express respect for people as reasoning (and reasonable) beings. That does seem an unqualified human good.

19 Feminist Critiques of the Rule of Law

Vanessa E. Munro

Introduction

It is a liberal truism that to live as a citizen in a society governed by "the rule of law" means both to be ruled *by* law and to be the ruler *of* law, at least insofar as submission is the consequence of a quasi-contractual or reciprocal exchange of chaos for order. The architecture of the rule of law ideal is built upon foundations of democratic legitimacy and popular sovereignty and, while the task of its authorship and enforcement may be collectively delegated, the fundamental mandate remains – so the theory goes – within the gift of individual citizens. For decades, however, critical scholars have questioned the legitimacy of this account, highlighting delusions of empowerment and the presence of micro-politics that mediate the relationship between what is authored in the name of citizens and the partial interests this may serve. This chapter takes its place within that critical frame, and, in particular, it examines some of the ways in which feminist analyses have posed questions about the foundations and operation of "the rule of law" – as a conceptual ideal, a principle of procedural ordering, and a material reality in women's daily lives.

For many feminists, the foundations of this notional "rule of law" transaction are premised on a problematic view of society and of the appropriate role and functioning of the individual within it. More specifically, it presupposes a self-serving and rational calculation in which unbounded freedom in respect of immediate wants and desires is knowingly and autonomously constrained in the service of longer term, higher order, functional preferences.[1] Moreover, the regime that is scaffolded upon this foundation is presumed to operate in a way that is rational,

[1] See, for example, Robin West, "Jurisprudence and Gender," *University of Chicago Law Review*, 55 (1988) 1–72; Martha Minow, "Foreword: Justice Engendered," *Harvard Law Review*, 101 (1987), 10–95; and Iris Marion Young Young, *Justice and the Politics of Difference* (Princeton: Princeton University Press, 1990).

coherent and predictable in its interventions.[2] The realities, of both life and law, are invariably more complicated than this. Denial of this complexity can have concrete effects in the lives of men as well as women, but the particular nature of women's historical and social condition means that they are peculiarly discounted and disadvantaged by a regime grounded on a veneered rhetoric of inclusivity and freedom. Using legal responses to sexual and gender-based violence in England and Wales as its concrete terrain, this chapter re-visits key areas of feminist consternation about the rule of law ideal, including its foundational assumption of equal participation, relationship to delineations of public/private, and alliance with rights frameworks that often constrain the parameters of possibility.

At the same time, however, feminism's relationship with the rule of law has been complicated. On the one hand, feminists have often insisted that its claims to equality, inclusivity and accountability are unfounded, disingenuous and designed – consciously or not – to ensure the preservation of a status quo in which gender is an axis of systematic and substantial oppression.[3] On the other hand, this very privileging of the ideals of equality, inclusivity, and accountability has positioned it as a valuable tool by which to subject to scrutiny by its own lights, and demand reform of, those rules and practices that operate to the particular disadvantage of women.[4] At a deeper level, this might be read as a commitment to the core ideals embodied in the rule of law, if only it could be made to transcend its partial and partisan operation, and as a rejection of any simplistic opposition to a dominant liberal ideology. Alternatively, it can be read as a strategic appropriation of tools, which – though acknowledged to be flawed – are nonetheless capable of bringing specific and contextual gains, albeit perhaps at the cost of longer-term ideological integrity or disruption to fundamental power asymmetries.

Legal responses to gender-based violence provide a powerful illustration of this multi-faceted and fluid engagement. Concerted feminist

[2] Nicola Lacey, *Unspeakable Subjects: Feminist Essays in Legal and Social Theory* (Oxford: Hart, 1998).

[3] Catharine A. MacKinnon, *Feminism Unmodified: Discourses in Life and Law* (Cambridge: Harvard University Press, 1987); Catharine A. MacKinnon, *Toward a Feminist Theory of State* (Cambridge: Harvard University Press, 1989).

[4] Martha Nussbaum, *Sex and Social Justice* (Oxford: Oxford University Press, 1999); Susan Muller Okin, "Justice and Gender: An Unfinished Debate," *Fordham Law Review*, 72 (2004), 1537–1567; Drucilla Cornell, *At the Heart of Freedom: Feminism, Sex and Equality* (Princeton: Princeton University Press, 1998).

campaigning has called for legal interventions that – amongst other things – mark the severity of gender-specific forms of abuse through robust punishment, ensure procedural protections to rape complainants in the trial process, or protect women from the peculiar forms of violation threatened both by individual men and the broader omnipresence of a "male gaze."[5] At the same time, however, an ambivalence remains in much feminist work regarding the futility (and counter-productivity) of seeking to dismantle "the master's house" with "the master's tools":[6] that is, there is a tangible skepticism which marks much feminist reform activity both as to the ability of law to produce meaningful and lasting social change in the concrete reality of women's daily lives and the potential for state cooption of feminist campaigning in the service of ulterior, and ultimately less progressive, agendas.[7]

This chapter can only provide a sketch of the long, multifaceted and rich nature of feminism's engagement with the rule of law, and its coverage is necessarily both restricted and selective. In the next section, I examine some of the key trajectories and tensions within feminist engagement with the liberal state and its rule of law ideal. I then expand on particular points of contention, namely those associated with the public/private dichotomy, the translation of relationships into a rights framework, and the risks and benefits of responding to "the siren call of law."[8] In the concluding section, I reflect briefly on where this leaves feminist scholarship on the rule of law ideal, and its potential to deliver greater social justice.

1 Feminism and the Illusory Nature of the Rule of Law

It has often been acknowledged and indeed celebrated that there is no such thing as a singular version of feminism, or of feminist jurisprudence. Understandings of the nature of gendered identity and experience, the

[5] See, further, Vanessa E. Munro, "Violence Against Women, 'Victimhood' and the (Neo) Liberal State," in Margaret Davies and Vanessa E. Munro, eds., *Ashgate Research Companion to Feminist Legal Theory* (Farnham: Ashgate, 2013), pp. 233–248.

[6] Audre Lorde, *Sister/Outsider* (New York: Crossing Press, 1984).

[7] Carol Smart, *Feminism and the Power of Law* (London: Routledge, 1989); Kristin Bumiller, *In an Abusive State: How Neoliberalism Appropriated the Feminist Movement Against Sexual Violence* (Durham: Duke Univerity Press, 2008); Vanessa E. Munro, *Law and Politics at the Perimeter: Re-Evaluating Key Debates in Feminist Theory* (Oxford: Hart, 2007).

[8] Carol Smart, *Feminism and the Power of Law* (London: Routledge, 1989), p. 160.

historical origins of and explanations for patriarchy, and the role of law and state in its preservation and/or dismantling in contemporary times have varied markedly across feminist interlocutors. At times, feminism has been much exercised by the existence of these disagreements, with considerable introspective energy being devoted to exploring their implications and seeking their resolution. Many mappings of feminist trajectories have etched boundaries upon the associated approaches of so-called "liberal," "cultural," "radical," and "postmodern" schools. But more contemporary feminist approaches have begun to embrace – albeit with some circumspection – a fluidity across these fault-lines and a more selective appropriation of lenses to suit specific purposes. Thus, feminist thought "is now increasingly a network of ideas and concepts which crystalise or recede according to context and strategy."[9]

Whether the underpinning tensions regarding how best to understand patriarchy, gender identity, the state, and their interrelation have been reconciled by this more pragmatic mind-set, it is also important to acknowledge that – even in the midst of their diversity – feminist approaches share a fundamental commonality in their commitment to explore and challenge "the modalities of power which produce gendered social existence."[10] These may be located in various sites, operate at multiple scales, and find sustenance in material, cultural or symbolic forms. But they are intimately bound up with assertions to authority and truth that perpetuate gender stereotypes or prop up manifestations of male privilege. When applied to the rule of law, moreover, these modalities are often cloaked in the formal insistence that "power is outside law, not structured, channeled or mediated by law; that law itself is a closed or at least relatively bounded system separated from the complex realities of everyday life; and that the legal subject is a rational and autonomous entity separate from and prior to the law."[11]

Shared feminist territory can be identified, therefore, in the claims that women's experiences and perspectives have been marginalized in the legal sphere and that this has had tangible effects upon their ability to engage on an equal and mutually respectful terrain alongside their male counterparts.

[9] Margaret Davies and Vanessa E. Munro, "Editors' Introduction," in idem, eds., *Ashgate Research Companion to Feminist Legal Theory*, p. 2.

[10] Davies and Munro "Editors' Introduction," p. 2.

[11] Margaret Davies, "Law's Truths and the Truth About Law: Interdisciplinary Refractions," in Davies and Munro, eds., *Ashgate Research Companion to Feminist Legal Theory*, p. 65.

The feminist claim, then, is not that women have been completely excluded from the legal form of life.[12] To the contrary, as Ngaire Naffine has observed, "the partial inclusion of women was, and remains, important for the law's legitimacy."[13] The essential point is that women have been recognized as legal persons only for certain purposes and often where that recognition has served to reinforce patriarchal structures. Some feminists argue that this is the result of historical exclusion or "unconscious bias," but others maintain that it results from the impossibility of ever realizing impartiality. As Iris Marion Young explains, situated perspectives derived from particular histories and experiences "rush to fill the vacuum created by counterfactual abstraction."[14] Some feminists have gone further, asserting that claims to neutrality are deliberately contrived to mask the truth of gender oppression.[15] Whatever the explanatory cause, this has meant that, even in contexts in which the law has recognized women as persons deserving of protection and empowerment, resulting interventions have often been "unconstructive to say the least."[16] This is amply illustrated in the context of sexual offenses, where laws have legitimated reliance on socio-sexual stereotypes under the guise of "everyday" concepts of consent and created the illusion of legal redress in a reality in which "mundane" complaints of acquaintance rape still face substantial hurdles to prosecution.[17] Likewise, notwithstanding a positive duty upon states to provide protection, laws against domestic abuse remain poorly enforced and guiding legal concepts and hierarchies of harm fail to reflect victims' own experiences.[18]

[12] Lucinda M. Finley, "Breaking Women's Silence in Law: The Dilemma of the Gendered Nature of Legal Reasoning," *Notre Dame Law Review*, 64 (1989), 886–910.

[13] Ngaire Naffine, "In Praise of Legal Feminism," *Legal Studies*, 22 (2002), 77–78.

[14] Young, *Justice and the Politics of Difference*, p. 115.

[15] See, for example, MacKinnon, *Toward a Feminist Theory of State*.

[16] Catharine A. MacKinnon, *Women's Lives, Men's Laws* (Cambridge: Harvard University Press, 2005), p. 33.

[17] See, further, Vanessa E. Munro, "Shifting Sands: Consent, Context and Vulnerability in Contemporary Sexual Offences Policy in England and Wales," *Social and Legal Studies*, 26 (2017), 417.

[18] See, for example, Charlotte Bishop and Vanessa Bettison, "Evidencing Domestic Violence, Including Behaviour that Falls Under the New Offence of Controlling or Coercive Behaviour," *International Journal of Evidence and Proof*, 22 (2017), 3; Vanessa E. Munro and Ruth Aitken, "Adding Insult to Injury? The Criminal Law's Response to Domestic Abuse Related Suicide in England and Wales," *Criminal Law Review*, 9 (2018), 732–741.

These concrete points of law's engagement with a gendered reality of precarity and violence illustrate the ways in which women's everyday experiences have been relegated to the periphery of the legal imaginary. Those who promote their inclusion have often encountered significant and structural obstacles to rendering them intelligible and of sufficient priority to male "others." For its feminist critics, the rule of law's averred commitment to impartial and rational regulation for the common good plays a pivotal role in masking, legitimating and maintaining this exclusion. In all its guises, feminist scholarship highlights the choices that underpin law's official story of coherence and neutrality. This scholarship promotes "an intellectual and political strategy – of exposing law's indeterminacy, of emphasizing its contingency, and of finding resources for its reconstruction in those doctrinal principles and discursive images which are less dominant, yet which fracture and complicate the seamless web imagined by orthodox legal scholarship."[19] But just as it would be inappropriate to solidify rigidly the contours of disagreement that mediate the broad terrain of feminist critique, so too it would do an injustice to the complexity of feminist engagement to *necessarily* cement it in opposition to the values, if not the historical and current practices, of liberalism and the rule of law.

Indeed, Martha Nussbaum has insisted that "the deepest and most central ideals of the liberal tradition are ideas of radical force and great theoretical and practical value ... although liberalism needs to learn from feminism if it is to formulate its own central insights in a fully adequate manner."[20] Similarly, scholars such as Susan Moller Okin and Drucilla Cornell have pointed to the productive potential of core liberal devices and ideals – including John Rawls's veil of ignorance and Ronald Dworkin's commitment to equal respect – which they suggest can be rescued and repurposed in pursuit of feminist objectives.[21] In previous work, I have also explored the feminist potential within liberalism, were it to be called upon in a more meaningful, situated and critically informed way, to live up to its averred ideals of democratic accountability, equality,

[19] Lacey, *Unspeakable Subjects*, p. 11. [20] Nussbaum, *Sex and Social Justice*, p. 56.

[21] Susan Muller Okin, "Reason and Feeling in Thinking about Justice," *Ethics*, 99 (1989), 229; Okin, "Justice and Gender," 1537; Cornell, *At the Heart of Freedom*.

and transparency.[22] To this extent, while feminism has every reason to be suspicious of the promises that the "rule of law" makes, it may also find itself hard-pressed to deny their attraction and should be cautious about jettisoning them, whether as ultimate goals or as high-political-currency vehicles for strategic gains.

The power potentially to be harnessed through such strategic and substantive engagement with the trappings of the rule of law is illustrated by various "feminist judgment" projects. Originating in the innovations of the Women's Court of Canada,[23] there has been an explosion of such engagements across jurisdictions or regions, including the United Kingdom, Australia, the United States, India and Africa.[24] Though the projects have varied in method and orientation, all involve feminists taking on the role of the judge. Pushing at the boundaries of the intelligibility of existing norms and practices in order to increase feminist resonance and relevance, authors have highlighted the choices made in the judgment process and the extent to which more progressive feminist outcomes could have been secured without breach of precedent, principle or policy. Though designed as a critique of the limits of legal liberalism, these projects also restore the potential for an alternative future still bound by a commitment to the rule of law.

In the following sections, I explore in more detail this dynamic and iterative relationship between critique and construction in contemporary feminist thought, focusing on three areas at the heart of the rule of law ideal and its operation: namely the public/private distinction, the regulation of individual relations through rights, and the faith in legal intervention to produce change.

[22] Munro, *Law and Politics at the Perimeter.*

[23] See, for example, Women's Court of Canada, "Native Women's Association of Canada v Canada," *Canadian Journal of Women and the Law*, 18 (2006), 76.

[24] Rosemary Hunter, Clare McGlynn, and Erika Rackley, eds., *Feminist Judgments: From Theory to Practice* (Oxford: Hart, 2010); H. Douglas et al., *Australian Feminist Judgments: Righting and Rewriting Law* (Oxford: Hart, 2014); Kathryn M. Stanchi, Linda L. Berger, and Bridget J. Crawford, eds., *Feminist Judgments: Rewritten Opinions of the United States Supreme Court* (Cambridge: Cambridge University Press, 2016); Máiréad Enright, Julie McCandless, and Aoife O'Donoghue, *Northern/Irish Feminist Judgments: Judges' Troubles and the Gendered Politics of Identity* (Oxford: Hart, 2017); Elisabeth McDonald et al., eds., *Feminist Judgments of Aotearoa New Zealand Te Rino: A Two Stranded Rope* (Oxford: Hart, 2017); Sharon Cowan, Chloë Kennedy, and Vanessa E. Munro, eds., *Scottish Feminist Judgments: (Re)Creating Law from the Outside In* (Oxford: Hart, 2019); Loveday Hodson and Troy Lavers, eds., *Feminist Judgments in International Law* (Oxford: Hart, 2019).

2 Public, Private, and Privilege in the Rule of Law

The exclusion or marginalization of women's experiences, which many feminist critics suggest has been masked by the rule of law ideology, often maps onto the structurally aligned notion of a distinction between public and private spheres. In an account in which a legal system is maintained by self-interested, autonomous individuals keen to maximise their ability to secure goals through an orchestrated social order, it is axiomatic that the state which oversees this legal system should restrict its interventions to those fields of activity in which citizen-agents interact with potentially competing objectives and interests. A corollary is that the state refrains from interfering in areas of life where there are no competing interest-bearers and/or where alternative forms of more localized ordering suffice to ensure functionality and value. In liberal terms, this has been translated into the conventional mantra that there is, and ought to remain, a distinction between so-called public and private spheres, and that the state's involvement should be limited to the former in order to maximize one's individual freedom in the latter.

Across feminist accounts, there are diverse views about the benefits and burdens associated with state intervention in women's lives. Drucilla Cornell's insistence upon an "imaginary domain" prior to law in which women have a meaningful freedom for self-determination, for example, endorses something akin to the conventional liberal logic.[25] But Martha Fineman's focus upon the innate vulnerability of the human condition calls for far greater intervention by the "responsive state" into the intimate terrain of people's daily lives.[26] These diverse accounts are framed, no doubt, by alternative visions in respect of the potential of the state to produce progressive outcomes, which will be taken up in the penultimate section. But what these, and other, feminist accounts agree on is the fundamentally constructed, artificial and political nature of the positioning of relationships, experiences, and opportunities across the public/private divide. In the words of Margot Young:

[25] Drucilla Cornell, *The Imaginary Domain: Abortion, Pornography and Sexual Harassment* (New York: Routledge, 1995).

[26] Martha Albertson Fineman, "The Vulnerable Subject: Anchoring Equality in the Human Condition," *Yale Journal of Law and Feminism*, 20 (2008), 1–23; Martha Albertson Fineman, "The Vulnerable Subject and the Responsive State," *Emory Law Journal*, 60 (2010), 251–275.

> preoccupied with the legitimacy of the coercive exercise of collective, central power over the free and autonomous individual, liberalism anxiously draws a line between public and private spheres. The public is the sphere open to configuration and regulation by collective power, to state authority; presented within the private are intimate and personal matters subject only to the mastery of the individual: heart and hearth, kith and kin … The divide is slippery, but functional in its ambiguity and manipulability.[27]

The boundaries of what constitute "public" and "private" may be presented as inevitable and natural; but under a feminist analysis it emerges either as reflective of unconscious bias and male privilege or of deliberate and systemic gender oppression. Those with power in society, mostly men, have typically relegated sexual and familial situations, in which women are often most vulnerable, to the private sphere. Reflective of that, the enforcement protocols and cultural values of state agencies – from criminal justice to health and social welfare – have been reluctant to investigate, take seriously and intervene in forms of physical and sexual abuse which occur in the family home or within domestic relationships, particularly those that fit the hetero-normative marriage or nuclear family frame.

A number of high-profile initiatives in England and Wales have sought to dislodge the primacy of the stranger rape within the popular and penal imagination, to encourage reporting of sexual and physical abuse irrespective of the context in which it takes place, to highlight the debilitating nature of coercive control as a non-physical form of domestic abuse, and to improve systems of multi-agency risk assessment and safety planning for domestic violence victims. But well-documented difficulties remain: attitudes which construct hierarchies of victimhood and rely on myths and misconceptions regarding gender and gendered violence have proven tenacious, resources for support services and police enforcement have shrunk in the face of austerity politics, and there is little confidence that the violence which continues to be perpetrated against women in households is adequately reported, prosecuted or punished. Though we have moved from an era in which a gentleman's home was his castle, and those who lived within it his private property, to a situation in which the state purports to address the harms that occur in the domestic sphere, the

[27] Margot E. Young, "Gender and Terrain: Feminists Theorize Citizenship," in Davies and Munro, eds., *Ashgate Research Companion to Feminist Legal Theory*, p. 184.

reality is that abuse experienced behind closed doors often remains invisible and goes unpunished.

But the solution to this does not lie merely or necessarily in marching onwards with the imposition of "public sphere" values, such as rights, justice and equality, upon domestic settings. This will produce progressive outcomes only if the surrounding infrastructure is in place to enable individuals to recognize themselves as the bearers of rights, identify their experiences as reflections of a broader inequality, and have access to sufficient resources for survival, let alone flourishing, outside the family. The retraction of the welfare state has brought these concerns into sharp relief. We have recently "witnessed the retrenchment of the welfare state, the dismantling of social programmes, the privatization of public assets and services, and the expansion of the market and voluntary sector to take over many welfare state functions, but under significantly different conditions."[28] Not only has this diminished the baseline resources available from the state, it has encouraged more individualized forms of problem-solving in which victims of abuse are expected to "take responsibility," for example, by attenuating personal vulnerabilities, taking safety precautions, reporting to the authorities immediately, and being a credible and relatable witness.[29] As Fine and Weis put it, "public sites of help have been appropriated into sites of surveillance" and responsibility for justice in the private sphere has often thereby been thrust "onto the bodies and souls of girls and women."[30] To this extent, permeating the constructed boundaries of the private sphere with the public gaze produces mixed results in the lives of individual women; it provides an avenue for challenging injustice, compelling protection, and punishing perpetrators, but it also invites a new infrastructure of surveillance and regulation, in a context of arguably diminishing resources for meaningful forms of rehabilitation.

The operation of the private sphere, of course, is not the only side of this dualism to be impacted by its deconstruction. "While some feminists have

[28] Rosemary Hunter, "Contesting the Dominant Paradigm: Feminist Critiques of Liberal Legalism," in Davies and Munro, eds., *Ashgate Research Companion to Feminist Legal Theory*, p. 20.

[29] Bumiller, *In an Abusive*; Munro, "Violence Against Women, 'Victimhood' and the (Neo) Liberal State," pp. 233–248.

[30] Michelle Fine and Lois Weis, "Disappearing Acts: The State and Violence Against Women in the Twentieth Century," *Signs*, 25 (2000), p. 1144.

argued that the damaging effects of the public/private distinction for women may be overcome by extending the 'public' values of justice, rights and equality to areas traditionally designated as 'private,'" notes Rosemary Hunter, "others have made the reverse argument, that values traditionally associated with the 'private', such as care, connection and empathy, should be extended to the public sphere."[31] In this respect, feminist attention has often been targeted at what might be characterized as the paradigm instrument of public ordering within the liberal frame: the rights-bearing individual. In the next section, I explore the ways in which this has been interrogated by feminist commentators, and its implications for a rule of law ideology constituted by, and constitutive of, such rights discourse.

3 Rights, Rules, and Reconstruction

The rule of law seeks to treat citizens equally, irrespective of status, power or resource. In a world in which access to such things is unevenly distributed, the transactional rationality of the many may support preserving this operational principle, albeit that its realization to date has been somewhat lacking (including in particular in respect of gender equality). Framing each individual as an abstract rights-bearer with an entitlement to receive equal respect and protection in exchange for reciprocal duties and responsibilities can facilitate this. Thus, the link between rights and the rule of law, within the liberal legal imaginary at least, is both descriptive *and* normative. Citizens hold and exercise rights because they hold equal interest in a collective enterprise and because that collective enterprise is directed by the state only on the basis of their consent.

But the way in which rights, and the interrelation between rights-bearers, have been conceptualized by the state remains a source of feminist concern. Liberal legalism, it is argued, has purported to analyze and address social problems by removing actors from their everyday environments, stripping them of the characteristics and relationships that influence their choices, and placing them in a sterile legal world where complex dilemmas are resolved by detached models of distributive justice. This, critics maintain, generates a hollow conception that fails to reflect the

[31] Hunter, "Contesting the Dominant Paradigm: Feminist Critiques of Liberal Legalism," p. 21.

realities of human subjectivity and perpetuates an unrealistic model for social justice. Such an atomistic vision sits at odds with the reality of our daily lives in which we do attribute significance to community and cannot fail to be interdependently situated in relational networks. Moreover, while the extent to which this connectivity is to be celebrated or lamented is much debated amongst feminist commentators, in a context in which women often find themselves particularly and peculiarly tied to the lives of others, it has had especially deleterious effects on their ability to see themselves within, and exercise the entitlements that arise from, an identity as a rights-bearer.

Feminist engagement with the notion of rights has therefore operated at two related levels. In more abstract terms, feminists have argued that a collective enterprise in which self-interested claims are enforced with a violence upon the vanquished (albeit within the trappings of rational, neutral and rule-bound procedural propriety) does not recognize the ethical engagements that ought to inform our conceptions of justice. Specifically, it does a disservice to the potential inherent in us all for a greater sense of community. As Robin West puts it, "if it is true ... that the act of caring for others to whom we are connected in some way is central to our moral lives, then our capacity for care should be at the centre of our understanding of our public and legal, as well as private and personal, virtues, and ... it should be central to the meaning of legal justice."[32] Thus, we should focus on reconciliation, communication, and empathy rather than entitlement, competition and self-interest; and legal systems should instill these values alongside those of equality and accountability. But this celebration of care, and the sacrifices that it calls for in the lives of many women, should not be uncritically valorized. Care, connection and compromise may have their virtues, but if they reflect a way of being made attractive to women primarily for its compatibility with traditional gender roles, and its associated potential to offer (limited) access to power within the constraints of patriarchal structures, they too require careful and critical attention to everyday lived experiences, micro-politics and broader structural dynamics.[33] Without this, it is impossible to

[32] Robin West, *Caring for Justice* (New York: New York University Press, 1997), p. 9.

[33] MacKinnon, for example, has questioned whether "women value care because men have valued us according to the care we give them" and "women think in relational terms becase our existence is defined in relation to men." See MacKinnon, *Feminism Unmodified*, p. 39.

know whether celebrating connection is to cement suppression, lauding care is to silence abuse, and advocating a concern for others is to prevent self-determination.

This speaks to the second level of feminist engagement, which examines how rights claims do, and do not, serve to empower women in individual contexts. A core concern here has related to whether rights analyses tend to (over)simplify complex power relations in ways that present them as amenable to legal solution, but which ultimately fail to engage with the problem as understood and experienced by those most affected and leave structural inequalities unchallenged.[34] Take, for example, the situation of a woman subjected to physical or sexual abuse by her cohabiting partner. Affording her the right not to be raped or beaten may be of little use if her partner's emotional or economic dominance within the relationship (or indeed the emotional or economic dominance of men in society more broadly) is not addressed. Though courts are often empowered to interfere with property entitlements to compel an abusive partner to vacate his home in preference for the victim, this is generally perceived to be a "draconian" and exceptional intervention; and in any event, petitioning for it may be beyond the financial and emotional means of many abused women. Moreover, while this may solve a problem framed in terms of wanting to be rid of an abusive partner, it renders unintelligible any desire to prevent violence whilst preserving the relationship. Thus, the right not to be abused may be both limited and limiting; and yet its mere presence functions to absolve the state of further responsibility and to place the onus for seeking and taking advantage of associated protections on to the individual herself. This can re-enforce rather than disrupt patterns of powerlessness and victim-blaming, and thus, as Martha Minow has observed, to the extent that "rights analysis offers release from hierarchy and subordination" only to those who can match the picture of the abstract, autonomous individual, its application can be "not only unresponsive but also punitive" to those "others."[35]

[34] Deborah L. Rhode, "Feminist Perspectives on Legal Ideology," in Juliet Mitchell and Ann Oakley, eds., *What is Feminism?* (Oxford: Blackwell, 1986); Mark Tushnet, "An Essay on Rights," *Texas Law Review*, 62 (1984), 1375; Stephanie Palmer, "Feminism and the Promise of Human Rights: Possibilities and Paradoxes," in Susan James and Stephanie Palmer, eds., *Visible Women: Essays on Feminist Legal Theory* (Oxford: Hart, 2002).

[35] Martha Minow, *Making All the Difference: Inclusion, Exclusion and American Law* (Ithaca: Cornell University Press, 1990), p. 147.

Operationalizing the rule of law through a rights framework thus offers both challenges and opportunities. To the extent that rights invoke individualism, abstraction and conflict, they may map more comfortably on to a male experience of social interaction and citizenship but redressing this bias simplistically through promotion of counter-values of connection, context and conciliation may play into, rather than challenge, broader patterns of gender oppression. The focus on entitlement and self-determination that lies at the heart of a rights claim – even if ethically impoverished – can have strategic and tangible benefits for the vulnerable and marginalized.[36] But the promise of this will be limited if the rights that are granted cannot answer the difficult questions they inevitably raise and cannot solve the underlying problem.[37]

4 Siren Calls and Legal Reform

Feminist ambivalence regarding rights analysis and its progressive potential for empowerment reflects, of course, but one concrete illustration of broader concerns regarding both the limits of legal reform as a mechanism for social change and the potential for cooption of feminism by liberal law.

From campaigns over suffrage and early "persons" cases, to gradual ceding of property entitlements and recognition of women's rights to sexual autonomy and bodily integrity, there is a narrative of steady and incremental progress that can be mapped upon feminist engagements with law reform. At the same time, however, battles that had been hard fought have been undermined or lost in practice, new forms of regulation and restriction have often filled the vacuums created, and the ongoing levels of discrimination and disadvantage experienced by women testifies to the slow rate of meaningful change. For some feminists, this is more than an illustration of the inevitably non-linear contours of progress and resistance; it is a reflection of the fundamental limits and impermeability of law as a site for progressive reform. Law, it is submitted, has engrained

[36] Elizabeth Kiss, "Alchemy or Fool's Gold? Assessing Feminist Doubts about Rights," in Mary Lyndon Shanley and Uma Narayan, eds., *Reconstructing Political Theory: Feminist Perspectives* (Philadelphia: Pennsylvania University Press, 1997); Mary Ann Glendon, *Rights Talk: The Impoverishment of Political Discourse* (New York: The Free Press, 1991).

[37] Frances Olsen, "Statutory Rape: A Feminist Critique of Rights Analysis," *Texas Law Review*, 63 (1984), 387–432; Vanessa E. Munro, "Square Pegs in Round Holes: The Dilemma of Conjoined Twins and Individual Rights," *Social and Legal Studies*, 10 (2001), 459–482.

techniques that limit and constrain feminist challenge and it is ill-equipped, or disinclined, to bring about social transformation. As Wishik has put it, "the analytical frames of patriarchal law are not the spaces within which to create visions of feminist futures."[38] On this account, the rule of law is ideological: its function is to mask, justify and paper over the cracks of a system driven fundamentally by patriarchal privilege. Engaging with the law as a site of resistance does not, and cannot, yield worthwhile change: at best, it provides empty and symbolic victories that occasionally, and only as a strategy to curb its own excesses, offer improvements in lived experience; at worst, it deceives those who turn to it with its rhetoric of equality, justice and rights whilst coopting feminist frames to give additional credence to this deceit. It is for this reason that Carol Smart has called on feminists to "de-center" law, to ignore its "siren call" and to pay attention to alternative sites of resistance and change.[39]

Though influential on much contemporary feminist thought, following through on this manifesto has proven almost impossible. For one thing, the inequalities and injustices perpetuated "on law's turf" are too glaring to be ignored and too jarring not to attract censure. As MacKinnon has observed, "one result of this turning away, however realistic its reasons, is that male power continues to own law unopposed."[40] Though engagement is a fraught and frustrating task, disengagement is all the more so; and its tendency to leave patriarchal privilege unchecked in modern society seems untenable. It is perhaps for this reason that, despite decades of trenchant critique of the inability of the liberal state to recognize the sexual violation of women from their own perspective, MacKinnon has continued to advocate for international law's condemnation of rape in times of both war and "peace."

Moreover, the parameters of law's power are far less tightly constrained than a conventional sovereign account might presume. As Martha Fineman has observed, legal power is "found not only in courts and cases, and legislatures and statutes, but in implementing institutions,

[38] Heather Ruth Wishik, "To Question Everything: The Inquiries of Feminist Jurisprudence," *Berkeley Women's Law Journal*, 1 (1985), 77.

[39] Smart, *Feminism and the Power of Law*. See also Martha L. Fineman, "Challenging Law, Establishing Difference: The Future of Feminist Legal Scholarship," *Florida Law Review*, 42 (1990), 25–43.

[40] Catharine A. MacKinnon, "The Power to Change," in idem, *Women's Lives, Men's Laws*, p. 107.

such as social work and law enforcement, as well."[41] The increasingly diffuse nature of legal power, and its implication in disciplinary frames of social welfare, health, and education, have been well-documented. This means both that the risks of cooption are diffused across multiple sites of engagement and that the interrelation of, and fluidity of power dynamics between, these regulatory regimes might create opportunities for strategic, localized but ultimately productive interventions.[42]

Thus, feminists may be well advised to remain skeptical regarding any positioning of law as having it within its gift to protect and empower women, and to recall that putting "women before the law is a dangerous undertaking" that always risks "re-authorising a legal system whose authority is ultimately self-legitimating."[43] But equally, they would be well advised not to foreclose the possibility of dialogue with law – both on its own and on substantively modified terms. Noting that it can be a wall, as well as a tool for taking down walls, Catharine MacKinnon has demanded that feminists continue to seek ways to make law into a door: "while legal change may not always make social change, sometimes it helps and law *un*changed can make social change impossible."[44]

This all speaks, of course, to a broader tension, which has plagued many critical movements – between exposing the dynamics of power, privilege and partiality which underpin and preserve the prima facie legitimacy of a legal system, and working within the processes and frames of that system to push at the boundaries of the intelligible and expose inconsistencies in internal standards. It is a tension between critique and reform, principle and practice, ideology and experience: and one that probably can never be completely reconciled. As I have suggested elsewhere, it is a tension that calls for a "permanent, unclosed perspective"[45] on the benefits and burdens of legal strategies; and, I would also argue, on "the rule of law" itself.

[41] Fineman, "Challenging Law, Establishing Difference," p. 34.

[42] Vanessa E. Munro Munro, "Legal Feminism and Foucault: A Critique of the Expulsion of Law," *Journal of Law and Society*, 28 (2001), 546–567; Ralph Sandland, "Between Truth and Difference: Poststructuralism, Law and the Power of Feminism," *Feminist Legal Studies*, 3 (1995), 2, 3–47.

[43] Drucilla Cornell, *The Imaginary Domain: Abortion, Pornography and Sexual Harassment* (London: Routledge, 1995), p. 235.

[44] MacKinnon, "The Power to Change," p. 103.

[45] Vanessa E. Munro and Carl F. Stychin, "Editors' Introduction," in idem V. Munro and C. Stychin, eds., *Sexuality and the Law: Feminist Engagements* (London: Routledge, 2007), p. xii.

Conclusion

In this chapter, I have provided a brief sketch of some of the key points of challenge that feminists – in their diversity – have raised against the claimed origins, operation, and benefits of the "rule of law," particularly as understood within the dominant liberal paradigm. Like feminism itself, of course, the "rule of law" is a site of contestation, operating at the scale of a pragmatic form of social ordering as well as a normative blue-print for substantive justice, and with its subtle shifting between these scales often making it a particularly difficult target for critique. Nonetheless, feminist analysis has highlighted – through careful attention to women's lived realities – the exclusions, excesses, and violence that law's rule has imposed and/or justified.

Feminism has demonstrated the repressive effects upon many women of living under the rule of law, and refused to accept its protestations of neutrality and concern in the face of these effects. But the aim here is not purely deconstructive – feminism is, after all, a progressive force, which pursues future flourishing. The hallmarks of equality, democratic accountability, and transparency – purported to be at the heart of the rule of law – are hard to jettison in this context, even where their pursuit has too often been road-blocked by patriarchal privilege and partiality. In this respect, then, while feminist critique has been cutting, significant, and urgent, it is also best understood as holding up a mirror to the "rule of law," demanding of it a more faithful account.

Critical Race Theory and the Rule of Law 20

Khiara M. Bridges*

Introduction

Two things are certain about the rule of law. First, it is not the rule of men.[1] Second, it is important: it protects those living under governments that are guided by it from authoritarianism, totalitarianism, and, quite possibly, "anarchy and the Hobbesian war of all against all."[2] Beyond those two certainties, however, much confusion reigns. Indeed, the rule of law is an "essentially contestable concept," and paradigmatically so.[3] There is no consensus around whether the rule of law requires certain features of government, such as judicial review or the separation of power among several branches of government. There is no consensus around whether the rule of law requires a particular approach to constitutional or statutory interpretation, such as originalism or textualism. And most relevant to the ensuing discussion, there is no consensus around whether the rule of law is solely an instrumental mandate or whether there are also substantive components to it.

This last point deserves elaboration. Consider Lon Fuller's influential account of the rule of law.[4] According to Fuller, the rule of law requires the law to be general, known and knowable to the public, prospective, clear,

* Thanks to Dick Fallon for his comments on an early draft of this chapter.

[1] Michel Rosenfeld, "The Rule of Law and the Legitimacy of Constitutional Democracy," *Southern California Law Review*, 74 (2001), 1313. Rosenfeld notes that the rule of law "is often contrasted to the 'rule of men'" and observes that this is usually taken to mean that the rule of law is incompatible with "unrestrained and potentially arbitrary personal rule by an unconstrained and perhaps unpredictable ruler." see also A. Scalia, "The Rule of Law as a Law of Rules," *University of Chicago Law Review*, 56 (1989), 1176, who notes the "dichotomy between 'general rule of law' and 'personal discretion to do justice'."

[2] See Richard H. Fallon, Jr., "'The Rule of Law' as a Concept in Constitutional Discourse," *Columbia Law Review*, 97 (1997), 2, where he notes "the familiar contrast between 'the Rule of Law' and 'the rule of men.'"

[3] See Jeremy Waldron, "Is the Rule of Law as an Essentially Contested Concept (in Florida)?" *Law and Philosophy*, 21 (2002), 137–164. See also idem, Chapter 6 in this volume.

[4] Lon L. Fuller, *The Morality of Law* (New Haven: Yale University Press, 1964).

consistent, capable of being obeyed, and stable; moreover, there has to be "congruence between the rules as announced and their actual administration."[5] Margaret Jane Radin observes that Fuller was most interested in offering a formulation of the rule of law that would effectively guide the behavior of subjects.[6] However, Radin suggests that Fuller offers an impoverished account of the rule of law inasmuch as "substantive ideals, like fairness or democracy, and autonomy or dignity of persons" are extraneous to the concept.[7] In a similar vein, Joseph Raz intimates toward the danger of excluding some substantive commitments – even if simply and solely to democracy – from a theory of the rule of law. He writes that if the rule of law was solely an instrumental aspiration – if it was only about inducing desired behaviors in the subjects of the law – then "[a] non-democratic legal system, based on the denial of human rights, on extensive poverty, on racial segregation, sexual inequalities and religious persecution may, in principle, conform to the requirements of the rule of law better than any of the legal systems of the more enlightened Western democracies."[8] To those concerned about human rights, poverty, racism, sexism, oppression on the basis of religion, and other issues of social justice, Raz's warning counsels that if the rule of law deserves to be venerated, there ought to be some substantive component to it.

However, theorists have also warned about the dangers of formulating the rule of law such that it contains a substantive element. Richard Fallon contends that including a substantive aspect in a theory of the rule of law is not entirely desirable inasmuch as it joins "questions about the meaning, existence, and requirements of the Rule of Law . . . to substantive disagreements about what the law ought to be."[9] And although he includes a substantive element in his own formulation of the rule of law, he argues that this element ought not to be prioritized over the other elements that he imagines a wholly actualized rule of law would embody.[10] Indeed, he

[5] Fuller, *The Morality of Law*, p. 21.

[6] Margaret J. Radin, "Reconsidering the Rule of Law," *Boston University Law Review*, 69 (1989).

[7] Radin, "Reconsidering the Rule of Law," at 786.

[8] Joseph Raz, "The Rule of Law and Its Virtue," in his *The Authority of Law: Essays on Law and Morality* (Oxford: Clarendon Press, 1979), pp. 210, 211.

[9] Fallon, "'The Rule of Law' as a Concept in Constitutional Discourse," 23.

[10] "Perfectly realized," writes Fallon, "the Rule of Law would be rule (i) in accordance with the originally intended and understood meaning of the directives of legitimate, democratically-accountable lawmaking authorities, (ii) cast in the form of intelligible rules binding on citizens, governmental officials, and judges alike, (iii) as identified and elucidated in an

believes that this substantive element ought to be "minimized," explaining:

First . . . [i]n a morally diverse society, law – and the regime of rights that require legal definition and enforcement to be meaningful – would be impossible if substantive, background controversies about what the law ought to be simply replicated themselves in jurisprudential disputes about what the law is. Second, a pervasively substantive conception of the Rule of Law would risk obliteration of the analytically and politically useful distinction between the Rule of Law, on the one hand, and a full theory of substantive justice, on the other. By linking the Rule of Law too closely to core positions in broader disputes about substantive justice, a strongly substantive conception would tend to deprive the ideal of the Rule of Law of independent analytical bite in assessing those desiderata of a legal system – including its efficacy in guiding the conduct of both private citizens and public officials – that Rule of Law virtues have traditionally measured.[11]

Fallon certainly is not the only theorist wary of a substantive conception of the rule of law.[12] What is important to note here, though, is that theorists have been receptive to the idea that the rule of law may embody *some* substantive commitments even if they also believe that those commitments ought to be subordinated to other requirements. In other words, the proposition that the rule of law coincides to some not insignificant degree with a particular substantive ideal – such as racial equality – is not unimaginable or unintelligible.[13] Quite the opposite, coherent arguments can be made that the rule of law requires the pursuit of certain noninstrumental,

interpretive process guided by publicly accessible norms and characterized by reason-giving, and (iv) consistent with legitimate public purposes and sound, shared principles of political morality." See his "'The Rule of Law' as a Concept in Constitutional Discourse," 38.

11 Fallon, "'The Rule of Law' as a Concept in Constitutional Discourse," 53, 54.

12 See, for example, William C. Whitford, "The Rule of Law," *Wisconsin Law Review* (2000), 742, who argues against formulating the rule of law such that it contains a substantive element, as such formulations "compromise the moral force of the ROL phrase by associating it with contestable ideals, weakening the force of the phrase when it is applied to its core meaning."

13 See Fallon, "'The Rule of Law' as a Concept in Constitutional Discourse," 24. According to Fallon, "substantive conceptions of the Rule of Law are clearly not precluded by any publicly agreed meaning of the term." See also Harry W. Jones, "The Rule of Law and the Welfare State," *Columbia Law Review*, 58 (1958), 151: "Although I, too, think of the [rule of law] as a primarily procedural one, I am by no means sure that a meaningful rule of law has nothing whatever to say concerning the substantive content of legally enforced principles. A good case can be made that the concepts of the rule of law and of natural rights are at least fraternal twins; I would not foreclose the possibility that they may be identical twins."

nonprocedural outcomes – like, for example, substantive equality between racial groups.

It is important to underscore at this point in the exposition that the rule of law is an ideal – albeit a contested one. As this part makes clear, theorists have disagreed with one another about the contours and the content of the ideal. Essentially, we are not exactly sure what the rule of law is. As such, it may confound things for anyone to assert that, as a general matter, the rule of law is corrupt, or biased, oppressive, or unjust. These assertions tend to confuse what the rule of law actually requires with a contested conception of what the rule of law requires. In other words, the ideal itself, when perfectly actualized, is unlikely to be corrupt or biased or oppressive or unjust. But particular formulations of the ideal (for example, Lon Fuller's account), or argued instantiations of the ideal (for example, the modern-day United States), may be all of those things.

Of what relevance is this to Critical Race Theory (CRT)? This chapter explains CRT's relationship to the rule of law. But first a brief introduction to CRT is needed.

1 What is Critical Race Theory?

Critical Race Theory emerged in the 1970s and 1980s at a time when most scholars conceptualized the law as uninvolved in creating and sustaining racial hierarchies. Prior to the advent of CRT, the reigning sense in the legal academy was that norms of fairness, equality, and justice guided the law. Accordingly, many legal academics found it difficult to contemplate that the law could be involved in creating a society that, racially speaking, is unfair, unequal, and unjust. The intellectual forefather of CRT, Derrick Bell, was one of the first to challenge this view. Bell devoted his scholarship to exploring how it came to be that black people remained on the bottom of practically every measure of social well-being in the post-civil rights era, even though the Civil Rights Movement had forced the passage of laws that ostensibly were designed to end black people's subordination.[14] Bell concluded that racial inequality endured because the vision of racial justice that civil rights lawyers had championed was a weak and impoverished

[14] Derrick A. Bell, Jr., "Serving Two Masters: Integration Ideals and Client Interests in School Desegregation Litigation," *Yale Law Review*, 85 (1976), 470–516.

one; he claimed that the result was that the civil rights laws that had been passed, which reflected this vision, were equally weak and impoverished. Thus, he argued that if racial inequality persisted in a post-civil rights era, then the law was central to explaining that persistence.

Bell's scholarship, along with the writings of others, eventually coalesced into CRT. Today, CRT is a body of scholarship and an analytical toolset for interrogating the relationship between law and racial inequality. The body of work that can be referred to as CRT scholarship is united by the questions that it asks about the law's role in constructing race. These questions include:

- If race is a social construction, what is the role of the law in constructing race?
- How has the law produced, reproduced, and protected racial inequality?
- How can the law be used to dismantle race, racism(s) and racial inequality?

While CRT is united by the questions it asks about the law, it is not united by the answers it gives. There is no CRT "solution" to what critical race theorists – who are a heterogeneous group engaging a range of different methodologies[15] – take to be the United States' race problem. Some critical race theorists believe that the solution lies in reparations. Others believe that legal reform is the answer. Still others reject incremental reform and champion revolution – taking it to the streets – as the remedy. While CRT theorists disagree about how to solve the problem of racial injustice, they all agree that there is a problem.

The architects of CRT have described the theory as a "left intervention into race discourse and a race intervention into left discourse."[16] By this, they are referring to CRT's emergence as a response to the perceived failures of two intellectual formations. On the one hand, those who would come to found CRT were disappointed with the fact that critical thinkers of the day – who had organized themselves as the Critical Legal Studies

[15] Kimberlé Williams Crenshaw, "The First Decade: Critical Reflections, or 'A Foot in the Closing Door'," *University of California Los Angeles Law Review*, 49 (2002), 1362. According to Crenshaw, critical race theorists are "fundamentally eclectic in many respects" and while CRT eventually "achieved some degree of intellectual coherence . . . the notion of CRT as a fully unified school of thought remains a fantasy of our critics."

[16] Kimberlé Crenshaw, Neil Gotanda, Gary Peller, and Kendall Thomas, "Introduction," in idem, eds., *Critical Race Theory: The Key Writings That Formed the Movement* (New York: The New Press, 1995), p. xix.

movement (CLS) – seemed uninterested in thinking about questions of race, racism, and racial justice. The adherents of CLS – or crits, as they came to be called – were a largely white, predominately male "collection of neo-Marxist intellectuals, former New Left activists, ex-counter-culturalists, and other varieties of oppositionists in law schools."[17] What united them was an interest in exposing the law's role in creating, sustaining, and naturalizing a society that they believed to be woefully oppressive and alienating. The crits brought an impressive catalog of theoretical tools to the task of critiquing the law, including "Marxian and neo-Marxian social theory, phenomenology, semiotics, structuralism, post-structuralism and the deconstructive techniques of post-modern literary criticism."[18] However, they largely did not use any of these tools to think about racial hierarchy and subordination. CRT ought to be understood as a reaction to CLS's perceived shortcomings in this regard.

The architects of CRT were also disappointed with the way political liberals had conceptualized racial hierarchy and subordination. These incipient critical race theorists felt that a dissatisfying conservatism had crept into liberal discourse around race as a result of its failure to adopt an avowedly critical stance to conceptualizing racial equality. To explain: liberal discourse around race typically defines racism as the fact of simply thinking about race.[19] This is what white supremacists did during the pre-civil rights era: they thought about race. They thought about race when they concluded that black people were unfit to sit in the same railway coaches as white people. They thought about race when they designated some schools for white children and other schools for black children. They thought about race when they declared that black people and white people ought not to marry and passed anti-miscegenation laws to criminalize such unholy unions. Liberal discourse around race identifies this constant race-thinking as the flaw of the pre-civil rights era. Thus, it prescribes never thinking about race – race unconsciousness – as the appropriate cognitive mode of the post-civil rights era. It designates colorblindness as the moral, legal, and political compass that ought to guide the nation.

[17] Crenshaw et al., "Introduction," pp. xvi–xvii.

[18] Elizabeth M. Iglesias, "LatCrit Theory: Some Preliminary Notes Towards a Transatlantic Dialogue," *University of Miami International and Comparative Law Review*, 9 (2001), 9.

[19] See Crenshaw et al., "Introduction," p. xv.

However, there are a number of consequences to understanding race consciousness to be racism and colorblindness to be the repudiation of racism. First, this understanding problematizes all race consciousness *equally*. Thus, for example, the white person who thinks about race when deciding to burn a cross on her black neighbor's lawn commits the identical cognitive and behavioral error as the black person who thinks about race when deciding to patronize a black-owned business in her neighborhood. CRT challenges the construction of equivalents between these two modes of thinking about race, disputing the suggestion that they are anything *like* one another. Surely, say critical race theorists, there is a difference between thinking about race in order to continue the exclusion of a group from spaces from which they have been historically excluded and thinking about race in order to finally bring that group into those spaces. There has to be a difference, they say, between thinking about race in order to maintain the dominance of a racial group and thinking about race in order to empower a subordinated racial group.

Secondly, if thinking about race is racist, then attempting to dismantle the nation's racial hierarchy by race-conscious means is racist. Accordingly, race consciousness when making school assignments in order or achieve mildly integrated schools, race consciousness in the construction of voting districts, race conscious affirmative action programs in hiring and university admissions, race consciousness when evaluating the impact of changes in voting laws or practices – all of these efforts become conceptualized as racist. Consequently, liberals – unwilling to challenge their conception of racism, but also committed to the existence of such remedial efforts – are forced to apologize for these programs. They are constrained to frame these programs as "necessary evils" – as "a merely 'exceptional' remedy for past injustice, a temporary tool to be used only until equal opportunity is achieved."[20] CRT proposes that there is something deeply problematic about styling such efforts as *evils*, albeit necessary ones. They certainly lose their moral force when they are conceptualized as evil. If they are evil, it becomes harder to argue that they are the *right* thing to do given our nation's history and present of racial subordination. Further, if such programs are evil, then it becomes easy to equate them with the evils of racial exclusion that the efforts are

[20] Crenshaw et al., "Introduction," p. xv.

attempting to address. One can just hear conservative opponents saying, "Well, two wrongs don't make a right . . ."

Critical race theorists unreservedly reject conceptualizing racism as race consciousness. They concede that race consciousness was a salient feature of the days of chattel slavery, Jim Crow, the Chinese Exclusion Act, the Japanese internment, Operation Wetback, and the requirement that one be a "free white person" in order to naturalize as a US citizen. However, they argue that the error practiced in those days was not simply thinking about race. Rather, it was thinking about race *in the service of white domination.* Thus, the race consciousness of Jim Crow and the race consciousness of affirmative action, for example, ought not to be lumped together in the same boat. CRT argues that they are on different continents, oceans away from each other.

Accordingly, critical race theorists embrace race consciousness *in the service of racial justice.* This acceptance of race-thinking – indeed, the unapologetic championing of race-thinking as necessary, right, and *good* – represents, perhaps, the most significant departure between CRT and liberal discourse around race.

Critical race theorists observe that both conservatives and liberals offer colorblindness as the best means for achieving racial equality. Conservatives and liberals mostly agree that if we simply stop thinking about race in the public sphere, people of color will be able to get decent educations, find competitive jobs, acquire wealth, be healthier, and live longer – things that the race consciousness of the pre-civil rights era denied them. But, CRT observes that if this is what colorblindness is supposed to do, it has not succeeded. Indeed, CRT understands colorblindness to be a "failed social policy."[21]

But, critical race theorists deride colorblindness for more than its simple failure to implement racial justice. They decry it because they are convinced that in an era of formal equality, colorblindness perpetuates racial oppression. So, yes: the "Whites Only" signs have been taken down. The covenants that forbid the sale of a home to a black person have been declared unenforceable. The bylaws that maintain that nonwhite people cannot be admitted into an organization have been removed. The persons who believe that nonwhite people are, as a rule, incompetent and

[21] Barbara J. Flagg, "'Was Blind, But Now I See': White Race Consciousness and the Requirement of Discriminatory Intent," *Michigan Law Review*, 91 (1993), 1014.

unqualified have had changes of heart, have been run out of public life, or have been advised that they can no longer make decisions in accordance with those beliefs. Critical race theorists' distaste for colorblindness results from their refusal to believe that some kind of social osmosis is going to happen and, in the absence of formal barriers, people of color are just going to float over into the neighborhoods, institutions, halls of government, and arenas of power from which they have been excluded. CRT proposes that we have to think about their race and actively move people of color into these spaces. Colorblindness prevents us from doing that.

2 CRT Critiques of the Rule of Law

CRT's relationship to the rule of law is not at all simple. In many respects, critical race theorists are big fans of the law. Indeed, they have much more confidence in law and the rule of law than their CLS counterparts. As mentioned above, CRT represents a departure from CLS. One of the reasons for the schism between CRT and CLS is critical race theorists' belief that CLS did not recognize the value of law. To many critical race theorists, the law had been a valuable tool in the struggle to improve the lives of people of color. Critical race theorists believed that CLS was too dismissive of the transformative potential of law, thinking of it as nothing more than an alienating, isolating, and subjugating force in the lives of all individuals.[22]

At the same time, critical race theorists have been highly critical of law and the rule of law. Acutely aware of the contested nature of the idea of the

[22] Unfortunately, many critics of CRT have not recognized the high regard, at least relatively speaking, that many critical race theorists have for law, and they have not recognized the hope that critical race theorists have for the rule of law. See Darren Lenard Hutchinson, "Critical Race Histories: In and Out," *American University Law Review*, 53 (2004), 1208–1209: "[M]any conservative critiques of CRT argue that CRT does not embrace the 'rule of law' and that it portrays the law as unable to bring about positive social change. The responses to the nihilism critique uncover the fallacies of these claims by pointing to the divergence of Critical Race Theorists from more radical forms of poststructuralism practiced by CLS scholars who engage in rights trashing." See also, Patricia J. Williams, *The Alchemy of Race and Rights: Diary of a Mad Law Professor* (Cambridge: Harvard University Press, 1991), p. 163: "To say that blacks never fully believed in rights is true. Yet it is also true that blacks believed in them so much and so hard that we gave them life where there was none before; we held onto them, put the hope of them in our wombs, mothered them."

rule of law, CRT is not disapproving of the rule of law as such. Rather, *CRT is critical of the way that the idea of the rule of law has been deployed to justify laws that frustrate the realization of racial justice.* This is how we ought to understand the critical stance many critical race theorists have taken with respect to the rule of law. Indeed, this is how we ought to understand the statement of Kimberlé Crenshaw and her coauthors that CRT endeavours "to understand how a regime of white supremacy and its subordination of people of color have been created and maintained in America, and, in particular, to examine the relationship between that social structure and professed ideas such as 'the rule of law.'"[23]

These theorists should not be read as declaring that the rule of law mandates "white supremacy and [the] subordination of people of color." Instead, they should be read as asserting that racial hierarchies have been defended under the banner of the rule of law. Indeed, some defenders have claimed that the rule of law *demands* the laws (like those that unduly restrict legal immigration and, consequently, produce the "undocumented immigrant") and legal approaches (like colorblindness in the interpretation of the equal protection clause and other antidiscrimination statutes) that have protected and perpetuated racial hierarchies. Thus, CRT is interested in critiquing the use of the language of "the rule of law" in the service of legitimating what it takes to be a racially unjust society.[24]

This is also how we ought to understand Paul Butler's rumination on the fact that "African-Americans were not afforded the benefit of the rule of law."[25] He continues:

[23] Crenshaw et al., "Introduction," p. xiii.

[24] Because CRT is as much of a critique of politically *liberal* discourse around race as it is a critique of politically conservative discourse around race, Crenshaw and her coauthors also criticize the way that observers have used the ideal of rule of law to defend the liberal approach to race and racism that the Warren Court embraced. See Crenshaw, et al., "Introduction," p. xvi: "[T]he law's 'embrace' of civil rights in the Warren Court is proclaimed as the very hallmark of justice under the rule of law." However, because Crenshaw and her coauthors believe that the "'legislation' of the civil rights movement and its integration into the mainstream commonsense assumptions in the late sixties and early seventies were premised on a tragically narrow and conservative picture of the goals of racial justice and the domains of racial power," they view the use of the ideal of the rule of law to validate the Warren Court's understanding of race and racism as another example of the way that the ideal of the rule of law has been deployed in ways that frustrate racial justice and legitimate racially unjust orders.

[25] Paul Butler, "Racially Based Jury Nullification: Black Power in the Criminal Justice System," *Yale Law Journal*, 105 (1995), 707.

Think, for example, of the existence of slavery in a republic purportedly dedicated to the proposition that all men are created equal, or the law's support of state-sponsored segregation even after the Fourteenth Amendment guaranteed blacks equal protection. That the rule of law ultimately corrected some of the large holes in the American fabric is evidence more of its malleability than of its virtue; the rule of law had, in the first instance, justified the holes.[26]

Here, Butler highlights the contested nature of the ideal of the rule of law. He observes that while the concept has been wielded to bring our nation closer to racial justice, it has also been wielded to defend, rationalize, and excuse racial injustice.[27] It is this latter use of the rule of law ideal – its use in the defense of racial hierarchy – that CRT critiques.[28]

While Butler and other critical race theorists might dismiss the concept of the rule of law because of its "malleability," this could amount to throwing out the proverbial baby with the bathwater. There is an alternative that is entirely in keeping with the general approach that CRT takes to legal critique: we critical race theorists might formulate, and insist upon, a rule of law that can produce a racially just society and against which a racially unjust society is fundamentally inconsistent. Or we might simply reject any formulation of the ideal that protects, legitimizes, or is compatible with white racial domination.

We should be aware, though, that some appraisals of the rule of law offered by critical race theorists have been quite damning, as when Anthony Paul Farley writes that "[t]here is no rule of law save as the disguise for the rule of one group over another."[29] Or when Francisco

[26] Butler, "Racially Based Jury Nullification," 707.

[27] Essentially, Butler is simply observing the indeterminacy of the rule of law. See Kimberlé Crenshaw and Gary Peller, "Reel Time/Real Justice," *Denver University Law Review*, 70 (1993), 291, who argue "the terms that guarantee the rule of law – terms like 'reasonable force' or 'equal protection' – are necessarily indeterminate" and that "[t]heir meaning must be socially constructed through narratives of place and time for there to be any meaning to them at all."

[28] See also Ruben J. Garcia, "Critical Race Theory and Proposition 187: The Racial Politics of Immigration Law," *Chicano-Latino Law Review*, 17 (1995), 132–133: "Proponents of Proposition 187 argue that undocumented immigrants have no claim to public entitlements because of their violation of United States immigration laws. Their assertions illustrate a type of 'rule of law' argument – that those who have entered the United States illegally in the past are worthy of punishment through the denial of public services. . . . The 'rule of law' is being used today in much the same way that 'sovereignty' functioned during Chinese Exclusion – as a concept that is inconsistently applied to exclude and penalize only nonwhites from American society."

[29] Anthony Paul Farley, "Accumulation," *Michigan Journal of Race and Law*, 11 (2005), 72. Farley here reflects on the faith that marginalized people have tended to have in the ability

Valdes and Sumi Cho write that racial domination exists and persists within the United States because "the self-serving 'rule of law' . . . cruelly declared formal (racial and social) equality while simultaneously limiting its reach."[30] Or when Butler, in the article discussed above, writes that "the idea of 'the rule of law' is more mythological than real" and that he has "more faith in the average black juror's idea of justice than [he does] in the idea that is embodied in the 'rule of law.'"[31]

It bears repeating, however, that the rule of law is a highly contested and contestable idea, with no general consensus having formed about its precise content and contours. Accordingly, when, for example, Cho and Valdes write that the rule of law has "cruelly declared formal (racial and social) equality while simultaneously limiting its reach," they are referring only to one formulation of the rule of law – a formulation that holds that the rule of law requires formal equality. The preceding discussion should make plain that *any* formulation of the rule of law, including one that appears to demand formal equality, is just one of many possible formulations. In other words, the "rule of law" does not demand formal equality. Instead, one contestable formulation of the rule of law demands formal equality.

As the preceding discussion should also make plain, it is not outside the bounds of reason for a critical race theorist to fold a substantive commitment to racial justice into her theorization of the rule of law and, consequently, reject formal equality as an element of the rule of law insofar as formal equality frustrates the achievement of racial justice.[32] Alternately,

of law to bring about their liberation. He writes that subjugated people conjure up "the idea of the rule of law" – understood as "equality of right and due process" – as the means by which they will be released from their subordinate status. Ibid., 54. However, because Farley is pessimistic about the capacity of law to bring about a full-throated racial justice – at least, within a capitalist economic system – he believes that hope in the rule of law functions to quiet the revolutionary demands of those who are dispossessed; he believes that it counsels them to delay the "General Strike" that will bring about their true liberation. As he writes, "The rule of law is the slaves' own creation. It is the sigh and submission of the oppressed creature . . . The slave's fundamentalist faith in the future good will of its master makes unnecessary the General Strike of tomorrow and tomorrow and tomorrow." Ibid., 67.

30 Francisco Valdes and Sumi Cho, "Critical Race Materialism, Theorizing Justice in the Wake of Global Neoliberalism," *Connecticut Law Review*, 43 (2011), 1521.

31 Butler, "Racially Based Jury Nullification," 706, 715.

32 It is worth noting here that it is unnecessary to reject formal equality as irreconcilable with racial justice. This is simply because what is meant by "formal equality" is subject to debate. If formal equality means that all persons ought to be treated the same without

a critical race theorist may elect to include formal equality as an element of the rule of law but subordinate it to a substantive commitment to racial justice; pursuant to this iteration of the rule of law, if formal equality precludes the achievement of substantive racial equality then the rule of law would require that it be suspended until such racial equality is achieved. Both these formulations of the rule of law are intelligible and defensible. Thus, when any critical race theorist criticizes the rule of law because he believes it to be incompatible with racial justice, the theorist assumes a constant, inherent, and inevitable characteristic of the rule of law that simply is not there.[33]

The above critiques of the rule of law levied by critical race theorists are apiece with a phenomenon that Fallon has observed, whereby the rule of law is invoked not to "describe an ideal," but rather to "condemn particular decisions, practices, rules, or legal systems as unacceptably distant from the ideal."[34] None of the critiques above describe a rule of law that would

regard to differences in ability, status, or the like, then formal equality might be irreconcilable with racial justice and, consequently, rejected by critical race theorists. Chantal Thomas describes this definition of formal equality, explaining that it "prevents legitimately differential treatment of groups to correct historical wrongs perpetrated upon them *qua* groups. Thus, the formal equality necessitated by the classical liberal understanding of the rule of law, though intended to secure justice, can perpetuate injustice by ignoring structural inequality in material conditions across groups." See Chantal Thomas, "Causes of Inequality in the International Economic Order: Critical Race Theory and Postcolonial Development," *Transnational Law and Contemporary Problems*, 9 (1999), 2. However, if formal equality means that similarly situated persons ought to be treated similarly – allowing for differently situated persons to be treated differently – then formal equality might be reconcilable with racial justice: understood in this way, it would allow for the different treatment of persons who are differently situated by virtue of different racial histories and racial presents.

33 Thus, when a critical race theorist, in her earnest youth, writes that CRT rejects "even the possibility of a rule of law – that is, a wholly objective and impartial legal system that can be blind to the social and political layers of each decision," we should understand the young theorist to be overstating the case. Khiara M. Bridges, "On the Commodification of the Black Female Body: The Critical Implications of a Market in Fetal Tissue," *Columbia Law Review*, 102 (2002), 131. A better presentation of the issue would be to state that critical race theorists, on the whole, reject even the possibility of a rule of law *when* it is understood to manifest itself as an objective and impartial legal system that purports to be blind to the social and political layers of each decision. This is because most critical race theorists embrace postmodernism's disbelief in the possibility of objectivity and impartiality, and they are convinced that most attempts "to speak of law or render legal decisions from a perspective of impartiality or neutrality [are] actually … exercise[s] in White supremacy." Ibid.

34 Fallon, "'The Rule of Law' as a Concept in Constitutional Discourse," 43.

produce the racial equality that theorists believe justice demands. Instead, they appear to assume that our current legal system and the mass of laws that it has produced – which they find to be complicit in the production and reproduction of racial inequality – is a manifestation of the rule of law. In condemning the current legal system for its role in protecting racial hierarchies, these theorists condemn "the rule of law." This wholesale condemnation is, I believe, unwarranted.

It is worth emphasizing again that critiques that would dismiss the rule of law as inescapably racist confuse what the ideal of the rule of law actually requires with someone's debatable notion of what the rule of law requires. If the rule of law actually demands racial justice – a perfectly reasonable demand – then the rule of law is not racist and does not countenance racism. If this is what the rule of law actually commands when it is perfectly realized, then some critical race theorists err when they decry it as an agent of racial oppression.

3 CRT as Incompatible with the Rule of Law

While some critical race theorists have, in my view, unnecessarily dismissed altogether the ideal of the rule of law as inherently and inevitably incompatible with a racially just social order, others have unfairly attacked CRT as inherently and inevitably incompatible with the rule of law. Jeffrey Rosen authored one widely read critique of CRT in the late 1990s in which he argued that CRT represented a dangerous threat to the rule of law.[35] While Rosen certainly takes issue with some critical race theorists' use of "storytelling"[36] in their scholarship, his biggest objection is CRT's rejection of colorblindness. He blames the acquittal of O. J. Simpson for the murder of his ex-wife, Nicole Brown Simpson, and her friend, Ron Goldman, on the

[35] Jeffrey Rosen, "The Bloods and the Crits: O. J. Simpson, Critical Race Theory, the Law, and the Triumph of Color in America," *New Republic*, December 9, 1996. (Rosen identifies a number of arguments that some critical race theorists have made, concluding that CRT amounts to "a stark challenge to the liberal ideal of the rule of law."

[36] Oddly enough, perhaps the most contested intervention that critical race theorists have made into legal scholarship is not substantive, but methodological: some have used narrative in their explorations of law. These narratives have taken many different forms, including "personal histories, parables, chronicles, dreams, stories, poetry, fiction, and revisionist histories." Mari J. Matsuda, Charles R. Lawrence III, Richard Delgado, and Kimberlé Williams Crenshaw *Words That Wound: Critical Race Theory, Assaultive Speech, and the First Amendment* (Boulder, CO: Westview Press, 1993), p. 5. The use of these narratives in legal scholarship is generally referred to as "storytelling."

refusal by Simpson's lawyers and the jurors in the case to be colorblind. He writes that "the defense strategy in the Simpson case was a textbook implementation of the premises of the critical race movement. [Simpson's lawyer] methodically selected an African American jury, predicting correctly that their racially fraught experiences with the police would influence their perception of the facts . . . He relentlessly pressed the claims of group solidarity and racial essentialism . . . And he ended his closing argument with an explicit call for race-based jury nullification, calling on African American jurors to ignore the evidence and 'send the message' to the racist police that letting a murderer go free was an appropriate payback for a legacy of state-sponsored oppression."[37] He concludes his essay by claiming that "[t]he prestige of color-blindness is diminishing in America, and not only among people of color. This is a disaster. For we will be blind to color or we will be blind to justice."[38] It is CRT's refusal to be blind to color that informs Rosen's conviction that CRT is inconsistent with the rule of law.

We can respond to Rosen by first noting that critical race theorists have never argued that we ought to be conscious of race whenever doing so would benefit any individual person of color. Rather, CRT proposes that we ought to be conscious of race *in the service of racial justice*. Thus, race consciousness might be appropriate when we are engaged in the distribution of opportunities – like seats in an incoming class or jobs – because it allows us to contextualize the accomplishments of an applicant, gain a nuanced understanding of what a candidate may bring to a position if hired, or remedy the effects of past societal discrimination. However, no self-identified critical race theorist has argued that race consciousness is appropriate when one endeavors to secure an acquittal in a murder trial. Certainly, CRT has asked us to be aware of the structural conditions that produce criminality. And it has also asked us to be skeptical about the propriety of pursuing incarceration as a method for addressing our social ills. But it has not asked us to "ignore the evidence" and acquit defendants of color accused of violent crimes simply because they are persons of color. Neither has it made an argument that racial justice demands that Simpson be acquitted of the murder of his ex-wife and her friend if he actually committed those murders.

[37] Rosen, "The Bloods and the Crits." [38] Rosen, "The Bloods and the Crits."

But, more importantly, our response to Rosen ought to recall the prior discussion about the error that some critical race theorists make when they equate the rule of law with a principle, like formal equality, that frustrates the achievement of racial justice. Just as critical race theorists err when they assume that the rule of law demands formal equality, Rosen errs when he assumes that the rule of law requires colorblindness.[39] The proposition that the rule of law demands colorblindness is one that critical race theorists might reject. Again, if the rule of law required substantive racial equality, and if colorblindness frustrates the achievement of substantive racial equality, then the principle of colorblindness might be rejected as incompatible with the rule of law; or the principle of colorblindness, if included as an element in the rule of law, might be subordinated to the command of substantive racial equality. Again, these theorizations of the rule of law are perfectly intelligible and reasonable.

What Rosen and similar-minded critics of CRT may be assuming is that the content of the rule of law is the political philosophy of liberalism and, further, that liberalism demands colorblindness; accordingly, the rule of law demands colorblindness. A response to this is to observe that it is not at all clear that liberalism requires colorblindness.[40] Until recently, a majority of the Justices

[39] Frank Michelman has offered a cogent articulation of this argument:

"Invocations of the rule of law against CRT can have multiple meanings. They may refer to the nonneutrality – the out-right partialism – of CRT's stance toward colorblindness ... To invoke against that stance the need for ruleness and "principle" in the law is obviously to beg the question of the moral apriorization of color-blindness itself. Racially partialist deviation from colorblindness is *lawless* only because and insofar as the law prohibits it, which is just what CRT is contesting; but a law permitting such deviation would not on that account alone be *unprincipled,* except in the possible sense in which "unprincipled" means unjust – to assert which would be tantamount to equating justice *a priori* with colorblind-ness in the law ... A principle that would, in some proposed application to a given context, defeat a conceded principle of justice for that context cannot itself be a principle of justice as thus applied in that context. Now, CRT has an *argument* that such is indeed the case with the principle of colorblindness as relentlessly applied to the American social context." Frank I. Michelman, "'Foreword: Racialism' and Reason," *Michigan Law Review,* 95 (1997), 734–735.

[40] With respect to the argument that liberalism requires colorblindness, it might be helpful to recall economist Friedrich A. Hayek's argument that liberalism required the absence of a welfare state. See F. A. Hayek, *The Road to Serfdom* (Chicago: University of Chicago Press, 1944). Because he also believed that liberalism formed the content of the rule of law, he believed that the welfare state was irreconcilable with the rule of law. See Jones, "The Rule of Law and the Welfare State," 146, who described Hayek as proposing that "the welfare state, by its inherent nature, is incompatible with the rule of law." Most will recognize as *political* the argument that the rule of law demands liberalism, and liberalism demands a small government and unfettered free-market capitalism. Similarly, we ought to recognize

on the US Supreme Court denied that the US Constitution mandates that state actors be colorblind. To argue that liberalism requires colorblindness is to argue that five Justices on the highest court in the country are illiberal in significant respects and would interpret the Constitution in ways that are disobedient to the rule of law.[41] This is an ambitious argument.

We might also respond to the argument that the substance of the rule of law is liberalism, which, in turn, requires colorblindness, by noting that even if we concede that liberalism requires colorblindness, we need not concede that the substance of the rule of law is liberalism. Indeed, many prominent formulations of the rule of law, including Lon Fuller's influential account, say nothing about liberalism.[42] This is not at all to deny that many theorizations certainly do associate the rule of law with liberalism.[43] It is simply to say that these theorizations are debatable. In this way, if CRT's position that color consciousness is the only means by which racial justice will be realized, their program might be incompatible with liberalism, but entirely compatible with the rule of law.

Conclusion

Critical race theorists offer a complicated assessment of the rule of law. On the one hand, critical race theorists disapprove of the way that the ideal of

as *political* the argument that the rule of law demands liberalism, and liberalism demands colorblindness. As Whitford writes, "The Rule of Law . . . phrase has been a slogan used for many political purposes." Whitford, "The Rule of Law," 723. Describing color consciousness as inconsistent with the rule of law is an undeniable example of the rule of law ideal being used as a political slogan and being put to political ends.

41 See *Parents Involved in Community Schools* v. *Seattle School District, No. 1*, 551 US 701, 788 (2007) (Kennedy, J, concurring): "The statement by Justice Harlan that '[o]ur Constitution is color-blind' was most certainly justified in the context of his dissent in *Plessy v. Ferguson* . . . [A]s an aspiration, Justice Harlan's axiom must command our assent. In the real world, it is regrettable to say, it cannot be a universal constitutional principle."

42 According to Fallon, Aristotle "equated the Rule of Law with the rule of reason," while "others have identified the Rule of Law with natural law or respect for transcendent rights." Fallon, "'The Rule of Law' as a Concept in Constitutional Discourse," 1.

43 "Within the Anglo-American tradition," according to Fallon," perhaps the most famous exposition [of the rule of law] came from a turn-of-the-century British lawyer, A. V. Dicey, who associated the Rule of Law with rights-based liberalism and judicial review of governmental action." See his "'The Rule of Law' as a Concept in Constitutional Discourse," 1. See also Radin, "Reconsidering the Rule of Law," 790: "The Rule of Law is grounded not on the bare claim of efficacy of behavioral control, but on the specific political vision of traditional liberalism."

the rule of law has been deployed to justify a racially unjust social order. On the other hand, the ideal contains emancipatory potential insofar as it might be theorized to embody a commitment to racial equality and justice. If it is understood in this way, critical race theorists might embrace it wholeheartedly.

But what if it the rule of law embodies no such commitment? What if the rule of law, when properly conceived, guarantees no more than efficient government? What if, when perfectly realized, the rule of law does no more than prevent anarchy, "allow people to plan their affairs with reasonable confidence that they can know in advance the legal consequences of various actions," and protect against "at least some types of official arbitrariness."[44] How would critical race theorists respond to that?

Because critical race theorists are a heterogeneous group, it is difficult to speak for all of them. Nevertheless, I believe that many would believe that if the rule of law is simply instrumental – containing no substantive commitment to an ardent *justice* – then the rule of law ought not to be revered as enthusiastically as it is.[45] This is especially true in light of the capacity of the ideal, when thinly wrought, to legitimize injustice. But, this is a pessimistic conclusion. Optimism might be more preferable. As Robert Williams asks:

> Do you believe in the rule of law, I mean really believe? Do you believe judges ought to decide like cases alike and treat people of equal worth and human dignity equally? Do you believe that slavery and servitude, or colonization and conquest, can never be justified by any court guided by the rule of law? Do you believe that the rule of law is a means to a greater end for humanity and justice for all?[46]

One can answer these questions in the affirmative. And if one does, then CRT ought to be a fervent champion of the ideal of the rule of law.

[44] Fallon, "'The Rule of Law' as a Concept in Constitutional Discourse," 7–8.

[45] See Rosenfeld, "The Rule of Law and the Legitimacy of Constitutional Democracy," 1314, who observes that the "rule of law in the narrow sense may be preferable to the rule of men, but it is ...... entirely compatible with legal regimes predicated on slavery, apartheid, or countless other oppressive and dehumanizing practices and policies grounded in law, shaped by law, and carried out through law." See also Jens Meierhenrich, *The Legacies of Law: Long-Run Consequences of Legal Development in South Africa, 1652–2000* (Cambridge: Cambridge University Press, 2008).

[46] Robert A. Williams, Jr., "Do You Believe in the Rule of Law?" *California Law Review*, 89 (2005), 1633.

Part V

Trajectories

(Economic) Development and the Rule of Law 21

Shane Chalmers and Sundhya Pahuja

Introduction

The "rule of law" is a relatively recent addition to the development project.[1] Only after the end of the 1980s, when the Cold War was over, history had ended,[2] and three worlds had putatively become "one," did it also become commonsensical for law, institutions and "governance" to be understood as integral to "development."[3] Since that time, not only have developmental institutions such as the World Bank, the International Monetary Fund and regional development banks explicitly taken up promotion of the rule of law as a core aspect of their mandates, but a significant marketplace of international, transnational, government, and domestic actors has emerged.[4] The result is a multi-billion dollar industry that is centrally concerned with "the rule of law" as instrument, end, and indicator of "development," positioned at the heart of state-making more broadly.

Yet, while the term "rule of law" may be a relative newcomer to the development project, this most recent form of developmental intervention continues in striking ways the nineteenth and early twentieth century

[1] On the idea of development as a project, see Sundhya Pahuja, *Decolonising International Law: Development, Economic Growth and the Politics of Universality* (New York: Cambridge University Press, 2011); Joseph Hodge, "Writing the History of Development, Part 1: The First Wave," *Humanity*, 6 (2015), 429–463; Joseph Hodge, "Writing the History of Development, Part 2: Longer, Deeper, Wider," *Humanity*, 7 (2016), 125–174.

[2] See, for example, Susan Marks, "The End of History? Reflections on some International Legal Theses," *European Journal of International Law*, 8 (1997), 449–477.

[3] Pahuja, *Decolonising International Law*, pp. 172–173.

[4] On the complex of actors involved in the rule of law promotion industry more generally, see Veronica Taylor, "The Rule of Law Bazaar," in Per Bergling, Jenny Ederlöf, and Veronica Taylor, eds., *Rule of Law Promotion: Global Perspectives, Local Applications* (Uppsala: Justus Förlag, 2009), 325–358. On the commercialization of this work, see also Veronica Taylor, "Big Rule of Law©®℠™(Pat.Pending): Branding and Certifying the Business of the Rule of Law," in Jeremy Farrall and Hilary Charlesworth, eds., *Strengthening the Rule of Law through the UN Security Council* (Abingdon: Routledge, 2016), pp. 27–42.

attempts to reshape the non-European world. In those earlier interventions, the "gift" of law was integral to the civilizing mission, promising both a "universal" mode of being in the world and a guide for realizing it.[5] Thus it was imagined by some that (European) law ("properly so-called") could spearhead efforts to turn the new world to account, by providing the technology by which its lands and peoples could become the property and propertied transactors of an emerging global economy. Law was imagined too as a pedagogy for constituting "modern" legal subjects, and as an institutional system for regulating and enforcing the new economic norms. To recall Fitzpatrick's analysis of this encounter, the promoters of this modern law "venture[d] forth to create the real, to endow [the 'new' world] with 'forms and norms.'"[6]

In this chapter we use the example of Liberia to illustrate the work that the "rule of law" does today in the context of developmental and state-making interventions,[7] as well as to draw out some of the continuities with earlier forms of intervention. We have chosen Liberia because of its extraordinary and yet all-too-ordinary experience of development throughout its colonial and postcolonial periods. And so, on one hand, Liberia's history is utterly unique. It was established at the beginning of the nineteenth century as a colony for free-born African-Americans and freed slaves under the governance of the American Colonization Society. In 1847, it became the first "black republic" in Africa and only the second in the world after Haiti. It survived the expansion of Europe's colonial empires in western Africa through the late-nineteenth and early-twentieth centuries, and yet wrought its own colonial violence on Africans in Liberia. That violence contributed to the downfall of the Americo-Liberian republic in 1980, and precipitated the civil wars of the 1990s and early 2000s in which a quarter of a million people were killed, many more displaced,[8] and immense damage was done to the institutions and infrastructure of the state.

[5] See Peter Fitzpatrick, *The Mythology of Modern Law* (London: Routledge, 1992), pp. 20–21; see also Pahuja, *Decolonising International Law*, ch. 5.

[6] Fitzpatrick, *The Mythology of Modern Law*, p. 42, citing Mircea Eliade, *The Myth of the Eternal Return: Cosmos and History* (Princeton: Princeton University Press, 1965), p. 10.

[7] Luis Eslava and Sundhya Pahuja, "The Nation-State and International Law: A Reading from the Global South," *Humanity*, 11 (2020), 118–138.

[8] See Shelly Dick, "FMO Country Guide: Liberia," *Refugee Studies Centre* (2003), p. 11 available at http://repository.forcedmigration.org/show_metadata.jsp?pid=fmo:5126.

And yet, on the other hand, despite this singular history, Liberia's experience of development, in both "colonial" and "postcolonial" terms, is startlingly familiar. This dynamic is central to our argument about the development project. Operating according to a logic of equivalences, what the development project encounters as unique and incomparable becomes stock-standard. At the same time, the "universal" "forms and norms" according to which the world is transformed and made equivalent are far from neutral. In describing Liberia's experience as at once extraordinary and ordinary, singular and exemplary, we aim to show how the putative universality of "the rule of law" in the development project is both economically inflected and Occidentally derived, and to highlight the violence of developmental interventions carried out in its name.[9]

To carry out this task, we begin in Section 2 by describing the institutional account of the rule of law most prevalent within the development project today. This is the rule of law as both means to, and end of, development. We outline the emergence of this version of "law and development" during the postwar period, and its re-emergence in the post-cold War period. Through this description, we suggest that as the "rule of law" was drawn into development as an idea, it was functionally (re)oriented primarily toward economic ends. But despite this orientation, it did not bring the promised growth which authorized the endeavor. In our account, the recurrent failure of this "(rule of) law" to bring (economic) development led to an intensification of the law and development project. The most recent turns to "legal pluralism" and "rule of law indicators" are just two of the latest fixes for a project that has failed to learn from its failures. In Section 3 we turn to Liberia to illustrate our account, and locate the precursors of "law and development" in the colonial period. In that section, we explore in more detail one example of the way that rule of law promotion and (economic) development have come together in the making and remaking of nation-states in the twentieth and twenty-first centuries. Through the example of Liberia, we see that developmental interventions continue the transformational violence of colonialism. Under the sign of a never-fulfilled convergence with an ideal, a unique history becomes a familiar (Third World) trajectory, rehearsing the tragedy of the (rule of law and) development story.

[9] See also Shane Chalmers, "The Mythology of International Rule of Law Promotion," *Law and Social Inquiry*, 44 (2019), 957–986.

1 Current Accounts

The Rule of Law as Means and End

In 2017 the World Bank released its latest World Development Report (WDR), *Governance and the Law*. At the core of the account of the world offered in the report lies "the rule of law," a concept that is described as both a means to, as well as a marker of, "development."[10] So, on the one hand, the World Bank is unequivocal that, "by its nature, law is a device," "a powerful instrument": "[f]ollowing Hart's classic legal theory, laws induce particular behaviors of individuals and firms through coercive power, coordination power, and legitimating power."[11] According to this naturalized legal positivism,[12] law (as the World Bank asserts) is a "rule system" that "order[s] behavior, authority, and contestation" ("[l]aw here means the *de jure* rules").[13] As such, law can be separate from, and govern over its subjects, providing a technology that is essential to "development." As the WDR confirms: "Ultimately, the *rule of law* – the impersonal and systematic application of known rules to government actors and citizens alike – is needed for a country to realize its full social and economic potential."[14] If any doubt remains about the essential role of this naturalized positive law for achieving such development, the World Bank reassures us with a mythic account of its origins: "[l]ong before the Code of Hammurabi set the law for ancient Mesopotamia, people subjected themselves – sometimes by cooperative agreement, sometimes under threat of force – to rules that would enable social and economic activities to be ordered."[15]

On the other hand, the World Bank is equally sure that "the rule of law" is an end goal of the development project, with "pragmatic policy design" capable of "mov[ing] countries on a trajectory toward a stronger rule of

[10] See also Jennifer Beard, *Political Economy of Desire: International Law, Development and the Nation State* (Abingdon: Routledge, 2007).

[11] World Bank, *World Development Report 2017: Governance and the Law* (Washington: World Bank, 2017), p. 13.

[12] On how "the ideal(ised) version of law in the development story is the law of the legal positivist," see further Sundhya Pahuja, "Beheading the Hydra: Legal Positivism and Development," *Law, Social Justice and Global Development*, 1 (2007), 3.

[13] World Bank, *World Development Report 2017*, p. 84.

[14] World Bank, *World Development Report 2017*, p. 14.

[15] World Bank, *World Development Report 2017*, p. 83.

law."[16] This of course takes "time – sometimes a very long time."[17] As the World Bank notes (tongue-in-cheek, citing then UK Prime Minister Gordon Brown): "[i]n establishing the rule of law, the first five centuries are always the hardest."[18] But the tongue is in the cheek for a reason: the World Bank, as this latest version of the WDR reveals, knows how to accelerate "transitions to the rule of law," so the joke is on History.[19] According to the World Bank, there are three basic stages to effecting the transition to the rule of law (although "other paths might be possible").[20] These are outlined in a table in the WDR credited to Francis Fukuyama.[21] First there is a "shift from a customary or pluralistic system (or both) to a codified modern one," which is seen to better serve the interests of the "elites" in society, "particularly their economic interests in expanded trade and investment." This is the stage of "rule *by* law." The second "shift to 'rule *of* law' occurs when the elites themselves accept the law's limitations." Why would the elites take this step and "accept the law's limitations"? The answer, we are told, is the emergence of "a powerful normative framework that makes elites respect the law as such." While it is far from clear what this "powerful normative framework" is – or more importantly from where and from whom it emanates – what is clear is that it is a temporary force. In order for the "elites" to remain docile, a third and final shift is necessary, to a stage in which the rule of law is sustained by "independent legal institutions." At that point, the imposing normative framework can be dispelled, with the rule of law held in place by "legal institutions that persist even after their normative foundations have disappeared." However, one must keep in mind that in countries into which these institutions have been imported – as part of the process of "acceleration" – "perhaps the most important variable determining success is the degree to which indigenous elites remain in control of the process and can tailor it to their society's own traditions."[22] As we discuss further below in relation to Liberia, this points to the projected understanding of development

[16] World Bank, World Development Report 2017, p. 14. On the circularity of this (the rule of law bringing about development; development bringing about the rule of law), see Pahuja, *Decolonising International Law*, p. 198.

[17] World Bank, *World Development Report 2017*, p. 14.

[18] World Bank, *World Development Report 2017*, p. 14.

[19] On the acceleration of history as part of "development" more generally, see Pahuja, *Decolonising International Law*, pp. 62, 117, 186–188.

[20] World Bank, *World Development Report 2017*, p. 14.

[21] World Bank, *World Development Report 2017*, Box 0.7.

[22] World Bank, *World Development Report 2017*, Box 0.7.

as an immanent process, imagined by the World Bank as emanating (universally) from within every (particular) society, inflected by that society's "traditions," and unfolding as part of its "own" history within History.

The World Bank is not alone in the developmental field of international rule of law promotion. In 2015, two years before publication of the WDR 2017, *Governance and the Law*, the UN General Assembly announced its post-2015 *Agenda for Sustainable Development*. The vision set out is one of global economic development: "[w]e envisage a world in which every country enjoys sustained, inclusive and sustainable economic growth."[23] Here too "the rule of law" is said to be "essential" for achieving such "sustainable development, including sustained and inclusive economic growth, social development, environmental protection and the eradication of poverty and hunger";[24] and here too "the rule of law" is said to mark the achievement of this development. This is most clearly articulated in the Sustainable Development Goals. If the world is to achieve these Goals, it must, according to the *Agenda for Sustainable Development*, hit a series of targets that include implementing "the rule of law at the national and international levels" (target 16.3), "effective, accountable and transparent institutions" (target 16.6; see also target 16.a), and "non-discriminatory laws and policies for sustainable development" (target 16.b).[25] If the rule of law was implicit in the Millennium Development Goals,[26] it is now both a fully fledged, explicit goal of development, as well as a means for achieving the Sustainable Development Goals as a whole.

Thus for the UN, as for the World Bank, "(economic) development" requires "the rule of law," while "the rule of law" is imagined as being brought about through "(economic) development." And as both the UN's *Agenda for Sustainable Development* and the World Bank's latest World Development Report make clear, achieving this virtuous circularity requires realizing certain institutional forms and legal norms. These "forms and norms" are supposedly immanent to every society – "emerging," according to the World Bank, "from a home-grown (endogenous) process of contestation."[27] And yet the resulting "ideal of the rule of

[23] UNGA Res. 70/1 (October 21, 2015), para. 9.

[24] UNGA Res. 70/1 (October 21, 2015), para. 9.

[25] UNGA Res. 70/1 (October 21, 2015), para. 9, pp. 25–26 ("Goal 16").

[26] See Pahuja, *Decolonising International Law*, pp. 231–232.

[27] World Bank, *World Development Report 2017*, p. 14 and also Box 0.7. On "forms and norms," see Fitzpatrick, *The Mythology of Modern Law*. On how the "forms and norms" of

law" that "emerges" from this immanent process is nonetheless universal, providing a transcendent mode of being as well as a guide to its realization that is without regard for the particularities of any society.[28] In other words, the relationship is less "virtuous circle" than an "impossible tautological-teleological developmental complex,"[29] in which a universal form precedes its particular realization at the same time as it is held to have emerged from the particular, in truly "speculative Hegelian" fashion.[30] As foreshadowed, this particular universality is distinctly economical, informed by a logic of equivalence that results from the solipsism of the market,[31] and aimed at generating private investment and economic growth.

The (PostColonial) Trajectory of (the Rule of) Law and (Economic) Development

What is typically regarded as the "first wave" of law and development began in Africa and Latin America in the 1960s and 1970s.[32] Framed by the Cold War, and led by a small group of legal academics, this US-led socio-legal experiment sought to "modernize" the legal systems of target states in the belief that this would both bring about economic growth and create the conditions for those states to develop into liberal democracies with advanced industrial-capitalist economies. As in earlier colonial interventions, they sought to achieve this in two main ways: by reforming the state's legal institutions, to bring about a structural

"the rule of law" are supposed to be immanent to every society according to the UN more generally, see also Chalmers, "The Mythology of International Rule of Law Promotion."

[28] World Bank, *World Development Report 2017*, p. 14. See also Pahuja, *Decolonising International Law*, ch. 5; Chalmers, "The Mythology of International Rule of Law Promotion."

[29] For another examination of how an "impossible tautological-teleological developmental complex" animates the "formal, paradoxical structure of international human rights law and the narrative of human personality development that it charters," see Joseph Slaughter, "Enabling Fictions and Novel Subjects: The *Bildungsroman* and International Human Rights Law," *PMLA* 121 (2006), 1405–1423, at 1412.

[30] Slavoj Žižek, *The Sublime Object of Ideology* (London: Verso, 2008), p. 29.

[31] See Alfred Sohn-Rethel, *Intellectual and Manual Labour: A Critique of Epistemology* (New York: Humanities Press, 1978), Part I; see also pp. 9–16.

[32] The following historical account of the "law and development" movement is informed in particular by David M. Trubek, "The Political Economy of the Rule of Law: The Challenge of the New Developmental State," *Hague Journal on the Rule of Law*, 1 (2009), 28–32; and idem, "Law and Development," in Neil Smelser and Paul Baltes, eds., *International Encyclopaedia of the Social and Behavioral Sciences* (New York: Elsevier, 2001), p. 8443.

transformation in the state; and by reforming the state's legal education system, to bring about a normative transformation in legal actors. The assumption, forged during colonial encounters,[33] was that Occidental modern law was the natural-historical end-point of legal development as well as the necessary means for achieving the political and economic transformations, and that transplanting the forms and norms of this law into Latin America and Africa would accelerate the "natural" historical progression of these countries.

By the late 1970s and 1980s, it was clear that the transplants had failed to take root as intended. The intended engineering of society through legal functionalism failed, and unintended consequences were produced, including facilitating authoritarian state-making.[34] At the same time as this first "law and development" movement was experiencing such failures, the broader development paradigm was also shifting. The 1980s saw the rise of what came to be shorthanded as "neoliberalism," signaling a move away from the economic "liberalism" of the 1950s and 1960s (which recognized a strong role for the government in the economy), and a shift toward "reducing" the role of the state in the economy, now imagined primarily as a (national) market.[35] Instead of emphasizing state-fostered industrialization, orthodox in the 1960s, by the 1980s, emphasis was placed on "opening" (developing) states up to export-led growth, foreign investment and global competition. This meant constraining the state from maintaining protective barriers against trade or continuing to subsidize national industries. It also meant constructing legal systems structurally and substantively oriented toward the protection of foreign investment and international trade. This double requirement of constraining particular forms of government action (through law), and protecting economic investments (through law), misleadingly dubbed "deregulation," found an ally in a particular conception of the "rule of law." This vision of the rule of law found its champions in the international economic institutions.

By the late 1980s, the World Bank and International Monetary Fund began to take an interest in "governance" and institutions – and the

[33] See Fitzpatrick, *The Mythology of Modern Law*.

[34] David M. Trubek and Marc Galanter, "Scholars in Self-Estrangement: Some Reflections on the Crisis in Law and Development Studies in the United States," *Wisconsin Law Review*, 4 (1974), 1062–1103.

[35] Anne Orford and Jennifer Beard, "Making the State Safe for the Market: The World Bank's *World Development Report 1997*," *Melbourne University Law Review*, 22 (1998), 195–216.

institutions of "the rule of law" in particular – and their role in the promotion of development.[36] Both political reforms, to bring about liberal democracies, and economic reforms, to bring about free-market economies, were packaged by these organizations as "good governance" and presented as necessary to stimulate growth and attract foreign investment, while "the rule of law" was held out as the necessary means for achieving these ends.

This shift to promoting "the rule of law" within states as an essential aspect of their economic development occurred at a moment when the Third World was actively asserting the rule of law between states, as part of the "decade of international law."[37] But in contrast to Third World attempts to renew the promise of a "classical" notion of formal sovereign equality, for the most powerful state(s) the end of the Cold War suggested much more evangelical possibilities. This evangelism took two forms. The first centered on the desire to "fulfill" a human rights project, mythically originating in the postwar moment,[38] whilst the second embraced a putative "realism" in which international law, and in particular rules around state legitimacy, should be modified to reflect the "empirical fact" of the triumph of the liberal democratic state.[39] Each asserted the universality of liberal democracy (as both normative and descriptive) in a new world order and centered that conception of democracy on "the rule of law."

Not only did this emphasis on the rule of law within states redirect the language of the rule of law toward developmental interventions, and away from its potentially critical role in relations between states, but it also worked to deflect attention away from the increasingly evident flaws in the orthodox models of development being operationalized by the

[36] On this turn, see, for example, Amanda Perry, "International Economic Organisations and the Modern Law and Development Movement," in Ann Seidman, Robert Seidman, and Thomas Wälde, eds., *Making Development Work: Legislative Reform for Institutional Transformation and Good Governance* (The Hague: Kluwer, 1999), p. 19. For the turn to governance, see also: World Bank, *Sub-Saharan Africa: From Crisis to Sustainable Growth* (Washington: World Bank, 1989); James Thuo Gathii, "Good Governance as a Counter-Insurgency Agenda to Oppositional and Transformative Social Projects in International Law," *Buffalo Human Rights Law Review*, 5 (1999), 107–174.

[37] Pahuja, *Decolonising International Law*, pp. 176–204.

[38] Pahuja, *Decolonising International Law*, pp. 179–181. See also Samuel Moyn, *The Last Utopia: Human Rights in History* (Cambridge: Belknap Press of Harvard University Press, 2012); Matthew Craven, Sundhya Pahuja, and Gerry Simpson, "Reading and Unreading a Historiography of Hiatus," in idem, eds., *International Law and the Cold War* (Cambridge University Press, 2019), pp. 1–24.

[39] Pahuja, *Decolonising International Law*, pp. 181–182.

international economic institutions. This deflection took place through a redescription of the causes of the breakdown of previous development strategies, now presented as failures of Third World legal and regulatory institutions, including the now-crucial "rule of law." Early institutional responses to the Asian Debt Crisis, for example, vindicated and amplified the diagnosis that the failure of development was due to a failure of legal institutions.[40] By the late 1990s this understanding was decisively embedded in development policy.

It was not long after this already significant shift that "the rule of law" began to appear as both means to as well as end of development. In a series of texts published in the mid-1990s, Ibrahim Shihata, then General Counsel to the World Bank, published a series of chapters, articles and papers outlining the World Bank's strategy on development and the rule of law.[41] It is in these papers that we first find the circularity of definition by which a proper "law" – as one which promotes "development" as a process – also indicates that an end-point of development has been reached insofar as such institutions as proper "law" can be found.[42] This logic manifests in its fullest form in the 1997 issue of the World Development Report on *The State in a Changing World*,[43] twenty years before the WDR 2017 on *Governance and the Law*.[44]

Learning from Failure?

As this account indicates, the development project in its late-nineteenth, twentieth, and now early-twenty-first century iterations has been marked by a recurrent failure to achieve its declared goals. Both the "law and development" movement of the 1960s and 1970s,[45] and the post-Cold War "rule of law promotion" movement of the 1990s and early 2000s,

40 See Sundhya Pahuja, "Technologies of Empire: IMF Conditionality and the Reinscription of the North/South Divide," *Leiden Journal of International Law*, 13 (2000), 749–813.

41 See Pahuja, *Decolonising International Law*, pp. 193–198.

42 On this point, see Thomas Carothers, "The Rule of Law Revival," in Thomas Carothers, ed., *Promoting the Rule of Law Abroad: In Search of Knowledge* (Washington: Carnegie Endowment for International Peace, 2006), pp. 3–14.

43 See James Wolfensohn, "Foreword," in World Bank, *World Development Report 1997: The State in a Changing World* (New York: Oxford University Press, 1997), p. iii. See also the passages on pp. 28, 32, and 99.

44 See also Orford and Beard, "Making the State Safe for the Market."

45 Trubek and Galanter, "Scholars in Self-Estrangement."

have given rise to famous self-critiques.[46] And yet, while these critiques posed important questions about the "legal" aspects of the interventions (questioning, for example, the efficacy of legal transplants and the focus on institution-building), they did not question the notion of development per se. Arguably, this framing of the failure of the development project (as a failure to understand how law develops, and how law contributes to the development of a society) manifested too in more mainstream assessments, and facilitated in part a new – and more vigorous – return of "law and development" after each failure.[47]

One manifestation of this expansion is in the more recent turn to "legal pluralism" in development. The critique of the "rule of law and development" movement of the 1990s and early 2000s was based in large part on a renewed awareness that law is not simply an objective ensemble of things (statutes, courts, lawyers, police, and so on), but is rather a subjective phenomenon that cannot be separated from its cultural, political, and indeed cosmological contexts. This was the "problem of knowledge" raised in Thomas Carothers's famous critique of the field: "the question of where the essence of the rule of law actually resides" – a question that turns on an understanding that "[l]aw is also a normative system that resides in the minds of the citizens of a society."[48] This understanding, combined with a mounting body of research showing that people in the places to be developed were largely ignoring the official state legal system and using their own "customary" or "traditional" or "informal" systems,[49] meant that development agencies including the World Bank could no longer simply ignore this plurality of laws, or what many call "legal pluralism."[50]

46 Thomas Carothers, ed., *Promoting the Rule of Law Abroad: In Search of Knowledge* (Washington: Carnegie Endowment for International Peace, 2006). For a thoughtful comparative reading of the two movements ("law and development" and "rule of law and development"), see Maxwell Chibundu, "Law in Development: On Tapping, Grounding and Serving Palm-Wine," *Case Western Reserve Journal of International Law*, 29 (1997), 167–261.

47 For further development of this argument, see Pahuja, "Beheading the Hydra."

48 Thomas Carothers, "The Problem of Knowledge," in idem, ed., *Promoting the Rule of Law Abroad*, pp. 19–21.

49 These systems are rarely given the name "law," and when they are, they remain underdeveloped versions of "modern" law that must undergo reform.

50 See, for example, the World Bank's Justice for the Poor program, which "operates in countries where legal pluralism presents a particular development challenge": World Bank, "Justice for the Poor," available at http://siteresources.worldbank.org/INTJUSFORPOOR/Resources/JusticeforthePoor-TwoPager.pdf; see also World Bank, "Legal Pluralism," available at http://go.worldbank.org/6OQAZODF70. On the turn to legal pluralism in development, see further

However, rather than the existence of a plurality of laws throwing into doubt the authority of a development project grounded in a telos of one (universal) law, "legal pluralism" has instead become cast as both a solution to the failures of (law and) development, as well as a problem that will be itself resolved through development, this time mediated through varying time-scales. So, on one hand, in the short-term, existing "informal" or "customary" systems are cast as providing a necessary supporting service to the state system that is cheap, efficient, timely, accessible, and effective. And, on the other hand, and in the longer-term, these systems are supposed to render themselves unnecessary by providing a "bridge" or transition to the formal state system. In this way, the "informal" or "customary" systems are both subordinated and rendered instrumental to the achievement of "development" through both providing and representing a kind of social-evolutionary link that enables a society to progress from a stage when these primitive forms of law are an historical necessity, to a stage when the most advanced "modern law" can take their place.[51] As discussed above, such a transition to the rule of law accords perfectly with the World Bank's understanding of development, as outlined in its WDR 2017, according to which the first "shift" is "from a customary or pluralistic system (or both) to a codified modern one."[52]

The contemporary turn to "rule of law indicators" is another manifestation of the way that the undeniable failures of *law and* development have led to an intensification of the development project. Again viewing the problem of development as a problem of knowledge, and in particular a problem of a lack of "empirical" knowledge,[53] the field turned in the early 2000s to new ways of measuring the results of development. As Taylor notes in her study of the international rule of law industry, such measurement provides a "mode of validation" that simultaneously establishes a "lack" in the rule of law as well as "proof" that the rule of law intervention has brought about change.[54] The

Brian Tamanaha, Caroline Sage, and Michael Woolcock, eds., *Legal Pluralism and Development: Scholars and Practitioners in Dialogue* (Cambridge: Cambridge University Press, 2012).

51 See also Pahuja, *Decolonising International Law*, pp. 197, 208.

52 See World Bank, *World Development Report 2017*, Box 0.7.

53 See also Erik Jensen and Thomas Heller, eds., *Beyond Common Knowledge: Empirical Approaches to the Rule of Law* (Stanford: Stanford University Press, 2003).

54 Taylor, "Big Rule of Law©®℠™(Pat.Pending)," p. 54. See also Elin Cohen, Kevin Fandl, Amanda Perry-Kessaris, and Veronica Taylor, "Truth and Consequences in Rule of Law: Interferences, Attribution and Evaluation," *Hague Journal on the Rule of Law*, 3 (2011), 106–129.

seductiveness of this technology can be seen in the proliferation of rule of law indicators over the past decade,[55] from the most ambitious attempts to measure, compare and track the progress of states in establishing "rule of law around the world," as the World Justice Project's *Rule of Law Index*® is designed to do,[56] to more nuanced tools such as the UN's *Rule of Law Indicators*, designed to support the UN's work in "building and strengthening the 'rule of law' in developing nations."[57] More targeted indicators include the World Bank's *Doing Business* index, which "provides objective measures of business regulations and their enforcement across 190 economies,"[58] and the *Business Climate, Legal and Institutional Reform (BizCLIR) Project* of the United States Agency for International Development (USAID), which has adapted the World Bank's *Doing Business* index to give "reformers a thorough understanding of the legal and institutional constraints to a better business environment."[59]

One way in which these rule of law indicators are used is through development agencies "embed[ding] them in procurement contracts and specify[ing] them as part of a design for a rule of law intervention."[60] However, as Taylor also observes, citing research by Perry-Kessaris, and Davis, Kingsbury and Merry, while the use of rule of law indicators in these projects might create "apparent certainty, transparency and commensurability" with regard

[55] See generally Sally Engle Merry, *The Seductions of Quantification: Measuring Human Rights, Gender Violence, and Sex Trafficking* (Chicago: University of Chicago Press, 2016); Sally Engle Merry, Kevin Davis, and Benedict Kingsbury, eds., *The Quiet Power of Indicators: Measuring Governance, Corruption, and Rule of Law* (Cambridge: Cambridge University Press, 2015).

[56] See World Justice Project, "About Us," available at https://worldjusticeproject.org/about-us. For critiques of the World Justice Project's Rule of Law Index, see Jothie Rajah, "'Rule of Law' as Transnational Legal Order," in Terence Halliday and Gregory Shaffer, eds., *Transnational Legal Orders* (Cambridge: Cambridge University Press, 2015), pp. 340–373; René Urueña, "Indicators and the Law: A Case Study of the Rule of Law Index," in Merry, Davis, and Kingsbury, eds., *Quiet Power of Indicators* pp. 75–102.

[57] United Nations, *The United Nations Rule of Law Indicators: Implementation Guide and Project Tools* (New York: United Nations, 2011), p. v.

[58] See World Bank, *Doing Business*, "About Us," available at www.doingbusiness.org/about-us.

[59] See USAID, "Improving Business Regulation," available at www.usaid.gov/what-we-do/economic-growth-and-trade/trade-and-regulatory-reform/improving-business-regulation. For a discussion of these and other rule of law indicators, see Taylor, "Big Rule of Law©®℠™(Pat.Pending)," pp. 55–57.

[60] The five indicators are: "Transparency International's *CPI* [*Corruption Perception Index*], the World Bank Institute's *Control of Corruption Indicator*, Freedom House's *Freedom in the World* rating, the Global Competitiveness Report, and Transparency International's *Global Corruption Barometer*": Taylor, "Big Rule of Law©®℠™(Pat.Pending)," p. 57.

to the rule of law, they also privilege interveners' "contributions to economic growth, rather than their responsiveness to citizens or achievements in social inclusion or economic distribution." And there remains very little evidence that the rule of law interventions are leading to the outcomes being measured by the indicators. What does "remain strong," nonetheless, according to Taylor, "is a desire on the part of financiers to reinforce the idea that rule of law interventions 'work.'"[61] The result is that rule of law indicators have become integral to "a mode of public/private co-production of branded and certified commodities designed to bolster the normative appeal of the transnational policy interventions that we call rule of law promotion."[62]

In this account of the rule of law, its transformations and expanding field of intervention are both continuous and discontinuous with the civilizational precursors of the development project. While most genealogies of "law and development" trace the field back to the mid-twentieth century, locating it in a putatively postcolonial moment, the core of what became known as "law and development" – and later still "rule of law promotion" – was forged in the experience of colonialism. As we will show in the case of Liberia in the next section of the chapter, European and US interventions in that country throughout the late-nineteenth and early-twentieth centuries sought both to reform the legal institutions of the state and to transform its "indigenous" peoples into proper legal subjects, with the express aim of achieving economic development. Liberia might have been an early recipient of the "gifts" of development, but it was far from alone, sharing its experience with both colonies and protectorates. Close attention to one example reveals the practices through which such "development" was authorized by the ideal of improving the colonized, but closely connected with turning the colonies themselves to account, and shaping colonial occupations into business opportunities.

2 The (Extra)ordinary Case of Liberia

Historical Trajectory: Developing Liberia

"Liberia" was conceived at the beginning of the nineteenth century by the American Colonization Society (ACS), a philanthropic organization

61 "Big Rule of Law©®℠™(Pat.Pending)," p. 57.
62 "Big Rule of Law©®℠™(Pat.Pending)," p. 61.

constituted by slave-owners and supporters, as well as abolitionists, for the purpose of "colonizing the free people of color" of the United States "in Africa, or elsewhere."[63] Presented by the ACS as an idea of liberty, Liberia was supposed to achieve two humanitarian ends: "real" emancipation of African-Americans – who remained "virtual slaves" in the United States despite their status as free people of color – and, through this, the emancipation of all of Africa.[64] This was the great development project of the day, "the hope of redeeming many millions of people from the lowest state of ignorance and superstition."[65] As one supporter of Liberia put it:

> When she shall have done the work, Sir, it will be seen that the new world will have sent back to the old, the most sublime empire of reason and law, ever known to mankind. She will have planted in a land, once illustrious, but long darkened by superstition and despotism, the institutions of civil and religious liberty; and savage men will feel their influence[66]

In 1847, Liberia's African-American settlers declared themselves a "Free, Sovereign and Independent State,"[67] making Liberia the only independent African republic at the time and the only other "black republic" in the world after Haiti. One of the main reasons for the Declaration of Independence was to gain legal personality so that the government could

[63] See Art. 2 of the Constitution of the American Society for Colonizing the Free People of Color of the United States, published in American Colonization Society, *A View of Exertions Lately Made for the Purpose of Colonizing the Free People of Color, in the United States, in Africa, or Elsewhere* (Washington: Jonathan Elliot, 1817), pp. 11–12. For histories of the American Colonization Society, see Eric Burin, *Slavery and the Peculiar Solution: A History of the American Colonization Society* (Gainesville: University Press of Florida, 2005); Amos Beyan, *The American Colonization Society and the Creation of the Liberian State: A Historical Perspective, 1822–1900* (Lanham: University Press of America, 1991); John Seh David, *The American Colonization Society and the Founding of the First African Republic* (Bloomington: iUniverse, 2014).

[64] Complicating this idea of liberty, for many in the ACS and its supporters, colonizing the free people of color of the US in Africa (or elsewhere) was also – and most importantly – supposed to secure the institution of slavery in the south of the country, by siphoning off a troubling demographic. See further Shane Chalmers, "Civil Death in the Dominion of Freedom: Liberia and the Logic of Capital," *Law and Critique*, 28 (2017), 152–154.

[65] Statement of Elias Caldwell, in American Colonization Society, *A View of Exertions Lately Made for the Purpose of Colonizing the Free People of Color, in the United States, in Africa, or Elsewhere*, p. 7. See also James Ciment, *Another America: The Story of Liberia and the Former Slaves Who Ruled It* (New York: Hill and Wang, 2013), p. 9.

[66] American Colonization Society, *Sixteenth Annual Report of the American Society for Colonizing the Free People of Color of the United States* (Washington: James Dunn, 1833) p. xvii.

[67] Declaration of Independence of Liberia (1847).

collect customs duties.[68] The Declaration succeeded in this, although European recognition of Liberia's status was qualified by two requirements. As the "scramble for Africa" intensified in the 1880s, Britain and France made clear that if Liberia was to subsist as a "free, sovereign and independent state," and not be annexed to either of their empires, then it would have to define its territorial borders, and "exercise dominion" over the peoples within that territory.[69]

The second of these requirements was formally met in 1904. Under the interior policy of President Arthur Barclay, the Constitution was amended to recognize Liberia's "indigenous peoples" as citizens. Although sufficient for the purposes of exercising "dominion," the recognition was not unqualified for those who were now granted the status of "uncivilized" citizens. The pathway to becoming full "civilized" citizens was dependent upon their development into subjects resembling the Americo-Liberians.[70]

At the same time, however, the interior of the country remained "effectively unoccupied."[71] For the first decade of the twentieth century the government struggled to extend its presence beyond Liberia's coastal settlements, in large part because it had no security forces to deploy in the interior and no funds to build infrastructure there.[72] In an attempt to match the formal assertion of sovereignty with effective occupation, the government entered into an agreement with the British-owned Liberian Development Company. From the government's perspective, the agreement was designed to achieve two aims. First, the Company would provide the government with a loan addressing its financial

[68] See Yekutiel Gershoni, "The Formation of Liberia's Boundaries, Part 1: Agreements," *Liberian Studies Journal*, 17 (1992), 25–45.

[69] Nnamdi Azikiwe describes this in terms of "the claws of imperialism": Nnamdi Azikiwe, *Liberia in World Politics* (Westport: Negro Universities Press, 1970), ch. 7.

[70] Achieved through a "book" education, conversion to a Christian world-view, among other things. See also Jean Comaroff and John Comaroff, *Of Revelation and Revolution*, Vol. 1: *Christianity, Colonialism, and Consciousness in South Africa* (Chicago: University of Chicago Press, 1991); and idem, *Of Revelation and Revolution*, Vol. 2 *The Dialectics of Modernity on a South African Frontier* (Chicago: Chicago University Press, 1997).

[71] According to the terms of the "declaration relative to the essential conditions to be observed in order that new occupations on the coasts of the African continent may be held to be effective," adopted by the *General Act of the Berlin Conference*, February 26, 1885. On what would constitute "effective occupation," see also *General Act of the Brussels Conference Relative to the African Slave Trade*, July 2, 1890.

[72] See Harrison Akingbade, "The Pacification of the Liberian Hinterland," *Journal of Negro History*, 79 (1994), 281.

problems,[73] and, secondly, the Company would carry out commercial (rubber) operations in the interior, which would count towards "effective occupation."[74]

Two years later, in 1906, the Liberian Development Company facilitated another large loan to the government from British bankers.[75] Within twelve months of this second loan, the government – by now heavily indebted, unable to make repayments, and still without control over the vast majority of its "citizens" – was forced to agree to a set of structural reforms under threat of colonization. As the British Consul put it, Liberia would have to "put her house in order, or be prepared, at no distant date, to disappear from the catalogue of independent countries."[76] "Putting her house in order" meant establishing a "frontier police force"; reforming the judiciary and Treasury under the supervision of Western advisors; appointing British customs officials; and granting the British Inspector-General of Customs a seat in the Cabinet of the Liberian Government "with a plenary power of veto over all expenditures."[77]

Following an ultimatum from the British Consul demanding implementation of the reforms, the government established the Liberian Frontier Force,[78] putting it under the command of a British army major and two other British officers.[79] The aim was not only to establish the authority of the state in the

[73] On Liberia's financial problems, see Azikiwe's discussion of Liberia's loans from 1871 through to the 1930s, which he describes (writing in the 1930s) as "one of the latest phases of imperialism." Azikiwe, *Liberia in World Politics*, ch. 8.

[74] See Akingbade, "The Pacification of the Liberian Hinterland," 280; see also *Brussels Conference Act* (1890), Art. 1.

[75] See also Gershoni, "The Formation of Liberia's Boundaries, Part 1," 36–37.

[76] As quoted in Monday Abasiattai, "European Intervention in Liberia with Special Reference to the 'Cadell Incident' of 1908–1909," *Liberian Studies Journal*, 14 (1989), 72–90.

[77] See Azikiwe, *Liberia in World Politics*, 114; Abasiattai, "European Intervention in Liberia with Special Reference to the 'Cadell Incident' of 1908–1909," 79.

[78] "Joint Resolution Providing for the Pay and Formation of a Frontier Police Force," in *Acts Passed by the Legislature of the Republic of Liberia during the Session 1907–1908* (Monrovia: Government Printing Office, 1908), 23, cited in Akingbade, "The Pacification of the Liberian Hinterland," 281–284. See also Azikiwe, *Liberia in World Politics*, p. 115. Azikiwe writes that Major Cadell, transferring from Sierra Leone, "brought with him about one-third of his soldiers from Sierra Leone, all uniformed in suits and caps stamped with the emblem of 'His Britannic Majesty's Service,'" and upon Cadell's arrival in Liberia, "immediately he requested the Municipality of Monrovia to recognise him as the Inspector-General of Police," before taking over "the positions of Street Commissioner, Tax Collector and Municipal Treasurer."

[79] See Abasiattai, "European Intervention in Liberia with Special Reference to the 'Cadell Incident' of 1908–1909," 79–85; Akingbade, "The Pacification of the Liberian Hinterland,"

interior and protect British and French economic interests around the border regions in order to secure Liberia's independent status, but also to accelerate the development of Liberia's "uncivilized citizens" into "civilized citizens." Writing in 1916, Charles King, then Liberian Secretary of State, asserted that, through the Frontier Force, Liberia "strikes at the very root of . . . political, religious and social institutions which are uncompromisingly antagonistic to the laws of humanity and civilization."[80] King would go on to become President of Liberia from 1920 to 1930, before being forced from office upon the release of a report by the League of Nations International Commission of Enquiry into "the existence of slavery and forced labour" in Liberia.[81]

African-Liberians' experience of "development" during this period was thus overwhelmingly abject. And yet the adverse consequences, highlighted in the Commission's report, were seen to result not from this colonial development, but from a failure by Liberians themselves, and especially African-Liberians, to properly *implement* the various proposals for development. "The now obvious fact," the Commission observed in prelude to its recommendations, is "that tropical Africa can never be developed, its agricultural, mineral, and other sources utilized, nor surplus Government funds be hoped for, without the willing co-operation and assistance of the indigenous population."[82] The cause of Liberia's problems, in other words, was African-Liberians' lack of cooperation and assistance, and Americo-Liberians' failure to secure that cooperation and assistance.

The Commission then recommended civilizing Liberia's uncivilized citizens.[83] This, the Commission asserted, would make the native truly

281; Azikiwe, *Liberia in World Politics*, pp. 114–117. Within a few years, the Frontier Force was put under US supervision and command. On the involvement of US officers in the Liberian Frontier Force between 1912 and 1927, see Timothy Rainey, "Buffalo Soldiers in Africa: The US Army and the Liberian Frontier Force, 1912–1927," *Liberian Studies Journal*, 21 (1996), 203–338.

80 "Secretary of State CDB King to James L Curtis, American Minister Resident" (May 26, 1916) RDSL 882.00/540, cited in Martin Ford, "Ethnic Relations and the Transformation of Leadership among the Dan of Nimba, Liberia (ca. 1900–1940)," Ph. D. dissertation, State University of New York, 1990, p. 93.

81 League of Nations, *Report of the International Commission of Enquiry into the Existence of Slavery and Forced Labour in the Republic of Liberia* (Geneva: League of Nations, 1930). The findings and recommendations are reprinted in International Commission of Enquiry, "The 1930 Enquiry Commission to Liberia," *Journal of the Royal African Society*, 30 (1931), 277–290. But compare Azikiwe, *Liberia in World Politics*, ch. 12.

82 International Commission of Enquiry, "The 1930 Enquiry Commission to Liberia," 281.

83 International Commission of Enquiry, "The 1930 Enquiry Commission to Liberia," 282.

useful to the economy: "[i]t is now becoming everywhere recognized by tropical African administrators that the first considerations towards financial competence must include provision for the civilization, education, and the gaining of the confidence of the native."[84]

> Schools are of the first importance, not merely for the purpose of teaching reading and writing, but for improving the native's sociological conditions; ... teaching him market values, and the use he can make of the innumerable economic products and raw materials around him. The unsophisticated native learns something of the outside world, and his wants are increased. The missionary, the school teacher, and the trader teach him what he may buy for money, and he then wants to learn what he can grow, what he should do, or where he should work to make some money, with the result that trade increases, the coast merchant flourishes, the revenues of Government expand, and money is forthcoming.[85]

The penalty for failing to act on these recommendations was, again, colonization. Just like Britain and France in previous decades, the Commission threatened that if the government did not civilize its natives, and reshape them into economic men, "Liberia may discover that its place in the community of civilized nations is jeopardized."[86]

At the time there was a shortage of labor in Europe's West African colonies, leading colonial administrations to erect barriers to keep domestic laborers within their colonies' borders. Against this policy the Liberian

[84] International Commission of Enquiry, "The 1930 Enquiry Commission to Liberia," 281.

[85] International Commission of Enquiry, "The 1930 Enquiry Commission to Liberia," 281.

[86] International Commission of Enquiry, "The 1930 Enquiry Commission to Liberia," 288. The Commission has been convincingly critiqued as an attempt to undermine the Black Republic as a model of African self-rule at a time of anti-colonial revolution across the continent. As Nnamadi Azikiwe wrote in 1932 in response to the International Commission of Enquiry and the coverage of its findings: "Liberia today is a winter resort for any artist who is interested in caricaturing Negro statehood." See his "In Defense of Liberia," *Journal of Negro History*, 17 (1932), 45. Azikiwe goes on to critique the "systematically organized propaganda that Liberia, Haiti, and Abyssinia are failures, and that they furnish evidence to prove the incapacity of the Negro for self-government in the tropical regions. Discarding all problems which sovereign states must face in order to maintain their *de jure* existence, most of the writers on Liberia, excepting Benjamin Brawley, McPherson, Froude, Jore, Cuthbert Christy, and Buell, have delighted themselves in seeing chaos, disorder, hopeless anarchy and failure of the Liberian 'experiment' whenever her case is before the bar of international opinion. Even Emmett J.Scott, of Howard University, holds that the usual charges of official corruption are not always true. This is generally done to take advantage of the people and pave way for economic exploitation": ibid., pp. 46–47. See also Azikiwe, *Liberia in World Politics*, chs. 12 and 14–17, in which Azikiwe notes how "all avenues and institutions of public opinion have been utilized to vilify it [Liberia] and to pave way for its extermination from the family of nations." Ibid., pp. 305–306.

government was committing two offenses. Not only was it failing to actualize the exchange value of its human resources by transforming them into productive (civilized) citizens, but it was also "leaking" laborers from neighboring colonies, especially Sierra Leone, by acting as a conduit for recruiters to ship them to the island of Fernando Pó.[87]

The Commission's intervention succeeded in stopping that "leak," satisfying British interests in Sierra Leone; but it also satisfied US interests by putting international pressure on Liberia to create a domestic labor market.[88] In 1926, four years before the finalization of its report, and around the time of the Commission's establishment "at the instigation of the United States Government,"[89] the US-owned Firestone Tire and Rubber Company had signed a planting agreement with the Liberian government to lease more than 1 million acres for rubber plantations, requiring a projected 350,000 laborers – laborers whom, the Company reminded the government, it had promised to make available.[90] What Firestone needed was workers to transform Liberia into a lucrative rubber plantation.[91] If the government did not ensure the supply of these human resources, Firestone's investment would fail.[92]

The League of Nations International Commission of Enquiry marked a turning point in the history of the Republic.[93] In 1944 the new

[87] See I. K. Sundiata, "Prelude to Scandal: Liberia and Fernando Po, 1880–1930," *Journal of African History*, 15 (1974), 110.

[88] See also Azikiwe, "In Defense of Liberia," 30. On the connection between the International Commission of Enquiry and the Firestone company/United States interests, see also W. E. B. Du Bois, "Liberia, the League and the United States," *Foreign Affairs*, 11 (1933) 682–695; Azikiwe, *Liberia in World Politics*, pp. 195–196.

[89] International Commission of Enquiry, "The 1930 Enquiry Commission," 277. Although the Liberian Government "requested" the League of Nations to conduct the International Commission of Enquiry, "in order to remove all doubts with respect to the existence of slavery as defined in the Slavery Conventions of 1926." Azikiwe, *Liberia in World Politics*, p. 189.

[90] Sundiata, "Liberia and Fernando Po," 108; Azikiwe, *Liberia in World Politics*, pp. 150, 153.

[91] For a discussion of the requirement of labor and the use of "forced labor" by the Firestone Company, see Azikiwe, *Liberia in World Politics*, ch. 10.

[92] In a letter to the US Secretary of State in 1931, Harvey S. Firestone, Sr also noted his "appreciation of the firm stand which our [US] Government is taking in demanding that Liberia take effective measures to abolish enforced labor ... As you know [... this] has seriously interfered with our obtaining free labor ... I cannot urge upon you too strongly that whatever steps are necessary to bring about the correction of the conditions outlined in the report [of the International Commission of Enquiry], should be taken with the least possible delay." As quoted in Azikiwe, *Liberia in World Politics*, pp. 206–207.

[93] On the "reconstruction of Liberia," undertaken by the Government in response to the International Commission of Enquiry, see Azikiwe, *Liberia in World Politics*, ch. 15. The

Government of President William V. S. Tubman launched its National Unification Policy. In line with the Commission's recommendations, the Policy promised equal economic development for all.[94] And yet, rather than marking a radical departure from the (proto)development policies of the nineteenth and early-twentieth centuries, National Unification represented the last great attempt of the twentieth century to realize the idea of Liberia. Informed by the same logic as before, African-Liberians remained objects to be liberated into a subject-hood that would serve the economic development of Liberia.

Little surprise, then, that Unification eventually erupted into its opposite: civil war. In the 1970s Liberia underwent a revolution led by young African-Liberians that culminated in a massive demonstration in 1979. A year later the Americo-Liberian Republic was brought to a bloody end with a *coup d'état* led by the "indigenous" man, Master-Sergeant Samuel Doe, who would become Liberia's first African-Liberian President. The *coup* also precipitated the civil wars of the 1990s and early 2000s that killed a quarter of a million people, displaced many more,[95] and destroyed the institutions and infrastructure of the state.

Contemporary Reconfigurations: "Establishing a State based on the Rule of Law"

The year 2018 marked fifteen years of postwar government in Liberia committed to instituting "the rule of law" as a core pillar of its twenty-first century development agenda. It also marked the withdrawal of a UN

changes made, summarized in a 1933 memorandum from the Liberian Government to the League of Nations, included reform of the "native policy ... in so far as criticism was justified,' including removal of "barriers between civilized and uncivilized Liberians." As quoted in Azikiwe, *Liberia in World Politics*, pp. 282–283.

94 Under the Policy, the government also promised to invest all Liberians with full citizenship; to abolish the jurisdictional distinction between "Americo-Liberian" and "tribal" African-Liberian, along with the corresponding territorial division between coastal "Counties" and hinterland "Provinces"; and to extend education and employment opportunities to Liberia's "indigenous" peoples. See also Yekutiel Gershoni, "Liberia's Unification Policy and Decolonization in Africa: A Parallel Process," *Asian and African Studies*, 16 (1982), 239–260.

95 According to one report, "virtually all of the country's approximately 3 million people had to flee their homes at one time or another, sometimes for a few weeks and in many cases for several years. However, official figures estimate that 1.2 million were internally displaced and 700,000 were refugees at the war's end." See Dick, "FMO Country Guide," p. 11.

peace operation that worked for fifteen years to support "the establishment of a State based on the rule of law"[96] alongside a teeming market of international, transnational, governmental, and domestic actors.[97] While the term "rule of law" is new, this most recent intervention in the formation of Liberia continues in important ways the nineteenth- and twentieth-century attempts to develop the lands and peoples of this country.

In 2012 the newly re-elected Government of President Ellen Johnson Sirleaf (herself a former officer of the World Bank and UNDP) launched its "development framework," the *Agenda for Transformation: Steps Toward Liberia Rising 2030*,[98] setting out the "long-term national vision" for Liberia to pursue in the years between 2012 and 2030, as well as an "action plan" for the first five years (2012–2017).[99] Like Liberia's first two post-civil war development programs,[100] the *Agenda for Transformation* was formulated according to the International Monetary Fund and World Bank standard "poverty reduction strategy."[101] As such, its core "pillars" include "economic transformation" (Pillar II), reformation of "governance and public institutions" (Pillar IV), promotion and protection of human rights (Pillars III and V), all of which are to be secured through the establishment of "the rule of law" (Pillar I).[102]

The overarching goal of "economic transformation" is "[t]o transform the economy so that it meets the demands of Liberians through development of the domestic private sector."[103] The vision is then set out in a paragraph that recalls the International Commission of Enquiry's

[96] UN Doc. S/Res./1509 (September 19, 2003), preambular para. 7.

[97] On the complex of actors involved in the rule of law promotion industry more generally, see Taylor, "Big Rule of Law©®℠™(Pat.Pending)."

[98] Republic of Liberia, *Agenda for Transformation: Steps Toward Liberia Rising 2030* (Monrovia: Republic of Liberia, 2012).

[99] Republic of Liberia, *Agenda for Transformation*, p. 29.

[100] Republic of Liberia, *Interim Poverty Reduction Strategy (2006–2008)* (Washington: International Monetary Fund, 2007); Republic of Liberia, *Poverty Reduction Strategy (2008–2011)* (Monrovia: Republic of Liberia, 2008).

[101] See World Bank, "What are PRSPs?," available at http://go.worldbank.org/CSTQBOF730; International Monetary Fund, "Factsheet: Poverty Reduction Strategy in IMF-supported Programs," available at www.imf.org/external/np/exr/facts/prsp.htm.

[102] For the argument that Pillar I is supposed to secure this development framework, see Shane Chalmers, *Liberia and the Dialectic of Law: Critical Theory, Pluralism, and the Rule of Law* (Abingdon: Routledge, 2018), ch. 4.

[103] Republic of Liberia, *Agenda for Transformation*, p. 54.

"recommendation" in 1930, that Liberia develop its labor and consumption capacity:[104]

> Ideally, households and individuals will have more opportunity to work or engage in their own enterprises, leading to improved income and the opportunity to purchase desired consumption. To support provision of public services and infrastructure, the private economy and concessions will generate tax and royalty revenue for the public sector.[105]

The central "pillar" of economic transformation is again "private sector development,"[106] and central to achieving this are "property rights and contract enforcement," in order "to attract investment by Liberians and foreigners."[107] This in turn requires once again reforming Liberia's land law as well as its state legal system more generally.[108]

To address the issue of property rights, in 2013 the government published its *Land Rights Policy*.[109] The Policy sets out a framework for creating four categories of rights: "public land," "government land," "private land," and "customary land." The last of these is the most transformative proposition, potentially converting the lands of Liberia – which largely remain in "traditional" legal forms that are not easily alienable – into a form of private property that would "liberate" them for the market.[110] As the Policy states: "Rights to Customary Land, including ownership rights, must be secured by

[104] "teach him what he may buy for money, and he then wants to learn what he can grow, what he should do, or where he should work to make some money, with the result that trade increases, the coast merchant flourishes, the revenues of Government expand, and money is forthcoming." International Commission of Enquiry, "The 1930 Enquiry Commission to Liberia," 281.

[105] Republic of Liberia, *Agenda for Transformation*, p. 54.

[106] Republic of Liberia, *Agenda for Transformation*, pp. 55–62.

[107] Republic of Liberia, *Agenda for Transformation*, pp. 56 and 61–62.

[108] On the extent of the dysfunction of Liberia's state legal system following the civil wars, see Deborah H. Isser, Stephen C. Lubkemann, and Saah N'Tow, *Looking for Justice: Liberian Experiences with and Perceptions of Local Justice Options* (Washington, DC: United States Institute of Peace, 2009).

[109] Republic of Liberia, *Land Rights Policy* (Monrovia: Land Commission, 2013). See also UN Secretary-General, *Thirty-Third Progress Report of the Secretary-General on the United Nations Mission in Liberia*, UN Doc. S/2017/510 (June 16, 2017), para. 18.

[110] See also Caleb Stevens, "The Legal History of Public Land in Liberia," *Journal of African Law*, 58 (2014), 250–265; Jon Unruh, "Land Rights in Postwar Liberia: The Volatile Part of the Peace Process," *Land Use Policy*, 26 (2009), 425–433. Hernando de Soto, *The Mystery of Capital: Why Capitalism Triumphs in the West and Fails Everywhere Else* (New York: Basic Books, 2000).

ensuring that these rights are equally protected as private land rights."[111] These private land rights would be held by "the community as a collective land owner," with "groups, families, and individuals within the community" also possessing certain rights.[112] However, in order to invest "a community" and "its customary land" with these rights, first corporate membership of "the community" would have to be clearly defined,[113] as would the boundaries of "its land."[114] Because such clear distinctions do not yet exist, any attempt at definition would create more conflict, not less.[115] Anticipating this, the government created a parallel policy for "land conflict management."[116] At the same time communities must themselves define their membership, lead the process of demarcating their boundaries, and have a large degree of regulatory autonomy over "Customary Land management, use, and allocation decisions."[117]

The policy thus grants communities a certain autonomy over the content of Liberia's new land regime, while imposing a particular form. And although avowedly granting autonomy, Liberia's history shows that such promises of "freedom" are never one-sided. In this case, the "other side" to these land reforms is an agenda for economic transformation that cares primarily for the exchange value of Liberia's peoples and their lands. The question for the government is how it will deal with this: how it will realize its *Agenda for Transformation* given the incipient violence of the logic that informs its economic "pillar."

The answer is "Pillar I" of the development framework: the rule of law. Following the cessation of armed conflict in 2003 and the signing of the Comprehensive Peace Agreement,[118] the UN Security Council established

[111] Republic of Liberia, *Land Rights Policy*, p. 15.

[112] Republic of Liberia, *Land Rights Policy*, p. 18.

[113] "[C]ommunity ownership of Customary Land will be formalized by the issuance of a deed to a legal entity, bearing the name of the community." Republic of Liberia, *Land Rights Policy*, p. 18.

[114] Republic of Liberia, *Land Rights Policy*, p. 19.

[115] See also Jon Unruh, "Catalyzing the Socio-Legal Space for Armed Conflict: Land and Legal Pluralism in Pre-War Liberia," *Journal of Legal Pluralism and Unofficial Law*, 40 (2008), 1–31.

[116] Chalmers interviews with officers of the Liberian Land Commission in Monrovia (August 14, 2013), Zorzor (August 29, 2013), and Harper (September 27, 2013). See also Liberian Land Commission, *2014 Annual Report* (Monrovia: Land Commission, 2014).

[117] Republic of Liberia, *Land Rights Policy*, p. 19.

[118] UN Doc. S/2003/850 (August 29, 2003). See also University of Notre Dame Kroc Institute for International Peace Studies, "Peace Accords Matrix," available at https://peaceaccords.nd.edu/accord/accra-peace-agreement.

the UN Mission in Liberia (UNMIL) with a mandate that included, as one of its "key priorities," "the establishment of a State based on the rule of law."[119] As UNMIL transitioned from a "peace-keeping" to a "peace-building" operation after the 2006 presidential elections, "the rule of law" became increasingly imbricated with its security objectives. By 2013 a securitized rule of law had become definitive of UNMIL's work to assist the government in implementing its *Agenda for Transformation.*[120] With the withdrawal of UNMIL on the horizon,[121] and fearful of a "security vacuum," especially in the interior,[122] the government had also begun to focus more intensively on building the capacity of its security apparatus.[123] To this end, as its flagship project the government proposed to build a network of five Regional Justice and Security Hubs covering the interior of Liberia.[124] While the purported rule of law aim would be to increase "access to justice" by co-locating police, customs, and judicial services in each of the five Hubs,[125] the design

[119] UN Doc. S/Res./1509 (September 19, 2003), preambular para. 1. As an operative matter, this meant assisting in "monitoring and restructuring the police force" (para. 3(n)); "reestablishment of national authority throughout the country" (para. 3(p)); "developing a strategy to consolidate governmental institutions, including a national legal framework and judicial and correctional institutions" (para. 3(q)); "restoring proper administration of natural resources" (para. 3(r)); while contributing "towards international efforts to protect and promote human rights" (paras. 3(l), 3(m)) – all with the aim of securing order and stability (see para. 1).

[120] On the securitization of "the rule of law" in Liberia, see Chalmers, *Liberia and the Dialectic of Law*, ch. 4; Shane Chalmers and Jeremy Farrall, "Securing the Rule of Law through United Nations Peace Operations," *Max Planck Yearbook of United Nations Law*, 18 (2014), 217–248.

[121] In 2013 UNMIL was in "the first phase of the second military draw down": Chalmers interview with United Nations Department of Peacekeeping Operations official, New York City, June 22, 2013. See also UN Doc. S/Res./2215 (April 2, 2015), paras. 1 and 3. The transfer of security responsibilities from UNMIL to Liberia's security services was completed on June 30, 2016, and a complete withdrawal of UNMIL has been scheduled for the end of April 2018: UN Doc. S/Res./2333 (December 23, 2016), para. 10.

[122] See Rory Keane, "Reviewing the Justice and Security Hub Modality as Piloted in Liberia," *Stability*, 1 (2012), 87.

[123] See UN Doc. S/2013/124 (February 28, 2013); UN Doc. S/2013/479 (August 12, 2013); UN Doc. S/2014/123 (February 18, 2014); UN Doc. S/2014/598 (August 15, 2014); UN Doc. S/2015/275 (April 23, 2015). Up until 2012 UNMIL's main security focus had been to provide operational support to the Liberian National Police and the Bureau of Immigration and Naturalization as part of its peacekeeping strategy rather than to develop the capacity of these agencies.

[124] Funded by the UN Peacebuilding Fund. See UN Doc. PBC/4/LBR/2 (November 16, 2010), with the Statement of Mutual Commitments between the Government of Liberia and the UN Peacebuilding Commission revised in UN Doc. PBC/6/LBR/2 (May 9, 2012).

[125] Justice and Security Joint Program, "Introduction," in *Gbarnga Regional Justice and Security Hub Report* (January 2012–January 2013), p. 3.

effectively provides "a rapid response forward operational base" for its security forces.[126]

While the government was building the capacity of its security sector, it was also beginning a process to reform the state legal system, to further increase "access to justice." For the government and its international supporters,[127] this has meant "modernizing" so-called customary and traditional legal systems, as a normative matter, and, as a structural matter, "harmonizing" them with the statutory legal system.[128] Alongside this, local and international nongovernment organizations have also been working to increase "access to justice" through "legal empowerment" projects.[129] What brings these otherwise distinct actors together is their

[126] Justice and Security Joint Program, "Introduction," p. 11. This is also in keeping with the government's original concept, on which the Hubs were based, to create regional command centers for the Liberian National Police to have forward operating bases in the interior. To obtain support from the UN Peacebuilding Commission and funding from the UN Peacebuilding Fund, the design was "scaled up" to include "justice" services as well. See also Keane, "Reviewing the Justice and Security Hub Modality as Piloted in Liberia", 88.

[127] UNMIL, the Carter Center in Liberia, the United States Institute of Peace, and the UNDP were instrumental in initiating and facilitating the "access to justice" legal system reform process: see Chalmers, *Liberia and the Dialectic of Law*, ch. 6. See also Amanda Rawls, *Policy Proposals for Justice Reform in Liberia: Opportunities under the Current Legal Framework to Expand Access to Justice* (Rome: International Development Law Organization, 2011).

[128] The term "statutory law" is used in Liberia to refer to the law articulated by Liberia's legislative and judicial organs of government. The term "customary law" refers to the law articulated by members of Liberia's executive organ of government, primarily in the Ministry of Interior, most frequently Chiefs. "Traditional law" by contrast refers to the law articulated by "unofficial" organs of government, such as the sacred institutions of *poro* and *sande*. On the government's "access to justice" legal system reforms, see Chalmers, *Liberia and the Dialectic of Law*, ch. 6, and, on the problem of "harmonization," see also ch. 5.

[129] The two most prominent NGOs in this field in 2013 were The Carter Center and the Liberian Catholic Justice and Peace Commission, working in partnership to provide legal advisory, education and dispute resolution services in communities. In the area of land, the Norwegian Refugee Council also pioneered a highly successful community-based dispute resolution and legal education program, and the Liberian Sustainable Development Initiative has been at the forefront of policy development on land rights and dispute resolution. Other local and international NGOs, as well as the UN in Liberia, government agencies and bilateral donors, have been carrying out similar work in the area of human rights. See further Chalmers, *Liberia and the Dialectic of Law*, ch. 6. On the "legal empowerment alternative" more generally, see Stephen Golub, "The Legal Empowerment Alternative," in Carothers, ed., *Promoting the Rule of Law Abroad*, pp. 105"136, and, in particular, Peter Chapman and Chelsea Payne, "'You Place the Old Mat with the New Mat': Legal Empowerment, Equitable Dispute Resolution, and Social Cohesion in Post-Conflict Liberia," in Open Society Justice Initiative, ed., *Justice*

approach to establishing the rule of law. At the heart of their work is the ambition to "bridge the gap" between different systems of law by increasing Liberians' knowledge of and material access to the state legal system. In doing so, they have a clear normative agenda: to change Liberians' worldviews and behavior according to a modern-liberal understanding of right, on the assumption, held by government, nongovernment and international actors alike, that Liberians are not using the state legal system in large part because they remain ignorant of it, and mired in their own superstitions.[130] Thus, just as the government is selective in its response to what "legal system reform" might look like – tolerating the idea of bringing other systems of law within the state legal system as long as they are "modernized" and "harmonized" with it in the process – the organizations working to support legal empowerment are selective in what can be "empowered" (with "international human rights" providing the standard threshold). In short, the "bridge" that is supposed to overcome the gap between Liberia's different systems of law is conceived as a one-way path to a Western liberal-modernity.

Such an approach is in keeping with the government's *Agenda for Transformation*, which would see Liberia become a "middle-income country" by 2030 based on an economic model of private sector development, requiring properly educated citizens to populate the new development state, and the rule of law to authorize and secure it. This is also in keeping with the "hope," expressed in 1817, "of redeeming many millions of people from the lowest state of ignorance and superstition" through the establishment of a "sublime empire of reason and law."[131]

Conclusion

Our aim in the final section of this chapter has been to show how (economic) development and the rule of law have come together in a particular case: the making and remaking of Liberia. The Liberian case is both

Initiatives: Legal Empowerment (New York: Open Society Justice Initiative, 2013), pp.15–29.

[130] For example, a dominant focus of the legal reform process has been to stop the use of popular forms of "trial by ordeal" that use magic in the resolution of disputes; see further Chalmers, *Liberia and the Dialectic of Law*, chs. 5 and 6.

[131] American Colonization Society, *A View of Exertions Lately Made for the Purpose of Colonizing the Free People of Color, in the United States, in Africa, or Elsewhere*, p. 7.

singular in its history, and unexceptional in its trajectory. As foreshadowed in the second section of the chapter, it is just one configuration of the field of economic development and the rule of law in which a complex of international, transnational, government and domestic actors work to authorize a particular kind of state by pursuing the various ends of "governance," "justice," "security," as well as more directly "economic development."

What this example illustrates is that beneath the postcolonial veneer of the "rule of law and development" project lies a colonial core. The most recent intervention in Liberia shows how contemporary reconfigurations of "economic development and the rule of law" continue much older and more overtly racist projects directed toward making Liberia's lands and peoples economically productive. Through the contemporary developmental rule of law, lands are transformed into private property and people are transformed into "modern" legal subjects capable of transacting in the globalized economy. This transformation is effected through interventions directed toward institutionalizing a legal system that is capable of both authorizing and enforcing the new developmental state, increasingly harnessed to facilitate the protection of (foreign) investments. The resonance between this contemporary project of development and its predecessors is strong. It recalls the unrelenting pressure that Europe and the United States put throughout the nineteenth and twentieth centuries on the Black Republic, to ensure its lands and peoples would be productive according to an Occidental economic model. This required, as a normative matter, converting African-Liberians into "civilized citizens" to make them useful to the North Atlantic economy; and, as a structural matter, it required reforming the institutions of government to secure European and US economic interests in West Africa.

In both historical and contemporary configurations, the express missions both to civilize and to "develop" have been overlaid by an invocation of "justice" that in turn authorizes interventions to actualize such "rule of law" and development. The confluence is aptly summarized by the Anglo-American painter Benjamin West. Commenting in 1805 on his painting, *The Treaty of Penn with the Indians, 1771–1772,* depicting one of the Provinces of Pennsylvania's founding jurisdictional acts, West noted: "[t]he great object I had in informing that composition was to express savages brought into harmony and peace by justice and benevolence, not by withholding from them what was their right, but giving to them what they were in want of."[132] Such "justice" is a concept of economic development *par excellence*, as the League of Nations International Commission of Enquiry was well aware (recall: "the unsophisticated native learns something of the outside world, and his wants are increased").[133] It is also at the heart of the Liberian Government's and its international supporters' work to bring about order and stability, or "harmony and peace," by establishing a state based on economic development and the rule of law.

[132] As quoted in Greg Lehman, "Benjamin Duterrau: The Art of Conciliation," *Journal of War and Culture Studies*, 8 (2015), 116.

[133] International Commission of Enquiry, "The 1930 Enquiry Commission to Liberia," 281.

22 Democracy and the Rule of Law

Martin Krygier

Introduction

Democracy and the rule of law are both "essentially contested concepts" in common use; indeed both are hurrah terms to which virtually everyone these days seeks to lay claim. In this brief chapter, rather than survey contestants I opt for stipulation. My stipulations are intended to be fairly undemanding, indeed deliberately unoriginal. They might well exclude legitimate contenders and not be uncontroversial, but they are intended to reflect not only my own preferences but central themes in long traditions of thought about these matters.[1]

In this chapter, "democracy" denotes a goal, specifically a political ideal variably and variously approached in practice, of a state of affairs in which citizens (not "subjects") and not hereditary or rich or sanctified or in any other way anointed individuals or castes of "rulers," are conceived of as ultimate authors, controllers and beneficiaries of the political order, significantly engaged in the exercise and/or control of the exercise of political power. What in practice that authorizing engagement in rule can and need involve in order to count as democratic, and how that is to be achieved, are subjects of long history[2] and wide-ranging controversy and debate. That such engagement in one form or another is central to and distinctive of democracy is not.

"Rule of law" also has to do with an ideal state of affairs, but one immediately focused on a different end: the institutionalized constraint and channeling of the exercise of significant power – some but not I would limit it to governmental power[3] – in ways that minimize its arbitrary

[1] See W. B. Gallie, " Essentially Contested Concepts," *Proceedings of the Aristotelian Society*, 56 (1956), 167–198; Jeremy Waldron, "Is the Rule of Law an Essentially Contested Concept (in Florida)?" *Law and Philosophy*, 21 (2002), 137–164; and idem, this volume, Chapter 6.

[2] See John Keane, *The Life and Death of Democracy* (London: Simon & Schuster, 2009).

[3] Cf. Paul Gowder, *The Rule of Law in the Real World* (Cambridge: Cambridge University Press, 2016); Martin Krygier, "Four Puzzles about the Rule of Law: Why, What, Where? And

exercise. Again, more can be said[4] but most would consider limiting the possibilities of arbitrary exercise of power a necessary, indeed central element. It is a common theme, especially in the Anglophone traditions from which the specific phrase derives,[5] and I believe a characteristic one in writings about the rule of law as an ideal. Whether it is sufficient is a question that can be pursued elsewhere.[6] It is enough for my purposes here that reduction of arbitrary power is understood to be a central and necessary purpose of the rule of law.

As a first cut and to put it crudely, as Isaiah Berlin has been criticized for putting it, democracy has to do with a particular and distinctive question, "Who governs me?"[7] Berlin took the democratic answer to that question – "we the people" – to appeal to what he called *positive* liberty ("freedom *to*") which, in a much questioned interpretation, he distinguished from *negative* liberty ("freedom *from*"), which he took to be another question altogether: "How far does government interfere with me?" He believed that excessive devotion to the former threatened to subvert the latter in practice, and needed to be kept conceptually separate from it, for reasons that went far beyond mental hygiene.

The distinction Berlin drew is much contested, and, it has been pointed out, does not exhaust the field, either of conceptions of liberty or of questions one can ask about power. For there is (at least) a third question that can be asked about the exercise of power, and partisans of the rule of

Who Cares?" in James E. Fleming, ed., *Getting to the Rule of Law: NOMOS L* (New York: New York University Press, 2011), pp. 64–104.

4 See Gianluigi Palombella, "Illiberal,Democratic and Non-Arbitrary?" *Hague Journal on the Rule of Law*, 10 (2018), 5–19.

5 See A. V. Dicey, *Introduction to the Study of the Law of the Constitution*, 8th ed. (Indianapolis: Liberty Fund, 1982), p. 110; and John Phillip Reid, *Rule of Law. The Jurisprudence of Liberty in the Seventeenth and Eighteenth Centuries* (DeKalb: Northern Illinois University Press, 2004). On differences between this tradition's conception of "the rule of law" and the influential German Rechtsstaat tradition, see Martin Krygier, "Rule of Law (and Rechtsstaat)," in James D. Wright, ed., *International Encyclopedia of the Social and Behavioral Sciences*, 2nd ed. (Oxford: Elsevier, 2015), pp. 780–787.

6 See, for one view, Joseph Raz, "The Rule of Law and Its Virtue," in idem, *The Authority of Law: Essays on Law and Morality*, 2nd ed. (Oxford: Oxford University Press, 2009), pp. 210–229, and for a contrary view Julian A. Sempill, "Ruler's Sword, Citizen's Shield: The Rule of Law and the Constitution of Power," *Journal of Law and Politics*, 31 (2016), 333–414. Also Martin Krygier, "The Rule of Law: Pasts, Presents, and Two Possible Futures," *Annual Review of Law and Social Science*, 12 (2016), esp. 203–208.

7 Isaiah Berlin, "Two Concepts of Liberty," in idem, *Four Essays on Liberty* (Oxford: Oxford University Press, 1969), p. 130.

law are disposed to ask it. This question is conceptually and in the first instance more closely related to negative than to positive liberty, but it is really an answer to a different question from either. Rather than "by whom?" or the question Berlin posed for negative liberty – "*how much*"[8] – the rule of law has to do with "*how* am I governed?" or, more broadly, "*how* is power exercised in relation to me?"[9] In particular, the rule of law has typically been counterposed to "arbitrary" power. If the answer to the "by whom?" question is "well, certainly not *the people*," then the ideal of democracy is challenged. If the answer to "how" is "arbitrarily," the challenge is to the central ideal of the rule of law.

I do not want to get bogged down in elaboration or defense of these stipulations, but there is one aspect of them both that warrants mention. Both conceptions are "teleological," rather than "anatomical" in character.[10] That is to say, they start from a postulated end in view, in both cases an end deemed by its partisans to be valuable, rather than a list of purported institutional attributes – "free and fair elections," the existence (or absence) of representative bodies of particular sorts with certain functions, say, in the case of democracy; prospective rules, independent judiciary, etc. in the case of the rule of law. Even if people reject my

[8] Isaiah Berlin, "Introduction," in idem, *Four Essays on Liberty,* p. xliii (emphasis added).

[9] According to Aurelian Craiutu, "By distinguishing between moderate and immoderate governments, Montesquieu departed from previous classifications. For him, the fundamental question was no longer *who* exercised power – one, the few, or the many – but *how* power was exercised, that is, moderately or immoderately. Political liberty, he argued, exists only in moderate goverments and only in those governments in which power is not chronically abused." See *A Virtue for Courageous Minds: Moderation in French Political Thought, 1748–1830* (Princeton: Princeton University Press, 2012), p. 40.

There is an overlap between this distinction (and much else in this chapter) and that developed in Philip Pettit's republican conception of freedom as non-domination. See his *Republicanism: A Theory of Freedom and Government* (Oxford: Oxford University Press, 1997). Like Pettit in that work, my objection is to arbitrary power, but whereas he starts from a philosophical commitment to a particular conception of freedom as non-domination and sees hostility to arbitrary power as an implication of it, I – and I think quite a few non-philosopher partisans of the rule of law – come at the problem less from the philosophical ground up, as it were, than from the empirical world down. We start by thinking about ways in which power has been and might be exercised and find arbitrary power distasteful for a host of reasons, including the fear, confusion, inequality, invasion of negative liberty, *as well as* domination, that it tends to sow. As I understand him, this is how Montesquieu comes to value "moderation" in the exercise of power.

[10] See Martin Krygier, "The Rule of Law. Legality, Teleology, Sociology," in Gianluigi Palombella and Neil Walker, eds., *Relocating the Rule of Law* (Oxford: Hart, 2009), pp. 45–69.

particular renditions of such ends, I would advocate starting by trying to sort them out, rather than directly engaging with the means thought possible to deliver them. One cannot stay with ends forever, and it is necessary to move seriously to consider how valued ends are to be operationalized and institutionalized. I only ask that we recognize that means are best assessed only after one has in view the ends they are (or were) supposed to help achieve.

Often discussion oscillates wordlessly between *telos* and anatomy, end and means, without distinction. One speaks of "the ideal of" democracy or the rule of law and then without pause cashes it out in (frequently nationally and institutionally parochial) listings of institutional arrangements, as though the ideal was uniquely to be identified with a particular notion of what might need to be in place to help attain it. The claim here, by contrast, is that it is preferable to approach these concepts by starting with what they are thought to be *for* and good for, why they and not some other accomplishment (oligarchy? rule *by* law?) is thought to matter, rather than by listing some institutional components or other supposed to identify the phenomena that warrant these labels – perhaps because they are also thought to serve such ends, or sometimes without further thought, just because particular institutions or practices have long been associated with a vaunted name. We can debate fruitfully how such ends might best be characterized, and my proposals above might not satisfy many. I am here less concerned about that (though I hope they satisfy someone) than I am to argue that some conception of the *teloi* of democracy and the rule of law is where we should *start*.

For democracy and the rule of law are both what Jeremy Waldron once described, in discussion of the latter, as "solution concepts."[11] If so, we should begin by asking what the problem is for which they are offered as solutions and, before we postulate what particular institutional arrangements might do the job, why "democracy" or "the rule of law" might offer such solutions.

Some questions in matters of governance are perennial, "by whom?" and "how?" among them. Historically there have been many answers to them. Some answers have a long life, but never as long or as uniform as the questions, for the answers, however obvious they appear in one or another culture, or to one or another generation, vary with circumstances,

[11] Waldron, "Is the Rule of Law an Essentially Contested Concept (in Florida)?" 158.

possibilities, cultures, beliefs and imaginations. And even where the answers have some longevity – for example, "the people (or the King, or the rich or the clever or the priests) should rule" – the institutional means we imagine might best embody them have relatively fleeting lives.

Both ideals and what we imagine will help us attain them, differ and change. Much as we might retrospectively want to puff up Magna Carta as the foundation of English democracy and the rule of law, that is not how the barons, the Church or the King saw it; our institutions are not theirs,[12] and they differ between societies and within them. It hardly seems warranted to insist that some specific institutional set-up, whether inherited or postulated by philosophers or political scientists or lawyers or anyone else, is a universal guarantee of the attainment of such ends in the many and varied circumstances, times and places we might hope for democracy and the rule of law. We should be open to the probability that institutional means are more contingent, various and negotiable than ultimate ends, unless we have more evidence than is typically adduced, or is likely to be adduced, to think otherwise.

And while of course ends require means for their achievement, and some familiar institutions might indeed turn out to be widely usable and useful, I venture that popular yearnings when expressed in terms of "democracy" or "the rule of law," are primarily concerned with the approximation of valued ends – who governs? and how? – rather than with specific, often technical means. Academics and promoters, by contrast, frequently enumerate institutional items as adding up to democracy or the rule of law, with little more than an intuitive leap from means to ends: we count votes without fudging them, so we have democracy; we are building courthouses so we are building the rule of law.

I am with the people. If conventionally enumerated democratic or legal institutions exist but do not work in ways that support, or work in ways that (often deliberately) subvert the ideals they are supposed to embody, we have a problem for democracy and the rule of law. And many countries today face just such problems where standard institutional nostrums seem to produce parodies of their desired ends: institutional ingredients listed by political scientists, lawyers, democracy and rule of law promoters are in abundance, but the ends people have sought from democracy and the rule

[12] See Martin Krygier, "Magna Carta and the Rule of Law Tradition," *Papers on Parliament*, 65 (2016), 11–29.

of law are far away, sometimes indeed driven further by abusive use of those very institutions.[13] To the extent this is the case, democracy and the rule of law are in bad shape, and would be even if the institutions themselves could be said to be in good shape. Conversely and perhaps hypothetically, were we to find polities and social orders which contrived to generate popular rule and constraint on possibilities of arbitrary power in ways and in circumstances that never occurred to us, it seems to me we should praise them in terms of the ideals of democracy and the rule of law, however they managed to do it. We might even learn something important from their exotic ways. Instead, it is more common to export particular political and legal institutions to benighted countries believed to be deficient in democracy and the rule of law, and then lament the ineffectiveness of the transplants to do what they were thought to do at home.

So this chapter seeks to address relationships between democracy and the rule of law understood as complex, practical ideals. They are complex, because a lot is needed even to approximate them and that lot varies and changes; practical because they are neither natural facts nor Utopian fantasies but goals intended to be made good (even if only partially) in the world, and they are ideals rather than simple descriptions. The concepts are normative. We need things in the world to achieve them, but what we need will depend first on what we want to achieve, then on the conditions and circumstances in which we seek to achieve them, and still then on whether whatever we have to offer is apt to deliver the former in the circumstances of the latter. Since such conditions, circumstances and offerings vary and change, so too might the best ways of attaining democracy and the rule of law.

1 Friends or Foes?

International promoters of democracy and the rule of law often speak of them together as though they are fond bed-fellows, indeed most happily to

[13] See David Landau, "Abusive Constitutionalism," *University of California Davis Law Review*, 47 (2013), 189–260; Kim Lane Scheppele, "Constitutional Coups in EU Law," in Maurice Adams, Anne Meuwese, and Ernst Hirsch Ballin, eds., *Constitutionalism and the Rule of Law: Bridging Idealism and Realism* (Cambridge: Cambridge University Press, 2017), pp. 446–478; Ozan Varol, "Stealth Authoritarianism," *Iowa Law Review*, 100 (2015), 1673–1742.

be joined in a *ménage* with a younger third, human rights. Country after country is exhorted to welcome "democracy, human rights and the rule of law,"[14] the assumption apparently being that they all bring each other joy, or at least do each other no harm. Indeed it is often said you cannot have one without the other.[15] Even if we restrict ourselves to the original couple, how plausible is that?

According to one popular reading of Benjamin Constant, one of the earliest great meditators on modernity and freedom, not very. Thus in his influential lecture on "the liberty of ancients compared with that of moderns" he argued that the form of democracy practised by "the ancients" – the Greek city states, and especially Sparta – was democracy *pur sang*, but lacked and had no appreciation of constraints on the power of the *demos*, which was necessary to ensure "the liberty of the moderns." Indeed it could not have coexisted in pure form with such constraints, to which few of the ancient Greeks in any case gave any thought; they were no part of the ancient ideal. One example can stand for many: "[O]stracism, that legal arbitrariness, extolled by all the legislators of the age; ostracism, which appears to us, and rightly so, a revolting iniquity, proves that the individual was much more subservient to the supremacy of the social body in Athens, than he is in any of the free states of Europe today."[16]

And so, as Constant famously argued:

among the ancients the individual, almost always sovereign in public affairs, was a slave in all his private relations. As a citizen, he decided on peace and war; as a private individual, he was constrained, watched and repressed in all his

[14] See, for example, Ken Macdonald, "Democracy and Human Rights Are Vital for the Rule of Law – and So Is Legality," available at www.scmp.com/comment/insight-opinion/article/2109596/democracy-and-human-rights-are-vital-rule-law-and-so; United States Agency for International Development, "Democracy, Human Rights, and the Rule of Law," available at www.usaid.gov/burma/our-work/democracy-human-rights-and-rule-law; Democracy International, "Human Rights, Democracy, and Rule of Law," www.democracy-international.org/human-rights; United Nations, High Commissioner for Refugees, "Rule of Law – Democracy and Human Rights," available at www.ohchr.org/EN/Issues/RuleOfLaw/Pages/Democracy.aspx; Council of Europe, "State of Democracy, Human Rights, and the Rule of Law 2017," available at https://edoc.coe.int/en/an-overview/7345-pdf-state-of-democracy-human-rights-and-the-rule-of-law.html.

[15] Democracy International, "Human Rights, Democracy, and Rule of Law," available at www.democracy-international.org/human-rights.

[16] Benjamin Constant, "The Liberty of the Ancients Compared with that of the Moderns," in idem, *Political Writings*, trans. and ed. Biancamaria Fontana (Cambridge: Cambridge University Press, [1819] 1988), p. 316.

movements; as a member of the collective body, he interrogated, dismissed, condemned, beggared, exiled, or sentenced to death his magistrates and superiors; as a subject of the collective body he could himself be deprived of his status, stripped of his privileges, banished, put to death, by the discretionary will of the whole to which he belonged. Among the moderns, on the contrary, the individual, independent in his private life, is, even in the freest of states, sovereign only in appearance. His sovereignty is restricted and almost always suspended. If, at fixed and rare intervals, in which he is again surrounded by precautions and obstacles, he exercises this sovereignty, it is always only to renounce it.[17]

As one modern scholar reads and reiterates Constant's argument, "[i]n Ancient Athens, the people, the Demos, *hoi polloi*, were politically dominant and nothing was there to restrain them. There was no Constitution, laws could be annulled or nullified by a temporary majority, there were no checks and balances. Athens was an illiberal democracy."[18]

However nostalgic we might feel for ancient liberty, Constant insists, after "the changes brought by two thousand years in the dispositions of mankind," it is beyond us: "[W]e can no longer enjoy the liberty of the ancients, which consisted in an active and constant participation in collective power. Our freedom must consist of peaceful enjoyment and private independence."[19] Those who claimed to resurrect ancient liberty in modern conditions, among whom he numbered Rousseau and the Jacobin authors of the French Revolutionary Terror, under the guise of democracy give succour to tyranny, which it was Constant's (and Berlin's) lifelong obsession to expose and to avoid. More generally, given that he saw "the main task of [modern] political theory as the discovery, in the absence of the king, of how to protect against arbitrariness ... to bind to principles," he believed democracy as the ancients understood it to be incompatible with the rule of law.[20]

Conversely, if there have been democracies which knew nothing of the rule of law it is hard to say that the ends of the rule of law – constraint on arbitrary power – are unattainable without democracy. Berlin had

[17] Constant, "The Liberty of the Ancients Compared with that of the Moderns," pp. 311–312.

[18] Aristides N. Hatzis, "The Illiberal Democracy of Ancient Athens," Unpublished paper, University of Athens, July 2016, p. 3.

[19] Constant, "The Liberty of the Ancients Compared with that of the Moderns," pp. 316; 317.

[20] Andreas Kalyvas and Ira Katznelson, *Liberal Beginnings: Making a Republic for the Moderns* (Cambridge: Cambridge University Press, 2008), p. 152, quoting Benjamin Constant, *Ecrits et discours politiques*, vol. 1, ed. Olivier. Pozzo di Borgo (Paris: Chez Jean-Jacques Pauvert, 1964), p. 82.

notoriously little to say in general about how values might be institutionalized and nothing much about law and the rule of law,[21] but he certainly believed that negative liberty "is not incompatible with some kinds of autocracy, or at any rate with the absence of self-government ... The connexion between democracy and individual liberty is a good deal more tenuous than it seemed to many advocates of both."[22] There was no conceptual connection, and only arguable practical links, between the two. Nothing in his arguments suggests he would think differently, had he thought at all, about how limitations on unwarranted intervention with the liberty he valued might be institutionalized.

Again, those eighteenth century "foreign observers of English manners" whom A. V. Dicey proudly quoted as finding England to be "a country governed, as is scarcely any other part of Europe, under the rule of law,"[23] were not praising it as a democracy, which it was not at all in the eighteenth century, and was only becoming in the nineteenth, and which few of them would have thought praiseworthy. But they had a point. In England over centuries power was less arbitrarily wielded, and law more of a constraint on rule than in, say, Russia (then or now) and than in many other states in the world, and the English had long considered that a public ideal.[24] There were numerous countervailing forces that tempered power in England, and that were praised for doing so, but the rule of the people was not until relatively recently among them. And, *pace* Dicey, England was not unique in having traditions, institutions, social arrangements and practices that effectively limited arbitrary power in the premodern and predemocratic era, which was long and full of more or less ruly autocracies. Think late-eighteenth- and nineteenth-century Prussia with Frederick the Great's Constitution declaring him "the first servant of the state," or the Austro-Hungarian empire; not democracies, but not tyrannies either. After democracy's ancient rise and demise, however, it took a much longer time for it to re-emerge and to be praised than did hostility to arbitrary power.[25]

[21] See Jeremy Waldron, "Isaiah Berlin's Neglect of Enlightenment Constitutionalism," in idem, *Political Political Theory: Essays on Institutions* (Cambridge: Harvard University Press, 2016), pp. 274–289.

[22] See Berlin, "Two Concepts of Liberty," 129–131.

[23] Dicey, *Introduction to the Study of the Law of the Constitution*, p. 108.

[24] See Richard Pipes, *Russia under the Old Regime* (Harmondsworth: Penguin, 1995); and Reid, *Rule of Law*.

[25] See Hilton Root, *Political Foundations of Markets in Old Regime France and England* (Berkeley: University of California Press, 1994).

Even where democracy and the rule of law coexist, moreover, the marriage has not always been easy. Many thinkers have argued that tensions between democracy and the rule of law are conceptually, or in principle, or in fact, hard-wired. On such views, the goals of democracy, to elevate the power of the people, are thought to be in structural tension with those of the rule of law, to constrain the exercise of power, even if it is that of the people. Where pursuit of the former requires the extension of the people's hold over institutions of power, the latter drives commitment to "curbs," "limits," "restraints," typically embodied in unelected institutions, some of the members of which are granted life or at least fixed tenure, precisely to shield them from influence by "the people" or their representatives.

Many democrats already complain that elections are inadequate reflections of the power of the people, and that they need to be supplemented by assorted measures of control responsive to them,[26] among them referenda. Some of them are even more hostile to institutions such as judicial review, often those most applauded by rule of lawyers, because of their unelected and therefore, so it is often thought, antidemocratic provenance and ways of working. Seven privileged, well-paid, (sometimes barely) live white male appointees, overruling the people's representatives? Nine? What sort of democracy is that?[27]

By contrast, Tocqueville and Mill worried about the "tyranny of the majority" in democracies, and some more recent partisans of the rule of law worry about "elective dictatorship,"[28] in circumstances where parliaments are commonly dominated by governments, who will stop at little to curry favor with electors. Such partisans of the rule of law seek to bolster what they see as the essential dyke-like functions of unelected judges, bills of rights, commissions of inquiry often headed by judges and staffed by experts, and other "independent" institutions, to stem the surging tides of

[26] See John Keane, *The Life and Death of Democracy*, pp. 690–691, on "monitory democracy" in "the age of surveys, focus groups, deliberative polling, online petitions and audience and customer voting."

[27] See Jeremy Waldron, *Democracy and Disagreement* (Oxford: Oxford University Press, 1999), part III.

[28] Lord Hailsham, *Elective Dictatorship* (London: BBC, 1976), and see Friedrich A. Hayek, *Law, Legislation ad Liberty*, vol. 3: *The Political Order of a Free People* (Chicago: University of Chicago Press, 1979), p. 101.

democratic and populist demands that wash against them. But it is hard, they say, when democracies press on politicians to "buy" their electoral favor.

Again, the democratic welfare and regulatory state came under challenge, especially from the 1970s, by neoliberals but not only by them. Among the grounds of these challenges was that its activities subverted the character and thereby the rule, of law. Apart from the neoliberal objection to the effects of modern intrusive state activity on market freedom, there was a separate critique of the character of transformations in the legal *means* used to provide welfare and regulation. Hayek, who thought more than many economists (and many neoliberals) about law, was influential here, but the argument came from many sides. For him, the rule of law required that the law be *clear, general, abstract, impersonal,* and *negative* rules of the game, "rules of just conduct,"[29] interpreted and enforced by independent arbiters, on the model of classical private and criminal law. It could not withstand blizzards of open-ended policy directives of public law, increasingly trying to keep up with popular demands, vague and unspecific in their terms, full of appeals to substantive criteria and specific social purposes to be achieved, open to discretionary implementation by goal-directed bureaucrats increasingly free (actually required) to adjust their interpretations to the specificity of particular cases in pursuit of governmentally prescribed specific ends. Bad goals in turn generate bad means, laws that do not guide, frameworks that keep being adjusted, prescriptions too vague and malleable to be followed, but altogether labile in the hands of their wielders. However well-meaning the motives of such activities, their pursuit was believed to exact a high price in terms of the ability of law to constrain power and contribute to coordination, even if their goals were likely to be achieved, which many such critics also doubted. A significant part of the cost of the pursuit, it was alleged, is borne by the rule of law.[30]

[29] Friedrich A. Hayek, *Law, Legislation and Liberty*, vol. 1: *Rules and Order* (Chicago: University of Chicago Press, 1976), p. 143.

[30] See, for example, Geoffrey de Q. Walker, *The Rule of Law: Foundation of Constitutional Democracy* (Melbourne: Melbourne University Press, 1988); Friedrich A. Hayek, *Law, Legislation and Liberty*, 3 vols. (Chicago: University of Chicago Press, 1973–1979); Eugene Kamenka and Alice Ehr-Soon Tay, "Beyond Bourgeois Individualism: The Contemporary Crisis in Law and Legal Ideology," in Eugene Kamenka and R. S. Neale, eds., *Feudalism, Capitalism and Beyond* (Canberra: ANU Press, 1975) pp. 126–144. And from a different political perspective, see Brian Tamanaha, *Law as a Means to an End:*

What of today? At the end of the twentieth century, Fareed Zakaria coined the term "illiberal democracy," a mutation that he feared was growing all around us.[31] While "for a century in the West, democracy has meant *liberal* democracy – a political system marked not only by free and fair elections, but also by the rule of law, a separation of powers, and the protection of basic liberties,"[32] this was decreasingly the case. Instead, "[t]oday the two strands of liberal democracy, interwoven in the Western political fabric, are coming apart in the rest of the world. Democracy is flourishing; constitutional liberalism is not."[33] As a result, though "we live in a democratic age,"[34] this is not necessarily something to boast about: "The tendency for a democratic government to believe it has absolute sovereignty (that is, power) can result in the centralization of authority, often by extra-constitutional means and with grim results."[35]

If that was a controversial observation in 1997, it had become less so under twenty years later. On the contrary, early twenty-first-century populist regimes in Hungary and Poland, which only a short time before had seemed to be paragons of newly won democracy and rule of law, came to boast of their democratic credentials while busily and often effectively subverting constraints on the power of "the sovereign people," or more accurately their elected representatives, wholesale. Central among such constraints were those traditionally associated with the rule of law, among them independent courts at virtually every level. Courting of the sovereign and winning support through elections and referenda, not all of them spurious, is popular among twenty-first-century populists. Legal (and other) constraints on their ability to wield arbitrary power are, by contrast, anathema to them: any such institutionalized intermediation would, it is often said, put unelected legal elites, "castes of jurists," typically in service

Threat to the Rule of Law (Cambridge: Cambridge University Press, 2007). More complex appraisals of such developments include Otto Kirchheimer, "The *Rechtsstaat* as Magic Wall," in idem, *Politics, Law, and Social Change*, ed., Frederic S. Burin, and Kurt L. Shell (New York: Columbia University Press, 1969), p. 428; Philippe Nonet and Philip Selznick, *Law and Society in Transition: Toward Responsive Law* (New Brunswick: Transaction Publishers, 2001); and, for a bracing critique of such "crisis talk," David Nelken, "Is There a Crisis in Law and Legal Ideology?" *Journal of Law and Society*, 9 (1982), 177–189. For a discussion of these writings on which this paragraph draws, see Martin Krygier, *Philip Selznick: Ideals in the World* (Palo Alto: Stanford University Press, 2012), ch. 8.

31 Fareed Zakaria, "Illiberal Democracy," *Foreign Affairs*, 76 (1997), 22–43.

32 Zakaria, "Illiberal Democracy," p. 22.

33 Zakaria, "Illiberal Democracy," p. 23.

34 Zakaria, "Illiberal Democracy," p. 42.

35 Zakaria, "Illiberal Democracy," p. 30.

of themselves and also monied or otherwise sullied elites, in the way of "the will of the people." And what democrat could support that?

This is not to say that legal and other institutions hitherto associated with the rule of law are automatically repudiated by populist leaders; on the contrary, they are commonly, indeed systematically, redirected to subverting the ideal of the rule of law. So courts, for example, are frequently emasculated, and then colonized and revived by populist leaders who find them useful, once suborned, to legitimize and cement their power. As any source of independent check or balance, however, they are denounced, evaded and ignored.[36] At the extreme, and it is increasingly easy to meet the extreme, populist "democrats" indulge shamelessly (literally: without shame) in "what political scientists call 'discriminatory legalism' (put simply: the idea of 'everything for my friends; for my enemies, the law')."[37] And so Viktor Orbán, architect of the "illiberal state"[38] in Hungary, has contrived to combine electoral victory, which he calls democracy, with sustained, systematic, incremental and direct assaults on the rule of law. This, by the way, is another reason to favor teleological over anatomical legal/formal conceptions of the rule of law: when populists make over legal institutions with cadres and legal ruses and purposes designed to lubricate their arbitrary sway over power, the ideal of the rule of law is being violated, even while forms familiar in rule of law institutional "laundry lists"[39] are being perpetuated, honored, so to say, in the breach.

[36] For a detailed account of such manoeuvres in Poland, see Wojciech Sadurski, *Poland's Constitutional Breakdown* (Oxford: Oxford University Press, 2019). On Hungary, see Ferenc Laczó, "The Illusion of Choice," available at http://visegradinsight.eu/the-illusion-of-choice/.

[37] Jan-Werner Müller, "Populism and Constitutionalism," in Cristóbal Rovira Kaltwasser, Paul Taggart, Paulina Ochoa Espejo, and Pierre Ostiguy, eds., *The Oxford Handbook of Populism* (Oxford: Oxford University Press, 2017), p. 597.

[38] Viktor Orbán, "Full text of Viktor Orbán's speech at Băile Tuşnad (Tusnádfürdő) of 26 July 2014," available at https://budapestbeacon.com/full-text-of-viktor-orbans-speech-at-baile-tusnad-tusnadfurdo-of-26-july-2014/.

[39] Jeremy Waldron's characterization of the lists of formal elements of rule of law rules compiled by Fuller, Raz and many others, to which he has added his own "procedural" list. See his, "The Rule of Law and the Importance of Procedure," in Fleming, ed., *Getting to the Rule of Law*, pp. 5–6. On uses of legal forms for anti-rule of law ends, see Landau, "Abusive Constitutionalism"; and Varol, "Stealth Authoritarianism." See also Julian A. Sempill, "Law, Dignity and the Elusive Promise of a Third Way," *Oxford Journal of Legal Studies*, 38 (2018), 217–245 on compatibilities between "procedural" institutional virtues and substantive vice.

If this section began with allegedly joyful copulations of democracy and the rule of law (not to mention human rights), then, it might be thought to have ended with recommendations for divorce. On such a view, it is easier to choose between one or other partner than to join them. At best, the union seems fated to a life of dramatic tension, both partners living at the other's expense. A sad story for partisans of them both.

2 Adjectives and Nouns

In the late years of European communism, and in those that immediately followed its collapse, it was common for dissidents and reformers to insist that they wanted democracy and the rule of law "without adjectives." It was easy to see what they meant, and to sympathize. After all, under communism, adjectives and nouns had a discomfiting tendency to devour each other, and not only each other. Millions of lives were destroyed, millions more were distorted, stunted, and in many other ways harmed. Consider the ravenous adjective in "socialist legality" and "socialist democracy," not to mention the gluttonous noun in "democratic centralism." Even now, Chinese citizens who deviate from political orthodoxy are likely to suffer quickly and severely from the qualifier in "the rule of law with Chinese characteristics."

The trouble is that democracy and the rule of law never come without adjectives, explicit or implicit, since they have yet to be realized in pure, unadulterated forms. Indeed, given the contested character of both concepts, we will only ever find them in some qualified form or another. More than that, following Constant there is reason to think that is a good thing. We should get used to it and ask questions about the quality of the partnerships on offer, rather than advocate celibacy for one or other partner. It might indeed be that once coupled we find that democracy and the rule of law are necessary for each other to flourish, rather than live at each other's expense, notwithstanding – as happens, after all, in many successful marriages – that there are unavoidable tensions between them.

That is my view, both as general caution and specific prescription. Generally, discussion of democracy and the rule of law (and many other important conceptual options, such as are often expressed in composite terms such as "liberal democracy," "constitutional democracy," "contestatory democracy," "monitory democracy") should avoid what Stephen Holmes calls "the tyranny of false polarities,"[40] among them between democracy and the rule of law. Rather than ask whether these different conceptions might enrich and support each other, those subjected to this (very common) conceptual tyranny are hounded to choose between them. That in general, and in this matter specifically, can be a misplaced demand, a false choice.

This was what, notwithstanding Berlin's misinterpretation of him, Constant believed. On his view, not only was it true that the unadulterated liberty of the ancients was incompatible with that of the moderns, and the pining for it dangerous. Direct participatory democracy is simply no longer available to citizens of large commercial societies. There are too many of them, scattered over huge expanses of territory. It is not possible for them all to deliberate, decide and legislate together in the detail required to govern such numbers over such spaces. Even were they fewer, they can no longer rely on slaves to do the work and leave them the time and leisure to devote their lives to matters of governance, nor, once commerce has supplanted law as the dominating activity of the society, do they have the time: "commerce does not, like war, leave in men's lives intervals of inactivity" which they can spend debating in the agora.

Instead, modern citizens must govern through representatives. That necessarily makes modern government *mediated*: it needs agents and they need institutions. The means have to be transformed, but the motivating ideal should be preserved. So while the liberty of the ancients in pure form is incompatible with that of the moderns, Constant insisted in this lecture and for the rest of his life that "political liberty," now in the form of representative democracy watched over by a vigilant people, was necessary for civil liberty, at least in the conditions of modernity:

[40] Stephen Holmes, *Passions and Constraint: On the Theory of Liberal Democracy* (Chicago: University of Chicago Press, 1995), p. 28. Holmes here echoes John Dewey's objections to "pernicious dualisms" and Maurice Cohen's "principle of polarity" that "stresses the interplay of contrasting ideas and standpoints, and the importance to good sense of showing how they involve each other." Philip Selznick, Unpublished lecture, as quoted in Martin Krygier, *Philip Selznick. Ideals in the World*, p. 250.

As you see, Gentlemen, my observations do not in the least tend to diminish the value of political liberty . . . It is not security which we must weaken; it is enjoyment which we must extend. It is not political liberty which I wish to renounce; it is civil liberty which I claim, along with other forms of political liberty. Governments, no more than they did before, have the right to arrogate to themselves an illegitimate power. But the governments which emanate from a legitimate source have even less right than before to exercise an arbitrary supremacy over individuals. . . . Therefore, Sirs, far from renouncing either of the two sorts of freedom which I have described to you, it is necessary, as I have shown, to learn to combine the two together.[41]

Underlying this position is the conviction that in modern conditions, democracy and the rule of law are not contradictory but complementary, indeed on some views mutually necessary, even mutually constitutive.

Thus Jürgen Habermas argues for an *internal* normative connection and also a practical empirical one between public rights anchored in popular sovereignty and democracy, and private rights protected by the rule of law. On the one hand, in the absence of premodern traditional moral sources of legitimation, Habermas argues that today we must answer "the legitimation question by referring, on the one hand, to the principle of *popular sovereignty* and, on the other, to the *rule of law* as guaranteed by human rights. The principle of popular sovereignty is expressed in rights of communication and participation that secure the public autonomy of citizens; the rule of law is expressed in those classical basic rights that guarantee the private autonomy of members of society."[42] Non-Habermasians might not be persuaded by this alleged implication from his discourse theory, but there is an insightful practical observation that undergirds it:

private and public autonomy mutually presuppose each other in such a way that neither human rights nor popular sovereignty can claim primacy over its counterpart.

This expresses the intuition that, on the one hand, citizens can make adequate use of their public autonomy only if, on the basis of their equally protected private autonomy, they are sufficiently independent; but that, on the other hand, they can

[41] Constant, "The Liberty of the Ancients Compared with that of the Moderns," pp. 323, 324, 327.

[42] Jürgen Habermas, "On the Internal Relation between Rule of Law and Democracy," *European Journal of Philosophy*, 3 (1995), 15–16. See also idem, *Between Facts and Norms:* Contributions to a Discourse Theory of Law and Democracy, trans. William Rehg (Cambridge: MIT Press, [1992] 1996), chs. 3 and 4.

arrive at a consensual regulation of their private autonomy only if they make adequate use of their political autonomy as enfranchised citizens.[43]

If the philosophical connection for which Habermas argues might stand or fall with the distinctive argumentation of the discourse theory in which it is embedded, the practical link can be appreciated from many points of view. Thus, Stephen Holmes has long argued that democracy is enabled by the rule of law, which in turn is supported by democracy. Thus, if the people are to be effectively engaged in rule, and not merely permitted to cast a vote every now and then for someone they do not know for reasons they do not understand, that will involve more than provision of polling booths. For citizens to be informed, to participate politically, to choose intelligently, to *engage* in political choice and maybe life, a lot is required. As Holmes explains:

The protection of private rights provides a crucial precondition for "positive liberty" in both senses. If the police can smash down doors at midnight and drag away families to unknown dungeons or graves, a citizen's chances for "personal fulfilment" will be drastically curtailed, as will his desire to participate actively in public life.[44]

On the other hand, democracy is a major potential source of check on arbitrary power. Maravall gets the point, though he somewhat simplifies it: "citizens have two insruments to protect them: first, to throw the rulers out of office at election time; second, to enforce, through institutions, legal limits to the political discretion of incumbents between elections. The first protection is provided by democracy; the second, by the rule of law."[45]

Indeed, not merely is it the case that democracy can support the ideal of the rule of law; on many views that, and not personal fulfillment or even political participation as a good in itself, is the primary good it offers. This is a central argument of Philip Pettit's republicanism. Election of governments is one function we expect from the demos, but it is not the only, nor necessarily the most important one: *contestation* is equally so.[46] For the first goal of political arrangements, on this reading, is non-domination. For

[43] Habermas, "On the Internal Relation between Rule of Law and Democracy," pp. 17, 18.

[44] Holmes, *Passions and Constraint*, pp. 28–29.

[45] José María Maravall, "The Rule of Law as a Political Weapon," in José María Maravall and Adam Preworski, eds., *Democracy and the Rule of Law* (Cambridge: Cambridge University Press, 2003), p. 261.

[46] See Philip Pettit, "Democracy, Electoral and Contestatory," in Jack Knight, ed., *Compromise: NOMOS LIX* (New York: New York University Press, 2000), pp. 105–144.

that to be freely available and readily accessed, the sway of arbitrary power is less than helpful; it is its perennial, indeed conceptual, antithesis. To be free *is* to be without subjection to arbitrary power.[47] They cannot live together. However, law is often not enough; the availability of popular contestation of public decision-making is crucial. So democracy and rule of law are helpmates not enemies. They are both necessary to freedom as non-domination. On this view, the role of the people is to be "trustor" and the state as "trustee":

> in particular it sees the people as trusting the state to ensure a dispensation of non-arbitrary rule. For this position direct democracy may often be a very bad thing, since it may ensure the ultimate form of arbitrariness: the tyranny of a majority. Democratic institutions of control will certainly be desirable and indispensable, but they are not the be-all and end-all of good government.[48]

In modern circumstances, as Constant insisted, direct rule is unavailable. Moreover, modern governments and other nongovernmental institutions as well can be awfully powerful. If that power is not to be exercised arbitrarily, a lot is required, not all of it likely to come from law on its own. The engagement of citizens in rule and control of their executive trustees who act in their name and ostensibly for their benefit is crucial. So "illiberal democracy" is an oxymoron, *inter alia* but centrally because its subversion of the rule of law stifles institutions to protect opportunities for autonomous popular opinion formation, not to mention genuine will formation, that are necessary for citizens to be "ultimate authors, controllers and beneficiaries of the political order." If democracy is not to slide, by sleight of word, in the direction of that self-contradictory phrase it needs to be buttressed by some "liberal" or "constitutional" or "republican" partner,

[47] In *On the People's Terms* (Cambridge: Cambridge University Press, 2012), p. 58, Pettit decides no longer to use the republican term "arbitrary," as he used to, since he believes it has strayed from referring above all to "uncontrolled" power as it did and as it does for him, and has come to be confused with "not subject to established rules" and "wrong or objectionable." He prefers to stick to "uncontrolled," and has come to prefer that word for clarity. I stick with "arbitrary," partly because it seems to me both to draw helpfully on a term deep and resonant in rule of law traditions, and to denote at least three forms of the exercise of power that different strands of those traditions have found objectionable: uncontrolled, unpredictable, and unrespectful See Martin Krygier, "The Rule of Law," 203–208. Notwithstanding this verbal difference, there is no substantive difference between us. We both object to uncontrolled exercise of power, and I have no doubt Pettit also objects to unpredictable and unrespectful power as well.

[48] Pettit, *Republicanism*, p. 58.

central to each of which is the rule of law. And for that to flourish in modern powerful states, the countervailing support of citizens is needed. So we should acknowledge, not only as the cliché aptly has it that "the price of liberty is eternal vigilance," but that the price of democracy is so also, and for closely interdependent and intertwined reasons.

23 Constitutionalism and the Rule of Law

Roberto Gargarella

Introduction

The concepts of the rule of law and constitutionalism are clearly interrelated, even though they do not mean the same thing or refer to the same phenomena. Although the two ideas are often equated, according to Ten "constitutionalism usually refers to specific constitutional devices and procedures, such as the separation of powers between the legislature, the executive and the judiciary, the independence of the judiciary, due process of fair hearings for those charged with criminal offences, and respect for individual rights, which are partly constitutive of a liberal democratic system of government." And the rule of law, by contrast, "embodies certain standards which define the characteristic virtues of a legal system as such."[1] In this chapter I shall examine three tensions between the rule of law and constitutionalism. The first concerns the connection between the rule of law and the principle of individual autonomy, the second the relation between the rule of law and private property, and the third between the rule of law and judicial review. In all three cases, as we shall see, democracy, and, with it, the corresponding value of self-government, is compromised.[2]

[1] C. L. Ten, "Constitutionalism and the Rule of Law," in Robert E. Goodin and Philip Pettit, eds., *A Companion to Contemporary Political Philosophy* (Oxford: Blackwell, 1993), pp. 394–404, p. 394.

[2] In what follows, I shall have in mind a particular conception of democracy that is related to so-called dialogic or "deliberative" approaches to it: Jon Elster, ed., *Deliberative Democracy* (Cambridge: Cambridge University Press, 1998); Jügen Habermas, *Between Facts and Norms: Contributions to a Discourse Theory of Law and Democracy*, trans. William Rehg (Cambridge: MIT Press, [1992] 1996); Carlos Santiago Nino, *The Constitution of Deliberative Democracy* (New Haven: Yale University Press, 1996); Cass R. Sunstein, *The Partial Constitution* (Cambridge: Harvard University Press, 1993). However, I assume that even a much more modest approach to democracy would suffice to ground most of the things I shall say in the following pages. According to this modest understanding of democracy, fundamental public issues should be the object of collective public debate and should ideally be decided by "all those potentially affected," rather than by legal elites or committees of experts.

1 Autonomy

Protecting Basic Liberties: Form and Substance

For many authors, the rule of law establishes legal principles aimed at protecting basic individual freedoms. This approach has been advanced, among others, by legal philosopher Joseph Raz, who presents the rule of law as having an "essentially … negative value."[3] The rule of law, he explains, is "designed to minimize the harm to freedom and dignity which the law may cause in its pursuit of its goals however laudable these may be."[4] This association between the rule of law and traditional liberal values is not only typical of authors advocating a formal approach; it is also endorsed by those who, like Ronald Dworkin, advocate a (so-called) *substantive approach* to the rule of law. For Dworkin, the rule of law cannot be limited to certain formal criteria which may be considered necessary for having a proper legal system in place, and this is so because individuals also have moral and political rights that need to be regularly enforced upon demand of individual citizens through courts.[5]

[3] Joseph Raz, "The Rule of Law and Its Virtue," in idem, *The Authority of Law: Essays on Law and Morality* (Oxford: Clarendon Press, 1979), p. 224. Raz here proposes a view of the rule of law which is linked to various fundamental values. These values are, above all, "the ability to choose styles and forms of life, to fix long-term goals and effectively direct one's life towards them," and its capacity to ensure "respect for human dignity," which included respecting individual autonomy. Ibid., p. 221.

[4] Raz, "The Rule of Law and Its Virtue," p. 228.

[5] Ronald Dworkin, *A Matter of Principle* (Cambridge: Harvard University Press, 1985), p. 11. Dworkin's approach to the rule of law has traditionally been considered a paradigmatic example of a "substantive view." Dworkin distinguished between what he called the "rule-book" conception of the rule of law, and the "rights" conception. According to the first, the power of the state should never be exercised against individual citizens "except in accordance with rules explicitly set out in a public rule book available to all." Ibid., p. 11. So, citizens and government officials need to adjust their behavior to these rules until they are changed in accordance with further rules. The idea is, in sum, very narrow and clearly non-substantive: "whatever rules are put in the book must be followed until changed." Ibid Substantive justice is here seen as something completely different and independent from the rule of law. In contrast with this first approach, Dworkin proposes an alternative one that he calls a "rights conception" of the rule of law, which he deems much more ambitious than the former one. Here, the rule of law and substantive justice are not strictly separated, as in the first approach. By contrast, the rules in the rule book need to "capture and enforce" moral rights. Ibid., p. 12. For a comparison between Dworkin and Dicey's view on the rule of law, see T. R. S. Allan, "Dworkin and Dicey: The Rule of Law as Integrity," *Oxford Journal of Legal Studies*, 8 (1988), pp. 266–277.

However, as Jeremy Waldron put it, most traditional advocates of the rule of law, even those more clearly associated with a *formal/procedural* view, also defend their (formal/procedural) criteria in the name of certain fundamental values.[6] Take, for instance, Fuller's eight principles defining the rule of law: generality, publicity, prospectivity, intelligibility, consistency, practicability, constancy, and congruence.[7] Fuller's association between certain formal principles, individual autonomy and classic liberal rights is clear: in those eight principles we find basic references to the due process, individual guarantees, and legal protections against the arbitrary and oppressive exercise of state power.

Albert V. Dicey's approach to the rule of law is similar. Dicey relates the notion of the rule of law to three principles of British constitutionalism. For the purposes of this paper, I shall address only the first, that "no man is punishable or can lawfully be made to suffer in body or goods except for a distinct breach of law established in the ordinary legal manner before the ordinary courts of the land."[8] In the same way that Fuller's eight principles appeared to be at the service of individual freedom ("human dignity and equality," in Waldron's view), Dicey's three principles were directed at honoring the idea of liberty.[9]

Autonomy versus Self-Government

This brief doctrinal review suggests that the most traditional approaches to the rule of law are grounded on typically liberal values, related to the

6 Jeremy Waldron, "Legislation and the Rule of Law," *Legisprudence*, 1 (2007), 91–123. Waldron here objects to the possibility of establishing a clear contrast between formal/procedural and substantive conceptions of the rule of law (at 115). He admits that there are more direct forms of pursuing certain values ("it is sensible to pursue them directly rather than through formalist or proceduralist strategies that might have only a contingent relation to the values in question": at 119). However, he considers it wrong to assume that there is a neat distinction between substantive and formal/procedural approaches. Waldron is in fact interested in exploring another distinction, namely the distinction between formal and procedural conceptions (conceptions that, in his opinion, are wrongly assimilated). The "procedural side of the Rule of Law" would be that which requires public institutions to "sponsor and facilitate reasoned arguments in human affairs," which for him implies associating the rule of law with the legal process "rather than with the form of the determinate norms that are supposed to emerge from that process." See his "The Rule of Law and the Importance of Procedure," in James E. Fleming, ed., *Getting to the Rule of Law*: NOMOS L (New York: New York University Press, 2011), p. 19.

7 Lon L. Fuller, *The Morality of Law* (New Haven: Yale University Press, 1964), p. 39.

8 A. V. Dicey, *Introduction to the Study of the Law of the Constitution* (London: Macmillan, 1885), pp. 188, 193, 195.

9 Waldron, "Legislation and the Rule of Law," 116.

notion of individual autonomy. Remarkably, these background values do not in any way refer to the other fundamental ideal of constitutionalism, which is the ideal of self-government. In fact, one could claim that in every modern constitution the value of individual autonomy plays the crucial role in the explanation and justification of the Bill of Rights, while the value of self-government does the main work in relation to that part of the constitution that defines the organization of powers. Bicameralism, the separation of powers, the system of "checks and balances" and the like, are mainly ways of expressing and putting in motion a certain understanding of the notion of self-government. In other words, such institutional mechanisms not only limit power but also organize the functioning of the "democratic machinery" of the constitution. Therefore, one could conclude that a proper notion of the rule of law should be able to include both concerns – the concern about individual autonomy and the one about collective self-government – within its essential formulation. Given that this is not the case, the question is: what then explains the focus on the former ideal – individual autonomy – rather than on the latter – collective self-government – in most approaches to the rule of law?

The preference for autonomy over self-government can perhaps be explained by the presence of a widespread historic fear of the tyrant, a discretional ruler exercising arbitrary power who oppressed individuals or undermined their fundamental rights. This fear, extending later to the fear of "majoritarian oppression," seems to explain the particular emphasis that the legal doctrine placed in the prevention of tyranny, whether of the one or the many. Consequently, the rule of law began to be characterized by its "negative value," that is, the value of preventing the violation of individual rights, rather than by its "positive value," namely making self-government possible.

An excellent illustration of this development appears in the work of Lon Fuller. Introducing his views about the rule of law and the "inner morality of the law,"[10] Fuller made use of a famous example, which was that of a totally discretional ruler, namely "King Rex." Life in this "unhappy reign

[10] For Waldron, Fuller's account of the rule of law requires "that the state should do whatever it wants to do in an orderly, predictable way, giving us plenty of advance notice by publicizing the general norms on which its actions will be based, and that it should then stick to those norms and not arbitrarily depart from the even if it seems politically advantageous to do so." Waldron, "The Concept and the Rule of Law," *Georgia Law Review*, 43 (2008), 7. This "inner morality" needs to be distinguished from what would

of a monarch" is used to illustrate the idea of the rule of law as a "barrier" against the tyranny of "one."[11] In other words, Fuller's formal principles can be explained by the fear of having society falling prey to the caprices of a (single) arbitrary ruler. Consequently, his eight principles are totally unrelated to the issue of self-government; all that matters is that the ruler does not exercise his powers whimsically.[12] But what about the offense posed by that political situation to our collective aspiration to self-government? In fact, the very existence of a regime that concentrates power in just one singular leader (whether or not a crazy king) should be seen as an insult to legitimate democratic ambitions.

The situation is similar when we examine Dicey's approach to the rule of law. Here, again, what really matters is that the ruler does not infringe fundamental rights and individual liberties. According to Dicey, individuals are protected from the arbitrary acts of the ruler through a series of individual rights or legal principles, which can be considered implicit in a proper legal order. The barriers that protect individuals from the caprices of power are constituted by defensive tools that define the contours of a "negative" legal system. But those defensive tools are in no way directed towards enabling citizens to exercise their self-governing capacities: those tools are simply aimed at preventing serious governmental oppressions. For this view, a legal system that respects the rule of law would be the one that prevents the curtailment of fundamental rights and liberties, whether or not the legal system contributed to the goal of self-government.

be the "external morality," which would be the substantive values that the legal system would seek to promote (Ten, "Constitutionalism and the Rule of Law," 397).

[11] Lon Fuller, *The Morality of Law*, p. 33.

[12] Fuller's approach on the subject has been the object of repeated criticisms. For instance, in his polemic with Fuller, Hart argued that even a dictatorial regime that violated fundamental rights would be capable of meeting Fuller's requirements. See H. L. A. Hart, "Positivism and the Separation of Law and Morals," *Harvard Law Review*, 71 (1958), 593–629. Also, for Judith Shklar, Fuller's eight criteria situate the rule of law in a "political vacuum" and make it compatible with an authoritarian government See her "Political Theory and the Rule of Law," in Stanley Hoffmann, ed., *Political Thought and Political Thinkers* (Chicago: Chicago University Press, [1987] 1998), pp. 21–37, at p. 33; Shannon C. Stimson, "Constitutionalism and the Rule of Law," in John S. Dryzek, Bonnie Honig, and Anne Phillips, eds., *The Oxford Handbook of Political Theory* (Oxford: Oxford University Press, 2009), p. 320. Fuller rejected those criticisms, assuming that the normal development of an authoritarian regime would take it – sooner or later – to pass retroactive laws or promote secret legislation in order to achieve its goals.

This neglect of the goal of self-government by those examined views of the rule of law renders such approaches unjustified. It seems indispensable that the legal system works to make the expression and execution of the deliberate will of the people possible.

2 Property

From Private Property to the Welfare State

The second issue to address concerns the relation between the rule of law and private property. Not all authors who promote the rule of law consider that this ideal requires respect for private property. However, it seems clear that many authors, including John Locke and Friedrich von Hayek, conceived of the rule of law in exactly those terms.

In the writings of John Locke we find both a serious concern for the preservation of the rule of law and a strong identification between the rule of law and private property. On the one hand, Locke refers to the need for a "settled law," an "established law," and a "standing law," which he sharply contrasts with "extemporary decrees," "arbitrary decrees," and "undetermined resolutions."[13] On the other hand, in all his references to the rule of law Locke alludes to the right to private property as a prepolitical right. His views on the topic probably represent the most significant and influential antecedent for different contemporary approaches on the matter. These more contemporary approaches also insist both on the fundamental importance of the right to private property and in establishing an inner connection between the right to property and the rule of law. Such views have become particularly prominent since the creation of the modern welfare state during the last century.[14]

13 Waldron, "The Rule of Law and the Importance of Procedure," p. 17.

14 In fact, according to some authors, the consolidation of the notion of the rule of law came between the end of the nineteenth century and the beginning of the twentieth, through the work of liberal jurists in Britain, Germany or France, who were all concerned with the threatening growth of the Welfare State. For Martin Loughlin, for instance, these jurists "were expressing particular concerns about the impact on the concept of law of the emergence of an extensive governmental system, charged with the tasks of regulating social life and promoting the welfare of the citizen through administrative resources." Martin Loughlin, *Foundations of Public Law* (Oxford: Oxford University Press, 2010), pp. 323–324.

Take, for instance, the work of A. V. Dicey. As we know, Dicey was a key figure in the modern development of the rule of law. Dicey's first principle of the rule of law established that no man was punishable or could be "lawfully made to suffer in body or goods except for a distinct breach of law established in the ordinary legal manner before the ordinary Courts of the land." It seems clear that the reference to "goods" in Dicey's first principle was intended to prevent restrictions on the use of property. Dicey was, at the time, particularly concerned about the growing levels of administrative discretion, which he considered contrary to a proper exercise of the law.[15]

The paradigmatic view that associates the rule of law with an antiregulatory approach is that of Friedrich von Hayek. For Hayek, the government had to be bound by rules fixed and announced beforehand. This was, for him, the essence of the rule of law. The main threat to a government by law, he felt, derived from a welfarist system trying to ensure distributive justice. In Hayek's view, an activist state is a state operating under discretionary rules: legislation trying to implement social justice required constant adjustments. For that reason, he suggested the size of government be reduced to a minimum, so as to increase individuals' personal freedom. In his words, "stripped of all technicalities this means that government in all its action is bound by rules fixed and announced beforehand – rules which make it possible to foresee with fair certainty how the authority will use its coercive powers in given circumstances, and to plan one's individual affairs on the basis of this knowledge."[16]

[15] A. V. Dicey, "The Development of Administrative Law in England," *Law Quarterly Review*, 31 (1915), 148.

[16] Friedrich A. Hayek, *The Road to Serfdom* (London: Routledge, 1944), p. 54. It could be argued that it is not clear how Hayek or other thinkers who developed similar views, "derived" such conclusions about the minimum State from the initial formulation about the rule of law. Their conclusions, in fact, seem instead to be derived from an independent principle that required an independent justification. For instance, according to Cass Sunstein, Hayek "identifies the rule of law with a norm of 'impartiality,'" whose "antonym" is "a system of 'planning' in which the state picks winners and losers." In this way, Hayek establishes a close association between the rule of law and free markets. However, Sunstein claims Hayek's approach is wrong in presenting his objections to the arbitrariness of state interventionism as if they derived from the notion of the rule of law. Hayek's judgment of "arbitrary" is "grounded in ideas about efficiency and liberty" that are not related to the rule of law but that require an independent defense. See Cass R. Sunstein, "Rules and Rulelessness," Coase-Sandor Institute for Law and Economics Working Paper No. 27, University of Chicago Law School 1994, 29–31. In addition, it is interesting to contrast Hayek's view of freedom with Raz's approach, according to which autonomy is not only

Hostility to Legislation

The views examined in the previous section share an approach to the rule of law that is in tension with basic democratic intuitions, intuitions that contemporary constitutional democracies hold. Those analyses are challenged by asking basic questions. Why should a democratic community be unable to freely deliberate and decide how to organize its basic institutions? Why should this community be unable to regulate private property? Why should that community be prohibited from organizing its institutions so as to secure both individual autonomy (for example, by preventing anyone to fall in situations of "dependency") and collective self-government (for example, by ensuring that all citizens become "full citizens," and consequently have the time and energy required to participate in politics)? The assumption according to which private property is a prepolitical right unreasonably prevents or obstructs these possibilities.

Dicey's views on the topic were heavily criticized precisely for his narrow understanding of law. British scholars such as William Robson (in his book *Justice and Administrative Law*) and Ivor Jennings (in his work *The Law and the Constitution,*) offered powerful objections that challenged Dicey's anticollectivist view, his resistance to the welfare state, his distrust of the then growing economic regulations, and his defense of *laissez-faire*. Contrary to Dicey, both Robson and Jennings were committed "to the expansion of the state's role in providing welfare and other social services."[17] According to Jeremy Waldron, traditional notions of the rule of law unjustifiably advance an approach which is "hostile to legislation": they understand the rule of law fundamentally at the service of economic development, where interferences or restrictions in the use of property or in the functioning of the market are seen as impermissible violations of the rule of law.[18]

opposed to a life of coerced choices, but also to a life of no choice or a life without one's capacity to choose, or a life without the collective good necessary for effective autonomy: Raz, *The Morality of Law*; Jeremy; Waldron, "The Rule of Law in Contemporary Liberal Theory," *Ratio Juris*, 2 (1989), 79–96, at 85–86.

[17] Jeffrey Jowell "The Rule of Law and its Underlying Values," in Jeffrey Jowell and Dawn Oliver, eds., *The Changing Constitution*, 7th ed. (Oxford: Oxford University Press, 2011), p. 14; T. R. S. Allan, "Dworkin and Dicey: The Rule of Law as Integrity," *Oxford Journal of Legal Studies*, 8 (1988), 267.

[18] Waldron illustrates such "hostile" views with scholar Robert Barro's suggestion that "democratization should take second place to legalization in nation-building," given that "legal protections for property rights and markets" should come first . See, "Legislation and the Rule of Law," 98. On this view, "the establishment of the rule of law is given priority over the

In various writings, Waldron has been arguing against this "hostility to legislation,"[19] explaining that there is something "deeply troubling" in the view that sees something "inherently unhealthy" about legislation, and particularly in legislation that goes "beyond the institution of property rights and the establishment and liberalization of markets."[20] According to those critics of welfare law, social and economic legislation is a perversion of the rule of law: regulatory laws are only accepted, when accepted, "as an indulgence to majoritarian democracy." Contrary to this approach, Waldron considers it unavoidable that "property rights will be affected over time by changes in circumstances, both in their character and in their distribution."[21]

Those hostile views not only prevent a democratic community doing what it should be allowed to do; they also wrongly conflate the concept of rule of law with the notion of economic efficiency,[22] and unjustifiably assume that

effective operation of elective institutions." Ibid. More recently, in his 2011 Hamlyn Lectures on "the measure of property," Waldron made reference to what he called "the World Bank Approach to the Rule of Law," more specifically to the indices that the World Bank has been using in order to rate countries according to what the institution considers to be respect to the rule of law, and for the benefit of investors and business people. According to those indexes, a particular society's score on its adherence to the rule of law is diminished by the enactment or enforcement of legislation whose tendency is "to interfere with market processes or to limit property rights or to make investment in society more precarious or in other ways less remunerative to outsiders." See Waldron, "The Hamlyn Lectures: The Rule of Law and the Measure of Property," Public Law and Legal Theory Research Paper Series, New York University School of Law, 2011, p. 54.

19 Waldron admits that formalist approaches to the rule of law do not necessarily imply denying that "societies have a legitimate aspiration to govern themselves through legislation." See "Legislation and the Rule of Law," 97. They may accept the need of an elected legislature, even recognizing this as part of the normal aspiration to democracy. However, they emphasize the distinction and separateness between those two ideals, and also recognize that they may be in tension. Waldron does not dispute these assumptions: although we cannot have democracy without the rule of law, he accepts that procedural democracy may eventually produce violations of the rule of law. What he does want to dispute is the idea that there is something like a "necessary incompatibility" between the two notions. He says: "Its denigration of legislation, particularly social and economic legislation, is associated with a sense of its being undesirable for the people of a country to act collectively even through the medium of . . . law to pursue social justice." ibid., 98.

20 Waldron, "Legislation and the Rule of Law," 121.

21 Waldron, "Legislation and the Rule of Law," 121.

22 For instance, presenting his own notion of the rule of law, Tom Bingham quotes among others, Alan Greenspan, the former chairman of the Federal Reserve Bank of the United States, recently saying that the most important contributor to economic growth was "the rule of law." He adds that "no one would choose to do business, perhaps involving large sums of money, in a country where parties, rights and obligations were undecided." See Bingham, *The Rule of Law* (London: Penguin, 2010), p. 38.

the legislative's power to regulate property necessarily derives in the adoption of sudden, hasty, passionate, or irrational decisions. In modern Western democracies, however, the opposite seems to be true: the basic principles that organize property tend to remain stable, even though it is sometimes the case that the more precise details of those regulations (say, specific taxes or incentives) may vary over time and according to contextual demands.

Before concluding this section, two final comments about the role of the legislative branch and the rule of law might be made. First, those who care about having a strong legislature and demand respect to the rule of law should not accept a simplistic approach to what enacting a democratic law means. The fact that a certain "x" number of representatives raise their hands at the same time saying "yes" to a certain legislative project should not suffice to call a bill "democratic." This norm should also be the product of a careful and respectful deliberation, where all the voices are heard and where the enacted norm is properly justified. In other words, we should be more demanding regarding issues of "legislative due process."[23]

The second comment refers not to the "internal" life of the legislature, but to its "external" sources. The "voice of the legislature" and "the voice of the people" should not be assumed to be synonymous.[24] For numerous reasons – including the fact that the institutional system has been designed for much simpler societies; the institutional difficulties that exist for making representatives accountable; the bureaucratization of politics; the undue influence of money in politics – our legislatures have become structurally incapable of representing the multiplicity of views and voices existing in

[23] In different works, Waldron made reference to the internal life of the legislature (Waldron, "The Rule of Law in Contemporary Liberal Theory," 99; "Legislation and the Rule of Law," 108), but only recently he presented a more detailed description of how this process could look. See his *Political Political Theory: Essays on Institutions* (Cambridge: Harvard University Press, 2016). In his references to the importance of "legislative due process," he admits that much legislation "is not in fact enacted scrupulously according to . . . forms and procedures." (Waldron, "Legislation and the Rule of Law," 108. He illustrates this case with the example of his home country, New Zealand, where the unicameral legislature commonly enacts laws "in a rush, in a mostly empty chamber, without any proper provision for careful deliberation and debate," in conditions where the legislative process "is wholly dominated by the executive and subject only to . . . executive convenience." ibid Those situations, he claims, call for criticisms, but a different thing is to jump to the conclusion that there is something like an intrinsic tension between the rule of law and the legislature.

[24] Bruce Ackerman, *We the People*, vol. 1: *Foundations* (Cambridge: Harvard University Press, 1991).

contemporary societies, and people tend to feel alienated from politics. Consequently, there is nothing particularly exciting in the fact of having contemporary constitutionalism in certain areas of the world slowly moving away from its traditional picture of pure judicial dominance and towards a different one where legislatures prevail. In this sense, for instance, I would resist both Jeremy Waldron's view of legislatures as the highest point of democracy, and his defense of representative over direct democracy.[25]

The problem is most clearly expressed by those who criticize the judiciary for its elitism, homogeneous attitudes, conservatism, or its defense of "private property and dislike of trade unions, [its] strong adherence to the maintenance of order, distaste for minority opinions, demonstrations and protests."[26] For those who object to the "politics of the judiciary" as a consequence of its profound elitism, the response should in no case be legislative elitism.

The distrust of both Congress or the Judiciary in no way speaks in favor of even less democratic alternatives, such as those based on Schmittian proposals for taking the Executive as the guardian of the political Constitution.[27] Despite the existing institutional difficulties, there are democratic reasons that still, and, may, make us prefer legislative dominance to judicial dominance. But the basic point is that for those who favor deliberative democracy, a system of legislative supremacy may be an improvement, but not a solution.

3 Judicial Review

An "Anti-Majoritarian" Judiciary

The third issue concerns the relation between the rule of law and judicial review. Probably as a result of one or both of the previously examined

[25] "People have assumed from my own work on judicial review, based as it is on principles of democratic legitimacy and democratic equality, that I, too must favor the people themselves voting directly as equals on the laws that are to govern them. It is sometimes said that if a democrat accepts anything short of that – any form of indirectness or representation – they have effectively given the game away because both representative authority and judicial authority involve the exercise of political power at some remove from the participation of ordinary citizen." Waldron, *Political Political Theory*, p. 135.

[26] J. A. G. Griffith, "The Political Constitution," *Modern Law Review*, 42 (1979), 1.

[27] David Dyzenhaus, "The Left and the Question of Law," *Canadian Journal of Law and Jurisprudence*, 17 (2004), 7–30.

concerns – protecting individual autonomy, preventing the "excesses" of the legislative branch – the judiciary has always been called upon to play an active role in what concerns the preservation of the rule of law.[28] Courts in general –and the practice of judicial review in particular – became essential components of any legal system seriously committed to the rule of law. A good illustration of this view can be found in the work of A. V. Dicey. For Dicey, the role of the courts in determining and interpreting the law provides "the foundation of constitutionalism."[29] Judges were, for Dicey, "the guardians of legality," in charge of protecting citizens' rights and freedoms from the boundless power of the legislature.[30] Nowadays, this view – more favorable to judicial review and judicial supremacy – seems better represented by the writings of scholars such as T. R. S. Allan, Larry Alexander, and Ronald Dworkin.

In a certain way, the fact that advocates of the rule of law treat judges as "guardians of the rule of law" is curious, particularly so in the light of the levels of discretion that tend to characterize the judicial function. Herein, I shall clearly be interested in examining (a variation of) the traditional "counter-democratic objection" to judicial review. However, the problems I shall address largely transcend those kinds of criticisms. In this respect, it should suffice to remember Jeremy Bentham's early criticisms of the role of judges, "Judges and co.," as he ironically referred to them. Bentham's positivism was in fact born in opposition to the common law's "lack of certainty and arbitrariness," which conferred extraordinary discretion on the judges, rendering the modern ideal of self-government impossible. For Bentham "it was impossible to infer any clear general rules, let alone public, consistent, or constant rules, from the activity of English judges."[31]

When we examine Joseph Raz's influential approach to the rule of law we can recognize both the centrality that his analysis assigns to judicial oversight and the tensions that this proposal generates in relation to the democratic ideal.

[28] "The rhetoric of the rule of law did live on into the twentieth century, but its message became more disparate. For some jurists, its claims are entirely illusory, serving only as a justification for the supremacy of the judge over governmental affairs." Loughlin, *Foundations of Public Law*, pp. 323–324.

[29] Allan, "Dworkin and Dicey," 269.

[30] Allan, "Dworkin and Dicey," 269. According to Martin Loughlin, "by claiming that the English possess a judge-made constitution, [Dicey] also promoted a highly conservative interpretation of constitutional history." See *Foundations of Public Law*, p. 317.

[31] Waldron, "Legislation and the Rule of Law," 109.

In "The Politics of the Rule of Law," Joseph Raz rejects two contemporary approaches to the justification of the rule of law, which he names the "bureaucratic model argument for the rule of law," and the "tradition-oriented" approach. The first sees the rule of law as a requirement of formal justice ("The law should be clearly and publicly laid down for all to see, so that people should be aware of it and will be able to plan their lives accordingly"), while the second focuses on the aspects of the rule of law which depend on an independent judiciary in charge of controlling the development of law. For this second approach, the common law would be "the purest manifestation of the rule of law."[32]

Raz rejects the first model, acknowledging that it "creates a gulf between the law and the people," by "making justice expansive" and by promoting a legal culture characterized by "legal categories which are far removed from the way ordinary people understand their conduct and interaction with others." The law becomes in this way "inaccessible and conceptually remove[d?] and alienating." Raz also questions the second model, which he considers "totally inadequate for societies which are in the process of fast social change."[33] The slow evolution of legal practices appears to be completely inapt for responding to pluralistic societies in continuous growth and change.

In contrast to those two approaches, he proposes a third view:

> the third view of the rule of law ... finds its core idea as principled faithful application of the law. Its major features are its insistence on an open, public administration of justice, which reasoned decisions by an independent judiciary, based on publicly promulgated, prospective, principled legislation. On this understanding the principle of the rule of law is directed primarily at the judiciary and other subordinate legal institutions ... It directs them to apply statutory and common law faithfully, openly and in a principled way.[34]

Even though Raz distinguishes this third approach from the second by saying that his view puts a "greater emphasis on the role of [democratic] legislation," the fact is that he himself emphasizes the "*anti-majoritarian*" character of his approach (italics added).[35] Courts, in his view, are required to "tame the democratic legislature in the light of existing legal doctrine"

[32] Joseph Raz, "The Politics of the Rule of Law," *Indian Journal of Constitutional Law*, 2 (2008), 2.

[33] Raz, "The Politics of the Rule of Law," 3.

[34] Raz, "The Politics of the Rule of Law," 5.

[35] Raz recognizes the "anti-majoritarian" character of his view, but adds that "no cogent political theory has ever found much merit in majoritarianism." See "The Politics of the Rule of Law," 8.

For him, the authority of courts to harness legislation to legal doctrine arises neither from their superior wisdom nor from any superior law of which they are custodians. Rather, their authority emerges from two considerations, namely coherence and tradition. On the one hand, courts need to "ensure coherence of purpose in the law, ensuring that its different parts do not fight each other."[36] On the other, courts need to ensure that "the fruits of long-established traditions" are mixed with "the urgencies of short term exigencies."[37] Legislatures by themselves could not ensure this, because of their "preoccupation with current problems" and the need of their members to secure re-election. Courts, then, mitigate the legislature's difficulties by becoming the "guardians of tradition."[38] In the end, Raz claims that his view of the rule of law ensures "a fine balance between the power of a democratic legislature and the force of tradition-based doctrine." The value of the rule of law thus lies in "curtailing arbitrary power, and in securing a well ordered society, subject to accountable, principled government."[39]

Democracy, Separation of Powers, and Judicial Review

The two reasons offered by Raz in support of judicial review/judicial supremacy are not without problems. Challenging them may also be a way of challenging other common and fundamentally similar approaches to this question. Concerning Raz's first argument, it is true that in a democratic society the assistance that courts may offer to legislators is invaluable: courts may help avoid inconsistencies and contradictions in the law-making process, force legislatures to consider relevant but improperly disregarded viewpoints, and may require them to clarify the reasons for enacting a certain law. All of these tasks, however, could and should be carried out in ways that are respectful of the legislators' superior authority. That is, there is no reason to assume that all those contributions require something like judicial supremacy, as Raz and many others seem to assume.

Recent developments in so-called *dialogic theory* – dialogic approaches to constitutionalism – allow us to recognize precisely this, namely that judicial review can be exercised in ways that do not imply judicial

[36] Raz, "The Politics of the Rule of Law," 7.

[37] Raz, "The Politics of the Rule of Law," 7. See also Ten, "Constitutionalism and the Rule of Law," 399.

[38] Raz, "The Politics of the Rule of Law."

[39] Raz, "The Politics of the Rule of Law," at 8.

supremacy. This means, in the end, that judicial review could be carried out in ways that make it perfectly compatible with even demanding understanding of democracy, particularly if judicial review were exercised in genuinely dialogic forms.[40]

These dialogical approaches also call for a renewed reading of the doctrine of the *separation of powers*. Dialogic approaches help us challenge what have so far been the most common understandings of that doctrine. On the one hand, they challenge the old version of the "strict separation," which was once promoted by radicals and republicans in the Anglo-American context and which assumed that the different branches of powers had to be strictly separated, and their functions clearly distinguished.[41] On the other hand, they challenge the Madisonian approach to the system of "checks and balances," which considered that the functions of the different branches partially overlapped: for this view, each branch was in charge of controlling the others, and had for that reason adequate means at its disposal – that is, the presidential veto, impeachment, etc. – to proceed in that way. In the face of these two views, dialogical approaches propose a third and alternative understanding of the separation of powers model which requires cooperation and "dialogue" between the different branches. For that reason, too, dialogical approaches call for institutional reforms designed to facilitate the cooperation between the branches. They assume that the prevalent system of "checks and balances" has (efficiently) been designed for the prevention

[40] On dialogic theory, see Christine Bateup, "Expanding the Conversation: American and Canadian Experiences of Constitutional Dialogue in Comparative Perspective," *Temple International and Comparative Law Journal*, 21 (2007), 1–57; Roberto Gargarella, "'We the People' Outside of the Constitution: The Dialogic Model of Constitutionalism and the System of Checks and Balances," *Current Legal Problems*, 67 (2014), 1–47; Stephen Gardbaum, *The New Commonwealth Model of Constitutionalism* (Cambridge: Cambridge University Press, 2013); Peter W. Hogg and Allison A. Bushell, "The *Charter* Dialogue Between Courts and Legislatures," *Osgoode Hall Law Journal*, 35 (1997), 75–124; Peter W. Hogg, Allison A. Bushell Thornton, and Wade K. Wright, "*Charter* Dialogue Revisited – Or 'Much Ado About Metaphors,'" *Osgoode Hall Law Journal*, 45 (2007), 1–65; Kent Roach, "Dialogic Judicial Review and its Critics," *Supreme Court Law Review*, 23 (2004), 49–104; Mark Tushnet, *Weak Courts, Strong Rights* (Princeton: Princeton University Press, 2008); idem, "Dialogic Judicial Review," *Arkansas Law Review*, 61 (2009), 205–216; and Katharine G. Young, *Constituting Economic and Social Rights* (Oxford: Oxford University Press, 2012).

[41] M. J. C. Vile, *Constitutionalism and the Separation of Powers* (Oxford: Clarendon Press, 1967).

of civil war, but not for the promotion of a "conversation" between the branches.[42]

Consider now Raz's second reason in favor of the (superior) authority of courts. Raz's second argument is similar to Alexander Bickel's famous justification for judicial review.[43] What we find in both cases is the idea that courts should be the custodians of long-standing values or traditions, which legislatures are not ready or able to protect, given the short-term objectives that they have, and the particular (political) needs of legislators (that is, increasing their popularity, achieving re-election, etc.). This argument is especially weak from the perspective of the rule of law since taking that suggestion would seriously undermine respect for the rule of law, given the level of uncertainty that it would add to the legal system. The reason is obvious: we profoundly disagree over the nature of our main traditions (or long-term commitments or values), their content and limits. This was, in fact, one of Thomas Paine's main arguments against Edmund Burke's defense of traditions: we all care about traditions, but disagree about their status and meaning. The "fact of disagreement" creates serious trouble for advocates of the rule of law who are eager to promote values such as those of legal certainty and stability.[44]

I doubt whether Ronald Dworkin's approach to judicial review/judicial supremacy, which constitutes one of the richest and more influential views on the matter, is more capable of resisting the usual criticisms of judicial discretion. Consider his famous "chain novel" example, which he uses in order to illustrate how precedents constrain judges. For Dworkin, a judge deciding a case is in a similar position to that of an author contributing a chapter to a "chain novel." In his example, "a group of novelists write a novel *seriatim*; each novelist in the chain interprets the chapters he has been given in order to write a new chapter, which is then added to what the next novelist receives, and so on." The participating authors "aim jointly to create, so far as they can, a single unified novel that is the best it can be." For that reason, each writer makes an effort to ensure that his or her his

[42] See Gargarella, "'We the People' Outside of the Constitution."

[43] Alexander M. Bickel, *The Least Dangerous Branch: The Supreme Court at the Bar of Politics* (New Haven: Yale University Press, 1962).

[44] I find this line of objection against judicial review very powerful. Contemporarily, that argument, which we could call the "disagreement-argument" has been strongly presented by authors such as Jeremy Waldron. That argument is Waldron's main objection against judicial review. See his *Law and Disagreement* (Oxford: Oxford University Press, 1999.

chapter "fits" well with the prior chapters.[45] The longer the chain, the more constrained the author is. The same would apply with the judge deciding a case: if he or she is to comply with the coherence requirement of "law as integrity," he or she is constrained to apply the principles that better fit the history of previous decisions.

Of course, Dworkin's analysis requires a more detailed analysis than the one I can present here. But in societies that are characterized by "the fact of disagreement," his approach is unable to eliminate or dissipate the reasonable fears that judicial discretion generates. What would be the best continuation of a "chain novel" on "equality," which wanted to incorporate a chapter on "affirmative action"? Should we consider, at least in principle, that affirmative action programs honor or offend our commitment to equality? What about the State's decision to expand public debate through measures such as those characterized by the so-called *fairness doctrine*?[46] Do such regulations undermine or strengthen "the principle that debate on public issues should be uninhibited, robust, and wide-open"?[47] And what about regulations concerning "campaign finance" – that is, the decision to limit the use of private money in the financing of political campaigns? Should we foster those regulations, in the name of democratic values, or rather prevent them, assuming that "money is speech" – as the US Court maintained, in the case *Buckley* v. *Valeo*, 424 US 1 (1976)?

The problem that affects Dworkin's approach is not that there are different possible continuations of the same initial story, that is the basic assumption of the metaphor. The relevant question is why judges should decide what the best continuation of the story is, in situations of profound and reasonable disagreement? Is it not the right of a democratic community to decide for itself, and through political means, what the best continuation of that story is: whether to adopt affirmative action programs; promote public debate through regulation of the media; limit the use of private money in political campaigns? The "public conversation" on those issues may reasonably develop through different means, and through the intervention of different institutions, but, in a plural democratic society, it

[45] Ronald Dworkin, *Law's Empire* (Cambridge: Belknap Press of Harvard University Press, 1986) pp. 229–31.

[46] The doctrine made two requirements for owners of broadcast licenses: first, to present issues of public importance, and then to do so in a manner that was equitable and balanced.

[47] This principle was affirmed by the US Court in *New York Times* v. *Sullivan*, 376 US 254, 1964. See Owen M. Fiss, *The Irony of Free Speech* (Cambridge: Harvard University Press, 1996).

is difficult to deny the community's right to have the "final say" on those matters. "We" all want to define the "best possible continuation" to the stories we write together, and it is not at all clear that judges, rather than "the people themselves," should be the ones in charge of deciding the reasonable disagreements we have.

Conclusion

This chapter has examined some problems affecting traditional approaches to the rule of law which are the object of discussion within contemporary constitutional theory. Those traditional approaches insist on a reading of the rule of law that remains deeply marked by features such as individualism, conservatism and elitism. In the face of those readings, it was suggested that an alternative, more democratic (or majoritarian) approach to the rule of law was possible .[48] According to this alternative reading, there is ample room to be explored between the defense of the ideal of the rule of law and the threat of "majoritarian" or democratic oppression. In other words, we should not simply assume that more democratic institutional arrangements would necessarily or obviously be conducive to tyranny, governmental oppression or "domination."[49] Our institutional system can and should be much more democratic than it actually is, and there is no reason to think that more democratic arrangements should work against the desired stability and certainty of our legal norms, or in any significant way undermine our commitment to individual rights and freedoms.

48 Roberto Gargarella, "The Majoritarian Reading of the Rule of Law," in José María Maravall and Adam Przeworski, eds., *Democracy and the Rule of Law* (Cambridge: Cambridge University Press, 2003), pp. 147–167.

49 Philip Pettit, *Republicanism: A Theory of Freedom and Government* (Oxford: Oxford University Press, 1997).

Punishment in the Rule of Law 24

Lindsay Farmer*

Introduction

State punishment, understood as hard treatment or the restriction of the liberty of the individual, has been central to modern debates about the rule of law. As a form of "dramatically coercive and burdensome" state action against the individual, punishment raises distinctive issues about the relationship between a state and its citizens, and as such requires particular justification.[1] These questions of justification are typically seen as questions of who may be punished, and for what, the identification of legitimate and illegitimate forms of punishment, and indeed of the processes that must consequently be respected by the state if it is to impose justified punishment.[2] It can therefore be seen that these questions are important not only in terms of justifying actual inflictions of punishment on particular individuals, but also in terms of legitimizing the institution of punishment more broadly. The definition of punishment in this way is also a means of distinguishing between legitimate (and hence justified) restrictions of liberty, and those which cannot be justified as a form of punishment, and which are prima facie illegitimate. Thus, forms of detention or of hard or oppressive treatment by the state (such as torture or the interrogation of suspects) which do not follow conviction for a crime will be understood to be illegitimate. The rule of law is central to this process as justified (or legitimate) state punishment is further understood as

* Thanks to Sarah Armstrong and Javier Velasco for their comments and assistance.

1 Antony Duff and Zachary Hoskins, "Legal Punishment," *Stanford Encyclopedia of Philosophy* available at https://plato.stanford.edu/archives/fall2017/entries/legal-punishment/.

2 H. L. A. Hart famously distinguished between the general justifying aim of the system of punishment and the justification of particular instances of punishment. See his "Prolegomenon to the Philosophy of Punishment," in idem, *Punishment and Responsibility* (Oxford: Oxford University Press, 1968), pp. 1–27.

punishment by right: defined in advance by law and imposed according to proper legal procedures.

Theories of the justification of punishment, distinguishing between the power to punish and the right to punish, have thus been central to codifying the limits of state power, understood in particular in terms of the relationship between state power and the individual citizen, in modernity. The first penal codes of the late eighteenth and early nineteenth centuries specifically aimed at limiting the power to punish of the state through the rule of law, and debates about the permissibility and justification of state action continue to be framed and understood in terms of theories of punishment. In this chapter I shall accordingly explore the terms in which this modern understanding of the relationship between punishment and the rule of law has developed. This chapter is in three sections. In the first section I examine the historical development of debates about the limiting of punishment, in particular the origins of the principle *nulla poena sine lege*. In the second section I explore contemporary theoretical dimensions of the principle of legality in criminal law and punishment. Then, in the final and concluding section I raise some questions about the limits of this approach to limiting punishment.

1 Historical Dimensions

A central figure in the development of the modern understanding of the relationship between punishment and the rule of law was Cesare Beccaria, whose work *Dei delitti e delle pene* (*On Crimes and Punishments*) was first published in Italian in 1764.[3] This short work had a wide influence and was quickly translated into a number of other European languages, in large part because of the enthusiastic reception and promotion of the book by Voltaire and the French *philosophes*. Beccaria became a celebrated figure in progressive intellectual circles and his treatise came to be regarded as the key enlightenment text on criminal law and punishment.

[3] For background, see Richard Bellamy, "Introduction," in Cesare Beccaria, *On Crimes and Punishments and Other Writings*, ed. Richard Bellamy, trans. Richard Davies (Cambridge: Cambridge University Press, [1764] 1995), pp. ix–xxx; Bernard E. Harcourt, "Beccaria's *On Crimes and Punishments*: A Mirror on the History of the Foundations of the Modern Criminal Law," in Markus D. Dubber, ed., *Foundational Texts in Modern Criminal Law* (Oxford: Oxford University Press, 2014), pp. 39–60.

The book took the form of a number of short chapters (often no more than a couple of pages long) which developed a critique of a range of contemporary penal practices, from secret denunciations and trials, to the use of torture, the death penalty and forms of unequal and arbitrary punishment. In the case of the death penalty, for example, he not only challenged the right of the state to kill, but went on to argue that capital punishment was ineffective; spectacular and savage punishments made less impression on the minds of people than "moderate and continuous" ones because the role of the law should be to exercise a "moderating influence on human conduct."[4] Torture was criticized as unjust because it was the punishment of someone before they had been found guilty, and as inefficient because the success of torture would depend on the constitution of the sufferer and, more broadly, would undermine the deterrent effect of punishment.[5] In place of arbitrary and unequal punishments he argued generally that punishment could only be effective if inflicted equally on all offenders, and only to the extent that punishment would deter future crime.

His critique was underpinned by the view that punishment must be justified on the basis of necessity, in the sense that the sovereign could only punish to the extent necessary to protect the security of society against the depredations of others. This was not a metaphysical principle but, he argued, was based both on the principles of the social contract and on human nature. The social contract was the source of the right to punish, as individuals would only agree to punishment (or the loss of liberty) to the extent that they had broken the terms of that contract; while identification of the degree and extent of punishment was to be determined by the deterrent effect it would have on the future conduct of citizens. The legislator could thus apply a "political arithmetic" to act on the motivations and emotions of men: punishments should be graded to create obstacles that would prevent particular forms of antisocial conduct.[6] Punishment in Beccaria's view was thus more than a response to crime; it was at the heart of a systematic and rational rearrangement of the powers and capacities of government.[7] Punishments, he argued, should be proportionate to crimes,

[4] Cesare Beccaria, "On Crimes and Punishments," in idem, *On Crimes and Punishments and Other Writings*, pp. 68 and 70. On the death penalty generally, see ch. 28.

[5] Beccaria, "On Crimes and Punishments," ch. 16.

[6] Beccaria, "On Crimes and Punishments," p. 19.

[7] Michel Foucault, *Discipline and Punish: The Birth of the Prison*, trans. Alan Sheridan (Harmondsworth: Penguin, [1975] 1977).

in the sense that they should be commensurate with the social harm caused by particular criminal acts, and that they should only be imposed to the extent that they were necessary for the security and good order of society.[8] Crucially, though, Beccaria argued that it followed from this that penal practices were only justified if authorized by law: "[L]aws alone can decree punishments for crimes, and . . . this authority resides only with the legislator, who represents the whole of society united by the social contract."[9] Criminal laws should be framed in general terms, applying equally to all members of society, and the laws should only be applied by an impartial magistrate.[10] He concluded the book by arguing that:

> In order that punishment not be an act of violence perpetrated by one or many upon a private citizen, it is essential that it should be public, speedy, necessary, the minimum possible in the given circumstances, proportionate to the crime, and determined by the law.[11]

Beccaria was not the first person to present such views, nor did he necessarily present the most philosophically rigorous defense of them.[12] However, the loose combination of social contract theory, utilitarianism and emergent ideas about political economy no doubt contributed greatly to the appeal of the book, as writers of such diverse opinions as Blackstone and Bentham were quick to praise Beccaria for his enlightened views on penal practices.[13] At the heart of his argument, though, was the commitment to subject penal practices to the rule of law, with three of the first five chapters of the book devoted to the consequences of his argument for law. In these chapters he argued punishments could only be established by law, and that magistrates should have no authority to impose greater

[8] Beccaria, *Crimes*, ch. 12.

[9] Beccaria, "On Crimes and Punishments," p. 12. Cf. Thomas Hobbes, *Leviathan* ed. Richard Tuck (Cambridge: Cambridge University Press, [1652] 1997), chs. 27 and 28, esp. p. 216: "Harme inflicted for a Fact done before there was a Law that forbad it, is not Punishment but an act of Hostility . . . For before the Law, there is no transgression of the Law."

[10] Beccaria, "On Crimes and Punishments," p. 12 and ch. 4.

[11] Beccaria, "On Crimes and Punishments," p. 113.

[12] Though cf. Bellamy, "Introduction," who suggests that it is part of a more coherent philosophical position.

[13] William Blackstone, *Commentaries on the Laws of England*, vol. 4 (Chicago: Chicago University Press, [1765] 1979), for example, at pp. 3, 16, and 18. This is further discussed in Simon Stern, "Blackstone's Criminal Law: Common Law Harmonization and Legislative Reform," in Dubber, ed., *Foundational Texts in Modern Criminal Law* pp. 69–74. On Bentham, see H. L. A. Hart, "Beccaria and Bentham," in idem, *Essays on Bentham: Jurisprudence and Political Theory* (Oxford: Clarendon Press, 1982), pp. 40–52.

punishment than that laid down by the legislator; that laws should be applied by impartial magistrates, whose only role was to establish the relevant facts; and that laws should be written in a clear language which is comprehensible to the mass of the people.[14] Law, then, was seen as both an instrument through which the power to punish could be made more effective, and also as the key framework for regulating social interaction between individuals and the state.[15] As his arguments were taken up and championed by penal reformers at the end of the eighteenth century, these claims about the relationship between law and punishment were captured in the Latin tag *nulla poena sine lege* (no punishment without law), otherwise known as the "principle of legality."

The principle of legality was subsequently incorporated in many of the penal and constitutional codes that were enacted at the end of the eighteenth century, framed as "a guarantee of civic liberty against the omnipotence and despotism of the State and of the judge."[16] Thus, for example, the principle was adopted in an Austrian law of 1787, before it was articulated in Article 8 of the much better-known French Declaration of the Rights of Man and the Citizen (1789) which declared that "no one shall suffer punishment except it be legally inflicted in virtue of a law passed and promulgated before the commission of the offense."[17] It was introduced into the Bavarian Penal Code of 1813 and then into the penal codes of a great number of other countries. These codes condemned legal uncertainty, unequal punishments and judicial discretion and sought to establish security through clearly promulgated laws. The recognition of the principle of legality, moreover, was not only a matter of legal formality, as it coincided with significant changes in penal practice, driven in large part by the desire to make punishment more certain and effective. Sanguinary displays of corporal and capital punishment were replaced by new institutions of police and punishment which offered the possibility of more

[14] Beccaria, "On Crimes and Punishments," chs. 3–5. There were later chapters addressing what we would call criminal procedure and evidence, for example, on witnesses, secret denunciations, evidence, oaths, etc. See also Montesquieu, *The Spirit of the Laws*, trans. and ed. Anne M. Cohler, Basia Carolyn Miller, and Harold Samuel Stone (Cambridge: Cambridge University Press, [1748] 1989), to whom Beccaria acknowledged his debt on these issues.

[15] Bellamy, "Introduction," p. xxiii.

[16] See Stefan Glaser, "Nullem Crimen Sine Lege," *Journal of Comparative Legislation and International Law*, 24 (1942), 30.

[17] Available at http://avalon.law.yale.edu/18th_century/rightsof.asp. This was subsequently incorporated in the Code Pénal of 1810.

certain detection of crime and the more measured infliction of punishment. Policing and punishment were reorganized around a preventive principle, aimed at securing order through law, and based on a conception of the rational, calculating individual who would be deterred from crime through the threat of legal punishment. This was a move towards the rational government of crime and through crime envisaged by reformers such as Beccaria, and it suggests that legality cannot be understood in isolation from the broader institutions of penal justice within which it operates.[18]

2 The Principle of Legality in Criminal Law and Punishment

> The essence of this principle of legality is limitation on penalization by the State's officials, effected by the prescription and application of specific rules.[19]

The modern principle of legality has two different dimensions.[20] On the one hand, it expresses the Beccarian idea that there should be no punishment without law (*nulla poena sine lege*): that the punishments attaching to certain crimes must be stated in advance in legislation, and not left to the discretion of the judge. However, the corollary of this is the idea that there should be no crimes without law (*nullum crimen sine lege*): that the definition of the crime should be clearly articulated in law in advance of any action by the state. Criminal laws, in other words, should not be retroactive. As we have seen, these ideas were originally driven by the idea of effective penal deterrence, but have subsequently received expression as constitutional principles protecting individual liberty against public officials claiming authority to criminalize conduct and inflict punishment in the name of the state – notably in the Universal Declaration of Human Rights Article 11(2) and in Article 7 of the

[18] Lindsay Farmer, *Making the Modern Criminal Law: Criminalization and Civil Order* (Oxford: Oxford University Press, 2016).

[19] Jerome Hall, *General Principles of Criminal Law*, 2nd ed. (Indianapolis: Bobbs-Merrill, 1960), p. 28.

[20] This division is normally attributed to Anselm von Feuerbach, *Lehrbuch des gemeinen in Deutschland geltenden Peinlichen Rechts* (Giessen: Georg Friedrich Heyer, 1801). He also formulated a third maxim, *nullum crimen sine poena legali* ("no crime without legal punishment"), though it is arguably not distinct from the other two. See further Hall, *General Principles of Criminal Law*, pp. 34–35. On von Feuerbach more generally, see Tatjana Hörnle, "PJA von Feuerbach and his Textbook of the Common Penal Law," in Dubber, ed., *Foundational Texts in Modern Criminal Law*, pp. 119–140.

European Convention on Human Rights and Fundamental Freedoms. These, and similar documents, show the broad acceptance of the principle of legality. However, the precise implications of the recognition of the principle, for either criminal law or for punishment, are substantially less clear – and reflect the inherent tension between the aims of deterrence and protection of individual liberty.

For the criminal law, the clearest articulation of the principle of legality is in the requirement that criminal laws should not have a directly retroactive effect.[21] The central idea is clear and easily grasped: that a person should not be criminalized for conduct that was not a crime at the time the conduct was carried out.[22] This might apply, say, where legislation is passed that criminalizes individuals for conduct which took place before the legislation came into force. This would be inconsistent both with the idea that criminal law should deter antisocial conduct, and with the belief that respect for individual liberty requires that individuals should be given fair warning of the content of the law in order that they might plan their conduct in advance so as to avoid breaking the law. The principle, though, has also been understood to include a cluster of other ideas, variously expressed as fair warning, the rules against vagueness, strict construction and so on, and it is not always clear whether these derive directly from the principle, or whether the principle has just become a convenient banner under which this collection of other rules or conventions of interpretation can be grouped.[23]

Taken together, these principles express the belief that there is a duty on the legislator to articulate criminal laws with the maximum degree of certainty, and that where there is uncertainty those rules should be interpreted in favor of the defendant or accused person.[24] It is argued that laws should emanate solely from the legislator, and that any scope for arbitrary judicial law-making should be clearly circumscribed, so as to respect the liberty and autonomy of the citizen. The code (or statute) is the sole source of law, and the courts should not be permitted to interpret the "code" in

[21] See, generally, Markus D. Dubber and T. Hörnle, *Criminal Law: A Comparative Approach* (Oxford: Oxford University Press, 2014), ch. 2.

[22] German Constitution, Art. 103, para. 2 Basic Law provides: "An act can be punished only if its punishability was specified by a law before the act was committed." See also Thomas Weigend, "Germany," in Kevin Jon Heller and Markus D. Dubber, eds., *The Handbook of Comparative Criminal Law* (Stanford: Stanford University Press, 2011), pp. 254–255.

[23] See, for example, Jeremy Horder, *Ashworth's Principles of Criminal Law*, 8th ed. (Oxford: Oxford University Press, 2016), pp. 82–89.

[24] *Kokkinakis* v. *Greece* (1994) 17 EHRR 397, para. 40.

a way which usurps that law-making function. This is sometimes described as a prohibition on extending the law by analogy.[25]

While legal systems have acknowledged these ideas, they have also recognized some scope for interpretation – often in ways which seem to undercut them. Thus, Dubber and Hörnle in their comparative review of the principle of legality in the United States and Germany point to a number of cases in both jurisdictions in which the courts have either upheld rules which have an apparently retroactive effect, or have asserted a power to interpret vague or incomplete norms in an expansive manner. Perhaps, the most famous of these recent cases is the so-called "Border Guard" case in which the German Federal Court of Justice upheld the convictions of two border guards who shot at and killed persons fleeing the German Democratic Republic (GDR), as was apparently permitted under GDR law at the time, on the grounds that there were higher obligations in law deriving from international human rights to which the GDR had signed up.[26] While the Court formally recognized the constitutional prohibition on retroactivity, this was only possible on the basis of a complex argument that appealed to norms of international law which, it was argued, took precedence over domestic law. This was an interpretation which would not necessarily have been obvious to the actors at the time – regardless of how reprehensible we regard their conduct as having been.

Profound difficulties also arise in relation to common law, where the courts have long had an acknowledged role in the development of the law. While the existence of an explicit power to "legislate," or create new crimes, is now usually disavowed by the courts, the principle of legality is not seen as being inconsistent with the idea that the courts can develop the common law.[27] In Scotland, for example, the "declaratory power" to create new criminal offenses claimed by the High Court of Justiciary is now regarded by most commentators as inconsistent with the principle of legality – but uncertainty remains over the capacity of the courts to continue to develop certain common law crimes. In recent case law in

[25] See, for example, Hall, *General Principles of Criminal Law*, pp. 36–48.

[26] BGHSt 39 (November 3, 1992), See Dubber and Hörnle, *Criminal Law*, pp. 76–81.

[27] See the discussions of whether the court could act as *custos morum*, or guardians of the morals, of the English people in *R* v. *Sedley*, 1663 1 Sid. 168; (1664) 82 ER 1036; *R* v. *Manley* [1933] 1 KB 529; and *Shaw* v. *DPP* [1962] AC 220. This was formally rejected in *Knuller* v. *DPP* [1973] AC 435.

relation to the Scottish crime of breach of the peace, the courts have sought to preempt the possibility of challenge under Article 7 of the European Convention on Human Rights by arguing that there are clear, identifiable principles underlying the development of the offense.[28] The argument of the courts is thus that while a certain degree of vagueness is inevitable, in areas such as public order law, the courts will only develop the law in ways which are consistent with the existing principles – and thus that a citizen should have reasonable expectations about what the scope of the law might be. This broad approach is also consistent with other developments in criminal jurisprudence, such as the removal of the marital rape immunity, where the European Court argued that there was a difference between the removal of an immunity protecting a limited class of persons (husbands) and the creation of a new offense.[29] This approach, it should be clear, leaves the courts in common law jurisdictions with considerable leeway in the interpretation of the law.

Similar problems are encountered in respect of the application of the principle to punishment. Once again, while there is acceptance of the general idea that punishment should not be arbitrary, or indeed unlimited, the precise application of this will depend on particular systems – and, as we shall see, on the definition of punishment itself. While many jurisdictions expressed a commitment to the legality principle in the nineteenth century, this was not necessarily seen as inconsistent with the move towards systems of punishment based on the idea of social protection, targeted at the offender rather than the offense. Indeed, as Pifferi has shown, the move towards rehabilitation and correctionalism in the early part of the twentieth century involved the modification and reinterpretation of the principle of legality in punishment, rather than its abandonment.[30] The 1970s and 1980s then saw a decisive reassertion of the classical interpretation of the principle of legality, under the banner of the "back to justice" movement, which explicitly appealed to the "classical"

[28] See notably *Smith* v. *Donnelly*, 2001 SLT 1007. For discussion see Fiona Leverick, "Breach of the Peace after *Smith v Donnelly*," *Scots Law Times*, 34 (2011), 257–262.

[29] *R* v. *R* (1996) 21 EHRR 363.

[30] Michele Pifferi, *Reinventing Punishment: A Comparative History of Criminology in the Nineteenth and Twentieth Centuries* (Oxford: Oxford University Press, 2016), esp. chs. 7 and 8 suggesting that in the US system the principle of *nullum crimen* was maintained in the finding of guilt, but that the weakened procedural legality of the sentencing phase permitted a weakening of *nulla poena* to support individualization of sentencing.

theories of those such as Beccaria. This attacked the individualization of punishment as contrary to the "classic" principles of criminal law, and focused in particular on the idea of proportionality in sentencing: the belief that the sentence for any crime must be proportional to the seriousness of the crime that had been committed (as opposed to any characteristics of the offender or the threat that they posed to society).[31]

Notwithstanding the intuitive appeal of the idea of proportionality as a limit on arbitrary punishment, there are none the less difficulties in trying to define exactly what it means. The central problem with the idea of proportionality is that "it leaves open what the elements are that must stand in appropriate relation to each other."[32] Should the crime be compared only to other similar acts? Should it be compared to the damage caused by the act, or to the threat posed by that class of actions? Should the mental state, motivation or past record of the offender also be taken into account? How should any preventive function of sentencing be taken into account? And if a particular crime (or class of crimes) is punished severely in a certain jurisdiction, then punishing proportionately to other offenses of this type may not have the potential to act as any kind of limit.[33] In attempting to address some of these questions, much of the theoretical literature now distinguishes between cardinal and ordinal proportionality.[34] Ordinal proportionality describes the relative seriousness of offences: whether, for example, burglary is to be regarded as more or less serious than other forms of property crime. Cardinal proportionality is then the term used to describe the relation between crimes and punishment: determining what kind of punishment would be proportionate to any particular offense. It is thus argued that by reflecting on the relation to these two different senses it should be possible to provide certain clear anchoring points and then distribute the punishment for other offenses around these on the basis of the relative seriousness of individual offenses.

[31] Francis A. Allen, *The Habits of Legality: Criminal Justice and the Rule of Law* (Oxford: Oxford University Press, 1996); Andrew von Hirsch, *Doing Justice: The Choice of Punishments* (New York: Hill and Wang, 1976).

[32] Ulfrid Neumann, "The 'Deserved' Punishment," in A. P. Simester, Antje Du Bois-Pedain, and Ulfrid Neumann, eds., *Liberal Criminal Theory: Essays for Andreas von Hirsch* (Oxford: Hart, 2014), p. 75.

[33] *US* v. *Angelos* (2004), cited in Dubber and Hörnle, *Criminal Law*, pp. 53–55, where a sentence of 61½ years for a minor drug offense was upheld after considering the issue of proportionality.

[34] For a classic analysis, see Andrew von Hirsch and Nils Jareborg, "Gauging Criminal Harm: A Living Standard Analysis," *Oxford Journal of Legal Studies*, 11 (1991), 1–38.

This is an ambitious attempt to resolve some of the problems associated with proportionality. However, as Ashworth points out, while it may be possible to determine the relative seriousness of certain offenses at particular points in time, there is always going to be a conventional and symbolic element to the relationship between offenses and punishment.[35] That is to say, while it may in principle be possible to construct a scale of relative seriousness (while recognizing, of course, that perceptions of seriousness might change over time), it is not clear why we should take any particular relationship between a crime and a punishment as an anchoring point for the scale. For example, life imprisonment might best be understood as a significant symbolic response to the crime of murder (a life for a life), rather than as reflecting any kind of necessary or inherent relationship between the crime of murder and its punishment – and it is not hard to conceive of other kinds of responses, ranging from capital punishment to forgiveness that might be seen as equally apposite. Crucially, it is not then apparent why proportionality would act as a limit on punishment, rather than just reinforcing existing penal practices or social understandings. Lacey and Pickard go further, arguing that proportionality should be seen as a "chimera."[36] They argue not only that the idea of proportionality between crime and punishment is "constructed," in the sense that there is no necessary relationship between any particular crime and punishment, but that proportionality only really "made sense" in societies where there existed conditions for broad agreement over the moral equivalences between crimes and punishments. In contemporary societies, they argue that the conditions for such agreement have broken down. This is in part because the understanding of proportionality is now more technical, depending on ideas of individual fault as well as the wrong committed, but mainly because the appeal to proportionality "simply defers the crucial and complicated processes of meaning-making, consensus-building and institutional development" which are necessary to building substantial limits to punishment.[37]

[35] Andrew Ashworth, *Sentencing and Criminal Justice*, 5th ed. (Cambridge: Cambridge University Press, 2010), p. 113.

[36] Nicola Lacey and Hannah Pickard, "The Chimera of Proportionality: Institutionalising Limits of Punishment in Contemporary Social and Political Systems," *Modern Law Review*, 78 (2015), 216–240.

[37] Lacey and Pickard, "The Chimera of Proportionality," 233. It is also the case that theories of proportionality treat the specific amount of pain inflicted by any given unit of punishment as specifiable and unproblematic.

One of the ways that certain jurisdictions have sought to institutionalize limits is by constitutionalizing the principle of proportionality as a requirement of the rule of law.[38] In Germany this takes the form of the "culpability principle," contained in §46(1) of the Penal Code, according to which culpability must be proportionate to the individual guilt of the offender, and is understood as an element of the rule of law protected by the Constitution.[39] While the purpose of punishment is thus broadly retributive, the Penal Code further provides that courts should take into account the effect of the sentence on the offender's future life in society – introducing considerations of the rehabilitative and preventive impact of the sentence into the deliberations of the court. The upshot, Krey argues, has been the development of a series of further principles surrounding sentencing, which focus on the appropriateness of particular punishments. The aims of the punishment must be broadly related to the means adopted; interference with fundamental rights must fit the purpose intended by that interference; the interference must be necessary, in the sense of there not being other more effective (and less intrusive) means available for achieving the ends; and the damage brought about by the interference should not be disproportionate to the intended purpose.[40] It is arguably the case that the sort of detailed jurisprudence which has given rise to these further considerations can, and does, act as a restraint on punitiveness in certain instances. The more abstract question that remains is whether the culpability principle acts as an "internal" limit on punishment (in the sense that an offender can only be punished to the extent of their culpable wrongdoing), or whether the introduction of further "social" considerations means that the potential to limit is diluted.[41]

Many of these issues arose in the case of *M* v. *Germany* (2009), which also demonstrates the limits of some of the constitutional protections, as it addressed questions of the balance, or proportion, between social

[38] See Franz Streng, "Sentencing in Germany: Basic Questions and New Developments," *German Law Journal*, 8 (2007), 153–171; Weigend, "Germany," p. 254. Cf. the approach in England and Wales, which has also sought to give more substantive content to the idea of proportionality See Ashworth, *Sentencing and Criminal Justice*, ch. 4.

[39] "The culpability principle is a specific expression of the proportionality principle, which is also a constitutional requirement of the 'rule of law.'" This is sometimes also referred to as *nulla poena sine culpa*. Streng, "Sentencing in Germany," p. 153.

[40] Volker Krey, "The Rule of Law in German Criminal Proceedings," *Rechtspolitisches Forum*, 43 (2008), 7.

[41] See, for example, discussion in Neumann, "The 'Deserved' Punishment."

protection and individual liberty.[42] In Germany, in common with many other jurisdictions, a distinction has been drawn between penal and nonpenal measures, with it being argued that nonpenal measures were not subject to the constitutional limitations on *ex post facto* punishment, because they were not penal in character.[43] In this case M had been held in preventive detention for a period of around eighteen years (since 1991) following the ending of his prison sentence, on the grounds that he presented a danger to the public. His challenge to this in his domestic courts was unsuccessful, and he appealed to the European Court of Human Rights, which overturned the judgment of the German Federal Constitutional Court on the legality of preventive detention. The Court held that they could look behind domestic classifications of whether a measure was penal or not, and concluded that in this case the measure was in fact a punishment, as it was only applied to those who had been convicted of serious crimes. They then recognized that it was justifiable for national systems to maintain systems of preventive detention, which might outweigh the right of the individual to freedom, but argued that these should be subject to certain restrictions: they should be used only as a last resort, and there should be treatment measures in place.

As Dubber and Hörnle point out, while the decision on the question of whether the detention was "really" penal criticizes the German government for failing to respect M's freedom, it does not really challenge the distinction between penal and nonpenal measures in itself.[44] This consequently does not challenge the widespread existence of schemes of preventive detention, or the jurisprudence which has grown up around the legitimation of these schemes. Something similar is seen in the recent UK Supreme Court case of *Brown* v. *Scottish Ministers*, which concerned a prisoner who spent a five-year period in prison, while imprisoned for a parole recall sentence of 40 days, due to unavailability of particular treatment programs and risk assessments.[45] He sought to challenge this under Article 5(1) of the European Convention of Human Rights, under which detention might be arbitrary if not for a legitimate purpose. After an extensive review of the

[42] *M.* v. *Germany*, No. 19359/04, paras. 7–12 (Eur. Ct. H.R. 2009).

[43] Cf. *Kansas* v. *Hendricks*, US Supreme Court, 521 US 346 (1997).

[44] Dubber and Hörnle, *Criminal Law*, pp. 69–70.

[45] *Brown* v. *The Parole Board for Scotland, the Scottish Ministers and another* [2017] UKSC 69.

authorities, the Court held that his detention (for parole recall) should not be categorized as indeterminate (and therefore triggering the requirement for access to rehabilitative programs), but as determinate – because it was within the period of his original sentence. The point here is that by focusing on the technical distinction (determinate/indeterminate) rather than looking at the question of whether the time spent in detention for violation of a parole condition was excessive in absolute terms, the potential impact of the limitations is further diluted.[46]

Conclusion

I have argued in this chapter that the rise of modern thinking about the rule of law was closely linked to the transformation of punishment that took place at the end of the eighteenth century. Thinking about civic liberty focused on the abuses of power that took place in criminal justice – in relation to torture, unauthorized detention and arbitrary punishment – and sought to curb these excesses by placing them within the legal framework of the "contract" between legislator and citizen. At the same time, though, the critique of criminal justice was focused on making punishment a more effective deterrent, by understanding humans as rational and calculating, and devising institutions that would harness this new understanding of human nature to a new kind of political arithmetic. So, in the field of criminal justice and punishment, the development of the principle of legality reflects the tension between liberty and the development of modern institutions of penal control. Or rather, it is not that there is a fundamental opposition between the two, but that modern understandings of the rule of law in punishment are intrinsically linked to the development of modern penal institutions. This means, as I have attempted to show in this chapter, that modern understandings of legality cannot be understood in wholly abstract terms, but must be understood in their relation to the kind of penal institutions that they seek to regulate.

The modern principle of legality has sought to limit, on the one hand, the law-making power, and, on the other, infliction of punishment, by identifying rules which would limit, or govern, the practices of law-making and

[46] See Sarah Armstrong, "Securing Prison through Human Rights: Unanticipated Implications of Rights-Based Penal Governance," *Howard Journal of Crime and Justice*, 57 (2018), 401–421.

punishment. In both cases it is clear that these rules are now clearly recognized in constitutional documents and penal codes, and have had a substantial impact on the practices they seek to regulate. Criminal laws which are vague or unclear might be struck down by the courts, and even in common law jurisdictions courts are wary about claiming an explicit power to create new laws for fear of falling foul of constitutional limits. And in relation to punishment, there is evidence of judicial sensitivity to the infliction of unauthorized or disproportionate forms of punishment. However, it is also clear that, notwithstanding these advances, there are areas in which the impact of rule of law restrictions has been rather more limited. Indeed, it is arguable that the institutionalization of the principle of legality has meant that courts have become more focused on the effectiveness of systems of criminal justice – through the drawing of sophisticated and increasingly fine-grained distinctions between authorized and unauthorized practices – rather than the prevention of overt injustices.

25 Populism and the Rule of Law

Nicola Lacey

Introduction

A wave of populism is now sweeping across the advanced democracies in the northern hemisphere, overturning the conventional sense that since the mid-twentieth century populism has been primarily a phenomenon of countries with personalized, presidential political systems and radical inequalities, with Latin American countries providing prominent examples. Populism evidently poses a major challenge to prevailing political systems, placing pressure in particular on established patterns of partisanship and hence on political parties. These factors, along with increasing reliance on "directly democratic" decision-making mechanisms such as referenda, raise questions about some very basic aspects of the rule of law and other features of modern constitutionalism. But while there is an emerging political theory and political science literature which seeks to explain the origins of populism and its implications for democracy, less has been written about its implications for the rule of law. Political science analyses have noted the tendency of populist regimes to exploit legal mechanism and subvert legal institutions, but jurists have been slower to focus on populism as a potential threat to the rule of law's integrity. Only in the last few years has this begun to change, largely as a result of some spectacular instances of the capacity of populist politics to put the rule of law under pressure even in countries in which its position had been largely seen as secure.

The aim of this chapter is to give some further analytic focus to these emerging concerns about the impact of populism on the rule of law by asking three questions. First, how many of the recent worrying developments with respect to the apparent erosion of the rule of law in Europe and North America are indeed associated with populism? Secondly, where such an association can be established, is it a contingent or analytic matter: does populism inevitably threaten the rule of law, or do other conditions intervene to shape its impact? Are some connections analytic but others contingent? And thirdly, what can we learn from this about the scope for minimizing the impact of rising populism on the rule of law?

In addressing these issues, I stray as a criminal lawyer into terrain primarily occupied by political scientists, political and legal theorists, and constitutional lawyers. I do so with a specific concern, one that will help me to carve out a manageable patch of territory within an enormous field. I am, in particular, concerned with the way that the design of some forms of political system, under conditions of declining stable partisanship, have rendered the law-making process highly responsive to populist considerations, whether through resort to mechanisms such as initiatives and referenda or simply through politicians' openness to popular concerns in shaping the legislative agenda, irrespective of the commitments made on electoral platforms and hence carrying democratic authority. Legislative populism, if I can put it in that way, has long been notable in relation to criminal law, and there is now a relevant comparative literature which considers how this change itself relates to broad shifts in political economy. A substantial part of this literature on changing patterns of criminalization and punishment – including a literature on the criminalization of migrants – is framed in terms of "penal populism" or "populist punitiveness."[1] The possibility broached in this literature – that differently configured political systems are more or less responsive to penal populist concerns – in turn opens up interesting general questions about whether these differences affect their capacity to absorb populist pressures without compromising values such as the rule of law and civil liberties.

The first and second sections of this chapter set out, respectively, how I understand the rule of law and populism for the purposes of my analysis. In the third section, I consider the issue of whether there are analytic links between populism and an erosion of the rule of law. In the fourth section, I consider a range of contingent links and examine the institutional and social conditions which conduce to strengthen or weaken them. In the fifth section, I consider the implications for contemporary criminalization,

[1] Ana Aliverti and Mary Bosworth, "Introduction: Criminal Justice Adjudication in an Age of Migration," *New Criminal Law Review,* 20 (2017)1–11, and the special issue their article introduces; Nicola Lacey, *The Prisoner's Dilemma: Punishment and Political Economy in Contemporary Democracies* (Cambridge: Cambridge University Press, 2008); J. Pratt, *Penal Populism* (London: Sage, 2006); Ian Loader, and Richard Sparks, "Penal Populism and Epistemic Crime Control," in Alison Liebling, Shadd Maruna, and Lesley McAra, eds., *The Oxford Handbook of Criminology*, 6th ed. (Oxford: Oxford University Press, 2017), pp. 98–115.

assessing how many of the factors producing what scholars have called "penal populism" or "overcriminalization" are truly a product of populism.

1 Approaching the Rule of Law

The vast literature on the rule of law has until relatively recently been preoccupied with a cluster of debates about its conceptual contours and scope. We can distinguish four broad approaches.

First, some scholars have taken a formal or "thin" conception of the rule of law. This position is most influentially set out by Joseph Raz, who argues that the rule of law inheres in a cluster of formal values such as clarity, nonretroactivity, publicity, universality of reach, possibility of compliance and congruence between expressed law and official enforcement.[2] Raz imagines the rule of law as a sharpener of law's "knife," hence expressing a distinctive and genuine "virtue" of law's *modus operandi* of, as Lon Fuller put it, "subjecting human conduct to the governance of rules."[3] It makes the law sharper and hence more effective; but the law's "sharp knife" may also be used for substantively immoral purposes. This formal conception of the rule of law is also dominant in a substantial public choice literature which ponders the conditions under which the rule of law is in equilibrium and hence a stable socio-political institutional framework and form of association.[4] In this literature, the possibility that the rule of law can be used as a political weapon is contemplated as one which presents no conceptual tension or contradiction.

Secondly, some scholars have seen the rule of law in procedural as well as formal terms. In Jeremy Waldron's view the rule of law expresses not merely formal constraints but procedural commitments which imply a certain interpersonal attitude.[5] A commitment such as equality before the law discloses a normative view of respect for persons as agents who

[2] Joseph Raz, "The Rule of Law and Its Virtue," in idem, *The Authority of Law: Essays on Law and Morality* (Oxford: Clarendon Press, 1979), pp. 210–229.

[3] Lon L. Fuller, *The Morality of Law* (New Haven: Yale University Press, 1964), p. 106.

[4] Stephen Holmes "Lineages of the Rule of Law," in José María Maravall and Adam Przeworski, eds., *Democracy and the Rule of Law* (Cambridge: Cambridge University Press, 2003), pp. 19–61.

[5] Jeremy Waldron, "The Rule of Law and the Importance of Procedure," in James E. Fleming, ed., *Getting to the Rule of Law: NOMOS L* (New York: New York University Press, 2011), pp. 3–31; cf. Judith Shklar, *Legalism: An Essay on Law, Morals and Politics* (Cambridge: Harvard University Press, 1964).

must be not only informed in advance of the content of legal norms so as to have the opportunity to adjust their conduct accordingly but also have a role in speaking and being heard by a neutral tribunal in any legal process in which they are concerned. Waldron here builds on Lon Fuller's eight canons of "the inner morality of law," a set of formal tenets to which Raz also subscribes but which Fuller saw as carrying moral quality as a mode of governance.

Thirdly, others have been inclined to conceptualize the rule of law in "thick" or "substantive" terms. In the view of scholars like Brian Tamanaha – but also of influential judges like Tom Bingham and Susanne Baer – the rule of law should be seen in terms not merely of the formal and procedural values enunciated by the first two conceptions but also of a wide range of institutional arrangements rooted in normative commitments strongly associated with liberal democracy.[6] In this substantive conception, concomitants of a rule of law worth the name include the values of constitutionalism: checks and balances, basic rights, judicial review, adequate access to justice and, ideally, an international legal order that upholds the rule of law and human rights. History presents many examples of oppressive things being done in conformity with the formal precepts of legalism but these jurists argue such a formal conception distorts the "true" meaning of the rule of law. If law is used merely as a means to an end, the distinctive mode of mutually respectful, agency-recognizing association reflected in the ideal of the rule of law is not present; if it is used for ends which are discriminatory, oppressive, arbitrary or otherwise unjust, this counts as "abusive" or "discriminatory" legalism or "autocratic" constitutionalism.[7]

Fourthly, some scholars have resisted the demand to conceptualize the rule of law in terms of either its form or its content. While recognizing that many of the procedural and institutional arrangements canvassed in the first three traditions will indeed be central to rule of law ideals and practices, scholars like Martin Krygier have taken a teleological or functional approach to the rule of law as a set of ideals and arrangements

[6] Brian Z. Tamanaha, *On the Rule of Law: History, Politics, Theory* (Cambridge: Cambridge University Press, 2012); Tom Bingham, *The Rule of Law* (London: Penguin, 2011); Susanne Baer, "The Rule of – and Not by Any – Law: On Constitutionalism," *Current Legal Problems* 71 (2018), 335–368.

[7] David Landau, "Abusive Constitutionalism," *University of California Davis Law Review*, 47 (2013), 189–260; Kim L. Scheppele, "Autocratic Legalism," *University of Chicago Law Review*, 85 (2018), 545–583.

oriented to tempering power.[8] Crucially, this will involve not only arrangements geared to limiting, constraining or rendering power accountable, but also enabling and strengthening power, not least by enhancing its legitimacy. A distinguishing feature of this cluster of approaches is their contextualism: the insistence that the values to which the rule of law aspires can only be met in terms of a close understanding of how particular social and political systems work.

Each of these approaches to the rule of law is born of their environment: the ideal takes its complexion both from perceived problems – whether arising from war, revolution, atrocities or ideological struggles – and from perceived institutional capacities. And this is key to unraveling the complex relationship between populism and the rule of law.

2 Approaching Populism

Like the literature on the rule of law, that on populism falls along a spectrum between positive political science,[9] and interpretive/normative political theory.[10] There are marked differences of view on whether populism is to be feared or applauded, a wide ideological spectrum between both those supporting and those fearing populism, varying approaches to the conditions which spawn populism, and specific disagreements on the relationship between populism and mechanisms of direct democracy. But there is broad agreement on the main conceptual components of populism as a form of political discourse.

Essentially, populism is a highly moralized approach to politics which pitches a homogeneous "we the people," often conceived in ethnic or national terms, embodied in a leader who speaks for and expresses the will of that undifferentiated collectivity, against a presumptively corrupt

8 Martin Krygier, "The Rule of Law: Legality, Teleology, Sociology," in Gianluigi Palombella and Neil Walker, eds., *Relocating the Rule of Law* (Oxford: Hart, 2009), pp. 45–69.

9 See, for example, Steven Levitsky and Daniel Ziblatt, *How Democracies Die* (New York: Crown, 2018); Cas Mudde and Cristóbal Rovira Kaltwasser, *Populism: A Very Short Introduction* (Oxford: Oxford University Press, 2017).

10 See, for example, Yascha Mounk, *The People vs Democracy: Why Our Freedom is in Danger and How to Save It* (Cambridge: Harvard University Press, 2018); Jan-Werner. Muller, *What is Populism?* (London: Penguin, 2017) Nadia Urbinati, *Democracy Disfigured: Opinion, Truth and the People* (Cambridge: Harvard University Press, 2014).

elite.[11] This implies that the particular shape of the "interpretive frame" through which actors comprehend the political world in a society influenced by populist discourse will be determined by a range of contingencies and can incorporate conflicting ideologies. Hence populism may take left- or right-wing forms and populists may aspire to realize some of the values which also characterize not only democracy but even liberalism. Yet populism is fundamentally at odds with liberal democracy because it is monistic rather than pluralistic, monarchic rather than diarchic, exclusive rather than inclusive, and with a vertical rather than a horizontal vision of power.

Populism may disfigure democracy but, arguably, it arises out of some irresolvable tensions within the liberal democratic ideal itself. As Urbinati observes, populism is, in some sense "parasitical" on representative democracy, from which it takes its image of the sovereign people; but it reacts against the inevitable tension within liberal representative democracy between the ideal of popular representation and the rules and conventions of constitutional arrangements that constrain the power of popular sovereignty.[12] Populism arises in part from the "broken promises" of democracy itself: since "the people" can never truly rule because of heterogeneity and conflicts of value and interest, some voices always prevail. Populism thus "exploits the tensions that are inherent to liberal democracy, which tries to find a harmonious equilibrium between majority rule and minority rights. This equilibrium is almost impossible."[13] But this also implies a contradiction at the heart of populism, and one which further illuminates its tendency towards authoritarianism and against democracy. For in order to preserve its highly moralized symbolic fantasy of a pure homogeneous "we the people," the real voices of dissent and variation must not be heard too loudly.

A significant spur to populism has been the perceived deficits and failures of liberal democracy to represent an adequate range of interests. This is particularly so in Europe, where the impulse of the reconstruction of democracy after World War II was to build structures to limit the sway of popular will, not least in its capacity to encroach on minorities. "In a world that is dominated by democracy and liberalism," Mudde and Rovira

[11] Mudde and Kaltwasser, *Populism*, p. 6. [12] Urbinati, *Democracy Disfigured*, p. 135.
[13] Mudde and Kaltwasser, *Populism*, p. 82.

Kaltwasser note, "populism has essentially become an illiberal democratic response to undemocratic liberalism."[14] The populist resurgence has undoubtedly been exacerbated by two further large facts. First, the fundamental restructuring of advanced political economies since the 1970s in the wake of de-industrialisation and under conditions of intensifying globalization has implied a dramatic decline in the relative economic and social standing of a large group, and a form of polarization and economic exclusion which has fostered widespread resentment and found expression in forms of identity politics such as nationalism and nativism. Secondly, elected governments have proved ineffective in countering these trends, and indeed are widely seen as having encouraged or exacerbated them by developing "neoliberal" economic policies focused on market competition in a globalizing economy.

It is important to remember, of course, that widespread though the emergence of populist political discourse, parties, leaders and agenda in both Europe and North America has been, the number of countries in which we can genuinely talk of a populist system of government remains small. The multi-party, parliamentary systems of Europe provide some protection as compared with presidential systems and the orientation to consensus and bargaining of the sectoral proportional representation systems of the coordinated market economies provides further protection.[15] And while the popular-democracy limiting and technocratic tendencies of the European Union and the highly integrated postwar constitutional settlements of countries like Germany may themselves have indirectly stoked populist resentment, they have also, as compared with the less coordinated systems of liberal market economies like the United Kingdom, provided some protection for the rule of law.[16]

The economic changes canvassed above have begun to erode the structure of the party system by fragmenting the sectoral interests or "pillars" on which the political systems of these countries depended. The limited extent

[14] Mudde and Kaltwasser, *Populism*, p. 82. p. 116.

[15] Peter A. Hall and David Soskice, eds., *Varieties of Capitalism: The Institutional Foundations of Comparative Advantage* (Oxford: Oxford University Press, 2001); Arend Lijphart, *Patterns of Democracy: Government Forms and Performance in Thirty-Six Countries* (New Haven: Yale University Press, 1999).

[16] Alan L. Bogg and Mark R. Freedland, "Labour Law in the Age of Populism: Towards Sustainable Democratic Engagement," *MPIL Research Paper* No. 2018–15 Max Planck Institute for Comparative Public Law and International Law, Heidelberg, July 2018.

of the model of party competition, compromise and pluralism, along with the liberal democratic constitutionalist mentality which institutionalizes it, in the postcommunist regimes of Central and Eastern Europe perhaps explains why the starkest European examples of populism come from that region.[17] The Orbán regime in Hungary is one example; the Polish government has also moved in a substantially populist direction; and the signs accumulate that, limited though US presidential powers over domestic policy have often been taken to be, Donald Trump's populist style of leadership has had a significant effect on US institutions beyond the presidency.

But the limited number of cases in which the hold of populism on political actors and institutions would justify our speaking in terms of a populist regime does not imply that populism has only limited relevance for politics and the rule of law in Europe and North America. For populism can affect the conduct and integrity of liberal democratic politics in a range of ways short of capturing the governing regime. The power of populism should be counted not merely in terms of the electoral votes a populist party or leader obtains, but also in terms of "the ability to put topics on the agenda . . . and the capacity to shape public policies."[18]

3 Analytic Links between Populism and Threats to the Rule of Law

Populism, then, is an ambivalent political discourse. There is, nonetheless, a straightforward analytic connection between the populist style of politics understood in the terms of the previous section and an impatience with the rule of law. This is because a populist leader claims to express the will of the "pure" people and any institutional structure which questions that political expression is liable to come into conflict with the populist leader. The populist leader's claim to express the people's will does not brook any system of checks and balances such as that envisaged by modern constitutionalism, for the latter is premised on a pluralist view of politics. Moreover the polarized and moralistic, friend/enemy, "pure us/corrupt

[17] Martin Krygier, "Institutionalisation and Its Discontents: Constitutionalism versus (Anti-) Constitutional Populism in East Central Europe." Paper presented at the Transnational Law Institute King's College, London, November 17, 2017.

[18] Mudde and Kaltwasser, *Populism*, p. 98.

them" tenor of populism tends to erode the usual norms of civility within political discourse. Accordingly, both constitutional rights and the institutions which protect them – notably the judiciary, but also the media – are often targets of populist criticism. Muller sees populism as a form of exclusionary identity politics which tends to undermine democracy.[19]

Populists do not necessarily eschew constitutionalism altogether. But populist constitutionalism is tricky, since the creation of separate and mutually checking governmental institutions necessarily gives rise to the possibility of conflict between them – a conflict which is inconsistent with the populist monarchic claim to express the people's will. Hence courts in particular are liable to populist suspicion, stemming from their capacity to constrain political power being reinforced by their standing as elitists or experts and their distance from "the people." Here, the availability of a purely formal conception of the rule of law – the rule of law not merely as useful "knife" but even as "weapon" – may become a tool in the hands of the populist constitutionalist. For the rule of law not only constrains but enables governmental power, and populist governments need law as much as any other regime.

Consequently, courts and other checking institutions need to be coopted, as they may be by court-packing, intimidation of the judiciary or other mechanisms such as those that have recently been deployed in Poland and Hungary. And once institutions such as the judiciary have been commandeered or coopted, we see what scholars have called forms of "abusive constitutionalism" or "discriminatory" or "autocratic legalism" in which the law itself is used to persecute minorities, to punish dissent, and to enforce executive power discursively legitimized as the people's will.[20] This can take the form of not only a corrupting politicization of the law and the judiciary but also of a "judicialization of politics," where the courts or other legal processes such as impeachment are used for political purposes. For not only adherents of substantive conceptions of the rule of law but also those who take a functional view of the rule of law as inherently concerned with tempering power, this amounts to a corruption of the rule of law, what might be called rule by

[19] Müller, *What is Populism?*, p. 8.

[20] José María Maravall, "The Rule of Law as a Political Weapon," in Maravall and Przeworski, eds., *Democracy and the Rule of Law*, pp. 261–301; Landau, "Abusive Constitutionalism"; Scheppele, "Autocratic Legalism."

law rather than the rule of law, albeit that the specific form which that subversion takes will vary across time and place.

4 Contingent Links between Populism and the Subversion of the Rule of Law

The analytic tensions between populism and the rule of law realize themselves primarily in populist regimes. Yet they are also of relevance to the much larger range of countries in which populists do not control government, but in which populist political movements have some significant presence: within the government, as in the case of the United States under the Trump presidency; as nationalist or otherwise populist parties, as with the French Front National or the German AfD; or as powerful factions within major parties, as with the vehemently anti-EU wing of the British Conservative Party; or even as popular social movements such as the Tea Party, Vote Leave, or Occupy. And in these countries, whether and how the links between populism and erosion of the rule of law announce themselves depends on many contingencies. Hence any full understanding of these links must be system- and context- specific.

The vulnerability of any system to populist-inspired erosion of the constraints on power offered by the rule of law will depend on such factors as: the structure of its political system and especially the electoral system and the internal rules of its political parties governing matters such as candidate selection and the election of a leader; the standing and the strength of the professional culture of its judiciary; the capacity of its legal, political and economic institutions to resolve social conflicts and to command reasonable levels of respect. It hence becomes possible to say something at a general level about the ways in which these very common, increasing, and partial forms of political populism may affect the robustness of the rule of law even in countries whose systems are fundamentally shaped in terms of liberal democratic values.

In this section, I distinguish four mechanisms, giving examples of each from Europe and the United States. The first two, those of agenda-setting and policy impact, have already been mentioned. A small populist faction within a large party, a small populist party, or a powerful populist who holds elected office, may be able to have a decisive impact on a country's political agenda and in specific policy terms. Probably the most spectacular example here is Donald Trump's power to set an isolationist agenda through trade and other aspects of foreign policy, in the name of "Making America Great Again."[21] Perhaps yet more worrying is the diffuse, yet hard to measure, impact of his populist and court-disrespecting rhetoric on practices at state and local level in relation to matters such as voter registration, redistricting, judicial appointments and indeed general law interpretation and enforcement.[22] The US constitutional structure which gives the President the right to nominate Supreme Court Justices and hence to shape the political complexion of the Court for decades – illustrated by the appointments of Justices Gorsuch and Kavanaugh – exemplifies a particular vulnerability.

In Europe – both in the European Union as a transnational political entity and also in particular nations – the inability to find a stable solution or even a broad consensus about the refugee crisis is another example of both the agenda-setting and policy impact of populist politics via erosion of the authority of the main political parties. And in Britain, the fear among MPs of the threat from UKIP/the Brexit Party in leave-voting constituencies has almost certainly shaped the Westminster Parliament's difficulty in reaching a compromise agreement on how to redefine Britain's relationship with the European Union. Such impacts come about in part through corrosive attitudinal changes. For example, evidence mounts that the Leave campaign exhibited a characteristically populist contempt for the electoral laws within which it should have been working, with Prime Minister Johnson's ambivalent acknowledgment concerning the authority of the Supreme Court's decision that his prorogation of parliament was unlawful – and the attempted prorogation itself – indicating that that mentality now has some influence at the heart of government.[23]

Two further potential and diffuse impacts of what might be called partial populism on the rule of law are also worthy of consideration. These are, first, the capacity of populism to affect the exercise of discretionary powers and, secondly, the upshot of what I will call "convention-trashing." Taking the example of discretionary powers, it is useful to focus on judges. It is widely recognized that judges enjoy a range of discretionary powers and considerable interpretive latitude. They are also, to state the obvious, human beings

[21] Levitsky and Ziblatt, *How Democracies Die.*

[22] Jason Zengerie, "How the Trump Administration is Remaking the Courts," *The New York Times Magazine*, August 26, 2018; Shira A. Scheindlin, "Trump's Hard-Right Judges Will Do Lasting Damage to America," *The Guardian*, July 5, 2018.

[23] *R (Miller)* v. *Prime Minister* [2019] UKSC 41.

who are subject to the usual range of pressures, albeit that their institutional role and their professional training and culture equip them, ideally, with some very particular capacities for independent judgment. It is hard not to worry, nonetheless, that incidents such as the infamous British *Daily Mail* "Enemies of the People" headline or Donald Trump's personal attacks on judges and law officers, will not in the longer term have some impact in inhibiting the full exercise of that independence.

This sort of impact on discretionary powers is hard to track empirically, but there is some evidence from the more discretionary aspects of judicial decision-making which gives it both indirect and direct support. One example is the upward travel of sentencing severity in both the United States and the United Kingdom during the era of so-called "penal populism."[24] Another is a recent study of the discretionary practice of domestic courts' citing international or transnational law, which suggests that in countries where populist hostility to supranational legal orders is strong, we may see a decline in such citations, a matter of concern because of the capacity of international law to provide extra protection for the rights of minorities, to strengthen pluralism and to counter polarization.[25] This argument applies, *a fortiori*, to the wide discretionary powers of a range of law enforcement and regulatory agencies.

Moving to the fourth potential upshot of partial populism for the rule of law, convention-trashing, we return to a theme which arose in our discussion of the rule of law: that the fullest expression of its aspiration depends upon a set of attitudes and an accepted mode of association which cannot be captured or completely enforced by rules. This implies that the internalization of the normative ideals associated with the rule of law by those who exercise power is key to its robustness. This is particularly evident in relation to the elaborate conventions which surround the operation of any constitution. Populist attitudes are, however, as we have seen, impatient of constraints. And where conventions or understandings are casually broken by populists, these can be very much harder to repair, and the relevant actors very much harder to discipline or restrain, than in the case of more blatant breaches of established constitutional norms.

24 David Garland, *The Culture of Control: Crime and Social Order in Contemporary Society* (New York: Oxford University Press, 2001).

25 Tamar Hostovsky. Brandes, "International Law in Domestic Courts in an Era of Populism," *International Journal of Constitutional Law*, 17 (2019), 576–596.

Recent examples include Trump's brazen flouting of the long-established conventions about conflicts of interest and nepotism, by failing effectively to separate himself from his business interests; his incontinent invective on Twitter; and his decision to move a large part of his family into the White House in positions of very significant executive power.[26] They also include the revelation arising from recent events in Hungary and Poland that while compliance with the rule of law is one of the conditions of accession to the European Union, continued compliance is a convention in the sense that it depends on self-restraint, with the EU possessing only relatively blunt tools to discipline countries which dismantle key aspects of it, notably the independence of the judiciary.[27] In the international perhaps yet more than the national sphere, the robustness of norms of legality, as of norms such as human rights, is substantially dependent on voluntary compliance.

5 Beyond Populism

The growth of populist sentiment and of populist political actors in Europe and North America has presented a number of challenges to the rule of law. But as Justice Susanne Baer notes, not all threats to the rule of law come from populist politics.[28] So it is relevant to consider how important populism has been in the recent development of criminalization and emergence of "penal populism."

Examples which fit the conception of populism adopted in this paper can be found. The origins of California's "three strikes and you're out" law, for example, was a product of California's system of direct democracy via citizen-initiated propositions.[29] And we could see legislative initiatives in England and Wales, ranging from corporate manslaughter to antisocial behaviour via dangerous dogs, as expressing a concern to show responsiveness to popular demands. More obliquely, we might see the concern with security which underlines the popularity of criminalization as itself

[26] Leah Litman, "How Trump Corrupts the Rule of Law," *The New York Times*, June 18, 2018.

[27] Kim Lane Scheppele, "Constitutional Coups in EU Law," in Maurice Adams, Anne Meuwese, and Ernst Hirsch Ballin, eds., *Constitutionalism and the Rule of Law: Bridging Idealism and Realism* (Cambridge: Cambridge University Press, 2017), pp. 446–478.

[28] Baer, "The Rule of – and Not by Any – Law."

[29] Franklin E. Zimring, Gordon Hawkins, and Sam Kamin, *Punishment and Democracy: Three Strikes and You're Out in California* (New York: Oxford University Press, 2001).

a product of a certain kind of disenchantment with the efficacy of government.[30]

But "penal populism" predates the populist resurgence which has been my main focus, and much of its drive comes from fear and insecurity attendant on crime, that fear and insecurity being projected onto "outsiders" in the form of offenders. There is a structural analogy with populism, but the outsiders are not necessarily the same as the enemy outsiders on which populism is currently focused. Indeed, they are disproportionately members of the groups whose economic dislocation and exclusion has fed the populist surge of recent years. So it is probably more accurate to see overcriminalization and penal severity as themselves products of some of the larger economic, social and political forces which have created populism itself: perceived weaknesses in national state sovereignty, prompting a resort to criminalization as one of the few tools of governance still within nation-state control; social conflict; a failure to ensure that an adequate majority feel that they have a stake in the prevailing order; and persistent inequality.

Likewise, in a self-reinforcing cycle, the failures of political leadership which stoke populism via distrust in government are in part a product of the erosion of party strength produced by populism itself. The causal linkages here are complex. For example, arguably one of the most urgent threats to the rule of law in the field of criminal law in England and Wales lies in the steady erosion of access to justice implied by swingeing cuts to court services, to the police and the Crown Prosecution Service, and to legal aid, which have been an offshoot of austerity policies. And austerity politics have both stoked populism by exacerbating economic exclusion and polarization and been fed by populist resentment of the reach of welfare benefits to "outsiders."

There are, however, two areas in which developments in criminalization might be thought to have been shaped by populism. The first is antiterrorism law, which in the United Kingdom as in several other countries deploys the notion of an alien "enemy within" on which populism feeds. Over the last two decades, we have seen a vivid case of the normalization of powers previously seen as exceptional, with a substantial amount of legislation

[30] Peter Ramsay, *The Insecurity State: Vulnerable Autonomy and the Right to Security in the Criminal Law* (Oxford: Oxford University Press, 2012); Lucia Zedner, *Security* (London: Routledge, 2009).

directly or indirectly geared to the criminalization of terrorism. The extraordinary events of September 2001 are, of course, an important part of the genesis of this new legislative concern. The antiterror reaction has created a wave of criminalization which expands the boundaries of criminal law, enhances police and prosecutorial power, weakens defense lawyers, curtails judicial discretion and, in some of its more radical "adjustments" to normal standards of procedure, directly undermines the rule of law by deploying some of the methods of terror itself.

Implicit in the structure of many of these terrorism offenses we see something akin to "enemy criminal law" or character responsibility: the idea that, on top of committing or planning acts of violence, there is something intrinsically wrong about being a certain kind of person engaged in a certain kind of activity – an aggravation of blameworthiness which justifies a special criminalization regime.[31] Much of the counterterrorism legislation of recent years is redolent of the criminalization of status. The implicit assumption is that there is a finite number of "bad people" who are "terrorists" and if we can simply detain them, the world will be a safer place for those of "good character," who alone deserve the full protection of the rule of law. But while these themes are reminiscent of aspects of populist discourse, they can hardly be said to have been driven by populist politics alone.

The other – and related – area of criminalization which on the face of it has been shaped by populism is so-called "crimmigration," the increasing resort to criminalization as a way of disciplining, excluding and expelling migrants or those seen as presumptively unentitled.[32] The blurring of the boundaries between administrative and criminal law, notably in the case of immigration detention, and of the boundaries between civil and criminal law, as in the use of a range of civil orders whose breach implies criminal liability, is of concern not only to migrants' and asylum seekers' human rights but also to erosion of the rule of law.[33]

[31] Nicola Lacey, *In Search of Criminal Responsibility: Ideas, Interests and Institutions* (Oxford: Oxford University Press, 2016), ch. 5.

[32] Juliet Stumpf, "The Crimmigration Crisis: Immigrants, Crime and Sovereign Power," *American University Law Review*, 56 (2006), 368–419; Aliverti and Bosworth, "Introduction."

[33] Lucia Zedner, "Penal Subversions: When Is Punishment Not Punishment, Who Decides and On What Grounds?," *Theoretical Criminology*, 20 (2016), 3–20.

Yet, even here, the causation may be more complex than at first appears. As Vanessa Barker has argued in a recent analysis of the emergence of "penal nationalism" in relation to migration in Sweden, "problems with pluralism, ethnic diversity and immigration are much more mainstream, long lasting and institutionalized than the current focus on populism allows."[34] So while the emergence of penal nationalism in countries such as Hungary and Poland may be genuinely driven by populism, this is not necessarily so: each case requires careful interpretation. In the case of Sweden, the clue is to be found in a concern to protect the Nordic welfare state. And although these exclusionary dynamics represent the less appealing underside of solidaristic Nordic conceptions of membership and belonging, they nonetheless differ from the forms of racist, antimigrant populism which characterize extremist parties in, for example, Austria, France or the Netherlands. Penal nationalism may most certainly threaten aspects of the rule of law including generality, publicity and congruence but it is not necessarily a straightforward result of populism.

Conclusion

Populism is currently creating significant risks to the rule of law in Europe and the United States through agenda-setting, policy impact, the shaping of discretionary decisions and convention-trashing. However, the specific force of these populist dynamics in particular countries is mediated by a range of contingencies. These contingencies concern social, political and economic history and the cultural mentalities which this history has engendered; legal, political and economic institutional frameworks; and the specific form which populism takes. The analytic tendency of populism in an anti–rule of law direction, then, can only be the start of any inquiry into the actual sway of populism in particular times and places.

[34] Vanessa Barker, *Nordic Nationalism and Penal Order: Walling the Welfare State* (London: Routledge, 2018), p. 53.

26 An "International Rule of Law Movement"?

Stephen Humphreys

> Could it be made actually to occur? . . . Were it to be established, an association in terms of the rule of law would certainly be a work of art . . . Of course the notion of setting up such an association *ex nihilo* . . . is absurd.
>
> Michael Oakeshott[1]

Introduction

Is there an "international rule of law movement"? Undoubtedly there exists a network of international bodies claiming to "work on" what are often called rule of law "issues," many of whom use this term and do so self-referentially.[2] These groups are not concerned with an "international rule of law," whatever that might be, or indeed with international law more broadly. They are "international" in the sense that they comprise cross-border networks, and in that they approach the "rule of law" in a quasi-constitutional sense, abstracted from any specific (national) polity. The groups that comprise this movement are numerous, networked and well-funded; they boast significant "presence" and share an understanding of the kind of work "rule of law" entails. That alone may be thought sufficient to claim there is an "international rule of law movement," in which case the task would merely be to describe its objectives, *modi operandi*, successes, and failures. And this is indeed what much literature on this supposed "movement" does.[3]

[1] Michael Oakeshott, "The Rule of Law," (1983), 163.

[2] See the contributions to David Marshall, ed., *The International Rule of Law Movement* (Cambridge: Harvard University Press, 2014).

[3] Among many examples, see Marshall, ed., *The International Rule of Law Movement*; Michael Zürn, André Nollkaemper, and Randall Peerenboom, eds., *Rule of Law Dynamics: In an Era of International and Transnational Governance* (Cambridge: Cambridge University Press, 2012); Marko Kmezic, *EU Rule of Law Promotion* (Abingdon: Routledge, 2017).

But to describe this self-proclaimed phenomenon on its own terms hardly tells us whether there *is*, in fact, an "international rule of law movement." If a movement is a politics articulated through motivated civic engagement, the question is whether the rule of law, however defined, qualifies as a political motive. At first blush, the fit seems good, given common assumptions about the rule of law—which is frequently thought to rest upon some form of "civil association." The task might then be to test the internal consistency of the bond between the protagonists (the "movement") and the occasion of their mobilization (something called the rule of law). Though we would still need to know whether a civil association can be international. We would also need to know how "rule of law" is conceived within this "movement" and, given the immense historical and theoretical work that has come to articulate this complex term of art, how persuasive that conception is.

In this chapter, I will first briefly describe the phenomenon itself, the entity that claims the rubric of an "international rule of law movement" – though my sketch will inevitably be over-simplified – and then guide it toward a case study, a body calling itself the World Justice Project (WJP).[4] Despite some differences of emphasis with other organizations in the field, the WJP is broadly representative of the contemporary trend. It is, moreover, well-suited to the question I am posing, as it is not an inter- or quasi-governmental body but an "association" of private actors who are "international" essentially in the sense of being unbounded by territorial constraints. The WJP presents itself as a "movement" – community-driven and human rights-focused – in a way that other rule of law organizations cannot.

I then compare the claims for the rule of law made within the field against Michael Oakeshott's distinctive account of the rule of law which, grounded in a detailed formulation of "civil association," provides an excellent foil for this inquiry. A more explicitly human-rights-friendly rule of law theorist – Joseph Raz or Lon Fuller, for example – might be thought better suited to the task I here assign Oakeshott, given the prevalence of human rights language and assertions running through the contemporary "movement." But Oakeshott's is a rigorously consistent explication of a historical and cultural (rather than merely legal or

[4] The phenomenon is described in detail in Stephen Humphreys, *Theatre of the Rule of Law: Transnational Legal Intervention in Theory and Practice* (Cambridge: Cambridge University Press, 2010); and Stephen Humphreys, "The Rule of Law as Morality Play," *Finnish Yearbook of International Law*, 23 (2012–2013), 3–44.

economic) concern, against which other versions may be tested. Moreover, despite an often gaping difference in rhetoric, the hostility to state-level policy that underlies Oakeshott's rule of law captures rather well the principal concern of contemporary practitioners: for three decades, recourse to the language of rule of law has been effectively mobilized to reduce the policy scope of the state.

1 The Lure of Law in Development

Promotion of something called "the rule of law" has comprised an element in the arsenal of international development since about 1989. As such, it flows between a group of countries characterized as "developed" and those characterized as "developing," the latter, of course, having often been previously colonized by the former. "Development," as many observers have noted, signifies a process internal to developing countries but already achieved in developed countries and so implicitly assumes the transfer of practices, ideas, and resources between these two groups of states. This evidently continues a process already underway prior to colonial independence, and rule of law promotion, too, continues a similar transfer of practices, insofar as certain ideas about law were transposed to "developing" countries, initially through the process of colonization itself.[5]

Nevertheless, since decolonization in the 1960s, notions of how development should be done have shifted, in the 1980s, away from state-centered, public-sector focused, centrally-planned economics toward what the World Bank calls "private sector development."[6] During this period, marked by the imposition of austerity-like policies ("structural adjustment") on many of the world's then indebted nations, the Bank was a principal actor adopting the language of "rule of law" in development policy; others quickly followed.[7] By the end of the 1990s, the notion that

5 Humphreys, *Theatre of the Rule of Law*, pp. 109–120; Sundhya Pahuja, *Decolonising International Law: Development, Economic Growth and the Politics of Universality* (Cambridge: Cambridge University Press, 2011).

6 Humphreys, *Theatre of the Rule of Law*, pp. 123–148. A key shift is often traced to the World Bank report, *Sub-Saharan Africa: From Crisis to Sustainable Growth*: World Bank, 1989).

7 See Ibrahim Shihata, *The World Bank in a Changing World: Selected Essays*, ed. Franziska Tschofen and Antonio Parra (Leiden: Martinus Nijhoff, 1991); Harry Blair and Garry Hansen, *Weighing in on the Scales of Justice: Strategic Approaches for Donor-Supported Rule of Law Programs* (Washington: USAID, 1994).

consolidation of "the rule of law" would assist developing countries to develop was widely shared across a diverse group of international actors, including dedicated development institutions such as the Bank and the International Monetary Fund (IMF), human rights organizations, "post-conflict and transitional justice" organizations, and some national development aid bodies, such as the United States Agency for International Development (USAID).[8] The language caught on more slowly at the United Nations (UN), only really taking off from 2004, when then Secretary General Kofi Annan adopted it in reference to post-conflict or "transitional justice" in the context of peacekeeping and what came to be called "peacebuilding."[9]

Rule of law language had become ubiquitous in international development circles by 2012, when a "High-Level Meeting" on "rule of law at national and international levels" was held under UN auspices, at which states "reaffirmed" their "commitment" to the rule of law as the "foundation of friendly and equitable relations between States and the basis on which just and fair societies are built."[10] The General Assembly Declaration asserts that "the rule of law and development are strongly interrelated and mutually reinforcing" and that the former is "essential for sustained and inclusive economic growth, sustainable development, the eradication of poverty and hunger and the full realization of all human rights."[11] Everyone was by now *for* the rule of law, whose curative reach seemed limitless.

But what did it mean in practice? As an economic discourse, the rule of law has been used to refer primarily to a set of measures aiming to reduce the role of government in economic life and sharpen the boundary between public and private interests.[12] State bodies were to be bound not only by strict rules ("governance") but also by policy restraint ("good" governance). Private – contractual and property – rights were to be strengthened, as was judicial independence, by removing discriminatory judicial practices motivated by state pressure, ideology, or corruption. As it expanded, rule of law discourse embraced the privatization of state enterprises and protections of investors'

[8] Thomas Carothers, ed., *Promoting the Rule of Law Abroad: In Search of Knowledge* (Washington: Carnegie Endowment for International Peace, 2006).

[9] Secretary General, *The Rule of Law and Transitional Justice in Conflict and Post-Conflict Societies*, UN Doc. S/2004/616 (August 23, 2004); Humphreys, *Theatre of the Rule of Law*, pp. 149–174.

[10] General Assembly, "Declaration of the High-level Meeting of the General Assembly on the Rule of Law at the National and International Levels," UN Doc. A/67/L/1 (September 19, 2012).

[11] UN Doc. A/67/L/1, para. 7.

[12] Humphreys, *Theatre of the Rule of Law*, pp. 175–218.

rights. The public sector, in rule of law language, grounds the polity but exercises restraint, assuring private *freedom.* Ultimately, the World Bank became one of many agencies compiling rule of law *indices*, comparing the prevalence of the rule of law in-country by reference to a set of standardized presumptively universal indicators. Lots of activity, then, but driven by international agencies and banks: is this an "international movement"?

2 The World Justice Project

If there is an "international rule of law movement," the World Justice Project, WJP, which claims to provide "the most comprehensive rule of law index," exemplifies it. The WJP index, based on "110,000 household surveys and 3,000 expert surveys in 113 countries and jurisdictions," comprises four "universal principles" ("accountability," "just laws," "open government," and "accessible and impartial dispute resolution"), eight "factors" and forty-four subfactors.[13] A WJP email of December 2017 states: "Together, we can build the movement to strengthen the rule of law worldwide."[14] "Effective rule of law," it continues, "reduces corruption, combats poverty and disease, and protects people from injustices large and small. It is the foundation for communities of equity, opportunity, and peace – underpinning development, accountable government, and respect for fundamental rights."[15] Together, the email goes on, "we can … grow our network of rule of law advocates, increase the public's understanding and appreciation for the rule of law, and inspire and foster more locally-led programs that extend the rule of law in communities around the globe."

Stirring stuff. But this is no grassroots NGO; the WJP is a veritable who's who of the great and the good. The Board of Directors is replete with prestigious persons, including the current President of Afghanistan, a former President of Bulgaria, the Chief Justice of the Gambian Supreme Court, and a sitting Minister in the Tunisian government.[16] The list of forty-one

[13] World Justice Project, *Rule of Law Index 2017–2018* (Washington: World Justice Project, 2018), pp. 2, 5, 16–17.

[14] Email from World Justice Project to Stephen Humphreys, subject: "Progress in 2017, but still much to do," sent Thursday, December 28, 2017 at 21:16:26 GMT.

[15] See also https://worldjusticeproject.org/.

[16] See https://worldjusticeproject.org/about-us/who-we-are/board-directors.

"honorary chairs" glitters with household names, including four former or sitting US Supreme Court Justices and the former chief justices of Britain and South Africa's highest courts.[17] The WJP is also well-resourced, listing 172 donors including Apple, Google, Wal-Mart, Boeing, and Nike,[18] and has an annual operating budget in the region of US$2–4 billion.[19] Two private donors top their 2014 annual report: the Bill Gates Foundation and the Neukom Family Foundation, each of whom provided the WJP with US$10 million.[20] These two are connected: William H. Neukom was for twenty-five years General Counsel of Microsoft. Neukom, the founder and President of the World Justice Project,[21] also contributed US$1 million to the WJP in his own name (as, coincidentally or not, did Microsoft).[22] All this private money notwithstanding, the WJP's third largest donor is the US government, whose State Department provided between US$5 million and US$7.5 million.[23]

Jose Luis and Urucum in the Favelas

The cover page of the 2014 annual report features a full-page picture of a favela dweller, Jose Luis, who was "evicted from his home in Alto de Paz, Brazil, with no notice or compensation."[24] Two decrepit boxes pictured next to him are "the only possessions he was able to remove from the rubble." "Jose Luis" (not his real name) looks disconsolately at the camera in t-shirt and jeans, a striking contrast with the suits, ties, open-collars-and-v-necks – and, in Neukom's case, a perennial bow-tie – that adorn the directors and donors lining the inside pages. Behind Jose Luis are breeze-blocks with photos masking-taped to what appears to be a boarded-up

[17] See https://worldjusticeproject.org/about-us/who-we-are/honorary-chairs. The list includes: Bill Gates, Mary Robinson, Madeleine Albright, Giuliano Amato, Cherie Blair, Jimmy Carter, Paul Volcker, James Baker, Richard Goldstone, Anthony Kennedy, Stephen Breyer, Sandra Day O'Connor, Ruth Bader Ginsburg, Harry Woolf, and Arthur Chaskalson.

[18] World Justice Project, *Annual Report 2014* (Washington: World Justice Project, 2015), pp. 23–24.

[19] World Justice Project, *Annual Report 2014*, pp. 21–22. This figure may be incorrect: the report does not in fact provide a currency unit for its financial figures.

[20] World Justice Project, *Annual Report 2014*, p. 23.

[21] See https://worldjusticeproject.org/about-us/who-we-are/board-directors.

[22] World Justice Project, *Annual Report 2014*, p. 23; also World Justice Project, *Annual Report 2013* (Washington: World Justice Project, 2014), p. 12. Neukom's net worth is estimated at US$850m: www.insidephilanthropy.com/guide-to-individual-donors/william-h-neukom.html.

[23] World Justice Project, *Annual Report 2014*, pp. 23–24. No exact figure is provided.

[24] World Justice Project, *Annual Report 2014*, p. 1.

window. The pictures show time-honored images of the oppressive state: the rubble of destroyed slums, figures in military and riot uniforms, a t-shirted man frog-marched, another forced to his knees with hands behind his head. These are apparently intended as pictures from the Alto de Paz eviction, though there is no explicit claim to that effect.[25]

What is the connection between Jose Luis and the contents of the otherwise dry annual report? According to the by-line, "WJP grantee Urucum – a collective of lawyers, journalists, and artists – is working with residents in favelas to help them understand their housing rights and change the way Brazilians interact with their government."[26] Urucum "is also working with favela residents to create their own maps; favelas are absent from the city maps."[27] "Creating these maps," we are told, "helps the residents feel visible as full citizens."[28] It seems Urucum was already a WJP grantee when Jose Luis's neighborhood was bulldozed in preparation for the 2014 World Cup. Urucum was alerted by residents as the eviction was underway and "rushed to the scene to help the displaced – including elderly residents and young children – find shelter and to document the eviction."[29] Documentation of this kind in a different favela reportedly led nine judges to visit the slum. Urucum also holds "awareness-raising" workshops with favela residents. Documentation, evidence-building and generating public interest is a key part of their strategy: "In a country with the second-largest number of Twitter users after the U.S., this can be a powerful tool for both government accountability and freedom of expression." (Despite all this, Urucum does not appear to have its own web presence.)

The brochure points out that Urucum is one of 80+ pilot programs funded by the WJP on five continents, to which WJP has provided "network connections and over $1,000,000 in funding."[30] They note

[25] Elsewhere on the WJP website, other favela dwellers are photographed against the same backdrop, but the background pictures differ: no frogmarching, riot gear, or kneeling. See: https://worldjusticeproject.org/photo-essays/right-remain. The same photos appear on the website of the photographer, Deborah Espinosa – although "Jose Luis" is there named Jean Paulo Teixeina Silva. See www.sameskyphoto.com/new-page-1/.

[26] World Justice Project, *Annual Report 2014*, p. 1.

[27] World Justice Project, *The Right to Remain: Brazil's Favelas vs. the World Cup and Olympics* (Washington: World Justice Project, 2015), p. 3.

[28] World Justice Project, *The Right to Remain*, p. 3.

[29] See https://worldjusticeproject.org/photo-essays/right-remain. Subsequent citations in this paragraph are from this source.

[30] World Justice Project, *The Right to Remain*, pp. 3–4. Subsequent citations in this paragraph are from this source.

that Urucum's approach "may seem unusual" in that it is not a "typical legal aid clinic." But "[i]t takes more than lawyers and judges to advance the rule of law; everyone in a community has a role to play and a shared interest in greater opportunity and equity." Urucum's approach thus "mirrors WJP's own approach to strengthening the rule of law – a strategy relying on collaboration between multiple sectors, professions, and disciplines."

What are we to make of this? Certainly the favelas make for striking photographs. No doubt it is nice to have judges visit your slum ("network connections") and Twitter is a fabulous platform upon which to place one's home(less) videos. Yet it is difficult to glean anything from these sources to show that slum dwellers have benefited in any material way from this project, other than "feel[ing] visible as full citizens" thanks to the maps. The donated money is a tiny drop in the ocean of the WJP millions and, faced with the evictions, the WJP has little in the way of concrete policy recommendations. Rather, we are told:

> There are no easy answers when it comes to the question of what to do about Brazil's favelas. Despite the complexities, WJP believes that approaches like Urucum's will help build a stronger culture of rule of law. The broader the collaboration, the more likely it is to take root and succeed over time.[31]

WJP does not, it seems, deal in "complexity"; it does not do "policy." It helps ordinary citizens "interact with their government." This is what a "stronger culture of the rule of law" looks like: collaboration, documentation, networks, maps, Twitter. The preference for procedure over policy in this account is symptomatic of "rule of law culture" as it appears in the pages of development organizations. It is the mode of engagement that matters here: the dispossessed do not react violently to the forced eviction visited upon them. They do not protest or rise up. Rather, they "document," they "network," they "map."

3 Associating with Oakeshott

In 1991, shortly after Michael Oakeshott died, Perry Anderson wrote that, although his passing had gone largely unnoticed in his native country, "he

[31] World Justice Project, *The Right to Remain*, p. 3.

was, in fact, one of the . . . outstanding European theorists . . . whose ideas now shape . . . a large pail of the mental world of end-of-the-century Western politics."[32] Indeed, beside the World Bank's explicitly Hayekian rule of law, there is much in the WJP literature that appears indebted to Oakeshott's account of the rule of law. The emphasis on a "culture" of the rule of law in the everyday interactions of "ordinary people" resonates strongly with Oakeshott's emphasis on rule of law as a "vernacular language" of moral association as does the distaste for policy,[33]and the whole notion of a "movement" appears consonant with the "civil association" at the heart of Oakeshott's rule of law. Oakeshott also has something to say about "development," the "poor" and human rights. I examine each theme in turn, beginning with Oakeshott's notion of association.

Societas against Society

The burgeoning invocations of the rule of law in recent declarations of the United Nations and organizations such as the WJP refer interchangeably to "societies" and states.[34] This assimilation of state to society is something Oakeshott does not countenance. Indeed the various cognate terms deriving from the Latin word *socius* (meaning "companion" or "friend") – *socii*, *societas*, association – perform complicated semantic definitional work in his writing.[35] As is well-known, Oakeshott distinguishes between "modes of association," defined by mutual adherence to sets of rules. Rule of law is associated with (in his varying terms) "civil association," *respublica*, or *civitas* – a "moral" (nonpurposive) association characterized by noninstrumental laws (which he terms *lex*) – as opposed to an "enterprise association," an association created to pursue an objective, be it wealth, pleasure, or faith; the beautiful, the true, the good.[36] In reference to the form of the state, he refines this distinction by recourse to a dichotomy between

[32] Perry Anderson, "The Intransigent Right at the End of the Century," *London Review of Books*, September 24, 1992. "It is," Anderson wrote, "alongside Carl Schmitt, Leo Strauss and Friedrich von Hayek that Michael Oakeshott is most appropriately seen."

[33] Michael Oakeshott, *On Human Conduct* (Oxford: Clarendon Press, 1975), pp. 78–81; Michael Oakeshott, "The Rule of Law," in idem, *On History and Other Essays* (Indianapolis: Liberty Fund, [1983] 1999), p. 144.

[34] UN Doc. A/67/L/1; World Justice Project, *Rule of Law Index 2017–2018.*

[35] *Oxford English Dictionary.*

[36] Oakeshott, *On Human Conduct*, pp. 201–206.

societas and *universitas*, with the rule of law, or *lex*, the mark of the former but not the latter.

With this distinction Oakeshott writes *against* "society," at least when conceived as coextensive with "state." This coextension, he says, cannot be correct as the fundamental distinction between a state and a society is that between a compulsory ("civil"/moral) and a voluntary ("enterprise"/purposive) association. In Oakeshott's vocabulary, the state conceived as *universitas* confuses these two: it is a compulsory enterprise association, with instrumental goal-oriented rules raised to law: "to make enterprise association compulsory would be to deprive an agent of that 'freedom' or 'autonomy' which is the condition of agency."[37] The compulsory association is, counterintuitively, founded on *consent* but consent to compulsion is conditional on the nonpurposiveness of the association, its "civil" or "moral" basis. Following Hobbes, he points out that the *cives* have *chosen* to be bound by law with a view to a "net gain in freedom," which Oakeshott calls "true freedom."[38] Oakeshott translates this notional Hobbesian "consent" to the sovereign into the actual rules that free agents in historical states might have accepted as compulsory in order to facilitate the freedom of what he calls "civil association."[39] The mark of the *civis* in a *civitas* is to treat these rules (i.e., laws or "*lex*") as obligatory, to accept their authority, even if she or he disagrees with them *in foro interno*.[40]

The condition that *lex* be noninstrumental necessitates the exclusion of any form of common enterprise or purpose. Civil association has no "common purpose" and were it to adopt one it would cease to be civil association and become enterprise association.[41] The "sole terms of [civil] relationship are the recognition of the authority or the authenticity of the laws."[42] The state as *societas*, therefore, does not have "social" objectives: "There is no such general relationship of agents corresponding to the word 'social.'"[43]

37 Oakeshott, *On Human Conduct*, p. 118.

38 Michael Oakeshott, *Hobbes on Civil Association* (Indianapolis: Liberty Fund, [1975] 2000), pp. 35–36.

39 In doing so, Oakeshott leans especially on Hegel. See Oakeshott, *On Human Conduct*, pp. 257–263.

40 Oakeshott, *On Human Conduct*, pp. 147–150. See also my discussion in Stephen Humphreys, "Conscience in the Datasphere," *Humanity*, 6 (2015), esp. 376–378.

41 Oakeshott, *On Human Conduct*, p. 119.

42 Oakeshott, "The Rule of Law," p. 149.

43 Oakeshott, *On Human Conduct*, p. 98.

In other words, and paradoxically, *societas* is opposed to the very notion of "society." For Oakeshott, there is no such thing as society: everything that smacks of common purposes, the common good, the *summum bonum* or *salus populi* – "managerialism" of any sort, "policy" *tout court* – deviates from the rule of law.[44] "An enterprise is a 'policy' and enterprise association is a managerial engagement."[45] They have their place, but not in the law of the land. "[B]ecause 'policy' . . . entails a command over the resources of the members of the state categorially different from that required to maintain the apparatus of the rule of law [it also entails] the destruction for the time being of the state as an association exclusively in terms of the rule of law."[46]

Development, Poverty, Human Rights

Among the most compelling passages in Oakeshott's writings is the last fifty pages of his essay on the modern European state, in which he bemoans the degree to which the state has been portrayed as *universitas* rather than *societas*.[47] Oakeshott concludes that "civil association" has not been the dominant form of the state anywhere and wherever it has existed, it has been "qualified" by entrepreneurial teleology.[48] Examples include the administrative state (as a vehicle of power); the mercantilist state (as a vehicle of proto-capitalism); the emergency state (as a vehicle of war); what he terms the Baconian technological state (as a vehicle of "enlightenment"); the socialist state (as a vehicle of welfare); and the colonial state (lordship by other means).[49] Development, a concern with poverty, and human rights, are all examples of the ineradicable tendency to qualify, confuse, or deny the rule of law.

Development: *Civitas Cupiditatis*

Oakeshott devotes considerable space to the "technological" conception of the state as posing the greatest threat to civil association.[50] The early

44 Oakeshott, *On Human Conduct*, p. 157. See also Oakeshott, "The Rule of Law," pp. 149–153.
45 Oakeshott, *On Human Conduct*, p. 115.
46 Oakeshott, "The Rule of Law," pp. 177–178. See also p. 176.
47 Oakeshott, *On Human Conduct*, pp. 263–313.
48 Oakeshott, *On Human Conduct*, p. 313.
49 Oakeshott, *On Human Conduct*, pp. 279–313.
50 Oakeshott, *On Human Conduct*, p. 286. The quotations in this paragraph are from pp. 286–289, except where indicated otherwise.

European states emerging from the religious wars, he says, were concerned to build "communities" on the basis of shared beliefs.[51] It took the "audacious imagination" of Francis Bacon to secularize this vehicle of community and "conceive of the state as a corporation aggregate concerned with the exploitation of the resources of an estate," one "recognised to be, and not merely to have, an economy." A state, on this telling, is "a circumstantially distinguished territory whose inhabitants, incorporated in the relentless exploitation of its resources, have a common interest in the continuous success of the enterprise."

Oakeshott's term for this developmental state is *civitas cupiditas*, a form of *universitas*.[52] However, he also identifies a related notion of the state as *societas cupiditas*, deviating only marginally from civil association and he contrasts this with *universitas cupiditas*, wherein civil association is "destroyed" by active redistribution of the fruits of the economy.[53] The implication is that the centrality of the economy to the state is not necessarily inimical to the rule of law in itself, but that the particular European approach to managing (i.e., *being* rather than *having*) an economy tended to *universitas* rather than *societas*. It is apparently the concept of "development" that marks this slippage and Oakeshott points with particular opprobrium to the notion of a "public interest" that underpins it, in whose name states are "transform[ed] into development corporations, whose members relate solely in terms of the enterprise and whose 'laws' are designed solely to promote its continuous success."[54]

The Poor: Individuals *Manqués*

The *civitas cupiditatis*, Oakeshott notes, "was an association appropriate for individuals *manqués* who had no choices of their own to make and needed the direction of official *lumières*."[55] The reference is to his characterization of *universitas* as a "compulsory enterprise association in which the office of government was not to rule subjects but to make substantive choices for those unable or indisposed to make them for

[51] Oakeshott, *On Human Conduct*, pp. 279, 283–286. Only England, according to Oakeshott, retained a predominant sense of state as *societas* during this period. Oakeshott, *On Human Conduct*, p. 282.

[52] See Oakeshott, *On Human Conduct*, pp. 290–291.

[53] Oakeshott, *On Human Conduct*, pp. 293–295.

[54] Oakeshott, *On Human Conduct*, p. 296.

[55] Oakeshott, *On Human Conduct*, p. 295.

themselves."[56] The individual *manqué* is a counterfigure to the persona animating *societas.* The latter is simply referred to as an "individual" having a certain "disposition" – "to transform ... 'freedom' of conduct from a postulate into an experience" – and whose appearance, marking the rise of *societas,* constitutes a "difficult achievement," "the outcome of an education, whose resources are collected in a self-understanding," a "cultivated self."[57] If the "early years of modern European history were distinguished by the confidence with which this disposition was embraced," it is Oakeshott's contention that "[p]ersons understanding themselves and understood in terms of this disposition postulate a state understood in terms of *societas.*"

Had this latter "disposition" been "the only character who walked the world in which the states of modern Europe emerged," European states "might have become unequivocal civil associations."[58] But not so: "there was another persona abroad," whose disposition could only be accommodated within the state-as-*universitas.* This is the "individual *manqué,*" the person who "could not respond" to the changing times. He or she is the "displaced labourer," the "dispossessed believer," the "helpless victim of an enclosure," emerging from some "combination of actual loss, debility, ignorance, timidity, poverty, loneliness, displacement, persecution or misfortune."[59] Although Oakeshott initially hesitates to identify these "individuals *manqués*" with "the poor," the "peasantry," or "the proletariat," he is comfortable identifying them with "the masses" given "their longing for the shelter of community."[60] But having ceded that "absence of possessions" marks this persona, he ultimately identifies "the emergence of the individual *manqué* [with] what may be called in the broadest sense the problem of the poor." It is this that led the "government of the modern state to a managerial engagement" with a resulting "unavoidable qualification of its character as a ruler of subjects."

Rivalry thus subsists at the heart of the modern European state between the libertarian (a "*libertin spirituel*")[61] and the masses, and this manifests in ongoing tension at the heart of the European state between *societas* and *universitas.* The rule of law exists in permanent competition with a vying

[56] Oakeshott, *On Human Conduct*, p. 274.

[57] The quotations in this paragraph are from Oakeshott, *On Human Conduct*, pp. 236–242.

[58] The quotations in this paragraph are from Oakeshott, *On Human Conduct*, pp. 274–278.

[59] Oakeshott, *On Human Conduct*, p. 275.

[60] Oakeshott, *On Human Conduct*, p. 276.

[61] Oakeshott, *On Human Conduct*, p. 275.

ideal – "the social," the collective, the welfare state. For Oakeshott, any concern with "the problem of the poor" is the mark of an unacceptable deviation from something called "the rule of law": indeed, the rule of law exists precisely to remove such problems from the purview of the state.[62]

Human Rights and Moral Idiocies

Towards the end of his account of the individual *manqué*, Oakeshott describes how this unfortunate, having "feelings rather than thoughts, impulses rather than opinions, inabilities rather than passions," needed to "be told what to think, to ask for, and to do."[63] The "natural submissiveness" of this character prompts "leaders" who had "nothing to offer" but were "merely advocates of his [sic] cause." These leaders "often confused the situation" by "formulating his so-called needs in terms of 'rights' to enjoy substantive benefits" while "concealing" from him "the modification of his status as a subject which the satisfaction of these needs by a government would entail." Rights-bearers, in short, lean on the state for substantive fulfillment of their rights, ultimately empowering the state at the expense of their own autonomy.

Oakeshott returns to the specific theme of the incompatibility of "human rights" and the rule of law in his 1983 essay, entitled "The Rule of Law." In a passage describing the futility of attempting to ground the *jus* of *lex* (that is, the "justice" of the law) in some "higher" (natural or divine) law, he picks out the notions of "fundamental values" and "human rights" as particular sources of "confusion."[64] "It is not at all clear," he writes, "how the necessarily conditional prescriptions of *lex* can derive their *jus* from their conformity . . . with a set of unconditional 'values,' 'rights' or 'liberties' . . . Indeed it is logically impossible that this should be the case."[65] To do so "denies to *lex* its character of a noninstrumental rule." Among the "current moral idiocies" with which the rule of law cannot concern itself are "spurious claims of conscientious objection, of minorities for special treatment," and of "so-called Bills of Rights (that is alleged unconditional principles of *jus* masquerading as themselves law)" or of "an independent

[62] Oakeshott, *On Human Conduct*, pp. 301, 304. See also idem, "The Rule of Law," p. 153.
[63] Oakeshott, *On Human Conduct*, pp. 277–278.
[64] Oakeshott, "The Rule of Law," pp. 154–155.
[65] Oakeshott, "The Rule of Law," p. 155.

office . . . authorized to declare a law to be inauthentic if it were found to be 'unjust.'"[66]

Although his writing on human rights is sparse, it is unambiguous. Oakeshott does not "list" the human rights reproduced in international law instruments that will later become a staple of organizations promoting something called the rule of law. But his examples are sufficiently varied and his critique sufficiently broad as to target the very idea of "human rights."

Conclusion

On each of the points I have chosen to highlight (society, development, poverty, human rights), Oakeshott presents an opposed position to what is today a near-consensual view of what the rule of law is deemed to comprise in the rhetoric of the United Nations and organizations like WJP: a guarantor of social and economic development and human rights and a necessary element of any effort to "make poverty history." And yet it seems right to say that Oakeshott's vision, idiosyncratic though it is, studiously articulates the intuitions underlying most accounts of the rule of law, including those of the WJP – eschewing an instrumental state engaging in "policy" in favor of some notion of "freedom" through "civil association." How can the disconnect be explained?

A first explanation is that there is nothing to explain: the disconnect is merely apparent. The WJP is evidently an enterprise association ("civil society") with the purpose of "promoting the rule of law" but its existence is not incompatible with "civil association," that is, with a rule of law *societas*, within which it would be embedded. On this account, the WJP's *raison d'être* is to work towards the construction of "civil associations" globally in contexts in which they are currently absent or deficient. But it does not itself represent *societas*. Presumably enterprise associations may deal with poverty and human rights and must, if they do, take the form of private associations such as WJP, a private organization prioritizing policy objectives in the public sphere.[67] Setting aside Oakeshott's profound, but idiosyncratic, opposition-in-principle to poverty reduction and human

[66] Oakeshott, "The Rule of Law," p. 156. [67] Oakeshott, *On Human Conduct*, p. 182.

rights, it is difficult to see why these outcomes should not be the objects of private, civil, politicking within a public *societas*.

A first objection to this view is easily dismissed. That is: we might query whether the rule of law can in fact be constructed in this fashion, as a matter of will or "*ex nihilo*."[68] Oakeshott believes it cannot, but immediately qualifies this in saying that the rule of law is evolutionary: "one can think of many . . . ways in which the legislative office might emerge and *acquire* authority."[69] Indeed the whole notion of rule of law as a "vernacular language" suggests it emerges "organically" from repeated interactions between *cives*. While nothing in Oakeshott's account suggests that civic agitation in a "movement" may form part of such a process he provides no reason in principle that it may not. As long as any such a "civic movement" does not emanate from the state, it may be purposive without infringing his criteria. At first blush, the WJP appears to fit the bill.

But three further objections present themselves. First is the suspicion that this "movement" is not free from governmental direction, evidenced not only by US State Department funding behind the WJP but also, more decisively, by the history of the larger "movement" within which it appears as a rare "private" actor. Indeed, viewed in the large – a by-now thirty-year history of rule of law promotion – this is a field conceived and guided by governmental and intergovernmental institutions. The WJP is rather a quasi-civic face of a fundamentally statal phenomenon. Moreover, the "civil space" is not the place from which it emerges but the body upon which it acts. It is as though reference to the "rule of law" here legitimates the very intervention into "policy" that this same register (of the rule of law) would ordinarily preclude.

A second objection is that the kind of rule of law the WJP aims to construct is, in Oakeshott's terms, *universitas* rather than *societas*. Indeed, there is no proposed *societas*, and this is true throughout the rule of law-in-development literature. The WJP's differences with Oakeshott are not confined to poverty eradication and human rights; they appear also in its insistence on "just laws" as a "universal principle" of the rule of law. Such a view flatly contradicts Oakeshott, for whom the distinctive specificity of the rule of law is precisely that it does not confuse "justice" and "law." *Lex* is "adverbial" not substantive. Not only is the WJP's proposed rule of law substantive rather than merely "procedural," but these

[68] Oakeshott, "The Rule of Law," p. 163.
[69] Oakeshott, "The Rule of Law," p. 136.

substantive goals appear in the rhetoric of the "movement" as a whole today. For Oakeshott, the addition of "policy" ingredients of this sort marks the dissolution of "the rule of law." It is the state as *universitas* that has been universalized.

The question then arises: why do the United Nations and WJP invoke the language of rule of law *at all* in reference to the programmatic objectives of ending poverty and fulfilling human rights?

Two possibilities. A first is that this aspirational rule of law language has now evolved beyond Oakeshott's account, such that its normative boundaries have expanded to embrace *universitas*. But if that were the case, it is unclear what remains specific to the term "rule of law." To put the point differently, the rise in "rule of law" rhetoric would mark its conceptual demise: the term becomes so capacious as to be meaningless.

The second possibility is more intriguing: perhaps it is the language of "poverty eradication" and "human rights" that is collapsing? On this view, the WJP are loading the term "rule of law" with rhetorical "objectives" that cannot possibly be delivered or even properly countenanced by a civil association in terms of the rule of law. Supporting this, it is noticeable about the WJP's engagement in the favelas that no substantive solutions are offered. Moreover, countries that have adopted the programmatic "policies" that justify themselves in terms of "rule of law" have *not* achieved the goals of human rights (other than in the narrowest sense) or poverty eradication: quite the reverse. Rule of law policies tend to withdraw government from the economy, champion private rights and privatization, and have in fact often exacerbated poverty.[70] The question would then be: what kind of "rule of law" does WJP imagine enhancing poverty eradication? There is no answer to this: WJP does not offer a coherent account of how "the rule of law" addresses poverty and neither does the United Nations, whose "declaration" does not even pretend an argument.[71] The claim appears to rely on the explicit assertion that a rule of law state generates wealth through increased investor confidence, but without the complementary assumption that a wealthier state might also be redistributive. Indeed, the latter assumption, precisely refuted by Oakeshott, is

[70] See Jason Hickel, *The Division* (London: William Heinemann, 2017).

[71] Cf. the World Bank, as discussed in Humphreys *Theatre of the Rule of Law*, pp. 78–88, 143. As well as Shihata, Anne Krueger, a former World Bank Chief Economist and IMF Director undertook this intellectual work. See, for example, Anne O. Krueger, "Aid in the Development Process," *Research Observer*, 1 (1986), 57–78.

generally disabled by the distaste for policy specifics that rule of law language consistently entails.[72] On this view, rather than risking semantic collapse, the language of the "rule of law" redefines the notions of "eradicating poverty" and "human rights" to render them nugatory or at best aspirational within a space in which the Oakeshottian bow-tied "individual" must always hold "egoistic" sway over the "individual *manqué*."[73] in t-shirt and jeans.

The third problem with the proposition that the WJP marks a civic "enterprise" movement with the objective of assisting in the "evolution" of a rule of law *societas* is territorial. The "rule of law" on every account maps onto states *qua* states.[74] Yet, while reverting to the state as the stage of its activity, WJP rhetoric of the rule of law maintains a curiously indistinct relationship between the territorial state and law. Its "international" donor-injected status seems to assume something other than a civic "organic vernacular." Rather it stands outside the state structure altogether, presenting itself as a "higher" authority representing a more "fundamental" value than the state, exactly the sort of thing Oakeshott dismisses.[75]

Hence the curious burden of the "international" in an "international rule of law movement." It may originate in the internationality of its multinational private members – their belonging, as it were, to an international "class" – but it pitches into a different sort of "international," that of its four "universal" principles. It is not "international" but supranational: global and universal. The international rule of law movement may provide no account or detail of the "legislative office" from which this rule of law flows but it does struggle towards a narrative in which "we," the *cives* of the world, might accept the "authenticity and authority" of rules to which we might consent, in a relationship that is increasingly compulsory. Here the language of human rights and development works to assist in the evolution of an authoritative consensus – notably in, for example, the UN Declaration on the Rule of Law – providing a vernacular that "we all" increasingly speak, globally, according to which we are willing to be bound in principle and through which we can then express our differences and engage in what Oakeshott calls "politics."[76]

[72] See Humphreys, "The Rule of Law as Morality Play."

[73] Oakeshott, *On Human Conduct*, p. 240, describing the "individual" as having "a masterful egoism almost as careless of the concerns of some others as it is of their opinions."

[74] Oakeshott, *On Human Conduct*, pp. 205–210 on jurisdiction.

[75] Oakeshott, "The Rule of Law," pp. 154–155.

[76] Oakeshott, *On Human Conduct*, pp. 158–182.

At this point, it may be useful to recall Oakeshott's Hobbesian roots. It is only apparently paradoxical that the promise of "development" (especially when framed minimally as poverty eradication) and of human rights (especially as minimal procedural standards) are at least evocative of the premise of Hobbesian self-preservation.[77] As in Hobbes, the "authority" and "authenticity" of the laws which bind our freedom are theoretically premised on the securing of a minimal space for individual freedom, with the promise that self-preservation is available if only we consent *in foro externo*. For members of the favela the promise is akin to *auto da fé*. Preoccupied with its World Cup and Olympics enterprises, the state may be a deficient guardian of "civil association" but the favela is networked within a larger international movement whose authority claims to be beyond the state. The "international rule of law movement" would then symbolize a Hobbesian covenant, but one in which sovereignty is uncoupled from the state.

Although this account differs fairly radically from Oakeshott's, it aligns at the critical juncture of the notion of authority. Authority is inscrutable in Oakeshott's writing: it cannot be subscribed to a "general will" or "social good" or "common purpose" or a "rule of recognition" and does not derive from rationality, or wisdom or charisma or science.[78] Rather (and tautologically), authority in a civil association arises as the mark of recognition of the existence of civil association: "a system of moral (not instrumental) rules, specifying its own jurisdiction, and recognised solely as rules."[79] Authority is "acquired merely by being acknowledged."[80] Extraordinarily, and notably in the provision of "specifying its own jurisdiction," this seems a relatively apt description of the "self-authenticating" imaginary of the international rule of law movement, attempting to elicit, on entering the favela, acknowledgment.[81]

What is most remarkable is that this putative accession to authority appears despite the fact that the "international rule of law movement" is

[77] Oakeshott stipulates that authority cannot be postulated "on account of its providing shelter from some of the uncertainties of a human life." This aside is clearly aimed at the welfare state rather than Hobbesian self-preservation. See Oakeshott, *On Human Conduct*, p. 152.

[78] The discussion is Oakeshott, *On Human Conduct*, pp. 149–154.

[79] Oakeshott, *On Human Conduct*, p. 153.

[80] Oakeshott, *On Human Conduct*, p. 154 fn. 1. See also p. 150: "The recognition of its [i.e., the *respublica*'s] authority begins in what may be called the recognition of the validity of its prescriptions."

[81] Oakeshott, *On Human Conduct*, p. 150.

neither in the usual sense "international" nor a "movement" and that it appears either confused or misguided about what "the rule of law" actually is or can be. The associations best served by the rule of law exhibited by this executive "movement" are undoubtedly those whose donations in fact keep the entire enterprise afloat.

27 Rule of Law Measurement

Tom Ginsburg and Mila Versteeg

Introduction

We live in an age of measurement and quantification which has produced cross-national indicators of concepts like gender equality, war and peace, and gross national happiness, to name just a few.[1] The rule of law (RoL) is no exception and recent years have seen a proliferation of indicators that are the subject of a nascent literature.[2] The literature points out that indicators inherently reduce complex social phenomena to simple measures with a corresponding loss of information but an increase in tractability.

Some of these indicators measure formal institutions, some measure behavior, while others measure beliefs. These differences are not always transparent. Indicators are also subject to various technical problems of aggregation and endogeneity that are not always clear. As one of us has noted, valid, reliable, and unbiased measures of institutional quality are extremely challenging to produce.[3] Objective measures, such as the number of court decisions that go against the government, are difficult to obtain and raise problems of comparison across countries. Survey data, on the other hand, raise concerns about validity and bias. While the general problems with RoL indicators are well documented, there has been limited

[1] Sally Merry, *The Seductions of Quantification: Measuring Human Rights, Gender Violence, and Sex Trafficking* (Chicago: University of Chicago Press, 2016).

[2] Kevin E. Davis, "What Can the Rule of Law Variable Tell Us About Rule of Law Reforms?" *Michigan Journal of International Law*, 26 (2004), 141–161; idem, "Legal Indicators: The Power of Quantitative Measures of Law," *Annual Review of Law and Social Science*, 10 (2014), 37–52; Jørgen Møller and Svend-Erik Skaaning, "On the Limited Interchangeability of Rule of Law Measures," *European Political Science Review*, 3 (2011), 371–394; Tom Ginsburg and Mila Versteeg, "Measuring the Rule of Law: A Comparison of Indicators," *Law and Social Inquiry*, 42 (2016), 100–137; Merry, *The Seductions of Quantification.*

[3] Tom Ginsburg, "Pitfalls of Measuring the Rule of Law," *Hague Journal on the Rule of Law*, 3 (2011), 269–280.

systematic inquiry into what these indicators actually capture and how they map onto underlying normative concepts.[4]

In this chapter, drawing on our other work, we take up this task and examine four of the most influential RoL indicators.[5] Specifically, we compare the attempts by the World Bank's World Governance Indicators project (WGI), the Heritage Foundation, Freedom House, and the World Justice Project (WJP) to quantify the RoL. These are not the only RoL indicators, but they are arguably the most prominent.[6] We show that these four indicators build significantly different substantive values into their definitions of the RoL. The WGI's RoL indicator focuses on the absence of crime, and the security of persons and their property, the Heritage Foundation's index emphasizes the protection of private property and the absence of corruption, and Freedom House's indicator focuses primarily on civil liberties and equality. The WJP's index uses the most comprehensive definition, which combines rights, crime and security, the absence of corruption, civil justice, and numerous other features into a single (multi-dimensional) indicator.

In addition to conceptualizing the RoL differently, the indicators use different coding methodologies. The Heritage Foundation and Freedom House both base their indicators on coding by country experts, whereas the WGI aggregates a range of existing variables into an overall RoL index. The WJP is unique in that it combines assessments from country experts with perceptions of ordinary citizens, based on nationally representative surveys.

[4] Exceptions include Svend-Erik Skaaning, "Measuring the Rule of Law," *Political Research Quarterly*, 63 (2010), 449–460; Stephan Haggard, Andrew MacIntyre, and Lydia Tiede, "The Rule of Law and Economic Development," *Annual Review of Political Science*, 29 (2008), 205–234; Stephan Haggard and Lydia Tiede, "The Rule of Law and Economic Growth: Where are We?" *World Development*, 39 (2011), 673–685; Møller and Skaaning, "On the Limited Interchangeability of Rule of Law Measures," 371–394.

[5] Ginsburg and Versteeg, "Measuring the Rule of Law"; Tom Ginsburg and Mila Versteeg, "Constitutional Correlates of the Rule of Law," in Maurice Adams and Anne Meuwese, eds., *Constitutionalism and Rule of Law; Bridging Idealism and Realism* (Cambridge: Cambridge University Press, 2017), pp. 506–525.

[6] One less well-known indicator is constructed by the Bertelsmann Foundation, and is explored in Skaaning, "Measuring the Rule of Law," 449–460; and Møller and Skaaning, "On the Limited Interchangeability of Rule of Law Measures," 371–394. Another indicator was recently constructed by Peter F. Nardulli, Buddy Peyton, and Joseph Bajjalieh, "Conceptualizing and Measuring Rule of Law Constructs, 1850–2010," *Journal of Law and Courts*, 1 (2013), 13–38. This measure, however, captures the RoL de jure rather than de facto.

Given their disparate conceptual approaches and measurement strategies, one might expect these different RoL indicators to be weakly correlated. However, we found that all four indicators are remarkably similar to each other. One could draw the inference from these findings that the four indices indeed capture the essence of the RoL and that the observed similarities suggest that they are all valid proxies of the underlying concept. If so, it would follow that, despite substantial theoretical disagreement over how to define the concept, the RoL is something that "you know when you see it" (to borrow Justice Potter Stewart's famous description of obscene images).[7] Yet, the stark differences in conceptualization and measurement raise considerable doubts about whether this is the case.

We therefore favor alternative explanations for the convergence between the indicators. Reporting on our other work, we find that the three RoL indicators that are nearly identical to each other are also nearly identical to Transparency International's (TI) Corruption Perceptions index (with the correlation between each of these three and TI's index all exceeding 0.95). By contrast, the indices are less similar to other indicators of human rights, democracy, constitutionalism, judicial independence, and GDP per capita. We speculate that the main theoretical link between perceptions of corruption and the RoL indicators is that both capture a deeper concept of impartial government. At the same time, the conceptual link between the two ideas does not explain why the substantive differences in RoL conceptualization fade out in RoL measurement.

Consequently, we explore a second set of more technical explanations that emphasize the role of experts and information constraints. All the RoL indicators are perception-based measures created by experts who rely on a limited set of information sources, including each other's assessments and past scores. The only exception is the WJP indicator, which also brings in popular perceptions of the RoL. We find that when we disaggregate the expert and population components of the WJP data, the country scores differ substantially from each other, especially regarding openness of government and civil justice. These discrepancies suggest that the similarities between the different RoL indicators and their similarity with the corruption indicator might result from the reliance on experts and the procedures they use to quantify the RoL.

[7] *Jacobellis* v. *Ohio*, 378 US 184 (1964) (Stewart, J., concurring).

We suggest that these two explanations might work together. Outside experts who rate the RoL utilize a limited set of resources and lack deep experience of the various environments in which the RoL operates. They may rely on an overall impression of the country's administration, which reduces the importance of definitional disagreements. The larger lesson, we conclude, is that measurement strategy, rather than conceptualization, seems to be the dominant factor shaping current RoL indicators.

1 Conceptualizing the Rule of Law

As Parts I-IV of this volume demonstrate, the rule of law is an essentially contested concept, with a whole range of different approaches. Different conceptualizations have implications for measurement. While most of the prominent RoL indicators start from the core formalist ideal that contrasts the rule of law with the "rule of man" (to paraphrase John Adams's famous description of the RoL from the Massachusetts Constitution), they each add different substantive values, such as public order, human rights, substantive equality, the security of private contracts, and property rights. Indeed, not a single pair of the four indicators reviewed in this contribution defines the RoL in the same way. Of course, this diversity is unsurprising given the disagreements in the theoretical literature.

We look at four indicators. The World Bank RoL index, part of the larger the World Governance Indicators project, is probably the most well-known and most commonly used in social science research.[8] According to the Bank, its rule of law indicator captures "perceptions of the extent to which agents have confidence in and abide by the rules of society, and in particular the quality of contract enforcement, property rights, the police, and the courts, as well as the likelihood of crime and violence."[9] This definition includes procedural elements (for example, whether "agents have confidence in and abide by the rules of society") but also adds substantive concepts (for example, security of property and private contracts).

[8] Daniel Kaufmann, Aart Kraay, and Massimo Mastruzzi, "The Worldwide Governance Indicators: Methodology and Analytical Issues," Policy Research Working Paper 5430, Development Research Group, World Bank, September 2010. For a critical review, see Melissa Thomas, "What Do the Worldwide Governance Indicators Measure?" *European Journal of Development Research*, 22 (2010), 31–54.

[9] To construct this RoL indicator, the World Bank draws on a range of existing indicators and aggregates their information into a single indicator.

As Ginsburg previously argued, the WGI's indicator "conflates many different notions into a single concept, including both crime and contract enforcement in the same framework."[10] Likewise, Thomas notes that the WGI's indicator lacks "content validity – it does not map onto a definition of the rule of law."[11] Not only is the World Bank's indicator the most widely used, it is also the most heavily criticized.

The Heritage Foundation, a conservative American think tank, constructs another prominent index that conceptualizes the RoL as one of four core economic freedoms, together with limited government, regulatory efficiency, and open markets. Compared to the WGI's indicator, the Heritage Foundation's RoL index is less focused on crime and the personal security and more focused on the security of property rights and the absence of corruption. The index assesses some formal components, such as "the independence of the judiciary, the existence of corruption within the judiciary, and the ability of individuals and businesses to enforce contracts."[12] Thus, like the WGI's indicator, the Heritage Foundation's index builds substantive values into its RoL definition, albeit different ones.

Freedom House, a US-based nongovernmental organization "dedicated to the expansion of freedom around the world," produces a third RoL measure. Unlike the World Bank and the Heritage Foundation, the Freedom House conceptualization of the RoL is heavily focused on human rights, using sub-concepts including: judicial independence; enforcement in courts and by police; personal liberty and security; and equal treatment. This definition also combines procedural elements (such as an independent judiciary and absence of abuse by state agents) with substantive elements (such as civil liberties, bodily integrity, and substantive equality). Unlike the WGI and the Heritage Foundation, however, the Freedom House Index does not capture the protection of private property rights or the security of private contracts.

A more recent initiative in measuring the RoL comes from the World Justice Project (WJP). The WJP is a nongovernmental organization founded with the mission "to advance the rule of law around the world,"

[10] Ginsburg, "Pitfalls of Measuring the Rule of Law," 271; Marcus J. Kurtz and Andrew Schrank, "Growth and Governance: Models, Measures, and Mechanisms," *Journal of Politics*, 69 (2007), 538–554.

[11] Thomas, "What Do the Worldwide Governance Indicators Measure?" 40.

[12] Heritage Foundation, *Property Rights*, November 2014, available at www.heritage.org/index/property-rights.

and its RoL indicator is by far the most ambitious effort to measure the rule of law globally. According to the WJP, its indicator "builds on years of development, intensive consultation, and vetting with academics, practitioners, and community leaders from over 100 countries and 17 professional disciplines."[13] The rule of law concept captured by the indicator is also the most comprehensive, defined as:

> The government and its officials and agents as well as individuals and private entities are accountable under the law. The laws are clear, publicized, stable, and just; are applied evenly; and protect fundamental rights, including the security of persons and property. The process by which the laws are enacted, administered, and enforced is accessible, fair, and efficient. Justice is delivered timely by competent, ethical, and independent representatives and neutrals who are of sufficient number, have adequate resources, and reflect the makeup of the communities they serve.

To provide further clarity to this definition, it scores countries on nine separate factors: (1) Constraints on Government Powers, (2) Absence of Corruption, (3) Open Government, (4) Fundamental Rights, (5) Order and Security, (6) Regulatory Enforcement, (7) Civil Justice, (8) Criminal Justice, and (9) Informal Justice (note however that the last component is not part of the published index).

Each of these nine factors has sub-dimensions, producing a total of forty-seven sub-dimensions. As this long list demonstrates, the WJP's index combines almost all of the substantive values that also feature in the other RoL indicators.[14] In addition, it adds a range of features not found in any of the other indicators. The WJP notes that its conceptualization of the RoL represents "an effort to strike a balance between what scholars call a 'thin' or minimalist conception of the rule of law that focuses on formal, procedural rules and a 'thick' conception that includes substantive characteristics, such as self-government and various fundamental rights and freedoms."[15] Despite an effort to strike a balance, the WJP's RoL index arguably adopts the thickest conception of the RoL among all RoL indicators. But it also has the distinct advantage of being modular: because there

[13] World Justice Project, *The World Justice Project Rule of Law Index 2014* (Washington: World Justice Project, 2014), p. 1, available at http://worldjusticeproject.org/sites/default/files/files/wjp_rule_of_law_index_2014_report.pdf

[14] World Justice Project, *The World Justice Project Rule of Law Index 2014*, p. 8.

[15] World Justice Project, *The World Justice Project Rule of Law Index 2014*, p. 5.

are forty-seven different dimensions, scholars can aggregate the data in different ways in accordance with their own definitions of the rule of law.[16]

Table 27.1 offers a more systematic comparison of how the four RoL indicators overlap and differ. Specifically, it offers an overview of all components that are found in at least two of the four RoL indicators. Ten such components were identified. Table 27.1 reveals that even when we concentrate on the components for which the indicators overlap, their emphases differ substantially.

At first glance, the WGI and WJP indicators appear to have considerable substantive overlap with the other RoL indicators. The WGI RoL indicator overlaps with at least one other indicator on all but one of the ten components (fundamental rights), and the WJP's RoL index overlaps with one or more indicators on all but two components (contract enforcement and control over the police). Importantly, however, both the WGI and WJP RoL indicators add a range of features not found in any of the other indicators. Table 27.1 also reveals that the Heritage Foundation's and Freedom House's indicators have a more distinctive focus. The Heritage Foundation's index overlaps with one or more indicators on only five of the ten components, and Freedom House's index overlaps with at least one indicator on six of the ten components. Notably, they are almost exact opposites of each other – Freedom House and the Heritage Foundation only overlap on judicial independence and judicial efficacy. Overall, there are substantial differences in the way the different indicators conceptualize the RoL.

In addition to defining the RoL differently, the four RoL indices use different methodologies to create their country scores. Two of the indicators – the Heritage Foundation and Freedom House – rely almost exclusively on country experts. Freedom House relies on "in-house and external analysts and expert advisers from the academic, think tank, and human rights communities."[17] The Heritage Foundation also relies upon expert assessments based on a standardized set of sources. The WGI indicator is different in that it is something of a meta-indicator. Using an unobserved components model, it aggregates information from thirty-two existing variables into a single rule of law indicator. The WGI indicator gives more weight to those variables that

[16] For one recent see example, Jerg Gutmann and Stefan Voigt, "The Rule of Law: Measurement and Deep Roots," *European Journal of Political Economy*, 54 (2018): 68–82.

[17] Freedom House, *Freedom in the World 2014: Methodology*, November 2014.

Table 27.1: Overview of Similarities and Differences Between Four RoL Indicators

	World Governance Indicators	Heritage Foundation	Freedom House	World Justice Project
Contract Enforcement	x	x		
Property Rights	x	x		x
Corruption	x	x		x
Crime and Violence	x		x	x
Judicial Independence	x	x	x	x
Judicial Efficacy	x	x	x	x
Separation of powers	x			x
Equality	x		x	x
Control over police	x		x	
Fundamental rights			x	x
Other	x			x

better fit within the underlying RoL component, thus reducing the importance of those variables less related to the RoL.

The Heritage Foundation, Freedom House, and WGI all ultimately rely on expert assessments of the RoL (the WGI indirectly relies on expert opinion by using existing variables that are based on expert coding). The WJP is more empirically ambitious than the other three initiatives. In contrast with the other indicators, the WJP supplements in-country expert views with original surveys of 1,000 respondents in the three largest cities of each country. One might expect that this distinct measurement approach would produce significantly different estimates from those RoL indicators that rely only on expert judgment.

2 An Empirical Comparison of Four Rule of Law Indicators

Since the RoL indicators by the Heritage Foundation, WGI, WJP, and Freedom House conceptualize the RoL differently and rely on different methods to score individual countries, one would expect to find that these indicators are only weakly correlated. Other studies of various RoL indicators have so found.[18] Møller and Skaaning, for example, observe that "the

[18] Skaaning, "Measuring the Rule of Law," 449–460; Møller and Skaaning, "On the Limited Interchangeability of Rule of Law Measures," 371–394; Jørgen Møller and Svend-Erik Skaaning, *The Rule of Law: Definitions, Measures, Patterns and Causes*

Table 27.2: Pairwise Correlations of Four RoL Indicators

	Heritage	WGI	WJP	Freedom House	Factor loading on factor 1
Heritage	–	0.958	0.953	0.769	0.97
WGI	0.958	–	0.958	0.819	0.98
WJP	0.953	0.967	–	0.834	0.98
Freedom House	0.768	0.819	0.834	–	0.90

empirical convergence of the rule of law indices is relatively low."[19] Haggard, MacIntyre, and Tiede, and Haggard and Tiede reach similar conclusions and emphasize the differences between different RoL components.[20]

However, in our analysis the four indicators turned out to be remarkably similar. Table 27.2 presents the pairwise correlations between the four RoL indicators from our 2016 study.[21] The Table reveals that the indicators produced by the Heritage Foundation, WGI, and WJP are almost identical to each other, with their pairwise correlations ranging between 0.95 and 0.97. The only distinct indicator is Freedom House's index, with lower correlations that are still fairly high.

The finding that most of the indices are largely identical to each other poses a puzzle: why do these indicators, with such different conceptualizations of the RoL and dissimilar measurement strategies, come up with similar country assessments? In theory, this could occur because all four indicators capture the essence of the RoL, notwithstanding definitional distinctions. In other words, a clear definition is not needed to identify whether or not a country possesses the RoL. It is also possible, though unlikely, that the different concepts introduced into the different measures just happen to be highly correlated. We explore these possibilities below.

(Houndmills: Palgrave, 2014); Haggard, MacIntyre, and Tiede, "The Rule of Law and Economic Development," 205–234; Haggard and Tiede, "The Rule of Law and Economic Growth: Where are We?" 673–685.

19 Møller and Skaaning, *The Rule of Law*, p. 66.

20 Haggard, MacIntyre, and Tiede, "The Rule of Law and Economic Development," 222; Haggard and Tiede, "The Rule of Law and Economic Growth, 673.

21 Ginsburg and Versteeg, "Measuring the Rule of Law."

3 The Rule of Law and Neighboring Concepts

A number of alternative explanations exist for the convergence between the four RoL indicators. First, it is possible that the RoL indicators are indistinguishable from related concepts such as democracy or human rights. Secondly, the convergence between the indicators might be driven by information constraints and practical obstacles faced by experts measuring the RoL. The idea here is that the stark differences in conceptualization fade out when measuring the RoL because the experts tasked with quantifying the RoL rely on a limited set of sources, possibly including each other's assessments and past impressions. These two explanations are of course related: information constraints might produce indicators that fail to capture something distinct. We nonetheless believe that it is useful to explore these explanations separately in order to gradually rule out different possibilities.

To explore whether the RoL indicators capture something distinct, we have compared them with measures of a number of related concepts. As noted, one of the main challenges in measuring the RoL is to define it in such a way that it is distinguishable from such neighboring concepts.[22] If the RoL is discrete and can be captured by the RoL indicators, then they should be distinct from indicators that capture neighboring concepts. However, if the RoL is defined so broadly that it incorporates a whole range of other values, such as democracy and human rights, it might become indistinguishable from those values. Another possible cause for convergence is measurement error caused by coders' impressions on the neighboring concepts. Indeed, the WGI's governance indicators have been criticized for suffering from a "halo-effect," meaning that general perceptions of economic and social development lead to higher governance scores.[23] Similar halo-effects could also make the RoL indicators harder to separate from related measures of countries' social and economic performance.

To explore the empirical validity of these explanations, we compared the four RoL measures with several related concepts: (1) democracy, (2) human

[22] Ginsburg, "Pitfalls of Measuring the Rule of Law," 269–280.

[23] Kurtz and Schrank, "Growth and Governance: Models, Measures, and Mechanisms," 538–554; Kaufmann, Kraay, and Mastruzzi, "The WorldWide Governance Indicators: Methodology and Analytical Issues," 15.

Table 27.3: Relationship of RoL with Neighboring Concepts

	Heritage	WGI	WJP	Freedom House	Scores on Factor 1
Democracy (Polity IV, 2010 values)	0.46	0.45	0.45	0.76	0.52
Human Rights (Fariss, 2010 values)	0.63	0.71	0.81	0.73	0.80
Constitutionalism (Law and Versteeg, 2009 values)	0.70	0.74	0.80	0.83	0.82
Judicial Independence (CIRI, 2010 values)	0.67	0.73	0.79	0.77	0.83
GDP per capita (World Development Indicators, 2010 values)	0.77	0.81	0.81	0.61	0.80
Corruption (Transparency International, 2011 values)	0.98	0.95	0.95	0.81	0.97
Impartial Government (Teorrell, Dahlstrom & Dahlberg 2011)	0.89	0.86	0.90	0.80	0.90

rights, (3) constitutionalism, (4) judicial independence, (5) GDP per capita, and (6) corruption.[24] Table 27.3 presents correlations with several leading indicators. We find that, in general, the RoL indicators appear to capture something distinct. They are only loosely correlated with democracy, human rights, constitutionalism, judicial independence, and GDP per capita. This means that the convergence between the indicators does not simply result from poor conceptualization or a halo-effect.

The notable exception, however, is corruption. Specifically, we find that the indicators by the Heritage Foundation, WGI, and WJP are largely identical to TI's Corruption Perceptions Index.[25] This raises the question

[24] See details in Ginsburg and Versteeg, "Measuring the Rule of Law."

[25] We perform a similar exercise for legal origins. Like GDP per capita, legal origins is perhaps better described as a determinant of RoL than a neighboring concept. There exists a substantial body of literature, spurred by the work of La Porta, Lopez de Silvanes, Shleifer, and Vishny (LLSV) that suggests that common law countries perform better in terms of a number of features, such as the quality of corporate law, the structure of equity and debt markets, judicial quality, and corruption, and others than their civil law counterparts. See Rafael La Porta, Florencio Lopez-de-Silvanes, Andrei Shleifer, and Robert W. Vishny, "Law and Finance," *Journal of Political Economy*, 106 (1998), 1113–1155. We found only very weak correlations between the RoL measures and the common law. The correlation was highest for the World Bank and the Heritage Foundation indices (both 0.14), while it is close to 0 for the WJP.

of whether the RoL indicators capture corruption rather than the RoL or perhaps a more general concept of government impartiality that encompasses both corruption and RoL.[26]

These close correlations raise the question of whether corruption and the RoL are theoretically distinct. Importantly, conceptual connections appear to exist between the two. While the classic discussions of the RoL focus on the risk of government arbitrariness and oppression, they do not specify the motives that might prompt such pathologies. Corruption, the misuse of public power for private gain, is surely one such motive, and so might be an important driver for low RoL. The result might be that, once operationalized in indicators, corruption and the RoL are indistinguishable from each other. Indeed, previous studies have also noted the close empirical link between RoL indicators and corruption indicators.[27]

Another possibility is that the indicators capture a more abstract concept that transcends the specifics of both corruption and the RoL. One such candidate is impartial government, as developed most prominently by Bo Rothstein.[28] According to Rothstein, both corruption and the RoL fit into a broader umbrella concept of impartiality. First, the idea of impartial government rules out all forms of corruption and several forms of particularism, including clientelism, patronage, and nepotism. Secondly, government impartiality implies the presence of the RoL. Since laws are the most general rules of society, an impartial application of the rules requires impartial application of law, a core feature of the thin definition of the RoL. Thus, government impartiality might be a higher order concept that connects corruption and the RoL and, accordingly, might constitute the essence of both indicators.

Teorell, Dahlstrom, and Dahlberg have attempted to measure Rothstein's notion of impartiality through a "low-cost web survey with public

[26] Bo Rothstein, "What is the Opposite of Corruption?" *Third World Quarterly*, 35 (2014), 737–752.

[27] Haggard, MacIntyre, and Tiede, "The Rule of Law and Economic Development," 205–234; Haggard and Tiede, "The Rule of Law and Economic Growth: Where are We?" 673–685.

[28] Rothstein, "What is the Opposite of Corruption?" 737–752; Bo Rothstein, *The Quality of Government: The Political Economy of Corruption, Social Trust, and Inequality in International Perspective* (Chicago: University of Chicago Press, 2011).

administration scholars."[29] If the RoL and corruption ultimately capture impartiality, we would expect the impartiality survey questions to correlate highly with both corruption and the RoL. The last row of Table 27.3 presents the correlation of the various RoL measures with Rothstein's impartiality data. It shows that the correlations are indeed quite high: ranging from 0.80 for Freedom House to 0.90 for the WJP. The correlation between Rothstein's impartiality measure and TI's corruptions perceptions index is 0.87. These results suggest that impartiality might be the core concept captured by these indicators, especially since the impartiality data is merely a shoestring effort to capture the concept.[30]

4 Experts and Information Constraints

The previous section argued that the RoL indicators capture something discrete from many neighboring concepts, but is nearly identical to the absence of corruption. While there are important theoretical links between corruption and the RoL, they are not identical and may be operationalized differently. This raises the possibility that technical obstacles and information constraints in the measurement process cause the convergence between the indicators.

One information constraint that could cause the four indices to converge is that they largely rely on the same sources of information for their coding. The indices are mostly based on the coding of experts, who appear to rely on a set of standardized sources, such as the Economist Intelligence Unit or US State Department Country Reports. In fact, there is some internal replication among the different indicators. For example, the Heritage Foundation draws on Transparency International's Corruption Perceptions Index as one of its components, and the WGI relies on Freedom House and the Heritage Foundation as two of its thirty-two components.[31] We should note, however, that the WJP and Freedom House do not explicitly rely on the other indicators in producing their

[29] Jan Teorell, Carl Dahlström, and Stefan Dahlberg, "The QoG Expert Survey Dataset" (University of Gothenburg: The Quality of Government Institute, 2011); Rothstein, *Quality of Government*, p. 32.

[30] Rothstein, "What is the Opposite of Corruption?" 737–752.

[31] The WJP is considered to be one of the nonrepresentative sources in the WGI indicator, and therefore plays a more minor role in constructing the index.

scores. But even the WJP's and Freedom House's country experts *might* take account of the information produced by the other RoL initiatives. Thus, experts who measure the RoL with access to a limited set of resources might cause convergence between the indicators.

Relatedly, experts might also rely on previous years' scores, which can create path dependency. Alternatively, these earlier ratings could affect other sources on which experts rely. For example, the Economist Intelligence Unit, the US Chamber of Commerce, or the US State Department might take previous RoL assessment into account when drafting their reports (that are subsequently coded by RoL experts). Indeed, RoL scores tend to vary only a little on a yearly basis.[32]

We can explore the importance of expert coding by contrasting expert assessments with perceptions of the general public, which should not be affected by the same constraints or source biases. At the same time, one obvious downside of relying on popular perceptions is that ordinary people simply have less information about some aspects of the RoL.

The WJP is the only RoL indicator that includes popular perceptions. The publicly available WJP data does not break down expert and population scores; instead, it only provides aggregate numbers based on both. The WJP granted us access to the disaggregated data, which we used to explore differences between expert opinion and popular perceptions. One complication is that, in many instances, the general population and the experts are asked somewhat different questions, but we were able to relate the two surveys for most of the topics.

We started by correlating the expert-based average and the population-based average for each of the nine overall categories in the WJP indicator, shown in the first column of Table 27.4. The exercise reveals substantial differences between the expert-based scores and the population-based scores. Open government and civil justice exhibit the largest differences, with correlations between the expert and population scores of 0.16 and 0.17, respectively. Agreement between the experts and general population is largest for corruption (with a correlation of 0.76).

The subsequent columns of Table 27.4 show the correlations between the WJP's population-based and expert-based RoL scores and the RoL indicators by the Heritage Foundation, the WGI, and Freedom House. For

[32] To illustrate, the correlation between the last available WB RoL score (2012) and the next-to-last available score (2011) is 0.997.

Table 27.4: Disaggregated WJP data by Population and Experts

	Correlation between WJP expert and population scores	Heritage		WGI		Freedom House		WJP overall	
		Pop	*Expert*	*Pop*	*Expert*	*Pop*	*Expert*	*Pop*	*Expert*
Constraints on Government Powers	0.69	0.76	0.87	0.74	0.88	0.64	0.87	0.76	0.89
Absence of Corruption	0.76	0.76	0.91	0.74	0.93	0.59	0.79	0.79	0.94
Open Government	0.16	0.35	0.89	0.28	0.90	0.16	0.81	0.28	0.92
Fundamental Rights	0.58	0.44	0.81	0.46	0.82	0.56	0.91	0.51	0.86
Order and Security	0.52	0.55	0.75	0.60	0.76	0.34	0.55	0.63	0.78
Regulatory Enforcement	0.58	0.63	0.93	0.62	0.93	0.44	0.81	0.66	0.96
Civil Justice	0.17	0.20	0.87	0.19	0.89	0.06	0.78	0.24	0.93
Criminal Justice	0.57	0.50	0.89	0.56	0.92	0.35	0.72	0.57	0.94

comparison, Table 27.4 lists the correlations with the overall WJP indicator. Even though we cannot disaggregate the other indicators along the same nine dimensions, Table 27.4 shows that the WJP's expert-based scores tend to have substantially higher correlations with the other RoL indicators than the WJP's population-based scores. The exercise thus suggests that it is the expert-based scores that are driving the convergence between the RoL indicators. It also suggests that the population-based assessments may ultimately play a small part in the construction of the overall WJP RoL indicator.[33]

On some topics, the WJP asked its country experts and the general population identical questions. We can use the identical questions to perform a more direct comparison between expert and popular perceptions of the RoL. Table 27.5 shows the correlations between the expert answers and the population answers for these questions. It also lists the average score across all countries for each question. Table 27.5 reveals substantial disagreements between the experts and the general population. On topics such as the role of ethnic minorities, religious minorities, and LGBT citizens in the criminal process, the availability of laws in a language that people understand, the ability to obtain compensation or sue government in case of expropriation, and worker's rights, the correlation is close to zero or even negative. There is more agreement for questions relating to corruption, though not nearly the same level of agreement between the overall corruption and RoL expert-based indicators.

Both disaggregation exercises suggest that the expert-based nature of the RoL indicators causes their convergence. While these exercises do not tell us whether the reliance on a limited set of sources, last year's scores, or other RoL indicators ultimately causes the stark similarities among the indicators, they show that we cannot rule out the possibility that these similarities have something to do with experts and their coding protocols.

It is worth emphasizing that expert assessments are ultimately based on perceptions, and necessarily so, since the RoL cannot be measured directly

[33] While the population and expert-based scores are weighted roughly equally for each subquestion, the population is only asked a small portion of the total number of questions that feature in WJP's index. As a result, the population-based scores end up having little impact on the overall index.

Table 27.5: Direct Comparison of Expert and Population Answers to Same Questions

	Expert mean	*Population mean*	*Correlation*
Courts are free of political influence	0.52	0.63	0.56
How likely to combat corruption by local government officials	0.55	0.43	0.44
How likely to combat corruption by higher ranking official when there is proof and it has reached the media	0.57	0.55	0.54
How likely to combat corruption by high-ranking police officer when there is enough proof	0.65	0.59	0.31
Police officers who commit crimes are punished	0.52	0.48	0.34
Local government officials are elected through a clean process	0.51	0.54	0.47
People can vote freely without feeling harassed or pressured	0.66	0.66	0.59
Need to pay bribe to register land or house	0.71	0.78	0.45
Need to pay bribe to obtain driver's licence	0.58	0.69	0.73
Need to pay bribe to register business or construction permit	0.78	0.67	0.57
Polluting company complies with Environmental Protection Agency	0.65	0.42	0.41
Corruption within police	0.57	0.51	0.57
Pay bribe to receive police services	0.63	0.72	0.61
Laws in language that people understand	0.43	0.50	0.06
Laws available in all official languages	0.63	0.62	0.47
People in neighborhood can get together with others and present concerns to local government officials	0.48	0.61	0.61
Poor people at disadvantage in criminal justice	0.38	0.32	0.34
Women at disadvantage in criminal justice	0.59	0.49	0.47
Ethnic minorities at disadvantage in criminal justice	0.52	0.49	0.05
Religious minorities at disadvantage in criminal justice	0.59	0.52	-0.12
Foreigners at disadvantage in criminal justice	0.51	0.52	0.12
LGBT people at disadvantage in criminal justice	0.52	0.49	0.06
Media can expose high-ranking government officials without fear of retaliation	0.57	0.51	0.58
Media can express opinions against government policies and actions without fear of retaliation	0.59	0.60	0.64
Civil society can express opinions against government policies and actions without fear of retaliation	0.63	0.65	0.63

Continued

Table 27.5: Cont.

	Expert mean	*Population mean*	*Correlation*
Political parties can express opinions against government policies and actions without fear of retaliation	0.67	0.70	0.75
Religious minorities can freely and publicly observe their holy days and religious events	0.68	0.69	0.78
People can freely join together with others to draw attention to an issue or sign a petition	0.65	0.72	0.62
People can freely join any political organization they want	0.75	0.63	0.52
Workers can freely form labor unions and bargain for their rights with their employers	0.68	0.66	0.45
Workers fired for promoting labor unions	0.77	0.47	0.20
Homeowners compensated when homes demolished because of public work project	0.80	0.93	0.16
Homeowners sue government in court	0.84	0.93	0.07
Corruption among judiciary	0.53	0.51	0.77

(like GDP per capita, for example). The WJP explicitly recognizes that its index is perception-based, since it is partly based on opinion poll data. But expert assessments are also perception-based, as the experts that measure the RoL possess few truly objective measures on which to rely. The same is true for corruption. Transparency International recognizes this and classifies its indicator as a subjective one: it does not purport to measure corruption directly, but rather relies on sources that capture perceptions of corruption.

We end by noting that our suggestion that expert perceptions cause convergence among the RoL indicators is consistent with our earlier finding that the RoL indicators might capture a concept at a higher level of abstraction (which, following Rothstein, we suggested might be government impartiality). Indeed, it seems plausible that the experts who rate the RoL based on a limited set of resources may ultimately rate countries based on their perceptions of government impartiality. Definitional disagreements thus fade out in the larger measurement enterprise, where limited resources prevent experts from capturing the nuances of their RoL definition. The result is that expert perceptions of government impartiality are highly correlated, even when measures purport to capture different aspects of government.

Conclusion

Measurement of the rule of law has become something of a cottage industry and it is likely that new measures will proliferate. In canvassing the various RoL indicators that have gained the most prominence, we were struck by the high degrees of correlation among them, notwithstanding different conceptualizations. We believe that the measures may be correlated: (1) because they are actually capturing a higher-order concept that subsumes all the differing conceptions of the RoL, such as Rothstein's notion of government impartiality; and/or (2) because the measures were derived from the same sources, cross-referenced, or path dependent.

We ultimately conclude that both of these explanations might operate together. The differences between expert and general population assessments of the RoL suggest that expert perceptions are a crucial determinant of the convergence between the indices. The lesson is that measurement strategy, rather than conceptualization, seems to be the dominant factor driving RoL indicators. We hope that progress will continue to be made on developing valid and reliable indicators in these areas.

Post-Conflict Rule of Law 28

Jane E. Stromseth

Introduction

We live at a time of sobering realism – indeed pessimism – regarding rule of law building after conflict. There are many reasons for this. The inherent difficulty of the endeavor itself is one fundamental factor. Although each country emerging from violent conflict is unique in its history, leadership, culture, and possibilities for progress, they often also face many common challenges. Governing institutions may be discredited, law enforcement and judiciaries may be distrusted, civilians may be recoiling from egregious injury, social divisions may run deep, infrastructure may be devastated, economic opportunities may be limited, and confidence in the very idea of the rule of law may be at an all-time low. Furthermore, the very concept of "post-conflict" itself can be misleading as countries may transition towards greater stability only to fall back into violence. The obstacles to navigating toward any enduring peace can be formidable and varied.

In addition, many global trends complicate the already enormously difficult work of post-conflict rule of law building. Rising nationalism and political polarization have eroded domestic support in donor states for overseas reconstruction efforts, while turmoil in long-standing alliances and international institutions has undercut cooperation in providing assistance. Countries that once stood together in funding and exporting rule of law assistance find themselves struggling with the fragility of the rule of law in their own societies as domestic cleavages over immigration, trade, jobs, budgets, and counterterrorism fester. Furthermore, the increasingly transnational nature of conflict itself – including organized crime, transnational terrorist networks, plundering of resources and trafficking of many kinds – adds more layers of difficulty to stabilizing countries emerging from long-standing conflict.

Even in promising post-conflict situations – where local leaders have widespread public support and legitimacy – the challenges can be immense.

Establishing basic security and civilian protection is often paramount. Building governance structures that are inclusive and enjoy ongoing public support can be as difficult as it is critical. Countering crime, predatory behavior, and corruption can be vital for stability. Building public confidence in recovering legal institutions by improving their fairness and capacity, and encouraging progressive reforms in traditional dispute resolution mechanisms, can be a central challenge. Empowering women and creating more equal economic and educational opportunities throughout society can be a crucial engine for progress and stability.

In the face of such multi-faceted challenges, it is not surprising that optimism about post-conflict rule of law building has given way to a more sober-minded realism. Even relatively large investments of resources and time have yielded far less progress than was hoped.[1] More modest assessments of what is possible, and what external actors realistically can contribute, now predominate.

Yet these very disappointments have also spurred reconsideration of conventional assumptions and approaches to post-conflict rule of law building. Indeed, much needed learning has occurred – learning reflected both in scholarship and in programs on the ground – that rule of law building is not a technocratic exercise but deeply complex politically and culturally. As the interconnectedness of law, politics, culture, justice and accountability for past abuses has become clearer, so has the importance of empowering ordinary people and civil society from the bottom up. All of this has helped to illuminate a range of positive, if modest, approaches worth building upon.

I will focus on four especially significant areas of learning and hope, all of which are marked by plenty of scholarly ferment, and all of which carry enormous and practical challenges on the ground. Yet, as I argue and explore below, each one offers some fruitful pathways forward even in the face of discouraging global trends and long-standing challenges.

The first area concerns rule of law aims and priorities. Fundamentally, what should be prioritized in post-conflict rule of law building? Are there new strategies that hold particular promise?

[1] Examples include Afghanistan and Iraq. United States Government, Special Inspector General for Afghanistan Reconstruction, *Quarterly Report to the United States Congress* (July 30, 2018), pp. 10–11; United States Government, Special Inspector General for Iraq Reconstruction, *Learning from Iraq: A Final Report* (2013).

The second area concerns culture and the rule of law. How does culture shape post-conflict rule of law building, and how can progressive, empowering change be encouraged?

A third and increasingly important area concerns transitional justice and rule of law building. How do efforts to seek justice for past atrocities influence rule of law going forward, and how can transformative synergies and reforms best be encouraged?

Fourth, and finally, is assessing impact. What do we actually know about the effects of rule of law building efforts in societies transitioning out of conflict, and are some approaches especially promising?

Through these four lenses, I aim to shed light on these fundamental questions by exploring recent experience and scholarship concerning rule of law building in the aftermath of conflict. In the end, I hope to show that there is reason for cautious optimism and hope even in the face of a sobering track record and pessimistic trends.

1 Rule of Law Priorities

Rule of law building has been central to post-conflict stabilization for decades and indeed much longer. Such work spans continents and cultures. From rule of law efforts in Germany and Japan after World War II, to post-Cold War interventions in Cambodia, Timor-Leste, Haiti, Kosovo, Iraq, Afghanistan, Sierra Leone, and elsewhere, to transitions from conflict in Latin America, to continuing ongoing struggles to bring stability to conflict-affected countries in regions around the globe, such as the Central African Republic, the Democratic Republic of the Congo, and Colombia.

Why is rule of law building so central after conflict? In many ways, the answer is straightforward. Whatever the rule of law entails, most would agree that some basic level of physical security allowing people to live and plan their lives is essential. So is stopping atrocities and erecting barriers to abusive, predatory behavior by private and public actors. So are credible governance structures and mechanisms for dispute resolution. In many societies wracked by conflict, these and other aspects of the rule of law may have completely broken down.

Given the urgent needs crying out for attention, it is no surprise that conceptualizing rule of law priorities usually gives way to responding to immediate needs. When a house is on fire, stopping the destruction and rescuing survivors takes precedence over plans for rebuilding the structure in flames. In addition to local leaders, civil society groups, and ordinary citizens on the ground, a cottage industry of external actors often rushes in to help. Ranging from United Nations representatives, regional organizations, the World Bank, foreign governments, NGOs, rule of law consultants, celebrities and more, they arrive to assist, each with their own objectives.

Yet efforts to coordinate and set priorities do exist, with the United Nations often playing the central role. Under the UN Charter, the UN Security Council acts on behalf of the international community in response to threats to the peace, authorizing collective responses that aim to restore international peace and security. In many conflict-affected situations, the UN Security Council has provided a mandate for peacekeeping, stabilization, reconstruction, and rule of law building – as in Iraq, Afghanistan, Timor-Leste, Sierra Leone, Haiti, and elsewhere. Sometimes regional organizations play a central role, as NATO and the European Union have done in Kosovo, or the African Union in Somalia. And all of this depends on the willingness of governments to contribute resources and personnel as they work with local leaders and civil society actors who know their home terrain best.

In this challenging labor, leaders at the United Nations and in governments have sought to clarify the aims of rule of law building after conflict. The UN Secretary-General set out an oft-referenced definition in 2004: "The 'rule of law' … refers to a principle of governance in which all persons, institutions and entities, public and private, including the State itself, are accountable to laws that are publicly promulgated, equally enforced and independently adjudicated, and which are consistent with international human rights norms and standards."[2] Additional requirements, the Secretary-General noted, include: "measures to ensure adherence to the principles of supremacy of law, equality before the law, accountability to the law, fairness in the application of the law, separation of powers, participation in decision-making, legal certainty, avoidance of arbitrariness and procedural and legal transparency."[3] This definition

[2] Report of the United Nations Secretary-General, *The Rule of Law and Transitional Justice in Conflict and Post-conflict Societies*, UN Doc. S/2004/616 (August 23, 2004), p. 4.

[3] Report of the United Nations Secretary-General, *The Rule of Law and Transitional Justice in Conflict and Post-conflict Societies*.

includes both substantive and formal elements and is on the "thicker" side of the spectrum with its understandable emphasis on laws that are consistent with international human rights – the advancement of which is one of the core purposes of the United Nations.

This definition resonates in key respects with others advanced by scholars and practitioners who focus on rule of law building after conflict.[4] Indeed, despite modest differences around the edges, more substantive conceptions of the rule of law are more common among those focused on post-conflict rule of law, likely because the fundamental needs are so evident. Moreover, there is often considerable convergence on key elements, such as: accountable governance, basic security, equality before the law, fair and impartial dispute resolution, and protection of fundamental human rights.[5]

Yet far more challenging than a definition of the aspired-for rule of law is the question of how to make it so. Concretely, what specifically should be prioritized in working to strengthen the rule of law *on the ground* in countries emerging from conflict? Is there any developing wisdom and learning on this question, whether in particular countries or more generally?

The United Nations's work in post-conflict societies has tended to focus on basic security and the justice system. Security and civilian protection is an immediate priority because it is persistent violence against civilians and pervasive insecurity that is generally the catalyst for UN-authorized collective action in the first place, and establishing some degree of order is the first step in restoring and rebuilding rule of law. Deployment of peacekeepers and civilian police[6] is often a crucial component of this endeavor, as part of moving toward longer-term

[4] See, for example, Jane Stromseth, David Wippman, and Rosa Brooks, *Can Might Make Rights? Building the Rule of Law After Military Interventions* (New York: Cambridge University Press, 2006), pp. 78–84; Rachel Kleinfeld, "Competing Definitions of the Rule of Law," in Thomas Carothers, ed., *Promoting the Rule of Law Abroad: In Search of Knowledge* (Washington: Carnegie Endowment for International Peace, 2012), pp. 34–46; United Nations Development Programme, *2017 Global Programme Annual Report: Strengthening the Rule of Law and Human Rights for Sustaining Peace and Fostering Development* (New York: United Nations, 2018); World Bank, *World Development Report 2017: Governance and the Law* (Washington: World Bank, 2017), ch. 3.

[5] Kleinfeld, "Competing Definitions of the Rule of Law," pp. 34–46.

[6] William J. Durch and Michelle Ker, "Police in UN Peacekeeping: Improving Selection, Recruitment, and Deployment," International Peace Institute, New York, November 2013.

assistance in "security sector reform."[7] Such assistance generally focuses on crucial military and police reforms as well as capacity-building in accountable governance and effective oversight of security actors. The UN and state contributors also typically concentrate on "cops, courts and corrections" or the people and institutional structures involved in law and order and formal dispute resolution, generally giving less attention to informal dispute resolution mechanisms although the population may use these more widely.[8] The formal state justice system nevertheless may play an important role in major cities, and developing its capacity for fairer adjudication and law enforcement can be a critical part of strengthening the rule of law over time. Substantive law reform – often with a focus on enacting improved criminal justice legislation – is also generally part of the mix.

None of this occurs in a political vacuum. On the contrary, all of this work can only be done effectively or sustainably if a governance arrangement, for example, a constitutional framework, that enjoys a basic degree of public support and legitimacy undergirds it. Yet such arrangements can be exceedingly difficult to negotiate and sustain in countries emerging from violent conflict, especially when deep-seated cleavages lead to precarious balances that often simply defer the hardest problems to another day.[9] But more inclusive governance foundations and frameworks can and must be striven for. Indeed, without them, the prospects of moving from fragility to stability are slim.[10]

Even in promising environments, post-conflict rule of law building is riven with enormous practical challenges. Local actors frequently point to the failure of international actors to fully understand the local terrain, to listen or consult widely enough to sufficiently appreciate domestic needs

[7] Paul Jackson, "Introduction: Second Generation Security Sector Reform," *Journal of Intervention and Statebuilding*, 12 (2018), 1–10; Geneva Centre for the Democratic Control of Armed Forces, *The Contribution and Role of SSR in the Prevention of Violent Conflict* (Geneva: Geneva Centre for the Democratic Control of Armed Forces, 2017).

[8] For a thoughtful critique of the UN's role, see David Marshall, "Reboot Required: The United Nations' Engagement in Rule of Law Reform in Postconflict and Fragile States," in idem, ed., *The International Rule of Law Movement: A Crisis of Legitimacy and the Way Forward* (Cambridge: Harvard University Press, 2014), ch. 3.

[9] Stromseth, Wippman, and Brooks, *Can Might Make Rights?*, ch. 4.

[10] David Cortright, Conor Seyle, and Kristen Wall, *Governance for Peace: How Inclusive, Participatory and Accountable Institutions Promote Peace and Prosperity* (Cambridge: Cambridge University Press, 2017); Conor Seyle, "Governance for Peace," One Earth Future, December 12, 2017.

and aspirations, or to adequately support local agency.[11] Similarly, many international actors are acutely aware of the limits of their role and the need for improvements informed by lessons learned. A number of overarching critiques and themes are worth highlighting.

Critiques of Existing Approaches

While offering critiques is easier than charting promising paths forward, thoughtful critiques help to illuminate weaknesses in existing approaches. More and better empirical information also helps to shed light on recurring difficulties as well as promising trends and approaches.

One particularly long-standing and prominent critique is that much post-conflict rule of law building focuses too narrowly on institutional reforms that just skim the surface of larger rule of law needs. Such initiatives, which might include holding judicial training sessions, providing computers, and refurbishing courthouses, may be easier to document for funders seeking concrete deliverables, but they may make little dent in larger problems of political influence in judicial decision-making or bolster public confidence in national courts.

Furthermore, critics argue that the heavy focus on criminal justice and security sector reform in post-conflict rule of law building too often neglects or crowds out other vital needs. David Marshall of the Office of the UN High Commissioner for Human Rights, who has years of experience in war-torn countries including South Sudan, argues that such "state-centric, top down" approaches can overlook crucial underlying "cultural attitudes, political inequalities" and "power dynamics" that profoundly affect criminal justice systems.[12] Marshall does not dispute the importance of establishing basic security, as this is crucial to protecting civilians and moving forward in building the rule of law. Without strengthening public confidence in police and law enforcement, or in dispute settlement mechanisms, many other aspects of the rule of law can be undercut. However, critics maintain that a fixation on state justice systems too often absorbs a disproportionate share of resources and attention at the

[11] David Alpher, "Learning from SIGIR's Final Report on Iraq Reconstruction," Middle East Institute, June 2013.

[12] David Marshall, "Introduction," in idem, ed., *The International Rule of Law Movement*, p. xv.

expense of other equally urgent priorities like empowering civil society advocacy, protecting fundamental human rights, and encouraging progressive reforms in traditional dispute resolution. Indeed, many scholars point to the relative neglect of customary dispute resolution, which is often the predominant mechanism relied on by the population.[13] So it is a question of emphasis and balance, and recalibration may be needed.

Even within the confines of the formal justice system there are numerous areas for improvement. Crucial priorities include better understanding of the historical role of police in a society and in communities, strengthening police accountability and transparency, safeguarding and empowering women more effectively, and building public trust.[14] One US general officer with years of experience in Afghanistan argues trenchantly that police capacity-building there has been far too top-down, neglecting to build upon community and tribal structures that would make for more sustainable capacity that enjoys greater local confidence and support.[15] Similar critiques have been made of aspects of rule of law building in Iraq.[16] Indeed, the tendency for much rule of law work to be overly top-down at the expense of building capacity and support from the bottom up is a recurring issue.

Yet as vital as bottom-up capacity building is, so too is appreciating the larger political context shaping prospects for change in areas such as judicial reform. Judiciaries often receive a lion's share of attention and funding, yet their embeddedness in the larger political system – and the often pervasive problems of political influence and corruption – makes meaningful improvements and sustainable reforms particularly difficult. Developing greater judicial professionalism and building norms of

[13] See, for example, Deborah H. Isser, ed., *Customary Justice and the Rule of Law in War-Torn Societies* (Washington: United States Institute of Peace Press, 2011); Geoffrey Swenson, "Legal Pluralism in Theory and Practice," *International Studies Review*, 20 (2018), 438–462; and idem, "Why U.S. Efforts to Promote the Rule of Law in Afghanistan Failed," *International Security*, 42 (2017), 114–151.

[14] Stromseth, Wippman and Brooks, *Can Might Make Rights?*, pp. 203–218; Charles T. Call, ed., *Constructing Justice and Security After War* (Washington: United States Institute of Peace Press 2007); Melanne A. Civic, "Rule of Law in Multi-Dimensional Peacekeeping: Lessons for Reform," United Nations Peacekeeping, April 2018; William G. O'Neill, "Police Reform in Post-Conflict Societies: What We Know and What We Still Need to Know," International Police Academy, April 2005.

[15] Brig. Gen. Donald Bolduc (ret.), "The Real Reasons We're Losing the Afghanistan War," *Daily Beast*, June 22, 2018.

[16] Alpher, "Learning from SIGIR's Final Report on Iraq Reconstruction."

fairness, impartiality, independence, and transparency are as important as they are challenging.[17]

Prisons generally get the short end of the stick, and yet poor treatment of prisoners can be both a humanitarian and security disaster. Problems of prolonged detention without legal process, awful conditions, including mistreatment, are all too common. Prisons can also be breeding grounds for extremists. For all these reasons, greater attention on prisons, including better training, compliance with human rights, and more resources, is crucial.[18]

The segmented and often stove-piped nature of reforms, whether in the justice sector or more broadly, is also a well-documented problem. Progress made on one aspect – such as training and building greater professionalism in police – can be undercut by relative neglect of other parts of a justice system. In Haiti, for example, although enormous initial progress was made in vetting and training the Haitian National Police during the UN mission following Jean-Bertrand Aristide's return to power, other parts of the justice system did not receive the same degree of assistance or pressure for reform.[19] As a result, some judges could be bribed to release suspects, and bad governance generally undermined the larger political system in which police operated. Large numbers of pre-trial detainees languished for months or years in squalid prisons without legal process. Little was done, moreover, to address the widespread suspicion among ordinary people that law is a vehicle of control and repression rather than of justice. And the initial police reforms were ultimately undercut most profoundly by the failure to build a more accountable political system in Haiti more generally. Similar problems occur in other post-conflict societies as well, highlighting the need to understand interrelationships among different institutions and to build local capacity synergistically across a number of related areas.

Local ownership and buy-in is also essential. Indeed, failure to adequately encourage and support local capacity – and **agency** – in key areas such as accountable governance and law-making, is another

[17] Stromseth, Wippman and Brooks, *Can Might Make Rights?*, pp. 230–246. For a comprehensive analysis of challenges in justice system reform, see Linn A. Hammergren, *Justice Reform and Development: Rethinking Donor Assistance to Developing and Transition Countries* (New York: Routledge, 2014).

[18] Stromseth, Wippman and Brooks, *Can Might Make Rights?*, pp. 218–226.

[19] Stromseth, Wippman and Brooks, *Can Might Make Rights?*, pp. 179–180, 214–218.

recurring critique of post-conflict rule of law building. Dropping model legal codes down from on high, for example, may seem "efficient" when serious gaps in criminal law exist. Yet the messier, slower work of nurturing an inclusive and responsive domestic law-making capacity – and the vital process of compromise it entails – is essential to sustainable reform. Precisely because legislation inevitably reflects cultural values and trade-offs, local participation in the process itself is as important as the content.

Ingredients for Progress

To be sure, strengthening the rule of law is always going to be a work in progress. The critiques above, together with many others, underscore the complexity and challenges involved. But promising approaches do exist.

One is to keep a clear focus on the ultimate ends of rule of law building. Rachel Kleinfeld reminds us to resist a too narrow focus on institutions alone and to keep the ultimate ends or aims of the rule of law in mind. These include, she argues: (1) a government bound by law; (2) equality before law; (3) law and order; (4) predictable and efficient rulings; and (5) human rights.[20] Building upon these insights, my coauthors and I advocate for a "synergistic" approach to rule of law building that is ends-based, adaptive and dynamic, and systemic.[21] This approach, guided by fundamental rule of law goals, seeks to constructively build upon the existing cultural and institutional resources for the rule of law, and takes a holistic perspective that appreciates how institutions intersect and operate as a system.[22] Such an orientation also encourages nurturing human capabilities, such as human dignity and freedom,[23] always keeping the ultimate ends of the rule of law in mind as the North Star to guide reform efforts.

Inclusive governance ought to be explicitly set forth as a crucial goal of rule of law building. Lack of it feeds conflict. Lack of it undercuts equality. Lack of it inhibits checks and balances. Lack of it breeds corruption and self-dealing. Inclusive governance is necessary to move effectively from

[20] Kleinfeld, "Competing Definitions of the Rule of Law."

[21] Stromseth, Wippman and Brooks, *Can Might Make Rights?*, pp. 78–83.

[22] Stromseth, Wippman and Brooks, *Can Might Make Rights?*, pp. 80–83.

[23] Lan Cao, *Culture in Law and Development: Nurturing Positive Change* (Oxford: Oxford University Press, 2016), pp. 27–28, 454–457 Cao engages with the work economist Amartya Sen and philosopher Martha Nussbaum on the importance of advancing human freedom and human capability.

conflict to stability and rights-protection.[24] It opens up space for civil society advocacy, supported by bottom-up empowerment.

Second, with such a vision in mind, it is critically important to better understand the rule of law landscape in a particular society. Fundamentally, this requires understanding the major issues of justice – and injustice –in a country.[25] For instance, how pervasive are injustices such as discrimination and violence against women, and discrimination directed against other segments of the population? How widespread is corruption by powerful figures? How central are disputes over land and property? Answering such questions requires going beyond capital cities and political elites to rural communities and local actors, and understanding the role of village leaders. It requires engaging with women, young people, and disadvantaged groups – and digging deep to understand the larger political, social and economic realities in a society.

Crucially, how do people typically resolve their disputes? To what extent does the public rely on or have confidence in national judicial institutions? Or are informal, traditional forms of dispute resolution – such as those conducted by tribal or village elders – more commonly used and trusted? Do these mechanisms have broad local legitimacy, or do they tend to privilege some segments of the population while disempowering others? And are local actors working for progressive reform of these mechanisms, whose work can be encouraged and reinforced? Addressing such questions can help with understanding the possibilities and obstacles to constructive change.

Third is the importance of citizen empowerment. As noted earlier, rule of law building often defaults to a top-down approach, with a focus on national leaders and elites and on building up state institutions. Ordinary people – particularly those living in rural areas and those with less power and status in society – too often are overlooked and shortchanged. Strategies focusing on legal empowerment, like those advocated by Stephen Golub and others, can help ensure that rule of law building reaches beyond capital cities and elite power-holders and embraces the needs and aspirations of a wider swath of society.[26] Such approaches include building

[24] Cortright, Seyle, and Wall, *Governance for Peace.*

[25] Louis-Alexandre Berg, Deborah Isser, and Douglas Porter, "Beyond Deficit and Dysfunction: Three Questions toward Just Development in Fragile and Conflict-Affected Settings," in Marshall, ed., *The International Rule of Law Movement*, pp. 272–274.

[26] Stephen Golub, "Beyond Rule of Law Orthodoxy: The Legal Empowerment Alternative," Carnegie Endowment for International Peace, October 2003; idem, ed., *Legal*

people's understanding of their rights, strengthening effective access to justice, improving local forms of dispute resolution, working to strengthen the property rights of women and other disadvantaged groups, and encouraging those who may not be as fully represented to seek leadership positions at all levels of society and governance. Such initiatives can help give people a stake in the law and encourage legal change from the bottom up.

Examples of these approaches illustrate their potential. In Sierra Leone, trained paralegals advise citizens about their options for dispute settlement, from traditional mechanisms involving village chiefs to formal state justice institutions, empowering people to make informed choices and, as a result, put constructive pressure on the institutions to improve the quality of justice that they deliver.[27] Legal clinics can train law students to assist vulnerable members of the community. Moreover, a focus on local community needs and on bottom-up capacity-building can be vital in areas such as policing, where overly top-down approaches are unlikely to be sustainable or enjoy the legitimacy and community support needed to be effective.

Fourth, and relatedly, is the need for both supply-side *and* demand-side rule of law capacity-building. Clearly, development of legal institutions and capacities (supply side) *and* development of public understanding and capabilities to advocate for basic rights and protections (demand side) are *both* important to building and sustaining the rule of law. Supply-side institution-building alone runs the risk of entrenching the powerful in positions of tremendous influence, often without sufficient checks and balances or transparency. Yet building demand for justice alone – without meaningful progress in reforming institutions – can be a recipe for deep

Empowerment: Practitioners' Perspectives (Rome: International Development Law Organization, 2010); Open Society Justice Initiative, ed., *Justice Initiatives: Legal Empowerment* (New York: Open Society Justice Initiative, 2013); Yash Ghai and Jill Cottrell, eds., *Marginalized Communities and Access to Justice* (New York: Routledge, 2010); Thomas Carothers, "Democracy Support Strategies: Leading with Women's Empowerment," Carnegie Endowment for International Peace, September 2016.

[27] Vivek Maru, "Between Law and Society: Paralegals and the Provision of Justice Services in Sierra Leone and Worldwide," *Yale Journal of International Law*, 31 (2006), 427–476. Creative civil society organizations such as Namati engage in this work around the world. See, for example, https://namati.org/ourwork/paralegals/.

public disappointment and frustration. So moving forward on both fronts is vital and ideally should be mutually reinforcing.

Concrete examples illustrate this point. In Timor-Leste, just as important as training judges and building a judiciary was the creation of the Judicial System Monitoring Program (JSMP), a nongovernmental organization that reviews the work of the justice system, shares valuable information with the public, and advocates for reforms.[28] Likewise, just as important as developing the capacity of executive branch ministries, such as defense and justice ministries, is developing capacity for legislative oversight of those ministries and for civil society scrutiny and advocacy on the policy issues they raise. Just as important as passing new laws addressing criminal justice is making sure that the public is informed about those laws and their rights. Such work is being done in a number of countries, including through radio programs and social media, providing greater transparency about the work of government and greater accessibility to civil society advocates for reform.

These promising approaches are among many that thoughtful practitioners and scholars are advancing. Some of the most fruitful insights and practical work, however, are emerging in the area of culture and the rule of law, the next area of focus in this essay.

2 Culture and the Rule of Law

A country's culture provides the context in which the rule of law is built. Leading scholars of law and development have long stressed the interrelatedness of law and culture.[29] Post-conflict rule of law building efforts, with their frequent focus on immediate needs and institutional reforms, run the risk of paying insufficient attention to the role of customary norms and practices – in a word, to culture. Furthermore, external actors may assume a centrality of certain institutions and practices that may not translate to a particular post-conflict setting. Also, they may underappreciate the potential ramifications of their

[28] The reports of the Judicial System Monitoring Program and additional information about its work are available on its website: http://jsmp.tl/publications/relatoriu/.

[29] Cao, *Culture in Law and Development*, chs. 1 and 3; Brian Z. Tamanaha, "The Primacy of Society and the Failures of Law and Development," *Cornell International Law Journal*, 44 (2011), 209–247; Stromseth, Wippman, and Brooks, *Can Might Make Rights?*, ch. 8.

own engagement, which may empower some actors and reinforce some practices at the expense of others.

Fortunately, the centrality of culture in post-conflict rule of law building is becoming better understood both as a general proposition and in concrete situations. This includes better understanding of positive cultural norms and practices but also those with negative effects, particularly on women; of the role of customary law and dispute resolution; of the ways in which power is exercised (in cities as well as rural areas); and of the possibilities for progressive change.[30] Increasing attention to these matters – both scholarly and practical – has generated a number of important suggestions and approaches.

First, there's a compelling need to better understand the divisions and flashpoints for social friction in countries transitioning out of conflict. These may include long-standing patterns of discrimination against certain groups, disputes over land tenure and property rights, gender-based violence, and economic inequality. Also crucial to appreciate, as mentioned earlier, is whether state justice institutions enjoy or warrant any degree of public confidence in particular societies. Even if these institutions exist beyond major cities, they may not be widely used or trusted due to corruption and their domination by powerful elites. Instead, "the law the people see" may predominantly be customary law and traditional dispute resolution mechanisms.[31] Thus understanding how these mechanisms work, their strengths and weaknesses including their treatment of marginalized groups, is crucial to working for their improvement.

While engaging sensitively with deeply rooted cultural practices can be difficult – particularly for outsiders – working closely with local reformers on the ground can help to engender positive change in those customary practices that may violate human dignity and human rights, particularly the rights of women.[32] Culture, as Lan Cao explains, is always fluid, changing, and contested.[33] But within a culture, there will be progressive strands on which to build and local change agents to support. Local leaders can spearhead reform from *within* the culture – while also navigating the

[30] Among the many thoughtful discussions, see, for example, Cao, *Culture in Law and Development*, and the essays in Isser, ed., *Customary Justice and the Rule of Law in War-Torn Societies*.

[31] Isser, ed., *Customary Justice and the Rule of Law in War-Torn Societies*.

[32] Cao, *Culture in Law and Development*.

[33] Cao, *Culture in Law and Development*.

dynamics and narrative of cultural change in the face of entrenched opposition.

Such efforts can be a vital part of post-conflict rule of law building. For instance, encouraging progressive reforms in traditional dispute settlement mechanisms can help move toward processes that warrant greater public trust and legitimacy, including among segments of the population that have not traditionally been as empowered or protected.[34]

Women's empowerment is absolutely crucial to positive culture change that advances the rule of law. Fundamentally important is the agency of women themselves. Working to change deeply rooted cultural barriers that discriminate against women and impede their equality, freedom and full participation in governance is vital both to women's human dignity and to strengthening the rule of law more broadly. Empowered and educated women contribute to a country's economic well-being, to the health and education of their children, and to decision-making in their communities and countries.[35]

External actors can play a valuable supporting role in nurturing positive culture change, but should do so with humility. They need to appreciate that their own cultural assumptions and approaches may not resonate in a particular local setting. But they should be prepared to stand up firmly for human dignity and human rights and work in partnership with constructive local actors who do so as well.

Post-conflict rule of law building that aims to encourage progressive culture change will need a wider scope than more narrowly focused institutional approaches.[36] Thinking creatively is essential. Some elements of a broader approach include:

- Getting to the grassroots by moving beyond cities, state institutions, and political elites to strengthen informal dispute resolution, build citizen's education, access to justice, and community organizing and advocacy programs.
- Strengthening civil society: including by helping to build independent, ethical and effective media and nongovernmental organizations.

[34] See, for example, the important work of the above mentioned NGO Namati.

[35] Cao, *Culture in Law and Development*, pp. 236–239; Carothers, "Democracy Support Strategies."

[36] This discussion draws on Stromseth, Wippman, and Brooks, *Can Might Make Rights?*, ch. 8.

- Focusing on the next generation: including through educational programs, cultural exchanges, service opportunities, and other initiatives.
- Giving people a stake in the law: involving them in planning new institutions and codes, and linking rule of law programs to development and antipoverty efforts.
- Including marginalized groups: engaging and empowering women, youth, and minorities.
- Being creative: using media, pop culture, and culturally resonant narratives and forms of communication to encourage progressive reforms.

These elements, combined, can spur innovative initiatives. In Haiti, for example, a dedicated priest has built a valuable legal aid clinic at a law school in a rural area. Law students in this clinic represent local residents in court cases, focusing on marginalized and disadvantaged people. The clinic empowers both students and clients alike, and puts constructive pressure on state justice institutions to be more responsive to the needs of community members. This approach gives students and community members a real stake in the law and a sense of power and hope for the future.[37]

Another promising approach to culture change is working to expose and counter corruption. Anticorruption work can be an illuminating lens and entry point for wider legal and political change.[38] Entrenched power holders through intimidation, bribery, and related means can thwart legal, political, and economic change that would benefit a country's people and its long-term future. Ordinary people may be willing to mobilize and rally for reforms, particularly when the pervasiveness and depth of corruption is exposed to the light of day. To be sure, corrupt leaders will resist challenges to their perks and self-dealing, and reformers can face grave risks in battling corruption. But external assistance to support greater transparency and accountability can provide an opening for change and enjoy considerable buy-in from the people.

One important example of such work is the International Commission Against Impunity in Guatemala (CICIG).[39] CICIG has been credited with

[37] Jessica Carew Kraft, "Establishing the Rule of Law in a Country Where Justice Hardly Exists," *The Atlantic*, April 22, 2015.

[38] Thomas Carothers and Christopher Carothers, "Seeking Political Stability Abroad? Fight Corruption," *The National Interest*, January 25, 2018; Michael Dziedzic, ed., *Criminalized Power Structures: The Overlooked Enemies of Peace* (Lanham: Rowman and Littlefield, 2016).

[39] Open Society Justice Initiative, *Against the Odds: CICIG in Guatemala* (New York: Open Society Justice Initiative, 2016).

advancing legal accountability for corruption and abuse of power in Guatemala, giving ordinary people greater confidence that even the powerful can be brought to justice – and building public demand for accountability of public leaders more generally.[40] Yet CICIG also confronted obstacles to its work and its future was undercut when Guatemala's President, himself under investigation, decided in August 2018 to terminate its mandate.[41] In Afghanistan and elsewhere, fighting corruption is a steep and crucial uphill climb,[42] but even modest steps are important.[43]

Corruption's pervasive and debilitating grip can profoundly thwart rule of law building. Yet tackling corruption can also be a gateway to other forms of justice and accountability, including for atrocity crimes, to which we now turn.

3 Transitional Justice and the Rule of Law

Countries emerging from sustained conflict frequently bear the scars of horrific violence directed against civilians. Victims and survivors – often targeted because of their ethnicity, tribe, religion, or gender – have every reason to be fearful and distrustful of the state's ability to protect them going forward. Impunity for such violence undercuts the very idea of the rule of law and erodes public confidence that the future will be different or that justice is even possible.

Holding perpetrators accountable for such crimes is thus an increasingly vital part of post-conflict rule of law building. At its core, "transitional justice" involves a country's willingness to address past atrocities and abuses as it navigates out of conflict toward a more rights-protecting

[40] Fernando Carrera, "Guatemala's International Commission Against Impunity: A Case Study of Institutions and Rule of Law," World Bank, 2017; Matthew M. Taylor, "Lessons from Guatemala's Commission Against Impunity," Council on Foreign Relations, June 2017; Human Rights Watch, "Guatemala: President Sabotages Fight for Justice," August 2018.

[41] Human Rights Watch, "Guatemala."

[42] Sarah Chayes, *Thieves of State: Why Corruption Threatens Global Security* (New York: W. W. Norton, 2015); George Clooney and John Prendergast, "The Key to Making Peace in Africa: Fighting Corruption Can Help End Conflict," *Foreign Affairs*, March 14, 2018.

[43] Pamela Constable, "Afghan Cases Target the Once-protected Elite," *Washington Post*, August 20, 2017; May Jeong, "The Impossible Job of Afghanistan's Attorney General," *The Atlantic*, March 9, 2017.

and stable future.[44] Seeking justice for victims and accountability for perpetrators – and truth about what happened and why – is essential to strengthening the rule of law going forward.

This is true for a number of reasons. To start with, atrocity crimes – such as deliberate targeting of civilians, mass rape, killing of people because of their religious beliefs or ethnic affiliation – violate fundamental norms of human conduct and fundamental rules of international humanitarian law. Demonstrating to perpetrators that such conduct is unacceptable and to victims that they are entitled to justice is about as basic to the rule of law as one can get. Fundamental rule of law principles are at stake, including protecting human dignity, equality before the law, government bound by law, due process, and the notion that the rule of law ultimately is more powerful than predatory violence.

Yet many obstacles can stand in the way of efforts to achieve meaningful justice and accountability. When violence and atrocities have been pervasive in a conflict, holding every perpetrator – or even most – criminally accountable is not likely to be possible. Conflicts settled by power-sharing agreements among warring factions may leave offenders in positions of authority able to thwart meaningful accountability. Furthermore, powerful actors often attempt to discredit justice efforts aimed at themselves or their affiliates; and risks of one-sided "victor's justice" may undercut fair prosecution.[45] Even when impartial and balanced prosecutions do occur, lingering resentments across ethnic, tribal, religious and other divides can undercut public confidence that justice is being fairly pursued. In the Balkans, for example, views about the work of the International Criminal Tribunal for the former Yugoslavia are deeply polarized along ethnic

[44] Jane Stromseth, "Peacebuilding and Transitional Justice: The Road Ahead," in Chester A. Crocker, Fen Osler Hampson, and Pamela Aall, eds., *Managing Conflict in a World Adrift* (Washington: United States Institute of Peace Press, 2015); Tricia D. Olsen, Leigh A. Payne, and Andrew G. Reiter, *Transitional Justice in Balance: Comparing Processes, Weighing Efficacy* (Washington: United States Institute of Peace, 2010); Ruti G. Teitel, *Transitional Justice* (Oxford: Oxford University Press, 2000). For current work in this field, see the International Center for Transitional Justice's website, www.ictj.org/ See also Jens Meierhenrich, Alexander Laban Hinton, and Lawrence Douglas, eds., *The Oxford Handbook of Transitional Justice* (Oxford: Oxford University Press, 2021).

[45] Victor Peskin, "Beyond Victor's Justice? The Challenge of Prosecuting the Winners at the International Criminal Tribunals for the Former Yugoslavia and Rwanda," *Journal of Human Rights*, 4 (2005), 213–231.

lines.[46] Moreover, securing evidence in a timely and effective manner or gaining custody of suspects can be difficult. For many victims and survivors, justice all too often can seem distant and sometimes unattainable.

Still, significant developments in relevant law and institutions since World War II have advanced the prospects of justice for atrocity crimes both legally and practically: from the Nuremberg Tribunal, which brought Nazi leaders to justice for egregious crimes, to the Geneva Conventions and Protocols; the Genocide Convention; and, in the post-Cold War era, the statutes and jurisprudence of numerous international and hybrid criminal tribunals. These tribunals include the International Criminal Tribunal for the former Yugoslavia (ICTY) and for Rwanda (ICTR), the International Criminal Court (ICC), the Special Court for Sierra Leone, the Cambodia Tribunal, and the joint African Union/Senegalese tribunal, among others.[47]

Together these courts – international, hybrid, and domestic – are helping to counter impunity for atrocity crimes. Although their track records are mixed, they are working to advance justice, and to demonstrate the growing expectation of justice and accountability for atrocity crimes. The United Nations, international and regional courts, and many governments have reinforced this message by clearly rejecting amnesties for these crimes.[48]

Countries recovering from conflict often pursue a combination of measures in tandem with criminal law approaches. Truth commissions, for instance – which can provide a full and public account of what transpired, documenting harms caused, patterns of abuse, responsibilities and root causes – can be vital both to survivors and the public more generally, and can illuminate priority areas for reform.[49] Moreover, vetting and institutional reforms, for example, changes in police and military hiring practices and oversight mechanisms, can be crucial in helping to prevent recurrence of atrocity crimes.

[46] Diane Orentlicher, *Some Kind of Justice: The ICTY's Impact in Bosnia and Serbia* (Oxford: Oxford University Press, 2018); Marko Milanović, "The Impact of the ICTY on the Former Yugoslavia: An Anticipatory Postmortem," *American Journal of International Law*, 110 (2016), 233–259 ; Mirko Klarin, "The Impact of the ICTY Trials on Public Opinion in the Former Yugoslavia," *Journal of International Criminal Justice*, 7 (2009), 89–96.

[47] Steven R. Ratner, Jason S. Abrams, and James L. Bischoff, *Accountability for Human Rights Atrocities in International Law: Beyond the Nuremberg Legacy*, 3rd ed. (Oxford: Oxford University Press, 2009).

[48] Stromseth, "Peacebuilding and Transitional Justice," 579–580.

[49] Priscilla B. Hayner, *Unspeakable Truths: Transitional Justice and the Challenge of Truth Commissions*, 2nd ed. (New York: Routledge, 2011).

As vital as justice for past atrocities can be for building the rule of law going forward, improvements are needed in a number of areas. One is strengthening the linkages between justice processes that focus on past atrocities and *ongoing* domestic justice capacity-building.[50] For example, hybrid courts located in directly affected societies have contributed to national capacity-building in multiple ways. They generally employ domestic investigators, prosecutors, defense counsel, judges, and administrators, many of whom go on to serve in the domestic justice system with enhanced skills in areas such as witness protection, investigations in complex criminal cases, due process in trial proceedings, and judicial opinion writing. Furthermore, relevant personnel at hybrid courts can offer lectures for legal professionals, internships for local law students, and other forms of training and community outreach.

International tribunals too can contribute tangibly to domestic capacity-building. The International Criminal Court (ICC), whose jurisdiction took effect in 2002, is deliberately designed to encourage and incentivize national accountability processes. A court of last resort, created by treaty (the Rome Statute), the ICC is complementary to domestic processes, which have primary responsibility to investigate and prosecute genocide, war crimes, and crimes against humanity. The ICC is able to step in, when it has jurisdiction, if states are unable or unwilling themselves genuinely to investigate or prosecute these crimes. This complementarity principle encourages justice to be done nationally in directly affected communities, and, hopefully, in the process build up domestic rule of law capacity as the first line of defense against atrocities. The ICC has helped to catalyze national investigation and prosecution for atrocity crimes in a number of instances.[51]

Community outreach efforts by court personnel warrant more attention as well. Explaining the justice process in the face of painful atrocities to affected communities is immensely challenging, particularly when they are deeply divided along political or ethnic lines and skeptical about the fairness or sufficiency of justice efforts.[52] These dialogues can be difficult

[50] Jane Stromseth, "Justice on the Ground: Can International Criminal Courts Strengthen Domestic Rule of Law in Post-Conflict Societies?" *Hague Journal on the Rule of Law*, 1 (2009), 87–97.

[51] Human Rights Watch, "Pressure Point: The ICC's Impact on National Justice," May 2018; Jane Stromseth, "Is the ICC Making a Difference?" *Just Security*, December 6, 2017.

[52] Stuart Ford, "A Social Psychology Model of the Perceived Legitimacy of International Criminal Courts: Implications for the Success of Transitional Justice Mechanisms," *Vanderbilt Journal of Transnational Law*, 45 (2014), 405–476.

and contested, and differing views about justice will persist. Yet these realities underscore how vital it is to listen to public concerns about justice, to answer questions forthrightly, and to communicate straightforwardly a tribunal's goals and procedures.

The Special Court for Sierra Leone's innovative outreach program provides a useful example. Outreach officers in town hall meetings across the country listened to the population's many critiques and sought to engage straightforwardly with often deeply skeptical domestic audiences. Facing criticism that the court was focusing only on "big fish" rather than on direct perpetrators next door, outreach officers explained the court's mandate to try those "most responsible" and why the tribunal was focusing on architects of the conflict's atrocities. They also stressed that no matter the cause there are legal rules limiting how a conflict should be fought – that no matter which side you are on, these legal rules apply.[53] This outreach helped build greater public understanding and appreciation for the court's work, with majorities ultimately viewing the court's contribution favorably. Moreover, learning from this experience, other tribunals are giving greater attention to meaningful outreach with affected populations and the wider public.

In working for accountability after conflict, it is crucial to keep in mind the overarching goals of transitional justice: obtaining justice for egregious atrocity crimes; preventing future atrocities; moving effectively toward more inclusive, human rights-respecting governance; and advancing the most fundamental underpinnings of the rule of law. To do this requires addressing deeper structural problems – inequalities, exploitation, corruption – that undercut building a more just society going forward. Realizing both how vital and how difficult aiming for "*transformative* justice" can be leads to our fourth and final area of focus: assessing impact.

4 Learning from Experience

Assessing the impact of rule of law building efforts in societies struggling to overcome conflict is inherently difficult and enormously challenging. Progress is generally not linear; the overall trajectory is often more back and forth than continuous. Setbacks in some areas can undercut progress

[53] Stromseth, "Justice on the Ground," 93–94.

in others, and whether we even have the right ways to "measure" it is unclear. Certainly, some crucial broad indicators, such as public trust in government institutions or women's equality, tell a key part of the story. But in difficult transitions out of conflict, crucial elements of the rule of law may be more apparent by their absence.

Another problem is the tendency of funders and implementers to focus on discrete activities that can be counted, even if they are neither the most important indicia of progress nor the most urgent rule of law priorities. As noted earlier, the number of training workshops held generally tells very little about advancements on deeper goals such as building a more impartial judiciary or a police force that enjoys public trust. Furthermore, the particular dynamics of the grant-making process for rule of law programs can incentivize eager grantees to overstate potential impacts and to focus on countable metrics to satisfy funders' documentation requirements, even if the ultimate result of this is likely to skim the surface of the most important rule of law needs.[54]

These problems, while often acknowledged, are not easy to fix and require casting a wider lens to measure and evaluate progress. Several steps can open pathways to promising entry points for rule of law building.

First, embracing human rights aims more clearly in rule of law programming can help build stronger rule of law foundations.[55] Not only do such approaches affirm human dignity, they can have important practical effects. For example, encouraging post-conflict governments to ratify key human rights treaties if they have not done so – and to strengthen domestic laws to better protect human rights – can be an impactful component of post-conflict rule of law building. Ratification and implementation of human rights treaties by transitioning states can empower domestic advocacy and change through agenda-setting, litigation, and mobilization by civil society, as Beth Simmons documents.[56] Even so, powerful cultural barriers to fair and equal treatment often persist even in the face of new and improved laws. Thus, working to change deep-seated cultural practices that marginalize and discriminate against women

[54] Erik G. Jensen, "Postscript: An Immodest Reflection," in Marshall, ed., *The International Rule of Law Movement*, p. 299.

[55] Marshall, "Reboot Required," pp. 87–88, 115–118.

[56] Beth A. Simmons, *Mobilizing for Human Rights: International Law in Domestic Politics* (Cambridge: Cambridge University Press, 2009).

and other disadvantaged groups will often be essential to protecting universal human rights and advancing human dignity tangibly on the ground.[57]

Second, empowerment approaches to rule of law building are also proving to be consequential in many ways. These include a wide array of programs to strengthen public access to justice, to provide education about rights and advocacy strategies, to support independent media and civil society organizations, and many other initiatives. Empirical research on legal empowerment finds notable impacts that include "increased legal knowledge" and "stronger agency" reflected in people's willingness to take action, as well as positive effects on conflict resolution, and on institutions, such as "changes in law, policy, or practice."[58]

Empowerment initiatives of different types can also be mutually reinforcing – including legal and economic empowerment. We can see this clearly in the impacts of empowering women. Women's economic empowerment not only helps to build more prosperous societies; it also can go a long way to advancing equality and protecting women from predatory violence. Amartya Sen's seminal work on "missing women," for example, illuminates how economic empowerment can help protect women from exploitation by enhancing their public visibility and agency in contributing to their communities and societies.[59] Women's political empowerment also has vital impacts and ensures that a wider range of issues and concerns are addressed in governance. The perspectives women bring to the table in peace negotiations have made a notable difference, with empirical studies showing that female participation enhances the prospects that a peace agreement will last.[60]

Furthermore, work on justice "systems" that includes education and empowerment strategies can have significant impacts in giving voice and agency to previously disadvantaged citizens more generally. This can put constructive pressure for reform on justice institutions. The training of

[57] Cao, *Culture in Law and Development.*

[58] Laura Goodwin and Vivek Maru, "What Do We Know about Legal Empowerment? Mapping the Evidence," *Hague Journal on the Rule of Law*, 9 (2017), 157–194.

[59] Amartya Sen, "More Than 100 Million Women Are Missing," *The New York Review of Books*, December 20, 1990; Cao, *Culture in Law and Development*, pp. 236–237.

[60] Catherine Powell, "How Women Could Save the World, If Only We Would Let Them: From Gender Essentialism to Inclusive Security," *Yale Journal of Law and Feminism*, 28 (2015), 271–325.

paralegals to help empower people to know their rights and their dispute resolution choices can incentivize both traditional and state leaders to improve the quality and fairness of the proceedings they offer.[61] Improvements in legal education, including clinical legal education as noted earlier, can help build skills from the bottom up, giving young people tools to work for meaningful change even in very difficult circumstances. Empowering civil society organizations, including media, can help nurture greater transparency and public knowledge of rights and of governance. Educating young people and students at all levels about human rights, including through innovative radio programming and social media platforms, can help build understanding of fundamental rights and strategies for effective reform.

Third, pursuing accountability for past atrocities through a combination of international and domestic mechanisms can help advance the rule of law. Political scientists have documented positive effects that the "justice cascade" is having in strengthening human rights and bolstering democracy in many countries, for example.[62] The ICC's impacts in catalyzing domestic accountability in post-conflict societies that are parties to the Court deserve thoughtful attention as part of this mix.[63] Even in countries that are not party to the ICC, growing public demand for justice and accountability can boost efforts to gather evidence of atrocity crimes and to seek or create judicial forums that have jurisdiction.[64]

Fourth, countering corruption is another area of critical need and tangible benefit in post-conflict rule of law building. Corruption can be a heavy albatross undermining progress in achieving rule of law goals. Corruption can be so deeply rooted and widespread that it undercuts public confidence in the very possibility of fair governance processes and legal institutions. Yet precisely because of corruption's pervasive influence in so many societies, tackling it can be an absolutely essential component of building more effective rule of law and increasing public trust.

[61] Maru, "Between Law and Society."

[62] Kathryn Sikkink, *Evidence for Hope: Making Human Rights Work in the 21st Century* (Princeton: Princeton University Press, 2017); Olsen, Payne, and Reiter, *Transitional Justice in Balance*.

[63] Human Rights Watch, "Pressure Point"; Geoff Dancy and Florencia Montal, "Unintended Positive Complementarity: Why ICC Investigations May Increase Domestic Human Rights Prosecutions," *American Journal of International Law*, 111 (2017), 689–723.

[64] Stromseth, "Is the ICC Making a Difference?"

Fifth, and finally, we must not lose sight of the big picture. Inclusive and effective governance is absolutely foundational to strengthening rule of law. So much else is linked to it: accountable leadership; civic participation and confidence in nonviolent conflict resolution; equality of opportunity; and meaningful checks and balances, among other vital matters. Research has shown that inclusive governance is central for a country to move from conflict to sustainable peace.[65] Governance foundations must be strong and fair for the rule of law to thrive.

Conclusion

The experience of post-conflict rule of law building over the last few decades is decidedly mixed. While there have been many disappointments on numerous levels, there has also been progress. Promising approaches have emerged even in the face of enormous challenges, including: greater focus on inclusive governance, human rights, and empowerment; clearer understandings of the importance of culture, customary dispute settlement mechanisms, and possibilities for progressive change; increasing attention to the need for meaningful justice and accountability for atrocity crimes; and growing knowledge of the impacts of different approaches to rule of law building after conflict. So there is a basis for hope even as there are also stubborn reasons for deep concern.

The wider, divisive political and economic trends on the global stage no doubt will complicate multilateral support for post-conflict rule of law building. But domestic actors on the ground who know their country best and have the deepest stake in its future hopefully will find partners – whether governments, NGOs, or individuals – who can help support progressive change, while also understanding the limits of what external actors realistically can contribute. Just as the struggle between pessimism and hope will persist in this vital work, so too will the struggle for justice.

[65] Cortright, Seyle, and Wall, *Governance for Peace*.

29 A Global Rule of Law

Anne Orford

Introduction

The view of international law as a profession committed to the spread of liberal ideas emerged in Europe and North America in the late nineteenth century.[1] One of those ideas was the rule of law. Attempts to realize a global rule of law and attempts to constitute an international community have long been linked. For many international lawyers, this gave international law a sense of forward movement and a clear *telos*, with the caveat that the reality of unequal power relations meant that international law could never be measured directly against a model borrowed from domestic law and politics.[2] Nonetheless, the gradual expansion of a system of codified law and international adjudication was seen as progress toward an international community founded on a global rule of law and away from a system of arbitrary power reliant upon the resort to force. For liberal international lawyers, the project of realizing the rule of law on a global scale is "a work in progress," to which judges and arbitrators contribute by the meticulous application of international law in an impartial manner to the disputes brought before them.[3]

[1] Martti Koskenniemi, *The Gentle Civilizer of Nations: The Rise and Fall of International Law 1870–1960* (Cambridge: Cambridge University Press, 2002).

[2] See, for example, Arthur Watts, "The International Rule of Law," *German Yearbook of International Law*, 36 (1993), 15–45; James Crawford, "International Law and the Rule of Law," *Adelaide Law Review*, 24 (2003), 3–12; Stéphane Beaulac, "The Rule of Law in International Law Today," in Gianluigi Palombella and Neil Walker, eds., *Relocating the Rule of Law* (Oxford: Hart, 2009), pp. 197–223; Rosalyn Higgins, "The Rule of Law: Some Sceptical Thoughts," in idem, *Themes and Theories*, vol. 2 (Oxford: Oxford University Press, 2009), p. 1330; Peter Tomka, "The Rule of Law and the Role of the International Court of Justice in World Affairs," Inaugural Hilding Eek Memorial Lecture, Stockholm Center for International Law and Justice, December 2, 2013.

[3] Higgins, "The Rule of Law," p. 1339.

Yet, as with many other liberal ideals, what it would mean in fact to realize the rule of a law on a global scale has never been certain or uncontested. In particular, liberal internationalists have imagined the project of realizing a global rule of law in two quite different ways. On the one hand, the claim that the conduct of relations between states should take place according to liberal ideals has shaped many of the principles that are often seen as foundational to the current international order, among them the principles of sovereign equality, self-determination, collective security, nonintervention in the internal affairs of other states, and the commitment to peaceful settlement of disputes. Thus while all states may not be "equal in absolute terms," they nonetheless "stand equally within the normative system."[4] Here the rule of law is translated into the international system to stand for reliance on law as opposed to arbitrary power as the dominant mechanism of rule in global politics, a commitment to settling disputes through arbitration rather than force, and the attempt to constrain the imperial ambitions or civilizing missions of powerful states.

On the other hand, liberal internationalists have also looked to law as a vehicle for transforming all states into liberal democracies, protecting the rights of individuals, entrenching market logic at the heart of government, and promoting freedom. That version of liberal internationalism saw itself as furthering a project of government that is founded upon certainty, nondiscrimination, and equal treatment before the law, in which the rights and duties of legal subjects are determined by independent and impartial arbitrators making reasoned and objective decisions on the basis of publicly available legal materials. The moral certainty underpinning that project sat uneasily with the pluralistic foundations of the thinner conception of international law expressed in documents such as the UN Charter. Those two visions of what it might mean to globalize the rule of law have often been in tension, particularly at moments when crusading liberal states have emerged as hegemonic.

As a result, while international lawyers and international institutions increasingly adopted the vocabulary of the rule of law to describe the goals of their work, it has never been clear in practice what it would mean to constitutionalize the rule of law on a global scale. This is perhaps unsurprising, given that the meaning of the rule of law is contested even within states in which there is a shared legal culture. As José Alvarez notes, "while

[4] Beaulac, "The Rule of Law in International Law Today," p. 210.

everyone is for the rule of law, this is made easier by the absence of a single definition of what it actually is, varying views about why it is relevant and to whom, and by the ever present (and sometimes hypocritical) tendency we have to apply whatever we think it is to others but not to ourselves."[5] The lack of agreement over what the global rule of law means has not, however, detracted from the tendency to treat debates about its application as evidencing a straightforward opposition between the international rule of law and arbitrary power, or between international law and politics.

Those patterns of international legal argumentation intensify aspects of rule of law discourse that have been criticized more generally. For example, the tendency to refer to a domestic standard of the rule of law as a starting point makes it seem that a fixed conception of the rule of law exists domestically, and that the only challenge to applying that conception globally is the lack of fit between domestic and international governance arrangements or the refusal of states to give up their sovereign prerogatives in the interests of realizing a shared vision of the common good. The question as to whether international law really conforms to the rule of law (or whether it is law at all) is not meant as a question about the rule of law more generally, but rather as a question about whether international law conforms to an otherwise self-evident model of the relation between law and power. Yet as generations of political and legal theorists have reminded us, the rule of law is an essentially contested concept, the content, use, and implications of which are historically indeterminate, politically fraught, and critically valuable.[6] Debates about what it might mean to create "a just world under law" involve foundational questions about the nature and purpose of the international legal system, including the proper relation between security and freedom or public order and human dignity, the role and function of the state, the tension between democratic decision-making and international obligations, the place of individuals and nonstate actors in a statist system, and the meaning of juridical equality in a world of substantive inequality.[7]

[5] José E. Alvarez, "International Organisations and the Rule of Law," *New Zealand Journal of Public and International Law*, 14 (2016), 7.

[6] Jeremy Waldron, "Is the Rule of Law an Essentially Contested Concept (in Florida)?" *Law and Philosophy*, 21 (2002), 137–164.

[7] Hilary Charlesworth and Donald Francis Donovan, "An Introduction: A Just World Under Law," *American Society of International Law Proceedings*, 100 (2006), xii–xiii.

The way in which the rule of law has been taken up by liberal advocates in debates about international law has also intensified the broad tendency of contemporary rule of law theories to formalize the concept and in doing so reduce it to a shopping list of appealing characteristics – generality, consistency, stability, equality before the law, and principled decision-making by impartial adjudicators in courts that are public and accessible to all. Rule of law proponents take as given that judges and arbitrators operating as a transnational guild of legal experts with discretion to shape the law should be preferred to other decision-makers. That approach to the rule of law removes and abstracts it from the broader political system within which the law is embedded.[8] Contemporary advocates of the global rule of law do not consider the relation of adjudication to the society within which it operates, nor its relation to that society's other institutions for control or coercion.[9] As Judith Shklar has argued about modern restatements of the rule of law more generally, the effect is "a level of abstraction so high as to make these models politically irrelevant."[10] There is little to accept or to reject in appeals to a global rule of law in the absence of any sense of the institutions or the political order within which law will rule.

If a form of government that depends upon authoritative legal determinations by international adjudicators is to prevail over other forms of politics, it must be founded on some compelling process of persuasion or of effective social control, and be part of a broader international order that is seen as legitimate. Instead, the successful creation of a network of international courts and tribunals that have lifted many issues out of the reach of domestic politics has given rise to forms of resistance and struggle which are proving difficult to routinize within international legal and political processes. For the first time in a generation, the backlash to international adjudication has required its advocates to articulate and defend the nature of the political system within which their project of realizing a global rule of law makes sense.

For decades, international lawyers and international institutions were able to present the rule of law as an abstract good that could be formalized and globalized because of the dominance of a particular liberal vision of

[8] See generally Judith N. Shklar, "Political Theory and the Rule of Law," in Stanley Hoffmann, ed., *Political Thought and Political Thinkers* (Chicago: University of Chicago Press, [1987] 1998), pp. 21–37.

[9] Shklar, "Political Theory and the Rule of Law," p. 33.

[10] Shklar, "Political Theory and the Rule of Law," p. 33.

the rule of law as the *telos* of international order. Those who opposed that project were portrayed as betraying a broader set of principles and values to which the rule of law was said to give expression. Today it is becoming more difficult to sustain the claim that the liberal world order is a project that operates outside politics. In order to grasp the work that the appeal to the global rule of law has done in shaping an international order, and the challenges posed to that order by the new politics of the rule of law, it is necessary first to consider how the global rule of law became so effectively equated with one particular liberal variant.

1 The UN Charter and the Thin Conception of the Rule of Law

The project of liberalizing international relations has over the centuries involved a broad set of institutional and conceptual commitments, including enabling free trade, reshaping the form of the absolutist or fiscal-military state, limiting the power of colonial and corporate monopolists, protecting rights, and confining the situations in which violence can be used, by whom, to what ends, and in what manner. Initially, that liberal project was also articulated in a thin conception of the international rule of law, which provided scope for state action while regularizing that action sufficiently to enable the growth of trade and commerce, freedom of movement, and the regularization of the rights and duties of belligerents and neutrals in ways that would enable commerce to continue during conflict. According to an increasingly dominant form of liberal internationalism, the juridicalization and judicialization of international affairs as part of that project was an unquestioned good.

The twin processes of juridification and judicialization have played a central role in the creation of a liberal international order since the nineteenth century. As international law began to take shape as a profession, international lawyers sought to defend international law's character as "law" through a move to developing treaties and codes as instruments to make their discipline more certain and establish its scientific character.[11] Organizations such as the *Institut de Droit International*

[11] Luigo Nuzzo and Miloš Vec, "The Birth of International Law as a Legal Discipline in the 19th Century," in Luigo Nuzzo and Miloš Vec, eds., *Constructing International Law: The Birth of a Discipline* (Frankfurt am Main: Vittorio Klostermann, 2012), pp. xiii–xiv.

promoted legal codification, and treaties began to be approached as potential law-making instruments that could be equated with domestic legislation rather than with private contracts.[12] International lawyers sought to interpret and systemize state practice into a set of claims and rules aimed at ensuring the maintenance of diplomatic relations, shaping the conduct of war, and structuring the acquisition of territory, while ensuring that (mainly European) sovereign states could largely pursue their own ends free from intervention.

The move to juridicalization was also accompanied by a push for the constitution and use of international courts and tribunals to ensure the peaceful settlement of disputes between states. The idea that the existence of courts was fundamental to "the function of law in the international community" was a core tenet of much internationalist thinking.[13] For Hersch Lauterpacht, an eloquent proponent of this approach, it was the Grotian tradition in international law that should be "identified with the progression of international law to a true system of law both in its legal and in its ethical content."[14] That tradition professed that "the totality of the relations between states" was subject to and governed by law.[15] For Lauterpacht, the refusal of states to recognize the compulsory jurisdiction and obligatory competence of courts in disputes between members of international society was a major barrier to the realization of the rule of law.[16] The international rule of law was an "instrument of peace," and the object of peace would be served by the compulsory judicial settlement of all disputes between states.[17] There was no principled reason why states should quarantine even the most sensitive aspects of sovereign decision-making from the purview of international tribunals.

The idea of a "legalist project for world order" was also forcefully sponsored in the early twentieth century by American international lawyers, who were an essential part of the foreign policy establishment and committed to reconciling universal principles with American power and its

[12] Martti Koskenniemi, "International Legislation Today: Limits and Possibilities," *Wisconsin International Law Journal*, 23 (2005), 61–92.

[13] Hersch Lauterpacht, *The Function of Law in the International Community* introd. Martti Koskenniemi (Oxford: Oxford University Press, [1933] 2011), p. 440.

[14] Hersch Lauterpacht, "The Grotian Tradition in International Law," *British Yearbook of International Law*, 23 (1946), 19.

[15] Lauterpacht, "The Grotian Tradition in International Law," 19.

[16] Lauterpacht, *The Function of Law in the International Community*, p. 440.

[17] Lauterpacht, *The Function of Law in the International Community*, p. 406.

projection into the region and later the globe.[18] Underpinning their project was the claim that a just world could be achieved under law, and that there was a moral imperative to pursue a global rule of law in order to structure world order, coordinate and secure interests, settle disputes in the present, and prevent conflicts in the future. These goals could be realized through the codification of legal rules, and the creation of courts and tribunals that would enable disputes to be settled authoritatively through arbitration by neutral experts.

The creation of the United Nations seemed to signal a step in that direction. The UN Charter expressed the commitment of members states to the principles of sovereign equality, nonuse of force, peaceful settlement of disputes, friendly relations, and peaceful coexistence, understood to form the minimalist foundation of the promotion of the rule of law amongst nations. In joining the UN, states gave up their right unilaterally to resort to force other than in self-defense, and pledged to use force only in the name of the international community. The principle of collective security meant not that force would be abolished, but that it would be "collectivized" or "denationalized."[19] International lawyers also advocated for the development of legislative machinery that would enable international law-making to become more like domestic law-making, understood to be the result of a rational and technical process rather than simply an outcome of political bargaining. The establishment of the International Law Commission (ILC) in 1947, tasked with the codification and progressive development of international law, was one result of that desire for a more scientific approach to international law-making.

In addition, while states still did not agree to compulsory jurisdiction or to submit all disputes to adjudication, the creation of the International Court of Justice (ICJ) to succeed the Permanent International Court of Justice and its inclusion in Article 92 of the Charter as "the principal judicial organ of the UN" was seen as significant.[20] The ICJ structure of fifteen full-time judges elected for nine-year terms, augmented by *ad hoc* judges where states in contentious proceedings had no judge of their nationality on the court, was thought to ensure the judicial independence

[18] Benjamin Allen Coates, *Legalist Empire: International Law and American Foreign Relations in the Early Twentieth Century* (Oxford: Oxford University Press, 2016), p. 3.

[19] Arnold D. McNair, "Collective Security," *British Yearbook of International Law*, 17 (1936), 161.

[20] Beaulac, "The Rule of Law in International Law Today," p. 212.

and impartiality of judges. Idealist international lawyers have argued that the "very existence" of such a court "must tend to be a factor of importance in maintaining the rule of law,"[21] and that as a result of its successful operation, "nobody nowadays would doubt that the conduct of states is ruled by law, that is to say by legal norms providing for certainty, predictability and stability."[22]

Yet where to draw the line between respect for sovereign equality and intervention to secure international order has never been straightforward. One example of that dilemma can be seen in debates over the meaning of the nonintervention principle that took place during the six-year negotiation of the 1970 *Declaration on Principles of International Law concerning Friendly Relations and Cooperation among States in accordance with the Charter of the United Nations* (Friendly Relations Declaration).[23] Throughout the early decades after the creation of the United Nations, states debated the status and scope of the nonintervention principle in the new international order. For the large number of postcolonial states that had joined the UN in the early 1960s, the principle of nonintervention meant that powerful states should be prevented from installing compliant leaders in newly independent states or coercing those states into adopting particular policies. At the same time, they considered that the principle should not prevent external support for anticolonial revolutionary movements. The USSR and its allies argued in favor of a strong norm against intervention between the Soviet and Western blocs, while at the same time arguing that intervention by the USSR to maintain the correct approach to socialism in Soviet bloc states did not violate the principle. Western states tried to limit the scope of the nonintervention principle still further, arguing that in an interdependent world, while the principle of sovereign equality was foundational, it was both inevitable and desirable that states be concerned with the actions and policies of other states, and try to influence them. The outcome of those negotiations was that the Friendly Relations Declaration did recognize the principle of nonintervention in general terms. Yet even that vague commitment was steadily eroded in the

21 Hersch Lauterpacht, *The Development of International Law by the International Court* (London: Stevens and Sons, 1958), p. 3.

22 Beaulac, "The Rule of Law in International Law Today," p. 221.

23 Edward McWhinney, "The 'New' Countries and the 'New' International Law: The United Nations' Special Conference on Friendly Relations and Co-operation among States," *American Journal of International Law*, 60 (1966), 1–33.

intervening decades, as more expansionist forms of international regulation began to be consolidated after the Cold War.

2 The Liberal Rule of Law and the End of History

With the end of the Cold War, Western states and their international lawyers began to advocate for a more substantive conception of what it meant to globalize the rule of law. Under that conception, it was argued that certain core principles of human rights, investment protection, and trade liberalization should be treated as foundational or constitutional. Liberal states had the right, or indeed the duty, to defend human rights and liberal values through military intervention when they deemed this necessary. As then British Prime Minister Tony Blair explained when justifying his country's support for the NATO bombing of Belgrade without Security Council authorization in 1999, the resort to force in such situations was motivated by a "subtle blend of mutual self interest and moral purpose in defending the values we cherish ... If we can establish and spread the values of liberty, the rule of law, human rights and an open society then that is in our national interests too."[24] Globalizing the rule of law was reconceived as a project aimed at protecting the economic liberty and property rights of individuals, preventing impunity, and punishing criminals, all directed to enhancing "the freedom of individual actors" through "stabilizing social relationships" and "creating a predictable environment in which actors can make meaningful choices."[25]

The idea that international law should play a role in protecting economic liberty and constraining the capacity of states to engage in forms of market intervention had long been mooted by a small but determined group of lawyers, liberal economists, and philosophers who were involved in think tanks including the Mont Pèlerin Society and the academic networks associated with Freiburg University, the London School of Economics and Political Science, and the Chicago School of Economics. Figures such as Wilhelm Röpke, Lionel Robbins, and Friedrich Hayek had developed

[24] Tony Blair, "Doctrine of the International Community," Speech given to the Economic Club of Chicago, Chicago, April 22, 1999.

[25] Mattias Kumm, "International Law in National Courts: The International Rule of Law and the Limits of the Internationalist Model," *Virginia Journal of International Law*, 44 (2003), 25–26.

proposals for constraining collectivism and developing the foundations of a new liberalism, in part through approaching the question of how to create a competitive market economy as one of international order.[26] For these liberal thinkers, liberalism and democracy were not necessarily compatible. Democratic states too easily become the prey of organized special interests. Threats to liberty were posed not only by communism and fascism, but also by the proposed post-war planned economies of the United Kingdom, the United States, and France, and of newly independent states.[27] Planning necessarily involved the "deliberate discrimination between particular needs of different people" and thus "the decline of the Rule of Law."[28] The form of transnational integration promoted after World War II offered one means through which liberal internationalists could address the "disintegration" of the international liberal order, by removing certain economic issues from deliberation or determination by domestic parliaments or legislatures.[29] The "solution" for "the problem of international order" depended upon institutionalizing "the genuinely liberal principle of the widest possible separation of the two spheres of government and economy, of sovereignty and economic exploitation, of Imperium and Dominium."[30] The "depoliticisation" of the economic sphere would reduce to a minimum the "economic significance of the coexistence of sovereign states."[31]

With the ending of the Cold War, that vision of the global rule of law began to be realized. Perhaps the most effective, and as a result the most contested, mechanism through which that took place was the creation of a transnational regime of investment protection. Home states had sought

[26] For the approach to economic ordering through international integration developed by Hayek, Röpke, and Robbins, and the ways it was furthered through the EU and the GATT/WTO, see Anne Orford, "Europe Reconstructed," *Modern Law Review*, 75 (2012), 275–286; idem, "Food Security, Free Trade, and the Battle for the State," *Journal of International Law and International Relations*, 11 (2015), 1–67; idem, "Theorizing Free Trade," in Anne Orford and Florian Hoffmann, eds., *The Oxford Handbook of the Theory of International Law* (Oxford: Oxford University Press, 2016), p. 701–737.

[27] Friedrich A. Hayek, *The Road to Serfdom* (Chicago: University of Chicago Press, [1944] 2007).

[28] Hayek, *The Road to Serfdom*, p. 82.

[29] Friedrich A. Hayek, "The Economic Conditions of Interstate Federalism," in idem, *Individualism and Economic Order* (Chicago: University of Chicago Press, [1939] 1948), p. 258.

[30] Wilhelm Röpke, "Economic Order and International Law," *Recueil des Cours*, 86 (1954), 203, at 223–224 (emphasis omitted).

[31] Röpke, "Economic Order and International Law," 224.

to internationalize the protection of foreign investment and justify the lawfulness of actions to protect private rights since the nineteenth century.[32] The creation of mixed commissions or tribunals to settle disputes concerning the property rights of aliens was not a new phenomenon,[33] and precedents also existed for granting standing to private investors to make claims before such tribunals. However, historically those international claims institutions had been the "stepchildren of war and rebellion," and were typically constituted by victorious states or aggrieved neutrals seeking compensation for their nationals.[34] States only consented to private actors bringing such claims in relation to "past, strictly circumscribed events in the aftermath of war or revolution,"[35] such as the capture, confiscation, or destruction of property, or the inability to collect debts during conflict. International claims practice was thus a "retributive instrument of international power politics,"[36] while also championed by the peace movement as a means of preventing further conflict.[37]

With decolonization, foreign investors and their home states perceived a threat to the security and profitability of investments in newly independent states, and sought to introduce greater protections for investments and private property. A key procedural step was the development by the World Bank of a form of international machinery to address disputes between states and investors. The resulting International Convention on the Settlement of Investment Disputes between States and Nationals of Other States (ICSID Convention) 1966 established a center for facilitating

[32] See generally Kate Miles, *The Origins of International Investment Law: Empire, Environment and the Safeguarding of Capital* (Cambridge: Cambridge University Press, 2013).

[33] Kathryn Greenman, "Aliens in Latin America: Intervention, Arbitration and State Responsibility for Rebels," *Leiden Journal of International Law*, 31 (2018), 617–639.

[34] David J. Bederman, "The United Nations Compensation Commission and the Tradition of International Claims Settlement," *New York University Journal of International Law and Politics*, 27 (1994), 3.

[35] Joost Paulweyn, "Rational Design or Accidental Evolution? The Emergence of International Investment Law," in Zachary Douglas, Joost Pauwelyn, and Jorge E. Viñuales, eds., *The Foundations of International Investment Law: Bringing Theory into Practice* (Oxford: Oxford University Press, 2014), p. 36.

[36] Bederman, "The United Nations Compensation Commission," 6.

[37] Heather L. Bray, "Understanding Change: Evolution from International Claims Commissions to Investment Treaty Arbitration," in Stephan W. Schill, Christian J. Tams, and Rainer Hofmann, eds., *International Investment Law and History* (Cheltenham: Edward Elgar, 2018), p. 119.

the settlement of disputes. Its proponents stressed that its operation would be founded upon state consent, that ICSID tribunals would only have jurisdiction over disputes that parties specifically agreed to submit for arbitration, and that states could carve out disputes they did not want to submit to ICSID.[38] However, what had seemed like a purely procedural commitment was later interpreted to provide grounds for jurisdiction.[39] In addition, as states entered into a growing number of bilateral investment treaties (BITs), broad interpretations of substantive provisions addressing direct or indirect "expropriation" served to protect investors against the effects on profits of new tax measures or routine government regulation aimed at protecting public health or the environment. Whereas in earlier eras international claims processes had been directed towards loss suffered during conflict, in the era of BITs the focus of arbitral scrutiny became the everyday conduct of government regulation and its impacts on the profits of foreign investors.[40] The result has been to disembed the economic relations of host states and foreign investors from the political situation in which investments are made, and to establish international arbitration as the principal mode of resolving investment disputes.

The creation of a transnational regime for investment protection was consolidated and expanded during the 1990s with the negotiation of many new BITs and other broad-reaching agreements such as the Energy Charter Treaty and the North American Free Trade Agreement (NAFTA). The number of investment treaties increased from approximately 500 in 1990 to 3,322 by the end of 2017 (of which 2,946 were BITs and 376 were treaties containing investment provisions).[41] A total of 855 known investor-state claims had been brought by the end of 2017, of which the majority were brought against "developing countries" or "transitional economies," and the majority brought by developed country investors (with 257 claimants from the United States and the Netherlands alone).[42] Arbitrators are

[38] Antonio R. Parra, *The History of ICSID* (Oxford: Oxford University Press, 2012), p. 25.

[39] In the "revolutionary" award of *AAPL* v. *Sri Lanka*, the tribunal found that the article of the UK–Sri Lanka BIT consenting to submit investment disputes to ICSID gave rights to investors to bring direct claims of treaty breach against Sri Lanka even in the absence of a contract between the investor and the government: *AAPL* v. *Sri Lanka*, ICSID/ARB/87/3 (1990). For the characterization of that award as revolutionary, see Paulweyn, "Rational Design or Accidental Evolution?" p. 31.

[40] Bray, "Understanding Change," pp. 104, 118.

[41] UNCTAD, *World Investment Report 2018* (Geneva: United Nations, 2018), p. 88.

[42] UNCTAD, *World Investment Report 2018*, p. 91.

appointed on a case-by-case basis, so that they do not have the security of tenure that is typically considered necessary to ensure independence and impartiality. Thirteen repeat arbitrators have been appointed to more than thirty tribunals each, of whom all but one were citizens of European or North American countries.[43] In cases decided in favor of the investor, the average amount claimed was US$1.3 billion and the average amount awarded was US$504 million.[44]

In addition, this period saw the creation of various other new international courts and tribunals as part of specialized regimes, including international criminal courts, regional economic courts, and regional human rights courts. The 1990s was the most fertile period for this process of judicialization. The creation in 1996 of the World Trade Organization with its compulsory dispute settlement system was heralded as replacing the ethos of diplomats with the rule of law.[45] The emergence of international criminal tribunals was welcomed as signaling the arrival of "a new world order based on the rule of international law," with the highpoint being the adoption in 1998 of the Rome Statute establishing the international criminal court.[46] The UN Convention on the Law of the Sea (UNCLOS) entered into force in 1994, and the International Tribunal for the Law of the Sea (ITLOS) began to operate in 1997, with commentators hailing the creation of a mandatory dispute settlement mechanism under UNCLOS as "one of the most significant developments in dispute settlement in international law, even as important as the entry into force of the United Nations Charter."[47] Regional human rights courts in Europe and Latin America became far more active and influential.

The end result was a form of uneven judicialization, with "a new paradigm of routinised litigation and judicial governance" developing alongside "the traditional paradigm of episodic international (inter-state)

[43] UNCTAD, *World Investment Report 2018*, p. 95.

[44] UNCTAD, *World Investment Report 2018*, p. 95.

[45] J. H. H. Weiler, "The Rule of Lawyers and the Ethos of Diplomats: Reflections on the Internal and External Legitimacy of WTO Dispute Settlement," *Journal of World Trade*, 35 (2001), 191–207.

[46] Antonio Cassese, "On the Current Trends Towards Criminal Prosecution and Punishment of Breaches of International Humanitarian Law," *European Journal of International Law*, 9 (1998), 8.

[47] Natalie Klein, *Dispute Settlement in the UN Convention on the Law of the Sea* (Cambridge: Cambridge University Press, 2009), p. 2.

dispute settlement by tribunals."[48] While in some areas, such as international trade and investment, litigation became almost routine, in other areas such as most military and intelligence activities, counterterrorism, migration, taxation, or most environmental policy, disputes rarely reached an international court or tribunal. The number of states recognizing the compulsory jurisdiction of the ICJ has remained steady at around one-third of UN member states. The United Kingdom is the only permanent member of the Security Council to have consistently consented to the ICJ's compulsory jurisdiction. The old idea that ICJ judges are impartial and independent was placed under pressure by the new practice of judges accepting appointment as arbitrators in investor-state disputes on an ad hoc basis during their ICJ terms.[49] In summary, the vision of the rule of law and the issues dealt with under that expanded regime of international adjudication were 'largely those of a global legal order dominated by liberal interests'.[50]

By the end of the 1990s, judicialization had been turned from an ambition into an accomplishment, 'helping to assuage Diceyan doubts' about the relevance of the rule of law to international law.[51] For some, the density, activity, and influence of the network of courts and tribunals was a major sign of progress. Sovereignty, including popular sovereignty, increasingly began to seem a dirty word. Cosmopolitan internationalists agreed that more and more of what had fleetingly been matters for decision by domestic parliaments must not be trusted to those bodies, now recast as sites of regulatory capture, special interests, or individuals gaming the system. Indeed, for the most committed of liberal internationalists, to the extent that this vision failed to deliver on the rule of law, it was because it did not go far enough. As an example, for scholars who saw the WTO as a vehicle for realizing the constitution of liberty, such as Ernst-Ulrich Petersmann or Anne Peters, the problem posed for the rule of law by WTO dispute settlement was the *lack* of direct access it made available to

[48] Benedict Kingsbury, "International Courts: Uneven Judicialisation in Global Order," in James Crawford and Martti Koskenniemi, eds., *The Cambridge Companion to International Law* (Cambridge: Cambridge University Press, 2012), p. 210.

[49] Nathalie Bernasconi-Osterwalder and Martin Dietrich Brauch, "Is 'Moonlighting' a Problem? The Role of ICJ Judges in ISDS," International Institute for Sustainable Development, November 2017. In 2018, the President of the ICJ announced that ICJ judges would no longer participate in investor–State arbitration.

[50] Kingsbury, "International Courts," p. 211.

[51] Kingsbury, "International Courts," p. 223.

business interests. The reliance of "business actors" on governments to initiate dispute settlement under the WTO was "neglectful of the rule of law," as it led to "unequal treatment of business actors."[52] Enabling "direct access of private parties would liberate business actors from the tutelage of their governments."[53] From that perspective, more remained to be done to "transform private interests into public interests by empowering citizens to act as agents of justice for the common good."[54] The true destiny of international law was "a world of liberal states."[55]

3 Plural Visions of the Global Rule of Law

The sense that liberal internationalism represented the end of history dominated the field of international law for the first decade after the Cold War. Much of the discipline and the field was organized around ideas about progress (or temporary barriers to progress) toward a rules-based international order. International law may have been a discipline organized around other people's crises, but international law itself was on the right side of history. Today a sense of history has reentered the field, both due to an external and an internal sense of rupture. The external sense resulted in part from the interrelated climate, refugee, financial, security, and food crises of the early twenty-first century, which gave a new urgency to questions about the direction of projects of international law and order. At the same time, an internal sense of rupture was caused by the challenges to and withdrawals from existing international regimes and treaties. The shifts signaled by the rise of China, the resurgence of nationalism and authoritarian populism in Europe and the United States, the accompanying backlash against the modes of regional and international integration associated with NAFTA, the EU, and the WTO, and the heated debates

[52] Anne Peters, "Membership in the Global Constitutional Community," in Jan Klabbers, Anne Peters, and Geir Ulfstein, *The Constitutionalization of International Law* (Oxford: Oxford University Press, 2009), p. 253.

[53] Peters, "Membership in the Global Constitutional Community," p. 253.

[54] Ernst-Ulrich Petersmann, "The Establishment of a GATT Office of Legal Affairs and the Limits of 'Public Reason' in the GATT/WTO dispute settlement system," in Gabrielle Marceau, ed., *A History of Law and Lawyers in the GATT/WTO: The Development of the Rule of Law in the Multilateral Trading System* (Cambridge: Cambridge University Press, 2015), pp. 183–184.

[55] Anne-Marie Slaughter, "International Law in a World of Liberal States," *European Journal of International Law*, 6 (1995), 503–538.

that accompanied attempts to negotiate the ambitious Trans-Pacific Partnership (TPP) and the Transatlantic Trade and Investment Partnership (TTIP) agreements served as reminders of the fragile nature of the consensus around dominant conceptions of the global rule of law as a public good.

In hindsight, it now appears that the decade of the 1990s was the high point for the project of liberal legalist international ordering. The relentless forward movement of that story first began to show some signs of faltering in the early twenty-first century, with the violent attacks on the United States of September 11, 2001, and the use of force in the global war on terror carried out in response. In particular, the invasion of Iraq by the US and its allies without Security Council authorization was perceived by some international lawyers as an attack on the consensual structure of the international order, with its basis in the principles of sovereign equality, nonintervention, and the prohibition on unilateral resort to force except in self-defense. Concern with resort to force absent Security Council authorization had already emerged in debates over the legitimacy of the NATO actions in Kosovo during 1999, as was made clear in collective statements issued by the Non-Aligned Movement, the Rio Group, and the Commonwealth of Independent States.[56]

During the lead-up to and in the aftermath of the US invasion of Iraq, a new split emerged over the question of unilateral resort to force, this time between Europe and the United States. The US was portrayed, particularly by European commentators, as a rogue hegemon whose actions threatened to undermine the rule of law in international affairs. As an example, Philippe Sands opened his influential critique of US conduct of the war on terror in *Lawless World* with the question: "How could it be that a country as profoundly attached to the rule of law and principles of constitutionality as the United States could have so little regard for international law?"[57] "Formalist" or "restrictive" legal scholars argued that the

[56] Movement of Non-Aligned Countries, Statement, Geneva, April 9, 1999; Declaration Adopted by the Inter-Parliamentary Assembly of States Members of the Commonwealth of Independent States, April 3, 1999, UN Doc. A/53/920-S/1999/461, Annex II, April 22, 1999, reprinted in Heike Krieger, ed., *The Kosovo Conflict and International Law: An Analytical Documentation 1974–1999* (Cambridge: Cambridge University Press, 2001), pp. 496–497.

[57] Philippe Sands, *Lawless World: Making and Breaking Global Rules* (New York: Viking, 2006), p. xv.

UN Charter established a "law against war."[58] The "right of a state to be free from attack" was seen as central to the global rule of law.[59] The US attempt to justify recourse to force as a form of international police action aimed at risk prevention signaled a movement "toward a fundamentally different kind of legal order."[60]

In contrast, American commentators framed US resort to force as itself a defense of the rule of law. According to that US position, depriving the international community of a "reasoned basis for using force" through a narrow reading of the Charter rules "threatens Charter interests and values, rather than supporting and advancing them."[61] The new era of political violence ushered in by September 11 required interpretations of the law that took the new context into account. US lawyers "rejected the proposition that the Charter is a value-free document" that "lends itself to a mechanical reading."[62] Instead, they argued that Charter provisions relating to the use of force "must be interpreted and applied in particular context."[63]

In addition, American commentators charged Europeans with failing to understand that the survival of the liberal international order depended upon the existence of a powerful state or states willing to assume the responsibility for its defense. That position was famously expressed by Robert Kagan,[64] whose essay on that theme was widely circulated and influential amongst Bush administration officials in the build-up to the invasion of Iraq.[65] According to Kagan, while Europe had entered

[58] Michael Bothe, "Terrorism and the Legality of Pre-emptive Force," *European Journal of International Law*, 14 (2003), 227–240; Olivier Corten, "The Controversies Over the Customary Prohibition on the Use of Force: A Methodological Debate," *European Journal of International Law*, 16 (2006), 802–833; Olivier Corten, *Le droit contre la guerre: l'interdiction du recours à la force en droit international contemporain* (Paris: Pedone, 2008); Jörg Kammerhofer, "Introduction: The Future of Restrictive Scholarship on the Use of Force," *Leiden Journal of International Law*, 29 (2016), 13–18.

[59] Georg Nolte, "Preventive Use of Force and Preventive Killings: Moves into a Different Legal Order," *Theoretical Inquiries in Law*, 5 (2004), 118.

[60] Nolte, "Preventive Use of Force and Preventive Killings." 113.

[61] Abraham Sofaer, "On the Necessity of Pre-Emption," *European Journal of International Law*, 14 (2003), 209–226.

[62] Sofaer, "On the Necessity of Pre-Emption," 212–213.

[63] Sofaer, "On the Necessity of Pre-Emption," 213.

[64] See Robert Kagan, *Paradise and Power: America and Europe in the New World Order* (London: Atlantic, 2003), which is an extended version of an article that first appeared in *Policy Review* in 2002.

[65] Jack L. Goldsmith, *The Terror Presidency: Law and Judgment Inside the Bush Administration* (New York: W.W. Norton, 2007), pp. 126–127.

a "post-historical paradise of peace and relative prosperity," the United States remained "mired in history," destined to operate in a Hobbesian world "where international laws and rules are unreliable, and where true security and the defense and promotion of a liberal order still depend on the possession and use of military might."[66] It was the effective exercise of American power "according to the rules of the old Hobbesian order" that had "made it possible for the Europeans to believe that power was no longer important."[67]

The idea that the international order is a Hobbesian state of nature, in which all actors seek to take advantage of each other at all times, has been at the heart of the rational choice and game theory approaches to security that have dominated elite US institutions for decades. Self-defense is the foundational principle for Hobbes, as it is for game theorists. Yet while Hobbes posits the agreement to create a commonwealth as the way in which self-preservation can be realized, for game theorists "'war' is the strictly dominant strategy" for every individual caught in the Hobbesian "prisoner's dilemma."[68] The state of nature cannot be sustained by the agreement to create a commonwealth, because actors will always be ready to defect from that agreement and choose war over peace. Thus, rather than realize self-preservation through mutual recognition and respect, as in the classical liberal posture, game theory assumes that self-preservation depends upon "credibly sustaining deterrent threats."[69] The arguments made by lawyers justifying the conduct of the war on terror since 2003 reveal just such a focus on expansive interpretations of the actions necessary to achieve individual and collective self-defense.[70] Those arguments signal the emergence of a trend away from a classically liberal, contractual model of international law-making and a respect for the autonomy of

[66] Kagan, *Paradise and Power*, p. 3. [67] Kagan, *Paradise and Power*, p. 73.

[68] See Shaun P. Hargreaves-Heap and Yanis Varoufakis, *Game Theory: A Critical Introduction*, 2nd ed. (London: Routledge, 2004), p. 174.

[69] S. M. Amadae, *Prisoners of Reason: Game Theory and Neoliberal Political Economy* (Cambridge: Cambridge University Press, 2015), p. 21.

[70] For discussions of the way in which what were initially seen as radical interpretations of individual and collective self-defense have increasingly gained ground since 2003, see Jack Goldsmith, "The Contributions of the Obama Administration to the Practice and Theory of International Law," *Harvard International Law Journal*, 57 (2016), 455–473; Victor Kattan, "Furthering the 'War on Terrorism' through International Law: How the United States and the United Kingdom Resurrected the Bush Doctrine on Using Preventive Military Force to Combat Terrorism," *Journal on the Use of Force and International Law*, 5 (2018), 97–144.

states, to a focus on effectiveness (including through unilateral action where necessary) in aligning international law with realizing the self-preservation and preference satisfaction of rational actors.[71]

Rather than see the stakes of those debates in terms of power politics versus the rule of law, the shift can better be understood as one politics of the rule of law challenging another politics of the rule of law. In the place of an older liberal rule of law framework that places state consent and sovereign equality at its heart, US scholars have set out a vision of the rule of law informed by rational choice and game theory approaches. The rule of law according to this neoliberal resolution of the freedom/security problematic depends upon the introduction of a state or state-like power that enforces the law by threatening sanctions on members of the polity (whether individuals or states) who will all "prefer to make an exception for themselves rather than voluntarily participate in upholding the social contract."[72]

A second front in the battle over which politics should inform the global rule of law has concerned the ambitious forms of property protection and economic integration that took shape under the network of trade agreements, investment agreements, and regional economic integration regimes. Throughout the twentieth century, the status and content of norms governing foreign investment had been fiercely contested, for example through the attempt by newly independent states to develop a systematic alternative to neoliberal globalization in the form of the New International Economic Order (NIEO).[73] The success of the judicialization project during the 1990s generated further resistance and contestation.

Criticisms were focused in part on the expansion of international adjudication to cover many areas formerly within the scope of domestic decision-making.[74] Critics expressed concern that as ever-broader

71 Nico Krisch, "The Decay of Consent: International Law in an Age of Global Public Goods," *American Journal of International Law*, 108 (2014), 1–40.

72 Amadae, *Prisoners of Reason*, p. 173.

73 For discussions of the legal aspects of the NIEO, see Mohammed Bedjaoui, *Towards a New International Economic Order* (New York: Holmes and Meier, 1979); Antony Anghie, "Legal Aspects of the New International Economic Order," *Humanity*, 6 (2015), 145–158.

74 Stephen Gill and A. Claire Cutler, eds., *New Constitutionalism and World Order* (Cambridge: Cambridge University Press, 2014); M. Sornarajah, *Resistance and Change in the International Law on Foreign Investment* (Cambridge: Cambridge University Press, 2015).

aspects of social and political life were recast as subject to economic logic, ever-broader areas of social and political decision-making were removed from democratic control.[75] In particular, expansive constraints and costs were placed on states seeking to implement environmental, labor, or health and safety measures, while corporate actors were empowered to challenge government decision-making in their role as foreign investors.[76] From that perspective, the lack of political institutions to provide checks and balances to international arbitrators,[77] the creation of a transnational guild of highly paid lawyers who moved between positions as advocates, ad hoc arbitrators, academic commentators, corporate counsel, and ICJ judges,[78] the secrecy of arbitral processes, and the substantive outcomes privileging property rights over human rights, environmental protection, public health, and equality, all signaled a shift away from, rather towards, a substantive commitment to the rule of law. The subject matter of investment disputes was intensely political, yet those arbitral regimes were not embedded within a broader set of political institutions.[79] Instead, the rule of international arbitrators was legitimized through the claim that judicial reason is exercised in service to apolitical external standards developed by transnational experts.[80] In the fields of international trade and investment law, the process of developing and interpreting the standards seen as necessary to secure the legal foundations of a capitalist economy was a "joint enterprise," carried out "by economists, international lawyers, and rational-choice political scientists" along with corporate and financial

[75] Orford, "Europe Reconstructed"; idem, "Theorizing Free Trade."

[76] Pia Eberhardt and Cecilia Olivet, *Profiting from Injustice: How Law Firms, Arbitrators and Financiers are Fuelling an Investment Arbitration Boom* (Amsterdam: Corporate Europe Observatory and the Transnational Institute, 2012).

[77] Nicolás M. Perrone, "The Governance of Foreign Investment at a Crossroad: Is an Overlapping Consensus the Way Forward," *Global Jurist*, 15 (2015), 1–28.

[78] Yves Dezalay and Bryant G. Garth, *Dealing in Virtue: International Commercial Arbitration and the Construction of a Transnational Legal Order* (Chicago: University of Chicago Press, 1996); Didier Bigo, "Sociology of Transnational Guilds," *International Political Sociology*, 10 (2016), 398–416; Bernasconi-Osterwalder and Brauch, "Is 'Moonlighting' a Problem?"

[79] Moritz Renner, "The Dialectics of Transnational Economic Constitutionalism," in Christian Joerges and Josef Falke, eds., *Karl Polanyi, Globalisation and the Potential of Law in Transnational Markets* (Oxford: Hart, 2011), 419–433.

[80] On this strategy and its limitations, see David Singh Grewal and Jedediah Purdy, "The Original Theory of Constitutionalism," *Yale Law Journal*, 127 (2018), 702–703.

stakeholders.[81] The legitimacy of the standards developed in that jurisprudence depended less on the role of state or democratic consent to their formulation and adoption, and more on claims to efficiency and problem-solving.[82] The resulting decisions regarding private property protection were couched in terms of technical correctness yet involved fundamental normative questions about the very meaning of property and how it was to be measured against other values.[83]

Finally, the sense that an interventionist liberal rule of law represented the end of history resulted in part from the emergence of the United States as the sole superpower at the end of the Cold War. That unipolar moment appears to have been relatively short-lived, given Russia's ambitions to regain world power status as suggested by its actions in Ukraine and Syria, and the growing assertiveness of China on the global stage. The approach to international order that Russia and China have sought to consolidate has also been expressed in legal terms. For example, in 2016 Russia and China jointly issued a declaration on the promotion of international law.[84] That declaration positioned Russia and China as the champions of the approach to the rule of law set out in the UN Charter and the Friendly Relations Declaration. In particular, the declaration stressed the centrality of the principle of sovereign equality to international stability, insisted on the need for all dispute settlement means and mechanisms to be based on consent, and condemned any interference by States in the internal affairs of other States. The Russian-Chinese Declaration made clear their disagreement with Western powers over "foundational constitutional principles of international law,"[85] and more generally over the vision of the rule of law that should underpin the future of international order.

[81] Anne van Aaken, "Rational Choice Theory," in Anthony Carty, ed., *Oxford Bibliographies Online: International Law* (Oxford: Oxford University Press, 2012). For a critical discussion, see Anne Orford, "Theorizing Free Trade."

[82] Andrew T. Guzman, "Against Consent," *Virginia Journal of International Law*, 52 (2012), 747–790; Laurence R. Helfer, "Nonconsensual International Lawmaking," *University of Illinois Law Review*, (2008), 71–126; Krisch, "The Decay of Consent."

[83] Perrone, "The Governance of Foreign Investment at a Crossroad," 17.

[84] Declaration of the Russian Federation and the People's Republic of China on the Promotion of International Law, Ministry of Foreign Affairs of the Russian Federation, June 25, 2016, available at www.mid.ru/en/foreign_policy/news/-/asset_publisher/cKNonkJE02Bw/content/id/2331698.

[85] Lauri Mälksoo, "Russia and China Challenge the Western Hegemony in the Interpretation of International Law," *EJIL: Talk!*, July 15, 2016.

All these tendencies came to a head in the second decade of the twenty-first century. Surprisingly rapidly, the complex architecture of international obligations and adjudication overseen by the transnational arbitrator class began to unravel. The "backlash" against the constitution of a global rule of law through international adjudication has been particularly marked in the areas of trade and investment law. In the field of investment law, both the procedural ICSID Convention and the substantive BITs and Energy Charter Treaty have been challenged. Bolivia, Ecuador, and Venezuela have denounced the ICSID Convention, while numerous states have withdrawn from or announced their intention to terminate some or all of their BITs, including Austria, Bolivia, the Czech Republic, Ecuador, India, Indonesia, Ireland, Italy, Poland, Russia, South Africa, and Venezuela. In the area of economic integration, the United States initiated a renegotiation of NAFTA, and the United Kingdom signaled its withdrawal from the European Union. In addition, the US "unsigned" the Trans-Pacific Partnership, and Russia withdrew from provisional application of the Energy Charter Treaty. According to UNCTAD, the investment treaty regime has "reached a turning point," with only eighteen new investment treaties concluded in 2017, the lowest number since 1983. Perhaps more significantly, for the first time the number of effective investment treaty terminations was higher than the number of new treaties concluded.[86]

That backlash against the process and substance of international adjudication has extended beyond economic matters. In the field of international criminal law, Burundi and the Philippines have withdrawn from the ICC and numerous African states have threatened to withdraw, Russia and the United States have withdrawn their signatures from the Rome Statute, and the African Union has adopted a coordinated "Withdrawal Strategy," arguing that the court had become a political instrument targeting Africans.[87] States in Europe and Latin America have argued that regional human rights courts have engaged in jurisdictional overreach. Finally, China has systematically refused to recognize the authority of ITLOS to hear the *South China Sea Arbitration* brought by the Philippines under UNCLOS. Chinese officials and legal scholars have consistently argued that the Tribunal's claim to jurisdiction ran "counter to the basic requirements

[86] UNCTAD, *World Investment Report 2018*, p. 88.

[87] African Union Assembly, Decision on the International Criminal Court, AU Doc. Assembly/AU/Dec.622 (XXVIII) January 30–31, 2017).

of the international rule of law" by infringing the right of China to choose the means by which it would peacefully settle disputes.[88]

In response to these challenges, liberal internationalism revealed itself as a politics. International lawyers have responded strongly to the current moment of withdrawal and "backlash." Many have sought to treat the decision to critique or withdraw from such regimes in the name of sovereignty as pathological, in contrast to the decision to join such regimes which is seen as a legitimate exercise of sovereignty.[89] Investment lawyers have rejected arguments that investment agreements interfere with the freedom of action of democratically elected governments, arguing instead that "the conclusion of a treaty is itself an exercise of sovereignty," and that investment protection treaties simply oblige states "to abide by the rule of law."[90] International lawyers have explained that "exiting" such agreements is not in fact as straightforward as it might appear.[91]

Indeed, for Harold Koh that is precisely the virtue of the "Kantian postwar system."[92] Writing in the aftermath of the election of US President Donald Trump, Koh argued that the liberal international order constrains governments (including US administrations with different policy agendas) that do not share the liberal internationalist view of where national interest lies. The United States is able to leverage international law with "other tools" such as "military force," "development," or "international institutions" to achieve foreign policy outcomes that could not have been achieved without "the legitimacy that international law bestows."[93] Global governance regimes also allow liberal internationalists to use international law against any "wilful president arriving at the White House with a self-proclaimed radical agenda to change how America engages the world."[94] A new president is faced with international legal obligations

[88] Chinese Society of International Law, "The South China Sea Arbitration Awards: A Critical Study," *Chinese Journal of International Law*, 17 (2018), 218.

[89] James Crawford, "The Current Political Discourse Concerning International Law," *Modern Law Review*, 81 (2018), 1–22.

[90] Charles N. Brower and Sadie Blanchard, "From 'Dealing in Virtue' to 'Profiting from Injustice': The Case Against Re-Statification of Investment Dispute Settlement," *Transnational Dispute Management*, 4 (2013), available at https://www.transnational-dispute-management.com.

[91] Crawford, "The Current Political Discourse Concerning International Law."

[92] Harold Hongju Koh, "The Trump Administration and International Law," *Washburn Law Journal*, 56 (2017), 415, 467.

[93] Koh, "The Trump Administration and International Law," 418.

[94] Koh, "The Trump Administration and International Law," 419.

that create "a persistent default path to compliance with pre-existing norms." Exiting multilateral regimes will be difficult, and if attempted, "will be challenged by transnational actors committed to the default agenda."[95] As a result, governments or democratic majorities that want to defeat the "default agenda" will have to ask themselves "how critical, really, are these policy changes and institutional exits?"[96] During the period when liberal internationalism was unchallenged, Koh had described his vision of "transnational legal process" as if it "operated automatically, organically, as a natural result of transnational interactions."[97] Faced with governments seeking to disrupt the liberal international order, he presented it as a "counter-strategy."[98] As a result, it is much easier to understand the politics of the liberal rule of law project.

The antibacklash literature has tended to treat all existing institutional arrangements collectively as part of progress toward the global rule of law. Critique or challenge of any one regime or institution is presented as an attack on this overall project. Isabel Hull, for example, has urged her readers to accept "that law matters and that international cooperation is not a utopia, but a functioning reality."[99] That "truth" has been difficult to hear above "the din produced by bad actors, like Putin and Trump, and by criticism of the neoliberal order from the left and the populist right, which obscures the positive effects of internationalism." Hull charges that while everyone benefits from international law and international institutions, "we have in recent decades neglected to explain or defend" them. She concludes that "we must stop lamenting and get up and do something."

4 The Politics of the Global Rule of Law

In response to attempts by US President Trump to disrupt his country's long-standing commitment to the liberal international order, one commentator asked: "What would it mean for the United States to abandon the liberal order? There's no other rules-based order to replace it with . . . The

[95] Koh, "The Trump Administration and International Law," 466.

[96] Koh, "The Trump Administration and International Law," 466.

[97] Craig Martin, "Symposium: The Assumptions of Koh's Transnational Legal Process as Counter-Strategy," *Opinio Juris*, February 26, 2018.

[98] Koh, "The Trump Administration and International Law," 413.

[99] Isabel Hull, "Anything Can Be Rescinded," *London Review of Books*, April 26, 2018.

alternative to an interconnected system of security partnerships and trade treaties is a return to the old system of unfettered power politics."[100] While, as that statement illustrates, for many liberal internationalists it seems there is no other rules-based order with which to replace the liberal variant, this is an effect of the dominance of that vision rather than a lack of alternatives historically or in contemporary politics.

International lawyers have participated in making the relation between liberal internationalism and the rule of law appear natural and inevitable. During the high point of liberal internationalism, the equation of the rule of law with that project seemed unquestionable, and those who disagreed or departed from those regimes were characterized as engaged in power politics in opposition to the rule of law. As the expansive architecture of international adjudication began to be challenged and to unravel, however, the dominance of the claim that liberal internationalism equates to the rule of law began in turn to diminish. International lawyers now have the disconcerting but exhilarating feeling of being flung back into history. Many of the old certainties about the nature of the liberal international order, its desirability, and its longevity seem to be changing, with the rise of China, the return of Russia, the disintegration of the European Union, the shifting fortunes of the United States under changing administrations, the intensification and expansion of the war on terror, and the destabilization of the Middle East. It is becoming clearer that the relation of liberal internationalism to the rule of law resulted from strategic calculations rather than historic inevitability, in part because its defenders have begun to articulate how the liberal architecture was constructed and how its relation to law was created. Today rival historical and contemporary accounts of what the global rule of law should look like are beginning to gain greater credibility and visibility.

The self-understanding of much scholarship about international law remains based upon an earlier era of liberalism, organized around notions of sovereign equality, constraints on the use of force, and nonintervention. That misunderstands what has been unfolding over the recent decades. A neoliberal approach to the global rule of law has been consolidated since the final decade of the twentieth century. That form of the rule of law differs from earlier liberal forms, in that rather than entrenching

[100] George Packer, "Donald Trump Goes Rogue," *The New Yorker*, June 25, 2018.

constraints on rulers through forms of constitutionalism legitimized by popular sovereignty, the global rule of law has been legitimized through reference to "humanity."[101] Sovereignty is rendered either a pathological threat to the constitution of liberty, or irrelevant as simply the agent or trustee overseeing the implementation of rational standards developed by experts on behalf of humanity.[102]

Here is where the return of attention to the rule of law in relation to a broader political order is valuable. The challenge to state sovereignty in the name of humanity is designed to limit the power of governments or rulers, but it does not do away with the problem of justifying political authority altogether.[103] Philosophical argument about individual rights has been at the center of rationalizations for certain kinds of political authority for centuries. While those rationalizations in earlier times served to empower states in the struggle against popes or emperors, today they serve to empower a diverse array of nonstate actors, from corporate investors and international adjudicators to criminal prosecutors and human rights NGOs. The claim to speak on behalf of humanity and to articulate its law is not a politically innocent claim, but is instead a claim that serves to found the jurisdiction, power, and authority of particular transnational elites. Whether this globalizing of the rule of law is a good or a bad thing cannot be assessed in a political vacuum that ignores these power relations.

The global rule of law has been invoked to justify a far-reaching system of international adjudication, which addresses fundamental questions about property, security, government, rights, and survival. That prioritizing of international adjudication over domestic political process inevitably embroils judges and arbitrators in serious controversies and political struggles. The claim of rationality is a fragile basis upon which to assert the legitimacy of that form of rule. Yet, rather than being seen as a problem, the removal of any political particularity or justification from the narrative about the global rule of law is seen to represent a step forward, precisely because in this worldview progress is achieved when politics is

[101] Anne Peters, "Humanity as the A and Ω of Sovereignty," *European Journal of International Law*, 20 (2009), 513–544.

[102] Eyal Benvenisti, "Sovereigns as Trustees of Humanity: On the Accountability of States to Foreign Stakeholders,"*American Journal of International Law*, 107 (2013), 295–333.

[103] Anne Orford, "Moral Internationalism and the Responsibility to Protect," *European Journal of International Law*, 24 (2013), 83–108.

eliminated.[104] Increasingly, "the appeal of a global rule of law lies in the promise of protection against the pathologies of internal domestic politics," and thus the very idea of a transnational rule of law "suggests a kind of internal depoliticization."[105] Disagreements over the application of the rule of law in specific situations have not shaken the conviction that the rule of law is a universally understood and agreed upon ideal that exists independently of ideology, politics, national interest, or substantive visions of the good.

Yet the recognition that there are plural visions of the rule of law globally is not the end of the story, but rather the beginning of a new chapter. A particular neoliberal model of the global rule of law triumphed in the late twentieth century. Its displacement poses challenges and opportunities for contemporary critical thinking about the role of law in international politics. Judicial systems must be "chosen and defended."[106] The return of history into this story is valuable because it allows us to experience that sense of choice and responsibility anew. The appeal to a global rule of law makes a strong political, moral or indeed ideological claim about the relation of law to desirable forms of rule globally, and an argument for why international order should be organized in particular ways. It involves not just ideas about law, but also surrounding beliefs about the role of law within political communities and the character of the institutions and the people who will be tasked with speaking and applying the law. Trying to grasp the stakes of these claims and counterclaims requires considering the political nature of the idea that the rule of law is a morally preferable form of rule historically and conceptually.

Conclusion

The process of constituting a global rule of law has winners and losers. The project that gained dominance in the final decade of the twentieth century and the first decade of the twenty-first separated winners and losers with

104 Friedrich Kratochwil, "Has the 'Rule of Law' Become a 'Rule of Lawyers'?," in Gianluigi Palombella and Neil Walker, eds., *Relocating the Rule of Law* (Oxford: Hart, 2009), 171–196.

105 Paul W. Kahn, "American Exceptionalism, Popular Sovereignty, and the Rule of Law," in Michael Ignatieff, ed., *American Exceptionalism and Human Rights* (Princeton: Princeton University Press, 2005), p. 198.

106 Shklar, "Political Theory and the Rule of Law," p. 25.

a vengeance. Liberal internationalists have defended that system in moral terms. An appeal to the rule of law has been central to that defense. International law has been a key vehicle for transmitting and constitutionalizing the doctrines, vocabularies, concepts, and practices that make sense of the relations between those who profit from the global economy and those rendered vulnerable by it. The appeal to the promotion of a global rule of law played a part in rationalizing why the forms of market relations embedded in trade and investment agreements and in projects of large-scale economic integration should be preferred to other relations, and thus why some people have entitlements to land, resources, profits, and security, and other people do not.

The call to continue defending this story has not abated, indeed it has only intensified, despite the signs that it has produced a world order that is not sustainable. Liberal internationalists continue to defend existing institutions, treaty regimes, and the actors they empower, seemingly unwilling or unable to take the opportunity to reflect critically upon the values, politics, ideologies, or accidents of history that produced existing international legal regimes, the substantive agendas they entrench and embed, and whether in fact they should be defended today. The appeal to a global rule of law works to disable conversations about those questions, treating any attempt to speak about the effects of particular institutions or legal regimes as somehow improperly contaminating a discussion of due process, neutral adjudication, clear rules, and legal authority with the messy stuff of politics, special interests, distribution, and power relations. Yet the form of contemporary international law cannot be that easily separated from the substantive agendas it furthers, and whether or not the global rule of law in its current form should be further consolidated and enforced cannot be considered without also examining the political choices, biases, or actors it enables.

Part VI

Conclusion

What the Rule of Law Is . . . and Is Not 30

Jens Meierhenrich

> The rule of law bakes no bread, it is unable to distribute loaves or fishes (it has none), and it cannot protect itself against external assault, but it remains the most civilized and least burdensome conception of a state yet to be devised.
>
> Michael Oakeshott[1]

> It would not be very difficult to show that the phrase "the rule of law" has become meaningless thanks to ideological abuse and general over-use. It may well have become just another one of those self-congratulatory rhetorical devices that grace the public utterances of Anglo-American politicians. No intellectual effort need therefore be wasted on this bit of ruling-class chatter.
>
> Judith Shklar[2]

> Big ideas are dramatic, borne to us by flights of unicorns. Sane ideas are often a sequence of smallness, rooted up in the mud by rhinos.
>
> Adam Gopnik[3]

Introduction

The rule of law is a sane idea gone big. Ever since Albert Venn Dicey, in 1885, popularized the phrase to describe the English way of law, it has left an indelible mark on societies the world over, and not always in a beneficial way.[4] Unmoored from the context in which – and for

[1] Michael Oakeshott, "The Rule of Law," in idem, *On History and Other Essays* (Indianapolis: Liberty Fund, [1983] 1999), p. 178.

[2] Judith N. Shklar, "Political Theory and the Rule of Law," in Allan C. Hutchinson and Patrick Monahan, eds., *The Rule of Law: Ideal or Ideology?* (Toronto: Carswell, 1987), p. 1.

[3] Adam Gopnik, *A Thousand Small Sanities: The Moral Adventure of Liberalism* (New York: Basic Books, 2019), p. 228.

[4] Its introduction into English constitutional discourse preceded Dicey's bestseller. Responsible for it was William Edward Hearn, who, in *The Government of England: Its Structure and Its Development* (London: Longmans, Green, Reader, and Dyer, 1867), wrote of "the undisputed supremacy of law," by which he meant "the submission of might to

which – it was first formulated, the idea has turned into a doctrine, some even think of it as an ideology. With its ancient origins, medieval roots, and modern instantiations, the idea of the rule of law – known by most, contested by many – has informed local and global ways of life like few other figments of our imagination.

Norms and institutions associated with the idea of the rule of law have lastingly shaped how societies govern, how governments rule, and how rulers are regarded by citizens and subjects. Leaders and ordinary people of all stripes routinely belt out the "fine sonorous phrase" with gusto, and many nations take it as their gospel.[5] The rule of law, or so it sometimes seems, is an idea too big to fail:

> Everyone seems to care about the rule of law. The rich and powerful governments of the world judge others by it; the poor and weak insist that they have it, and thus are entitled to the respect and commercial opportunities offered by the developed world; the United Nations, the World Bank, and nongovernmental organizations galore try to promote it, and philosophers praise it.[6]

Not unlike the word "democracy," to which it is often tethered, the slogan of the rule of law "resonates in people's minds and springs from their lips as they struggle for freedom and a better way of life."[7] Alas, the notion is as ambiguous in conception as it is ubiquitous in practice. Upon closer inspection, it becomes clear that the history of the rule of law is far less glittering than it appears at first glance, that it is shot through with violence. The rule of law is a conceit tainted by deceit.

Like the concept of democracy, the rule of law is an idea "whose meaning we must discern if it is to be of any use in guiding political analysis and practice."[8] The need to do so is pressing at a time when liberalism – the intellectual movement with which the idea of the rule of law in the last few

right." Ibid., p. 88. Two decades before Dicey, Hearn found that law ruled in nineteenth-century England, that it had become "the usual and natural state of things." Ibid., p. 89. See also Martin Loughlin, *Martin Loughlin, Foundations of Public Law* (Oxford: Oxford University Press, 2010), p. 315.

5 I borrowed the formulation from R. M. Jackson, *The Machinery of Justice in England*, 4th ed. (Cambridge: Cambridge University Press, [1964] 2015), p. 373.

6 Paul Gowder, *The Rule of Law in the Real World* (Cambridge: Cambridge University Press, 2016), p. 1.

7 Philippe C. Schmitter and Terry Lynn Karl, "What Democracy Is . . . and Is Not," *Journal of Democracy*, 2 (1991), 3.

8 Schmitter and Karl, "What Democracy Is . . . and Is Not," 3.

centuries has become closely associated – is seen by many as "the god that failed."[9] In an age of crumbling certainties about what makes the world hang together, the rule of law, too, requires unbiased scrutinty. The growing number of transitions to authoritarian rule, and the rise of cascading social movements – from Black Lives Matter in the United States to the insurgent citizens of Hong Kong, the latter protesting loudly against the introduction by the Chinese government of draconian national security legislation in the former British colony – for some are indications that the rule of law is on the wane, that populism has outmaneuvered legalism.[10] Before one can begin to ascertain whether that is so, however, one must gain clarity about what the rule of law is – and what it is not.

This chapter takes a stab at the task. Several questions are addressed: What is the rule of law? What should it be? Is the rule of law worth having if it cannot sustain the liberty of all citizens? Is it worth promoting if it helps to sustain not just democracy but autocracy as well? What can be done about the rule of law? What can be done *with* it? What is the virtue of the rule of law? And is much of it left?

Whatever one makes of the rule of law, as an invented tradition, it is under siege once more.[11] Allan Hutchinson and Patrick Monahan, who took stock of the rule of law in the final years of the Cold War, expressed a sentiment with clear echoes in the twenty-first century. Writing in the 1980s, Hutchinson and Monahan were convinced that the achievements of the rule of law would never – *could* never – amount to more than the "shuffling [of] power among elite groups," that its promotion was always going to be little more than "moralistic window-dressing."[12] An equitable society, they argued, was impossible to build on the foundation of a rule of law, by which they meant a legal system that relieved heavily on

[9] John Feffer, quoted in Ivan Krastev and Stephen Holmes, *The Light That Failed: A Reckoning* (London: Allen Lane, 2019), p. 20.

[10] On the vicissitudes of democracy around the world, see Larry Diamond, Marc F. Plattner, and Christopher Walker, eds., *Authoritarianism Goes Global: The Challenge to Democracy* (Baltimore: Johns Hopkins University Press, 2016); "Is Democracy Dying? A Global Report," *Foreign Affairs*, 97 (2018), 10–56; and, most recently, Pippa Norris and Ronald Inglehart, *Cultural Backlash: Trump, Brexit, and Authoritarian Populism* (Cambridge: Cambridge University Press, 2019).

[11] Cf. William E. Scheuerman, ed., *The Rule of Law under Siege: Selected Essays of Franz L. Neumann and Otto Kirchheimer* (Berkeley: University of California Press, 1996).

[12] Allan C. Hutchinson and Patrick Monahan, "Democracy and the Rule of Law," in idem, eds., *The Rule of Law: Ideal or Ideology?* (Toronto: Carswell, 1987), p. 100.

"constitutional adjudication," the kind of judicial review for which the US Supreme Court is known, but traces of which can also be found in the widely hailed jurisprudence of Germany's *Bundesverfassungsgericht* as well as in that of the equally admired Constitutional Court of South Africa.[13] Hutchinson and Monahan set out to subvert conceptions of the rule of law that portrayed it as "the butler of democracy."[14] They would have regarded the production of what Roger Berkowitz, in the post-apartheid context of South Africa, admiringly called "dignity jurisprudence" as facadist.[15] To Hutchinson and Monahan, the rule of law is, at best, conducive to elite democracy, never to truly representative democracy, the kind that advances the welfare of all. José María Maravall, reflecting on the rule of law in the decade *after* the demise of the Soviet Union, was less disillusioned than Hutchinson and Monahan about the promise of the rule of law. But he, too, was reluctant to sing its praises, noting instead that "getting rid of adversaries through the rule of law" was *de rigueur* also in consolidated democracies.[16] With reference to his native Spain, he reminded his readers that throughout history democracy had been subverted "with the rule of law," that the rule of law was not just a cherished trope in the Western canon but also "a political weapon."[17]

If one goes by the news headlines and social media posts in the twentieth year of the second millennium, the number of democracy-demanding forces – from Causeway Bay to Portland to Moscow – who are questioning the achievements of the rule of law are growing. Those marching in the streets point to the perverse incentives to which the rule of law in the real world can, and does, give rise. They excoriate the violence

[13] Allan C. Hutchinson and Patrick Monahan, "Introduction," in idem, eds., *The Rule of Law*, p. xii. On the relationship between constitutional review and the *Rechtsstaat* in Germany and the rule of law in South Africa, see, for example, Matthias Jestaedt, Oliver Lepsius, Christoph Möllers, and Christoph Schönberger, *The German Federal Constitutional Court: The Court without Limits*, trans. Jeff Seitzer (Oxford: Oxford University Press, 2020); Theunis Roux, *The Politics of Principle: The First South African Constitutional Court, 1995–2005* (Cambridge: Cambridge University Press, 2013).

[14] Hutchinson and Monahan, "Introduction," p. xii.

[15] Roger Berkowitz, "Dignity Jurisprudence: Building a New Law on Earth," in Drucilla Cornell, Stu Woolman, Sam Fuller, Jason Brickhill, Michael Bishop, and Diana Dunbar, eds., *The Dignity Jurisprudence of the Constitutional Court of South Africa: Cases and Materials*, vol. 1. (New York: Fordham University Press, 2013), p. 65.

[16] José María Maravall, "The Rule of Law as a Political Weapon," in José María Maravall and Adam Przeworski, eds., *Democracy and the Rule of Law* (Cambridge: Cambridge University Press, 2003), p. 283.

[17] Maravall, "The Rule of Law as a Political Weapon," pp. 261, 273.

done in its name. They question the violence and the word, as Robert Cover once put it.

If it is true, as Cover argued, that "[b]etween the idea and the reality of common meaning falls the shadow of the violence of law, itself," ours is an opportune moment at which to ask anew what the rule of law is – and what contribution, if any, it can make to the creation and maintenance of social order.[18] In this collection, we invited thought-provoking scholars from around the globe to help us pose the question. Their stimulating and diverse attempts to address it demonstrate that the rule of law as a category of practice is considerably more complex than conventional wisdom has it. Neither is its meaning fixed, nor its virtue obvious, to anyone who writes rigorously – be it theoretically or empirically – about the rule of law, this most confounding of protean ideals.[19]

1 A Protean Ideal

Theorizing the rule of law was an intellectual preoccupation long before Dicey gave a name to the phenomenon. For centuries scholars have been busy delineating what the rule of law is – by which they mean what it *should* be. Theirs has been a quest for an elusive ideal. Virtually all who partake proceed in a deductive fashion. They reason from principles, often beginning with the concept of law itself before thinking about its rule. They have their eyes trained on manufacturing a universal standard. In recent years, a phenomenological turn in the study of law has cast doubt on the value of globalism. Those behind it have questioned much of what we thought we knew about the rule of law, including the wisdom of searching for an universally applicable standard of what it means. They foreground practices, not principles. They wonder aloud

[18] See generally, Robert M. Cover, "Violence and the Word," *Yale Law Journal*, 95 (1986), 1601–1629.

[19] A recent example of what I consider "rigorous" rule of law scholarship is Frank Lovett, *A Republic of Law* (Cambridge: Cambridge University Press, 2016), a treatment located firmly on the theoretical side of things. For empirically driven examples, see Sally Engle Merry, *Colonizing Hawai'i: The Cultural Power of Law* (Princeton: Princeton University Press, 2000); R. W. Kostal, *A Jurisprudence of Power: Victorian Empire and the Rule of Law* (Cambridge: Cambridge University Press, 2005); and Michael Lobban, *Imperial Incarceration: Detention without Trial in the Making of British Colonial Africa* (Cambridge: Cambridge University Press, 2021).

whether "global norms with a local face" are possible, and what such everyday justice looks like – and feels like and sounds like.[20]

The latest generation of rule of law scholars has achieved analytical rigor by blending theoretical *and* empirical sophistication. The resultant literature is considerably richer – and more diverse – than what for the longest time passed for leading scholarship about the rule of law.[21] In imaginative books and articles its authors have called into question conventional wisdom about the meanings – and workings – of the rule of law. In closly observed, thickly described studies, they have demonstrated that one or a few cases can yield tremendous theoretical gains. From Chile to Egypt, and from Russia to South Africa, they also showed, more disconcertingly, that authoritarianism and the rule of law are not the strange bedfellows they long were made out to be.[22] This finding did not come as a surprise to some, like Joseph Raz, for whom "many forms of arbitrary rule are compatible with the rule of law."[23] But it did ruffle the feathers of the late Lord Bingham and other rule of law enthusiasts who thought the idea unimpeachable and the concept of the "authoritarian rule of law" a preposterous proposition.[24] And yet, the available evidence is unambiguous: "authoritarian regimes switch to the rule of

[20] Lisbeth Zimmermann, *Global Norms with a Local Face: Rule of Law Promotion and Norm Translation* (Cambridge: Cambridge University Press, 2017).

[21] Notable titles include Tamir Moustafa, *The Struggle for Constitutional Power: Law, Politics, and Economic Reform in Egypt* (Cambridge: Cambridge University Press, 2007); Lisa Hilbink, *Judges beyond Politics in Democracy and Dictatorship: Lessons from Chile* (Cambridge: Cambridge University Press, 2007); Jens Meierhenrich, *The Legacies of Law: Long-Run Consequences of Legal Development in South Africa, 1652–2000* (Cambridge: Cambridge University Press, 2008); Stephen Humphreys, *Theatre of the Rule of Law: Transnational Legal Intervention in Theory and Practice* (Cambridge: Cambridge University Press, 2010); Mark Fathi Massoud, *Law's Fragile State: Colonial, Authoritarian, and Humanitarian Legacies in Sudan* (Cambridge: Cambridge University Press, 2013); Didier Fassin, *Enforcing Order: An Ethnography of Urban Policing*, trans. Rachel Gomme (Cambridge: Polity 2013); Nick Cheesman, *Opposing the Rule of Law: How Myanmar's Courts Make Law and Order* (Cambridge: Cambridge University Press, 2015); Kathryn Hendley, *Everyday Law in Russia* (Ithaca: Cornell University Press, 2017); Alexander Laban Hinton, *The Justice Facade: Trials of Transition in Cambodia* (Oxford: Oxford University Press, 2018); Mark Fathi Massoud, *Shari'a, Inshallah: Finding God in Somali Legal Politics* (Cambridge: Cambridge University Press, 2021); and Jens Meierhenrich, *The Violence of Law: The Formation and Deformation of* Gacaca *Courts in Rwanda, 1994–2019* (Cambridge: Cambridge University Press, 2021).

[22] See also Jens Meierhenrich, ed., *Dual States: A Global History* (Cambridge: Cambridge University Press, forthcoming).

[23] Joseph Raz, "The Rule of Law and its Virtue," in idem, *The Authority of Law: Essays on Law and Morality* (Oxford: Clarendon Press, 1979), p. 219.

[24] Tom Bingham, *The Rule of Law* (London: Penguin, 2011).

law as a legitimizing narrative" and have done so from the moment Dicey came up with his memorable phrase.[25] Often, the rule of law is merely facade. Kim Lane Scheppele has described Hungary under Viktor Orbán as the "archetypal case" of "autocratic legalism," a term she reserves for the performance of a sham legalism by charismatic leaders who "masquerade as democrats" while they carve out a "destructive path" leading to authoritarian rule.[26] "For such legitimizing functions to succeed, however, judicial institutions must enjoy some degree of real autonomy from the executive, and they must, at least on occasion, strike against the expressed will of the regime."[27]

From colonial times to the present, the rule of law was not just a utopian idea. It was also a dystopian one. R. W. Kostal has shown in granular detail why and how the mid-Victorian English elite broadcast a "jurisprudence of power" in its overseas territories in the name of the rule of law. Contemporary authors like William Finlason labored tirelessly to forge "a credible theoretical synthesis of expansive imperialism and the rule of law."[28] Take the case of the so-called Jamaica affair, the violent suppression in October 1865 of the Morant Bay uprising in the island colony. Edward Eyre, the Governor of Jamaica, along with his senior officers and like-minded apologists in England, "fervently maintained that the suppression had taken place in strict accordance with the law. Specifically, Eyre and his allies claimed that even the most ruthless measures – the whippings, burnings, and hangings – were perfectly legal under the English law of martial law."[29]

The argumentation is remarkably similar to that which, in the spring of 2020, came out of Washington, DC, where the administration of US President Donald Trump sought to justify the deployment of militarized federal forces to the city of Portland. There, a US Senator warned, America was "staring down the barrel of martial law."[30] Another described the Trump administration's use of the rule of law as "an all-out assault in military-style fashion."[31] From the

[25] Tamir Moustafa and Tom Ginsburg, "Introduction: The Function of Courts in Authoritarian Politics," in Tom Ginsburg and Tamir Moustafa, eds., *Rule by Law: The Politics of Courts in Authoritarian Regimes* (Cambridge: Cambridge University Press, 2008), p. 6.

[26] Kim Lane Scheppele, "Autocratic Legalism," *University of Chicago Law Review*, 85 (2018), 549.

[27] Moustafa and Ginsburg, "Introduction," p. 6.

[28] Kostal, *A Jurisprudence of Power*, p. 481.

[29] Kostal, *A Jurisprudence of Power*, p. 465.

[30] As quoted in David Smith and Daniel Strauss, "America 'Staring Down the Barrel of Martial Law', Oregon Senator Warns," *The Guardian*, July 25, 2020.

[31] As quoted in Smith and Strauss, "America 'Staring Down the Barrel of Martial Law'." See also Josh Gerstein, "Feds Assemble 'Operation Diligent Valor' Force to Battle Portland Unrest," *Politico*, July 22, 2020.

colony to the postcolony, democratic regimes in the world's most advanced countries have used the rule of law for questionable ends, which poignantly illustrates Maravall's argument about the rule of law as a political weapon.

These, and many other unexpected findings like it, underline the need to thoroughly revisit the rule of law, this most influential of modern social imaginaries. We must ask anew: What, if anything, is the rule of law good for? Can we embrace it knowing full well that a self-described "civilized nation" like Great Britain, "one emphatically committed to the principle of the rule of law over men," used the institutions tied to this principle to govern a burgeoning empire?[32] It is undeniable, as Brian Tamanaha and scores of others have pointed out, "that the USA adhered to the rule of law even when slavery was legally enforced, and racial segregation legally imposed."[33] Must we therefire give up on the rule of law? Can the rule of law *ever* be more than organized hypocrisy? Does it matter if it can't?

I do not have a definitive anwer, but I have a stopgap solution: Let us puncture the inflated expectations that are weighing down the idea of the rule of law. Let us *not* think of the rule of law as an ideal. Let us *not* think of it as an ideology either. Let us think of it as a *social imaginary*. Let us see it for what it is, where it is. If we readjusted our legal imagination in a small but consequential way, we might, eventually, be able to access – and repair – our legal unconscious.[34] For judging by the histories and moralities – and the pathologies and trajectories – that our contributors catalogued, the unknowing and unintentional reenactment of cultural trauma has undeniably been a pernicious byproduct of marketing the rule of law.

2 A Social Imaginary

For Charles Taylor, the eminent philosopher, a "social imaginary" is that common understanding that makes possible collective endeavors and which is reinforced by them. Taylor's focus is on "the ways people imagine their social existence, how they fit together with others, how things go on between them and their fellows, the expectations that are normally met,

[32] Kostal, *A Jurisprudence of Power*, p. 461.

[33] Brian Z. Tamanaha, *On the Rule of Law: History, Politics, Theory* (Cambridge: Cambridge University Press, 2004), p. 93.

[34] Shoshona Felman, *The Juridical Unconscious: Trials and Traumas in the Twentieth Century* (Cambridge: Harvard University Press, 2002).

and the deeper normative notions and images that underlie these expectations."[35] Taylor is adamant that social imaginaries "are never just ideology," which is why his heuristic trope is so useful for thinking about the rule of law.[36]

A social imaginary, as Taylor understands it, is both factual *and* normative, which is a useful starting point for thinking about the rule of law. For, as many of the chapters in this collection make plain, it is the practices of the rule of law that say more about the idea than the principles often tacked to it. Judith Shklar said as much as early as 1964, when she bemoaned "the sterile game of defining law, morals, and politics in order to separate them as concepts both 'pure' and empty, divorced from each other and from their common historical past and contemporary setting."[37] The tendency to think of the rule of law as a discreet entity that is "there," I, too, consider misguided. Thinking of the rule of law as a social imaginary is a more promising way of developing an understanding of the diverse manifestations of its rule, and its constitutive role – both locally and globally – in the making and remaking of the modern world.

Another reason why I conceive of the rule of law as a social imaginary is to make explicit the moralities that feed into it, "to criticize," as Shklar put it, "those of its traditional adherents who, in their determination to preserve law from politics, fail to recognize that they too have made a choice among political values."[38] In our time there is a greater awareness than existed in hers of the manifold ways in which the norms and institutions of liberalism have been implicated in the subjugation – not just liberation – of individuals and groups. The rule of law is *primus inter pares* among these norms and institutions, as scholars affiliated with Critical Legal Studies, Feminist Legal Theory, Critical Race Theory, and other intellectual movements of critical inquiry have argued *ad nauseum* for generations. Constitutionalism and parliamentarism are two other institutions tained by the odious scourge of illiberalism. This brings us back to Taylor.

Whether with reference to the rule of law or any other phenomenon, gaining an "understanding of what we're doing right now," Taylor insists,

[35] Charles Taylor, *Modern Social Imaginaries* (Durham: Duke University Press, 2004), p. 23.

[36] Taylor, *Modern Social Imaginaries*, p. 183.

[37] Judith N. Shklar, *Legalism: Law, Morals, and Political Trials* (Cambridge: Harvard University Press, 1964), p. 3.

[38] Shklar, *Legalism*, p. 8.

> makes the sense it does because of our grasp on the wider predicament: how we continuously stand or have stood in relation to others and to power. This, in turn, opens out wider perspectives on where we stand in space and time: our relationship to other nations and peoples (for example, to external models of democratic life we are trying to imitate, or of tyrrany we are trying to distance ourselves from) and also where we stand in our history, in the narrative of our becoming.[39]

In the final analysis, it is of little consequence whether we think of the rule of law as an ideal or an ideology or something in-between, as long as we appreciate that our social imagination has been – and always will be – the source of this invented tradition. The rule of law does not – cannot – exist abstractly. Whether it originated *in* a place, or was octroyed *on* a place, its social meaning(s) will always develop in relation *to* a place. We must place law in *space* to talk about its rule in context. Looking for varieties of legalism *in concreto* "serves to identify the distinctly legal elements" of the rule of law, "it helps us to isolate their characteristics and analyse their role and significance, an exercise that is often enhanced by comparison between empirical examples."[40] Space matters, as does time. We must place law in *time* to be able to say anything meaningful about the logic and long-run consequences of its rule.[41] "Over time, social arrangements build through, on top of, and around legal arrangements, interconnecting law within the whole culture, economy, and polity, mutually supporting and anchoring one another."[42] The formation, deformation, and transformation of rule of law practices tend to happen piecemeal in the real world,

> with selected alterations absorbed and fitted within pre-existing legal arrangements, in turn affecting related social arrangements. People may alter their actions to conform to new legal requirements – responding to the costs, benefits, or normative authority attached to the law – or people may be unaware of, disregard, or circumvent legal requirements.[43]

It follows that we should be concerned with the changing character of the rule of law. We should not be engaged in a forever war about the essential

[39] Taylor, *Modern Social Imaginaries*, p. 27.

[40] Fernanda Pirie, *The Anthropology of Law* (Oxford: Oxford University Press, 2013), p. 212.

[41] Paul Pierson, *Politics in Time: History, Institutions, and Social Analysis* (Princeton: Princeton University Press, 2004).

[42] Brian Z. Tamanaha, *A Realistic Theory of Law* (Cambridge: Cambridge University Press, 2017), p. 196.

[43] Tamanaha, *A Realistic Theory of Law*, pp. 196–197.

properties of a deductive model – whether philosophical or game-theoretical – about what that rule entails. The rule of law is what actors make of it. Only time will tell what, in a given place, that is or was.

The late Douglass North, Nobel Laureate and leading thinker of what is known as the New Institutional Economics, once admonished an entire discipline – one with a long track record of studying the rule of law parsimoniously – for not giving temporality its due in institutional theory: "Without a deep understanding of time, you will be lousy political scientists, because time is the dimension in which ideas and institutions and beliefs evolve."[44] Tracing its real-world practices, which invariably are messy and confounding, is a surer way of making progress in our understanding of the rule of law than "reading off its requirements from some canonical definition."[45]

3 The Rule That Was

If and when law, as an institution, is at the heart of a polity's social imaginary, it stands to reason that it "rules." *That* law rules tells us little about how and why it does, and for whose benefit. We do not know, without further investigation, whether, in a setting where law rules, we are dealing with an instance of the democratic rule of law or the authoritarian rule of law or a theatrical enactment. All we know is that law, where it rules, is an important parameter to choice. That knowledge is more valuable than it may seem at first glance. Why? Because the facticity of law's rule, while it may not tell us anything about the validity of this rule, is frequently suggestive of a polity's mores more generally, of the "sense-giving features" that lurk in the background of legalism, international and otherwise.[46] This legal unconscious, culturally determined, is worth probing for insights about the sources – and depths – of a given polity's fidelity to law.

[44] Douglass North, "In Anticipation of the Marriage of Political and Economic Theory," in James E. Alt, Margaret Levi, and Elinor Ostrom, eds., *Competition and Cooperation: Conversations with Nobelists about Economics and Political Science* (New York: Russell Sage Foundation, 1999), p. 316.

[45] Jeremy Waldron, "Rule *by* Law: A Much Maligned Proposition," Public Law and Legal Theory Research Paper Series, New York University School of Law, June 2019, 22.

[46] Taylor, *Modern Social Imaginaries*, p. 28. For an illustration with evidence from the eras of segregation and apartheid in South Africa, see Meierhenrich, *The Legacies of Law*, esp. pp. 219–267. On facticity (*Faktizität*) and validity (*Geltung*), see Jürgen Habermas, *Between Facts and Norms: Contributions to a Discourse Theory of Law and Democracy*, trans. William Rehg (Cambridge: MIT Press, [1992] 1996).

"[I]t is the practice that carries the understanding," Taylor tells us, by which he means that we can only grasp the reach of, say, law's authority, if we relate it to "that largely unstructured and inarticulate understanding of our whole situation, within which particular features of our world," such as legalism, "show up for us in the sense they have."[47] Starting with practices – not principles – is anathema to conventional approaches to the rule of law, however.

Policy-oriented studies render technical what the rule of law requires. Philosophical treatments are no less reductionist – and anachronistic. Both approaches to the rule of law – the abstract and the applied – have in common a misplaced faith in universality.[48] "[S]tandard contemporary discussions of the rule of law," as Lovett points out, "approach the problem from the wrong end. They begin with a laundry-list of principles such as generality, prospectivity, stability, and so forth. Often it is unclear what the grounds are for preferring one list to another: each list seems to represent the particular's author's intuitive sense of the formal or substantive virtues law should ideally possess."[49] The same is true for the increasingly popular rule of law indices on which organizations such as the World Justice Project or the World Bank rely.[50] The problem with an emphasis on generalization – whether placed by legal theorists or legal practitioners – is that it has a *disciplining effect*. It conditions our way of seeing the rule of law. We recognize it before we look. A criterial rendering of the rule of law, one informed by data or deduction alone, is bound to be flat. A flattening of reality is the last thing a world caught in the throes of populism needs.[51]

The rule of law used to be easy to define. Before the realization set in that the cherished institution also was "the cutting edge of colonialism, an instrument of the power of an alien state and part of the process of coercion," the rule of law was like the proverbial mansion on the hill: something to strive for, an ideal place of being, the hallmark of *civitas*.[52]

[47] Taylor, *Modern Social Imaginaries*, p. 25.

[48] For an interesting, if dated, intervention from a time when subaltern critiques of liberal legalism were not as common as they are today, see Surya Prakash Sinha, "Non-Universality of Law," *Archiv für Rechts- und Sozialphilosophie*, 81 (1995), 185–214.

[49] Lovett, *A Republic of Law*, p. 26.

[50] See, for example, Tom Ginsburg and Mila Versteeg, "Rule of Law Measurement," in this volume.

[51] For global data, patterns, and trends, see Norris and Inglehart, *Cultural Backlash*.

[52] Martin Chanock, *Law, Custom and Social Order: The Colonial Experience in Malawi and Zambia* (Cambridge: Cambridge University Press, 1985), p. 4.

However, the rule of law that used to be on most everyone's lips was but a version of the rule of law, a historically inaccurate, one-dimensional rendering that sprang from a very particular modern social imaginery: liberalism. For a sizable portion of the world's population, the rule of law has meant something else. Many did not cherish but feared it, just like any other technology of rule. Grasping this darker side of virtue – the vices of the rule of law – is indispensable for making the idea comprehensible – and for transplanting it intelligently – as we come to terms in the twenty-first century at long last with the legacies of "racial liberalism."[53]

Speaking of the uses of law for political ends, some equate the rule *of* law with rule *by* law, "whether that law be good, bad, or indifferent."[54] Frank Lovett, Yuhua Wang, and Jemery Waldron, for example, question the analytical value of conceptual differentiation. "If it were up to me, we would drop or downplay the contrast between *rule of law* and *rule by law*. It is more trouble than it is worth," writes Waldron:

> Of course we should acknowledge that legal means can be used sometimes to undermine the rule of law, and that that ideal is not satisfied simply by enforcing commands that have the words law pasted on to them. But equally not every instrumental use of law is disqualified under this acknowledgment. Law is an instrument for the public good, legality is not just political cover for the law-makers. And using law as an instrument of rule is already the acceptance of a demanding discipline – formally, procedurally, and in the acceptance of a need for legal authorization for government action. It already implicates government in a compact of legality – where citizens' subjection to law is matched with an assurance that the rules laid down in advance are the ones that will be applied to her conduct and applied as law, with legal procedures and legal safeguards. This is not a minimal assurance. Though you can array it under the heading 'rule by law' if you like, it already captures a considerable element of what the rule of law is supposed to involve.[55]

Regardless of whether a given regime aims for good or for ill, I assume, "it will always be better at least for those subject to that regime if it rules by law rather than by other means."[56] The following is a prolegomenon to a realistic theory of the rule of law. It is a conceptual contribution to

[53] Charles W. Mills, *Black Rights/White Wrongs: The Critique of Racial Liberalism* (Oxford: Oxford University Press, 2017). See also Jens Meierhenrich, "Racial Legalism," *Annual Review of Law and Social Science*, vol. 18 (forthcoming).

[54] Lovett, *A Republic of Law*, p. 113.

[55] Waldron, "Rule *by* Law," 22, 23. (emphases omitted).

[56] Lovett, *A Republic of Law*, p. 123.

consider alongside – or in lieu of – the criterial concepts of the rule of law that have long dominated theory and practice.

4 The Intelligibility of the Rule of Law

Across the centuries, it was usually legal theorists, sometimes trained as philosophers, more often as political theorists, who contemplated the rule of law, who defined it "through requirements" for those working at the coalface of law.[57] Legal theory is concerned with the features that law "generally needs in order to rule."[58] This concern has given rise to a criterial approach to the rule of law.[59] The long-standing quest for the essence of the rule of law – for its intelligibility – has led to rival taxonomies. Perhaps the most famous of these is Lon Fuller's account of the "inner morality of law," which many twenty-first century thinkers outside of legal theory have embraced as a useful approximation of the rule of law.[60]

When Judith Shklar, many years ago, set out to make the rule of law intelligible, she did not think Fuller had all that much to offer. The eminent political theorist lumped Fuller's procedural theory rule of law together with Ronald Dworkin's theory of adjudication and declared both (along with Dicey's "unfortunate outburst of Anglo-Saxon parochialism") flawed for mistaking "the rule of courts" for the rule of law.[61] Not at all taken with twentieth-century legal theory, Shklar figured she

[57] Gianluigi Palombella, "The Rule of Law and Its Core," in Gianluigi Palombella and Neil Walker, eds., *Relocating the Rule of Law* (Oxford: Hart, 2009), p. 35.

[58] Palombella, "The Rule of Law and Its Core," p. 35.

[59] For a social-scientific instantiation of this approach, see, for example, Jørgen Møller and Svend-Erik Skaaning, *The Rule of Law: Definitions, Measures, Patterns and Causes* (London: Palgrave, 2014).

[60] Lon L. Fuller, *The Morality of Law*, 2nd rev. ed. (New Haven: Yale University Press, 1969). On Fuller's reception, see, for the domestic realm, among many others, Gillian K. Hadfield, *Rules for a Flat World: Why Humans Invented Law and How to Reinvent It for a Complex Global Economy* (Oxford: Oxford University Press, 2017). Concerning the international realm, see, for example, Jutta Brunnée and Stephen J. Toope, *Legitimacy and Legality in International Law: An Interactional Account* (Cambridge: Cambridge University Press, 2010). See also Kristen Rundle, "The Morality of the Rule of Law: Lon L. Fuller," in this volume.

[61] Shklar, "Political Theory and the Rule of Law," pp. 5, 6. For an updated, and considerably more refined, argument for conceiving of the rule of law in terms of, *inter alia*, "the existence and operation of the sorts of institutions we call courts," see Jeremy Waldron, "The Concept and the Rule of Law," *Georgia Law Review*, 43 (2008), 20.

had better go back in time – and take sides. To one side stood Aristotle (of whom Fuller and Dworkin reminded her). On the other she noticed Montesquieu. Aristotle's rule of law, Shklar pointed out, was "perfectly compatible not only with the slave society of ancient Athens, but with the modern 'dual state.'"[62] On this ancient conception, the rule of law was the rule of reason. What Shklar found unconvincing about Aristotle's understanding of the rule of law, however, was not the compatibility of its morality with the possible reality of authoritarian rule, but, rather, "its concentration on the judging agent, the dispenser of legal justice."[63] The extraordinary amount of virtue that Aristotle required (and Fuller and Dworkin in his wake) of rule of law practitioners, Shklar thought, made for an unrealistic theory of the rule of law – which is why she threw her lot in with Montesquieu.

For Montesquieu, as Leslie Green reminds us, "the fear of violence and the threat of arbitrary government provides an essential context in which the rule of law takes its meaning."[64] Shklar was sold on this idea. She described it as the authentic core of the rule of law: "If one . . . begins with the fear of violence, the insecurity of arbitrary government and the discriminations of injustice one may work one's way up to finding a significant place for the Rule of Law, and for the boundaries it has historically set upon these the most enduring of our political troubles."[65] Throughout her career, Shklar gathered building blocks for a realistic theory of the rule of law. A political theorist with "the historian's faith that ideals must be tried in the court of world history," she was gearing up for a critique of contemporary legal theory.[66]

Shklar found wanting philosophical accounts of the rule of law because their authors "have tended to ignore every political reality outside the courtroom or hurled the notion of ruling into such abstraction that it appears to occur in no recognizable context."[67] Her scorn was directed

[62] Shklar, "Political Theory and the Rule of Law," p. 2. On the modern "dual state," see Ernst Fraenkel, *The Dual State: A Contribution to the Theory of Dictatorship* (Oxford: Oxford University Press, [1941] 2017), trans. E. A. Shils, with an Introduction by Jens Meierhenrich. For comparisons and extensions, see Meierhenrich, *The Remnants of the Rechtsstaat*, esp. pp. 225–252.

[63] Shklar, "Political Theory and the Rule of Law," p. 4.

[64] Leslie Green, "Law's Rule," *Osgoode Hall Law Journal*, 24 (1986), 1026. See also Sharon R. Krause, "The Rule of Law in Montesquieu," in this volume.

[65] Shklar, "Political Theory and the Rule of Law," p. 16. [66] Green, "Law's Rule," 1026.

[67] Shklar, "Political Theory and the Rule of Law," p. 3.

primarily at Fuller and Dworkin but also indirectly at the influence of John Rawls, whose subordination in *A Theory of Justice* of political philosophy to moral philosophy had trickle-down effects on discursive formations about the rule of law.[68] Other eminent theorists of the rule of law did not escape Shklar's critique unscathed either. She also chided Dicey, then Friedrich Hayek on the right and Roberto Unger on the left, for ignoring Montesquieu's major conceptual advances on the ancient idea of the rule of law. The way Shklar saw it, Hayek's faith in general and prospective rules was hanging "on an unverifiable claim about the necessary consequences of human ignorance."[69] She chided Unger in her refreshingly frank prose for offering "warmed-over Max Weber as substitute for serious history and for being dangerously utopian."[70] Shklar's "negative, non-utopian approach" which she applied to the idea of the rule of law as well as to other invented traditions of liberalism, "not only avoids the apolitical conclusions of mainstream liberal theories" and those of upstream critical theories but "proves the inherently realist thrust of her liberalism."[71]

Shklar's was a lone voice in the late twentieth century. Debates about the intelligibility of the rule of law were all the rage in her time, abstraction the highest mark of theoretical achievement. Thinking parsimoniously, not contextually, was par for the course of becoming a quotable theorist of the rule of law.[72] Hayek for a while was one of the most quotable. His "moral science" informed for decades the way in which the World Bank and International Monetary Fund approached the rule of law.[73] There was a natural affinity between the libertarian economist and the guardians of

[68] For a lasting critique of Rawls giving "priority of the moral over the political" in the philosophy of liberalism, see Bernard Williams, "From Freedom to Liberty: The Construction of a Political Value," in Bernard Williams and Geoffrey Hawthorn, eds., *In the Beginning was the Deed: Realism and Moralism in Political Argument* (Princeton: Princeton University Press, 2005), pp. 75–96. For a history of the lasting and also pernicious influence of Rawlsian liberalism on global thought, see Katrina Forrester, *In the Shadow of Justice: Postwar Liberalism and the Remaking of Political Philosophy* (Princeton: Princeton University Press, 2019).

[69] Green, "Law's Rule," 1026. [70] Green, "Law's Rule," 1026.

[71] Katharina Kaufmann, "Conflict in Political Liberalism: Judith Shklar's Liberalism of Fear," *Res Publica*, 26 (2020), 577–595.

[72] While Shklar's *Legalism*, published in 1964, has long enjoyed canonical status in certain quarters of the law, the social sciences, and humanities – and amassed thousands of citations there – her observations about the rule of law, domestic and international, never were mainstream fare in the male-dominated world of legal theory.

[73] Timothy Fuller, "Friedrich Hayek's Moral Science," *Ratio Juris*, 2 (1989), 17–26.

the international economic order. In thinking about the rule of law, Hayek, like them, veered "in a more international direction" than theorists of justice like Rawls – and Dicey before him – who turned inward.[74] Hayek believed it was impossible to defend the rule of law "without retreating to the kind of nationalist position he saw as the main threat to the idea of a liberal political order."[75] From this article of faith sprang Hayek's project – never fully realized – of developing a universally applicable theory of the rule of law.[76]

Hayek's account of the rule of law underwent notable changes over the course of his life, but, in essence, it amounted to a defense of a law of rules.[77] The "main point" of the rule of law, Hayek opined in 1953, as the world transitioned from World War to Cold War,

> is that in the use of its coercive powers, the discretion of the authorities should be so strictly bound by laws laid down beforehand that the individual can foresee with fair certainty how these powers will be used in particular instances; and that the laws themselves are truly general and create no privileges for class or person because they are made in view of their long-run effects and therefore in necessary ignorance of who will be the particular individuals who will be benefited or harmed by them.[78]

"Since this Rule of Law," Hayek continued, "is a rule for the legislator, a rule about what the law ought to be, it can, of course, never be a rule of the positive law of any land. The legislator can never effectively limit his own powers. The rule is rather a meta-legal principle which can operate only through its action on public opinion. So long as it is generally believed in, it will keep legislation within the bounds of the Rule of Law. Once it ceases to be accepted or understood by public opinion, soon the law itself will be in conflict with the Rule of Law."[79]

Abstraction was Hayek's technique, generalizability the glittering prize. In 1973, in the first installment of *Law, Legislation and Liberty*, Hayek argued that the system of rules he was articulating, and the norms of

[74] Chandran Kukathas, "Hayek and the State," in David Dyzenhaus and Thomas Poole, eds., *Law, Liberty and State: Oakeshot, Hayek and Schmitt on the Rule of Law* (Cambridge: Cambridge University Press, 2015), p. 292.

[75] Kukathas, "Hayek and the State," p. 292.

[76] Kukathas, "Hayek and the State," p. 292.

[77] See also Antonin Scalia, "The Rule of Law as a Law of Rules," *University of Chicago Law Review*, 56 (1989), 1175–1188.

[78] Friedrich A. Hayek, "Decline of the Rule of Law, Part 1," *The Freeman*, April 20, 1953. See also idem, "Decline of the Rule of Law, Part 2," *The Freeman*, May 4, 1953.

[79] Hayek, "Decline of the Rule of Law, Part 1."

institutions that belonged to it, would achieve "their intended effect of securing the formation of an abstract order of actions only through their universal application, while their application in the particular instance cannot be said to have a specific purpose distinct from the purpose of the system of rules as a whole."[80] Hayek's minimalism was nonetheless moralistic because he regarded commitment to it a categorical imperative. "Commitment to the rule of law restrains the preoccupation with material success without condemning it," is how one interpreter summarized Hayek's position.[81] To be sure, Hayek wanted to protect the freedom of markets, which is why he emphasized early on in his oeuvre the centrality of property rights. But he also cared about the rule of law *as such.* To him what it represented was both end *and* means. In Hayek's account of the rule of law, writes Timothy Fuller, "[m]utuality and self-interest are shown to be reconcilable."[82] Fuller summarizes the Hayekian position thus:

> If we can become better off materially in consequence of the commitment to the rule of law, that is all to the good; but if we believe that the commitment to the rule of law should stand or fall on such considerations, we sow the seeds for undermining that commitment in all those who perceive advantages to themselves in abandoning the rule of law – and there are always advantages to some in so doing.[83]

Hayek was an institutionalist of "spontaneous order."[84] The rule of law, for him, was a rationalist solution to the problem of collection action. He especially welcomed in the evolution of law over the centuries the "transition from specificity and concreteness to increasing generality and abstractness."[85] For him the legalization of politics was the way forward, its judicialization a neutral safeguard. We can be ruled by law, Hayek wrote in *The Constitution of Liberty,* "in the sense in which 'to rule' means the enforcement of general rules, laid down irrespective of the particular case and equally applicable to all."[86] What he called the "law of liberty" he regarded as an awesome institutional design, a moral achievement,

[80] Friedrich A. Hayek, *Law, Legislation and Liberty,* vol. 1: *Rules and Order* (Chicago: University of Chicago Press, 1973), p. 122.

[81] Fuller, "Friedrich Hayek's Moral Science," 19.

[82] Fuller, "Friedrich Hayek's Moral Science," 18.

[83] Fuller, "Friedrich Hayek's Moral Science," 19.

[84] Hayek, *Law, Legislation and Liberty,* vol. 1, esp. pp. 35–54.

[85] Friedrich A. Hayek, *The Collected Works of F. A. Hayek,* vol. 17: *The Constitution of Liberty,* ed. Ronald Hamowy (Chicago: University of Chicago Press, [1960] 2011), p. 219.

[86] Hayek, *The Collected Works of F. A. Hayek,* vol. 17, p. 224.

because it secured and ring-fenced well into the future for an untold number of individuals and groups "a known range within which" they could decide on their actions in that society, thereby enabling them "to make the fullest use" of their knowledge.[87] The virtue of the rule of law, as Hayek saw it, was its ability "to accord universal recognition of human worth without falling into chaos or arbitrariness."[88] Morality per se had nothing to do with this virtue of the rule of law in his account. On this point Hayek was adamant: "orderliness cannot be the result of a unified direction."[89] In that direction, he was certain, serfdom lay.

Late in life, however, Hayek had second thoughts. Gradually he came "to recognize the limitations of [the] institutional solutions" he had once advocated.[90] He was "much more sceptical about the possibility of a limited state."[91] Right after World War II, the rule of law for Hayek held the appeal of "a noble ideal."[92] At the end of his career he was all but certain "it was doomed to failure."[93] Is the rule of law doomed, as the late Hayek feared? Or did the Austrian economist as a young man, this rational moralist, simply expect too much from the rule of law?

The fallacy of positivism in the philosophy of law (and the philosophy of the social sciences) is the exclusive focus on the *rules* of the rule of law – on the rule of law as a law of rules, as Antonin Scalia once put it.[94] Among legal positivists this manifests as a preoccupation with "the command-and-control aspect" of law.[95] Positivists in the social sciences (where they are known as positive political theorists or, more simply, as rationalists) emphasize the central importance of so-called rules of the game, rules that legal norms and institutions, if they rule, help to define – and *qua* system – to uphold.[96] Cass Sunstein, like Hayek, has also made the case for rules, although his is a more

[87] Hayek, *The Collected Works of F. A. Hayek*, vol. 17, p. 224.

[88] Fuller, "Friedrich Hayek's Moral Science," 18.

[89] Hayek, *The Collected Works of F. A. Hayek*, vol. 17, p. 229.

[90] Kukathas, "Hayek and the State," p. 294.

[91] Kukathas, "Hayek and the State," p. 294.

[92] Kukathas, "Hayek and the State," p. 294.

[93] Kukathas, "Hayek and the State," p. 294.

[94] Scalia, "The Rule of Law as a Law of Rules."

[95] Waldron, "The Concept and the Rule of Law," 56.

[96] Hayek's aside, the most cited treatment of the rule of law by a rationalist is Barry R. Weingast, "The Political Foundations of Democracy and the Rule of the Law," *American Political Science Review*, 91 (1997), 245–263. Even more influential has been his earlier, co-authored piece with Douglass North, "Constitutions and Commitment: The Evolution of Institutions Governing Public Choice in Seventeenth-Century England," *Journal of Economic History*, Vol. 49 (1989), 803-832. See also Yoram Barzel, *A Theory of the State: Economic Rights, Legal Rights, and the Scope of the State* (Cambridge: Cambridge University Press, 2002). Most recently, see Gillian K.

modest argument for them. He thinks the rule of law requires a system of rules. The systematization of rules for him is "the signal virtue of a regime of law."[97] Why? Because rules, according to Sunstein, often function as precommitment strategies that overcome "predictable problems with ruleless decisions."[98] Yet Sunstein, contrary to Hayek (as well as left-leaning critics of the Austrian economist), does not see any reason to align the rule of law as closely with free markets, with what in the 1990s became known as the "Washington Consensus" about neoliberalism, as Hayek did. "The rule of law does not have the features that Hayek and his Marxist opponents understand it to have," Sunstein contends.[99] "The rule of law has many virtues, but we should not overstate what it entails," he cautioned, because "the virtues of rules are inseparable from the vices of rules."[100]

These vices are not always easy to spot. And we do not always look for them. Even when we do, they are difficult to identify in the rule of law, says Waldron, "without any reference to the culture of argument that it frames, sponsors, and institutionalizes."[101] To truly grasp the rule of law, then – to pinpoint it accurately at one of the many conceivable points of its operation – requires us to think of it as a social imaginary. This entails situating it concretely, not just abstractly, in the lifeworlds of those who are touched by the rule of law, violently or otherwise.

The preoccupation ever since World War II with taxonomies of the rule of law – an epistemological way of representing the rule of law that originated in legal philosophy, then found mathematical expression in political science, and in recent decades has manifested – often paternalistically, sometimes perversely – in the form of technical identi-kits disseminated by the international community to construct in unfamiliar cultures a composite likeness of the rule of law to aid the distant needy – has retarded not advanced understanding of the rule of law.[102] The dogged

Hadfield, Jens Meierhenrich, and Barry R. Weingast, "A Positive Theory of the Rule of Law," in this volume.

97 Cass R. Sunstein, *Legal Reasoning and Political Conflict* (New York: Oxford University Press, 1996), p. 102.

98 Sunstein, *Legal Reasoning and Political Conflict*, p. 110.

99 Sunstein, *Legal Reasoning and Political Conflict*, p. 120.

100 Sunstein, *Legal Reasoning and Political Conflict*, p. 120.

101 Waldron, "The Concept and the Rule of Law," 56.

102 On the continued salience of the tool-kit-approach in international rule of law efforts, see, most recently, European Commission, "The EU's Rule of Law Toolbox," Factsheet, April 2019, available at https://ec.europa.eu/info/sites/info/files/rule_of_law_factsheet_1

search for a quantifiable essence of the rule of law, and the inflated expectations that this search created, has obscured the idea of the rule of law more than it has illuminated it.

An "unavoidable cliché," the rule of law now means "so many different things to so many different people," Martin Krygier complained, "it is hard to say just what this rhetorical balloon is full of, or indeed where it might float next."[103] Worst of all, worries he, "people continue to blow warm air into the concept."[104] I am mindful of avoiding this trap. The "current rule of law effusions" are helping no one except authoritarian rulers who know how to manipulate the technologies of the rule of law just like their democratic counterparts.[105] Seeing that the rule of law is hopelessly contested, this begs the question: Does the rule of law *need* to be intelligible?

5 The Phenomenology of the Rule of Law

The rule of law is contested – and essentially so – because of a disagreement among three broad constituencies.[106] Let us call them *positivists*, *normativists*, and *empiricists*. We encountered some the most influential positivists and normativists in the previous section. Their disagreements are about the relationship between law and morals in conceptions of the (rule of) law.[107] For the longest time, empiricists, by which

.pdf; International Bar Association, *Toolkit for Lawyers at Risk*, January 2020, available at www.ibanet.org/Human_Rights_Institute/Toolkit-on-Lawyers-at-Risk-project.aspx. See also *Office of the United Nations High Commissioner for Human Rights, Rule of Law Tools for Post-Conflict States: National Consultations on Transitional Justice* (New York: United Nations, 2009). For a sustained critique, see Humphreys, *Theatre of the Rule of Law*. See also David M. Trubek and Alvaro Santos, eds., *The New Law and Economic Development: A Critical Appraisal* (Cambridge: Cambridge University Press, 2006).

[103] Martin Krygier, "The Rule of Law: Pasts, Presents, and Two Possible Futures," *Annual Review of Law and Social Science*, 12 (2016), 200.

[104] Krygier, "The Rule of Law," 200. [105] Krygier, "The Rule of Law," 200.

[106] See also Jeremy Waldron, "The Rule of Law as an Essentially Contested Concept," in this volume. The first scholar to describe the rule of law – and the Rechtsstaat – as "essentially contested concepts" was Neil MacCormick. See his "Der Rechtsstaat und die rule of law," *Juristenzeitung*, 39 (1984), 66, 69.

[107] The de-emphasis in the philosophy of law on the so-called Hart–Fuller debate coincided with "skepticism about the idea that inquiries into the nature of law" – investigations that, some say, are separate from and must precede any discussion of its rule – "should be framed, either exclusively or predominantly, as exercises in 'conceptual analysis.'" John Tasioulas, "Introduction," in idem, ed., *The Cambridge Companion to the Philosophy of Law* (Cambridge: Cambridge University Press, 2020), p. 5.

I mean scholars and practitioners who work with the rule of law concretely not just abstractly, played a minor role in the debate about intelligibility. The data they brought to the topic, whether interpretive or quantitative, were too vast or unwieldy to be made to fit – except as parables or vignettes – into the models of the twentieth-century philosopher kings who held forth about the rule of law.[108] Lest I be misunderstood, I think eminently useful some of these models. They discipline the mind. They have enlarged our sense of the rule of law as utopia. But instead of asking in perpetuity, with recurring references to Western legal thought, what the rule of law is – and is not – it might be time to abandon the quest for intelligibility.

I think there is life left in the idea of the rule of law. And, as some say, "we make progress by arguing about it."[109] But I want to think differently about intelligibility than Ernest Weinrib, who has made the strongest case for a criterial approach to the rule of law.[110] Weinrib's is a self-consciously formal theory of the rule of law. The result of a purely internal inquiry, his is a highly stylized conception of the rule of law, one concerned solely with inner normativity. It is an account of the immanence of the rule of law. Leaning on Aristotle's characterization of law as "intelligence without appetite," Weinrib wants us to understand the rule of law formally, not instrumentally.[111] "To understand something in this way is to understand it unconditionally in the literal sense, i.e., as something whose intelligibility is not conditioned by or dependent upon anything extrinsic."[112] The intelligibility of the rule of law *stands apart* from that of any dispositional virtues and vices. Goals frequently associated with the rule of law Weinrib is keen to dissasociate from the concept include, *inter alia*, the maximization of liberty, prosperity, and solidarity, and, more specifically, the pursuit of such utilitarian policy objectives as free markets, human rights, or economic development.

108 See, *pars pro toto*, Ronald Dworkin, *Law's Empire* (Cambridge: Belknap Press of Harvard University Press, 1986).

109 Waldron, "Rule *by* Law," 22.

110 Ernest J. Weinrib, "The Intelligibility of the Rule of Law," in Allan C. Hutchinson and Patrick Monahan, eds., *The Rule of Law: Ideal or Ideology?* (Toronto: Carswell, 1987), pp. 59–84.

111 See also Ernest J. Weinrib, "Aristotle's Forms of Justice," *Ratio Juris*, 2 (1989), 211–226. Here he defends legal formalism against Hans Kelsen's charge of emptiness. Cf. Hans Kelsen, "Aristotle's Doctrine of Justice," in idem, *What is Justice? Justice, Law and Politics in the Mirror of Science* (Berkeley: University of California Press, 1957), pp. 110–136.

112 Ernest J. Weinrib, "Legal Formalism: On the Immanent Rationality of the Law," *Yale Law Journal*, 97 (1988), 956–957.

Weinrib insists that the meaning of the rule of law is immanent to the idea itself. What some regard as a tautological way of thinking about the rule of law, he and other formalists regard as indispensable in a world riven by contending moralities. "By suggesting that the rationality of law lies in a moral order immanent to legal material, formalism postulates that juridical content can somehow sustain itself from within."[113] The rule of law, or so the argument goes, has no need for external validation. It is what it is, and it is good. There is virtue in coherence, which is why Weinrib's argument about the rule of law is all about form: "Form is the organizing idea latent in the content of a sophisticated culture, and the ultimate test for legal content is its adequacy to the form it expresses."[114] As he writes,

> When we seek the intelligibility of something, we want to know what the something is. This search for "whatness" presupposes that the something is a *this* and not a *that*, that it has, in other words, a determinate content. This content is determinate because it sets the matter apart from other matters and prevents it from falling back into the chaos of unintelligible indeterminacy that its identification as a something denies. The content has thus both a positive and a negative significance: It makes the matter in question what it is, and it differentiates it from what it is not.[115]

By abstracting from reality, formal theorists of the rule of law, like Weinrib, draw "a circle of thought that feeds upon its own unfolding explicitness."[116] In other words, they conjure a self-referential world. This mode of thinking about the rule of law, for all its technical mastery, is impervious to the real world, which renders it unhelpful as a guide to thinking about the rule of law. "Like Moses and Marx," as one interlocutor put it, "Weinrib is a discoverer who declares the good and urges its controlling power on the world."[117] But the rule of law is not just something that we discern; it is also, and primarily, something we *do*. This brings us back to the tension of thought versus practice in articulations of the rule of law.

Pace Weinrib and other advocates of noninstrumental conceptions of the rule of law who take the idea out of context, scrub the concept free of all contaminants it picked up in countless histories, and make it look pristine,

[113] Weinrib, "Legal Formalism," 955.

[114] Weinrib, "Legal Formalism," 974. See also Ernest Weinrib, *The Idea of Private Law* (Cambridge: Harvard University Press, 1995), esp. p. 25.

[115] Weinrib, "Legal Formalism," 958.

[116] Weinrib, "Legal Formalism," 974.

[117] Allan C. Hutchinson, "The Importance of Not Being Ernest," *McGill Law Journal*, 34 (1989), 238.

I seek to re-complexify the rule of law. I am attuned to its grubbier side, to the darkness on the edge of law. Instead of trying to achieve intelligibility *nomothetically*, mine is an argument for trying to approximate intelligibility *ideographically*, in the vernacular. By thinking about what the rule of law means in translation, we free ourselves from the shackles of preconceived notions. We reach an improved position from which to assess the power – and pathologies – of the rule of law and its discursive formations.[118]

I am not the first to suggest that the rule of law no longer has, if it ever did, "a specific or even any documentary anchor or focal point."[119] My previous explorations of the rule of law in the real world have convinced me that, conceptually speaking, less is more.[120] In my ongoing quest to approximate what the rule of law "is," I continue to find value in Joseph Raz's much-debated account, which he recently revisited – and once more defended.[121] "There is no point in verbal disputes about which ideals deserve to be called the rule of law."[122] In the real world, legal practices, implicitly or otherwise, are governed by "a variety of moral principles."[123] According to Raz, "[t]he rule of law is one of them, but not the only one."[124] Instead of debating the place of morality *in* the concept of the rule of law, Raz seems to be saying, we should recognize the rule of law *as* morality.

I assume, with Raz, that the rule of law is the specific virtue of legality. I propose legality, as a structuring device, will be consequential to the extent there exists in a given society a propensity for "a legal way of doing things."[125] A commitment to legalism – as opposed to, say, decisionism – in the creation and maintenance of rule, whether democratic or authoritarian or a hybrid form, is nothing to be sniffed at, at least not outright. In post-Soviet Russia, for example, the rule of "everyday law" has proved so durable, and has successfully structured so many aspects of ordinary

[118] See also Frederic C. Schaffer, *Democracy in Translation: Understanding Politics in an Unfamiliar Culture* (Ithaca: Cornell University Press, 1998).

[119] Martin Krygier, "Tempering Power," in Maurice Adams, Anne Meuwese, and Ernst Hirsch Ballin, eds., *Constitutionalism and the Rule of Law: Bridging Idealism and Realism* (Cambridge: Cambridge University Press, 2017), p. 39.

[120] See also Paul Gowder, *The Rule of Law in the Real World* (Cambridge: Cambridge University Press, 2016).

[121] Joseph Raz, "The Law's Own Virtue," *Oxford Journal of Legal Studies*, 39 (2019), 1–15.

[122] Raz, "The Law's Own Virtue," 2. [123] Raz, "The Law's Own Virtue," 9.

[124] Raz, "The Law's Own Virtue," 9.

[125] On the conceptualization and operationalization of this seemingly vague indicator, see Meierhenrich, *The Legacies of Law*.

lifeworlds – notably through so-called justice-of-the-peace courts (*mirovye sudy*) – that it would be churlish, and empirically distortive, to claim that law did not rule in this authoritarian regime. Scholars like Marina Kurkchiyan have long bemoaned the existence of a "negative myth of the rule of law" in the international discourse about Russia's supposed lawlessness.[126]

In addition to taking a leaf from Raz, I assume, with Krygier, that the specific virtue of the rule of law is the moderation it can inspire. Few have written more insightfully, or copiously, about the rule of law in recent decades than Krygier. One of his most lasting contributions to its theory, it seems to me, will be his careful precising of why, first, "arbitrary power" is the quintessential problem of social order; and why, secondly, we should regard "tempering power" as the most useful contribution the rule of law can provide to solving it. Krygier's intellectual refinement and integration of centuries' worth of theoretical argumentation by the good and the great, from Aristotle to Montesquieu, and, in our time, Stephen Holmes, allowed Krygier to put front and center once again an institutional logic that long ago had been relegated to the margins of rule of law theorizing – what in Roman legal thought was known as *temperantia*, a legal transplant that can be traced back to the even earlier Greek idea of σωφροσύνη, or temperance.[127] The ancient concern, not unlike today's, was to create disincentives for arbitrary rule, to avoid *pleonexia*, that is, the greed, avarice, and covetousness that Aristotle (and much later also Thomas Hobbes, in Chapter XV of *Leviathan*) identified as a recipe for lawlessness.[128]

One of the keys to moderation, says Krygier, updating Montesquieu's solution to the problem of "immoderate" rule, is a streamlined conception of the rule of law, one that is neither too permissive nor too prohibitive. "[C]ontrary to what many say about the rule of law," Montesquieu "clearly saw the aim of moderating or tempering power as

[126] Marina Kurkchiyan, "The Illegitimacy of Law in Post-Soviet Societies," in Denis J. Galligan and Marina Kurkchiyan, eds., *Law and Informal Practices: The Post-Communist Experience* (Oxford: Oxford University Press, 2003), p. 30. More recently, see Marina Kurkchiyan and Agnieszka Kubal, eds., *A Sociology of Justice in Russia* (Cambridge: Cambridge University Press, 2018); and Hendley, *Everyday Law in Russia.*

[127] Krygier, "The Rule of Law," 206.

[128] See also Karen Margrethe Nielsen, "The Tyrant's Vice: *Pleonexia* and Lawlessness in Plato's *Republic*," *Ethics*, 33 (2019), 146–169.

not to shackle government but to channel its activities to what it needs to do, and in the process make it able to do such things better, and not do things it should not do."[129] For Krygier, the rule of law is about "enabling constraints," as Holmes uses the term.[130] By bringing "'negative' realism" to the rule of law, Krygier has updated in a convincing fashion Shklar's argument from what she famously called "the liberalism of fear."[131] Inviting us to treat "hostility to arbitrariness" as *the* central aspect of the rule of law, the connective tissue that links duelling concepts, Krygier shows, rather convincingly, that the value of the rule of law, if thought about with modest expectations, is not only "immanent and generic" but also "intrinsic to the ideal of the rule of law" and "relevant across the board."[132]

Neither Krygier nor Raz, who arrived in the same destination via a different route, are naïve. Both are realistic about the potentials of the rule of law to temper power. "It would be foolish to claim that conformity to the rule of law," defined minimally, "can completely eliminate arbitrary use of power, or other forms of abuse of legal power. It merely helps to do so."[133] A conception encouraging inflated expectations this is not. This is to be applauded. I favor arguments about the rule of law that foreground the contribution of its norms and institutions to reducing arbitrariness, and therewith uncertainty when it comes to bargaining for mutual advantage. But I have a friendly amendment. It seems to me, Krygier's argument from arbitrariness could be strengthened if he – and all of us – paid attention to the social mechanism by which the rule of law reduces uncertainty.

One conceivable way of accomplishing this is to bring the idea of coordination back in. In the 1980s, philosophers and game theorists built theories of the rule of law that foregrounded the value of cooperation. Although John Finnis, who joined the effort from the philosophical camp, insisted, oddly yet stridently, that the game-theoretical concept of a coordination problem was "inappropriate for use in legal theory" and "not an adequate model for explaining the emergence and features of law," including its rule, there is much to be said for thinking rigorously about the rule of law.[134] Indeed, the

[129] Krygier, "The Rule of Law," 206.

[130] Stephen Holmes, *Passions and Constraint: On the Theory of Liberal Democracy* (Chicago: University of Chicago Press, 1995), p. xi.

[131] Krygier, "Tempering Power," pp. 41–46. [132] Krygier, "The Rule of Law," 216.

[133] Raz, "The Law's Own Virtue," 14.

[134] For this argument, see, for example, Hadfield, Meierhenrich, and Weingast, "A Positive Theory of the Rule of Law."

question of coordination (and the broader idea of cooperation) lend themselves to bridging the epistemological divide between law and the humanities in studies of the rule of law.[135]

In fact, Finnis, despite his protestations about the supposed incompatibility of philosophical and game-theoretical approaches to law, has already done the heavy lifting – by sketching a procedural logic that John Ferejohn, Richard Posner, Barry Weingast and other proponents of positive political theory would have no trouble endorsing. Neither would Hayek. Notice that in *The Constitution of Liberty*, Hayek approvingly quoted Emil Brunner, a Swiss theologian and philosopher of natural law.[136] For Brunner, the rule of law was "order by foresight."[137] In his forgotten account from 1945, "that is the service" the rule of law renders, "it is also its burden and its danger."[138] The rule of law, theorized Brunner, "offers protection from the arbitrary; it gives a feeling of reliability, of security, it takes from the future its ominous darkness."[139] Brunner's is one of the most realistic conceptions of the rule of law on offer. It is worth reclaiming for the present. Hayek certainly did in *his* present: "Order with reference to society," he wrote, "means essentially that individual action is guided by successful foresight, that people not only make effective use of their knowledge but can also foresee with a high degree of confidence what collaboration they can expect from others."[140]

The rule of law, in this conception, gains its virtue from the moral association it enables by way of the social imaginary it enacts. We may not approve of these moralities, but it would be methodologically misguided, as the historian Claudia Koonz reminds us, to deny to abhorrent moralities the empirical status as belief systems, especially if these belief systems made a difference to – and through – law.[141] James

[135] John M. Finnis, "Law as Co-ordination," *Ratio Juris*, 2 (1989), 97, 98. For one such effort, one that tried to integrate insights from rational choice institutionalism and historical institutionalism, see Meierhenrich, *The Legacies of Law*.

[136] Hayek, *The Collected Works of F. A. Hayek*, vol. 17, p. 231 fn. 28.

[137] Emil Brunner, *Justice and the Social Order*, trans. Mary Hottinger (New York: Harper, 1945), p. 22.

[138] Brunner, *Justice and the Social Order*, p. 22.

[139] Brunner, *Justice and the Social Order*, p. 22.

[140] Hayek, *The Collected Works of F. A. Hayek*, vol. 17, p. 229.

[141] Claudia Koonz, *The Nazi Conscience* (Cambridge: Belknap Press of Harvard University Press, 2003). For similar arguments with an exclusive focus on Nazi law, see Meierhenrich, *The Remnants of the Rechtsstaat*; and Herlinde Pauer-Studer, *Justifying Injustice: Legal Theory in Nazi Germany* (Cambridge: Cambridge University Press, 2020).

Whitman has shown that the idea of Jim Crow segregation was sufficiently coherent in normative terms to serve as a mental model in the making of Nazi race law.[142]

My conceptual move relates morality to the rule of law *without* making it a defining attribute of the concept of the rule of law. For understanding the rule of law, it is significant by association, not by definition. The concept of the rule of law, thought of in minimalist terms, can be married to varieties of morality – to moralities.[143] "[H]ostility to arbitrariness might stem from a commitment to liberty, moral equality, or dignity."[144] In methodological terms, hostility to arbitrariness is also a virtue that is recognizable, and therewith traceable, in less frequently studied settings, from small-scale societies to unfamiliar cultures or bygone eras, including those that do not look back on a long tradition of the rule of law as it has been conventionally understood in the capitals of "the West." As Fernanda Pirie writes, "The power and appeal of law are inevitably taking new forms in the modern world, but if we look widely it is evident that historic patterns are re-emerging. Law has often been regarded as superior to the ruler, embodying higher standards with which he or she ought to comply: the ideal of the 'rule of law.'"[145]

By holding fast to the constitutive function of law, a phenomenological approach that expects nothing else from the rule of law other than a hostility to arbitrariness captures authentically what, at the beginning of the legal universe, caused the invention of what one might be tempted to think of as the *telos* of the rule of law. The demand for such a *telos*, whether local, regional, national, international, or global, arguably grew out of a realization – here, there, and everywhere – what an *absence* of law-governed rule has always meant for dispute resolution, whether small-scale or vast-scale, namely "the presence of resolution by will, volition, choice."[146] That kind of rule is "an exertion of sway," it is prerogative rule.[147] It is the antithesis of the law of rules, of normative rule, of the rule of law. What the rule of law implies is that law "is not essentially *voluntas* but *ratio*," that it is capable of guiding – more

[142] James Q. Whitman, *Hitler's American Model: The United States and the Making of Nazi Race Law* (Princeton: Princeton University Press, 2017).

[143] See also Part III of this volume.

[144] Krygier, "The Rule of Law," 216.

[145] Pirie, *The Anthropology of Law*, p. 220.

[146] Lewis D. Sargentich, *Liberal Legality: A Unified Theory of Our Law* (Cambridge: Cambridge University Press, 2018), p. 141.

[147] Sargentich, Liberal Legality, p. 141. See also Meierhenrich, *The Remnants of the Rechtsstaat.*

or less generally – politics, the economy, and society.[148] Stated thus, "the virtues of a rule-system, as differentiated from orders and commands," are related to the incentives it produces.[149]

Take the example of ancient Athens, which illustrates nicely this logic of incentives in everyday law. Owing to Greek political thinkers from the fourth century, Plato and Aristotle foremost among them, the city-state is still the setting of a confected, widely rehearsed but empirically inaccurate origin story about the rule of law. Plato and Aristotle dreamt up utopias of the rule of law, ignoring the realities of the rule of law on their doorstep. They favored intelligibility over phenomenology. The reception of their philosophies has for centuries distorted conventional wisdom about the classical way of law. In the city state's radical approach to the rule of law, the kinds of virtues that Aristotle's writings persuaded us moderns to cherish – generality being the most conspicuous – had little to do with everyday law in the *polis*, with how law actually ruled. Metatheory and microhistory, in the case of ancient Athens, produced conflicting portrayals of what the ancient rule of law was. This dissonance points to a need to distinguish between ancient legal thought and ancient legal practice, an important difference that is often elided.[150] The study of legal thought alone is insufficient for making sound inferences about the social meanings of law: about the *role* of its rule.

The Athenian city-state did not have *the* rule of law, but its citizens undoubtedly possessed *a* rule of law. Law there ruled in the sense that it gradually, organically developed into one of the polity's most relevant institutions for making ancient democracy work. As Adriaan Lanni has shown, "Athenian legal institutions, though very different from the straightforward mechanisms that dominate modern legal systems, played an important role in maintaining order."[151] But because classical Athens was "a highly participatory democracy run primarily by amateurs," its rule of law lacked certainty.[152] It was neither consistently codified nor reliably

[148] Loughlin, *Foundations of Public Law*, p. 333.

[149] Loughlin, *Foundations of Public Law*, p. 335.

[150] For a recent, wide-ranging survey of the former, see Larry May, *Ancient Legal Thought: Equity, Justice, and Humaneness from Hammurabi and the Pharaohs to Justinian and the Talmud* (Cambridge: Cambridge University Press, 2019).

[151] Adriaan Lanni, *Law and Order in Ancient Athens* (Cambridge: Cambridge University Press, 2016), pp. 4–5.

[152] Lanni, *Law and Order in Ancient Athens*, p. 8.

backed by sanctions. And yet its rule was accepted, furthered, and sought out. It had authority. In Athens, the function of the ancient rule of law was *expressive*, it communicated a social imaginary, a finding that ties in with my argument about the phenomenology of the rule of law in modern times.

Lanni found that Athenian statutes, counterintuitively, fostered compliance with law in the absence of direct enforcement. The force of law was symbolic, its effect on behavior indirect. As "well-publicized expressions of community sentiment," the polity's legal norms and institutions, according to the latest scholarship, achieved acceptance because they derived from, and were constitutive of, the same social imaginary.[153] If we did not take into account this lifeworld, if we measured the polity's legalism instead with a criterial concept of the rule of law, we would miss much that was distinctive – and effective – about the Athenian way of law.

The Venetian Republic is another case to consider as we think phenomenologically about the rule of law. Law ruled in the Italian city-state, a commercial republic, for five hundred years. Between 1297 and 1797, government business in Venice was public business, scrupulously conducted through, by, and under law. In 1474, to give an example, the oligarchy of mechants and aristocrats adopted the first statutory patent system in Europe, possibly the earliest codified such system in the world. But law mattered throughout the civic reign. It was a fundamental building block in the institutional foundations of republicanism there. Crucially, however, as Waldron recently pointed out, Venetian legal practices were not associated "with any idea of active entitlement by ordinary members of the public to demand an account from officials of how public business was being conducted."[154] In this example, hostility to arbitrariness was the "central animating idea," so to speak, in the institutional design of a legal system that over a five-hundred-year period reduced, more or less reliably, the transactions costs for commercial activity.[155]

Faith in the sovereignty of the market, not the people, was the sense-giving feature in the Venetian imaginary of the of law. *Civitas*, not citizens, counted. Rules were designed for the community of citizens, as represented

153 Lanni, *Law and Order in Ancient Athens*, p. 13.

154 Jeremy Waldron, *Political Political Theory: Essays on Institutions* (Cambridge: Harvard University Press, 2016), p. 176.

155 On the helpful notion of the "central animating idea" in institutional design, see Robert E. Goodin, "Institutions and Their Design," in idem, ed., *The Theory of Institutional Design* (Cambridge: Cambridge University Press, 1996), pp. 26–27.

by the elites who governed them. "[T]he publicness of public business was not personified in an entity conceived of as entitled to actively demand an account. Instead, officials were held to the rule of law, and both they and those who evaluated their actions were expected to exercise and apply standards of civic virtue. It was in the rule of law and in the standards of virtue that the publicness of the republic was represented."[156] The law of Venice functioned not as a curb but as a coordination device, an enabling constraint. This I submit is what the rule of law, first and foremost, is.

The rule of law is *not* a limit. But it is not liberty either. It sits betwixt and between, a liminal institution, serviceable by anyone who cares about predictability, including dictators like Augusto Pinochet or Americans governing authoritarian enclaves in the Deep South during Jim Crow. The rule of law, then, is, in one sense,

> the requirement that government action must, by and large, be conducted under the auspices of law, which means that, unless there is very good reason to the contrary, law should be created in advance to authorize the actions that government is going to have to perform. This usually means an articulated process . . . so that the various aspects of lawmaking and legally authorized action are not just run together in a single gestalt.[157]

But the rule of law also exists *outside* of government action. Data about the everyday life of law from all areas of the the globe attest to this finding, a fact that has escaped many a metatheorist.[158]

Rules of law can survive, function, even thrive in the interstices of prerogative rule. In democratic regimes, the value of the rule of law is typically greatest in the nongovernmental realm, where it tends to structure a vastly larger number of social interactions (think contract law, corporate law, equity and trusts, family law, mergers and acquisitions, and tort law alone) than in the governmental sphere. What the rule of law is *not* is "an extemporere or off-the-cuff use of political authority."[159] That would be arbitrary rule. Such rule may possess charismatic, traditional, or another form of authority. It may even be couched in legal language, such as Executive Order 13768 of January 25, 2017, entitled "Enhancing Public Safety in the Interior of the United States," which is worth a brief mention. US District Judge William Orrick III declared the

[156] Waldron, *Political Political Theory*, pp. 176–177.
[157] Waldron, *Political Political Theory*, p. 63.
[158] See, most recently, Hendley, *Everyday Law in Russia.*
[159] Waldron, *Political Political Theory*, p. 65.

order unconstitutional in part, issuing a nationwide permanent injunction against the implementation of the order. What had happened is this: In a case of presidential overreach, the US administration of Donald Trump had sought to deny funding to so-called sanctuary cities, municipalities like San Francisco that refused to cooperate with federal immigration officials in the deportation of undocumented immigrants. A San Francisco City attorney hailed the permanent injunction, a swift judicial response to executive arbitrariness, a victory for the "rule of law."[160]

If one defines the rule of law solely in terms of hostility to arbitrariness, as I do, it is conceivable that "an odious regime" may use the idea "to legitimate its tyranny by pointing out – ominously – that there are even more tyrannical possibilities. To see formal legality as moral in itself can have hazardous consequences for a populace."[161] This is true, and borne out by an abundance of empirical data. But it is also true, and equally demonstrable, that law, as a resource for justifying power, if and when it rules, "invites argument over the nature of the authority it defines; it requires explanation."[162] Unless the rule of law is entirely facadist, it "does not enable the ruler to exercise power, so much as justify its use, and for the same reason can be used to resist or control it."[163] Thurgood Marshall recognized this, E. P. Thompson did, too, and so did "others" like Nelson Mandela, who, in the apartheid theater of the rule of law performed stunning acts of legal sabotage, wielding the authoritarian rule of law as an offensive weapon of the weak.[164]

160 As quoted in E. Rosenberg, "Federal Judge Blocks Trump's Executive Order on Denying Funds to Sanctuary Cities," *Washington Post*, November 21, 2017.

161 Tamanaha, *On the Rule of Law*, p. 96.

162 Fernanda Pirie and Judith Scheele, "Justice, Community, and Law," in idem, eds., *Legalism: Community and Justice* (Oxford: Oxford University Press, 2014), p. 10. See also James Boyd White, *Heracles' Bow* (Madison: University of Wisconsin Press, 1985), pp. 238–242.

163 Pirie, *The Anthropology of Law*, p. 229.

164 Kenneth W. Mack, *Representing the Race: The Creation of the Civil Rights Lawyer* (Cambridge: Harvard University Press, 2012); Jens Meierhenrich and Catherine M. Cole, "In the Theater of the Rule of Law: Performing the Rivonia Trial in South Africa, 1963–1964," in Jens Meierhenrich and Devin O. Pendas, eds., *Political Trials in Theory and History* (Cambridge: Cambridge University Press, 2016), pp. 229–262; and E. P. Thompson, *Whigs and Hunters: The Origin of the Black Act* (New York: Pantheon, 1975). See also Richard Abel, *Politics by Other Means: Law in the Struggle against Apartheid, 1980–1994* (London: Routledge, 1995); Meierhenrich, *The Legacies of Law*; and, farther afield, Douglas Morris, *Legal Sabotage: Ernst Fraenkel in Hitler's Germany* (Cambridge: Cambridge University Press, 2020). On the rule of law as a defensive weapon of the weak and beleagured in this century, see, for example, Richard L. Abel's two-volume account: *Law's Wars: The Fate of the Rule of*

Despite Lon Fuller's spending decades at the epicenter of the philosophical debate about "the concept and the rule of law," he was, somewhat surprisingly, less keen than most in jurisprudence on pure abstraction.[165] In a reply to his critics, appended to the revised edition of *The Morality of Law*, Fuller was full of hope that "[p]erhaps in time legal philosophers will cease to be preoccupied with building 'conceptual models' to represent legal phenomena, will give up their endless debate about definitions, and will turn instead to an analysis of the social processes that constitute the reality of law."[166] Fuller's reply, to my knowledge, was one of the very few occasions on which he used explicitly the phrase "the rule of law," a formulation he was at pains to avoid his entire working life, presumably because of the sloganeering and facile blather that he felt it regularly inspired. As other observers have noted, "the ideology of the legal profession during the first half of the twentieth century, particularly in America," whence Fuller wrote, reduced the idea of the rule of law "to slogans in the cause of liberty and human rights," a portrayal that, according to this observer, "was full of unrecognised contradictions, and probably confused issues more than it developed them."[167]

The early twenty-first century is an opportune time to take down the rule of law from the pedestal on which it – certainly in North America and Western Europe – still stands a little too proudly. But I am in no rush to assign the rule of law to the dustbin of theory. Despite its well-documented pathologies (see Part IV of this collection), I think the rule of law a desirable ingredient in the soup of politics, domestic and international.[168] It may not be "an unqualified human good," as E. P. Thompson thought, but a worthwhile human good it is.[169] And it is this chiefly on account of its procedural ethos. Justice Felix Frankfurter, of the US Supreme Court, in *Uveges* v. *Commonwealth of Pennsylvania*, a 1948 case, found it necessary to remind his country of this very specific virtue of law's rule. "[T]he law," he argued, joined by Justices Robert Jackson and Harold Burton, in a dissenting opinion in what was a case revolving around a minor's right to due process, "is essentially legalistic in the

Law in the U.S. "War on Terror" (Cambridge: Cambridge University Press, 2018); and *Law's Trials: The Performance of Legal Institutions in the U.S. "War on Terror"* (Cambridge: Cambridge University Press, 2018).

165 Waldron, "The Concept and the Rule of Law." 166 Fuller, *The Morality of Law*, p. 242.

167 Noel B. Reynolds, "Grounding the Rule of Law," *Ratio Juris*, 2 (1989), 2.

168 Waldron, "The Concept and the Rule of Law," 5.

169 Thompson, *Whigs and Hunters*, p. 266. See also Douglas Hay, "E. P. Thompson and the Rule of Law: Qualifying the 'Unqualified Good,'" in this volume.

sense that observance of well-recognized procedure is, on the balance, socially desirable."[170] But a caveat is in order. Law may be socially desirable – "in that it is a stabilizing force in society" where it rules – but it will *never* be "neutral."[171] To claim otherwise is to inflate expectations about what the rule of law is – and what difference it can make in life. That is where hubris lies.

The rule of law is a noble lie, albeit a lie one can believe in. It can lengthen the shadow of the future for most anyone because it "is designed to promote the security of expectations."[172] But we would do well to remember, at the same time, that "[f]or all its responsiveness to social changes it remains a conservatizing influence. It is not a mere method capable of applying every sort of social purpose. It tends to preserve and order."[173] It is a sane idea, with proceduralism as its USP – its unique selling point. Defining the rule of law procedurally is, in fact, about substance. "The 'procedures' of law are also a social policy, as much so as any act of Congress," is how Judith Shklar put it in her defense of legalism: "Its so called 'purely procedural' aspects have the most direct social consequences. They are nothing if not substantive in their social impact."[174]

What the rule of law can add – even where it is creaky or compromised – is balance, sometimes only a modicum, at other times a far greater measure. In my pared-down conception of the rule of law, it is capable, in the right circumstances, of moderating the way we are governed – nothing more but also nothing less. "[A]lthough tempered power is not necessarily or always more important than other goals, it has a specific focus and a general importance not reducible to other things," as Krygier writes.[175] "There are many ways to exercise power, and doing so in a way that is not, and routinely can be expected not to be, arbitrary is salutary."[176] I concur with Krygier. If an additional authority were needed to bolster our case, Michael Oakeshott is it.

6 A Kind of Literacy

Oakeshott's contribution to thinking about the rule of law is little known. This is regrettable but not surprising. After all, Oakeshott only ever

170 *Uveges* v. *Commonwealth of Pennsylvania*, 435 US 437, 449 (1948) (dissenting opinion).
171 Judith N. Shklar, "In Defense of Legalism," *Journal of Legal Education*, 19 (1966), 57.
172 Shklar, "In Defense of Legalism," 57.
173 Shklar, "In Defense of Legalism," 57.
174 Shklar, "In Defense of Legalism," 57, 58.
175 Krygier, "The Rule of Law," 218.
176 Krygier, "The Rule of Law," 218.

published one essay on the topic. Although he is "virtually ignored" in the philosophy of law as a result – and his contribution left no lasting mark, except among a handful of cognoscenti, on the literature about the rule of law – his take is one of the most insightful we possess.[177] David Dyzenhaus certainly thinks so. He credits Oakeshott with having made "one of the most important contributions" to the subject since World War II.[178] Shirley Letwin thought similarly about Oakeshott's significance for thinking about the rule of law. She credits him for having transcended the debate over the intelligibility of the rule of law, which, as we have seen, centered endlessly on the relationship between law and morals. In her reading of Oakeshott's writings about the rule of law, he single-handedly resolved the differences between positivists and normativists:

> He makes it unambiguously clear that association under law is a moral relationship, that it is a relationship in terms of rules which lay down considerations to be taken into account by independent agents, and that the authority of those rules is distinct from their rightness. But even though he insists on the moral character of the rule of law, Oakeshott does not join the normativist opposition to positivism. He is engaged rather in filling the gap left by the failure of positivist philosophers to explain the moral character of law and he does not in the least deny the positivist contention that law consists of authorized rules and that the obligation to obey them rests on their authority, not the justice of their provisions.[179]

Oakeshott's was a "skeptical jurisprudence."[180] His signal contribution, evidently inspired by his conviction, developed elsewhere in his oeuvre, that "experience" needed to be taken seriously, was to appreciate the changing character of the rule of law. He believed in both the rationality *and* morality of rules but he stood the ancient and modern approaches to both on their head:

> Oakeshott succeeded in making a complete break with the ancient pantheism by redefining reason as a purely human, but creative power. To avoid any suggestion of a cosmic principle, he speaks of "rationality" . . . rather than reason. Oakeshott's "rationality" is neither a capacity to discover indisputable truths or universal and

[177] David Dyzenhaus, "Dreaming the Rule of Law," in David Dyzenhaus and Thomas Poole, eds., *Law, Liberty and State: Oakeshott, Hayek and Schmitt on the Rule of Law* (Cambridge: Cambridge University Press, 2015), p. 235.

[178] Dyzenhaus, "Dreaming the Rule of Law," 236.

[179] Shirley Robin Letwin, "Morality and Law," *Ratio Juris*, 2 (1989), 61.

[180] Shirley Robin Letwin, *On the History of the Idea of Law*, ed. Noel B. Reynolds (Cambridge: Cambridge University Press, 2005), p. 307.

eternal patterns [about the rule of law], as in the ancient picture, nor is rationality a slave of the passions or a calculating power, as in the modern picture. As understood by Oakeshott, rationality is a faculty for inventing interpretations of and responses to experience.[181]

Oakeshott's call for a new way of seeing the rule of law is of a kind with my plea for a phenomenological approach to studying it. Oakeshott's insistence in his other writings that the "whole of interlocking meanings" matters for understanding human conduct is what makes his rule of law essay especially valuable in the twenty-first century at a time when the intellectual appetite for universal truths is on the wane.[182] Oakeshott's sophisticated argument reminds of the "webs of significance" that the anthropologist Clifford Geertz wanted us to notice.[183] Oakeshott's approach also has an affinity with what is known as practice theory, a long-standing, increasingly influential, though still underappreciated approach to studying life – including the lives of the law – in context. It gives pride of place to the particular in politics, to the granular in law.[184] Like practice theorists – and unlike philosophers of law – Oakeshott favored concreteness over abstraction. He was a phenomenologist of the rule of law *avant la lettre.*

Here is what Oakeshott thought the rule of law was:

The expression "the rule of law," taken precisely, stands for a mode of moral association exclusively in terms of the recognition of the authority of known, noninstrumental rules (that is, laws) which impose obligations to subscribe to adverbial conditions in the performance of the self-chosen actions of all who fall within their jurisdiction. This mode of association may be opprobriously branded as "legalistic" and other modes may be considered more interesting or more profitable, but this I think is what the rule of law must mean.[185]

By virtue of its legality, Oakeshott maintained, the rule of law enabled human beings to enter into "an exclusive, specifiable mode of relationship," one whose substance was up for grabs.[186] Oakeshott, in this

[181] Letwin, *On the History of the Idea of Law*, p. 309.

[182] Michael Oakeshott, *The Voice of Liberal Learning* (Indianapolis: Liberty Fund, [1989] 2001), p. 38.

[183] Clifford Geertz, "Thick Description: Toward an Interpretive Theory of Culture," in idem, *The Interpretation of Cultures: Selected Essays* (New York: Basic Books, 1973), p. 5.

[184] See, for example, Jens Meierhenrich, "The Practice of International Law: A Theoretical Analysis," *Law and Contemporary Problems*, 76 (2013), 1–83.

[185] Oakeshott, "The Rule of Law," p. 148.

[186] Oakeshott, "The Rule of Law," pp. 129, 149.

definition, and in his elaboration thereof, foregoes entirely the path of conceptualization through requirements. His theoretical intervention differs noticeably, and refreshingly, from what Paul Gowder has described as "the standard normative theory accounts of the concept of the rule of law," which, he rightly points out, are "quite abstract and difficult to connect to observable phenomena of the sorts that can be tested by social scientists, yet simultaneously extensive and demanding, generating lengthy laundry lists of requirements that states must satisfy."[187] Although he is partial to conceptual analysis, Oakeshott finds wanting attempts to achieve the intelligibility of the rule of law.

Erika Kiss has a neat take on what we stand to gain from rethinking the rule of law by paying attention to Oakeshott. She has identified two metaphors that, she believes, are hidden in Oakeshott's unusual definition of the rule of law: (1) the rule of law "as a game"; and (2) the rule of law "as social tissue."[188] What Kiss is suggesting, in essence, is this: Defining the rule of law in terms of rules is a necessary conceptual step, but not a sufficient one because the meaning of rules, and their validity, is empirically contingent. The rules of the rule of law, as a game, says Oakeshott, "are identified," and must thus be interpreted, "not only with respect to the desirability of the conditions they prescribe, but also with respect to their authenticity."[189] An association "in terms of the rule of law," Oakeshott wrote, in what may well be the most thoughtful commentary on the idea ever committed to paper,

> recognizes the formal principles of a legal order, which may be said to be themselves principles of "justice." And beyond this it may float upon the acknowledgment that the considerations in terms of which the *jus* of *lex* may be discerned are neither arbitrary, nor unchanging, nor uncontentious, and that they are the product of moral experience which is never without tensions and internal discrepancies. What this mode of association requires for determining the *jus* of a law is not a set of abstract criteria but an appropriately argumentative form of discourse

[187] Paul Gowder, *The Rule of Law in the Real World* (Cambridge: Cambridge University Press, 2016), p. 3.

[188] Erika A. Kiss, "The Rules of the Game: Stochastic Rationality in Oakeshott's Rule of Law Theory," in Dyzenhaus and Poole, eds., *Law, Liberty, and the State* p. 222.

[189] Loughlin, *Foundations of Public Law*, p. 326. See also idem, "Michael Oakeshott's Republican Theory of the Rule of Law," in this volume.

> in which to deliberate the matter; that is, a form of moral discourse, not concerned generally with right and wrong in human conduct, but focused narrowly upon the kind of conditional obligations a law may impose, undistracted by prudential and consequential considerations, and insulated from ... moral idiocies.[190]

This treatment is arresting, at least to me, because it manages to say something about the rule of law that may well be universally true without being universalizing. It is an example of theorizing without proselytizing. In his theoretical account, Oakeshott achieves parsimony without blinders. For him, the rule of law was both produced by *and* constitutive of the context in which it was invented, to which it was transplanted, on which it was octroyed. For this reason, believed he, "the rule of law requires the same sensitivity for nuances from its examiner as literature does from its critic," which is a call not dissimilar to mine for a phenomenology of the rule of law.[191]

But it is worth noting that Oakeshott adds a level of theoretical sophistication that is missing from many anthropological accounts of the rule of law in context, that is, accounts in which phenomenological ways of seeing are most common. As Kiss writes,

> Oakeshott uses the notion of *Rechtsgefühl* (through his analogy between vernacular language and the rule of law) to criticize a game-theoretical approach to the rule of law. He insists that the rule of law is not stochastic in the sense of a chess or cricket game, whose system of rules is invented in a more or less arbitrary fashion, but as a vernacular-language game, whose rules are like those of a natural language. A vernacular-language game is imbedded in heterogeneous vernacular practices based upon the kind of stochastic conduct that relies on a historically acquired and analytically obscure feeling for stochastic approximation. Analytical (incuding game-theory) approaches to the rule of law – Oakeshott argues – are based upon the false assumptions of finiteness, commensurability and the concept of mathematical probability as opposed to real-life likelihood.[192]

Literally, the German idea of *Rechtsgefühl* translates as "feeling for the rule of law." Oakeshott's use of it ties in with the sense-giving features of the rule of law as a social imaginary with which I began. In thinking about the rule of law, Oakeshott was wary, like I am, of "the rigidity of a morality reduced to rules."[193] Viewing the rule of law and its rules dynamically (in

[190] Oakeshott, "The Rule of Law," pp. 155–156.
[191] Kiss, "The Rules of the Game," p. 219. [192] Kiss, "The Rules of the Game," p. 219.
[193] Oakeshott, "The Rule of Law," p. 134.

socio-legal terms), not statically (in formalist terms), circumvents the problem of rigidity in relation to morality. Oakeshott is useful in this regard because his treatment of the rule of law sits astride the debate over the relationship between law and morals. In thinking about the rule of law anew, "he indicated a possibility" of theorizing it "that is different from both procedural legitimacy and compliance with a substantive morality."[194] Oakeshott, more than any other twentieth-century theorist of the rule of law, created the cognitive space necessary for thinking theoretically about the rule of law without being constrained by the corset of jurisprudence.

Oakeshott crafted an analytical framework that can accommodate positivists, normativists, and empiricists. He related the real to the ideal in a way that no theorist before him or since has quite managed. Interestingly, Oakeshott hitched his conception of the rule of law, at least in part, to early ideas of the *Rechtsstaat*. His description thereof is in line with the modest expectations he had of the rule of law: "[T]he character of a state in terms of the rule of law which appears in the writings of numerous eighteenth-century jurists and especially the early exponents of the *Rechtsstaat*," he wrote, was "a state ruled by *lex*, the authority of which lies in its *jus*."[195] But *jus*, for Oakeshott as well as for most eighteenth-century theorists in Germany, was a procedural *jus*. The kind of rule that the law enabled "was something less than the promise of the fulfilment of the dream of being, at last, ruled by incontestable 'justice,' and something more than the mere extrapolation of a current tendency."[196] Or, as he put it, the *jus* of the conditions the rule of law creates hinges on "their absolute faithfulness to the formal character of law and to their moral-legal acceptability, itself a reflection of the moral-legal self-understanding" of the association that it governs, which is another way of saying that the rule of law is a social imaginary, both abstractly *and* concretely.[197]

To defend the rule of law normatively, all that is needed is a factual catalogue of the thousand small sanities the idea – despite its well-documented imbrications with violence – has made possible over the centuries.

[194] Dyzenhaus, "Dreaming about the Rule of Law," p. 242.

[195] Oakeshott, "The Rule of Law," p. 169. See also Jens Meierhenrich, *The Idea of the Rechtsstaat: An Intellectual History* (Oxford: Oxford University Press, forthcoming); and idem, "*Rechtsstaat* versus the Rule of Law," in this volume.

[196] Oakeshott, "The Rule of Law," pp. 169, 173–174.

[197] Oakeshott, "The Rule of Law," p. 174.

7 A Thousand Small Sanities

If we believe Adam Gopnik, "[s]ane ideas are often a sequence of smallness."[198] In recent years the World Bank has come around, sort of, to a sane view of the rule of law, to regarding it from where Oakeshott stood. Its 2017 World Development Report, by the title *Governance and the Law*, provides tentative evidence that the international organization may have learned from its and others' extremely modest successes – and the many more outright failures – in promoting the rule of law abroad. The new vademecum the World Bank has given itself is suggestive of more than a trivial change in policy: "Think not only about the rule of law, but also about the *role of law*."[199]

What the economists on H Street have in mind are the many ways in which "groups and individuals in society use law as a means of promoting, enforcing, and institutionalizing interests or objectives."[200] Like me, and with Oakeshott, the World Bank accepts the problems that arise when morality is reduced to rules. It is noticeably less confident than it used to be about pronouncing on the nature of the rule of law, and its function in economic development. The so-called second-generation of rule of law practitioners – in Washington, DC, and elsewhere – appears to have understood that universalizing conceptions of the rule of law are not only impractical but also Pareto-inefficient, or suboptimal. In recognition, the World Bank has embraced a contingent approach to law, defining the rule of law as

> a device that provides a particular language, structure, and formality for ordering things, and this characteristic gives it the potential to become a force independent of the initial powers and intentions behind it.[201]

On the World Bank's latest procedural definition, the law rules insofar as it enjoys the status of a fundamental institution of (international) society. To govern, its values or practices must be constitutive in a major way of social life. They must be meaningful. This is to say they must have a structuring effect on societal outcomes – not on all of these outcomes, but on a sizable chunk of them. The rule of law still matters, on a systemic

198 Gopnik, *A Thousand Small Sanities*, p. 228.

199 World Bank, *World Development Report 2017: Governance and the Law* (Washington: World Bank, 2017), p. 29.

200 World Bank, *World Development Report 2017*, p. 96.

201 World Bank, *World Development Report 2017*, p. 13.

level. But how *exactly* it matters, and with what long-run effects, where and when, depends on the experience-near.

The rule of law anywhere is the result of a commitment – whether expressively nurtured from within or transmitted instrumentally from without – to institutionalism, to playing *by* and *with* rules. This is where Hayek comes back in, for whom the aim of legal rules is merely to prevent as much as possible, by drawing boundaries, the actions of different individuals from interfering with each other; they cannot alone determine, and also therefore cannot be concerned with, what the results for different individuals will be."[202] This does not mean Hayek was agnostic or callous. But he was less successful in keeping ideology at bay in thinking about the rule of law than Oakeshott.

Having pinpointed areas of theoretical affinity between conventional and phenomenological approaches to the rule of law, it stands to reason that the "antithesis" between rule-bound and value-bound theorists of the rule of law – between positivists and "purposivists" – may have been overstated.[203] The idea of the rule of law, as I want to understand it in this chapter, is neither the sole preserve of liberalism nor of realism, nor of any other "-ism." I believe the rule of law is present where a legal order is "in legally good shape," to repurpose John Finnis's formulation. Law rules where it has factual, demonstrable authority. It follows from this that "acknowledging the authority of law does not entail approval of what it prescribes."[204] Facticity and authority, more so than legitimacy, ought to be the touchstones of the rule of law.[205] As Hayek wrote, "there can never be a science of law that is purely a science of norms and takes no account of the factual order at which it aims."[206] Here is another way of putting it: "The rule of law captures those features of a legal order that are needed for

[202] Hayek, *Law, Legislation and Liberty*, vol. 1, p. 108.

[203] Cf. Brian Z. Tamanaha,*Law as a Means to an End: Threat to the Rule of Law* (Cambridge: Cambridge University Press, 2006).

[204] Letwin, *On the History of the Idea of Law*, p. 316. For a recent illustration of this insight in the case of Nazi Germany, with which the so-called Radbruch theses were concerned, and around which the Hart–Fuller debate centrally revolved, see Meierhenrich, *The Remnants of the Rechtsstaat*, esp. ch. 1. See also Stanley L. Paulson, "Lon L. Fuller, Gustav Radbruch, and the 'Positivist' Theses," *Law and Philosophy*, 13 (1994), 313–359.

[205] John Finnis, *Natural Law and Natural Rights*, 2nd ed. (Oxford: Oxford University Press), p. 270.

[206] Hayek, *Law, Legislation and Liberty*, vol. 1, p. 105.

that order to function well," figures Nick Barber. "The rule of law," he writes,

requires that law make the difference it purports to make; the principle focuses on the interplay between the formal demands of law – the rules found in statutes and other official pronouncements – and the reality of the rules that structure power within a community. To some extent, adherence to the rule of law is necessary for a legal order to exist; there are aspects of the principle that must be present in a system to be governed by law – and, in societies like ours, this is clearly the case – the rule of law amounts to a normative demand, a requirement that a certain set of mechanisms for the coercion and regulation of law is desirable, the demands of the rule of law stretch beyond the bare minimum necessary for law's existence.[207]

The upshot of this account, which bears a resemblance to Fuller's argument about "the inner morality of law," is this: the rule of law operates on two separate levels.

Some of the demands of the rule of law relate to features that are necessary for the very existence of the legal order; in their absence, the community is not governed by law. Other requirements of the principle move beyond this, and speak to the flourishing of the legal order; these demands relate to elements that are needed for the rule of law, as an ideal, to be fulfilled, and there is often a range of ways that these elements might be manifested within a legal order. There are plenty of real world legal orders that succeed in meeting the minimum demands of the principle but which still fall far short of the ideal.[208]

I agree, which is why mine is an argument for giving up on the rule of law in the singular – for abandoning the search for *the* rule of law in a diverse world that is losing patience after centuries of legal orientalism, one in which the Eurocentric conception of the rule of law, with its moral pretences, has outlived its usefulness. As already mentioned, I think it best to scale back conceptual ambition, to start with the *realities* of the rule of law. I think it advisable to take a step back from grand theories, to let go of first principles, and to start practice tracing *rules of law*, to appreciate the many legalities there always have been – and forever will be – in the real world. As Christopher Tomlins wrote, with early America in mind,

[207] N. W. Barber, *The Principles of Constitutionalism* (Oxford: Oxford University Press, 2018), p. 85.

[208] *Barber, The Principles of Constitutionalism*, p. 85. On Fuller, see, most recently, Rundle, "The Morality of the Rule of Law: Lon L. Fuller," in this volume.

legalities are the symbols, signs, and instantiations of formal law's classificatory impulse, the outcomes of its specialized practices, the products of its institutions. They are the means of effecting law's discourses, the mechanisms through which law names, blames, and claims. But legalities are not produced in formal settings alone. They are social products, generated in the course of virtually any repetitive practice of wide acceptance within a specific locale, call the result rule, custom, tradition, folkway or pastime, popular belief or protest.[209]

The rule of law, in other words, is what actors make of it. If that is so, why not give up on imagining the rule of law as either ideal or ideology, and start thinking of it as an *ideal type*?

The heuristic instrument of the *Idealtypus*, which Max Weber pioneered over a century ago, needs no introduction. It has long been a staple of the methodology of the social sciences. Unfortuntately, it has fallen out of favor, is rarely utilized anymore. The promise I see is this: Ideal typical constructions of the rule of law satisfy, to some extent, the craving for "conceptual purity" ("*begriffliche Reinheit*") on the part of rule of law scholars who, as we have seen, are after intelligibility, while also being commensurable with the kind of interpretive scholarship that has a keen interest in the phenomenology of the rule of law.[210] As Weber pointed out, in 1904, ideal types are cognitive tools, manufactured by conceptually heightening certain aspects of reality.[211] Whatever content the ideal type is given, its function is illumination, *not* idealization. Ideal types do not exist in reality. The point is to measure empirical reality *against* this imaginary standard in order to determine, interpretively, the distance or degree of approximation between, in our case, the reality of the rule of law and its ideal type.[212] Keith Tribe recently elaborated the methodological function thus:

The Weberian "ideal type" is not actually an idealisation of a given form or institution, but rather a *Gedankenbild*, a thought-image of the leading

[209] Christopher Tomlins, "The Many Legalities of Colonization: A Manifesto of Destiny for Early American Legal History," in Christopher L. Tomlins and Bruce H. Mann, eds., *The Many Legalities of Early America* (Chapel Hill: University of North Carolina Press, 2001), pp. 2–3.

[210] Max Weber, "Die 'Objektivität' sozialwissenschaftlicher und sozialpolitischer Erkenntnis," in idem, *Gesammelte Aufsätze zur Wissenschaftslehre* (Tübingen: Mohr, [1904] 1922), p. 191.

[211] Weber, "Die 'Objektivität' sozialwissenschaftlicher und sozialpolitischer Erkenntnis," pp. 190, 191.

[212] See also Fritz Ringer, *Max Weber's Methodology: The Unification of the Cultural and Social Sciences* (Chicago: University of Chicago Press, 1997), pp. 110–121.

characteristics associated with a form or institution used in historical investigation, and not the outcome of such investigation. It is not a model of a given historical reality, nor is it the essential nature of that reality; it is far looser, unhierarchised, and preliminary than that would suggest.[213]

The heuristic payoff of ideal typical constructions, especially of the rule of law, lies in accumulating knowledge of "concrete cultural phenomena in their interconnections, their causes, and their meanings."[214] For Weber, constructing them was not the purpose of inquiry. Instead they served as his maps on the path to knowledge; they told him where to go next.

I regard the ideal type as a focal point where nomothetic and ideographic approaches to the rule of law can be made to intersect. It marks a spot where unclaimed cognitive space is still available. Speaking of space, Gopnik, in his defense of liberalism observed that "liberals have become planetary. We think in a global way. We feel at home in the world. This is an extraordinarily positive idea for so many – it's an extension of liberal cosmopolitanism."[215] "But," he warned, "we can't ignore or look past the profound reality that human beings live in *places*. We can't fix the world around us by looking past the room we're in because the world begins in that room. The world is *made* of rooms – the world is the room, times many millions."[216] To stay with the metaphor, the rule of law, too, is made of rooms, times a few hundred. We must deal with rules of law, with all kinds of traditions, all over the place, all invented at one point or another. As Lauren Benton put it for one formative period of world history – the one during which Dicey popularized the famous phrase this collection is all about – "we should label legal transformations in the long nineteenth century not as the rise of the rule of law but as an iterative cultural politics centering on rules about law."[217]

[213] Keith Tribe, "Appendix A: Translation Appendix," in Max Weber, *Economy and Society: A New Translation*, trans. and ed. Keith Tribe (Cambridge: Harvard University Press, [1922] 2019), p. 473.

[214] Weber, "Die 'Objektivität' sozialwissenschaftlicher und sozialpolitischer Erkenntnis," p. 193.

[215] Gopnik, *A Thousand Small Sanities*, p. 232.

[216] Gopnik, *A Thousand Small Sanities*, p. 232.

[217] Lauren Benton, *Law and Colonial Cultures: Legal Regimes in World History, 1400–1900* (Cambridge: Cambridge University Press, 2001), p. 264.

To be able to think more realistically, and less idealistically, about the rule of law, we may want to pay greater heed to singular trajectories, to longitudinal inquiry. Comparisons matter, but singular experiences do as well. One or a few cases *can* yield theoretical gains.[218] The potted histories of ancient, medieval, or modern cases that have long adorned quantitative and philosophical studies of the rule of law are almost always inadequate.[219] Far too often, these snapshots are hampered by a lack of historiographical grounding or empirical understanding. Almost always are they hamstrung by a reductionist standard of the rule of law.[220] If we let go of this standard, and focus on the thousand small sanities the rule of law can bring, we will see more clearly why Thompson thought it an unqualified human good, notwithstanding the evidence to the contrary. However, in order to notice at all the many small sanities that have always been associated with rule of law practices, we must rid the concept of its utopian baggage. Doing so would clear the path for a liberalism without illusions.[221] As Tamanaha reminds us,

> the rule of law originated prior to liberalism and can exist independent of liberalism. Liberals tend to obscure this in their jealous identification of the rule of law with liberalism. From a broader perspective, the singular achievement of the rule of law is its insistence that governments must act in accordance with the law – an essential restraint that is valuable in all societies regardless of their

[218] For the argument from historical institutionalism, see Dietrich Rueschemeyer, "Can One or a Few Cases Yield Theoretical Gains?" in James Mahoney and Dietrich Rueschemeyer, eds., *Comparative Historical Analysis in the Social Sciences* (Cambridge: Cambridge University Press, 2003), pp. 305–336. For the argument from rational choice institutionalism, see Bates et al., *Analytic Narratives*. For a methodological primer, see John Gerring, *Case Study Research*, 2nd ed. (Cambridge: Cambridge University Press, 2017). For the argument from ethnography, see Edward Schatz, ed., *Political Ethnography: What Immersion Contributes to the Study of Power* (Chicago: University of Chicago Press, 2009). For an exploration of the latter in the study of the rule of law, see Nick Cheesman, "Rule of Law Ethnography," *Annual Review of Law and Social Science*, 14 (2018), 167–184.

[219] Qualitative approaches, too, can lead to potted histories. See, for example, the World Justice Project's White Paper "History and Importance of the Rule of Law," authored by Theo J. Angelis and Jonathan H. Harrison in 2003 to inform the policy deliberations of the American Bar Association's rule of law task force. Their teleological account can be accessed at https://worldjusticeproject.org/our-work/publications/working-papers/history-and-importance-rule-law.

[220] See, for example, Stephan Haggard and Lydia Tiede, "The Rule of Law and Economic Growth: Where are We?" *World Development*, 39 (2011), 673–685.

[221] Related, see Bernard Yack, ed., *Liberalism without Illusions: Essays on Liberal Theory and the Political Vision of Judith N. Shklar* (Chicago: University of Chicago Press, 1996); and Judith N. Shklar, *After Utopia: The Decline of Political Faith*, with a new foreword Samuel Moyn (Princeton: Princeton University Press, [1957] 2020).

social, cultural, economic, or political orientation. In view of the awesome power and resources governments can wield, holding the government to legal restraints is a universal good.[222]

I agree.

8 Rules of Law

Thinking about the rule of law in multiples makes thinking about the idea both more difficult and less. It makes it *more* difficult because we lose the certainty of convention. By abandoning the search for a universal standard for the rule of law, it makes it *easier* because we gain much-needed perspective that keeps rule of law practices at a remove from rule of law theories. If we ground our thinking about the rule of law actively in the everyday, where instantiations of the idea have always structured life-worlds in all kinds of messy ways, we arguably stand a better chance of advancing it – and eventually giving substance to it – than by continuing to tether it from the outset to the ideology of liberalism.[223]

The international community might also improve its track record in promoting the rule of law if it recognized the intellectual logjam in which almost all of its rule of law programs have for decades been stuck. "The 'rule of law' promises an alternative – a domain of expertise, a program for action – which obscures the need for distributional choices or for clarity about how distributing things one way rather than another will, in fact, lead to development. Unfortunately, this turns out to be a false promise."[224] If the international community, as represented, for example, by the United Nations, World Bank, IMF, and EU, scaled back its ambition for the rule of law, and recognized how group think, and the streamlining of epistemic communities, have long exercised a stranglehold on the

[222] Brian Z. Tamanaha, "The Dark Side of the Relationship between the Rule of Law and Liberalism," *New York University Journal of Law and Liberty*, 3 (2008), 546.

[223] For an influential treatment of liberalism alongside other ideologies, with particular reference to the international sphere, see Michael. W. Doyle, *Ways of War and Peace: Realism, Liberalism, and Socialism* (New York: W. W. Norton, 1997). On the role of neoliberalism in that sphere, see Joseph E. Stiglitz, *Globalization and Its Discontents Revisited: Anti-Globalization in the Era of Trump*, 2nd ed. (London: Penguin, 2017).

[224] David Kennedy, *The Dark Sides of Virtue: Reassessing International Humanitarianism* (Princeton: Princeton University Press, 2004), p. 155. See also Shane Chalmers and Sundhya Pahuja, "(Economic) Development and the Rule of Law," in this volume.

international rule of law discourse, and thus its agenda, much would be won. As it stands, "[t]he risk in recent developments is that the rule of law is ripe to be tainted by its close indentification with liberalism, particularly in developing countries."[225] Why should this be so?

Because international development organizations as well as governmental organizations such as the United States Agency for International Development and the UK Department for International Development for many years introduced the rule of law as the "front man" in their marketing of neoliberal reforms.[226] If and when these reforms backfire, as they often do, or just lead to social dislocation, as they always do, the norms and institutions of the rule of law are at risk of being deemed guilty by association. For example, "if courts are perceived to defend the rich who enjoy increasing wealth while most in society are left wanting, the rule of law may be held responsible or tarnished, viewed by the populace with suspicion or cynicism – making it all the harder to implant and build the rule of law. It would be a tragic paradox if the great liberal advocates for the rule of law contributed to preventing it from taking hold and spreading around the world."[227] The comparative-historical evidence is conclusive. As far as the rule of law is concerned, the international community through the ages has overpromised and underdelivered. What if it changed tactics?

Moving toward a phenomenology of the rule of law would be one way to get there. By keeping it real, this approach ensures we steer clear of what the polyglot Alfred North Whitehead termed "the fallacy of misplaced concreteness," a formulation with which he alerted his readers to the danger of mistaking abstract schemes – of which the invented tradition of the rule of law is a perfect example – for reality itself. The cases of ancient Athens and Nazi Germany, which I touched on briefly, are two in the study of which a preoccupation with pure abstraction has long stood in the way of serviceable knowledge about the legal origins of dictatorship and democracy.[228]

[225] Tamanaha, "The Dark Side of the Relationship between the Rule of Law and Liberalism," 546.

[226] Tamanaha, "The Dark Side of the Relationship between the Rule of Law and Liberalism," 547.

[227] Tamanaha, "The Dark Side of the Relationship between the Rule of Law and Liberalism," 547.

[228] Cf. Barrington Moore, Jr., *Social Origins of Dictatorship and Democracy: Lord and Peasant in the Making of the Modern World* (Boston: Beacon Press, 1966); Daron Acemoglu, and James A. Robinson, *Economic Origins of Dictatorship and Democracy* (Cambridge: Cambridge University Press, 2006).

Let us make the rule of law strange again, let us try to see it anew, unvarnished – as if for the first time. That certainly has been the mission in this volume. Collectively, we have reassessed the promise of the rule of law and its limits. Together with our thirty-two distinguished contributors, we paid attention to its bright sides, but also to the perverse outcomes that it, if practiced odiously, is equally capable of producing. Shining a light on, and to be frank about, these pathologies is imperative lest the rule of law in the twenty-first centry lose even more of its lustre than it already has.[229]

Conclusion

"What is remarkable," E. P. Thompson noted in *Whigs and Hunters*, his account of the Black Act of 1723, "is not that the laws were bent" in Hanoverian Britain, "but the fact that there was, anywhere in the eighteenth century, a Rule of Law at all."[230] Thompson's finding stood out in the left-leaning intellectual currents in which he swam – and tried to stay afloat. As he mused at the time, "I stand on a very narrow ledge, watching the tides come up. Or, to be more explicit, I sit here in my study, at the age of fifty, the desk and the floor piled high with five years of notes, xeroxes, rejected drafts, the clock once again moving into the small hours, and see myself, in a lucid instant, as an anachronism."[231] Thompson felt like the odd one out in the 1970s. His study of the rule of law in the vernacular – of the everyday life of law – was out of kilter with the metatheoretical critiques that were *en currant* at the time.[232] His turn to microhistory made him see clearly that the strident Marxists in his circle needed to acknowledge that there was more to the rule of law than meets the eye, to wit, that rule of law essentialism was as pronounced on the left as it was among liberals in the center and conservatives on the right. Thompson

[229] For an illustration from a high-profile case that has dominated the news cycle, and the activities of the European Union, for several years, see Wojciech Sadurski, *Poland's Constitutional Breakdown* (Oxford: Oxford University Press, 2019).

[230] *Thompson, Whigs and Hunters.* [231] Thompson, *Whigs and Hunters*, p. 260.

[232] See, for example, Bob Fine, who, in *Democracy and the Rule of Law: Liberal Ideals and Marxist Critiques* (London: Pluto Press, 1984), argued that Thompson, by rejecting vulgar Marxist conceptions of law in *Whigs and Hunters*, had come "close to abandoning Marxist criticism of the rule of law in its entirety in favor of a resuscitated liberalism." Ibid., p. 175.

issued a broadside against reductionist perspectives on the left that is of continued relevance, especially given the appeal in the study of foreign, comparative, and international law of arguments from "legal orientalism."[233] What, then, is the rule of law?

The rule of law, regardless of how we define it, is neither unqualifiedly good nor inherently treacherous. Whether we think it an ideal, an ideology, or an ideal type, the idea of the rule of law "would not have received such applause," and in some many diverse settings for so long, "if no one thought it was good for anything."[234] Most fundamentally, the idea encapsulates hostility to arbitrary power, a disposition to rule that is common to *all* regime types. Even dictatorships on occasion curb arbitrariness by law to sustain the violent orders of their making. Often such efforts are facadist to manipulate what political scientists call audience costs, but sometimes they are not, or not completely so.[235] Sometimes such efforts are dualistic.[236]

The constitutionalization of Chile's military junta in the early 1980s is a case in point: "The Chilean dictatorship was subject to and constrained by legal institutions of its own making," according to Robert Barros.[237] "From March 11, 1981 through the dissolution of the military regime exactly nine years later, the military dictatorship was subject to and limited by constitutional constraints."[238] The so-called decree-laws on which the authoritarian regime came to rest were an expressive act of collective self-binding to serve an instrumental end – regime survival – performed by a junta that in the mid-1970s was increasingly consumed by mistrust. They were designed "to prevent any one junta member, in particular Pinochet, from concentrating all power in the regime. Rules were instituted to bind each junta member to agreed-on procedures, not to tie the hands of the Junta as a whole."[239]

[233] See, for example, Teemu Ruskola, *Legal Orientalism: China, the United States, and Modern Law* (Cambridge: Harvard University Press, 2013).

[234] Krygier, "The Rule of Law," 215.

[235] See, for example, Kenneth A. Schultz, "Why We Needed Audience Costs and What We Need Now," *Security Studies*, 21 (2012), 369–375.

[236] Fraenkel, *The Dual State*; Meierhenrich, *The Legacies of Law*; Meierhenrich, *The Remnants of the Rechtsstaat*; Hendley, *Everyday Law in Russia*.

[237] Robert Barros, *Constitutionalism and Dictatorship: Pinochet, the Junta, and the 1980 Constitution* (Cambridge: Cambridge University Press, 2002), p. 313.

[238] Barros, *Constitutionalism and Dictatorship*, p. 315.

[239] Barros, *Constitutionalism and Dictatorship*, p. 317.

The remnants of the *Rechtsstaat* that occasionally constrained the Nazi dictatorship in the early years of the "Third Reich" is another case worth rethinking from a more realistic perspective on the rule of law than is usually taken when the case is considered. I have shown that the Nazi rule of violence was not one of lawlessness, at least not entirely. Up until 1938, when authoritarianism turned into totalitarianism, the functional equivalent of an authoritarian rule of law structured politics and society and also the economy. What this means is that a legal way of doing things for several years coexisted with the use of physical violence. Audience costs played a role but the expressive function of law played a larger role: "Many of the elite jurists in the Third Reich were genuinely committed to broadening their country's legal imagination – however repulsive this Nazi legal conscience is by almost any standard. They certainty were self-interested actors, but whether as nemesis or katechon, the *Rechtsstaat* mattered to almost every one of them expressively."[240]

A realistic theory of the rule of law would hesitate to exclude cases like Nazi Germany and Chile from its purview. It would be reluctant to assign them, and more recent cases like Hungary and China, to the catch-all category of "rule by law," this negative conceptual space where legal philosophers park morally odious cases until further notice. "Theories that center on law within social and historical contexts," Tamanaha recently complained, "have been all but banished from jurisprudence," that is, from that branch of legal inquiry where for longest time almost all debates about the rule of law were staged.[241] Why this is problematic Tamanaha also explains, reinforcing our argument for approaching the rule of law phenomenologically, not philosophically: "Legal philosophers abstract law from history and from society to present theories of law as timeless and universally true," he chides.[242] "Natural law theorists concentrate on objective principles of morality and their implications for law."[243] Legal positivists, not unlike game theorists in economics and political science, assert those features of the rule that they think law must necessarily possess. But Tamanaha is not just down on those who believe in the intelligibility of the rule of law. He also finds fault with other

[240] Meierhenrich, *The Remnants of the Rechtsstaat*, p. 111.
[241] Tamanaha, *A Realistic Theory of Law*, p. 1.
[242] Tamanaha, *A Realistic Theory of Law*, p. 1.
[243] Tamanaha, *A Realistic Theory of Law*, p. 1.

approaches to the rule of law. "Beyond these two main branches of legal theory lies a jumble of schools of thought: legal realism, law and economics, critical legal studies, critical feminism, critical race theory, legal pragmatism, and so on. These various theoretical approaches have particular angles and concerns – none considers law in its social totality."[244] Tamanaha's gripe is with the metatheoretical discourse about the rule of law, especially philosophical contributions to it. Many of these discursive formations are rigid, others rickety. Not infrequently are they cobbled together parsimoniously hundreds or thousands of miles removed from the realities of the rule of law.

Talk of the rule of law has illocutionary force. As an utterance, the concept espouses a distinct, governmental rationality. The "four clipped syllables, two iambs, two hard nouns," as Stephen Humphreys writes, conjure "a magical, or at least talismanic, role" whenever they are invoked in the name of humanity, as they were, to give a recent example, by the Commission on Legal Empowerment of the Poor that Madeleine Albright and Hernando de Soto led to uproot poverty in the twenty-first century. The plan of action the twenty-one commissioners presented after three years of study is noteworthy because of its blind faith in formality.[245] In it, shibboleths about the rule of law abound. Always virtuous, never vicious, the vision of the rule of law the Commission on Legal Empowerment of the Poor performed for the world was that of a harbinger of modernization.

> [F]our billion people around the world are robbed of the chance to better their lives and climb out of poverty, because they are excluded from the rule of law. Whether

[244] Tamanaha, *A Realistic Theory of Law*, p. 1. *Pace* Tamanaha, a few exceptions do exist. See, for example, Mahmood Mamdani, *Citizen and Subject: Contemporary Africa and the Legacy of Late Colonialism* (Princeton: Princeton University Press, 1996); Stuart Banner, *Possessing the Pacific: Land, Settlers, and Indigenous People from Australia to Alaska* (Cambridge: Harvard University Press, 2007); Inga Markovits, *Justice in Lüritz: Experiencing Socialist Law in East Germany* (Princeton: Princeton University Press, 2010); Naomi Murakawa, *The First Civil Right: How Liberals Built Prison America* (Oxford: Oxford University Press, 2014); and Cheesman, *Opposing the Rule of Law*; Hinton, *The Justice Facade*; Massoud, *Shari'a, Inshallah*; and Meierhenrich, *The Violence of Law*. Although it lurks in the background, and only occasionally appears in the foreground, the rule of law is the *topos* of all of these books. It is addressed in them in its social totality. in its social totality.

[245] See generally, Arthur L. Stinchcombe, *When Formality Works: Authority and Abstraction in Law and Organizations* (Chicago: University of Chicago Press, 2001).

living below or slightly above the poverty line, these men, women, and children lack the protections and rights afforded by the law. They may be citizens of the country in which they live, but their resources, modest at best, can neither be properly protected nor leveraged. Thus it is not the absence of assets or lack of work that holds them back, but the fact that the assets and work are insecure, unprotected, and far less productive than they might be.[246]

The trope to "strengthen the rule of law," which the Commission on Legal Empowerment of the Poor rehearsed, performed, and reinscribed, is a simplified lesson, and a vacuous directive. It is the mindless product of rote learning by generations of policy-makers of one of liberalism's most pernicious morality tales: the story of progress. To be sure, outcomes of improvement – from "modernization schemes" to "development projects" to "empowerment programs" – are not always deleterious. But inasmuch as "[p]rograms of improvement often bring changes that people want – more roads and bridges, fewer floods and diseases, less corruption and waste," the history of the modern world is full of litanies about cases in which the triumph of the will to improve retarded well-being – best laid plans notwithstanding.[247] The history of the rule of law is no exception.

I have argued in this chapter that "the rule of law means ruling by law and not by other means."[248] What sounds like a truism, isn't. Rather, it describes both accurately and pithily what the rule of law, in the final analysis, *is*. When all is said and done, our *explanandum* is an institution of rule grounded in an idea about reducing arbitrariness in the exercise of government that can be made fit for any purpose – and by any type of regime – under the sun. It rules if and when it is accorded, for expressive or instrumental reasons or both, central significance as a primary institution of order.[249]

[246] Commission on Legal Empowerment of the Poor, *Making the Law Work for Everyone*, vol. 1: *Report of the Commission on Legal Empowerment of the Poor* (New York: Commission on Legal Empowerment of the Poor and United Nations Development Programme, 2008), pp. 1–2.

[247] Tania Murray Li, *The Will to Improve: Governmentality, Development, and the Practice of Politics* (Durham: Duke University Press, 2007), p. 1.

[248] Lovett, *A Republic of Law*, p. 127.

[249] Lest I sow conceptual confusion, my use of the term "primary institution" was inspired not by H. L. A. Hart's distinction between law's "primary" and "secondary" rules, but, rather, by English School thinking about the primary institutions of international society. See H. L. A Hart, *The Concept of Law*, 2nd ed. (Oxford: Clarendon Press, 1994), esp. pp. 79-99; and, for a summation of the underdeveloped international thought about the nature and role of primary institutions, Barry Buzan, *From International to World Society? English*

I do not think it possible, nor analytically desirable, for the reasons set out above, to draw static boundaries around the rule of law, to fix its meaning by trading attributes. With the late, great Judith Shklar I do not think of the rule of law as something "that can be understood simply by defining it."[250] Like her I think a social phenomenon such as the rule of law "must be seen in its various concrete manifestations, in its diverse applications, and in the many degrees of intensity with which men" and other genders "in different places and conditions have abided by it."[251] For this reason Shklar thought the rule of law "a complex of human qualities, not a quantity to be measured and labeled."[252] One would be hard-pressed to find a conception of the rule of law more frustratingly vague than Shklar's. One would be equally hard-pressed to come across one more universally true. What in the twenty-first century can realistically be said about the rule of law is this: The rule of law is phenomenologically complex. What it is *not* is philosophically intelligible. We would be well advised to think of the rule of law neither as a criterial concept nor a universally shared standard of the good life. The rule of law is – and always has been – what actors make of it.

School Theory and the Social Structure of Globalisation (Cambridge: Cambridge University Press, 2004), ch. 6.

[250] Shklar, *Legalism*, p. 1. [251] Shklar, *Legalism*, p. 1. [252] Shklar, *Legalism*, p. 1.

Bibliography

Abasiattai, Monday, "European Intervention in Liberia with Special Reference to the 'Cadell Incident' of 1908–1909," *Liberian Studies Journal*, 14 (1989), 72–90.

Abel, Richard, *Politics by Other Means: Law in the Struggle against Apartheid, 1980–1994* (London: Routledge, 1995).

Abel, Richard L., *Law's Wars: The Fate of the Rule of Law in the U.S. "War on Terror"* (Cambridge: Cambridge University Press, 2018).

Abel, Richard L., *Law's Trials: The Performance of Legal Institutions in the U.S. "War on Terror"* (Cambridge: Cambridge University Press, 2018).

Abelove, Henry, Betsy Blackmar, Peter Dimock, and Jonathan Schneer, eds., *Visions of History* (Manchester: Manchester University Press, 1983).

Acemoglu, Daron, and James A. Robinson, *Economic Origins of Dictatorship and Democracy* (Cambridge: Cambridge University Press, 2006).

Ackerman, Bruce, *We the People: Foundations* (Cambridge: Harvard University Press, 1991).

Adams, Maurice, Anne Meuwese, and Ernst Hirsch Ballin, eds., *Constitutionalism and the Rule of Law: Bridging Idealism and Realism* (Cambridge: Cambridge University Press, 2017).

Akingbade, Harrison, "The Pacification of the Liberian Hinterland," *Journal of Negro History*, 79 (1994), 277–296.

Alexander, Jeffrey C., *The Meanings of Social Life: A Cultural Sociology* (Oxford: Oxford University Press, 2003).

Aliverti, Any, and Mary Bosworth, "Introduction: Criminal Justice Adjudication in an Age of Migration," *New Criminal Law Review*, 20 (2017), 1–11.

Allan, T.R.S., "Dworkin and Dicey: The Rule of Law as Integrity," *Oxford Journal of Legal Studies*, 8 (1988), 266–277.

Allan, T. R. S., *Law, Liberty, and Justice: The Legal Foundations of British Constitutionalism* (Oxford: Clarendon Press, 1993).

Allan, T. R. S., "Rule of Law (Rechtsstaat)," in Edward Craig, ed., *The Routledge Encyclopedia of Philosophy*, vol. 8 (London: Routledge, 1998), pp. 388–391.

Allan, T. R. S., *Constitutional Justice: A Liberal Theory of the Rule of Law* (Oxford: Oxford University Press, 2001).

Allan, T. R. S., *The Sovereignty of Law: Freedom, Constitution, and Common Law* (Oxford: Oxford University Press, 2013).

Allan, T. R. S., "The Rule of Law," in David Dyzenhaus and Malcolm Thorburn, eds., *Philosophical Foundations of Constitutional Law* (Oxford: Oxford University Press, 2016), pp. 201–221.

Allen, C. K., *Law in the Making*, 7th ed. (Oxford: Clarendon Press, 1964).

Allen, Francis A., *The Habits of Legality: Criminal Justice and the Rule of Law* (New York: Oxford University Press, 1996).

Alpher, David, "Learning from SIGIR's Final Report on Iraq Reconstruction," Middle East Institute, June 12, 2013.

Alvarez, José E., "International Organisations and the Rule of Law," *New Zealand Journal of Public and International Law*, 14 (2016), 3–46.

Amadae, S. M., *Prisoners of Reason: Game Theory and Neoliberal Political Economy* (Cambridge: Cambridge University Press, 2015).

American Colonization Society, *A View of Exertions Lately Made for the Purpose of Colonizing the Free People of Color, in the United States, in Africa, or Elsewhere* (Washington: Jonathan Elliot, 1817).

American Colonization Society, *Sixteenth Annual Report of the American Society for Colonizing the Free People of Colour of the United States* (Washington: James Dunn, 1833).

Anderson, Perry, *Arguments Within English Marxism* (London: Verso, 1980).

Anderson, Perry, "The Intransigent Right at the End of the Century," *London Review of Books*, September 24, 1992.

Angelis, Theo J., and Jonathan H. Harrison, "History and Importance of the Rule of Law," World Justice Project, 2003.

Anghie, Antony, *Imperialism, Sovereignty, and the Making of International Law* (Cambridge: Cambridge University Press, 2005).

Anghie, Antony, "Legal Aspects of the New International Economic Order," *Humanity*, 6 (2015), 145–158.

Annas, Julia, "Virtue and Law in Plato," in Christopher Bobonich, ed., *Plato's Laws: A Critical Guide* (Cambridge: Cambridge University Press, 2010), pp. 71–91.

Arendt, Hannah, *The Human Condition* (Chicago: University of Chicago Press, [1958] 1973).

Arendt, Hannah, *Eichmann in Jerusalem: A Report on the Banality of Evil*, rev. and enlarged ed. (New York: Penguin, [1963] 1992).

Aristotle, *The Politics*, trans. and ed. Stephen Everson (Cambridge: Cambridge University Press, 1988).

Armstrong, S., "Securing Prison through Human Rights: Unanticipated Implications of Rights-Based Penal Reform," *Howard Journal of Crime and Justice*, 57 (2018), 401–421.

Arndt, H. W., "The Origins of Dicey's Concept of the Rule of Law," *Australian Law Journal*, 31 (1957), 117–123.

Arneson, Richard J., "Mill versus Paternalism," *Ethics*, 90 (1980), 470–489.

Ashworth, A., *Sentencing and Criminal Justice*, 5th ed. (Cambridge: Cambridge University Press, 2010).

Aumann, Francis R., "Book Review: *Legalism* by Judith N. Shklar," *Journal of Politics*, 27 (1965), 703–705.

Austin, John, *The Province of Jurisprudence Determined*, 2nd ed. (London: John Murray, 1861).

Austin, John, *Lectures on Jurisprudence*, vol. 2 (London: John Murray, 1863).

Axelrod, Robert, *The Complexity of Cooperation: Agent-Based Models of Competition and Collaboration* (Princeton: Princeton University Press, 1997).

Azad, Ghulam Murtaza, "Conduct and Qualities of a Qadi," *Islamic Studies*, 24 (1985), 51–61.

Azikiwe, Nnamdi, "In Defense of Liberia," *Journal of Negro History*, 17 (1932), 30–50.

Azikiwe, Nnamdi, *Liberia in World Politics* (Westport: Negro Universities Press, 1970).

Baer, Susanne, "The Rule of – and Not by Any – Law: On Constitutionalism," *Current Legal Problems*, 71 (2018), 335–368.

Balot, Ryan K., *Greek Political Thought* (Oxford: Blackwell, 2006).

Banner, Stuart, *Possessing the Pacific: Land, Settlers, and Indigenous People from Australia to Alaska* (Cambridge: Harvard University Press, 2007).

Barber, N. W., "The *Rechtsstaat* and the Rule of Law," *University of Toronto Law Journal*, 53 (2003), 443–454.

Barber, N. W., *The Principles of Constitutionalism* (Oxford: Oxford University Press, 2018).

Bar-Gill, Oren, and Chaim Fershtman, "Law and Preferences," *Journal of Law, Economics, and Organization*, 20 (2004), 331–352.

Barkan, Joshua, *Corporate Sovereignty: Law and Government Under Capitalism* (Minneapolis: University of Minnesota Press, 2013).

Barker, Vanessa, *Nordic Nationalism and Penal Order: Walling the Welfare State* (London: Routledge, 2018).

Barkey, Karen, "Aspects of Legal Pluralism in the Ottoman Empire," in Lauren Benton and Richard J. Ross, eds., *Legal Pluralism and Empires, 1500–1850* (New York: New York University Press, 2013) pp. 83–107.

Barnett, Michael N., ed., *Paternalism beyond Borders* (Cambridge: Cambridge University Press, 2016).

Barrière, Pierre, *Un grand provincial: Charles-Louis de Secondat baron de La Brède et de Montesquieu* (Bordeaux: Delmas, 1946).

Barros, Robert, *Constitutionalism and Dictatorship: Pinochet, the Junta, and the 1980 Constitution* (Cambridge: Cambridge University Press, 2002).

Barzel, Yoram, *A Theory of the State: Economic Rights, Legal Rights, and the Scope of the State* (Cambridge: Cambridge University Press, 2002).

Bates, Robert H., Avner Greif, Margaret Levi, Jean-Laurent Rosenthal, and Barry R. Weingast Bates, *Analytic Narratives* (Princeton: Princeton University Press, 1998).

Basu, Kaushik, *Prelude to Political Economy: A Study of the Social and Political Foundations of Economics* (Oxford: Oxford University Press, 2000).

Bateup, Christine, "Expanding the Conversation: American and Canadian Experiences of Constitutional Dialogue in Comparative Perspective," *Temple International and Comparative Law Journal*, 21 (2007), 1–57.

Baxter, Hugh, *Habermas: The Discourse Theory of Law and Democracy* (Stanford: Stanford University Press, 2011).

Bayly, Christopher, *Imperial Meridian: The British Empire and the World 1780–1830* (London: Longman, 1989).

Baynes, Kenneth, and Rene von Schomburg, eds., *Discourse and Democracy: Essays on* Between Facts and Norms (Albany: State University of New York Press, 2002).

Beard, Jennifer, *Political Economy of Desire: International Law, Development and the Nation State* (Abingdon: Routledge, 2007).

Beaud, Olivier, and Erk Volkmar Heyen, eds., *Eine deutsch-französische Rechtswissenschaft? Une science juridique franco-allemande?* (Baden-Baden: Nomos, 1999).

Beaulac, Stéphane, "The Rule of Law in International Law Today," in Gianluigi Palombella and Neil Walker, eds., *Relocating the Rule of Law* (Oxford: Hart, 2009), pp. 197–223.

Beccaria, Cesare, *On Crimes and Punishments and Other Writings*, ed. Richard Bellamy, trans. Richard Davies (Cambridge: Cambridge University Press, [1764] 1995).

Bedau, H. A., "Book Review: *Legalism* by Judith N. Shklar," *Philosophical Review*, 76 (1967), 129–130.

Bederman, David J., "The United Nations Compensation Commission and the Tradition of International Claims Settlement," *New York University Journal of International Law and Politics*, 27 (1994), 1–42.

Bedjaoui, Mohammed, *Towards a New International Economic Order* (New York: Holmes & Meier, 1979).

Begon, Jessica, "Paternalism,"*Analysis*, 76 (2016), 355–373.

Beinart, Ben, "The Rule of Law," *Acta Juridica* (1962), 99–114.

Bell, Derrick A., Jr., "Serving Two Masters: Integration Ideals and Client Interests in School Desegregation Litigation," *Yale Law Journal*, 85 (1976), 470–516.

Bellamy, Richard, "Introduction," in Cesare Beccaria, *On Crimes and Punishments and Other Writings*, ed. Richard Bellamy, trans. Richard Davies (Cambridge: Cambridge University Press, [1764] 1995), pp. ix–xxx.

Benhabib, Seyla, "International Law and Human Plurality in the Shadow of Totalitarianism: Hannah Arendt and Raphael Lemkin," in idem, ed., *Dignity in Adversity: Human Rights in Troubled Times* (Cambridge: Polity, 2011), pp. 41–57.

Benrekassa, Georges, *Montesquieu: La liberté et l'histoire* (Paris: Librairie Générale Française, 1987).

Bentham, Jeremy, *A Fragment on Government* (London: T. Payne, P. Elmsly, E. Brooke, 1776).

Benton, Lauren, *Law and Colonial Cultures: Legal Regimes in World History, 1400–1900* (Cambridge: Cambridge University Press, 2001).

Benton, Lauren, and Lisa Ford, *Rage for Order: The British Empire and the Origins of International Law, 1800–1850* (Cambridge: Harvard University Press, 2016).

Benton, Lauren, and Richard J. Ross, eds., *Legal Pluralism and Empires, 1500–1850* (New York: New York University Press, 2013).

Benvenisti, Eyal, "Sovereigns as Trustees of Humanity: On the Accountability of States to Foreign Stakeholders," *American Journal of International Law*, 107 (2013), 295–333.

Berg, Louis-Alexandre, Deborah Isser, and Douglas Porter, "Beyond Deficit and Dysfunction: Three Questions toward Just Development in Fragile and Conflict-Affected Settings," in David Marshall, ed., *The International Rule of Law Movement: A Crisis of Legitimacy and the Way Forward* (Cambridge: Harvard University Press, 2014), pp. 267–294.

Berkowitz, Roger, "Dignity Jurisprudence: Building a New Law on Earth," in Drucilla Cornell, Stu Woolman, Sam Fuller, Jason Brickhill, Michael Bishop, and Diana Dunbar, eds., *The Dignity Jurisprudence of the Constitutional Court of South Africa: Cases and Materials*, vol. 1 (New York: Fordham University Press, 2013), pp. 65–72.

Berlin, Isaiah, *Four Essays on Liberty* (Oxford: Oxford University Press, 1969).

Berlin, Isaiah, *Against the Current: Essays in the History of Ideas* (New York: Viking, 1980).

Berman, Harold J., *Law and Revolution: The Formation of the Western Legal Tradition* (Cambridge: Harvard University Press, 1983).

Bernasconi-Osterwalder, Nathalie, and Martin Dietrich Brauch, "Is 'Moonlighting' a Problem? The Role of ICJ Judges in ISDS," International Institute for Sustainable Development, November 2017.

Besson, Samantha, and José Luis Martí, eds., *Legal Republicanism: National and International Perspectives* (Oxford: Oxford University Press, 2009).

Beyan, Amos, *The American Colonization Society and the Creation of the Liberian State: A Historical Perspective, 1822–1900* (Lanham: University Press of America, 1991).

Beyme, Klaus von, *Politische Theorien im Zeitalter der Ideologien* (Wiesbaden: Verlag für Sozialwissenschaften, 2002).

Bhat, Girish N., "Recovering the Historical *Rechtsstaat*," *Review of Central and East European Law*, 32 (2007), 65–97.

Bickel, Alexander M., *The Least Dangerous Branch: The Supreme Court at the Bar of Politics* (New Haven: Yale University Press, 1962).

Bigo, Didier, "Sociology of Transnational Guilds," *International Political Sociology*, 10 (2016), pp. 398–416.

Bingham, Tom, *The Rule of Law* (London: Penguin, 2011).

Binoche, Bertrand, *Introduction à De l'esprit des lois de Montesquieu* (Paris: PUF, 1998).

Bishop, Charlotte, and Vanessa Bettison, "Evidencing Domestic Violence, Including Behaviour that Falls Under the New Offence of Controlling or Coercive Behaviour," *International Journal of Evidence and Proof*, 22 (2017), 3–29.

Blackstone, William, *Commentaries on the Laws of England*, vol. 4 (Chicago: Chicago University Press, [1765] 1979).

Blair, Harry, and Garry Hansen, *Weighing in on the Scales of Justice: Strategic Approaches for Donor-Supported Rule of Law Programs* (Washington: US Agency for International Development, 1994).

Blaau, Loammi C., "The *Rechtsstaat* Idea Compared with the Rule of Law as a Paradigm for Protecting Rights," *South African Law Journal*, 107 (1990), 76–96.

Bobbio, Norberto, *Thomas Hobbes and the Natural Law Tradition*, trans. Daniela Gobetti (Chicago: Chicago University Press, 1993).

Böckenförde, Ernst-Wolfgang, "Lorenz von Stein als Theoretiker der Bewegung von Staat und Gesellschaft zum Sozialstaat," in idem, *Staat, Gesellschaft, Freiheit: Studien zur Staatstheorie und zum Verfassungsrecht* (Frankfurt am Main: Suhrkamp, [1963] 1976), pp. 146–185.

Böckenförde, Ernst-Wolfgang, "Entstehung und Wandel des Rechtsstaatsbegriffs," in idem, *Recht, Staat, Freiheit: Studien zu Rechtsphilosophie, Staatstheorie und Verfassungsgeschichte*, Expanded ed. (Frankfurt am Main: Suhrkamp, [1969] 2006), pp. 65–92.

Böckenförde, Ernst-Wolfgang, "The Origin and Development of the Concept of the Rechtsstaat," in idem, *State, Society and Liberty: Studies in Political Theory and Constitutional Law*, trans. J. A. Underwood (New York: Berg, [1969] 1991), pp. 47–70.

Böckenförde, Ernst-Wolfgang, "The Concept of the Political: A Key to Understanding Carl Schmitt's Constitutional Theory," in idem, *Constitutional and Political Theory: Selected Writings*, eds. Mirjam Künkler and Tine Stein (Oxford: Oxford University Press, [1988] 2018), pp. 69–85.

Boesche, Roger, "Fearing Monarchs and Merchants: Montesquieu's Two Theories of Despotism," *Western Political Science Quarterly*, 43 (1990), 741–761.

Bogg, Alan L, and Mark R. Freedland, "Labour Law in the Age of Populism: Towards Sustainable Democratic Engagement," *Research Paper*. No. 2018–15, Max Planck Institute for Comparative Public Law and International Law, Heidelberg, July 2018.

Bongiovanni, Giorgio, "*Rechtsstaat* and Constitutional Justice in Austria: Hans Kelsen's Contribution," in Pietro Costa and Danilo Zolo, eds., *The Rule of Law: History, Theory and Criticism* (Dordrecht: Springer, 2007), pp. 293–319.

Bothe, Michael, "Terrorism and the Legality of Pre-emptive Force," *European Journal of International Law*, 14 (2003), 227–240.

Boucher, David, "The Rule of Law in the Modern European State: Oakeshott and the Enlargement of Europe," *European Journal of Political Theory*, 4 (2005), 89–107.

Brandes, Tamar Hostovsky, "International Law in Domestic Courts in an Era of Populism," *International Journal of Constitutional Law*, 17 (2019), 576–596.

Bray, Heather L., "Understanding Change: Evolution from International Claims Commissions to Investment Treaty Arbitration," in Stephan W. Schill, Christian J. Tams, and Rainer Hofmann, eds., *International Investment Law and History* (Cheltenham: Edward Elgar, 2018), pp. 102–135.

Bridges, Khiara M., "On the Commodification of the Black Female Body: The Critical Implications of a Market in Fetal Tissue," *Columbia Law Review*, 102 (2002), 123–167.

Brower, Charles N., and Sadie Blanchard, "From 'Dealing in Virtue' to 'Profiting from Injustice': The Case Against Re-Statification of Investment Dispute Settlement," *Transnational Dispute Management*, 4 (2013), available at https://www.transnational-dispute-management.com.

Brown, Brendan F., "Book Review: *Legalism* by Judith N. Shklar," *University of Toronto Law Journal*, 17 (1967), 218–225.

Brown, Mark, "'An Unqualified Human Good'? On Rule of Law, Globalization, and Imperialism," *Law and Social Inquiry*, 43 (2018), 1391–1426.

Brown, Nathan J., *The Rule of Law in the Arab World: Courts in Egypt and the Gulf* (Cambridge: Cambridge University Press, 1997).

Brunnée, Jutta, and Stephen J. Toope, *Legitimacy and Legality in International Law: An Interactional Account* (Cambridge: Cambridge University Press, 2010).

Brunner, Emil, *Justice and the Social Order*, trans. Mary Hottinger (New York: Harper, 1945).

Bumiller, Kristin, *In an Abusive State: How Neoliberalism Appropriated the Feminist Movement Against Sexual Violence* (Durham: Duke University Press, 2008).

Burin, Eric, *Slavery and the Peculiar Solution: A History of the American Colonization Society* (Gainesville: University Press of Florida, 2005).

Burin, Frederick, and Kurt Shell, eds., *Politics, Law, and Social Change: Selected Essays of Otto Kirchheimer* (New York: Columbia University Press, 1969).

Burke, Edmund, *Reflections on the Revolution in France* (Indianapolis: Hackett, [1790] 1987).

Burrow, J. W., *Whigs and Liberals: Continuity and Change in English Political Thought* (Oxford: Clarendon Press, 1988).

Butler, Paul, "Racially Based Jury Nullification: Black Power in the Criminal Justice System," *Yale Law Journal*, 105 (1995), 677–725.

Calafat, Guillaume, "Jurisdictional Pluralism in a Litigious Sea (1590–1630): Hard Cases, Multi-Sited Trials and Legal Enforcement between North Africa and Italy," *Past and Present*, 242 (2019), 142–178.

Caldwell, Peter C., "National Socialism and Constitutional Law: Carl Schmitt, Otto Koellreutter, and the Debate over the Nature of the Nazi State," *Cardozo Law Review*, 16 (1994), 399–427.

Caldwell, Peter C., "Ernst Forsthoff and the Legacy of Radical Conservative State Theory in the Federal Republic of Germany," *History of Political Thought*, 15 (1994), 615–641.

Caldwell, Peter C., *Popular Sovereignty and the Crisis of German Constitutional Law* (Durham: Duke University Press, 1997).

Caldwell, Peter C., "Ernst Forsthoff in Frankfurt: Political Mobilization and the Abandonment of Scholarly Responsibility," in Moritz Epple, Johannes Fried, Raphael Gross, and Janus Gudian, eds., *"Politisierung der Wissenschaft": Jüdische Wissenschaftler und ihre Gegner an der Universität Frankfurt am*

Main vor und nach 1933 (Frankfurt am Main: Wallstein Verlag, 2014), pp. 249–283.

Call, Charles T., ed., *Constructing Justice and Security After War* (Washington: United States Institute of Peace Press, 2007).

Callanan, Keegan, "Liberal Constitutionalism and Political Particularism in Montesquieu's *Spirit of the Laws*," *Political Research Quarterly*, 67 (2014), 589–602.

Callot, Emile, *La philosophie de la vie au XVIIIe siècle* (Paris: Éditions Marcel Rivière, 1965).

Cao, Lan, *Culture in Law and Development: Nurturing Positive Change* (Oxford: Oxford University Press 2016).

Carothers, Thomas, *Promoting the Rule of Law Abroad: In Search of Knowledge* (Washington: Carnegie Endowment for International Peace, 2006).

Carothers, Thomas, "The Problem of Knowledge," in idem, ed., *Promoting the Rule of Law Abroad: In Search of Knowledge* (Washington: Carnegie Endowment for International Peace, 2006), pp. 15–28.

Carothers, Thomas, "The Rule of Law Revival," in idem, ed., *Promoting the Rule of Law Abroad: In Search of Knowledge* (Washington: Carnegie Endowment for International Peace, 2006), pp. 3–13.

Carothers, Thomas, "Democracy Support Strategies: Leading with Women's Empowerment," Carnegie Endowment for International Peace, September 2016.

Carothers, Thomas, and Christopher Carothers, "Seeking Political Stability Abroad? Fight Corruption," *National Interest*, January 25, 2018.

Carpano, Eric, *État de droit et droits européens* (Paris: L'Harmattan, 2006).

Carrera, Fernando, "Guatemala's International Commission Against Impunity: A Case Study of Institutions and Rule of Law," World Bank, 2017.

Carrese, Paul, *Democracy in Moderation* (Cambridge: Cambridge University Press, 2016).

Carrithers, David W., "Montesquieu's Philosophy of Punishment," *History of Political Thought*, 19 (1998), 213–240.

Cartledge, Paul, *Ancient Greek Political Thought in Practice* (Cambridge: Cambridge University Press, 2009).

Cartledge, Paul, and Matt Edge, "'Rights,' Individuals, and Communities in Ancient Greece," in Ryan K. Balot, ed., *A Companion to Greek and Roman Political Thought* (Oxford: Blackwell, 2009), pp. 149–163.

Cass, Ronald A., "Ignorance of the Law: A Maxim Reexamined," *William and Mary Law Review*, 17 (1976), 671–700.

Cassell, Per, *Grounds of Judgment: Extraterritoriality and Imperial Power in Nineteenth-Century China and Japan* (Oxford: Oxford University Press, 2012).

Cassese, Antonio, "On the Current Trends Towards Criminal Prosecution and Punishment of Breaches of International Humanitarian Law," *European Journal of International Law*, 9 (1998), 2–17.

Chalmers, Shane, "Civil Death in the Dominion of Freedom: Liberia and the Logic of Capital," *Law and Critique*, 28 (2017), 145–165.

Chalmers, Shane, *Liberia and the Dialectic of Law: Critical Theory, Pluralism, and the Rule of Law* (Abingdon: Routledge, 2018).

Chalmers, Shane, "The Mythology of International Rule of Law Promotion," *Law and Social Inquiry*, 44 (2019), 957–986.

Chalmers, Shane, and Jeremy Farrall, "Securing the Rule of Law through United Nations Peace Operations," *Max Planck Yearbook of United Nations Law*, 18 (2014), 217–248.

Chanock, Martin, Law, *Custom and Social Order: The Colonial Experience in Malawi and Zambia* (Cambridge: Cambridge University Press, 1985).

Chapman, Peter, and Chelsea Payne, "'You Place the Old Mat with the New Mat': Legal Empowerment, Equitable Dispute Resolution, and Social Cohesion in Post-Conflict Liberia," in Open Society Justice Initiative, ed., *Justice Initiatives: Legal Empowerment* (New York: Open Society Justice Initiative, 2013), pp.15–29.

Charlesworth, Hilary, and Donald Francis Donovan, "An Introduction: A Just World Under Law," *American Society of International Law Proceedings*, 100 (2006), xii–xiii.

Chayes, Sarah, *Thieves of State: Why Corruption Threatens Global Security* (New York: W. W. Norton, 2015).

Cheesman, Nick, *Opposing the Rule of Law: How Myanmar's Courts Make Law and Order* (Cambridge: Cambridge University Press, 2015).

Cheesman, Nick, "Rule of Law Ethnography," *Annual Review of Law and Social Science*, 14 (2018), 167–184.

Chen, Li, *Chinese Law in Imperial Eyes: Sovereignty, Justice, and Transcultural Politics* (New York: Columbia University Press, 2016).

Chesterman, Simon, 2008, "An International Rule of Law?" *American Journal of Comparative Law*, 56 (2008), 331–361.

Chevallier, Jacques, *L'État de droit*, 6th ed. (Issy-les-Moulineaux: LGDJ, 2017).

Chibundu, Maxwell, "Law in Development: On Tapping, Grounding and Serving Palm-Wine," *Case Western Reserve Journal of International Law*, 29 (1997), 167–261.

Chinese Society of International Law, "The South China Sea Arbitration Awards: A Critical Study," *Chinese Journal of International Law*, 17 (2018), 207–748.

Christ, Matthew R., *The Litigious Athenian* (Baltimore: Johns Hopkins Press, 1998).

Christov, Theodore, *Before Anarchy: Hobbes and His Critics in Modern International Thought* (Cambridge: Cambridge University Press, 2015).

Chwe, Michael Suk-Young, *Rational Ritual: Culture, Coordination, and Common Knowledge* (Princeton: Princeton University Press, 2001).

Ciment, James, *Another America: The Story of Liberia and the Former Slaves Who Ruled It* (New York: Hill and Wang, 2013).

Civic, Melanne A., "Rule of Law in Multi-dimensional Peacekeeping: Lessons for Reform," *United Nations Peacekeeping*, April 2018.

Clendinnen, Inga, "Understanding the Heathen at Home: E. P. Thompson and His School," *Historical Studies*, 18 (1979), 435–440.

Coates, Benjamin Allen, *Legalist Empire: International Law and American Foreign Relations in the Early Twentieth Century* (Oxford: Oxford University Press, 2016).

Cohen, David, *Theft in Athenian Law* (Munich: C. H. Beck, 1983).

Cohen, David, *Law, Violence, and Community in Classical Athens* (Cambridge: Cambridge University Press, 1995).

Cohen, Elin, Kevin Fandl, Amanda Perry-Kessaris, and Veronica Taylor, "Truth and Consequences in Rule of Law: Interferences, Attribution and Evaluation," *Hague Journal on the Rule of Law*, 3 (2011), 106–129.

Coke, Thomas, *The Selected Writings and Speeches of Sir Edmund Coke*, vol. 1 ed. Steve Sheppard (Carmel: Liberty Fund, [1600] 2003).

Cole, Daniel H., "'An Unqualified Human Good': E. P. Thompson and the Rule of Law," *Journal of Law and Society*, 28 (2001), 177–203.

Comaroff, Jean, and John Comaroff, *Of Revelation and Revolution*, vol. 1: *Christianity, Colonialism, and Consciousness in South Africa* (Chicago: University of Chicago Press, 1991).

Comaroff, Jean, and John Comaroff, *Of Revelation and Revolution*, vol. 2: *The Dialectics of Modernity on a South African Frontier* (Chicago: Chicago University Press, 1997).

Commission on Legal Empowerment of the Poor, *Making the Law Work for Everyone*, vol. 1: *Report of the Commission on Legal Empowerment of the Poor* (New York: Commission on Legal Empowerment of the Poor and United Nations Development Programme, 2008).

Conover, Kellam, *Bribery in Classical Athens*, Ph.D. dissertation, Princeton University, 2010.

Constant, Benjamin, "The Liberty of the Ancients Compared with that of the Moderns," in idem, *Political Writings*, trans. and ed. Biancamaria Fontana (Cambridge: Cambridge University Press, 1988), pp. 309–328.

Coons, Christian, and Michael Weber, eds., *Paternalism: Theory and Practice* (Cambridge: Cambridge University Press, 2013).

Cornell, Drucilla, *The Imaginary Domain: Abortion, Pornography and Sexual Harassment* (New York: Routledge, 1995).

Cornell, Drucilla, *At the Heart of Freedom: Feminism, Sex and Equality* (Princeton: Princeton University Press, 1998).

Corten, Olivier, "The Controversies Over the Customary Prohibition on the Use of Force: A Methodological Debate," *European Journal of International Law*, 16 (2006), 803–822.

Corten, Olivier, *Le droit contre la guerre: l'interdiction du recours à la force en droit international contemporain* (Paris: Pedone, 2008).

Cortright, David, Conor Seyle, and Kristen Wall, *Governance for Peace: How Inclusive, Participatory and Accountable Institutions Promote Peace and Prosperity* (Cambridge: Cambridge University Press, 2017).

Coulson, Noel, *A History of Islamic Law* (Edinburgh: Edinburgh University Press, 1965).

Courtney, C. P., "Montesquieu and Natural Law," in David W. Carrithers, Michael A. Mosher, and Paul A. Rahe, eds., *Montesquieu's Science of Politics: Essays on The Spirit of Laws* (Lanham Rowman & Littlefield, 2001), pp. 41–68.

Cover, Robert M., "Violence and the Word," *Yale Law Journal*, 95 (1986), 1601–1629.

Cowan, Sharon, Chloë Kennedy, and Vanessa E. Munro, eds., *Scottish Feminist Judgments: (Re)Creating Law from the Outside In* (Oxford: Hart, 2019).

Cox, Iris, *Montesquieu and the History of French Laws* (Oxford: Voltaire Foundation, 1983).

Craig, Paul, "Formal and Substantive Conceptions of the Rule of Law: An Analytical Framework," *Public Law* (1997), pp. 467–487.

Craiutu, Aurelian, *A Virtue for Courageous Minds. Moderation in French Political Thought, 1748–1830* (Princeton: Princeton University Press, 2012).

Craven, Matthew, Sundhya Pahuja, and Gerry Simpson, "Reading and Unreading a Historiography of Hiatus," in idem, eds., *International Law and the Cold War* (Cambridge: Cambridge University Press, 2019), pp. 1–24.

Crawford, James, "International Law and the Rule of Law," *Adelaide Law Review*, 24 (2003), 3–12.

Crawford, James, "The Current Political Discourse Concerning International Law," *Modern Law Review*, 81 (2018), 1–22.

Crenshaw, Kimberlé, Neil Gotanda, Gary Peller, and Kendall Thomas, "Introduction," in idem, eds., *Critical Race Theory*, pp. xiii–xxxii.

Crenshaw, Kimberlé Williams, "The First Decade: Critical Reflections, or 'A Foot in the Closing Door,'" *University of California Los Angeles Law Review*, 49 (2002), 1343–1372.

Crenshaw, Kimberlé and Gary Peller, "Reel Time/Real Justice," *Denver University Law Review*, 70 (1993), 283–296.

Crenshaw, Kimberlé, Neil Gotanda, Gary Peller, and Kendall Thomas, eds., *Critical Race Theory: The Key Writings That Formed the Movement* (New York: The New Press, 1995).

Cromartie, Alan, *The Constitutionalist Revolution: An Essay on the History of England, 1450–1642* (Cambridge: Cambridge University Press, 2006).

Cromwell, Oliver, *The Letters and Speeches of Oliver Cromwell, with Elucidations by Thomas Carlyle*, vol. 2, ed. S. C. Lomas (London: Methuen, 1904).

Cromwell, Oliver, *The Letters and Speeches of Oliver Cromwell, with Elucidations by Thomas Carlyle*, vol. 3, ed. S. C. Lomas (London: Methuen, 1904).

Cromwell, Oliver, *The Writings and Speeches of Oliver Cromwell*, vol. 4: *The Protectorate 1655–1658*, ed. Wilbur Cortez Abbott (Cambridge: Harvard University Press, 1947).

Cruz Villalón, Pedro, "Das Grundgesetz im internationalen Wirkungszusammenhang der Verfassungen: Bericht Spanien," in Ulrich Battis, Ernst Gottfried Mahrenholz, and Dimitris Tsatsos, eds., *Das Grundgesetz im internationalen Wirkungszusammenhang der Verfassungen: 40 Jahre Grundgesetz* (Berlin: Duncker und Humblot, 1990), pp. 93–108.

Cupit, Geoffrey, *Justice as Fittingness* (Oxford: Clarendon Press, 1996).

Dancy, Geoff, and Florencia Montal, "Unintended Positive Complementarity: Why ICC Investigations May Increase Domestic Human Rights Prosecutions," *American Journal of International Law*, 111 (2017), 689–703.

Darley, John M., Kevin M. Carlsmith, and Paul H. Robinson, "The Ex Ante Function of the Criminal Law," *Law and Society Review*, 35 (2001), 165–190.

David, John Seh, *The American Colonization Society and the Founding of the First African Republic* (Bloomington: iUniverse, 2014).

Davies, Margaret, "Law's Truths and the Truth about Law: Interdisciplinary Refractions," in Margaret Davies and Vanessa E. Munro, eds., *The Ashgate Research Companion to Feminist Legal Theory* (Farnham: Ashgate, 2013), pp. 65–81.

Davies, Margaret, and Vanessa E. Munro, "Editors' Introduction," in Margaret Davies and Vanessa E. Munro, eds., *The Ashgate Research Companion to Feminist Legal Theory* (Farnham: Ashgate, 2013), pp. 1–10.

Davis, Kenneth Culp, *Discretionary Justice: A Preliminary Inquiry* (Baton Rouge: Louisiana State University Press, 1969).

Davis, Kevin E., "What Can the Rule of Law Variable Tell Us About Rule of Law Reforms?" *Michigan Journal of International Law*, 26 (2004), 141–161.

Davis, Kevin E., "Legal Indicators: The Power of Quantitative Measures of Law," *Annual Review of Law and Social Science*, 10 (2014), 9–34.

Dawkins, Richard, *The Selfish Gene*, 2nd ed. (Oxford: Oxford University Press, 1990).

de Dijn, Annelien, "Aristocratic Liberalism in Post-Revolutionary France," *Historical Journal*, 48 (2005), 661–681.

de Dijn, Annelien, "Montesquieu's Controversial Context: *The Spirit of the Laws* as a Monarchist Tract," *History of Political Thought*, 34 (2013), 66–88.

Denzau, Arthur T., and Douglass C. North, "Shared Mental Models: Ideologies and Institutions," *Kyklos*, 47 (1994), 3–31.

Derrida, Jacques, "Force of Law: The Mystical Foundation of Authority," in Drucilla Cornell, Michael Rosenfeld, and David Gray Carlson, eds., *Deconstruction and the Possibility of Justice* (New York: Routledge, 1992), pp. 3–67.

de Soto, Hernando, *The Mystery of Capital: Why Capitalism Triumphs in the West and Fails Everywhere Else* (New York: Basic Books, 2000).

Dezalay, Yves, and Bryant G. Garth, *Dealing in Virtue: International Commercial Arbitration and the Construction of a Transnational Legal Order* (Chicago: University of Chicago Press, 1996).

Diamond, Larry, Marc F. Plattner, and Christopher Walker, eds., *Authoritarianism Goes Global: The Challenge to Democracy* (Baltimore: Johns Hopkins University Press, 2016).

Dicey, A. V., *The Privy Council: The Arnold Prize Essay, 1860* (Oxford: T. & G. Shrimpton, 1860).

Dicey, A. V., "The Development of the Common Law," *Macmillan's Magazine*, 24 (1871), 287–296.

Dicey, A. V., "Stubbs's Constitutional History of England," *Nation*, 20 (1875), 152–154.

Dicey, A. V., "Digby on History of English Law," *Nation*, 21 (1875), 373–374.

Dicey, A. V., "How Is the Law to be Enforced in Ireland?" *Fortnightly Review*, 30 (1881), 537–552.

Dicey, A. V., *Introduction to the Study of the Law of the Constitution* (London: Macmillan, 1885).

Dicey, A. V., *A Digest of the Law of England with reference to the Conflict of Laws* (London: Stevens & Son, 1896).

Dicey, A. V., "*Droit Administratif* in Modern French Law," *Law Quarterly Review*, 17 (1901), 302–318.

Dicey, A. V., *Law and Public Opinion in England during the Nineteenth Century* (London: Macmillan, 1905).

Dicey, A. V., "Woman Suffrage," *Quarterly Review*, 210 (1909), 276–304.

Dicey, A. V., *Introduction to the Study of the Law of the Constitution*, 8th ed. (London: Macmillan, 1915).

Dicey, A. V., "The Development of Administrative Law in England," *Law Quarterly Review*, (1915), 31. TBC

Dicey, A. V., *Introduction to the Study of the Law of the Constitution*, 8th ed. (London: Macmillan, 1915).

Dick, Shelly, "FMO Country Guide: Liberia," *Refugee Studies Centre*, 2003.

Dickson, Tiphaine, "Shklar's Legalism and the Liberal Paradox," *Constellations*, 22 (2015), 188–198.

Donovan, James M., *Juries and the Transformation of Criminal Justice in France in the Nineteenth and Twentieth Centuries* (Chapel Hill: University of North Carolina Press, 2010).

Douglas, Heather, Francesca Bartlett, Trish Luker, and Rosemary Hunter, eds., *Australian Feminist Judgments: Righting and Rewriting Law* (Oxford: Hart, 2014).

Douglass, Robin, "Montesquieu and Modern Republicanism," *Political Studies*, 60 (2012), 703–719.

Doyle, Michael W., *Ways of War and Peace: Realism, Liberalism, and Socialism* (New York: W. W. Norton, 1997).

Du Bois, W. E. B., *The Souls of Black Folk*, ed. Brent Hayes Edwards (Oxford: Oxford University Press, [1903] 2007).

Du Bois, W. E. B., "Liberia, the League and the United States," *Foreign Affairs*, 11 (1933), 682–695.

Dubber, Markus D., and Tatjana Hörnle, *Criminal Law: A Comparative Approach* (Oxford: Oxford University Press, 2014).

Duff, Antony, and Zachary Hoskins, "Legal Punishment," *Stanford Encyclopedia of Philosophy*, available at https://plato.stanford.edu/archives/fall2017/entries/legal-punishment/.

Dupret, Baudoin, ed., *Standing Trial: Law and the Person in the Modern Middle East* (London, I. B. Tauris, 2004).

Durch, William J., and Michelle Ker, "Police in UN Peacekeeping: Improving Selection, Recruitment, and Deployment," International Peace Institute, New York, November 2013.

Dworkin, Gerald, "Moral Paternalism," *Law and Philosophy*, 24 (2005), 305–319.

Dworkin, Ronald, *Taking Rights Seriously* (Cambridge: Harvard University Press, 1977).

Dworkin, Ronald, "Political Judges and the Rule of Law," *Proceedings of the British Academy*, 64 (1978), 259–287.

Dworkin, Ronald, *A Matter of Principle* (Cambridge: Harvard University Press, 1985).

Dworkin, Ronald, *Law's Empire* (Cambridge: Belknap Press of Harvard University Press, 1986).

Dworkin, Ronald, *Justice in Robes* (Cambridge: Belknap Press of Harvard University Press, 2006).

Dyzenhaus, David, "The Politics of Deference: Judicial Review and Democracy," in Michael Taggart, ed., *The Province of Administrative Law* (Oxford: Hart, 1997), pp. 279–307.

Dyzenhaus, David, "Form and Substance in the Rule of Law: A Democratic Justification for Judicial Review," in Christopher Forsyth, ed., *Judicial Review and the Constitution* (Oxford: Hart, 2000), pp. 141–167.

Dyzenhaus, David, "The Left and the Question of Law", *Canadian Journal of Law and Jurisprudence*, 17 (2004), 7–30.

Dyzenhaus, David, "How Hobbes met the 'Hobbes Challenge,'" *Modern Law Review*, 72 (2009), 488–506.

Dyzenhaus, David, "Hobbes on the Authority of Law", in David Dyzenhaus and Thomas Poole, eds., *Hobbes and the Law* (Cambridge: Cambridge University Press, 2012), pp. 186–209.

Dyzenhaus, David, "Dreaming the Rule of Law," in David Dyzenhaus and Thomas Poole, eds., *Law, Liberty and State: Oakeshot, Hayek and Schmitt on the Rule of Law* (Cambridge: Cambridge University Press, 2015), pp. 234–260.

Dziedzic, Michael, ed., *Criminalized Power Structures: The Overlooked Enemies of Peace* (Lanham: Rowman & Littlefield, 2016).

Eberhardt, Pia, and Cecilia Olivet, *Profiting from Injustice: How Law Firms, Arbitrators and Financiers are Fuelling an Investment Arbitration Boom* (Amsterdam: Corporate Europe Observatory and the Transnational Institute, 2012).

Edelstein, Dan, Stefanos Geroulanos, and Natasha Wheatley, eds., *Power and Time: Temporalities in Conflict and the Making of History* (Chicago: University of Chicago Press, 2020).

Efstathiou, Christos, *E. P. Thompson: A Twentieth-Century Romantic* (London: Merlin Press, 2015).

Ehrard, Jean, *Politique de Montesquieu* (Paris: Armand Colin, 1965).

Eliade, Mircea, *The Myth of the Eternal Return: Cosmos and History* (Princeton: Princeton University Press, 1965).

Elon, Amos, *The Pity of It All: A History of Jews in Germany, 1743–1933* (New York: Henry Holt, 2002).

Elster, Jon, ed., *Deliberative Democracy* (Cambridge: Cambridge University Press,1998).

Enright, Máiréad M., Julie McCandless, and Aoife O'Donoghue, eds., *Northern/Irish Feminist Judgments: Judges' Troubles and the Gendered Politics of Identity* (Oxford: Hart, 2017).

Ensley, Michael J., and Michael C. Munger, "Ideological Competition and Institutions: Why 'Cultural' Explanations of Development Patterns Are Not Nonsense," in Ram Mudambi, Pietro Navarra, and Giuseppe Sobbrio, eds., *Rules and Reason: Perspectives on Constitutional Political Economy* (Cambridge: Cambridge University Press, 2001), pp. 107–121.

Errera, Roger, "Dicey and French Administrative Law," *Public Law* (1985), pp. 695–709.

Eslava, Luis, and Sundhya Pahuja, "The Nation-State and International Law: A Reading from the Global South," *Humanity*, 11 (2020), 118–138.

Faber, Karl-Georg, "Macht, Gewalt: Liberale Lehre von der Staatsgewalt," in Otto Brunner, Werner Conze, and Reinhart Koselleck, eds., *Geschichtliche Grundbegriffe* (Studienausgabe), vol. 3 (Stuttgart: Klett-Cotta, 2004), pp. 817–935.

Faguet, Emile, *La politique comparée de Montesquieu, Rousseau et Voltaire* (Paris: Société Française d'Imprimérie et de Librairie, 1902).

Fallon, Richard H., Jr., "'The Rule of Law' as a Concept in Constitutional Discourse," *Columbia Law Review*, 97 (1997), 1–56.

Farley, Anthony Paul, "Accumulation," *Michigan Journal of Race and Law*, 11 (2005), 51–73.

Farmer, Lindsay, *Making the Modern Criminal Law: Criminalization and Civil Order* (Oxford: Oxford University Press, 2016).

Fassin, Didier, *Enforcing Order: An Ethnography of Urban Policing*, trans. Rachel Gomme (Cambridge: Polity 2013).

Feinberg, Joel, "Legal Paternalism," *Canadian Journal of Philosophy*, 1 (1971), 105–124.

Felman, Shoshona, *The Juridical Unconscious: Trials and Traumas in the Twentieth Century* (Cambridge: Harvard University Press, 2002).

Feuerbach, Anselm von, *Lehrbuch des gemeinen in Deutschland geltenden Peinlichen Rechts* (Giessen: Georg Friedrich Heyer, 1801)

Fine, Michelle, and Lois Weis, "Disappearing Acts: The State and Violence against Women in the Twentieth Century," *Signs*, 25 (2000), 1139–1146.

Fine, Bob, *Democracy and the Rule of Law: Liberal Ideals and Marxist Critiques* (London: Pluto Press, 1984).

Fine, Robert, "The Rule of Law and Muggletonian Marxism: The Perplexities of Edward Thompson," *Journal of Law and Society*, 21 (1994), 193–213.

Fineman, Martha L., "Challenging Law, Establishing Difference: The Future of Feminist Legal Scholarship," *Florida Law Review*, 42 (1990), 25–43.

Fineman, Martha Albertson, "The Vulnerable Subject: Anchoring Equality in the Human Condition," *Yale Journal of Law and Feminism*, 20 (2008), pp. 1–23.

Fineman, Martha Albertson, "The Vulnerable Subject and the Responsive State," *Emory Law Journal*, 60 (2010), pp. 251–275.

Finley, Lucinda M., "Breaking Women's Silence in Law: The Dilemma of the Gendered Nature of Legal Reasoning," *Notre Dame Law Review*, 64 (1989), 886–910.

Finnis, John, *Natural Law and Natural Rights* (Oxford: Oxford University Press, 1980).

Finnis, John M., "Law as Co-ordination," *Ratio Juris*, 2 (1989), 97–1.

Finnis, John, *Natural Law and Natural Rights*, 2nd ed. (Oxford: Oxford University Press, 2011).

Fiss, Owen M., "Death of the Law?," *Cornell Law Review*, 72 (1986), 1–16.

Fiss, Owen M., *The Irony of Free Speech* (Cambridge: Harvard University Press, 1996).

Fitzpatrick, Peter, *The Mythology of Modern Law* (London: Routledge, 1992).

Flagg, Barbara J., "'Was Blind But Now I See': White Race Consciousness and the Requirement of Discriminatory Intent," *Michigan Law Review*, 91 (1993), 953–1017.

Flewers, Paul, and John McIlroy, eds., *1956: John Saville, E. P. Thompson and* The Reasoner (London: Merlin Press, 2016).

Flogaïtis, Spyridon, *Administrative law et droit administratif* (Paris: R. Pichon et R. Durand-Auzias, 1986).

Ford, Franklin, *Robe and Sword: The Regrouping of the French Aristocracy after Louis XIV* (Cambridge: Harvard University Press, 1953).

Ford, Lisa, *Settler Sovereignty: Jurisdiction and Indigenous People in America and Australia, 1788–1836* (Cambridge: Harvard University Press, 2010).

Ford, Martin, "Ethnic Relations and the Transformation of Leadership among the Dan of Nimba, Liberia (ca. 1900–1940)," Ph.D. dissertation, State University of New York, 1990.

Ford, Stuart, "A Social Psychology Model of the Perceived Legitimacy of International Criminal Courts: Implications for the Success of Transitional Justice Mechanisms," *Vanderbilt Journal of Transnational Law*, 45 (2014), 405–476.

Forrester, Katrina, *In the Shadow of Justice: Postwar Liberalism and the Remaking of Political Philosophy* (Princeton: Princeton University Press, 2019).

Forsdyke, Sara, "Ancient and Modern Conceptions of the Rule of Law," in Mirko Canevaro, Andrew Erskine, Benjamin Gray, and Josiah Ober, eds., *Ancient Greek History and Contemporary Social Science* (Edinburgh: Edinburgh University Press, 2018), pp. 184–212.

Forsthoff, Ernst, “Führung und Bürokratie: Einige grundsätzliche Erwägungen,” *Deutsches Adelsblatt*, 53 (1935), 1339–1340.

Forsthoff, Ernst, ed., *Rechtsstaatlichkeit und Sozialstaatlichkeit* (Darmstadt: Wissenschaftliche Buchgesellschaft, 1968).

Fortescue, John, *De Laudibus Legum Anglie*, trans. and ed. S. B. Chrimes (Cambridge: Cambridge University Press, 1949 [1471]).

Foucault, Michel, *Discipline and Punish: The Birth of the Prison*, trans. Alan Sheridan (Harmondsworth: Penguin, [1975] 1977).

Fraenkel, Ernst, *The Dual State: A Contribution to the Theory of Dictatorship*, trans. E. A. Shils, with an Introduction by Jens Meierhenrich (Oxford: Oxford University Press, [1941] 2017).

Freedom House, *Freedom in the World 2014: Methodology*, November 2014.

Friedman, Barry, “Taking Law Seriously” *Perspectives on Politics*, 4 (2006), 261–276.

Fromont, Michel, “Les mythes du droit public français: séparation des pouvoirs et État de droit,” in Patrick Charlot, ed., *Utopies: Études en hommages à Claude Courvoisier* (Dijon: Éditions universitaires, 2005), pp. 293–302.

Fukuyama, Francis, “Transitions to the Rule of Law,” *Journal of Democracy*, 21 (2010), 33–44.

Fuller, Lon L., “Reason and Fiat in Case Law,” *Harvard Law Review*, 59 (1946), 376–395.

Fuller, Lon L., “American Legal Philosophy at Mid-Century: A Review of Edwin W. Patterson’s *Jurisprudence, Men and Ideas of the Law*,” *Journal of Legal Education*, 6 (1954), 457–485.

Fuller, Lon L., “Human Purpose and Natural Law,” *Journal of Philosophy*, 53 (1956), 697–705.

Fuller, Lon L., “Positivism and Fidelity to Law – A Reply to Professor Hart,” *Harvard Law Review*, 71 (1958), 630–672.

Fuller, Lon L., *The Morality of Law* (New Haven: Yale University Press, 1964).

Fuller, Lon L., “Reply to Professors Cohen and Dworkin,” *Villanova Law Review*, 10 (1965), 655–666.

Fuller, Lon L, *The Morality of Law*, 2nd rev. ed. (New Haven: Yale University Press, 1969).

Fuller, Lon L., “The Forms and Limits of Adjudication,” *Harvard Law Review*, 92 (1978), 353–409.

Fuller, Timothy, “Friedrich Hayek’s Moral Science,” *Ratio Juris*, 2 (1989), 17–26.

Funk, David A., “Traditional Islamic Jurisprudence: Justifying Islamic Law and Government,” *Southern University Law Review*, 20 (1993), 213–294.

Gabel, Peter, et al., “Critical Legal Studies Symposium,” *Stanford Law Review*, 36 (1984), 1–674.

Gagarin, Michael, “Law, Politics, and the Question of Relevance in the Case on the Crown,” *Classical Antiquity*, 31 (2012), 293–314.

Gallie, W. B., "Essentially Contested Concepts," *Proceedings of the Aristotelian Society*, 56 (1956), 167–198.

Garcia, Ruben J., "Critical Race Theory and Proposition 187: The Racial Politics of Immigration Law," *Chicano-Latino Law Review*, 17 (1995), 118–148.

Gardbaum, Stephen, *The New Commonwealth Model of Constitutionalism* (Cambridge: Cambridge University Press, 2013).

Gargarella, Roberto, "The Majoritarian Reading of the Rule of Law," in José María Maravall and Adam Przeworski, eds., *Democracy and the Rule of Law* (Cambridge: Cambridge University Press, 2003), pp. 147–167.

Gargarella, Roberto, "'We the People' Outside of the Constitution: The Dialogic Model of Constitutionalism and the System of Checks and Balances," *Current Legal Problems*, 67 (2014), 1–47.

Garland, David, *The Culture of Control Crime and Social Order in Contemporary Society* (New York: Oxford University Press, 2001).

Gathii, James Thuo, "Good Governance as a Counter-Insurgency Agenda to Oppositional and Transformative Social Projects in International Law," *Buffalo Human Rights Law Review*, 5 (1999), 107–174.

Geertz, Clifford, "Thick Description: Toward an Interpretive Theory of Culture," in idem, *The Interpretation of Cultures: Selected Essays* (New York: Basic Books, 1973), pp. 3–30.

Geneva Centre for the Democratic Control of Armed Forces, *The Contribution and Role of SSR in the Prevention of Violent Conflict* (Geneva: Geneva Centre for the Democratic Control of Armed Forces, 2017).

Gennaioli, Nicola, and Andrei Shleifer, "The Evolution of Common Law," *Journal of Political Economy*, 115 (2007), 43–68.

Gennaioli, Nicola, and Andrei Shleifer, "Overruling and the Instability of Law," *Journal of Comparative Economics*, 35 (2007), 309–328.

Gerring, John, *Case Study Research*, 2nd ed. (Cambridge: Cambridge University Press, 2017).

Gershoni, Yekutiel, "Liberia's Unification Policy and Decolonization in Africa: A Parallel Process," *Asian and African Studies*, 16 (1982), 239–260.

Gershoni, Yekutiel, "The Formation of Liberia's Boundaries, Part 1: Agreements," *Liberian Studies Journal*, 17 (1992), 25–45.

Ghai, Yash, and Jill Cottrell, eds., *Marginalized Communities and Access to Justice* (New York: Routledge, 2010).

Gill, Stephen, and A. Claire Cutler, eds., *New Constitutionalism and World Order* (Cambridge: Cambridge University Press, 2014).

Ginsburg, Tom, "Does Law Matter for Economic Development?" *Law and Society Review*, 34 (2000), 829–856.

Ginsburg, Tom, "Constitutional Afterlife: The Continuing Impact of Thailand's Postpolitical Constitution," *International Journal of Constitutional Law*, 7 (2009), 83–105.

Ginsburg, Tom, "Pitfalls of Measuring the Rule of Law," *Hague Journal on the Rule of Law*, 3 (2011), 269–280.

Ginsburg, Tom, and Tamir Moustafa, "Introduction: The Functions of Courts in Authoritarian Politics," in Tamir Moustafa and Tom Ginsburg, eds., *Rule by Law: The Politics of Courts in Authoritarian Regimes* (Cambridge: Cambridge University Press 2008), pp. 1–22.

Ginsburg, Tom, and Tamir Moustafa, eds., *Rule by Law: The Politics of Courts in Authoritarian Regimes* (Cambridge: Cambridge University Press, 2008).

Ginsburg, Tom, and Mila Versteeg, "Measuring the Rule of Law: A Comparison of Indicators," *Law and Social Inquiry*, 42 (2016), 100–137.

Ginsburg, Tom, and Mila Versteeg, "Constitutional Correlates of the Rule of Law," in Maurice Adams and Anne Meuwese, eds., *Constitutionalism and Rule of Law: Bridging Idealism and Realism* (Cambridge University Press, 2017), pp. 506–525.

Glaser, Stefan, "Nullem Crimen Sine Lege," *Journal of Comparative Legislation and International Law*, 24 (1942), 29–37.

Glendon, Mary Ann, *Rights Talk: The Impoverishment of Political Discourse* (New York: The Free Press, 1991).

Gneist, Rudolf, *Verwaltung-Justiz-Rechtsweg: Staatsverwaltung und Selbstverwaltung nach englischen und deutschen Verhältnissen mit besonderer Rücksicht auf Verwaltungsformen und Kreis-Ordnungen in Preußen* (Berlin: Springer, 1869).

Gneist, Rudolf, *Der Rechtsstaat und die Verwaltungsgerichte in Deutschland*, 2nd ed. (Berlin: Springer, 1879).

Goldsmith, Jack L., *The Terror Presidency: Law and Judgment Inside the Bush Administration* (New York: W. W. Norton, 2007).

Goldsmith, Jack, "The Contributions of the Obama Administration to the Practice and Theory of International Law," *Harvard International Law Journal*, 57 (2016), 455–473.

Golub, Stephen, "Beyond Rule of Law Orthodoxy: The Legal Empowerment Alternative," Carnegie Endowment for International Peace, October 2003.

Golub, Stephen, "The Legal Empowerment Alternative," in Thomas Carothers, ed., *Promoting the Rule of Law Abroad: In Search of Knowledge* (Washington, DC: Carnegie Endowment for International Peace, 2006), pp. 161–187.

Golub, Stephen, ed., *Legal Empowerment: Practitioners' Perspectives* (Rome: International Development Law Organization, 2010).

Goodin, Robert E., "Institutions and Their Design," in idem, ed., *The Theory of Institutional Design* (Cambridge: Cambridge University Press, 1996), pp. 26–27.

Goodrich, Peter, *Languages of Law: From Logics of Memory to Nomadic Masks* (Cambridge: Cambridge University Press, 1990).

Goodwin, Laura, and Vivek Maru, "What Do We Know about Legal Empowerment? Mapping the Evidence," *Hague Journal on the Rule of Law*, 9 (2017), 1–38.

Gopnik, Adam, *A Thousand Small Sanities: The Moral Adventure of Liberalism* (New York: Basic Books, 2019).

Gordon, Robert W., "E. P. Thompson's Legacies," *Georgetown Law Journal*, 82 (1994), 2005–2011.

Gordon, Robert W., "The Role of Lawyers in Producing the Rule of Law: Some Critical Reflections," *Theoretical Inquiries in Law*, 11 (2010), 441–468.

Gowder, Paul, *The Rule of Law in the Real World* (Cambridge: Cambridge University Press, 2016).

Goyard-Fabre, Simone, *La philosophie du droit de Montesquieu* (Paris: Librairie C. Klincksieck, 1973).

Gozzi, Gustavo, "*Rechtsstaat* and Individual Rights in German Constitutional History," in Pietro Costa and Danilo Zolo, eds., *The Rule of Law: History, Theory and Criticism* (Dordrecht: Springer, 2007), pp. 237–259.

Gray, John, "Political Power, Social Theory, and Essential Contestability," in David Miller and Larry Siedentop, eds., *The Nature of Political Theory* (Oxford: Oxford University Press, 1983), 75–101.

Green, Jonathan Allen, "Edmund Burke's German Readers at the End of Enlightenment, 1790–1815," Ph.D. dissertation, University of Cambridge, 2017.

Green, Leslie, "Law's Rule," *Osgoode Hall Law Journal*, 24 (1986), 1023–1042.

Greenman, Kathryn, "Aliens in Latin America: Intervention, Arbitration and State Responsibility for Rebels," *Leiden Journal of International Law*, 31 (2018), 617–639.

Greer, Allan, *Property and Dispossession: Natives, Empires and Land in Early Modern North America* (Cambridge: Cambridge University Press, 2018).

Greif, Avner, and David D. Laitin, "A Theory of Endogenous Institutional Change," *American Political Science Review*, 98 (2004), 633–652.

Grewal, David Singh, and Jedediah Purdy, "The Original Theory of Constitutionalism," *Yale Law Journal*, 127 (2018), 664–705.

Grewe, Constance, "Das deutsche Grundgesetz aus französischer Sicht," *Jahrbuch des öffentlichen Rechts der Gegenwart*, 58 (2010), 1–14.

Griffith, J. A. G., "The Political Constitution," *Modern Law Review*, 42 (1979), 1–21.

Grimm, Dieter, *Deutsche Verfassungsgeschichte 1776–1866* (Frankfurt am Main: Suhrkamp, 1988).

Grosrichard, Alain, *Structure du sérail: La fiction du despotisme asiatique dans l'occident classique* (Paris: Éditions du seuil, 1979).

Gross, Raphael, *Carl Schmitt and the Jews*, trans. Joel Golb (Madison: University of Wisconsin Press, 2007).

Guzman, Andrew T., "Against Consent," *Virginia Journal of International Law*, 52 (2012), 747–790.

Habermas, Jürgen, "Zum Begriff der politischen Beteiligung," in Jürgen Habermas, Ludwig Friedeburg, Christoph von Oehler, and Friedrich Weltz, eds., *Student und Politik* (Neuwied: Luchterhand, 1961), pp. 13–55.

Habermas, Jürgen, *The Structural Transformation of the Public Sphere: An Inquiry into a Category of Bourgeois Society*, trans. Thomas Burger (Cambridge: MIT Press, [1962] 1989).

Habermas, Jürgen, *Between Facts and Norms: Contributions to a Discourse Theory of Law and Democracy*, trans. William Rehg (Cambridge: MIT Press, [1992] 1996).

Habermas, Jürgen, "Natural Law and Revolution," in idem, *Theory and Practice*, trans. John Viertel (Boston: Beacon Press, [1963] 1974), pp. 82–120.

Habermas, Jürgen, *Rekonstruktion des Historischen Materialismus* (Frankfurt am Main: Suhrkamp, 1976).

Habermas, Jürgen, *Theory of Communicative Action*, vol. 2, trans. Thomas McCarthy (Boston: Beacon Press, [1985] 1987).

Habermas, Jürgen, "Law and Morality," in Sterling M. McMurrin, ed., *The Tanner Lectures on Human Values* (Salt Lake City: University of Utah Press, 1988), pp. 219–279.

Habermas, Jürgen, "On the Internal Relation between Rule of Law and Democracy," *European Journal of Philosophy*, 3 (1995), 12–20.

Hadfield, Gillian K., *Rules for a Flat World: Why Humans Invented Law and How to Reinvent It for a Complex Global Economy* (Oxford: Oxford University Press, 2017).

Hadfield, Gillian K., and Jamie Heine, "Law in the Law-Thick World: The Legal Resource Landscape for Ordinary Americans," in Samuel Estreicher and Joy Radice, eds., *Beyond Elite Law: Access to Civil Justice for Ordinary Americans* (New York: Cambridge University Press, 2016), pp. 21–52.

Hadfield, Gillian K., and Barry R. Weingast, "What Is Law? A Coordination Model of the Characteristics of Legal Order," *Journal of Legal Analysis*, 4 (2012), 471–514.

Hadfield, Gillian K., and Barry R. Weingast, "Law without the State: Legal Attributes and the Coordination of Decentralized Collective Punishment," *Journal of Law and Courts*, 1 (2013), 3–34.

Hadfield, Gillian K., and Barry R. Weingast, "Microfoundations of the Rule of Law," *Annual Review of Political Science*, 17 (2014), 21–42.

Haggard, Stephan, and Lydia Tiede, "The Rule of Law and Economic Growth: Where are We?" *World Development*, 39 (2011), 673–685.

Haggard, Stephan, Andrew MacIntyre, and Lydia Tiede, "The Rule of Law and Economic Development," *Annual Review of Political Science*, 11 (2008), 205–234.

Hailsham, Lord, *Elective Dictatorship* (London: BBC, 1976).

Hall, Jerome, *General Principles of Criminal Law*, 2nd ed. (Indianapolis: Bobbs-Merrill, 1960).

Hall, Livingston, and Selig J. Seligman, "Mistake of Law and Mens Rea," *University of Chicago Law Review*, 8 (1941), 641–683.

Hall, Peter A., and David Soskice, eds., *Varieties of Capitalism: The Institutional Foundations of Comparative Advantage* (Oxford: Oxford University Press, 2001).

Hallaq, Wael, *A History of Islamic Legal Theories* (Cambridge: Cambridge University Press, 1999).

Hamilton, Scott, *The Crisis of Theory: E. P. Thompson, the New Left, and Postwar British Politics* (Manchester: Manchester University Press, 2011).

Hammergren, Linn A., *Justice Reform and Development: Rethinking Donor Assistance to Developing and Transition Countries* (New York: Routledge, 2014).

Hamson, C. J., *Executive Discretion and Judicial Control: An Aspect of the French Conseil d'État* (London: Stevens & Sons, 1954).

Hansen, Mogens Herman, *The Athenian Democracy in the Age of Demosthenes* (Oxford: Blackwell, 1991).

Harcourt, Bernard E., "Beccaria's *On Crimes and Punishments*: A Mirror on the History of the Foundations of the Modern Criminal Law," in Markus D. Dubber, *Foundational Texts in Modern Criminal Law* (Oxford: Oxford University Press, 2014), pp. 39–60.

Hardin, Russell, "Law and Social Order," *Philosophical Issues*, 11 (2010), 61–86.

Hargreaves Heap, Shaun P., and Yanis Varoufakis, *Game Theory: A Critical Introduction*, 2nd ed. (London: Routledge, 2004).

Harrington, James, *The Common-Wealth of Oceana* (London: J. Streater, 1656).

Harris, Edward, *The Rule of Law in Action in Democratic Athens* (Oxford: Oxford University Press, 2013).

Hart, H. L. A. "Positivism and the Separation of Law and Morals," *Harvard Law Review*, 71 (1958), 593–629.

Hart, H. L. A., "Book Review: *The Morality of Law* by Lon L. Fuller," *Harvard Law Review*, 78 (1965), 1281–1296.

Hart, H. L. A., "Prolegomenon to the Philosophy of Punishment," in idem, *Punishment and Responsibility* (Oxford: Oxford University Press, 1968), pp. 1–27.

Hart, H. L. A., "Beccaria and Bentham," in idem, *Essays on Bentham: Jurisprudence and Political Theory* (Oxford: Clarendon Press, 1982), pp. 40–52.

Hart, H. L. A., *The Concept of Law*, 2nd ed. (Oxford: Clarendon Press, 1994).

Hart, Henry M., Jr., and Albert M. Sacks, *The Legal Process: Basic Problems in the Making and Application of Law*, eds. William N. Eskridge, Jr., and Philip P. Frickey (Westbury: Foundation Press 1994).

Harvey, W. Burnett, "The Rule of Law in Historical Perspective," *Michigan Law Review*, 59 (1961), 487–500.

Hatzis, Aristides N., "The Illiberal Democracy of Ancient Athens," Unpublished paper, University of Athens, July 2016.

Hauriou, Maurice, *Précis de droit administratif et droit public*, 8th ed. (Paris: Recueil Sirey, 1914).

Hauriou, Maurice, *La jurisprudence administrative de 1892 à 1929*, vol. 1 (Paris: Recueil Sirey, 1929).

Haverkate, Georg, "Staat und Soveränität: Rechtsstaat," in Otto Brunner, Werner Conze, and Reinhart Koselleck, eds., *Geschichtliche Grundbegriffe* (Studienausgabe), vol. 6 (Stuttgart: Klett-Cotta, 2004), pp. 1–154.

Hay, Douglas, "Moral Economy, Political Economy, and Law," in Adrian Randall and Andrew Charlesworth, eds., *Moral Economy and Popular Protest: Crowds, Conflict and Authority* (Manchester: Manchester University Press, 1999), pp. 93–122.

Hay, Douglas, "The State and the Market: Lord Kenyon and Mr Waddington," *Past and Present*, 162 (1999), 101–162.

Hay, Douglas, and Nicholas Rogers, *Eighteenth-Century English Society: Shuttles and Swords* (Oxford: Oxford University Press, 1997).

Hay, Douglas, Peter Linebaugh, John G. Rule, E. P. Thompson, and Cal Winslow, *Albion's Fatal Tree: Crime and Society in Eighteenth-Century England*, 2nd ed. (London: Verso, 2011).

Hayek, Friedrich A., "The Economic Conditions of Interstate Federalism," in idem, *Individualism and Economic Order* (Chicago: University of Chicago Press, [1939] 1948), pp. 255–273.

Hayek, Friedrich A., *The Road to Serfdom* (Chicago: University of Chicago Press, [1944] 2007).

Hayek, Friedrich A., "Decline of the Rule of Law, Part 1," *The Freeman*, April 20, 1953.

Hayek, Friedrich A., "Decline of the Rule of Law, Part 2," *The Freeman*, May 4, 1953.

Hayek, Friedrich A., *The Collected Works of F. A. Hayek*, vol. 17: *The Constitution of Liberty*, ed. Ronald Hamowy (Chicago: University of Chicago Press, [1960] 2011).

Hayek, Friedrich A., *Law, Legislation and Liberty*, 3 vols. (Chicago: University of Chicago Press, 1973–1979).

Hayner, Priscilla B., *Unspeakable Truths: Transitional Justice and the Challenge of Truth Commissions*, 2nd ed. (New York: Routledge, 2011).

Hearn, William Edward, *The Government of England: Its Structure and Its Development* (London: Longmans, Green, Reader, & Dyer, 1867).

Hegel, G. W. F., *Elements of the Philosophy of Right*, trans. H. B. Nisbet, ed. Allen W. Wood (Cambridge: Cambridge University Press, [1820] 1991).

Helfer, Laurence R., "Nonconsensual International Lawmaking," *University of Illinois Law Review*, 2008 (2008), 71–125.

Hendley, Kathryn, *Everyday Law in Russia* (Ithaca: Cornell University Press, 2017).

Heritage Foundation, *Property Rights*, November 2014, available at www.heritage.org/index/property-rights.

Heuschling, Luc, *État de droit, Rechtsstaat, Rule of Law* (Paris: Dalloz, 2002).

Heuschling, Luc, "Book Review: *Eine deutsch-französische Rechtswissenschaft? Une science juridique franco-allemande?* by Olivier Beaud and Erk Volkmar Heyen," *Revue internationale de droit compare*, 55 (2003), 995–1000.

Heuschling, Luc, "État de droit," in Loïc Cadiet, ed., *Dictionnaire de la Justice* (Paris: PUF, 2004), pp. 455–461.

Heuschling, Luc, "Why Should Judges Be Independent? Reflections on Coke, Montesquieu and the French Tradition of Judicial Dependence," in Katja Ziegler, Denis Baranger, and Anthony Bradley, eds., *Constitutionalism and the Role of Parliaments* (Oxford: Hart, 2007), pp. 199–223.

Heuschling, Luc, "État de droit: Étude de linguistique, de théorie et de dogmatique juridiques comparées," in Hartmut Bauer and Christian Calliess, eds., *Verfassungsprinzipien in Europa – Constitutional Principles in Europe – Principes constitutionnels en Europe* (Athens/Berlin/Brussels: Sakkoulas/Berliner Wissenschafts-Verlag/Bruylant, 2008), pp. 103–155.

Heuschling, Luc, "Le regard d'un comparatiste: L'État de droit *dans* et *au-delà* des cultures juridiques nationales," in Société française de droit international, ed., *L'État de droit en droit international* (Paris: Pédone, 2009), pp. 41–67.

Heuschling, Luc, "État de droit," in Jean-Bernard Auby, ed., *L'influence du droit européen sur les catégories juridiques du droit public français* (Paris: Dalloz, 2010), pp. 541–552.

Hewart, Lord, *The New Despotism* (London: Ernest Benn, 1929).

Hickel, Jason, *The Division* (London: William Heinemann, 2017).

Higgins, Rosalyn, "The Rule of Law: Some Sceptical Thoughts," in idem, *Themes and Theories: Selected Essays, Speeches and Writings in International Law,* vol. 2 (Oxford: Oxford University Press, 2009), pp. 1330–1339.

Hilbink, Lisa, *Judges beyond Politics in Democracy and Dictatorship: Lessons from Chile* (Cambridge: Cambridge University Press, 2007).

Hildebrandt, Mireille, "Radbruch's *Rechtsstaat* and Schmitt's Legal Order: Legalism, Legality, and the Institution of Law," *Critical Analysis of Law*, 2 (2015), 42–63.

Hill, George Birkbeck Norman, and L. F. Powell, eds., *Boswell's Life of Johnson,* vol. 1: *The Life (1709–1765)* (Oxford: Oxford University Press, 1934).

Hinton, Alexander Laban, *The Justice Facade: Trials of Transition in Cambodia* (Oxford: Oxford University Press, 2018).

Hirsch, Philipp-Alexander, *Freiheit und Staatlichkeit bei Kant: Die autonomietheoretische Begründung von Recht und Staat und das Widerstandsproblem* (Berlin: de Gruyter, 2017).

Hirschl, Ran, *Towards Juristocracy: The Origins and Consequences of the New Constitutionalism* (Cambridge: Harvard University Press, 2004).

Hitz, Zena, "Plato on the Sovereignty of Law," in Ryan K. Balot, ed., *A Companion to Greek and Roman Political Thought* (Oxford: Blackwell, 2009), pp. 367–381.

Hobbes, Thomas, *Leviathan*, ed. Richard Tuck (Cambridge: Cambridge University Press, [1652] 1997).

Hobbes, Thomas, *A Dialogue Between a Philosopher and a Student, of the Common Laws of England*, in idem, *The Clarendon Edition of the Works of Thomas Hobbes*, vol 11: *Writings on Common Law and Hereditary Right*, eds. Alan Cromartie and Quentin Skinner (Oxford: Clarendon Press, [1681] 2005), pp. 1–146.

Hodge, Joseph, "Writing the History of Development, Part 1: The First Wave," *Humanity*, 6 (2015), 429–463.

Hodge, Joseph, "Writing the History of Development, Part 2: Longer, Deeper, Wider," *Humanity*, 7 (2016), 125–174.

Hodson, Loveday, and Troy Lavers, eds., *Feminist Judgments in International Law* (Oxford: Hart, 2019).

Hogg, Peter W., and Allison A. Bushell, "The *Charter* Dialogue Between Courts and Legislatures," *Osgoode Hall Law Journal*, 35 (1997), 75–124.

Hogg, Peter W., Allison A. Bushell Thornton, and Wade K. Wright, "*Charter* Dialogue Revisited – Or Much Ado About Metaphors," *Osgoode Hall Law Journal*, 45 (2007), 1–65.

Holmes, Oliver Wendell, Jr., *The Common Law*, introd. G. Edward White (Cambridge: Belknap Press of Harvard University Press, [1881] 2009).

Holmes, Stephen, *Benjamin Constant and the Making of Modern Liberalism* (New Haven: Yale University Press, 1984).

Holmes, Stephen, *Passions and Constraint: On the Theory of Liberal Democracy* (Chicago: University of Chicago Press, 1995).

Holmes, Stephen, "Lineages of the Rule of Law," in José María Maravall and Adam Przeworski, eds., *Democracy and the Rule of Law* (Cambridge: Cambridge University Press, 2003), pp. 19–61.

Holt, Wythe, "Tilt," *George Washington Law Review*, 52 (1983), 280–288.

Horder, Jeremy, *Ashworth's Principles of Criminal Law*, 8th ed. (Oxford: Oxford University Press, 2016).

Hörnle, Tatjana, "PJA von Feuerbach and his Textbook of the Common Penal Law," in Markus D. Dubber, ed., *Foundational Texts in Criminal Law* (Oxford: Oxford University Press, 2014) pp. 119–140.

Horwitz, Morton J., "The Rule of Law: An Unqualified Human Good?," *Yale Law Journal*, 86 (1977), 561–566.

Hull, Isabel V., *A Scrap of Paper: Breaking and Making International Law during the Great War* (Ithaca: Cornell University Press, 2014).

Hull, Isabel, "Anything Can Be Rescinded," *London Review of Books*, April 26, 2018.

Hulliung, Mark, *Montesquieu and the Old Regime* (Berkeley: University of California Press, 1976).

Hulsebosch, Daniel, *Constituting Empire: New York and the Transformation of Constitutionalism in the Atlantic World, 1664–1830* (Chapel Hill: University of North Carolina Press, 2006).

Human Rights Watch, "Pressure Point: The ICC's Impact on National Justice," May 2018.

Human Rights Watch, "Guatemala: President Sabotages Fight for Justice," August 2018.

Humphreys, Stephen, *Theatre of the Rule of Law: Transnational Legal Intervention in Theory and Practice* (Cambridge: Cambridge University Press, 2010).

Humphreys, Stephen, "The Rule of Law as Morality Play," *Finnish Yearbook of International Law*, 23 (2012–2013), 3–44.

Humphreys, Stephen, "Conscience in the Datasphere," *Humanity*, 6 (2015), 361–386.

Hunter, Ian, *Rival Enlightenments: Civil and Metaphysical Philosophy in Early Modern Germany* (Cambridge: Cambridge University Press, 2001).

Hunter, Rosemary, "Contesting the Dominant Paradigm: Feminist Critiques of Liberal Legalism," in Margaret Davies and Vanessa E. Munro, eds., *The Ashgate Research Companion to Feminist Legal Theory* (Farnham: Ashgate, 2013), pp. 13–30.

Hunter, Rosemary, Clare McGlynn, and Erika Rackley, eds., *Feminist Judgments: From Theory to Practice* (Oxford: Hart, 2010).

Husak, Douglas N., "Paternalism and Autonomy," *Philosophy and Public Affairs*, 10 (1981), 27–46.

Hutchinson, Allan C., "The Importance of Not Being Ernest," *McGill Law Journal*, 34 (1989), 234–263.

Hutchinson, Allan C., and Patrick Monahan, "Introduction," in idem, eds., *The Rule of Law: Ideal or Ideology?* (Toronto: Carswell, 1987), pp. iv–xiv.

Hutchinson, Allan C., and Patrick Monahan, "Democracy and the Rule of Law," in idem, eds., *The Rule of Law: Ideal or Ideology?* (Toronto: Carswell, 1987), pp. 97–123.

Hutchinson, D. L., "Critical Race Histories: In and Out," *American University Law Review*, 53 (2004), 1187–1215.

Iglesias, Elizabeth M., "LatCrit Theory: Some Preliminary Notes Towards a Transatlantic Dialogue," *University of Miami International and Comparative Law Review*, 9 (2001), 1–32.

Ingrao, Charles, "The Problem of 'Enlightened Absolutism' and the German States," *Journal of Modern History*, 58 (1986), S161–S180.

International Commission of Enquiry, "The 1930 Enquiry Commission to Liberia," *Journal of the Royal African Society*, 30 (1931), 277–290.

Ireland, Paddy, "History, Critical Legal Studies, and the Mysterious Disappearance of Capitalism," *Modern Law Review*, 65 (2002), 120–140.

"Is Democracy Dying? A Global Report," *Foreign Affairs*, 97 (2018), 10–56.

Isser, Deborah H., ed., *Customary Justice and the Rule of Law in War-Torn Societies* (Washington: United States Institute of Peace Press, 2011).

Isser, Deborah H., Stephen C. Lubkemann, and Saah N'Tow, *Looking for Justice: Liberian Experiences with and Perceptions of Local Justice Options* (Washington: United States Institute of Peace, 2009).

Jackson, Paul, "Introduction: Second Generation Security Sector Reform," *Journal of Intervention and Statebuilding*, 12 (2018), 1–10.

Jackson, R. M., *The Machinery of Justice in England*, 4th ed. (Cambridge: Cambridge University Press, [1964] 2015).

James of Viterbo, "Is It Better to Be Ruled by the Best Man than by the Best Laws?," in Arthur Stephen McGrade, John Kilcullen, and Matthew Kempshall, eds., *The Cambridge Translations of Medieval Philosophical Texts*, vol. 2: *Ethics and Political Philosophy* (Cambridge: Cambridge University Press, [1295–1296] 2001), 321–325.

Jellinek, Georg, *Allgemeine Staatslehre*, 3rd ed. (Berlin: Springer, 1921).

Jennings, W. Ivor, *Local Government in the Modern Constitution* (London: University of London Press, 1931).

Jennings, W. Ivor, *The Law and the Constitution* (London: University of London Press, 1933).

Jennings, W. Ivor, "Courts and Administrative Law: The Experience of English Housing Legislation," *Harvard Law Review*, 49 (1936), 426–454.

Jensen, Erik G., "Postscript: An Immodest Reflection," in David Marshall, ed., *The International Rule of Law Movement: A Crisis of Legitimacy and the Way Forward* (Cambridge: Harvard University Press, 2014), pp. 295–303.

Jensen, Erik, and Thomas Heller, eds., *Beyond Common Knowledge: Empirical Approaches to the Rule of Law* (Stanford: Stanford University Press, 2003).

Jeong, May, "The Impossible Job of Afghanistan's Attorney General," *The Atlantic*, March 9, 2017.

Jestaedt, Matthias, Oliver Lepsius, Christoph Möllers, and Christoph Schönberger, *The German Federal Constitutional Court: The Court without Limits*, trans. Jeff Seitzer (Oxford: Oxford University Press, 2020).

Jhering, Rudolph von, *The Struggle for Law*, trans. John J. Lalor, 5th ed. (Chicago: Callaghan, 1879).

Johansen, Baber, "Sacred and Religious Element in Hanafite Law – Function and Limits of the Absolute Character of Government Authority," in Ernest Gellner and Jean-Claude Vatin, eds., *Islam et politique au Maghreb* (Paris: Éditions du Centre National de la Recherche Scientifique, 1981), pp. 281–303.

Johnstone, Steven, *Disputes and Democracy: The Consequences of Litigation in Ancient Athens* (Austin: University of Texas Press, 1999).

Jones, Harry W., "The Rule of Law and the Welfare State," *Columbia Law Review*, 58 (1958), 143–156.

Jouanjan, Olivier, ed., *Figures de l'État de droit: Le Rechtsstaat dans l'histoire intellectuelle et constitutionnelle de l'Allemagne* (Strasbourg: Presses universitaires de Strasbourg, 2001).

Jouanjan, Olivier, "État de droit," in Denis Alland and Stéphane Rials, eds., *Dictionnaire de la culture juridique* (Paris: PUF, 2003), pp. 649–653.

Jouanjan, Olivier, "Le Conseil constitutionnel est-il une institution libérale?," *Droits*, 43 (2006), 73–90.

Jowell, Jeffrey, "The Rule of Law and Its Underlying Values," in Jeffrey Jowell and Dawn Oliver, eds., *The Changing Constitution*, 7th ed. (Oxford: Oxford University Press, 2011), pp. 11–34.

Kagan, Robert, *Paradise and Power: America and Europe in the New World Order* (Atlantic: Atlantic, 2003).

Kahn, Paul W., *The Cultural Study of Law: Reconstructing Legal Scholarship* (Chicago: University of Chicago Press, 1999).

Kahn, Paul W., "American Exceptionalism, Popular Sovereignty, and the Rule of Law," in Michael Ignatieff, ed., *American Exceptionalism and Human Rights* (Princeton: Princeton University Press, 2005), pp. 198–222.

Kalyvas, Andreas, and Ira Katznelson, *Liberal Beginnings: Making a Republic for the Moderns* (Cambridge: Cambridge University Press, 2008).

Kamenka, Eugene, and Alice Erh-Soon Tay, "Beyond Bourgeois Individualism – The Contemporary Crisis in Law and Legal Ideology," in Eugene Kamenka and R. S. Neale, eds., *Feudalism, Capitalism and Beyond* (Canberra: ANU Press, 1975), pp. 126–144.

Kammerhofer, Jörg, "Introduction: The Future of Restrictive Scholarship on the Use of Force," *Leiden Journal of International Law*, 29 (2016), 13–18.

Kant, Immanuel, *Werkausgabe*, vol. 8: *Die Metaphysik der Sitten*, ed. Wilhelm Weischedel (Frankfurt am Main: Suhrkamp, [1797] 1977).

Kassem, Badreddine, *Décadence et absolutisme dans l'oeuvre de Montesquieu* (Paris: Librairie Minard, 1960).

Kattan, Victor, "Furthering the 'War on Terrorism' through International Law: How the United States and the United Kingdom Resurrected the Bush Doctrine on Using Preventive Military Force to Combat Terrorism," *Journal on the Use of Force and International Law*, 5 (2018), 97–144.

Kaufmann, Daniel, Aart Kraay, and Massimo Mastruzzi, "The Worldwide Governance Indicators: Methodology and Analytical Issues," Policy Research Working Paper 5430, Development Research Group, World Bank, September 2010.

Kaufmann, Katharina, "Conflict in Political Liberalism: Judith Shklar's Liberalism of Fear," *Res Publica*, 26 (2020), 577–595.

Kayaoglu, Turan, *Legal Imperialism: Sovereignty and Extraterritoriality in Japan, the Ottoman Empire, and China* (Cambridge: Cambridge University Press, 2014).

Kaye, Harvey J., *The British Marxist Historians* (London: Macmillan, [1984] 1995).

Kaye, Harvey J., and Keith McClelland, eds., *E. P. Thompson: Critical Perspectives* (Cambridge: Polity, 1990).

Keane, John, *The Life and Death of Democracy* (London: Simon & Schuster, 2009).

Keane, Rory, "Reviewing the Justice and Security Hub Modality as Piloted in Liberia," *Stability*, 1 (2012), 87–91.

Keedy, Edwin R., "Ignorance and Mistake in the Criminal Law," *Harvard Law Review*, 22 (1908), 75–96.

Kelsen, Hans, *Vom Wesen der Demokratie* (Tübingen: Mohr, 1920).

Kelsen, Hans, *General Theory of Law and State*, trans. Anders Wedberg (Cambridge: Harvard University Press, [1925] 1949).

Kelsen, Hans, *Introduction to the Problems of Legal Theory: A Translation of the First Edition of the Reine Rechtslehre or Pure Theory of Law*, trans. Bonnie Litschewski Paulson and Stanley L. Paulson (Oxford: Clarendon Press [1934] 1992).

Kelsen, Hans, "Aristotle's Doctrine of Justice," in idem, *What is Justice? Justice, Law and Politics in the Mirror of Science* (Berkeley: University of California Press, 1957), pp. 110–136.

Kennedy, David, *The Dark Sides of Virtue: Reassessing International Humanitarianism* (Princeton: Princeton University Press, 2004).

Kennedy, Duncan, *A Critique of Adjudication: fin de siècle* (Cambridge: Harvard University Press, 1998).

Kenny, Michael, *The First New Left: British Intellectuals After Stalin* (London: Lawrence & Wishart, 1995).

Keohane, Nannerl O., *Philosophy and the State in France* (Princeton: Princeton University Press, 1980).

Kim, Pauline T., "Bargaining with Imperfect Information: A Study of Worker Perceptions of Legal Protection in an At-Will World," *Cornell Law Review*, 83 (1998), 105–160.

Kingsbury, Benedict, "International Courts: Uneven Judicialisation in Global Order," in James Crawford and Martti Koskenniemi, eds., *The Cambridge Companion to International Law* (Cambridge: Cambridge University Press, 2012), pp. 203–227.

Kingston, Rebecca, *Montesquieu and the Parlement of Bordeaux* (Geneva: Librairie Droz, 1996).

Kingston, Rebecca, "Parlement de Bordeux," in Catherine Volpilhac-Auger, ed., *Dictionnaire Montesquieu* (Lyons: ENS, 2013), available at

Kirchheimer, Otto, "The *Rechtsstaat* as Magic Wall," in William E. Scheuerman, ed., *The Rule of Law under Siege: Selected Essays of Franz L. Neumann and Otto Kirchheimer* (Berkeley: University of California Press, [1967] 1996), pp. 243–266.

Kirchheimer, Otto, *Von der Weimarer Republik zum Faschismus: Die Auflösung der demokratischen Rechtsordnung* (Frankfurt am Main: Suhrkamp, 1976).

Kiss, Elizabeth, "Alchemy or Fool's Gold? Assessing Feminist Doubts about Rights," in Mary Lyndon Shanley and Uma Narayan, eds., *Reconstructing Political Theory: Feminist Perspectives* (Philadelphia: Pennsylvania University Press, 1997), pp. 1–24.

Kiss, Erika A., "The Rules of the Game: Stochastic Rationality in Oakeshott's Rule of Law Theory," in David Dyzenhaus and Thomas Poole, eds., *Law, Liberty, and the State: Oakeshott, Hayek and Schmitt on the Rule of Law* (Cambridge: Cambridge University Press, 2015), pp. 214–233.

Klarin, Mirko, "The Impact of the ICTY Trials on Public Opinion in the Former Yugoslavia," *Journal of International Criminal Justice*, 7 (2009), 89–96.

Klein, Friedrich, "Bonner Grundgesetz und Rechtsstaat," *Zeitschrift für die gesamte Staatswissenschaft*, 106 (1950), 390–411.

Klein, Natalie, *Dispute Settlement in the UN Convention on the Law of the Sea* (Cambridge: Cambridge University Press, 2009).

Kleinfeld, Rachel, "Competing Definitions of the Rule of Law," in Thomas Carothers, ed., *Promoting the Rule of Law Abroad: In Search of Knowledge* (Washington: Carnegie Endowment for International Peace, 2012), pp. 34–46.

Kmezic, Marko, *EU Rule of Law Promotion* (Abingdon: Routledge, 2017).

Koditschek, Theodore, "The Possibilities of Theory: Thompson's Marxist History," in Roger Fieldhouse and Richard K. S. Taylor, eds., *E. P. Thompson and English Radicalism* (Manchester: Manchester University Press, 2013), pp. 70–95.

Koh, Harold Hongju, "The Trump Administration and International Law," *Washburn Law Journal*, 56 (2017), pp. 413–469.

Kohler, Richard E., "Ignorance or Mistake of Law as a Defense in Criminal Cases," *Dickinson Law Review*, 40 (1935), 113–122.

Koonz, Claudia, *The Nazi Conscience* (Cambridge: Belknap Press of Harvard University Press, 2003).

Koskenniemi, Martti, *The Gentle Civilizer of Nations: The Rise and Fall of International Law 1870–1960* (Cambridge: Cambridge University Press, 2002).

Koskenniemi, Martti, "International Legislation Today: Limits and Possibilities," *Wisconsin International Law Journal*, 23 (2005), 61–92.

Kostal, R. W., *A Jurisprudence of Power: Victorian Empire and the Rule of Law* (Cambridge: Cambridge University Press, 2005).

Kurkchiyan, Marina, "The Illegitimacy of Law in Post-Soviet Societies," in Denis J. Galligan and Marina Kurkchiyan, eds., *Law and Informal Practices: The Post-Communist Experience* (Oxford: Oxford University Press, 2003), pp. 25–47.

Kurkchiyan, Marina, and Agnieszka Kubal, eds., *A Sociology of Justice in Russia* (Cambridge: Cambridge University Press, 2018).

Kraft, Jessica Carew, "Establishing the Rule of Law in a Country Where Justice Hardly Exists," *The Atlantic*, April 22, 2015.

Krastev, Ivan, and Stephen Holmes, *The Light That Failed: A Reckoning* (London: Allen Lane, 2019).

Kratochwil, Friedrich, "Has the 'Rule of Law' Become a 'Rule of Lawyers'?" in Gianluigi Palombella and Neil Walker, eds., *Relocating the Rule of Law* (Oxford: Hart, 2009), pp. 171–196.

Krause, Sharon R., "Despotism in *The Spirit of Laws*," in David W. Carrithers, Michael A. Mosher, and Paul A. Rahe, eds., *Montesquieu's Science of Politics: Essays on The Spirit of Laws* (Lanham: Rowman & Littlefield, 2001), pp. 231–272.

Krause, Sharon R., *Liberalism with Honor* (Cambridge: Harvard University Press, 2002).

Krause, Sharon R., "Laws, Passions, and the Attractions of Right Action in Montesquieu," *Philosophy and Social Criticism*, 32 (2006), 211–230.

Krey, Volker, "The Rule of Law in German Criminal Proceedings," *Rechtspolitisches Forum*, 43 (2008), 1–26.

Krieger, Heike, ed., *The Kosovo Conflict and International Law: An Analytical Documentation 1974–1999* (Cambridge: Cambridge University Press, 2001).

Krieger, Leonard, *The German Idea of Freedom: History of a Political Tradition* (Boston: Beacon Press, 1957).

Krisch, Nico, "The Decay of Consent: International Law in an Age of Global Public Goods," *American Journal of International Law*, 108 (2014), 1–40.

Krueger, Anne O., "Aid in the Development Process," *Research Observer*, 1 (1986), 57–78.

Krygier, Martin, "The Hart–Fuller Debate, Transitional Societies and the Rule of Law," in Peter Cane, ed., *The Hart–Fuller Debate in the Twenty-first Century* (Oxford: Hart, 2009), 107–134.

Krygier, Martin, "The Rule of Law: Legality, Teleology, Sociology," in Gianluigi Palombella and Neil Walker, eds., *Relocating the Rule of Law* (Oxford: Hart, 2009), pp. 45–69.

Krygier, Martin, "Four Puzzles about the Rule of Law: Why, What, Where? And Who Cares?" in James E. Fleming, ed., *Getting to the Rule of Law: NOMOS L* (New York: New York University Press, 2011), pp. 64–104.

Krygier, Martin, *Philip Selznick: Ideals in the World* (Palo Alto: Stanford University Press, 2012).

Krygier, Martin, "Rule of Law (and *Rechtsstaat*)," in James R. Silkenat, James E. Hickey Jr., and Peter D. Barenboim, eds., *The Legal Doctrines of the Rule of Law and the Legal State (Rechtsstaat)* (New York: Springer, 2014), pp. 45–59.

Krygier, Martin, "Rule of Law (and Rechtsstaat)," in James D. Wright, ed., *International Encyclopedia of the Social and Behavioral Sciences*, 2nd ed. (Oxford: Elsevier, 2015), pp. 780–787.

Krygier, Martin, "Magna Carta and the Rule of Law Tradition," *Papers on Parliament*, 65 (2016), 11–29.

Krygier, Martin, "The Rule of Law: Pasts, Presents, and Two Possible Futures," *Annual Review of Law and Social Science*, 12 (2016), 199–229.

Krygier, Martin, "Institutionalisation and Its Discontents: Constitutionalism versus (Anti-)Constitutional Populism in East Central Europe." Paper presented at the Transnational Law King's College, London, November 17, 2017.

Krygier, Martin, "Tempering Power," in Maurice Adams, Anne Meuwese, and Ernst Hirsch Ballin, eds., *Constitutionalism and the Rule of Law: Bridging Idealism and Realism* (Cambridge: Cambridge University Press, 2017), pp. 35–49.

Krynen, Jacques, *L'État de justice: France, XIIIe-XXe siècle*, 2 vols. (Paris: Gallimard, 2009 and 2012).

Kukathas, Chandran, "Hayek and the State," in David Dyzenhaus and Thomas Poole, eds., *Law, Liberty and State: Oakeshot, Hayek and Schmitt on the Rule of Law* (Cambridge: Cambridge University Press, 2015), pp. 281–294.

Kumm, Mattias, "International Law in National Courts: The International Rule of Law and the Limits of the Internationalist Model," *Virginia Journal of International Law*, 44 (2003), 19–32.

Kurtz, Marcus J., and Andrew Schrank, "Growth and Governance: Models, Measures, and Mechanisms," *Journal of Politics*, 69 (2007), 538–554.

Laband, Paul, *Das Staatsrecht des Deutschen Reiches*, vol. 2 (Tübingen: Laupp, 1878).

Laborde, Cécile, and Maynor, John, eds., *Republicanism and Political Theory* (Oxford: Blackwell, 2007).

Lacey, Nicola, *Unspeakable Subjects: Feminist Essays in Legal and Social Theory* (Oxford: Hart, 1998).

Lacey, Nicola, *The Prisoners' Dilemma: Punishment and Political Economy in Contemporary Democracies* (Cambridge: Cambridge University Press, 2008).

Lacey, Nicola, *In Search of Criminal Responsibility: Ideas, Interests and Institutions* (Oxford: Oxford University Press, 2016).

Lacey, Nicola and Pickard, Hanna, "The Chimera of Proportionality: Institutionalising Limits of Punishment in Contemporary Social and Political Systems," *Modern Law Review*, 78 (2015), 216–240.

Landau, David, "Abusive Constitutionalism," *University of California Davis Law Review*, 47 (2013), 189–260.

Lanni, Adriaan, "Arguing from 'Precedent': Modern Perspectives Athenian Practice," in Edward M. Harris and Lene Rubinstein, eds., *The Law and the Courts in Ancient Greece* (London: Bristol Classical Press, 2004), pp. 159–171.

Lanni, Adriaan, *Law and Justice in the Courts of Classical Athens* (Cambridge: Cambridge University Press, 2006).

Lanni, Adriaan, "Judicial Review and the Athenian Constitution," in Mogens Herman Hansen, ed., *Démocratie athénienne-démocratie modern: tradition et influences* (Geneva: Fondation Hardt, 2010), pp. 235–263.

Lanni, Adriaan, *Law and Order in Ancient Athens* (Cambridge: Cambridge University Press, 2016).

La Porta, Rafael, Florencio Lopez-de-Silanes, Andrei Shleifer, and Robert W. Vishny, "Law and Finance," *Journal of Political Economy*, 106 (1998), 1113–1155.

Laquièze, Alain, "État de droit and National Sovereignty in France," in Pietro Costa and Danilo Zolo, eds., *The Rule of Law: History, Theory and Criticism* (Springer, 2017), pp. 261–291.

Larrère, Catherine, "Montesquieu on Economics and Commerce," in David W. Carrithers, Michael A. Mosher, and Paul A. Rahe, eds., *Montesquieu's Science of Politics: Essays on The Spirit of Laws* (Lanham: Rowman & Littlefield, 2001), pp. 335–374.

Lasson, Adolf, *Das Culturideal und der Krieg* (Berlin: Moeser, 1868).

Latour, Bruno, *The Making of Law: An Ethnography of the Conseil d'État*, trans. Marina Brilman and Alain Pottage (Cambridge: Polity, [2002] 2010).

Lauterpacht, Hersch, *The Function of Law in the International Community*, with an Introduction by Martti Koskenniemi (Oxford: Oxford University Press, [1933] 2011).

Lauterpacht, Hersch, "The Grotian Tradition in International Law," *British Yearbook of International Law*, 23 (1946), 1–53.

Lauterpacht, Hersch, *The Development of International Law by the International Court* (London: Stevens & Sons, 1958).

Lauterpacht, Hersch, "Is International Law a Part of the Law of England?," in idem, *International Law: Being the Collected Papers of Hersch Lauterpacht*, vol. 2: *The Law of Peace, Part I*, ed. Elihu Lauterpacht (Cambridge: Cambridge University Press, 1975), pp. 537–569.

Lauth, Hans-Joachim, and Jennifer Sehring, "Putting Deficient *Rechtsstaat* on the Research Agenda: Reflections on Diminished Subtypes," *Comparative Sociology*, 8 (2009), 185–201.

Lax, Jeffrey R. "Political Constraints on Legal Doctrine: How Hierarchy Shapes the Law," *Journal of Politics*, 74 (2012), 765–781.

League of Nations, *Report of the International Commission of Enquiry into the Existence of Slavery and Forced Labour in the Republic of Liberia* (Geneva: League of Nations, 1930).

Ledford, Kenneth, "Formalizing the Rule of Law in Prussia: The Supreme Administrative Law Court, 1876–1914," *Central European History*, 37 (2004), 203–224.

Lehman, Greg, "Benjamin Duterrau: The Art of Conciliation," *Journal of War and Culture Studies*, 8 (2015), 109–124.

Letwin, Shirley Robin, "Morality and Law," *Ratio Juris*, 2 (1989), 55–65.

Letwin, Shirley Robin, *On the History of the Idea of Law*, ed. Noel B. Reynolds (Cambridge: Cambridge University Press, 2005).

Li, Tania Murray, *The Will to Improve: Governmentality, Development, and the Practice of Politics* (Durham: Duke University Press, 2007).

Leverick, Fiona, "Breach of the Peace after *Smith v Donnelly*," *Scots Law Times*, 34 (2011), 257–262.

Levitsky, Steven, and Daniel Ziblatt, *How Democracies Die* (New York: Crown, 2018).

Levy, Jacob, "Montesquieu's Constitutional Legacies," in Rebecca Kingston, ed., *Montesquieu and His Legacy* (Albany: State University of New York, 2008), pp. 115–138.

Liberian Land Commission, *2014 Annual Report* (Monrovia: Land Commission, 2014).

Lijphart, Arend, *Patterns of Democracy: Government Forms and Performance in Thirty-Six Countries* (New Haven: Yale University Press, 1999).

Llewellyn, Karl, *The Bramble Bush: The Classic Lectures on the Law and Law School*, ed. Steve Sheppard (New York: Oxford University Press, [1951] 2008).

Loader, Ian, and Richard Sparks, "Penal Populism and Epistemic Crime Control," in Alison Liebling, Shadd Maruna, and Lesley McAra, eds., *The Oxford Handbook of Criminology*, 6th ed. (Oxford: Oxford University Press, 2017), pp. 98–115.

Lobban, Michael, *White Man's Justice: South African Political Trials in the Black Consciousness Era* (Oxford: Clarendon Press, 1996).

Lobban, Michael, *Imperial Incarceration: Detention without Trial in the Making of British Colonial Africa* (Cambridge: Cambridge University Press, 2021).

Locke, John, *Second Treatise of Government*, ed. C. B. Macpherson (Indianapolis: Hackett, 1980).

Loiselle, Marc, "Le concept d'État de droit dans la doctrine juridique française," Ph.D. dissertation, Université Paris II Panthéon-Assas, 2000.
Lorde, Audre, *Sister/Outsider* (New York: Crossing, 1984).
Loughlin, Martin, *Public Law and Political Theory* (Oxford: Clarendon Press, 1992).
Loughlin, Martin, "The Functionalist Style in Public Law," *University of Toronto Law Journal*, 55 (2005), 361–403.
Loughlin, Martin, *Foundations of Public Law* (Oxford: Oxford University Press, 2010).
Lovett, Frank, *A Republic of Law* (Cambridge: Cambridge University Press, 2016).
Lowenthal, David, "Book I of Montesquieu's *The Spirit of the Laws*," *American Political Science Review*, 53 (1959), 485–498.
Lugosi, Charles I., "Rule of Law or Rule by Law: The Detention of Yaser Hamdi," *American Journal of Criminal Law*, 30 (2003), 225–278.
Luhmann, Niklas, *Das Recht der Gesellschaft* (Frankfurt am Main: Suhrkamp, 1993).
Luhmann, Niklas, *Politische Soziologie* (Berlin: Suhrkamp, 2010).
MacCormick, Neil, "Jurisprudence and the Constitution," *Current Legal Problems*, 36 (1983), 13-30.
MacCormick, D. Neil, "Der Rechtsstaat und die rule of law," *Juristenzeitung*, 39 (1984), 65–70.
Mack, Kenneth W., *Representing the Race: The Creation of the Civil Rights Lawyer* (Cambridge: Harvard University Press, 2012).
MacKinnon, Catharine A., *Feminism Unmodified: Discourses in Life and Law* (Cambridge: Harvard University Press, 1987).
MacKinnon, Catharine A., *Toward a Feminist Theory of State* (Cambridge: Harvard University Press, 1989).
MacKinnon, Catharine A., *Women's Lives, Men's Laws* (Cambridge: Harvard University Press, 2005).
MacKinnon, Catharine A., "The Power to Change," in idem, *Women's Lives, Men's Laws* (Cambridge: Harvard University Press, 2005), pp. 103–108.
MacMillan, Ken, *The Atlantic Imperial Constitution: Center and Periphery in the English Atlantic World* (New York: Palgrave Macmillan, 2011).
Macpherson, C. B., *The Political Theory of Possessive Liberalism: From Hobbes to Locke* (Oxford: Oxford University Press, 1962).
Maistre, Joseph de, "Study on Sovereignty," in idem, *The Works of Joseph de Maistre*, selected, trans., and with an Introduction by Jack Lively (New York: Schocken, [1794–1796] 1971), pp. 93–129.
Maistre, Joseph de, "Essay on the Generative Principle of Political Constitutions," in idem, *The Works of Joseph de Maistre*, selected, trans., and with an Introduction by Jack Lively (New York: Schocken, [1814] 1971), pp. 147–181.
Maistre, Joseph de, "The Pope," in idem, *The Works of Joseph de Maistre*, selected, trans., and with an Introduction by Jack Lively (New York: Schocken, [1819] 1971), pp. 131–146.

Maliks, Reidar, "Revolutionary Epigones: Kant and his Radical Followers," *History of Political Thought*, 33 (2012), 647–671.

Mälksoo, Lauri, "Russia and China Challenge the Western Hegemony in the Interpretation of International Law," *EJIL: Talk!*, July 15, 2016.

Mamdani, Mahmood, *Citizen and Subject: Contemporary Africa and the Legacy of Late Colonialism* (Princeton: Princeton University Press, 1996).

Mannheim, Karl, *Konservatismus: Ein Beitrag zur Soziologie des Wissens* (Frankfurt am Main: Suhrkamp, 1984).

Mantzavinos, C., *Individuals, Institutions, and Markets* (Cambridge: Cambridge University Press, 2001).

Mantzavinos, C., Douglass C. North, and Syed Shariq, "Learning, Institutions, and Economic Performance," *Perspectives on Politics*, 2 (2004), 75–84.

Maravall, José María, "The Rule of Law as a Political Weapon," in José María Maravall and Adam Przeworski, eds., *Democracy and the Rule of Law* (Cambridge: Cambridge University Press, 2003), pp. 261–301.

Maravall, José María, and Adam Przeworski, eds., *Democracy and the Rule of Law* (Cambridge: Cambridge University Press, 2003).

Marglin, Jessica M., *Across Legal Lines: Jews and Muslims in Modern Morocco* (New Haven: Yale University Press, 2016).

Markovits, Inga, *Justice in Lüritz: Experiencing Socialist Law in East Germany* (Princeton: Princeton University Press, 2010).

Marks, Susan, "The End of History? Reflections on some International Legal Theses," *European Journal of International Law*, 8 (1997), 449–477.

Marmor, Andrei, "The Rule of Law and Its Limits," *Law and Philosophy*, 24 (2004),1–43.

Marshall, David, "Introduction," in idem, ed., *The International Rule of Law Movement: A Crisis of Legitimacy and the Way Forward* (Cambridge: Harvard Law School, 2014), pp. xiii–xxiii.

Marshall, David, "Reboot Required: The United Nations' Engagement in Rule of Law Reform in Postconflict and Fragile States," in idem, ed., *The International Rule of Law Movement: A Crisis of Legitimacy and the Way Forward* (Cambridge: Harvard University Press, 2014), pp. 85–133.

Marshall, David, ed., *The International Rule of Law Movement: A Crisis of Legitimacy and the Way Forward* (Cambridge: Harvard Law School, 2014).

Marshall, Geoffrey, *Constitutional Theory* (Oxford: Clarendon Press, 1971).

Martin, Craig, "Symposium: The Assumptions of Koh's Transnational Legal Process as Counter-Strategy," *Opinio Juris*, February 26, 2018.

Martindale, Don, ed., *Functionalism in the Social Sciences: The Strength and Limits of Functionalism in Anthropology, Economics, Political Science, and Sociology* (Philadelphia: American Academy of Political and Social Science, 1965).

Maru, Vivek, "Between Law and Society: Paralegals and the Provision of Justice Services in Sierra Leone and Worldwide," *Yale Journal of International Law*, 31 (2006), 427–476.

Massoud, Mark Fathi, *Law's Fragile State: Colonial, Authoritarian, and Humanitarian Legacies in Sudan* (Cambridge: Cambridge University Press, 2013).

Massoud, Mark Fathi, *Shari'a, Inshallah: Finding God in Somali Legal Politics* (Cambridge: Cambridge University Press, 2021).

Matsuda, Mari J., Charles R. Lawrence III, Richard Delgado, and Kimberlé Williams Crenshaw, et al., *Words That Wound: Critical Race Theory, Assaultive Speech, and the First Amendment* (Boulder, CO: Westview Press, 1993).

Maus, Ingeborg, *Zur Aufklärung der Demokratietheorie: Rechts- und demokratietheoretische Überlegungen im Anschluß an Kant* (Frankfurt am Main: Suhrkamp, 1994).

May, Larry, *Ancient Legal Thought: Equity, Justice, and Humaneness from Hammurabi and the Pharaos to Justinian and the Talmud* (Cambridge: Cambridge University Press, 2019).

McAdams, Richard H., "An Attitudinal Theory of Expressive Law," *Oregon Law Review*, 79 (2000), 339–390.

McCormick, John P., "Identifying or Exploiting the Paradoxes of Constitutional Democracy? An Introduction to Carl Schmitt's *Legality and Legitimacy*," in Carl Schmitt, *Legality and Legitimacy*, trans. and ed. Jeffrey Seitzer, with an Introduction by John P. McCormick (Durham: Duke University Press, [1932] 2004), pp. xiii–xliii.

McDonald, Elisabeth, Rhonda Powell, Mamari Stephens, and, Rosemary Hunter, eds., *Feminist Judgments of Aotearoa New Zealand Te Rino: A Two Stranded Rope* (Oxford: Hart, 2017).

McNair, Arnold D., "Collective Security," *British Yearbook of International Law*, 17 (1936), 150–164.

McWhinney, Edward, "The 'New' Countries and the 'New' International Law: The United Nations' Special Conference on Friendly Relations and Cooperation among States," *American Journal of International Law*, 60 (1966), 1–33.

Meierhenrich, Jens, *The Legacies of Law: Long-Run Consequences of Legal Development in South Africa, 1652–2000* (Cambridge: Cambridge University Press, 2008).

Meierhenrich, Jens, "The Practice of International Law: A Theoretical Analysis," *Law and Contemporary Problems*, 76 (2013), 1–83.

Meierhenrich, Jens, *The Remnants of the Rechtsstaat: An Ethnography of Nazi Law* (Oxford: Oxford University Press, 2018).

Meierhenrich, Jens, *The Violence of Law: The Formation and Deformation of* Gacaca *Courts in Rwanda, 1994–2019* (Cambridge: Cambridge University Press, 2021).

Meierhenrich, Jens, *Lawfare: A Genealogy* (Cambridge: Cambridge University Press, forthcoming).

Meierhenrich, Jens, "The Rule of Law Imaginary: Regarding *Iustitia*," in Michael Sevel, ed., *The Routledge Handbook of the Rule of Law* (London: Routledge, forthcoming).

Meierhenrich, Jens, *The Idea of the Rechtsstaat: An Intellectual History* (Oxford: Oxford University Press, forthcoming).

Meierhenrich, Jens, "Racial Legalism," *Annual Review of Law and Social Science*, 18 (forthcoming).

Meierhenrich, Jens, ed., *Dual States: A Global History* (Cambridge: Cambridge University Press, forthcoming).

Meierhenrich, Jens, and Catherine M. Cole, "In the Theater of the Rule of Law: Performing the Rivonia Trial in South Africa, 1963–1964," in Jens Meierhenrich and Devin O. Pendas, eds., *Political Trials in Theory and History* (Cambridge: Cambridge University Press, 2016), pp. 229–262.

Meierhenrich, Jens, Alexander Laban Hinton, and Lawrence Douglas, eds., *The Oxford Handbook of Transitional Justice* (Oxford: Oxford University Press, 2021).

Meineke, J., "Gesetzinterpretation und Gesetzanwendung im Attischen Zivilprozess," *Revue Internationale des Droits de l'Antiquité*, 18 (1971), 275–360.

Meinel, Florian, *Der Jurist in der industriellen Gesellschaft: Ernst Forsthoff und seine Zeit* (Berlin: Akademie Verlag, 2011).

Merritt, Adrian, "The Nature and Function of Law: A Criticism of E. P. Thompson's 'Whigs and Hunters,'" *British Journal of Law and Society*, 7 (1980), 194–214.

Merry, Sally Engle, *The Seductions of Quantification: Measuring Human Rights, Gender Violence, and Sex Trafficking* (Chicago: University of Chicago Press, 2016).

Merry, Sally Engle, Kevin Davis, and Benedict Kingsbury, eds., *The Quiet Power of Indicators: Measuring Governance, Corruption, and Rule of Law* (Cambridge: Cambridge University Press, 2015).

Merton, Robert K., *Social Theory and Social Structure* (New York: The Free Press, 1957).

Meyer-Laurin, Harald, *Gesetz und Billigkeit im attischen Prozess* (Weimar: Böhlaus Nachfolger, 1965).

Michelman, Frank I., "Foreword: 'Racialism' and Reason," *Michigan Law Review*, 95 (1997), 723–740.

Migdal, Joel, "Studying the State," in Mark Irving Lichbach and Alan S. Zuckerman, eds., *Comparative Politics: Rationality, Culture, and Structure* (Cambridge: Cambridge University Press, 1997), pp. 208–235.

Migdal, Joel S., *The State in Society: Studying How States and Societies Transform and Constitute One Another* (Cambridge: Cambridge University Press, 2001).

Milanović, Marko, "The Impact of the ICTY on the Former Yugoslavia: An Anticipatory Postmortem," *American Journal of International Law*, 110 (2016), 233–259.

Miles, Kate, *The Origins of International Investment Law: Empire, Environment and the Safeguarding of Capital* (Cambridge: Cambridge University Press, 2013).

Mill, John Stuart, *Considerations on Representative Government* (London: Parker, Son & Bourn, 1861).

Mill, John Stuart, *The Subjection of Women* (Indianapolis: Hackett, [1869] 1988).

Mills, Charles W., *Black Rights/White Wrongs: The Critique of Racial Liberalism* (Oxford: Oxford University Press, 2017).

Minow, Martha, "Justice Engendered," *Harvard Law Review*, 101 (1987), 10–95.

Minow, Martha, *Making All the Difference: Inclusion, Exclusion, and American Law* (Ithaca: Cornell University Press, 1990).

Møller, Jørgen, and Svend-Erik Skaaning, "On the Limited Interchangeability of Rule of Law Measures," *European Political Science Review*, 3 (2011), 371–394.

Møller, Jørgen, and Svend-Erik Skaaning, "Systematizing Thin and Thick Conceptions of the Rule of Law," *Justice System Journal*, 33 (2012), 136–153.

Møller, Jørgen, and Svend-Erik Skaaning, *The Rule of Law: Definitions, Measures, Patterns and Causes* (London: Palgrave, 2014).

Mona, Martino, "The Normative Content of the Notion of the *Rechtsstaat* in Late Modernity," *Punishment and Society*, 15 (2013), 412–419.

Montesquieu, *De l'esprit des lois* in *Oeuvres complètes*, vol. 2 ed. Roger Caillois (Paris: Pléiade, 1951).

Montesquieu, *The Spirit of the Laws*, trans. and ed. Anne M. Cohler, Basia Carolyn Miller, and Harold Samuel Stone (Cambridge: Cambridge University Press, [1748] 1989).

Moore, Barrington, Jr., *Social Origins of Dictatorship and Democracy: Lord and Peasant in the Making of the Modern World* (Boston: Beacon Press, 1966).

Moores, Christopher, *Civil Liberties and Human Rights in Twentieth-Century Britain* (Cambridge: Cambridge University Press, 2017).

Morrall, John B., *Political Thought in Medieval Times* (Toronto: University of Toronto Press, 1980).

Morrill, John, "The Stuarts (1603–1688)," in Kenneth O. Morgan, ed., *The Oxford Illustrated History of Britain* (Oxford: Oxford University Press, 1984), pp. 286–351.

Morris, Douglas, *Legal Sabotage: Ernst Fraenkel in Hitler's Germany* (Cambridge: Cambridge University Press, 2020).

Morris, William, *News from Nowhere*, ed. James Redmond (London: Routledge and Kegan Paul, [1890] 1970).

Mosher, Michael A., "Monarchy's Paradox: Honor in the Face of Sovereign Power," in David W. Carrithers, Michael A. Mosher, and Paul A. Rahe, eds., *Montesquieu's Science of Politics: Essays on The Spirit of Laws* (Lanham: Rowman & Littlefield, 2001), pp. 159–230.

Mosher, Michael A., "What Montesquieu Taught: Perfection Does not Concern Men or Things Universally," in Rebecca Kingston, ed., *Montesquieu and His Legacy* (Albany: State University of New York, 2008), pp. 7–30.

Mounk, Yascha, *The People vs Democracy: Why Our Freedom Is in Danger and How to Save It* (Cambridge: Harvard University Press, 2018).

Moustafa, Tamir, *The Struggle for Constitutional Power: Law, Politics, and Economic Reform in Egypt* (Cambridge: Cambridge University Press, 2007).

Moustafa, Tamir, and Tom Ginsburg, "Introduction: The Function of Courts in Authoritarian Politics," in Tom Ginsburg and Tamir Moustafa, eds., *Rule by Law: The Politics of Courts in Authoritarian Regimes* (Cambridge: Cambridge University Press, 2008), pp. 1–21.

Moyn, Samuel, *The Last Utopia: Human Rights in History* (Cambridge: Belknap Press of Harvard University Press, 2010).

Moyn, Samuel, "Judith Shklar versus the International Criminal Court," *Humanity*, 4 (2013) 473–500.

Mudde, Cas, and Cristóbal Rovira Kaltwasser, *Populism: A Very Short Introduction* (Oxford: Oxford University Press, 2017).

Müller, Ingo, *Hitler's Justice: The Courts of the Third Reich* (Cambridge: Harvard University Press, [1987] 1991).

Müller, Jan-Werner, *What is Populism?* ((London: Penguin, 2017).

Müller, Jan-Werner, "Populism and Constitutionalism," in Cristóbal Rovira Kaltwasser, Paul Taggart, Paulina Ochoa Espejo, and Pierre Ostiguy, eds., *The Oxford Handbook of Populism* (Oxford: Oxford University Press, 2017).

Munro, Vanessa E., "Legal Feminism and Foucault – A Critique of the Expulsion of Law," *Journal of Law and Society*, 28 (2001), 546–567.

Munro, Vanessa E., "Square Pegs in Round Holes: The Dilemma of Conjoined Twins and Individual Rights," *Social and Legal Studies*, 10 (2001), 459–482.

Munro, Vanessa E., *Law and Politics at the Perimeter: Re-Evaluating Key Debates in Feminist Theory* (Oxford: Hart, 2007).

Munro, Vanessa E., "Violence against Women, 'Victimhood' and the (Neo)Liberal State," in Margaret Davies and Vanessa E. Munro, eds., *The Ashgate Research Companion to Feminist Legal Theory* (Farnham: Ashgate, 2013), pp. 233–248.

Munro, Vanessa E., "Shifting Sands: Consent, Context and Vulnerability in Contemporary Sexual Offences Policy in England and Wales," *Social and Legal Studies*, 26 (2017), 417–440.

Munro, Vanessa E., and Ruth Aiken, "Adding Insult to Injury? The Criminal Law's Response to Domestic Abuse-related Suicide in England and Wales," *Criminal Law Review*, 9 (2018), 732–741.

Munro, Vanessa E., and Carl F. Stychin, "Editors' Introduction," in idem, eds., *Sexuality and the Law: Feminist Engagements* (London: Routledge, 2007), pp. xi–xvii.

Murakawa, Naomi, *The First Civil Right: How Liberals Built Prison America* (Oxford: Oxford University Press, 2014).

Murphy, Colleen, "Lon Fuller and the Moral Value of the Rule of Law," *Law and Philosophy*, 24 (2005), 246–252.

Murphy, Mark C., "Was Hobbes a Legal Positivist?" *Ethics*, 105 (1995), 846–873.

Myerson, Roger B., "Justice, Institutions, and Multiple Equilibria," *Chicago Journal of International Law*, 5 (2004), 91–107.

Naffine, Ngaire, "In Praise of Legal Feminism," *Legal Studies*, 22 (2002), 71–101.

Nardulli, Peter F., Buddy Peyton, and Joseph Bajjalieh, "Conceptualizing and Measuring Rule of Law Constructs, 1850–2010," *Journal of Law and Courts*, 1 (2013), 13–38.

Neeson, J. M., *Commoners: Common Right, Enclosure and Social Change in England, 1700–1820* (Cambridge: Cambridge University Press, 1993).

Nielsen, Karen Margrethe, "The Tyrant's Vice: *Pleonexia* and Lawlessness in Plato's *Republic*," *Ethics*, 33 (2019), 146–169.

Nelken, David, "Is there a Crisis in Law and Legal Ideology?" *Journal of Law and Society*, 9 (1982), 177–189.

Neumann, Franz L., *Behemoth: The Structure and Practice of National Socialism 1933–1944*, 2nd ed. (New York: Harper & Row, 1944).

Neumann, Franz L., "Types of Natural Law," in idem, *The Democratic and the Authoritarian State* (New York: The Free Press, [1940] 1957), pp. 69–95.

Neumann, Franz L., *The Rule of Law: Political Theory and the Legal System of Modern Society* (Leamington Spa: Berg, [1936] 1986).

Neumann, Franz L., "Labor Law in Modern Society," in William E. Scheuerman, ed., *The Rule of Law Under Siege* (Berkeley: University of California Press, [1951] 1996), pp. 231–242.

Neumann, Franz L. "The Concept of Political Freedom," in William E. Scheuerman, ed., *The Rule of Law Under Siege* (Berkeley: University of California Press, [1953] 1996), pp. 195–230.

Neumann, Franz L., "The Change in the Function of Law in Modern Society," in William E. Scheuerman, ed., *The Rule of Law Under Siege* (Berkeley: University of California Press, [1937] 1996), pp. 195–230.

Neumann, Ulfrid, "The 'Deserved' Punishment," in A. P. Simester, Antje Du Bois-Pedain, and Ulfrid Neumann, eds., *Liberal Criminal Theory: Essays for Andreas von Hirsch* (Oxford: Hart, 2014), pp. 67–86.

Nino, Carlos Santiago, *The Constitution of Deliberative Democracy* (New Haven: Yale University Press, 1996).

Nolte, Georg, "Preventive Use of Force and Preventive Killings: Moves into a Different Legal Order," *Theoretical Inquiries in Law*, 5 (2004), 111–129.

Nonet, Philippe, and Philip Selznick, *Law and Society in Transition: Toward Responsive Law* (New Brunswick: Transaction Publishers, 2001).

Norris, Pippa, and Ronald Inglehart, *Cultural Backlash: Trump, Brexit, and Authoritarian Populism* (Cambridge: Cambridge University Press, 2019).

North, Douglass C., *Institutions, Institutional Change and Economic Performance* (Cambridge: Cambridge University Press, 1990).

North, Douglass C., "In Anticipation of the Marriage of Political and Economic Theory," in James E. Alt, Margaret Levi, and Elinor Ostrom, eds., *Competition and Cooperation: Conversations with Nobelists about Economics and Political Science* (New York: Russell Sage Foundation, 1999), pp. 314–317.

North, Douglass C., *Understanding the Process of Economic Change* (Princeton: Princeton University Press, 2005).

North, Douglass C., and Robert Paul Thomas, *The Rise of the Western World: A New Economic History* (Cambridge: Cambridge University Press, 1973).

North, Douglass C., John Joseph Wallis, and Barry R. Weingast, *Violence and Social Orders: A Conceptual Framework for Interpreting Recorded Human History* (Cambridge: Cambridge University Press, 2009).

North, Douglass C., and Barry R. Weingast, "Constitutions and Commitment: The Evolution of Institutions Governing Public Choice in Seventeenth-Century England," *Journal of Economic History*, 49 (1989), 803–832.

Nussbaum, Martha, *Sex and Social Justice* (Oxford: Oxford University Press, 1999).

Nussbaum, Martha C., The Cosmopolitan Tradition: *A Noble but Flawed Ideal* (Cambridge: Belknap Press of Harvard University Press, 2019).

Nuzzo, Luigo, and Miloš Vec, "The Birth of International Law as a Legal Discipline in the 19th Century," in Luigo Nuzzo and Miloš Vec, eds., *Constructing International Law: The Birth of a Discipline* (Frankfurt am Main: Vittorio Klostermann, 2012), pp. 25–50.

Oakeshott, Michael, "The Vocabulary of a Modern European State," *Political Studies*, 23 (1975), 319–341.

Oakeshott, Michael, *On Human Conduct* (Oxford: Clarendon Press, 1975).

Oakeshott, Michael, *Hobbes on Civil Association* (Indianapolis: Liberty Fund, [1975] 2000).

Oakeshott, Michael, "The Rule of Law," in idem, *On History and Other Essays* (Indianapolis: Liberty Fund, [1983] 1999), pp. 129–178.

Oakeshott, Michael, *The Voice of Liberal Learning* (Indianapolis: Liberty Fund, [1989] 2001).

Oakeshott, Michael, "Law," in idem, *What is History? and Other Essays*, ed. Luke O'Sullivan (Exeter: Imprint Academic, 2004), pp. 423–427.

Oakeshott, Michael, *Lectures in the History of Political Thought*, eds. Terry Nardin and Luke O'Sullivan (Exeter: Imprint Academic, 2006).

Ober, Josiah, *Mass and Elite in Democratic Athens: Rhetoric, Ideology, and the Power of the People* (Princeton: Princeton University Press, 1990).

Office of the United Nations High Commissioner for Human Rights, *Rule of Law Tools for Post-Conflict States: National Consultations on Transitional Justice* (New York: United Nations, 2009).

Ogden, C. K., and I. A. Richards, *The Meaning of Meaning: A Study of the Influence of Language upon Thought and of the Science of Symbolism*, 2nd ed. (London: Kegan Paul, 1927).

Okin, Susan Moller, "Reason and Feeling in Thinking about Justice," *Ethics*, 99 (1989), 229–249.

Okin, Susan Moller, "Justice and Gender: An Unfinished Debate," *Fordham Law Review*, 72 (2004), 1537–1568.

Olsen, Frances, "Statutory Rape: A Feminist Critique of Rights Analysis," *Texas Law Review*, 63 (1984), 387–432.

Olsen, Tricia D., Leigh A. Payne, and Andrew G. Reiter, *Transitional Justice in Balance: Comparing Processes, Weighing Efficacy* (Washington: United States Institute of Peace Press, 2010).

O'Neill, William G., "Police Reform in Post-Conflict Societies: What We Know and What We Still Need to Know," International Police Academy, April 2005.

Open Society Justice Initiative, ed., *Justice Initiatives: Legal Empowerment* (New York: Open Society Justice Initiative, 2013).

Open Society Justice Initiative, *Against the Odds: CICIG in Guatemala* (New York: Open Society Justice Initiative, 2016).

Oppenheim, Felix, *Political Concepts: A Reconstruction* (Oxford: Blackwell, 1981).

Orentlicher, Diane, *Some Kind of Justice: The ICTY's Impact in Bosnia and Serbia* (Oxford: Oxford University Press, 2018).

Orford, Anne, "Europe Reconstructed," *Modern Law Review*, 75 (2012), 275–286.

Orford, Anne, "Moral Internationalism and the Responsibility to Protect," *European Journal of International Law*, 24 (2013), 83–108.

Orford, Anne, "Food Security, Free Trade, and the Battle for the State," *Journal of International Law and International Relations*, 11 (2015), 1–67.

Orford, Anne, "Theorizing Free Trade," in Anne Orford and Florian Hoffmann, eds., *The Oxford Handbook of the Theory of International Law* (Oxford: Oxford University Press, 2016), pp. 701–737.

Orford, Anne, and Jennifer Beard, "Making the State Safe for the Market: The World Bank's World Development Report 1997," *Melbourne University Law Review*, 22 (1998), 195–216.

Osborne, Robin, "Law in Action in Classical Athens," *Journal of Hellenic Studies*, 105 (1985), 40–58.

Osterhammel, Jürgen, "Britain and China, 1842–1914," in Andrew Porter, ed., The *Oxford History of the British Empire*, vol 3: *The Nineteenth Century* (Oxford: Oxford University Press, 2009), pp. 146–169.

Ostwald, Martin, *From Popular Sovereignty to the Sovereignty of Law: Law, Society and Politics in Fifth-Century Athens* (Berkeley: University of California Press, 1986).

Owensby, Brian, *Empire of Law and Indian Justice in Colonial Mexico* (Stanford: Stanford University Press, 2008).

Packer, George, "Donald Trump Goes Rogue," *The New Yorker*, June 25, 2018.

Padoa-Schioppa, Antonio, "Conclusions: Models, Instruments, Principles," in idem, ed., *The Origins of the Modern State in Europe, 13th to 18th Centuries*, vol. 3: *Legislation and Justice* (Oxford: Clarendon Press, 1997), pp. 335–369.

Pahuja, Sundhya, "Technologies of Empire: IMF Conditionality and the Reinscription of the North/South Divide," *Leiden Journal of International Law*, 13 (2000), pp. 749–813.

Pahuja, Sundhya, "Beheading the Hydra: Legal Positivism and Development," *Law, Social Justice and Global Development*, 1 (2007), 1–19.

Pahuja, Sundhya, *Decolonising International Law: Development, Economic Growth and the Politics of Universality* (Cambridge: Cambridge University Press, 2011).

Palmer, Bryan D., *E. P. Thompson: Objections and Oppositions* (London: Verso, 1994).

Palmer, Stephanie, "Feminism and the Promise of Human Rights: Possibilities and Paradoxes," in Susan James and Stephanie Palmer, eds., *Visible Women: Essays on Feminist Legal Theory* (Oxford: Hart, 2002), pp. 91–116.

Palombella, Gianluigi, "The Rule of Law and Its Core," in Gianluigi Palombella and Neil Walker, eds., *Relocating the Rule of Law* (Oxford: Hart 2009), pp. 17–42.

Palombella, Gianluigi, "Illiberal, Democratic and Non-Arbitrary?" *Hague Journal on the Rule of Law*, 10 (2018), 5–19.

Pangle, Thomas, *Montesquieu's Philosophy of Liberalism: A Commentary on The Spirit of the Laws* (Chicago: University of Chicago Press, 1973).

Pangle, Thomas, *The Theological Basis of Liberal Modernity in Montesquieu's Spirit of the Laws* (Chicago: University of Chicago Press, 2010).

Pauer-Studer, Herlinde, *Justifying Injustice: Legal Theory in Nazi Germany* (Cambridge: Cambridge University Press, 2020).

Paulson, Stanley L., "Lon L. Fuller, Gustav Radbruch, and the 'Positivist' Theses," *Law and Philosophy*, 13 (1994), 313–359.

Paulweyn, Joost, "Rational Design or Accidental Evolution? The Emergence of International Investment Law," in Zachary Douglas, Joost Pauwelyn, and Jorge E. Viñuales, eds, *The Foundations of International Investment Law: Bringing Theory into Practice* (Oxford: Oxford University Press, 2014), pp. 11–14.

Perrone, Nicolás M., "The Governance of Foreign Investment at a Crossroad: Is an Overlapping Consensus the Way Forward?" *Global Jurist*, 15 (2015), 1–28.

Perry, Amanda, "International Economic Organisations and the Modern Law and Development Movement," in Ann Seidman, Robert Seidman, and Thomas Wälde, eds., *Making Development Work: Legislative Reform for Institutional Transformation and Good Governance* (The Hague: Kluwer, 1999), pp. 19–32.

Peskin, Victor, "Beyond Victor's Justice? The Challenge of Prosecuting the Winners at the International Criminal Tribunals for the Former Yugoslavia and Rwanda," *Journal of Human Rights*, 4 (2005), 213–231.

Peters, Anne, "Humanity as the A and Ω of Sovereignty," *European Journal of International Law*, 20 (2009), 513–544.

Peters, Anne, "Membership in the Global Constitutional Community," in Jan Klabbers, Anne Peters, and Geir Ulfstein, *The Constitutionalization of International Law* (Oxford: Oxford University Press, 2009), pp. 253–262.

Petersmann, Ernst-Ulrich, "The Establishment of a GATT Office of Legal Affairs and the Limits of 'Public Reason' in the GATT/WTO Dispute Settlement System," in Gabrielle Marceau, ed., *A History of Law and Lawyers in the GATT/ WTO: The*

Development of the Rule of Law in the Multilateral Trading System (Cambridge: Cambridge University Press, 2015), pp. 182–207.

Pettit, Philip, *Republicanism: A Theory of Freedom and Government* (Oxford: Oxford University Press, 1997).

Pettit, Philip, "Democracy, Electoral and Contestatory," in Jack Knight, ed., *Compromise: NOMOS LIX* (New York: New York University Press, 2000), pp. 105–144.

Pettit, Philip, *On the People's Terms* (Cambridge: Cambridge University Press, 2012).

Pfersmann, Otto, "Prolégomènes pour une théorie normativiste de 'l'État de droit,'" in Olivier Jouanjan, ed., *Figures de l'État de droit* (Strasbourg: Presses universitaires de Strasbourg, 2001), pp. 53–78.

Phillips, O. Hood, *The Principles of English Law and the Constitution* (London: Sweet & Maxwell, 1939).

Pierson, Paul, *Politics in Time: History, Institutions, and Social Analysis* (Princeton: Princeton University Press, 2004).

Pifferi, Michele, *Reinventing Punishment* (Oxford: Oxford University Press, 2016).

Pilbeam, Pamela, *The Constitutional Monarchy in France, 1814–48* (London: Routledge, 2000).

Pipes, Richard, *Russia under the Old Regime* (Harmondsworth: Penguin, 1995).

Pirie, Fernanda, *The Anthropology of Law* (Oxford: Oxford University Press, 2013).

Pirie, Fernanda, and Judith Scheele, "Justice, Community, and Law," in idem, eds., *Legalism: Community and Justice* (Oxford: Oxford University Press, 2014), pp. 1–24.

Placidus, Johann Wilhelm, *Litteratur der Staatslehre: Ein Versuch* (Stuttgart: Metzler, 1798).

Pocock, J. G. A., *The Ancient Constitution and the Feudal Law* (Cambridge: Cambridge University Press, 1957).

Poole, Thomas, "Hobbes on Law and Prerogative", in David Dyzenhaus and Thomas Poole, eds., *Hobbes and the Law* (Cambridge: Cambridge: University Press, 2012), pp. 68–96.

Postema, Gerald J., "Coordination and Convention at the Foundation of Law," *Journal of Legal Studies*, 11 (1982), 165–203.

Powell, Catherine, "How Women Could Save the World, If Only We Would Let Them: From Gender Essentialism to Inclusive Security," *Yale Journal of Law and Feminism*, 28 (2015), 271–325.

Pratt, J., *Penal Populism* (London: Sage, 2006).

Radin, M. J., "Reconsidering the Rule of Law," *Boston University Law Review*, 69 (1989), 781–819.

Raeff, Marc, "The Well-Ordered Police State and the Development of Modernity in Seventeenth- and Eighteenth-Century Europe: An Attempt at a Comparative Approach," *American Historical Review*, 80 (1975), 1221–1243.

Rahe, Paul, *Montesquieu and the Logic of Liberty* (New Haven: Yale University Press, 2010).

Rainey, Timothy, "Buffalo Soldiers in Africa: The US Army and the Liberian Frontier Force, 1912–1927," *Liberian Studies Journal*, 21 (1996), 203–338.

Rait, Robert S., *Memorials of Albert Venn Dicey, Being Chiefly Letters and Diaries* (London: Macmillan, 1925).

Rajah, Jothie, *Authoritarian Rule of Law: Legislation, Discourse and Legitimacy in Singapore* (Cambridge: Cambridge University Press, 2012).

Rajah, Jothie, "'Rule of Law' as Transnational Legal Order," in Terence Halliday and Gregory Shaffer, eds., *Transnational Legal Orders* (Cambridge: Cambridge University Press, 2015), pp. 340–373.

Ramsay, Peter, *The Insecurity State: Vulnerable Autonomy and the Right to Security in the Criminal Law* (Oxford: Oxford University Press, 2012).

Rasmussen, Dennis, *The Pragmatic Enlightenment* (Cambridge: Cambridge University Press, 2014).

Ratner, Steven R., Jason S. Abrams, and James L. Bischoff, *Accountability for Human Rights Atrocities in International Law: Beyond the Nuremberg Legacy*, 3rd ed. (Oxford: Oxford University Press, 2009).

Rawls, Amanda C., *Policy Proposals for Justice Reform in Liberia: Opportunities under the Current Legal Framework to Expand Access to Justice* (Rome: International Development Law Organization, 2011).

Raz, Joseph, "The Rule of Law and Its Virtue," *Law Quarterly Review*, 93 (1977), 195–211.

Raz, Joseph, "The Rule of Law and Its Virtue," in idem, *The Authority of Law: Essays on Law and Morality* (Oxford: Clarendon Press, 1979), pp. 210–229.

Raz, Joseph, *The Concept of a Legal System: An Introduction to the Theory of a Legal System*, 2nd ed. (Oxford: Clarendon Press, 1980).

Raz, Joseph, *The Morality of Freedom* (Oxford: Oxford University Press, 1986).

Raz, Joseph, "The Politics of the Rule of Law," *Indian Journal of Constitutional Law*, 2 (2008), 1.

Raz, Joseph, "The Law's Own Virtue," *Oxford Journal of Legal Studies*, 39 (2019), 1–15.

Reid, John Phillip, *Rule of Law: The Jurisprudence of Liberty in the Seventeenth and Eighteenth Centuries* (DeKalb: Northern Illinois University Press, 2004).

Renner, Moritz, "The Dialectics of Transnational Economic Constitutionalism," in Christian Joerges and Josef Falke, eds., *Karl Polanyi, Globalisation and the Potential of Law in Transnational Markets* (Oxford: Hart, 2011), pp. 419–433.

Republic of Liberia, *Acts Passed by the Legislature of the Republic of Liberia during the Session 1907–1908* (Monrovia: Government Printing Office, 1908).

Republic of Liberia, *Interim Poverty Reduction Strategy (2006–2008)* (Washington: International Monetary Fund, 2007).

Republic of Liberia, *Poverty Reduction Strategy (2008–2011)* (Monrovia: Republic of Liberia, 2008).

Republic of Liberia, *Agenda for Transformation: Steps Toward Liberia Rising 2030* (Monrovia: Republic of Liberia, 2012).

Republic of Liberia, *Land Rights Policy* (Monrovia: Land Commission, 2013).

Reynolds, Noel B., "Grounding the Rule of Law," *Ratio Juris*, 2 (1989), 1–16.

Rhode, Deborah L., "Feminist Perspectives on Legal Ideology," in Juliet Mitchell and Ann Oakley, eds., *What is Feminism?* (Oxford: Blackwell, 1986), pp. 151–160.

Richter, Melvin, "Montesquieu and the Concept of Civil Society," *European Legacy*, 3 (1998), 33–41.

Riess, Werner, *Performing Interpersonal Violence: Court, Curse, and Comedy in Fourth-Century BCE Athens* (Berlin: de Gruyter, 2012).

Ringer, Fritz K., *Max Weber's Methodology: The Unification of the Cultural and Social Sciences* (Cambridge: Harvard University Press, 1997).

Roach, Kent, "Dialogic Judicial Review and its Critics," *Supreme Court Law Review*, 23 (2004), 49–104.

Robson, William, "The Report of the Committee on Ministers' Powers," *Political Quarterly*, 3 (1932), 346–364.

Root, Hilton, *Political Foundations of Markets in Old Regime France and England*, (Berkeley: University of California Press, 1994).

Röpke, Wilhelm, "Economic Order and International Law," *Recueil des Cours*, 86 (1954), 203–273.

Rosanvallon, Pierre, *La démocratie inachevée: Histoire de la souveraineté du people en France* (Paris: Gallimard, 2000).

Rosen, Jeffrey, "The Bloods and the Crits: O.J. Simpson, Critical Race Theory, the Law, and the Triumph of Color in America," *New Republic*, December 9, 1996.

Rosen, Lawrence, *The Justice of Islam: Comparative Perspectives on Islamic Law and Society* (Oxford: Oxford University Press, 2000).

Rosen, Lawrence, *Islam and the Rule of Justice: Image and Reality in Muslim Law and Culture* (Chicago: University of Chicago Press, 2018).

Rosenberg, Alexander, *Philosophy of Social Science*, 3rd ed. (Boulder: Westview Press, 2008).

Rosenfeld, Michel, "The Rule of Law and the Legitimacy of Constitutional Democracy," *Southern California Law Review*, 74 (2001), 1307–1352.

Rothstein, Bo, *The Quality of Government: The Political Economy of Corruption, Social Trust and Inequality in an International Comparative Perspective* (Chicago: University of Chicago Press, 2011).

Rothstein, Bo, "What is the Opposite of Corruption?" *Third World Quarterly*, 35 (2014), 737–752.

Rousseau, Jean-Jacques, *The Social Contract and Other Later Political Writings*, ed. Victor Gourevitch (Cambridge: Cambridge University Press, 1997).

Roux, Theunis, *The Politics of Principle: The First South African Constitutional Court, 1995–2005* (Cambridge: Cambridge University Press, 2013).

Rowland, David, *Manual of the English Constitution* (London: John Murray, 1859).

Royer, Jean Pierre, Nicolas Derasse, Jean Pierre Allinne, Bernard Durand, and Jean-Paul Jean, *Histoire de la justice en France du XVIIIe siècle à nos jours*, 5th ed. (Paris: PUF, 2016).

Rubin, Edward L., "Law and Legislation in the Administrative State," *Columbia Law Review*, 89 (1989), 369–426.

Rueschemeyer, Dietrich, "Can One or a Few Cases Yield Theoretical Gains?" in James Mahoney and Dietrich Rueschemeyer, eds., *Comparative Historical Analysis in the Social Sciences* (Cambridge: Cambridge University Press, 2003), pp. 305–336.

Rule, John, and Robert Malcolmson, eds., *Protest and Survival: Essays for E. P. Thompson* (London: Merlin Press, 1993).

Rundle, Kristen, *Forms Liberate: Reclaiming the Jurisprudence of Lon L. Fuller* (Oxford: Hart, 2012).

Rundle, Kristen, "Form and Agency in Raz's Legal Positivism," *Law and Philosophy*, 32 (2013), 767–791.

Rundle, Kristen, "Opening the Doors of Inquiry: Lon Fuller and the Natural Law Tradition," in Robert P. George and George Duke, eds., *The Cambridge Companion to Natural Law Jurisprudence* (Cambridge: Cambridge University Press, 2017), 428–456.

Rundle, Kristen, "Fuller's Relationships," in Hirohide Takikawa, ed., *The Rule of Law and Democracy: The 12th Kobe Lecture and the 1st IVR Japan International Conference, Kyoto, July 2018* (Stuttgart: Franz Steiner Verlag, 2020), pp. 17–40.

Ruskola, Teemu, *Legal Orientalism: China, the United States, and Modern Law* (Cambridge: Harvard University Press, 2013).

Rutherford, Samuel, *Lex, Rex: The Law and the Prince* (London: John Field, 1644).

Sadurski, Wojciech, *Poland's Constitutional Breakdown* (Oxford: Oxford University Press, 2019).

Sandland, Ralph, "Between Truth and Difference: Poststructuralism, Law and the Power of Feminism," *Feminist Legal Studies*, 3 (1995), 3–47.

Sands, Philippe, *Lawless World: Making and Breaking Global Rules* (New York: Viking, 2006).

Sargentich, Lewis D., *Liberal Legality: A Unified Theory of Our Law* (Cambridge: Cambridge University Press, 2018).

Sartre, Jean-Paul, "Preface," in Frantz Fanon, *The Wretched of the Earth*, trans. Constance Farrington (London: Penguin [1961] 1990), pp. 7–26.

Scafuro, Adele C., *The Forensic Stage: Settling Disputes in Graeco-Roman New Comedy* (Cambridge: Cambridge University Press, 1997).

Scalia, Antonin, "The Rule of Law as a Law of Rules," *University of Chicago Law Review*, 56 (1989), 1175–1188.

Schaffer, Frederic C., *Democracy in Translation: Understanding Politics in an Unfamiliar Culture* (Ithaca: Cornell University Press, 1998).

Schatz, Edward, ed., *Political Ethnography: What Immersion Contributes to the Study of Power* (Chicago: University of Chicago Press, 2009).

Scheppele, Kim Lane, "Constitutional Coups in EU Law," in Maurice Adams, Anne Meuwese, and Ernst Hirsch Ballin, eds., *Constitutionalism and the Rule of Law: Bridging Idealism and Realism* (Cambridge: Cambridge University Press, 2017), pp. 446–478.

Scheppele, Kim Lane, "Autocratic Legalism," *University of Chicago Law Review*, 85 (2018), 545–583.

Scheuerman, William E., *Between the Norm and the Exception: The Frankfurt School and the Rule of Law* (Cambridge: MIT Press, 1994).

Scheuerman, William E., ed., *The Rule of Law under Siege: Selected Essays of Franz L. Neumann and Otto Kirchheimer* (Berkeley: University of California Press, 1996).

Scheuerman, William E., *The End of Law: Carl Schmitt in the Twenty-First Century* (London: Rowman & Littlefield, 2019)

Schmitt, Carl, *Political Theology: Four Chapters on the Concept of Sovereignty*, trans. with an Introduction by George Schwab (Cambridge: MIT Press, [1922] 1985).

Schmitt, Carl, *The Crisis of Parliamentary Democracy*, trans. with an Introduction by Ellen Kennedy (Cambridge: MIT Press, [1923/1926] 1985).

Schmitt, Carl, *Constitutional Theory*, trans. and ed. Jeffrey Seitzer (Durham: Duke University Press, [1928] 2008).

Schmitt, Carl, "The Guardian of the Constitution," in Lars Vinx, ed., *The Guardian of the Constitution: Hans Kelsen and Carl Schmitt on the Limits of Constitutional Law* (Cambridge: Cambridge University Press, [1929] 2015), pp. 79–173.

Schmitt, Carl "Die Wendung zum totalen Staat," in idem, *Positionen und Begriffe im Kampf mit Weimar-Genf-Versailles* (Hamburg: Hanseatische Verlagsanstalt, [1931] 1940), pp. 146–57.

Schmitt, Carl, *Legality and Legitimacy*, trans. and ed. Jeffrey Seitzer, with an Introduction by John P. McCormick (Durham: Duke University Press, [1932] 2004).

Schmitt, Carl, *The Concept of the Political*, trans. George Schwab (New Brunswick: Rutgers University Press, [1932] 1976).

Schmitt, Carl, *Staat, Bewegung, Volk: Die Dreigliederung der politischen Einheit* (Hamburg: Hanseatische Verlagsanstalt, 1933).

Schmitt, Carl, "Die deutsche Rechtswissenschaft im Kampf gegen den jüdischen Geist, " *Deutsche Juristen-Zeitung*, 41 (1936), 1193–1199.

Schmitt, Carl, *The Leviathan in the State Theory of Thomas Hobbes: Meaning and Failure of a Political Symbol*, trans. George Schwab and Erna Hilfstein (Westport: Greenwood, [1938] 1996).

Schmitter, Philippe C., and Terry Lynn Karl, "What Democracy Is . . . and Is Not," *Journal of Democracy*, 2 (1991), 75–88.

Schnapper, Bernard, *Voies nouvelles en histoire du droit: la justice, la famille, la répression pénale (XVIème – XXème siècles)* (Paris: PUF, 1991).

Schofield, Norman, "Anarchy, Altruism, and Cooperation: A Review," *Social Choice and Welfare*, 2 (1985), 207–219.

Schönberger, Christoph, "Der Begriff des Staates im Begriff des Politischen," in Reinhard Mehring, ed., *Carl Schmitt: Der Begriff des Politischen* (Berlin: Akademie Verlag, 2003), pp. 21–44.

Schultz, Kenneth A., "Why We Needed Audience Costs and What We Need Now," *Security Studies*, 21 (2012), 369–375.

Scott, James Brown, *A Survey of International Relations between the United States and Germany* (New York: Oxford University Press, 1917).

Searby, Peter, John Rule, and Robert Malcolmson, "Edward Thompson as a Teacher: Yorkshire and Warwick," in John Rule and Robert Malcolmson, eds., *Protest and Survival: Essays for E. P. Thompson* (London: Merlin Press, 1993), pp. 1–23.

Seiberth, Gabriel, *Anwalt des Reiches: Carl Schmitt und der Prozess "Preußen contra Reich" vor dem Staatsgerichtshof* (Berlin: Duncker und Humblot, 2001).

Sempill, Julian, "Ruler's Sword, Citizen's Shield: The Rule of Law and the Constitution of Power," *Journal of Law and Politics*, 31 (2016), 333–414.

Sempill, Julian A., "Law, Dignity and the Elusive Promise of a Third Way," *Oxford Journal of Legal Studies*, 38 (2018), 217–245.

Sen, Amartya, "More Than 100 Million Women Are Missing," *New York Review of Books*, December 20, 1990.

Seyle, Conor, "Governance for Peace," *One Earth Future*, December 12, 2017.

Shackleton, Robert, *Montesquieu: A Critical Biography* (Oxford: Oxford University Press, 1961).

Shafer-Landau, Russ, "Liberalism and Paternalism," *Legal Theory*, 11 (2005), 169–191.

Shapiro, Ian, ed., *The Rule of Law: NOMOS XXXVI* (New York: New York University Press, 1994).

Sherlock, William, *The Case of Resistance of the Supreme Powers Stated and Resolved, According to the Doctrine of the Holy Scriptures* (London: Gardiner, 1684).

Shihata, Ibrahim, *The World Bank in a Changing World: Selected Essays*, ed. Franziska Tschofen and Antonio Parra (Leiden: Martinus Nijhoff, 1991).

Shklar, Judith N., *After Utopia: The Decline of Political Faith*, with a new Foreword by Samuel Moyn (Princeton: Princeton University Press, [1957] 2020).

Shklar, Judith N., *Legalism:* An Essay on *Law, Morals, and Political Trials* (Cambridge: Harvard University Press, 1964).

Shklar, Judith N., "In Defense of Legalism," *Journal of Legal Education*, 19 (1966), 51–58.

Shklar, Judith N., *Freedom and Independence: A Study of the Political Ideas of Hegel's Phenomenology of Mind* (Cambridge: Cambridge University Press, 1976).

Shklar, Judith N., *Montesquieu* (Oxford: Oxford University Press, 1987).

Shklar, Judith N., "Political Theory and the Rule of Law," in Allan C. Hutchinson and Patrick Monahan, eds., *The Rule of Law: Ideal or Ideology?* (Toronto: Carswell, 1987), pp. 1–16.

Shklar, Judith N., "Political Theory and the Rule of Law," in Stanley Hoffmann, ed., *Political Thought and Political Thinkers* (Chicago: University of Chicago Press, [1987] 1998), pp. 21–37.

Shklar, Judith N., "A Life of Learning," in Bernard Yack, ed., *Liberalism without Illusions: Essays on Liberal Theory and the Political Vision of Judith N. Shklar* (Chicago: University of Chicago Press, 1996), pp. 263–281.

Shore, Cris, "The Crown as Proxy for the State? Opening up the Black Box of Constitutional Monarchy," *The Round Table*, 107 (2018), 401–416.

Sikkink, Kathryn, *Evidence for Hope: Making Human Rights Work in the 21st Century* (Princeton: Princeton University Press, 2017).

Simard, Augustin, "Tocqueville, Dicey et le 'problème' du droit administratif," *Tocqueville Review*, 38 (2017), 270–298.

Simmons, Beth A., *Mobilizing for Human Rights: International Law in Domestic Politics* (Cambridge: Cambridge University Press, 2009).

Simmonds, Nigel, "Reply: The Nature and Virtue of Law," *Jurisprudence*, 1 (2010), 277–293.

Singha, Radhika, *A Despotism of Law: Crime and Justice in Early Colonial India* (Delhi: Oxford University Press, 1998).

Sinha, Surya Prakash, "Non-Universality of Law," *Archiv für Rechts- und Sozialphilosophie*, 81 (1995), 185–214.

Skaaning, Svend-Erik, "Measuring the Rule of Law," *Political Research Quarterly*, 63 (2010), 449–460.

Skinner, Quentin, *Liberty before Liberalism* (Cambridge: Cambridge University Press, 1998).

Skinner, Quentin, *Visions of Politics*, vol. 3: *Renaissance Virtues* (Cambridge: Cambridge University Press, 2002).

Slaughter, Anne-Marie, "International Law in a World of Liberal States," *European Journal of International Law*, 6 (1995), 503–538.

Slaughter, Joseph R., "Enabling Fictions and Novel Subjects: The *Bildungsroman* and International Human Rights Law, " *PMLA*, 121 (2006), 1405–1423.

Smart, Carol, *Feminism and the Power of Law* (London: Routledge, 1989).

Smith, David L., "Editor's Introduction," in idem, ed., *Cromwell and the Interregnum: The Essential Readings* (Oxford: Blackwell, 2003), pp. 1–14.

Société française de droit international, ed., L'État de droit en droit international (Paris: Pédone, 2009)

Sofaer, Abraham, "On the Necessity of Pre-Emption," *European Journal of International Law*, 14 (2003), 209–226.

Sohn-Rethel, Alfred, *Intellectual and Manual Labour: A Critique of Epistemology* (New York: Humanities Press, 1978).

Sorel, Georges, *Reflections on Violence*, trans. T. E. Hulme and J. Roth (Mineola: Dover, [1916] 2004).

Sornarajah, M., *Resistance and Change in the International Law on Foreign Investment* (Cambridge: Cambridge University Press, 2015).

Stahl, Friedrich Julius, *Die Philosophie des Rechts*, vol. 2: *Rechts- und Staatslehre auf der Grundlage christlicher Weltanschauung*, 3rd ed. (Heidelberg: Mohr, 1856).

Stanchi, Kathryn M., Linda L. Berger, and Bridget J. Crawford, eds., *Feminist Judgments: Rewritten Opinions of the United States Supreme Court* (Cambridge: Cambridge University Press, 2016).

Stein, Mitchell C., "Bringing Professors Hay and Thompson to the Bargaining Table," *Boston University Law Review*, 68 (1988), 621–651.

Steinberg, Jonathan, *Bismarck: A Life* (New York: Oxford University Press, 2011).

Stern, Stefan, "Blackstone's Criminal Law: Common Law Harmonization and Legislative Reform," in Markus D. Dubber, ed., *Foundational Texts in Criminal Law* (Oxford: Oxford University Press, 2014) pp. 61–78.

Stevens, Caleb, "The Legal History of Public Land in Liberia," *Journal of African Law*, 58 (2014), 250–265.

Stiglitz, Joseph E., *Globalization and Its Discontents Revisited: Anti-Globalization in the Era of Trump*, 2nd ed. (London: Penguin, 2017).

Stimson, Shannon C., "Constitutionalism and the Rule of Law," in John S. Dryzek, Bonnie Honig, and Anne Phillips, eds., *The Oxford Handbook of Political Theory* (Oxford: Oxford University Press, 2009).

Stinchcombe, Arthur L., *When Formality Works: Authority and Abstraction in Law and Organizations* (Chicago: University of Chicago Press, 2001).

Stolleis, *Michael, Geschichte des öffentlichen Rechts in Deutschland, vol. 2: Staatsrechtslehre und Verwaltungswissenschaft 1800–1914* (Munich: C. H. Beck, 1992).

Strayer, Joseph R., *On the Medieval Origins of the Modern State* (Princeton: Princeton University Press, 1970).

Stromseth, Jane E., "Justice on the Ground: Can International Criminal Courts Strengthen Domestic Rule of Law in Post-Conflict Societies?" *Hague Journal on the Rule of Law*, 1 (2009), 87–97.

Stromseth, Jane E., "Peacebuilding and Transitional Justice: The Road Ahead," in Chester A. Crocker, Fen Osler Hampson, and Pamela Aall, eds., *Managing Conflict in a World Adrift* (Washington: United States Institute of Peace Press, 2015), pp. 571–591.

Stromseth, Jane E., "Is the ICC Making a Difference?" *Just Security*, December 6, 2017.

Stromseth, Jane E., David Wippman, and Rosa Brooks, *Can Might Make Rights? Building the Rule of Law After Military Interventions* (New York: Cambridge University Press, 2006).

Stubbs, William, *The Constitutional History of England in Its Origin and Development*, vol. 1 (London: Macmillan & Co., 1874).

Stumpf, Juliet, "The Crimmigration Crisis: Immigrants, Crime and Sovereign Power," *American University Law Review*, 56 (2006), 368–419.

Streng, Franz, "Sentencing in Germany: Basic Questions and New Developments," *German Law Journal*, 8 (2007), 153–171.

Sugarman, David, "The Legal Boundaries of Liberty: Dicey, Liberalism and Legal Science," *Modern Law Review*, 46 (1983), 102–111.

Sullivan, Vickie B., "Criminal Procedure as the Most Important Knowledge and the Distinction between Human and Divine Justice in Montesquieu's *Spirit of the Laws*," in Ann Ward and Lee Ward, eds., *Natural Right and Political Philosophy: Essays in Honor of Catherine Zuckert and Michael Zuckert* (Notre Dame: Notre Dame University Press, 2017), pp. 153–173.

Sullivan, Vickie B., *Montesquieu and the Despotic Ideas of Europe* (Chicago: University of Chicago Press, 2017).

Sundiata, I. K., "Prelude to Scandal: Liberia and Fernando Po, 1880–1930," *Journal of African History*, 15 (1974), 97–112.

Sunstein, Cass R., *The Partial Constitution* (Cambridge: Harvard University Press, 1993).

Sunstein, Cass R., "Rules and Rulelessness," Coase-Sandor Institute for Law and Economics Working Paper No. 27, University of Chicago Law School, 1994.

Sunstein, Cass R., *Legal Reasoning and Political Conflict* (New York: Oxford University Press, 1996).

Sunstein, Cass R., and Richard H. Thaler, "Libertarian Paternalism Is Not an Oxymoron," *University of Chicago Law Review*, 70 (2003), 1159–1202.

Swenson, Geoffrey, "Why US Efforts to Promote the Rule of Law in Afghanistan Failed," *International Security*, 42 (2017), 114–151.

Swenson, Geoffrey, "Legal Pluralism in Theory and Practice," *International Studies Review*, 20 (2018), 438–462.

Sypnowich, Christine, *The Concept of Socialist Law* (Oxford: Clarendon Press, 1990).

Sypnowich, Christine, "Utopia and the Rule of Law," in David Dyzenhaus, ed., *Recrafting the Rule of Law: The Limits of Legal Order* (Oxford: Hart, 1999), pp. 178–195.

Tamanaha, Brian Z., *On the Rule of Law: History, Politics, Theory* (Cambridge: Cambridge University Press, 2004).

Tamanaha, Brian Z., *Law as a Means to an End: Threat to the Rule of Law* (Cambridge: Cambridge University Press, 2006).

Tamanaha, Brian Z., "The Dark Side of the Relationship Between the Rule of Law and Liberalism," *New York University Journal of Law and Liberty*, 3 (2008), 516–547.

Tamanaha, Brian Z., "The Primacy of Society and the Failures of Law and Development," *Cornell International Law Journal*, 44 (2011), 216–247.

Tamanaha, Brian Z., *A Realistic Theory of Law* (Cambridge: Cambridge University Press, 2017).

Tamanaha, Brian Z., "Law's Evolving Emergent Phenomena: From Rules of Social Intercourse to Rule of Law Society," *Washington University Law Review*, 95 (2018), 1–39.

Tamanaha, Brian, Caroline Sage, and Michael Woolcock, eds., *Legal Pluralism and Development: Scholars and Practitioners in Dialogue* (Cambridge: Cambridge University Press, 2012).

Tasioulas, John, "Introduction," in idem, *The Cambridge Companion to the Philosophy of Law* (Cambridge: Cambridge University Press, 2020), pp. 1–14.

Taylor, Charles, *Modern Social Imaginaries* (Durham: Duke University Press, 2004).

Taylor, Matthew M., "Lessons from Guatemala's Commission Against Impunity," Council on Foreign Relations, June 2017.

Taylor, Veronica, "The Rule of Law Bazaar," in Per Bergling, Jenny Ederlöf, and Veronica Taylor, eds., *Rule of Law Promotion: Global Perspectives, Local Applications* (Uppsala: Justus Förlag, 2009), pp. 325–358.

Taylor, Veronica, "Big Rule of Law©®SM™(Pat.Pending): Branding and Certifying the Business of the Rule of Law," in Jeremy Farrall and Hilary Charlesworth, eds., *Strengthening the Rule of Law through the UN Security Council* (Abingdon: Routledge, 2016), pp. 27–42.

Teitel, Ruti G., *Transitional Justice* (Oxford: Oxford University Press, 2000).

Ten, C., "Constitutionalism and the Rule of Law," in Robert E. Goodin and Philip Pettit, eds., *A Companion to Contemporary Political Philosophy* (Oxford: Blackwell, 1993), pp. 394–404.

Teorell, Jan, Carl Dahlström, and Stefan Dahlberg, "The QoG Expert Survey Dataset," (University of Gothenburg: The Quality of Government Institute, 2011).

Thomas, Chantal, "Causes of Inequality in the International Economic Order: Critical Race Theory and Postcolonial Development," *Transnational Law and Contemporary Problems*, 9 (1999), 1–15.

Thomas, Melissa, "What Do the Worldwide Governance Indicators Measure?" *European Journal of Development Research*, 22 (2010), 31–54.

Thompson, E. P., *William Morris: Romantic to Revolutionary* rev. ed. (Pontypool: Merlin Press, [1955] 1976 2011).

Thompson, E. P., "Socialist Humanism," *The New Reasoner*, 1 (1957), 105–143.

Thompson, E. P., *The Making of the English Working Class* (London: Victor Gollanz, 1963.

Thompson, E. P., "The Peculiarities of the English," *The Socialist Register*, reprinted in idem, *The Poverty of Theory and Other Essays* (London: Merlin Press, [1965] 1978), pp. 35–91.

Thompson, E. P., "An Open Letter to Leszek Kolakowski," *The Socialist Register* reprinted in idem, *The Poverty of Theory and Other Essays* (London: Merlin Press, [1973] 1978), pp. 93–192.

Thompson, E. P., "Patrician Society, Plebian Culture," *Journal of Social History*, 7 (1974), 382–405.

Thompson, E. P., *Whigs and Hunters: The Origin of the Black Act* (New York: Pantheon, 1975).

Thompson, E. P., "The Grid of Inheritance: A Comment," in Jack Goody, Joan Thirsk, and E. P. Thompson, eds., *Family and Inheritance: Rural Society in Western Europe, 1200–1800* (Cambridge University Press, 1978), pp. 328–360.

Thompson, E. P., "Eighteenth-Century English Society: Class Struggle without Class," *Social History*, 3 (1978), 133–165.

Thompson, E. P., *The Poverty of Theory and Other Essays* (London: Merlin Press, 1978).

Thompson, E. P., *Writing by Candlelight* (London: Merlin Press, 1980).

Thompson, E. P., *Double Exposure* (London: Merlin Press, 1985).

Thompson, E. P., *The Heavy Dancers* (London: Merlin Press, 1985).

Thompson, E. P., *Customs in Common* (London: Merlin Press, 1991).

Thompson, E. P., *Witness Against the Beast: William Blake and the Moral Law* (Cambridge: Cambridge University Press, 1993).

Thompson, E. P., *Persons and Polemics: Historical Essays* (London: Merlin Press, 1994).

Thompson, E. P., *The Essential E. P. Thompson*, ed. Dorothy Thompson (New York: The New Press, 2001).

Todd, Stephen, "Lysias Against Nikomachos: The Fate of the Expert in Athenian Law," in Lin Foxhall and A. D. E. Lewis, eds., *Greek Law in its Political Setting: Justifications not Justice* (Oxford: Oxford University Press, 1996), pp. 101–131.

Todorov, Tzvetan, *On Human* Diversity, trans. Catherine Porter (Cambridge: Harvard University Press, 1993).

Tomlins, Christopher, "The Many Legalities of Colonization: A Manifesto of Destiny for Early American Legal History," in Christopher L. Tomlins and Bruce H. Mann, eds., *The Many Legalities of Early America* (Chapel Hill: University of North Carolina Press, 2001), pp. 1–20.

Totani, Yuma, *The Tokyo War Crimes Trial: The Pursuit of Justice in the Wake of World War II* (Cambridge: Harvard University Press, 2008).

Treitschke, Heinrich von, *Politik*, ed. Max Cornicelius (Leipzig: W. Hirzl, 1897).

Tribe, Keith, "Appendix A: Translation Appendix," in Max Weber, *Economy and Society: A New Translation*, trans. and ed. Keith Tribe (Cambridge: Harvard University Press, [1922] 2019), pp. 459–487.

Trigger, Bruce G., *Understanding Early Civilizations* (Cambridge: Cambridge University Press, 2003).

Troper, Michel, "Le concept d'État de droit," *Droits*, 15 (1992), 51–63.

Trubek, David M., "Max Weber on Law and the Rise of Capitalism," *Wisconsin Law Review* (1972), 720–753.

Trubek, David M., "Law and Development," in Neil Smelser and Paul Baltes, eds., *International Encyclopaedia of the Social and Behavioral Sciences* (New York: Elsevier, 2001), pp. 8443–8446.

Trubek, David M., "The Political Economy of the Rule of Law: The Challenge of the New Developmental State," *Hague Journal on the Rule of Law* 1 (2009), 28–32.

Trubek, David M., and Marc Galanter, "Scholars in Self-Estrangement: Some Reflections on the Crisis in Law and Development Studies in the United States," *Wisconsin Law Review*, 4 (1974), 1062–1103.

Trubek, David M., and Alvaro Santos, eds., *The New Law and Economic Development: A Critical Appraisal* (Cambridge: Cambridge University Press, 2006).

Tunc, Andre, "The Royal Will and the Rule of Law," in Arthur E. Sutherland, ed., *Government under Law* (Cambridge: Harvard University Press, 1956), pp. 401–422.

Turner, Jonathan H., *Human Institutions: A Theory of Societal Evolution* (Lanham: Rowman & Littlefield Publishers, 2003).

Tushnet, Mark, "An Essay on Rights," *Texas Law Review*, 62 (1984), 1363–1403.

Tushnet, Mark, "Defending the Indeterminacy Thesis," *Quinnipiac Law Review*, 16 (1996), 339–356.

Tushnet, Mark *Weak Courts, Strong Rights* (Princeton: Princeton University Press, 2008).

Tushnet, Mark, "Dialogic Judicial Review," *Arkansas Law Review*, 61 (2009), 205–216.

UNCTAD, *World Investment Report 2018* (Geneva: United Nations, 2018).

Unger, Roberto Mangebeira, *Law in Modern Society: Toward a Criticism of Social Theory* (New York: The Free Press, 1976).

Unger, Roberto Mangabeira, *The Critical Legal Studies Movement* (Cambridge: Harvard University Press, 1986).

United Nations, *The United Nations Rule of Law Indicators: Implementation Guide and Project Tools* (New York: United Nations, 2011).

United Nations Development Programme, *2017 Global Programme Annual Report: Strengthening the Rule of Law and Human Rights for Sustaining Peace and Fostering Development* (New York: United Nations, 2018).

United Nations General Assembly, *Declaration of the High-level Meeting of the General Assembly on the Rule of Law at the National and International Levels*, UN Doc. A/67/L/1, September 19, 2012.

United Nations, High Commissioner for Refugees, "Rule of Law – Democracy and Human Rights," available at www.ohchr.org/EN/Issues/RuleOfLaw/Pages/Democracy.aspx.

United Nations Secretary General, *The Rule of Law and Transitional Justice in Conflict and Post-Conflict Societies*, UN Doc. S/2004/616, August 23, 2004.

United States Government, Special Inspector General for Afghanistan Reconstruction, *Quarterly Report to the United States Congress*, July 30, 2018.

United States Government, Special Inspector General for Iraq Reconstruction, *Learning from Iraq: A Final Report* (Washington: Government Printing Service, 2013).

Unruh, Jon D., "Catalyzing the Socio-Legal Space for Armed Conflict: Land and Legal Pluralism in Pre-War Liberia," *Journal of Legal Pluralism and Unofficial Law*, 40 (2008), 1–31.

Unruh, Jon D., "Land Rights in Postwar Liberia: The Volatile Part of the Peace Process," *Land Use Policy*, 26 (2009), 425–433.

Upham, Frank, "Mythmaking in the Rule of Law Orthodoxy," in Thomas Carothers, ed., *Promoting the Rule of Law Abroad: In Search of Knowledge* (Washington: Carnegie Endowment for International Peace, 2006), pp. 75–104.

Urbinati, Nadia, *Democracy Disfigured: Opinion, Truth and the People* (Cambridge: Harvard University Press, 2014).

Urueña, René, "Indicators and the Law: A Case Study of the Rule of Law Index," in Sally Engle Merry, Kevin Davis, and Benedict Kingsbury, eds., *The Quiet Power of Indicators: Measuring Governance, Corruption, and Rule of Law* (Cambridge: Cambridge University Press, 2015), pp. 75–102.

Valdes, Francisco, and Sumi Cho, "Critical Race Materialism, Theorizing Justice in the Wake of Global Neoliberalism," *Connecticut Law Review*, 43 (2011), 1513–1572.

van Caenegem, R. C., *Legal History: A European Perspective* (London: Hambledon Press, 1991).

Varol, Ozan, "Stealth Authoritarianism," *Iowa Law Review*, 100 (2015), 1673–1742.

Vile, M. J. C., *Constitutionalism and the Separation of Powers* (Indianapolis: Liberty Fund, 1967).

Vinx, Lars, "Constitutional Indifferentism and Republican Freedom," *Political Theory*, 38 (2010), 809–837.

Viroli, Maurizio, *Republicanism* (New York: Hill & Wang, 2002).

Volkov, Shulamit, "Antisemitism as a Cultural Code," *Leo Baeck Institute Yearbook*, 23 (1978), 25–46.

Volpi, Frédéric, "Pseudo-democracy in the Muslim World," *Third World Quarterly*, 25 (2004), 1061–1078.

von Hirsch, Andrew, *Doing Justice: The Choice of Punishments: Report of the Committee for the Study of Incarceration* (New York: Hill and Wang, 1976).

von Hirsch, Andrew, and Nils Jareborg, "Gauging Criminal Harm: A Living Standard Analysis," *Oxford Journal of Legal Studies*, 11 (1991), 1–38.

von Jhering, Rudolph, *The Struggle for Law*, 5th ed. trans. John J. Lalor (Chicago: Callaghan, 1879)

Waddicor, Mark, *Montesquieu and the Philosophy of Natural Law* (The Hague: Martinus Nijhoff, 1970).

Wade, E. C. S., and G. Godfrey Phillips, *Constitutional Law* (London: Longmans, Green & Co., 1931).

Waldron, Jeremy, "The Rule of Law in Contemporary Liberal Theory," *Ratio Juris*, 2 (1989), 79–96.

Waldron, Jeremy, *Law and Disagreement* (Oxford: Oxford University Press, 1999).

Waldron, Jeremy, "Is the Rule of Law an Essentially Contested Concept (in Florida)?" *Law and Philosophy*, 21 (2002), 137–164.

Waldron, Jeremy, "Legislation and the Rule of Law," *Legisprudence*, 1 (2007), 91–123.

Waldron, Jeremy, "The Hamlyn Lectures: The Rule of Law and the Measure of Property," Public Law and Legal Theory Research Paper Series, New York University School of Law, 2011.

Waldron, Jeremy, "Positivism and Legality: Hart's Equivocal Response to Fuller," *New York University Law Review*, 83 (2008), 1135–1169.

Waldron, Jeremy, "The Concept and the Rule of Law," *Georgia Law Review*, 43 (2008), 1–61.

Waldron, Jeremy, "Are Sovereigns Entitled to the Benefit of the Rule of Law?" *European Journal of International Law*, 22 (2011), 315–343.

Waldron, Jeremy, "The Rule of Law and the Importance of Procedure," in James E. Fleming, ed., *Getting to the Rule of Law* NOMOS L (New York: New York University Press, 2011), pp. 3–31.

Waldron, Jeremy, *The Rule of Law and the Measure of Property* (Cambridge: Cambridge University Press, 2012).

Waldron, Jeremy, *Political Political Theory: Essays on Institutions* (Cambridge: Harvard University Press, 2016).

Waldron, Jeremy, "Rule *by* Law: A Much Maligned Proposition," Public Law and Legal Theory Research Paper Series, New York University School of Law, June 2019.

Walker, Geoffrey de Q., *The Rule of Law: Foundation of Constitutional Democracy* (Melbourne: Melbourne University Press, 1988).

Wallace, Robert W., "When the Athenians Did Not Enforce their Laws," in Bernard Legras and Gerhard Thür, eds., *Symposion 2011: Vorträge zur griechischen und hellenistischen Rechtsgeschichte* (Vienna: Austrian Academy of Sciences Press, 2012), pp. 115–125.

Walters, Mark D., "Public Law and Ordinary Legal Method: Revisiting Dicey's Approach to *Droit Administratif*," *University of Toronto Law Journal*, 66 (2016), 1–30.

Walters, Mark D., "The Unwritten Constitution as a Legal Concept," in David Dyzenhaus and Malcolm Thorburn, eds., *The Philosophical Foundations of Constitutional Law* (Oxford: Oxford University Press, 2016), 33–52.

Wang, Yuhua, *Tying the Autocrat's Hand: The Rise of the Rule of Law in China* (Cambridge: Cambridge University Press, 2015).

Watts, Arthur, "The International Rule of Law, " *German Yearbook of International Law*, 36 (1993), 15–45.

Weber, Max, "Die 'Objektivität' sozialwissenschaftlicher und sozialpolitischer Erkenntnis," in idem, *Gesammelte Aufsätze zur Wissenschaftslehre* (Tübingen: Mohr, [1904] 1922), pp. 146–214.

Weber, Max, *On Law in Economy and Society* ed. and introduced by Max Rheinstein, trans. Edward A. Shils and Max Rheinstein (Cambridge: Harvard University Press, 1954).

Weber, Max, *Economy and Society: An Outline of Interpretive Sociology*, vol. 2, ed. Guenther Roth and Claus Wittich (Berkeley: University of California Press, [1922] 1978).

Weigend, Thomas, "Germany," in Kevin Jon Heller and Markus D. Dubber, eds., *The Handbook of Comparative Criminal Law* (Stanford: Stanford University Press, 2011) pp. 252–287.

Weil, Françoise, "Montesquieu et le Despotisme," in *Actes du congrès Montesquieu réuni à Bordeaux du 23 au 26 mai 1955 pour commémorer le deuxièm centenaire de la mort de Montesquieu* (Bordeaux: Imprimeries Delmas, 1956), pp. 191–215.

Weiler, J. H. H., "The Rule of Lawyers and the Ethos of Diplomats: Reflections on the Internal and External Legitimacy of WTO Dispute Settlement," *Journal of World Trade*, 35 (2001), 191–207.

Weingast, Barry R., "The Political Foundations of Democracy and the Rule of the Law," *American Political Science Review*, 91 (1997), 245–263.

Weinrib, Ernest J., "The Intelligibility of the Rule of Law," in Allan C. Hutchinson and Patrick Monahan, eds., *The Rule of Law: Ideal or Ideology?* (Toronto: Carswell, 1987), pp. 59–84.

Weinrib, Ernest J., "Legal Formalism: On the Immanent Rationality of the Law," *Yale Law Journal*, 97 (1988), 949–1016.

Weinrib, Ernest J., "Aristotle's Forms of Justice, " *Ratio Juris*, 2 (1989), 211–226.

Weinrib, Ernest J., *The Idea of Private Law* (Cambridge: Harvard University Press, 1995).

Welldon, J. E. C., *The Politics of Aristotle* (London: Macmillan & Co., 1883).

West, Robin, "Jurisprudence and Gender," *University of Chicago Law Review*, 55 (1988), 1–72.

West, Robin, *Caring for Justice* (New York: New York University Press, 1997).

West, Robin, "Reconsidering Legalism," *Minnesota Law Review*, 88 (2003), 119–158.

White, Steven, *Political Theory and Postmodernism* (New York: Cambridge University Press, 1991).

White, James Boyd, *Heracles' Bow* (Madison: University of Wisconsin Press, 1985).

Whitford, William C., "The Rule of Law," *Wisconsin Law Review* (2000), 723–742.

Whitman, James Q., *Hitler's American Model: The United States and the Making of Nazi Race Law* (Princeton: Princeton University Press, 2017).

Williams, Bernard, "Realism and Moralism in Political Theory," in Bernard Williams and Geoffrey Hawthorn, eds., *In the Beginning was the Deed: Realism and Moralism in Political Argument* (Princeton: Princeton University Press, 2005), pp. 1–17.

Williams, Bernard, "From Freedom to Liberty: The Construction of a Political Value," in Bernard Williams and Geoffrey Hawthorn, eds., *In the Beginning was the Deed: Realism and Moralism in Political Argument* (Princeton: Princeton University Press, 2005), pp. 75–96.

Williams, David Lay, "Political Ontology and Institutional Design in Montesquieu and Rousseau," *American Journal of Political Science*, 54 (2010), 527–531.

Williams, Patricia J., *The Alchemy of Race and Rights: Diary of a Mad Law Professor* (Cambridge: Harvard University Press, 1991).

Williams, Robert A., Jr., "Do You Believe in the Rule of Law?" *California Law Review*, 89 (2005), 1633–1640.

Willis, John, "Three Approaches to Administrative Law: The Judicial, the Conceptual, and the Functional," *University of Toronto Law Journal*, 1 (1935), 53–81.

Wishik, Heather Ruth, "To Question Everything: The Inquiries of Feminist Jurisprudence, " *Berkeley Women's Law Journal*, 1 (1985), 64–77.

Wolfensohn, James, "Foreword," in World Bank, *World Development Report 1997: The State in a Changing World* (New York: Oxford University Press, 1997), pp. iii–iv.

Wolff, Kurt H., *The Sociology of Georg Simmel* (New York: Simon & Schuster, 1950).

Women's Court of Canada, "Native Women's Association of Canada v Canada," *Canadian Journal of Women and the Law*, 18 (2006), 76–119.

Wood, Ellen Meiksins, "Falling through the Cracks: E. P. Thompson and the debate on base and superstructure," in Harvey J. Kaye and Keith McClelland, eds., *E. P. Thompson: Critical Perspectives* (Cambridge: Polity, 1990), pp. 125–152.

World Bank, *Sub-Saharan Africa: From Crisis to Sustainable Growth. A Long-Term Perspective Study* (Washington: World Bank, 1989).

World Bank, *World Development Report 2017: Governance and the Law* (Washington: World Bank, 2017).

World Justice Project, *Annual Report 2013* (Washington: World Justice Project, 2014).

World Justice Project, *Annual Report 2014* (Washington: World Justice Project, 2015).

World Justice Project, *The Right to Remain: Brazil's Favelas vs. the World Cup and Olympics* (Washington: World Justice Project, 2015).

Wouters, Arno, "The Function Debate in Philosophy," *Acta Biotheoretica*, 53 (2005), 123–151.

Yack, Bernard, "The Rationality of Hegel's Concept of Monarchy," *American Political Science Review*, 74 (1980), 709–720.

Young, David, "Montesquieu's View of Despotism and His Use of Travel Literature," *Review of Politics*, 40 (1978), 392–405.

Young, Iris Marion, *Justice and the Politics of Difference* (Princeton: Princeton University Press, 1990).

Young, Katharine G., *Constituting Economic and Social Rights* (Oxford: Oxford University Press, 2012).

Young, Margot, "Gender and Terrain: Feminists Theorize Citizenship," in Margaret Davies and Vanessa E. Munro, eds., *The Ashgate Research Companion to Feminist Legal Theory* (Farnham: Ashgate, 2013), pp. 177–195.

Zakaria, Fareed, "Illiberal Democracy," *Foreign Affairs*, 76 (1997), 22–43.

Zedner, Lucia, *Security* (London: Routledge, 2009).

Zedner, Lucia, "Penal Subversions: When Is Punishment Not Punishment, Who Decides and On What Grounds?" *Theoretical Criminology*, 20 (2016), 3–20.

Zengerie, Jason, "How the Trump Administration is Remaking the Courts," *The New York Times Magazine*, August 26, 2018.

Zimmermann, Lisbeth, *Global Norms with a Local Face: Rule of Law Promotion and Norm Translation* (Cambridge: Cambridge University Press, 2017).

Zimmermann, Reinhard, and Daniel Visser, eds., *Southern Cross: Civil Law and Common Law in South Africa* (Oxford: Clarendon Press, 1996).

Zimring, Franklin E., Gordon. Hawkins, and Sam Kamin, *Punishment and Democracy: Three Strikes and You're Out in California* (New York: Oxford University Press, 2001).

Žižek, Slavoj, *The Sublime Object of Ideology* (London: Verso, 2008).

Zuckert, Michael, "Natural Law, Natural Rights, and Classical Liberalism: Montesquieu's Critique of Hobbes," *Social Philosophy and Policy*, 18 (2001), 227–251.

Zürn, Michael, André Nollkaemper, and Randall Peerenboom, eds., *Rule of Law Dynamics: In an Era of International and Transnational Governance* (Cambridge: Cambridge University Press, 2012).

Zweigert, Konrad, and Hein Kötz, *Introduction to Comparative Law*, 3rd ed., trans. Tony Weir (Oxford: Clarendon Press, 1998).

Index

Tables are indicated by page numbers in *italic* type.

CPSIA information can be obtained
at www.ICGtesting.com
Printed in the USA
BVHW042009030821
613544BV00008B/42